THE WILLIAM STALLINGS BOOKS ON COMPUTER AND DATA COMMUNICATIONS TECHNOLOGY

OPERATING SYSTEMS

A state-of-the art survey of operating system principles. Covers fundamental technology as well as contemporary design issues, such as threads, real-time systems, multiprocessor scheduling, distributed systems, and security.

HANDBOOK OF COMPUTER-COMMUNICATIONS STANDARDS VOLUME 1
THE OPEN SYSTEMS INTERCONNECTION (OSI) MODEL AND OSI-RELATED STANDARDS, SECOND EDITION

A description of the master plan for all computer-communications standards: the OSI model. The book also provides a detailed presentation of OSI-related standards at all 7 layers, including HDLC, X.25, ISO internet, ISO transport, ISO session, ISO presentation, Abstract Syntax ONE (ASN.1), and common application service elements (CASE).

HANDBOOK OF COMPUTER-COMMUNICATIONS STANDARDS VOLUME 2
LOCAL AREA NETWORK STANDARDS, SECOND EDITION

A detailed examination of all current local network standards, including logical link control (LLC, IEEE 802.2), CSMA/CD (IEEE 802.3), token bus (IEEE 802.4), token ring (IEEE 802.5), and fiber distributed data interface (FDDI, ANS X3T9.5).

HANDBOOK OF COMPUTER-COMMUNICATIONS STANDARDS VOLUME 3
THE TCP/IP PROTOCOL SUITE, SECOND EDITION

A description of the protocol standards that are mandated on all DOD computer procurements and are becoming increasingly popular on commercial local network products, including TCP, IP, FTP, SMTP, and TELNET. The network management standards, SNMP and CMOT, are also presented.

W9-AZU-012

Data and
Computer
Communications

DATA AND COMPUTER COMMUNICATIONS

FOURTH EDITION

William Stallings, Ph.D.

MACMILLAN PUBLISHING COMPANY
New York
MAXWELL MACMILLAN CANADA
Toronto
MAXWELL MACMILLAN INTERNATIONAL
New York   Oxford   Singapore   Sydney

To my loving wife, Tricia

Editor: Betsy Jones
Production Supervisor: John Travis
Production Manager: Aliza Greenblatt
Cover Designer: Robert Freese
Cover Art: Slide Graphics of New England

This book was set in Palatino by Clarinda
and was printed and bound by R. R. Donnelley & Sons
The cover was printed by Phoenix Color Corp.

Macmillan Publishing Company
866 Third Avenue, New York, New York 10022

Macmillan Publishing Company is part
of the Maxwell Communication Group of Companies.

Maxwell Macmillan Canada, Inc.
1200 Eglinton Avenue East
Suite 200
Don Mills, Ontario M3C 3N1

Library of Congress Cataloging-in-Publication Data

Stallings, William.
    Data and computer communications / William Stallings.— 4th ed.
        p.   cm.
    Includes bibliographical references and index.
    ISBN 0-02-415441-5
    1. Data transmission systems.   2. Computer networks.   I. Title.
TK5105.S73   1994
004.6—dc20   93-15050
                                                                    CIP

Printing: 2 3 4 5 6 7 8   Year: 4 5 6 7 8 9 0 1 2

Preface

The 1970's and early 1980's saw a merger of the fields of computer science and data communications that profoundly changed the technology, products, and companies of the now combined computer-communications industry. Although the consequences of this revolutionary merger are still being worked out, it is safe to say that the revolution occurred, and any investigation of the field of data communications must be made within this new context.

Objectives

It is the ambitious purpose of this book to provide a unified view of the broad field of data and computer communications. The organization of the book reflects an attempt to break this massive subject into comprehensible parts and to build, piece by piece, a survey of the state of the art. The book emphasizes basic principles and topics of fundamental importance concerning the technology and architecture of data and computer communications.

The book explores the key topics in the field in the following general categories:

- *Principles:* Although the scope of this book is broad, there are a number of basic principles that appear repeatedly as themes which unify this field. Examples are multiplexing, flow control, and error control. The book highlights these principles and contrasts their application in specific areas of technology.
- *Design approaches:* The book examines alternative approaches to meeting specific communication requirements. The discussion is bolstered with examples from existing implementations.
- *Standards:* Standards have come to assume an increasingly important, not to say dominant, role in this field. An understanding of the current status and future direction of the technology is not possible without a comprehensive discussion of the role and nature of the related standards.

The subject, and therefore this book, is highly technical. Nevertheless, an attempt has been made to make the book self-contained. Part I, in particular, draws upon the disciplines of probability and electrical engineering, but the emphasis is on results rather than derivations. In general, a building-block ap-

v

proach is taken. The principles of data communications are carefully and thoroughly explored. These principles are then applied to the complex systems found in communication networks and computer-communications architectures.

Intended Audience

The book is intended for a broad range of readers interested in data and computer communications:

- *Students and professionals in data processing and data communications:* This book is intended as both a textbook for study and a basic reference volume for this exciting and complex field.
- *Designers and implementers:* The book discusses the critical design issues and explores alternative approaches to meeting user requirements.
- *Computer and communication system customers and managers:* The book provides the reader with an understanding of what features and structure are needed in a communications capability, as well as a knowledge of current and evolving standards. This information provides a mean of assessing specific implementations and vendor offerings.

Plan of the Text

The book is organized to clarify the unifying and differentiating concepts underlying the field of data and computer communications. It is divided into four parts:

I *Data communications:* This part is concerned primarily with the exchange of data between two directly-connected devices. Within this restricted environment, the key aspects of transmission, interfacing, link control, and multiplexing are examined.

II *Data communication networking:* This part examines the internal mechanisms by which communication networks provide a data transfer service for attached devices.

III *Computer communications architecture:* This part explores both the architectural principles and the specific mechanisms required for the exchange of data among computers, terminals and other data processing devices.

IV *Integrated Services Digital Networks:* This part introduces ISDN and broadband ISDN, which are emerging worldwide digital telecommunications facilities. This part pulls together many of the concepts examined throughout the book.

The organization of the chapters is as follows:

1. *Introduction:* Provides an overview of the book as well as a discussion of the roles of the various standards-making organizations.
2. *Data transmission:* Explores the behavior of signals propagated through a transmission medium.

3. *Data encoding:* Describes the techniques used for encoding analog and digital data as either analog or digital signals.

4. *Digital data communication techniques:* Examines interfacing and synchronization issues.

5. *Data link control:* Describes the techniques used for converting an unreliable transmission link into a reliable communications link.

6. *Multiplexing:* Examines frequency-division multiplexing and both synchronous and statistical time-division multiplexing.

7. *Circuit switching:* Discusses circuit-switching mechanisms and network design.

8. *Packet switching:* Examines the mechanisms of packet switched networking, including routing and traffic control; introduces X.25.

9. *Local and metropolitan area networks:* Examines alternative approaches in the areas of transmission medium, topology, and medium access control technique.

10. *Protocols and architecture:* Defines communications protocols and motivates the need for a communications architecture.

11. *Internetworking:* Explores alternative techniques for communicating across multiple networks.

12. *Transport protocols:* Provides a detailed analysis of the most complex and important class of communications protocols.

13. *Session services and protocols:* Examines the services provided for the user to manage a logical communications connection, and looks at the protocol mechanisms to support those services.

14. *Presentation facilities:* Introduces Abstract Syntax Notation One (ASN.1) and examines several examples of presentation-level facilities, including encryption and virtual terminal protocols.

15. *Distributed Applications:* Provides examples of application-level protocols, including SNMPv2, FTAM, and X.400.

16. *ISDN and broadband ISDN:* A survey of the networking technology and design that represents the culmination of the computer-communications revolution.

17. *Frame relay and cell relay:* Examines the new data transmission technologies that are having a profound impact on network design.

In addition, the book includes an extensive glossary, a list of frequently-used acronyms, and a bibliography. Each chapter includes problems and suggestions for further reading.

The four parts of the book are sufficiently independent to enable the design of shorter courses using parts of this book. For example, a course on fundamentals of data communications could cover just Part I, the first section of Chapters 7, 8, and 9, and Chapter 10. A course on communications networks could cover Parts II and IV. A course on communications architecture could cover Chapters 4 and 5, the first section of Chapters 7 and 8, and Part III.

The book is intended for both an academic and a professional audience. As a textbook, it is intended as a one-semester course. It covers the material in the

Computer Communication Networks course of The Joint ACM/IEEE Computing Curricula 1991.

The book also serves as a basic reference volume and is suitable for self-study. For the reader with little or no background in data communications, a brief primer is included.

Related Materials

The author has prepared three collections of reprints that cover topics in this book:

- Computer Communications: Architectures, Protocols, and Standards, Third Edition (1992)
- Advances in ISDN and Broadband ISDN (1992)
- Advances in Local and Metropolitan Area Networks (1993)

Each collection includes key references that cover important aspects of data and computer communications. All of the books are published by the IEEE Computer Society Press, 10662 Los Vaqueros Circle, P.O. Box 3014, Los Alamitos, CA 90720, telephone 714-821-8380.

A set of videotape courses specifically designed for use with this book is available from The Media Group, Boston University, 565 Commonwealth Avenue, Boston, MA 02215; telephone (617) 353-3227.

Networking Standards: A Guide to OSI, ISDN, LAN and MAN Standards (Addison-Wesley, 1993) covers the leading-edge standards that are defining the networks and distributed applications recently introduced or currently under development.

The Fourth Edition

This fourth edition is seeing the light of day just nine short years after the publication of the first edition. Much has happened during those years. Indeed, the pace of change, if anything, is increasing. The result is that this revision is more comprehensive and thorough than any of the previous ones. As an indication of this, over one-fourth of the figures (93 out of 346) and one-fifth of the tables (24 out of 123) in this edition are new. Every chapter has been revised, and new chapters have been added.

To begin, the third edition of this book was extensively reviewed by a number of professors who taught from that edition. The result is that, in many places, the narrative has been clarified and tightened and illustrations have been improved. Also, a number of new "field-tested" problems have been added.

Beyond these refinements to improve pedagogy and user-friendliness, there have been major substantive changes throughout the book. In Part II, coverage of the use of optical fiber has been expanded, and the new metropolitan area network (MAN) scheme, the IEEE 802.6 DQDB standard, is described.

One of the most important, and perhaps the most important, addition to the book is an extensive treatment in Part III of the Abstract Syntax Notation One (ASN.1), which has become the *lingua franca* of computer communications. Work in both OSI and TCP/IP development relies heavily on the use of ASN.1. It is vital for students in this area to be able to understand and use ASN.1. Part III also includes expanded coverage of lightweight transport protocols, a technology of growing importance in this era of very-high-speed networks. Part III now includes coverage of network security and network management, both of which have become indispensable components of a communications architecture. For network management, the most important protocol, SNMPv2, is covered in some detail. Also in Part III, the coverage of the TCP/IP protocol suite has been expanded, recognizing the continuing and growing importance of this architecture.

Part IV on ISDN has been expanded to include greater coverage of broadband ISDN. In addition, an entire chapter is devoted to the new technologies of frame relay and cell relay. These new transmission technologies are having a dramatic impact on network design, and no serious student of data and computer communications should be unfamiliar with them.

The revision of this text has been an interesting and rewarding experience for the author, and it is hoped that its readers find it a useful guide to this fascinating field.

W.S.

Contents

CHAPTER 12

Transport Protocols   539

CHAPTER 13

Session Services and Protocols   603

CHAPTER 14

Presentation Facilities   636

CHAPTER 15

Distributed Applications   701

PART IV

INTEGRATED SERVICES DIGITAL NETWORKS

CHAPTER 16

ISDN and Broadband ISDN   751

CHAPTER 17

Frame Relay and Cell Relay   799

CHAPTER 1

Introduction

1.1

THE COMPUTER–COMMUNICATIONS REVOLUTION

The 1970s and early 1980s saw a merger of the fields of computer science and data communications that profoundly changed the technology, products, and companies of the now combined computer–communications industry. Although the consequences of this revolutionary merger are still being worked out, it is safe to say that the revolution has occurred, and any investigation of the field of data communications must be made within this new context.

The computer–communications revolution has produced several remarkable facts:

- There is no fundamental difference between data processing (computers) and data communications (transmission and switching equipment).
- There are no fundamental differences among data, voice, and video communications.
- The lines between single-processor computer, multi-processor computer, local network, metropolitan network, and long-haul network have blurred.

One effect of these trends has been a growing overlap of the computer and communications industries, from component fabrication to system integration. Another result is the development of integrated systems that transmit and process all types of data and information. Both the technology and the technical standards organizations are driving toward a single public system that integrates all communications and makes virtually all data and information sources around the world easily and uniformly accessible.

It is the ambitious purpose of this book to provide a unified view of the broad field of data and computer communications. The organization of the book reflects an attempt to break this massive subject into comprehensible parts and to build, piece by piece, a survey of the state of the art. This introductory chapter begins with a general model of communications. Then, a brief discussion introduces each of the four major parts of this book. Next, the all-important role of standards is introduced. Finally, a brief outline of the rest of the book is provided.

A COMMUNICATIONS MODEL

We begin our study with a simple model of communications. A block diagram of this model appears as Figure 1.1.

The fundamental purpose of data communications is to exchange information between two agents. In Figure 1.1, the information to be exchanged is a message labeled m. This information is represented as data g and is generally presented to a transmitter in the form of a time-varying signal, $g(t)$.

The terms data and information are defined in Table 1.1. These definitions seem rather academic, but for our purpose they might be given the following interpretation: Data can be identified; data can be described; data do not necessarily represent something physical in terms of the measurable world; but above all, data can be and should be used, namely for producing information. They also imply that data to one person may appear as information to another. Information is born when data are interpreted. To exchange information, then, requires access to elements of data and the ability to transmit them.

Returning now to Figure 1.1, the signal $g(t)$ is to be transmitted. Generally, the signal will not be in a form suitable for transmission and must be converted to a signal $s(t)$ that is in some sense matched to the characteristics of the transmission medium. The signal is then transmitted across the medium. On the other end, a signal $r(t)$, which may differ from $s(t)$, is received. This signal is then converted by a receiver into a form suitable for output. The converted signal $\tilde{g}(t)$, or data $\tilde{g}$, is an approximation or estimate of the input. Finally, the output device presents the estimated message, $\tilde{m}$, to the destination agent.

This simple narrative conceals a wealth of technical complexity. To attempt to elaborate, we present two examples, one using electronic mail, the other a telephone conversation.

For the case of electronic mail, consider that the input device and transmitter are components of a personal computer. The agent is a user who wishes to send a message to another user, for example, "The meeting scheduled for

FIGURE 1.1. Simplified communications block diagram.

TABLE 1.1   Data and Information

Data	A representation of facts, concepts, or instructions in a formalized manner suitable for communication, interpretation, or processing by human beings or by automatic means
Information	The meaning that is currently assigned to data by means of the conventions applied to those data

Source: [ANSI90].

March 25 is canceled'' (m). This string of characters is the information. The user activates the electronic mail package on the personal computer and enters the message via the keyboard (input device). The character string is briefly buffered in main memory. We can view it as a sequence of characters (g) or, more literally, a sequence of bits (g) in memory. The personal computer is connected to some transmission medium, such as a local network or a telephone line, by an I/O device (transmitter), such as a local network transceiver or a modem. The input data are transferred to the transmitter as a sequence of bits [$g(t)$] or, more literally, a sequence of voltage shifts [$g(t)$] on some communications bus or cable. The transmitter is connected directly to the medium and converts the incoming bits [$g(t)$] into a signal [$s(t)$] suitable for transmission; specific alternatives will be described in Chapter 3.

The transmitted signal $s(t)$ presented to the medium is subject to a number of impairments, discussed in Chapter 2, before it reaches the receiver. Thus the received signal $r(t)$ may differ to some degree from $s(t)$. The receiver will attempt to estimate the nature of $s(t)$, based on $r(t)$ and its knowledge of the medium, producing a sequence of bits $\tilde{g}(t)$. These bits are sent to the output personal computer, where they are briefly buffered in memory as a block of bits or characters ($\tilde{g}$). In many cases, the destination system will attempt to determine if an error has occurred and, if so, cooperate with the source system to eventually obtain a complete, error-free block of data. These data are then presented to the user via an output device, such as a printer or screen. The message ($\tilde{m}$) as viewed by the user will usually be an exact copy of the original message (m).

A variation is worth mentioning. The agent at either end may be a computer process rather than a human user. For example, messages might be stored on disk or tape to be automatically sent when a certain condition occurs (e.g., in the evening, when phone rates are lower). Or a message might be received when the user is unavailable and stored on disk or tape for later retrieval.

Now consider a telephone conversation. The agent in this case is the speaker, who generates a message (m) in the form of sound waves. The sound waves are converted by the telephone into electrical signals of the same frequency. These signals are transmitted without modification over the telephone line. Hence the input signal $g(t)$ and the transmitted signal $s(t)$ are identical. The signal $s(t)$ will suffer some distortion over the medium, so that $r(t)$ will not be identical to $s(t)$. Nevertheless, the signal $r(t)$ is converted back into a sound wave with no attempt at correction or improvement of signal quality. Thus $\tilde{m}$ is not an exact replica of m. However, the received sound message is generally comprehensible to the listener.

Again, we mention a variation. In so-called digital telephones, the input signal $g(t)$ is digitized (i.e., converted into a sequence of bits). It is this sequence of bits, in the form of a sequence of voltage shifts, that is transmitted as $s(t)$.

These two examples give some idea of the nature of data communications. Another view is expressed in Table 1.2, which lists key tasks that must be performed in a data communications system. The list is somewhat arbitrary: Elements could be added; items on the list could be merged; and some items represent several tasks that are performed at different "levels" of the system. However, the list as it stands is suggestive of the scope of this book.

The first item, *transmission system utilization*, refers to the need to make efficient use of transmission facilities that are typically shared among a number of communicating devices. Various techniques (referred to as *multiplexing*) are used to allocate the total capacity of a transmission medium among a number of users. Congestion control techniques may be required to assure that the system is not overwhelmed by excessive demand for transmission services.

In order to communicate, a device must *interface* with the transmission system. All the forms of communication discussed in this book depend, at bottom, on the use of electromagnetic signals propagated over a transmission medium. Thus, once an interface is established, *signal generation* is required for communication. The properties of the signal, such as form and intensity, must be such that they are (1) capable of being propagated through the transmission system, and (2) interpretable as data at the receiver.

Not only must the signals be generated to conform to the requirements of the transmission system and receiver, but there must be some form of *synchronization* between transmitter and receiver. The receiver must be able to deter-

TABLE 1.2   Communication Tasks

Transmission system utilization
Interfacing
Signal generation
Synchronization
Exchange management
Error detection and correction
Flow control
Addressing
Routing
Recovery
Message formatting
Protection
System management

mine when a signal begins to arrive and when it ends. It must also know the duration of each signal element.

Beyond the basic matter of deciding on the nature and timing of signals, there are a variety of requirements for communication between two parties that might be collected under the term *exchange management*. If data are to be exchanged in both directions over a period of time, the two parties must cooperate. For example, for two parties to engage in a telephone conversation, one party must dial the number of the other, causing signals to be generated that result in the ringing of the called phone. The called party completes a connection by lifting the receiver. For data processing devices, more will be needed than simply establishing a connection; certain conventions must be decided upon. These conventions may include whether both devices may transmit simultaneously or must take turns, the amount of data to be sent at one time, the format of the data, and what to do if certain contingencies such as an error arise.

The next two items might have been included under exchange management, but they seem important enough to list separately. *Error detection and correction* are required in circumstances where errors cannot be tolerated. This is usually the case with data processing systems. For example, in transferring a file from one computer to another, it is simply not acceptable for the contents of the file to be accidentally altered. *Flow control* is required to assure that the source does not overwhelm the destination by sending data faster than they can be processed and absorbed.

Next, we mention the related but distinct concepts of *addressing* and *routing*. When a transmission facility is shared by more than two devices, a source system must somehow indicate the identity of the intended destination. The transmission system must assure that the destination system, and only that system, receives the data. Further, the transmission system may itself be a network through which various paths may be taken. A specific route through this network must be chosen.

Recovery is a concept distinct from that of error correction. Recovery techniques are needed in situations in which an information exchange, such as a data base transaction or file transfer, is interrupted due to a fault somewhere in the system. The objective is either to be able to resume activity at the point of interruption or at least to restore the state of the systems involved to the condition prior to the beginning of the exchange.

Message formatting has to do with an agreement between two parties as to the form of the data to be exchanged or transmitted. For example, both sides must use the same binary code for characters.

Frequently, it is important to provide some measure of *protection* in a data communications system. The sender of data may wish to be assured that only the intended receiver actually receives the data. And the receiver of data may wish to be assured that the received data have not been altered in transit and that the data actually come from the purported sender.

Finally, a data communications facility is a complex system that cannot create or run itself. *System management* capabilities are needed to configure the system, monitor its status, react to failures and overloads, and plan intelligently for future growth.

Thus we have gone from the simple idea of data communication between source and destination, to a six-stage model (Figure 1.1) of data communications, to a rather formidable list of data communications tasks. In this book, we further elaborate this list of tasks to describe and encompass the entire set of activities that can be classified under data and computer communications.

1.3

DATA COMMUNICATIONS

This book is organized into four parts. The first part deals primarily with the portion of Figure 1.1 between points 2 and 5. For want of a better name, we have given Part I the title "Data Communications," although that term arguably encompasses some or even all of the topics of Parts II, III, and IV.

Since the purpose of this chapter is merely to preview the remainder of the book, little needs to be added to the discussion of the preceding section to introduce Part I. The topics that will be covered are

- Data transmission.
- Data encoding.
- Digital data communication techniques.
- Data link control.
- Multiplexing.

Data transmission deals with the portion of Figure 1.1 between points 3 and 4. As was mentioned, the received signal will differ from the transmitted signal due to distortions, or transmission impairments. These distortions are in large part determined by the nature of the transmission medium used. *Data encoding* is the process of transforming input data or signals into signals that can be transmitted. The encoding technique is tailored to the method of data transmission to optimize performance.

The next two topics, *digital data communications techniques* and *data link control*, move the discussion from the simple transmission of data signals to true data communications. Referring again to Figure 1.1, the objective is to transfer data from the input device to the output device, with these two devices cooperating to minimize or eliminate error and to coordinate their actions. We will see that some rather complex techniques are required to achieve these objectives.

Finally, *multiplexing* refers to a variety of techniques used to make more efficient use of a transmission facility. In many cases, the capacity of a transmission facility exceeds the requirements for the transfer of data between two devices. That capacity can be shared among multiple transmitters by multiplexing a number of signals onto the same medium. In this case, the actual transmission path is referred to as a *circuit* or *link*, and the portion of capacity dedicated to each pair of transmitter/receivers is referred to as a *channel*.

DATA COMMUNICATION NETWORKING

In its simplest form, data communication takes place between two devices that are directly connected by some form of point-to-point transmission medium. Often, however, it is impractical for two devices to be directly, point-to-point connected. This is so for one (or both) of the following contingencies:

- The devices are very far apart. It would be inordinately expensive, for example, to string a dedicated link between two devices thousands of miles apart.
- There is a set of devices, each of which may require a link to many of the others at various times. Examples are all of the telephones in the world and all of the terminals and computers owned by a single organization. Except for the case of a very few devices, it is impractical to provide a dedicated wire between each pair of devices.

The solution to this problem is to attach each device to a *communication network*. Figure 1.2 illustrates this concept in a general way. We have a collection of devices that wish to communicate; we will refer to them generically as *sta-*

◯ = Communication network node

▢ = Network station

FIGURE 1.2.   Interconnection via a communication network.

tions. The stations may be computers, terminals, telephones, or other communicating devices. Each station attaches to a network *node.* The set of nodes to which stations attach is the boundary of a communication network that is capable of transferring data between pairs of stations.

Communication networks may be categorized based on the architecture and techniques used to transfer data. In this book we will be concerned with the following types of communication networks:

- Switched networks.
  - Circuit-switched networks.
  - Packet-switched networks.
- Broadcast networks.
  - Packet radio networks.
  - Satellite networks.
  - Local networks.

In a *switched communication network* (Figure 1.3), data are transferred from source to destination through a series of intermediate nodes. These nodes (including the boundary nodes) are not concerned with the content of the data; rather, their purpose is to provide a switching facility that will move the data from node to node until they reach their destination.

In a *circuit-switched network,* a dedicated communications path is established between two stations through the nodes of the network. That path is a connected sequence of physical links between nodes. On each link, a logical channel is dedicated to the connection. Data generated by the source station are transmitted along the dedicated path as rapidly as possible. At each node, incoming data are routed or switched to the appropriate outgoing channel

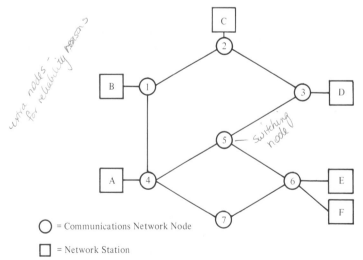

○ = Communications Network Node

□ = Network Station

FIGURE 1.3.   Generic switching network.

without delay. The most common example of circuit switching is the telephone network.

A quite different approach is used in a *packet-switched network*. In this case, it is not necessary to dedicate transmission capacity along a path through the network. Rather, data are sent out in a sequence of small chunks, called *packets*. Each packet is passed through the network from node to node along some path leading from source to destination. At each node, the entire packet is received, stored briefly, and then transmitted to the next node. Packet-switched networks are commonly used for terminal-to-computer and computer-to-computer communications.

With a *broadcast communication network*, there are no intermediate switching nodes (Figure 1.4). At each station, there is a transmitter/receiver that communicates over a medium shared by other stations. A transmission from any one station is broadcast to and received by all other stations. A simple example of this is a CB radio system, in which all users tuned to the same channel may

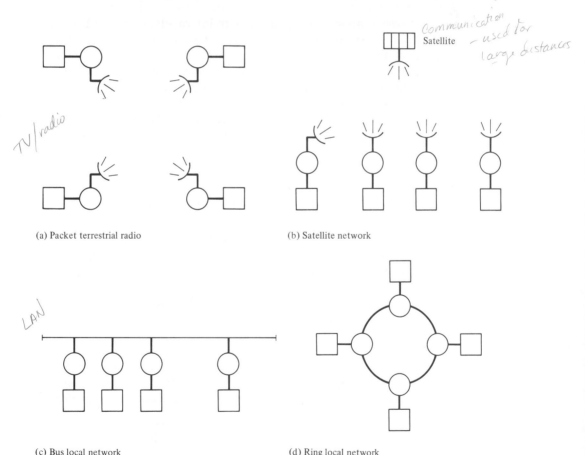

(a) Packet terrestrial radio

(b) Satellite network

(c) Bus local network

(d) Ring local network

FIGURE 1.4.   Broadcast communication networks.

communicate. We will be more concerned with networks used to link terminals and computers. In the latter case, data are often transmitted in packets. Since the medium is shared, only one station at a time can transmit a packet.

Two similar types of broadcast networks are packet radio networks and satellite networks. In both cases, stations transmit and receive via antenna, and all stations share the same channel or radio frequency. In a *packet radio network*, stations are within transmission range of each other and broadcast directly to each other. In a *satellite network*, data are not transferred directly from transmitter to receiver but are relayed via satellite: each station transmits to the satellite and receives from the satellite.

Two common instances of broadcasting are local area networks (LANs) and metropolitan area networks (MANs). A LAN is a communication network that is confined to a small area, such as a single building or a small cluster of buildings. A MAN encompasses a larger area, such as a building complex or urban area. The two most common types of LANs and MANs are depicted in Figure 1.4c and d. In a *bus local network*, all stations are attached to a common wire or cable. A transmission by any one station propagates the length of the medium in both directions and can be received by all other stations. The *ring network* consists of a closed loop, with each station attached to a repeating element. A transmission from any station circulates around the ring past all other stations and can be received by each station as it goes by.

Each of these types of communication network, in its own fashion, overcomes the problems cited at the beginning of this section. A detailed discussion of these networks comprises Part II of this book.

1.5

COMPUTER COMMUNICATIONS ARCHITECTURE

As we have mentioned, the term "data communications" as used in this book refers primarily to the area between points 2 and 5 of Figure 1.1. That is, it is concerned with the transfer of a signal or set of data between two points, with no regard for the meaning or intent of those data. Similarly, communication networks are concerned primarily with such a data transfer, again with no regard for data content.

However, when computers, terminals, and/or other data processing devices exchange data, the scope of concern is much broader. Consider, for example, the transfer of a file between two computers. There must be a data path between the two computers, either directly (Figure 1.1) or via a communication network (Figure 1.2). But more is needed. Typical tasks to be performed:

1. The source system must either activate the direct data communication path or inform the communication network of the identity of the desired destination system.

2. The source system must ascertain that the destination system is prepared to receive data.
3. The file transfer application on the source system must ascertain that the file management program on the destination system is prepared to accept and store the file for this particular user.
4. If the file formats used on the two systems are incompatible, one or the other system must perform a format translation function.

It is clear that there must be a high degree of cooperation between the two computer systems. The exchange of information between computers for the purpose of cooperative action is generally referred to as *computer communications*. Similarly, when two or more computers are interconnected via a communication network, the set of computer stations is referred to as a *computer network*. Since a similar level of cooperation is required between a user at a terminal and a computer, these terms are often used when some of the communicating entities are terminals.

In discussing computer communications and computer networks, two concepts are paramount:

- Protocols.
- Computer–communications architecture.

A protocol is used for communication between entities in different systems. The terms "entity" and "system" are used in a very general sense. Examples of entities are user application programs, file transfer packages, data-base management systems, electronic mail facilities, and terminals. Examples of systems are computers, terminals, and remote sensors. Note that in some cases the entity and the system in which it resides are coextensive (e.g., terminals). In general, an *entity* is anything capable of sending or receiving information, and a *system* is a physically distinct object that contains one or more entities. For two entities to communicate successfully, they must "speak the same language." What is communicated, how it is communicated, and when it is communicated must conform to some mutually acceptable conventions between the entities involved. The conventions are referred to as a *protocol*, which may be defined as a set of rules governing the exchange of data between two entities. The key elements of a protocol are

- *Syntax:* includes such things as data format and signal levels.
- *Semantics:* includes control information for coordination and error handling.
- *Timing:* includes speed matching and sequencing.

Having introduced the concept of a protocol, we can now introduce the concept of a computer–communications architecture. It is clear that there must be a high degree of cooperation between the two computers. Instead of implementing the logic for this as a single module, the task is broken up into subtasks, each of which is implemented separately. As an example, Figure 1.5 suggests the way in which a file transfer facility could be implemented. Three

FIGURE 1.5.   A simplified architecture for file transfer.

modules are used. Tasks 3 and 4 in the preceding list could be performed by a file transfer module. The two modules on the two systems exchange files and commands. However, rather than requiring the file transfer module to deal with the details of actually transferring data and commands, the file transfer modules each rely on a communications service module. This module is responsible for making sure that the file transfer commands and data are reliably exchanged between systems. Among other things, this module would perform task 2. Now the nature of the exchange between systems is independent of the nature of the network that interconnects them. Therefore, rather than building details of the network interface into the communications service module, it makes sense to have a third module, a network access module, that performs task 1 by interacting with the network.

Let us try to summarize the motivation for the three modules in Figure 1.5. The file transfer module contains all of the logic that is unique to the file transfer application, such as transmitting passwords, file commands, and file records. There is a need to transmit these files and commands reliably. However, the same sorts of reliability requirements are relevant to a variety of applications (e.g., electronic mail, document transfer). Therefore, these requirements are met by a separate communications service module that can be used by a variety of applications. The communications service module is concerned with assuring that the two computer systems are active and ready for data transfer and for keeping track of the data that are being exchanged to assure delivery. However, these tasks are independent of the type of network that is being used. Therefore, the logic for actually dealing with the network is separated out into a separate network access module. That way, if the network to be used is changed, only the network access module is affected.

Thus, instead of a single module for performing communications, there is a structured set of modules that implements the communications function. That structure is referred to as a **communications architecture.** In the remainder of this section, we generalize the preceding example to present a simplified communications architecture. Following that, we look at more complex, real-world examples.

A Three-Layer Model

In very general terms, communications can be said to involve three agents: applications, computers, and networks. One example of an application is a file transfer operation. These applications execute on computers that can often support multiple simultaneous applications. Computers are connected to networks, and the data to be exchanged are transferred by the network from one computer to another. Thus, the transfer of data from one application to another involves first getting the data to the computer in which the application resides and then getting it to the intended application within the computer.

With these concepts in mind, it appears natural to organize the communication task into three relatively independent layers:

- Network access layer.
- Transport layer.
- Application layer.

The *network access layer* is concerned with the exchange of data between a computer and the network to which it is attached. The sending computer must provide the network with the address of the destination computer, so that the network may route the data to the appropriate destination. The sending computer may wish to invoke certain services, such as priority, that might be provided by the network. The specific software used at this layer depends on the type of network to be used; different standards have been developed for circuit switching, packet switching, local area networks, and others. Thus it makes sense to separate those functions having to do with network access into a separate layer. By doing this, the remainder of the communications software, above the network access layer, need not be concerned about the specifics of the network to be used. The same higher-layer software should function properly regardless of the particular network to which the computer is attached.

Regardless of the nature of the applications that are exchanging data, there is usually a requirement that data be exchanged reliably. That is, we would like to be assured that all of the data arrive at the destination application and that the data arrive in the same order in which they were sent. As we shall see, the mechanisms for providing reliability are essentially independent of the nature of the applications. Thus, it makes sense to collect those mechanisms in a common layer shared by all applications; this is referred to as the transport layer.

Finally, the application layer contains the logic needed to support the various user applications. For each different type of application, such as file transfer, a separate module is needed that is peculiar to that application.

Figures 1.6 and 1.7 illustrate this simple architecture. Figure 1.6 shows three computers connected to a network. Each computer contains software at the network access and transport layers and software at the application layer for one or more applications. For successful communication, every entity in the

FIGURE 1.6.   Communications architectures and networks.

overall system must have a unique address. Actually, two levels of addressing are needed. Each computer on the network must have a unique network address; this allows the network to deliver data to the proper computer. Each application on a computer must have an address that is unique within that computer; this allows the transport layer to deliver data to the proper application. These latter addresses are known as *service access points* (SAPs), connoting the fact that each application is individually accessing the services of the transport layer.

Figure 1.7 indicates the way in which modules at the same level on different computers communicate with each other: by means of a protocol. A protocol is the set of rules or conventions governing the ways in which two entities

FIGURE 1.7.   Protocols in a simplified architecture.

cooperate to exchange data. A protocol specification details the control functions that may be performed, the formats and control codes used to communicate those functions, and the procedures that the two entities must follow.

Let us trace a simple operation. Suppose that an application, associated with SAP 1 at computer A, wishes to send a message to another application, associated with SAP 2 at computer B. The application at A hands the message over to its transport layer with instructions to send it to SAP 2 on computer B. The transport layer hands the message over to the network access layer, which instructs the network to send the message to computer B. Note that the network need not be told the identity of the destination service access point. All that it needs to know is that the data are intended for computer B.

To control this operation, control information, as well as user data, must be transmitted, as suggested in Figure 1.8. Let us say that the sending application generates a block of data and passes this to the transport layer. The transport layer may break this block into two smaller pieces to make it more manageable. To each of these pieces the transport layer appends a transport header, containing protocol control information. The combination of data from the next higher layer and control information is known as a protocol data unit (PDU); in this case, it is referred to as a transport protocol data unit. The header in each transport PDU contains control information to be used by the peer transport protocol at computer B. Examples of items that may be stored in this header include

- *Destination SAP:* When the destination transport layer receives the transport protocol data unit, it must know to whom the data are to be delivered.
- *Sequence number:* Since the transport protocol is sending a sequence of protocol data units, it numbers them sequentially so that if they arrive out of order, the destination transport entity may reorder them.
- *Error-detection code:* The sending transport entity may include a code that is a function of the contents of the remainder of the PDU. The receiving transport

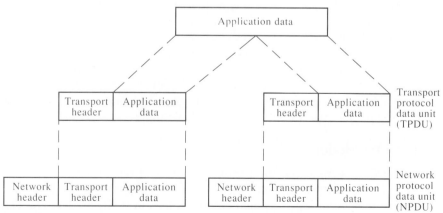

FIGURE 1.8. Protocol data units.

protocol performs the same calculation and compares the result with the incoming code. A discrepancy results if there has been some error in transmission. In that case, the receiver can discard the PDU and take corrective action.

The next step is for the transport layer to hand each protocol data unit over to the network layer, with instructions to transmit it to the destination computer. To satisfy this request, the network access protocol must present the data to the network with a request for transmission. As before, this operation requires the use of control information. In this case, the network access protocol appends a network access header to the data it receives from the transport layer, creating a network-access PDU. Examples of the items that may be stored in the header include

- *Destination computer address:* The network must know to whom (which computer on the network) the data are to be delivered.
- *Facilities requests:* The network access protocol might want the network to make use of certain facilities, such as priority.

Figure 1.9 puts all of these concepts together, showing the interaction between modules to transfer one block of data. Let us say that the file transfer module in computer X is transferring a file one record at a time to computer Y. Each record is handed over to the transport layer module. We can picture this action as being in the form of a command or procedure call, A-SEND (application-send). The arguments of this procedure call include the destination computer address, the destination service access point, and the record. The transport layer appends the destination service access point and other control information to the record to create a transport PDU. This is then handed down to the network access layer in a T-SEND command. In this case, the arguments for the command are the destination computer address and the transport protocol data unit. The network access layer uses this information to construct a network PDU. The transport protocol data unit is the data field of the network PDY, and the network PDU header includes information concerning the source and destination computer addresses.

The network accepts the network PDU from X and delivers it to Y. The network access module in Y receives the PDU, strips off the header, and transfers the enclosed transport PDU to X's transport layer module. The transport layer examines the transport protocol data unit header and, on the basis of the SAP field in the header, delivers the enclosed record to the appropriate application, in this case the file transfer module in Y.

The OSI Model

Figure 1.7 suggests that the various elements of the structured set of protocols are layered, or form a hierarchy. This concept is also evident in Figure 1.10, which depicts the open systems interconnection (OSI) model. The OSI model was developed by the International Organization for Standardization as a

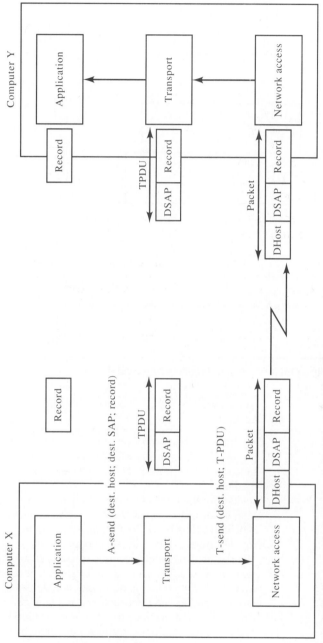

FIGURE 1.9. Operation of a communications architecture.

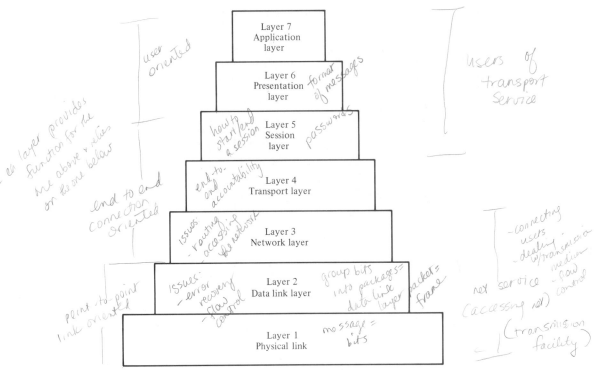

FIGURE 1.10.   Open systems interconnection model.

Created by ISO

TABLE 1.3   The OSI Layers

1. Physical	Concerned with transmission of unstructured bit stream over physical medium; deals with the mechanical, electrical, functional, and procedural characteristics to access the physical medium
2. Data link	Provides for the reliable transfer of information across the physical link; sends blocks of data (frames) with the necessary synchronization, error control, and flow control
3. Network	Provides upper layers with independence from the data transmission and switching technologies used to connect systems; responsible for establishing, maintaining, and terminating connections
4. Transport	Provides reliable, transparent transfer of data between end points; provides end-to-end error recovery and flow control
5. Session	Provides the control structure for communication between applications; establishes, manages, and terminates connections (sessions) between cooperating applications
6. Presentation	Provides independence to the application processes from differences in data representation (syntax)
7. Application	Provides access to the OSI environment for users and also provides distributed information services

model for a computer communications architecture, and as a framework for developing protocol standards. Table 1.3 briefly defines the functions performed at each layer. The intent of the OSI model is that protocols be developed to perform the functions of each layer. Part III of this book will examine protocols in detail and make use of this model for that purpose.

1.6

STANDARDS-MAKING ORGANIZATIONS

It has long been accepted in the communications industry that standards are required to govern the physical, electrical, and procedural characteristics of communication equipment. In the past, this view has not been embraced by the computer industry. Whereas communication equipment vendors recognize that their equipment will generally interface to and communicate with other vendors' equipment, computer vendors have traditionally attempted to monopolize their customers. The proliferation of computers and distributed processing has made that an untenable position. Computers from different vendors must communicate with each other and, with the ongoing evolution of protocol standards, customers will no longer accept special-purpose protocol conversion software development. The result is that standards now permeate all of the areas of technology discussed in this book.

Throughout the book, especially in Part III, we will describe the most important standards that are in use or being developed for various aspects of data and computer communications. The appendix to this chapter looks at the key organizations involved with the development of standards.

There are a number of advantages and disadvantages to the standards-making process. We list here the most striking ones. The principal advantages of standards are

- A standard assures that there will be a large market for a particular piece of equipment or software. This encourages mass production and, in some cases, the use of large-scale-integration (LSI) or very-large-scale-integration (VLSI) techniques, resulting in lower costs.
- A standard allows products from multiple vendors to communicate, giving the purchaser more flexibility in equipment selection and use.

The principal disadvantages are

- A standard tends to freeze the technology. By the time a standard is developed, subjected to review and compromise, and promulgated, more efficient techniques are possible.
- There are multiple standards for the same thing. This is not a disadvantage of standards per se, but of the current way things are done. Fortunately, in recent years the various standards-making organizations have begun to co-

operate more closely. Nevertheless, there are still areas where multiple conflicting standards exist.

Interesting discussion of this topic can be found in [CERN84] and [CARG89].

OUTLINE OF THE BOOK

Chapter Summary

This chapter, of course, serves as an introduction to the entire book. A brief synopsis of the remaining chapters follows.

Data Transmission

The principles of data transmission underlie all of the concepts and techniques presented in this book. To understand the need for encoding, multiplexing, switching, error control, and so on, the reader must understand the behavior of data signals propagated through a transmission medium. Chapter 2 provides an understanding of the distinction between digital and analog data and digital and analog transmission. Concepts of attenuation and noise are introduced, and the various transmission media described.

Data Encoding

Data come in both analog (continuous) and digital (discrete) form. For transmission, input data (point 2, Figure 1.1) must be encoded as an electrical signal (point 3, Figure 1.1) that is tailored to the characteristics of the transmission medium. Both analog and digital data can be represented by either analog or digital signals; each of the four cases is discussed in Chapter 3.

Digital Data Communication Techniques

In Chapter 4 the emphasis shifts from data transmission to data communications. For two devices linked by a transmission medium to exchange digital data, a high degree of cooperation is required. Typically, data are transmitted one bit at a time over the medium. The timing (rate, duration, spacing) of these bits must be the same for transmitter and receiver. Two common communication techniques—asynchronous and synchronous—are explored. This chapter also looks at techniques for detecting bit errors. Finally in this chapter, we look at transmission line interfaces. Typically, digital data devices do not attach to and signal across a transmission medium directly. Rather, this process is mediated through a standardized interface.

Data Link Control

True cooperative exchange of digital data between two devices requires some form of data link control. Chapter 5 examines the fundamental techniques common to all data link control protocols and then examines the most commonly used protocol, HDLC.

Multiplexing

Transmission facilities are, by and large, expensive. It is often the case that two communication stations will not utilize the full capacity of a data link. For efficiency, it should be possible to share that capacity. The generic term for such sharing is multiplexing.

Chapter 6 concentrates on the three most common types of multiplexing techniques. The first, frequency-division multiplexing (FDM), is the most widespread and is familiar to anyone who has ever used a radio or television set. The second is a particular case of time-division multiplexing (TDM) often known as synchronous TDM. This is commonly used for multiplexing digitized voice streams. The third type is another form of TDM that is more complex but potentially more efficient than synchronous TDM; it is referred to as statistical or asynchronous TDM.

Circuit Switching

Any treatment of the technology and architecture of circuit-switched networks must of necessity focus on the internal operation of a single switch. This is in contrast to packet-switched networks, which are best explained by the collective behavior of the set of switches that make up a network. Thus Chapter 7 begins by examining digital switching concepts, including space- and time-division switching. This leads to a discussion of the devices most commonly used to build circuit-switched local networks (although these are rarely thought of as "true" local networks): digital data switches. We are then ready to look at the digital private branch exchange, which supports both digital data devices and telephones. Finally, the concepts of a multinode circuit-switched network are discussed; the topics of routing and control signaling are covered.

Packet Switching

There are two main technical problems associated with a packet-switched network, and each is examined in Chapter 8:

- *Routing:* Since the source and destination station are not directly connected, the network must route each packet, from node to node, through the network.
- *Traffic control:* The amount of traffic entering and transiting the network must be regulated for efficient, stable, and fair performance.

The key design issues in both of these areas are presented and analyzed; the discussion is supported by examples from specific networks. In addition, a key packet-switching interface standard, X.25, is described.

Local and Metropolitan Area Networks

The design of a local area network (LAN) or metropolitan area network (MAN) is determined primarily by three factors: transmission medium, topology, and medium access control (MAC) technique. The bulk of Chapter 9 is devoted to these topics, together with a look at LAN/MAN performance. Throughout, reference is made to standards for LANs and MANs. These are summarized at the end of the chapter.

Protocols and Architecture

Chapter 12 introduces the subject of computer–communications architecture and motivates the need for a layered architecture with protocols defined at each layer. The concept of protocol is defined, and the important features of protocols are discussed.

The three most important communications architectures are introduced in this chapter. The open systems interconnection (OSI) model is described in some detail. Although the OSI model is almost universally accepted as the framework for discourse in this area, an equally important architecture is the TCP/IP protocol suite, which is the basis for many commercially available interoperable products. Finally, the most important proprietary architecture is IBM's system network architecture (SNA).

Internetworking

With the proliferation of networks, internetworking facilities have become essential components of network design. Chapter 11 begins with an examination of the requirements for an internetworking facility and the various design approaches that can be taken to satisfy those requirements. Next, the use of bridges is examined, including a discussion of bridge routing algorithms. The remainder of the chapter deals with the use of routers for internetworking. The internet protocol (IP) and the ISO connectionless network protocol (CLNP) are used as examples; various routing protocols are also described.

Transport Protocols

The transport protocol is the keystone of the whole concept of a computer communications architecture. It can also be one of the most complex of protocols. Chapter 12 examines in detail transport protocol mechanisms and then introduces two important examples, the ISO family of transport protocol and TCP. Finally, the chapter analyzes lightweight transport protocols, which are designed to enable efficient use of high-speed networks.

Session Services and Protocols

A session protocol is used to control the dialogue between two applications. Chapter 16 focuses on the ISO standards, which define a range of services that can be provided and specify session protocol mechanisms to support those services.

Presentation Facilities

Presentation facilities deal with the representation and transformation of information of concern to applications. Chapter 14 begins with a detailed presentation of Abstract Syntax Notation One (ASN.1); a familiarity with this language is almost essential for understanding the current work in computer communications. Then, two important presentation facilities are examined: encryption and virtual terminal protocols. For the former, the increasingly important MD5 authentication standard is used as an example; for the latter, the examples are TELNET and the ISO standard.

Distributed Applications

The purpose of a communications architecture is to support distributed applications. Chapter 15 examines three of the most important of these applications; in each case, general principles are discussed, followed by a specific example. The applications discussed are network management, file transfer, and electronic mail. The corresponding examples are SNMPv2, FTAM, and X.400.

ISDN and Broadband ISDN

The integrated services digital network (ISDN) is a projected worldwide public telecommunications network that is designed to service a variety of user needs. Broadband ISDN is an enhancement of ISDN that can support very high data rates. This chapter looks at the architecture, design principles, and standards for ISDN and broadband ISDN.

Frame Relay and Cell Relay

Perhaps the most significant development in communication networking over the past few years has been the introduction of frame relay and cell relay (also known as asynchronous transfer mode or ATM) technologies into various networking and communications products. Chapter 17 examines these two technologies and contrasts them with each other and with traditional packet switching.

Relationship of Chapter Organization to the OSI Model

Roughly speaking, this book is organized along the lines of the OSI architecture, going from the bottom (physical) to the top (application) layer. However, for the sake of clarity of presentation, a strict mapping of chapters to successive layers has not been followed.

Figure 1.11 indicates the relationship. Most of Part I deals with the fundamentals of data communications and corresponds to OSI layer 1. The exception

				16–ISDN and BISDN 17–Frame relay and cell relay
Physical	2–Data transmission 3–Data encoding 4–Digital data communication techniques	6–Multiplexing	7–Circuit switching 8–Packet switching 9–LANs and MANs	10–Protocols and architecture
Data Link	5–Data link control			
Network				11–Inter-networking
Transport				12–Transport protocols
Session				13–Session services and protocols
Presentation				14–Presentation facilities
Application				15–Distributed applications

FIGURE 1.11. Relationship of chapters to the OSI model.

is Chapter 5, on data link control, which covers functions assigned to OSI layer 2. This material is introduced before multiplexing in Chapter 6, which is a layer 1 concern, because of the implications for multiplexing with respect to data link control frame structure.

Part II deals with communications networks. Thus, much of the material in this part is concerned with functions assigned to OSI layer 3. However, the design and functioning of a network involve consideration of layer 1 and 2 issues as well. Thus, it is fair to say that Part II covers OSI layers 1 through 3.

Part III begins with an overview of protocols and communications architectures in Chapter 10, covering the entire seven-layer architecture. Chapter 11 is devoted to a specific layer-3 function referred to as internetworking. Chapters 12 through 15 cover layers 4, 5, 6, and 7, respectively.

Finally, Part IV covers ISDN. Since ISDN is a communication network, it too maps into layers 1 through 3.

APPENDIX 1A

Standards Organizations

Throughout this book, especially in Parts III and IV, we describe the most important standards in use or being developed for various aspects of data and computer communications. Various organizations have been involved in the development or promotion of these standards. This appendix provides a brief description of the most important (in the current context) of these organizations.

1A.1 Standards-Making Organizations

International Organization for Standardization (ISO)   ISO is an international agency for the development of standards on a wide range of subjects. It is a voluntary, nontreaty organization whose members are designated standards bodies of participating nations, plus nonvoting observer organizations. Although ISO is not a governmental body, more than 70 percent of ISO member bodies are governmental standards institutions or organizations incorporated by public law. Most of the remainder have close links with the public administrations in their own countries. The United States member body is the American National Standards Institute (ANSI), described later in this section.

ISO was founded in 1946 and has issued more than 5000 standards in a broad range of areas. Its purpose is to promote the development of standardization and related activities to facilitate international exchange of goods and services and to develop cooperation in the sphere of intellectual, scientific, technological, and economic activity. Standards have been issued to cover everything from screw threads to solar energy. One important area of standardization deals with the open systems interconnection (OSI) communications architecture and the standards at each layer of the OSI architecture.

In the areas of interest in this book, ISO standards are actually developed in a joint effort with another standards body, the International Electrotechnical Commission (IEC). IEC is primarily concerned with electrical and electronic engineering standards. In the area of information technology, the interests of the two groups overlap, with IEC emphasizing hardware and ISO focusing on software. In 1987, the two groups formed the Joint Technical Committee 1 (JTC 1). This committee has the responsibility of developing the documents that ultimately become ISO (and IEC) standards in the area of information technology.

The development of an ISO standard from first proposal to actual publication of the standard follows a seven-step process. The objective is to ensure that the final result is acceptable to as many countries as possible. The steps are briefly described here (time limits are the minimum time in which voting could be accomplished, and amendments require extended time):

1. A new work item is assigned to the appropriate technical committee, and within that technical committee, to the appropriate working group. The working group prepares the technical specifications for the proposed standard and publishes these as a **draft proposal** (DP). The DP is circulated among interested members for balloting and technical comment. At least three months are allowed, and there may be iterations. When there is substantial agreement, the DP is sent to the administrative arm of ISO, known as the Central Secretariat.
2. The DP is registered at the Central Secretariat within two months of its final approval by the technical committee.
3. The Central Secretariat edits the document to ensure conformity with ISO practices; no technical changes are made. The edited document is then issued as a **draft international standard** (DIS).
4. The DIS is circulated for a six-month balloting period. For approval, the DIS must receive a majority approval by the technical committee members and 75 percent approval of all voting members. Revisions may occur to resolve any negative vote. If more than two negative votes remain, it is unlikely that the DIS will be published as a final standard.
5. The approved, possibly revised, DIS is returned within three months to the Central Secretariat for submission to the ISO Council, which acts as the board of directors of ISO.
6. The DIS is accepted by the Council as an **international standard** (IS).
7. The IS is published by ISO.

As can be seen, the process of issuing a standard is a slow one. Certainly, it would be desirable to issue standards as quickly as the technical details can be worked out, but ISO must ensure that the standard will receive widespread support.

International Telegraph and Telephone Consultative Committee (CCITT) CCITT is a committee of the International Telecommunications Union (ITU), which is itself a United Nations treaty organization. Hence the members of CCITT are governments. The U.S. representation is housed in the Department of State. The charter of CCITT is "to study and issue recommendations on technical, operating, and tariff questions relating to telegraphy and telephony." Its primary objective is to standardize, to the extent necessary, techniques and operations in telecommunications to achieve end-to-end compatibility of international telecommunication connections, regardless of the countries of origin and destination.

CCITT is organized into 15 study groups that prepare standards, called Recommendations by CCITT. There are three areas of activity concerned with ISDN matters (see Part IV): data communications, telematic services, and integrated services digital networks (ISDN). Telematic services are user-oriented services that involve information transfer, query, and update.

Work within CCITT is conducted in four-year cycles. Every four years, a Plenary Assembly is held. The work program for the next four years is established at the assembly in the form of questions submitted by the various study groups, based on requests made to the study groups by their members. The assembly assesses the questions, reviews the scope of the study groups, creates new or abolishes existing study groups, and allocates questions to them.

Based on these questions, each study group prepares draft recommendations to be submitted to the next assembly, four years hence. After approval by the assembly, these are published as CCITT Recommendations. If a certain draft recommendation is very urgent, a study group may employ a balloting procedure to gain approval before the end of the four years. In general, however, the process of standardization within CCITT is a slow one.

Within the fields of data communications and information processing, there has traditionally been a split between the interests of CCITT and ISO. CCITT has primarily been concerned with data transmission and communication network issues. Roughly, these occupy the lower three levels of the OSI architecture. ISO has traditionally been concerned with computer communications and distributed processing issues, which correspond roughly to layers 4 through 7. The increasing merger of the fields of data processing and data communications, however, has resulted in considerable overlap in the areas of concern of these two organizations. Fortunately, the growth of the overlap has been accompanied by a growth in cooperation, so that competing standards are not being used.

The American National Standards Institute (ANSI)   ANSI is a nonprofit, nongovernment federation of standards-making and standards-using organizations. Its members include professional societies, trade associations, governmental and regulatory bodies, industrial companies, and consumer groups. ANSI is the national clearinghouse for voluntary standards in the United States and is also the United States-designated voting member of the ISO.

ANSI publishes national standards but does not develop them. Rather, standards are developed by other groups that are accredited to develop standards for ANSI consideration. Much of this work is done directly by ANSI member organizations, such as the Institute of Electrical and Electronics Engineers (IEEE), which developed the IEEE 802 local area network standards. Additionally, an important group of standards is developed by quasi-independent committees, known as Accredited Standards Committees, which are administered by ANSI member organizations. In either case, once a consensus is reached on the content of a standard within a committee, it is published by ANSI for open public review and comment. If and when ANSI determines that there is a consensus, the proposal is adopted as an American National Standard. The federal government frequently uses ANSI standards in its procurement specifications.

Other Standards-Making Organizations Other groups are also involved in the publication of standards for telecommunications and computer communications. Among the most important:

- *National Institute of Standards and Technology:* Part of the Department of Commerce, it was until 1988 called the National Bureau of Standards. It issues Federal Information Processing Standards (FIPS) for equipment sold to the federal government. The concerns of NIST are broad, encompassing the areas of interest of both CCITT and ISO. NIST is attempting to satisfy federal government requirements with standards that, as far as possible, are compatible with international standards.
- *Defense Communications Agency:* Promulgates communications-related military standards (MIL-STD). DOD feels that its requirements in some areas are unique, and this is reflected in standards that are unlike those used elsewhere. However, the agency works closely with NIST to attempt to have military requirements satisfied by broader-based standards.
- *Electronics Industries Association (EIA):* Trade association of electronics firms and a member of ANSI. It is concerned primarily with standards that fit into OSI layer 1 (physical).
- *Institute of Electrical and Electronics Engineers (IEEE):* Professional society and also a member of ANSI. Their concerns have primarily been with the lowest two layers of the OSI model (physical and data link).

1A.2 Standards-Related Organizations

The success of standards related to OSI depends not only on the development of timely, technically appropriate standards, but on their acceptance by the vendors who supply and the customers who buy equipment that conforms to the standards. One of the most promising developments in recent years is the creation of a number of organizations whose goal is to ensure that acceptance. In this subsection, we briefly mention three of these organizations.

MAP/TOP Users' Group   The Manufacturing Automation Protocol (MAP) is an effort begun by General Motors in 1982; it since has been taken over by the MAP/TOP Users' Group, administered by the Society of Manufacturing Engineers. The objective of MAP is to define a local area network and associated protocols for terminals, computing resources, programmable devices, and robots within a plant or a factory. It sets standards for procurement and provides a specification for use by vendors who want to build networking products for factory use that are acceptable to MAP participants. The strategy has three parts:

1. For cases in which international standards exist, select those alternatives and options that best suit the needs of the MAP participants.
2. For standards currently under development, participate in the standards-making process to represent the requirements of the MAP participants.
3. In those cases where no appropriate standard exists, devise interim MAP standards until the international standards are developed.

Thus, MAP is intended to specify those standards and options within standards appropriate for the factory environment. Because of the widespread support for MAP among manufacturing companies, this guarantees a large market for products that conform to those standards.

A similar effort, called Technical and Office Protocols (TOP), addresses the needs of the office and engineering environments. Like MAP, TOP specifies standards and options within standards and has received widespread support. TOP was begun by Boeing and is now, together with MAP, part of the MAP/TOP Users' Group.

Corporation for Open Systems   An equally important development is the creation, in 1986, of the Corporation for Open Systems (COS). COS is a nonprofit joint venture of more than 100 of the major suppliers of data processing and data communications equipment. Its purpose is

> to provide a vehicle for acceleration of the introduction of interoperable, multi-vendor products and services operating under agreed-to OSI, ISDN, and related international standards to assure widespread customer acceptance of an open network architecture in world markets.

COS is involved in a number of standards-related activities. Its most important activity is the development of a single consistent set of test methods, test facilities, and certification procedures. This will allow vendors to certify that their products do in fact meet the international standards and will work with certified equipment from other vendors.

U.S. Government OSI Users' Committee   A final significant development worth noting is the creation in 1986 of the U.S. Government OSI Users' Committee. The U.S. government is the world's largest user of computers and thus has a profound impact on the product plans of many of the vendors. The objectives of the committee are to

- Develop implementable OSI specifications.
- Coordinate cooperative efforts between government agencies and industry to introduce products that meet government needs and are compliant with international standards.
- Define unique agency requirements and work for OSI incorporation.

The most important outcome of this committee's efforts has been the government open systems profile (GOSIP). Like MAP and TOP, GOSIP specifies standards and options within standards that are suitable for government use. Furthermore, GOSIP provides detailed implementation guidelines that should help assure that products from different vendors do in fact work together. GOSIP is now a federal information-processing standard (FIPS) and is mandatory for use on government procurements. This, together with the MAP/TOP and COS efforts, guarantees the widespread availability of products that conform to international OSI-related standards.

PART I

DATA COMMUNICATIONS

T his first part of the book deals with the transfer of data between two devices that are directly connected; that is, the two devices are linked by a single transmission path rather than a network.

Chapter 2 looks at the key aspects of data transmission. A distinction is drawn between the concepts of analog and digital, in the context of data, signaling, and transmission. The effect of impairments and choice of medium on transmission are also examined. Chapter 3 then reviews the various means of encoding data for transmission.

With Chapter 4, the text moves from the simple transmission of data to the additional processing required to achieve true data communications. This chapter introduces some of the basic data communication processing techniques. Chapter 5 examines data link control procedures, which are designed to turn an unreliable transmission medium into a reliable data link. Chapter 6 examines various methods of multiplexing data signals to achieve more efficient utilization of the transmission medium.

Data Transmission

The successful transmission of data depends principally on two factors: the quality of the signal being transmitted and the characteristics of the transmission medium. The objective of this chapter is to provide the reader with an intuitive feeling for the nature of these two factors.

The first section presents some concepts and terms from the field of electrical engineering. This should provide sufficient background to deal with the remainder of the chapter. Section 2.2 clarifies the use of the terms *analog* and *digital*. Either analog or digital data may be transmitted using either analog or digital signals. Furthermore, it is common for intermediate processing to be performed between source and destination, and this processing has either an analog or digital character.

Section 2.3 looks at the various impairments that may introduce errors into the data during transmission. The chief impairments are attenuation, delay distortion, and the various forms of noise.

Finally, Section 2.4 looks at the most common types of transmission media and the behavior of signals on those media.

2.1

CONCEPTS AND TERMINOLOGY

In this section we introduce some concepts and terms that will be referred to throughout the rest of the chapter and, indeed, throughout Part I.

Transmission Terminology

Data transmission occurs between transmitter and receiver over some *transmission medium*. Transmission media may be classified as guided or unguided. In both cases, communication is in the form of electromagnetic waves. With *guided media*, the waves are guided along a physical path; examples of guided media are twisted pair, coaxial cable, and optical fiber. *Unguided media* provide a means for transmitting electromagnetic waves but do not guide them; examples are propagation through air, vacuum, and seawater.

The term *direct link* is used to refer to the transmission path between two devices in which signals propagate directly from transmitter to receiver with no intermediate devices, other than amplifiers or repeaters used to increase signal strength. Both parts of Figure 2.1 depict a direct link. Note that this term can apply to both guided and unguided media.

A guided transmission medium is *point-to-point* if it provides a direct link between two devices and those are the only two devices sharing the medium (Figure 2.1a). In a *multipoint* guided configuration, more than two devices share the same medium (Figure 2.1b).

A transmission may be simplex, half-duplex, or full duplex. In *simplex* transmission, signals are transmitted in only one direction; one station is transmitter and the other is receiver. In *half-duplex* operation, both stations may transmit, but only one at a time. In *full-duplex* operation, both stations may transmit simultaneously. In the latter case, the medium is carrying signals in both directions at the same time. How this can be is explained in due course.

We should note that the definitions just given are the ones in common use in the United States (ANSI definitions). In Europe (CCITT definitions), the term "simplex" is used to correspond to half-duplex as defined above, and "duplex" is used to correspond to full-duplex as defined above.

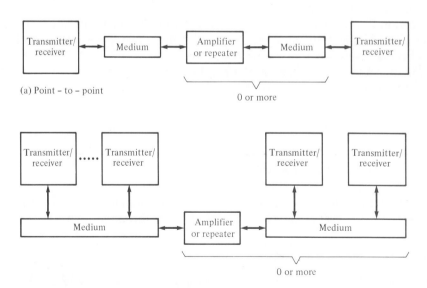

FIGURE 2.1.   Guided transmission configurations.

Frequency, Spectrum, and Bandwidth

At point 3 in Figure 1.1, a signal is generated by the transmitter and transmitted over a medium. The signal is a function of time, but it can also be expressed as a function of frequency; that is, the signal consists of components of different frequencies. It turns out that the "frequency-domain" view of a signal is far more important to an understanding of data transmission than a "time domain" view. Both views are introduced here.

Time-Domain Concepts

We begin by looking at a signal as a function of time. A signal $s(t)$ is *continuous* if

$$\lim_{t \to a} s(t) = s(a)$$

for all a. In words, there are no breaks or discontinuities in the signal. A signal is *discrete* if it takes on only a finite number of values. Figure 2.2 shows exam-

(a) Continuous

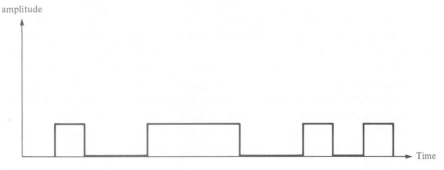

(b) Discrete

FIGURE 2.2.   Continuous and discrete signals.

Amplitude

(a) Sine wave

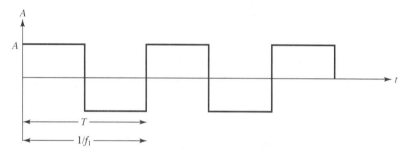

(b) Square wave

FIGURE 2.3.   Example of periodic signals.

ples of both kinds of signals. The continuous signal might represent speech, and the discrete signal might represent binary 1's and 0's.

A signal $s(t)$ is *periodic* if and only if

$$s(t + T) = s(t) \quad -\infty < t < +\infty$$

where the constant T is the *period* of the signal (T must be the smallest value that satisfies the equation). Otherwise, a signal is aperiodic.

Figure 2.3 displays portions of two periodic signals, the sine wave and the square wave. Three important characteristics of a periodic signal are amplitude, frequency, and phase. The *amplitude* is the instantaneous value of a signal at any time. Since the signals discussed in this book are all electrical or electro-magnetic waves, amplitude is measured in volts. The *frequency* is the inverse of the period ($1/T$), or the number of repetitions of the period per second; it is expressed in cycles per second, or hertz (Hz). *Phase* is a measure of the relative position in time within a single period of a signal. As an example, Figure 2.4 shows two signals that are out of phase by $\pi/2$ radians (2π radians $= 360° = 1$ period).

Thus we can express a sinusoid as

$$s(t) = A \sin(2\pi f_1 t + \theta)$$

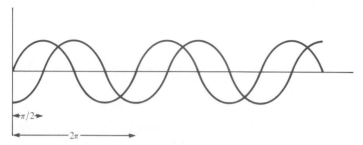

FIGURE 2.4.   Example of a phase difference.

where A is the maximum amplitude, f_1 is the frequency, and θ is the phase. Note that the sine wave in Figure 2.3 can be expressed as either

$$s(t) = A \sin(2\pi f_1 t)$$

or

$$s(t) = A \cos(2\pi f_1 t - \pi/2)$$

Frequency Domain Concepts

So far, we have viewed a signal as a function of time. But any signal can also be viewed as a function of frequency. For example, the signal

$$s(t) = \sin(2\pi f_1 t) + \frac{1}{3} \sin(2\pi(3f_1)t)$$

is shown in Figure 2.5. The components of this signal are just sine waves of frequencies f_1 and $3f_1$; parts a and b of the figure show these individual components. There are several interesting points that can be made about this figure:

- The second frequency is an integer multiple of the first frequency. When all of the frequency components of a signal are integer multiples of one frequency, the latter frequency is referred to as the fundamental frequency.
- The period of the total signal is equal to the period of the fundamental frequency. The period of the component $\sin(2\pi f_1 t)$ is $T = 1/f_1$, and the period of $s(t)$ is also T, as can be seen from Figure 2.5c.

It can be shown, using a discipline known as Fourier analysis, that any signal is made up of components at various frequencies, in which each component is a sinusoid. This result is of tremendous importance because the effects of various transmission media on a signal can be expressed in terms of frequencies, as is discussed later in this chapter. For the interested reader, the subject of Fourier analysis is introduced in Appendix 2A at the end of this chapter.

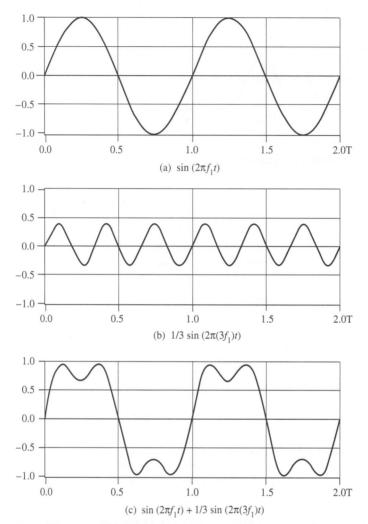

(a) $\sin (2\pi f_1 t)$

(b) $1/3 \sin (2\pi(3f_1)t)$

(c) $\sin (2\pi f_1 t) + 1/3 \sin (2\pi(3f_1)t)$

FIGURE 2.5.   Addition of frequency components ($T = 1/f_1$).

So we can say that for each signal, there is a time-domain function $s(t)$ that specifies the amplitude of the signal at each instant in time. Similarly, there is a frequency-domain function $S(f)$ that specifies the constituent frequencies of the signal. Figure 2.6a shows the frequency-domain function for the signal of Figure 2.5c. Note that, in this case, $S(f)$ is discrete. Figure 2.6b shows the frequency domain function for a single square pulse that has the value 1 between $-X/2$ and $X/2$, and is 0 elsewhere. Note that in this case $S(f)$ is continuous and that it has nonzero values indefinitely, although the magnitude of the frequency components becomes smaller for larger f. These characteristics are common for real signals.

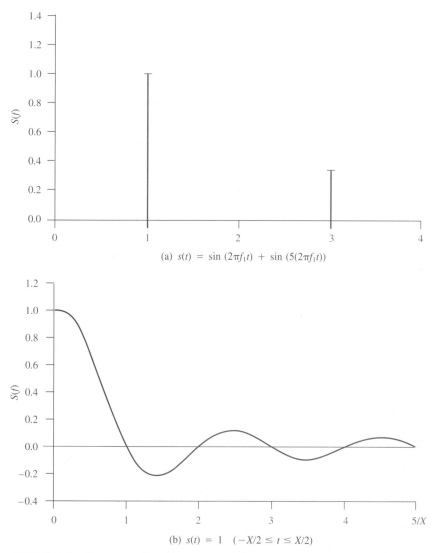

(a) $s(t) = \sin(2\pi f_1 t) + \sin(5(2\pi f_1 t))$

(b) $s(t) = 1 \quad (-X/2 \leq t \leq X/2)$

FIGURE 2.6.   Frequency-domain representations.

The *spectrum* of a signal is the range of frequencies that it contains. For the signal of Figure 2.5c, the spectrum extends from f_1 to $3f_1$. The *absolute bandwidth* of a signal is the width of the spectrum. In the case of Figure 2.5c, the bandwidth is $2f_1$. Many signals, such as that of Figure 2.6b, have an infinite bandwidth. However, most of the energy in the signal is contained in a relatively narrow band of frequencies. This band is referred to as the *effective bandwidth*, or just *bandwidth*.

One final term to define is *dc component*. If a signal includes a component of zero frequency, that component is a direct current (dc) or constant component.

For example, Figure 2.7 shows the result of adding a dc component to the signal of Figure 2.6. With no dc component, a signal has an average amplitude of zero, as seen in the time domain. With a dc component, it has a frequency term at $f = 0$ and a nonzero average amplitude.

Relationship Between Data Rate and Bandwidth

The concept of effective bandwidth is a somewhat fuzzy one. We have said that it is the band within which most of the signal energy is confined. The term *most* in this context is somewhat arbitrary. The important issue here is

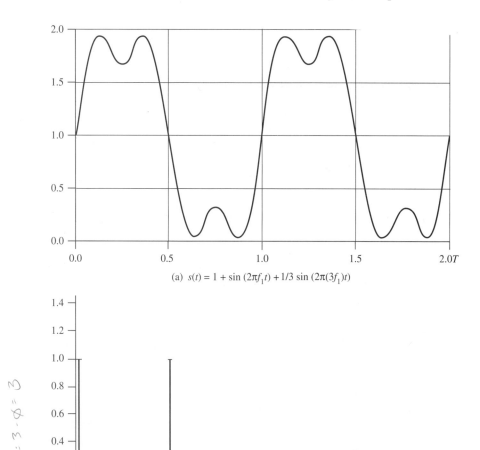

(a) $s(t) = 1 + \sin(2\pi f_1 t) + 1/3 \sin(2\pi(3f_1)t)$

(b) $S(f)$

FIGURE 2.7. Signal with dc component.

that, although a given waveform may contain frequencies over a very broad range, as a practical matter any transmission medium that is used will be able to accommodate only a limited band of frequencies. This in turn limits the data rate that can be carried on the transmission medium.

To try to explain these relationships, consider the square wave of Figure 2.3b. Suppose that we let a positive pulse represent binary 1 and a negative pulse represent binary 0. Then, the waveform represents the binary stream 1010 . . . The duration of each pulse is $1/2f_1$; thus, the data rate is $2f_1$ bits per second (bps). What are the frequency components of this signal? To answer this question, consider again Figure 2.5. By adding together sine waves at frequencies f_1 and $3f_1$, we get a waveform that resembles the square wave. Let us continue this process by adding a sine wave of frequency $5f_1$, as shown in Figure 2.8a, and then adding a sine wave of frequency $7f_1$, as shown in Figure 2.8b. As we add additional odd multiples of f_1, suitably scaled, the resulting waveform approaches that of a square wave more and more closely.

Indeed, it can be shown that the frequency components of the square wave can be expressed as follows:

$$s(t) = A \times \sum_{k=1}^{\infty} \frac{1}{k} \sin(2\pi k f_1 t)$$

Thus, this waveform has an infinite number of frequency components and hence an infinite bandwidth. However, the amplitude of the kth frequency component, kf_1, is only $1/k$, so most of the energy in this waveform is in the first few frequency components. What happens if we limit the bandwidth to just the first three frequency components? We have already seen the answer, in Figure 2.8a. As we can see, the shape of the resulting waveform is reasonably close to that of the original square wave.

We can use Figures 2.5 and 2.8 to illustrate the relationship between data rate and bandwidth. Suppose that we are using a digital transmission system that is capable of transmitting signals with a bandwidth of 4 MHz. Let us attempt to transmit a sequence of alternating 1s and 0s as the square wave of Figure 2.8c. What data rate can be achieved? Well, let us approximate our square wave with the waveform of Figure 2.8a. Although this waveform is a "distorted" square wave, it is sufficiently close to the square wave that a receiver should be able to discriminate between a binary 0 and a binary 1. Now, if we let $f_1 = 10^6$ cycles/second = 1 MHz, then the bandwidth of the signal

$$s(t) = \sin((2\pi \times 10^6)t) + \frac{1}{3} \sin((2\pi \times 3 \times 10^6)t) + \frac{1}{5} \sin((2\pi \times 5 \times 10^6)t)$$

is $(5 \times 10^6) - 10^6 = 4$ MHz. Note that for $f_1 = 1$ MHz, the period of the fundamental frequency is $T = 1/10^6 = 10^{-6} = 1$ μsec. Thus, if we treat this waveform as a bit string of 1s and 0s, one bit occurs every 0.5 μsec, for a data rate of $2 \times 10^6 = 2$ Mbps. Thus, for a bandwidth of 4 MHz, a data rate of 2 Mbps is achieved.

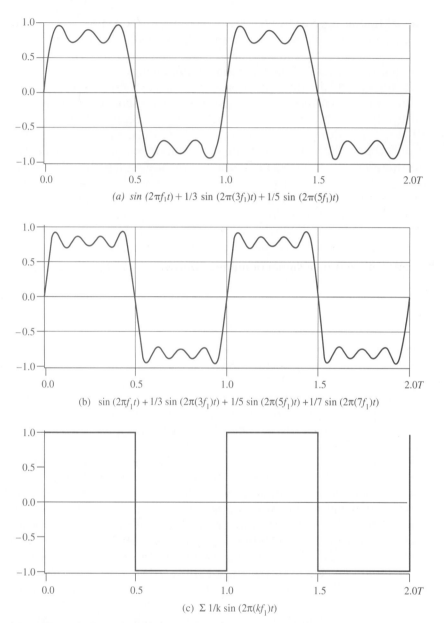

(a) $\sin(2\pi f_1 t) + 1/3 \sin(2\pi(3f_1)t) + 1/5 \sin(2\pi(5f_1)t)$

(b) $\sin(2\pi f_1 t) + 1/3 \sin(2\pi(3f_1)t) + 1/5 \sin(2\pi(5f_1)t) + 1/7 \sin(2\pi(7f_1)t)$

(c) $\Sigma\ 1/k \sin(2\pi(kf_1)t)$

FIGURE 2.8. Frequency components of a square wave $(T = 1/f_1)$.

Now suppose that we have a bandwidth of 8 MHz. Let us look again at Figure 2.8a, but now with $f_1 = 2$ MHz. Using the same line of reasoning as before, the bandwidth of the signal is $(5 \times 2 \times 10^6) - (2 \times 10^6) = 8$ MHz. But in this case $T = 1/f_1 = 0.5\ \mu\text{sec}$. As a result, one bit occurs every $0.25\ \mu\text{sec}$ for a data rate of 4 Mbps. Thus, other things being equal, by doubling the bandwidth, we double the potential data rate.

But now suppose that the waveform of Figure 2.5c is considered adequate for approximating a square wave. That is, the difference between a positive and negative pulse in Figure 2.5c is sufficiently distinct that the waveform can be successfully used to represent a sequence of 1s and 0s. Now, let $f_1 = 2$ MHz. Using the same line of reasoning as before, the bandwidth of the signal of Figure 2.5c is $(3 \times 2 \times 10^6) - (2 \times 10^6) = 4$ MHz. But in this case $T = 1/f_1 = 0.5$ μsec. As a result, one bit occurs every 0.25 μsec for a data rate of 4 Mbps. Thus, a given bandwidth can support various data rates, depending on the requirements of the receiver.

We can draw the following general conclusions from the preceding observations. In general, any digital waveform will have infinite bandwidth. If we attempt to transmit this waveform as a signal over any medium, the nature of the medium will limit the bandwidth that can be transmitted. Furthermore, for any given medium, the greater the bandwidth transmitted, the greater the cost. Thus, on the one hand, economic and practical reasons dictate that digital information be approximated by a signal of limited bandwidth. On the other hand, limiting the bandwidth creates distortions, which makes the task of interpreting the received signal more difficult. The more limited the bandwidth, the greater the distortion, and the greater the potential for error by the receiver.

One more illustration should serve to reinforce these concepts. Figure 2.9 shows a digital bit stream with a data rate of 2000 bits per second. With a bandwidth of 1700 to 2500 Hz, the representation is quite good. With a bandwidth of 4000 Hz, the representation is very good. Furthermore, we can generalize these results. If the data rate of the digital signal is W bps, then a very good representation can be achieved with a bandwidth of 2W Hz.

Thus, there is a direct relationship between data rate and bandwidth: the higher the data rate of a signal, the greater is its effective bandwidth. Looked at the other way, the greater the bandwidth of a transmission system, the higher is the data rate that can be transmitted over that system.

Another observation worth making is this: If we think of the bandwidth of a signal as being centered about some frequency, referred to as the *center frequency*, then the higher the center frequency, the higher the potential bandwidth and therefore the higher the potential data rate. Consider that if a signal is centered at 2000 Hz, its maximum bandwidth is 4000 Hz. As the center frequency increases, so does the potential bandwidth, and hence the potential data rate.

We will return to a discussion of the relationship between bandwidth and data rate later in this chapter, after a consideration of transmission impairments.

Signal Strength

An important parameter in any transmission system is the strength of the signal being transmitted. As a signal propagates along a transmission medium, there will be a loss, or *attenuation*, of signal strength. To compensate, amplifiers may be inserted at various points to impart a gain in signal strength.

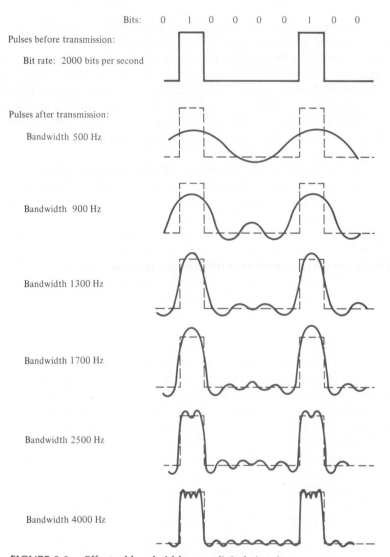

Bits: 0   1   0   0   0   0   1   0   0

Pulses before transmission:

Bit rate: 2000 bits per second

Pulses after transmission:

Bandwidth 500 Hz

Bandwidth 900 Hz

Bandwidth 1300 Hz

Bandwidth 1700 Hz

Bandwidth 2500 Hz

Bandwidth 4000 Hz

FIGURE 2.9.   Effect of bandwidth on a digital signal.

It is customary to express gains, losses, and relative levels in decibels because

- Signal strength often falls off logarithmically, so loss is easily expressed in terms of the decibel, which is a logarithmic unit.
- Gains and losses in a cascaded transmission path can be calculated with simple addition and subtraction.

The decibel is a measure of the difference in two power levels:

$$N_{dB} = 10 \log_{10} \frac{P_1}{P_2}$$

where

N_{dB} = number of decibels
$P_{1,2}$ = power values
$\log_{10}$ = logarithm to the base 10 (from now on, we will simply use log to mean $\log_{10}$)

For example, if a signal with a power of 10 mW is inserted onto a transmission line and the measured power some distance away is 5 mW, the loss can be expressed as

$$\text{LOSS} = 10 \log(5/10) = 10(-0.3) = -3 \text{ dB}$$

Note that the decibel is a measure of relative, not absolute, difference. A loss from 1000 W to 500 W is also a -3dB loss. Thus, a loss of 3 dB halves the magnitude; similarly, a gain of 3 dB doubles the magnitude.

The decibel is also used to measure the difference in voltage, taking into account that power is proportional to the square of the voltage:

$$P = \frac{V^2}{R}$$

where

P = power dissipated across resistance R
V = voltage across resistance R

Thus

$$N_{dB} = 10 \log \frac{P_1}{P_2} = 10 \log \frac{V_1^2/R}{V_2^2/R} = 20 \log \frac{V_1}{V_2}$$

Decibel values refer to relative magnitudes or changes in magnitude, not to an absolute level. It is convenient to be able to refer to an absolute level of power or voltage in decibels so that gain and losses may be easily calculated. Thus several derived units are in common use.

The dBW (decibel-watt) is used extensively in microwave applications. The value of 1 W is selected as reference and defined to be 0 dBW. The absolute decibel level of power in dBW is defined as

$$\text{Power(dBW)} = 10 \log \frac{\text{Power(W)}}{1 \text{ W}}$$

For example, a power of 1000 W is 30 dBW. A power of 1 mW is -30 dBW.

The dBmV (decibel-millivolt) is used in video applications and is an absolute decibel unit with 0 dBmV equivalent to 1 mV. Thus

$$\text{Voltage(dBmV)} = 20 \log_{10} \frac{\text{Voltage(mV)}}{1 \text{ mV}}$$

The voltage levels are assumed to be across a 75-ohm resistance.

The decibel is convenient for determining overall gain or loss in a system. For example, consider a point-to-point link that consists of a transmission line with a single amplifier partway along. If the loss on the first portion of line is 13 dB, the gain of the amplifier is 30 dB, and the loss on the second portion of line is 40 dB, then the overall gain (loss) is $-13 + 30 - 40 = -23$ dB. If the original signal strength is -30 dBW, the received signal strength is -53 dBW.

ANALOG AND DIGITAL DATA TRANSMISSION

In transmitting data from a source to a destination, one must be concerned with the nature of the data, the actual physical means used to propagate the data, and what processing or adjustments may be required along the way to assure that the received data are intelligible. For all of these considerations, the crucial point is whether we are dealing with analog or digital entities.

The terms *analog* and *digital* correspond, roughly, to continuous and discrete, respectively. These two terms are used frequently in data communications in at least three contexts:

- Data.
- Signaling.
- Transmission.

We discussed data, as distinct from information, in Chapter 1. For present purposes, we define *data* as entities that convey meaning. *Signals* are electric or electromagnetic encoding of data. *Signaling* is the act of propagating the signal along a suitable medium. Finally, *transmission* is the communication of data by the propagation and processing of signals. In what follows, we try to make these abstract concepts clear by discussing the terms "analog" and "digital" in these three contexts.

Data

The concepts of analog and digital data are simple enough. *Analog data* take on continuous values on some interval. For example, voice and video are continuously varying patterns of intensity. Most data collected by sensors, such as temperature and pressure, are continuous-valued. *Digital data* take on discrete values; examples are text and integers.

The most familiar example of analog data is audio or acoustic data, which, in the form of sound waves, can be perceived directly by human beings. Figure 2.10 shows the acoustic spectrum for human speech. Frequency components of speech may be found between 20 Hz and 20 kHz. Although much of the energy in speech is concentrated at the lower frequencies, tests have shown

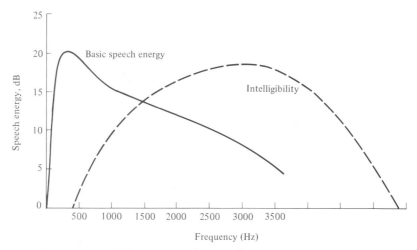

FIGURE 2.10.   Acoustic spectrum for speech. Source: [FREE89]

that frequencies up to 600 to 700 Hz add very little to the intelligibility of speech to the human ear. The dashed line more accurately reflects the intelligibility or emotional content of speech.

Another common example of analog data is video. Here it is easier to characterize the data in terms of the viewer (destination) of the TV screen rather than the original scene (source) that is recorded by the TV camera. To produce a picture on the screen, an electron beam scans across the surface of the screen from left to right and top to bottom. For black-and-white television, the amount of illumination produced (on a scale from black to white) at any point is proportional to the intensity of the beam as it passes that point. Thus at any instant in time the beam takes on an analog value of intensity to produce the desired brightness at that point on the screen. Further, as the beam scans, the analog value changes. Thus the video image can be viewed as a time-varying analog signal.

Figure 2.11a depicts the scanning process. At the end of each scan line, the beam is swept rapidly back to the left (horizontal retrace). When the beam reaches the bottom, it is swept rapidly back to the top (vertical retrace). The beam is turned off (blanked out) during the retrace intervals.

To achieve adequate resolution, the beam produces a total of 483 horizontal lines at a rate of 30 complete scans of the screen per second. Tests have shown that this rate will produce a sensation of flicker rather than smooth motion. However, the flicker is eliminated by a process of interlacing, as depicted in Figure 2.11b. The electron beam scans across the screen starting at the far left, very near the top. The beam reaches the bottom at the middle after $241\frac{1}{2}$ lines. At this point, the beam is quickly repositioned at the top of the screen and, beginning in the middle, produces an additional $241\frac{1}{2}$ lines interlaced with the original set. Thus the screen is refreshed 60 times per second rather than 30,

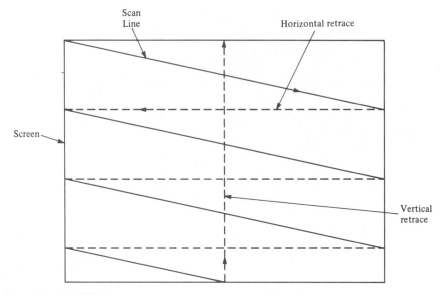

Scan Line

Horizontal retrace

Screen

Vertical retrace

(a) Composition of a TV field

Lines 5 through 238 of first field and lines 267 through 500 of second field not shown here.

Lines 242 through 262 and lines 505 through 525 are not part of raster; they occur while beam is shut off during vertical retrace.

(b) Video interlacing technique

FIGURE 2.11. TV picture production.

and flicker is avoided. Note that the total count of lines is 525. Of these, 42 are blanked out during the vertical retrace interval, leaving 483 actually visible on the screen.

A familiar example of digital data is text or character strings. While textual data are most convenient for human beings, they cannot, in character form, be easily stored or transmitted by data processing and communications systems. Such systems are designed for binary data. Thus a number of codes have been devised by which characters are represented by a sequence of bits. Perhaps the earliest common example of this is the Morse code. Today, the most commonly used code in the United States is the ASCII (American Standard Code for Information Interchange) code (Table 2.1) promulgated by ANSI. ASCII is also widely used outside the United States. Each character in this code is represented by a unique 7-bit pattern; thus 128 different characters can be represented. This is a larger number than is necessary, and some of the patterns represent "control" characters. Some of these control characters have to do with controlling the printing of characters on a page. Others are concerned with communications procedures and will be discussed later. ASCII-encoded characters are almost always stored and transmitted using 8 bits per character (a block of 8 bits is referred to as an *octet* or a *byte*). The eighth bit is a parity bit used for error detection. This bit is set such that the total number of binary 1's in each octet is always odd (odd parity) or always even (even parity). Thus a transmission error that changes a single bit can be detected.

Signals

In a communications system, data are propagated from one point to another by means of electric signals. An *analog signal* is a continuously varying electromagnetic wave that may be propagated over a variety of media, depending on spectrum; examples are wire media, such as twisted pair and coaxial cable, fiber optic cable, and atmosphere or space propagation. A *digital signal* is a sequence of voltage pulses that may be transmitted over a wire medium; for example, a constant positive voltage level may represent binary 1 and a constant negative voltage level may represent binary 0.

In what follows, we first look at some specific examples of signal types and then discuss the relationship between data and signals.

Examples

Let us return to our three examples of the preceding subsection. For each example, we will describe the signal and estimate its bandwidth.

In the case of acoustic data (voice), the data can be represented directly by an electromagnetic signal occupying the same spectrum. However, there is a need to compromise between the fidelity of the sound as transmitted electrically and the cost of transmission, which increases with increasing bandwidth. Although, as mentioned, the spectrum of speech is approximately 20 Hz to

TABLE 2.1   The American Standard Code for Information Interchange (ASCII)

Bit position

$b_7 b_6 b_5$ \ $b_4 b_3 b_2 b_1$	000	001	010	011	100	101	110	111
0 0 0 0	NUL	DLE	SP	0	@	P	`	p
0 0 0 1	SOH	DC1	!	1	A	Q	a	q
0 0 1 0	STX	DC2	"	2	B	R	b	r
0 0 1 1	ETX	DC3	#	3	C	S	c	s
0 1 0 0	EOT	DC4	$	4	D	T	d	t
0 1 0 1	ENQ	NAK	%	5	E	U	e	u
0 1 1 0	ACK	SYN	&	6	F	V	f	v
0 1 1 1	BEL	ETB	'	7	G	W	g	w
1 0 0 0	BS	CAN	(	8	H	X	h	x
1 0 0 1	HT	EM	)	9	I	Y	i	y
1 0 1 0	LF	SUB	*	:	J	Z	j	z
1 0 1 1	VT	ESC	+	;	K	[	k	{
1 1 0 0	FF	FS	,	<	L	\	l	|
1 1 0 1	CR	GS	-	=	M	]	m	}
1 1 1 0	SO	RS	.	>	N	^	n	~
1 1 1 1	SI	US	/	?	O	_	o	DEL

This is the U.S. national version of CCITT International Alphabet Number 5 (T.50). The control characters are explained below and opposite.

Format Control

BS (Backspace): Indicates movement of the printing mechanism or display cursor backwards in one position.

HT (Horizontal Tab): Indicates movement of the printing mechanism or display cursor forward to the next preassigned "tab" or stopping position.

LF (Line Feed): Indicates movement of the printing mechanism or display cursor to the start of the next line.

VT (Vertical Tab): Indicates movement of the printing mechanism or display cursor to the next of a series of preassigned printing lines.

FF (Form Feed): Indicates movement of the printing mechanism or display cursor to the starting position of the next page, form, or screen.

CR (Carriage Return): Indicates movement of the printing mechanism or display cursor to the starting position of the same line.

TABLE 2.1 (continued)

Transmission Control

SOH (Start of Heading): Used to indicate the start of a heading which may contain address or routing information.

STX (Start of Text): Used to indicate the start of the text and so also indicates the end of the heading.

ETX (End of Text): Used to terminate the text which was started with STX.

EOT (End of Transmission): Indicates the end of a transmission which may have included one or more "texts" with their headings.

ENQ (Enquiry): A request for a response from a remote station. It may be used as a "WHO ARE YOU?" request for a station to identify itself.

ACK (Acknowledge): A character transmitted by a receiving device as an affirmation response to a sender. It is used as a positive response to polling messages.

NAK (Negative Acknowledgment): A character transmitted by a receiving device as a negative response to a sender. It is used as a negative response to polling messages.

SYN (Synchronous/Idle): Used by a synchronous transmission system to achieve synchronization. When no data is being sent a synchronous transmission system may send SYN characters continuously.

ETB (End of Transmission Block): Indicates the end of a block of data for communication purposes. It is used for blocking data where the block structure is not necessarily related to the processing format.

Information Separator

FS (File Separator):
GS (Group Separator):
RS (Record Separator):
US (United Separator):

Information separators to be used in an optional manner except that their hierarchy shall be FS (the most inclusive) to US (the least inclusive).

Miscellaneous

NUL (Null): No character. Used for filling in time or filling space on tape when there is no data.

BEL (Bell): Used when there is need to call human attention. It may control alarm or attention devices.

SO (Shift Out): Indicates that the code combinations which follow shall be interpreted as *outside* of the standard character set until a SHIFT IN character is reached.

SI (Shift In): Indicates that the code combinations which follow shall be interpreted according to the standard character set.

DEL (Delete): Used to obliterate unwanted characters (for example, on paper tape by punching a hole in *every* bit position).

SP (Space): A nonprinting character used to separate words, or to move the printing mechanism or display cursor forward by one position.

DLE (Data Link Escape): A character which shall change the meaning of one or more contiguously following characters. It can provide supplementary controls, or permits the sending of data characters having any bit combination.

DC1, DC2, DC3 and DC4 (Device Controls): Characters for the control of ancillary devices or special terminal features.

CAN (Cancel): Indicates that the data which precede it in a message or block should be disregarded (usually because an error has been detected).

EM (End of Medium): Indicates the physical end of a card, tape or other medium, or the end of the required or used portion of the medium.

SUB (Substitute): Substituted for a character that is found to be erroneous or invalid.

ESC (Escape): A character intended to provide code extension in that it gives a specified number of contiguously following characters an alternate meaning.

20 kHz, a much narrower bandwidth will produce acceptable voice reproduction. The standard spectrum for a voice signal is 300 to 3400 Hz. This is adequate for voice reproduction, minimizes required transmission capacity, and allows the use of rather inexpensive telephone sets. Thus the telephone transmitter converts the incoming acoustic voice signal into an electromagnetic signal over the range 300 to 3400 Hz. This signal is then transmitted through the telephone system to a receiver, which reproduces an acoustic signal from the incoming electromagnetic signal.

Now, let us look at the video signal, which, interestingly, consists of both analog and digital components. To produce a video signal, a TV camera, which performs similar functions to the TV receiver, is used. One component of the camera is a photosensitive plate, upon which a scene is optically focused. An electron beam sweeps across the plate from left to right and top to bottom, in the same fashion as depicted in Figure 2.11 for the receiver. As the beam sweeps, an analog electric signal is developed proportional to the brightness of the scene at a particular spot.

Now we are in a position to describe the video signal. Figure 2.12a shows three lines of a video signal; in this diagram, white is represented by a small positive voltage and black by a much larger positive voltage. So, for example, line 3 is at a medium gray level most of the way across with a blacker portion in the middle. Once the beam has completed a scan from left to right, it must retrace to the left edge to scan the next line. During this period, the picture should be blanked out (on both camera and receiver). This is done with a digital "horizontal blanking pulse." Also, to maintain transmitter–receiver synchronization, a synchronization (sync) pulse is sent between every line of video signal. This horizontal sync pulse rides on top of the blanking pulse, creating a staircase-shaped digital signal between adjacent analog video signals. Finally, when the beam reaches the bottom of the screen, it must return to the top, with a somewhat longer blanking interval required. This is shown in Figure 2.12b. The vertical blanking pulse is actually a series of synchronization and blanking pulses, whose details need not concern us here.

Next, consider the timing of the system. We mentioned that a total of 483 lines are scanned at a rate of 30 complete scans per second. This is an approximate number taking into account the time lost during the vertical retrace interval. The actual U.S. standard is 525 lines, but of these about 42 are lost during vertical retrace. Thus the horizontal scanning frequency is 525 lines $\div$ $\frac{1}{30}$ s/scan = 15,750 lines per second, or 63.5 μs/line. Of this 63.5 μs, about 11 μs are allowed for horizontal retrace, leaving a total of 52.5 μs per video line.

Finally, we are in a position to estimate the bandwidth required for the video signal. To do this we must estimate the upper (maximum) and lower (minimum) frequency of the band. We use the following reasoning to arrive at the maximum frequency: The maximum frequency would occur during the horizontal scan if the scene were alternating between black and white as rapidly as possible. We can estimate this maximum value by considering the resolution of the video image. In the vertical dimension, there are 483 lines, so the maxi-

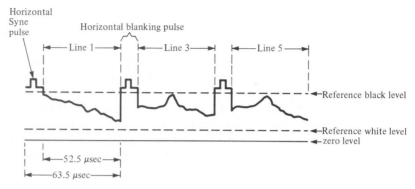

(a) Horizontal lines of video

(b) Vertical blanking signal

FIGURE 2.12. Video signal (different scales for a and b).

mum vertical resolution would be 483. Experiments have shown [CUNN80] that the actual subjective resolution is about 70 percent of that number, or about 338 lines. In the interest of a balanced picture, the horizontal and vertical resolutions should be about the same. Since the ratio of width to height of a TV screen is 4:3, the horizontal resolution should be about $\frac{4}{3} \times 338 = 450$ lines. As a worst case, a scanning line would be made up of 450 elements alternating black and white. The scan would result in a wave with each cycle of the wave consisting of one higher (black) and one lower (white) voltage level. Thus there would be $450/2 = 225$ cycles of the wave in 52.5 μs, for a maximum frequency of about 4 MHz. This rough reasoning, in fact, is fairly accurate. Thus the maximum frequency is 4 MHz. The lower limit will be a dc or zero frequency, where the dc component corresponds to the average illumination of the scene (the average value by which the signal exceeds the reference white level). Thus the bandwidth of the video signal is approximately 4 MHz − 0 = 4 MHz.

The foregoing discussion did not consider color or audio components of the signal. It turns out that, with these included, the bandwidth remains about 4 MHz.

Finally, the third example described above is the general case of binary digital data. A commonly used signal for such data uses two constant (dc) voltage levels, one level for binary 1 and one level for binary 0. (In Chapter 3, we shall see that this is but one alternative, referred to as NRZ.) Again, we are interested in the bandwidth of such a signal. This will depend, in any specific case, on the exact shape of the waveform and the sequence of 1's and 0's. We can obtain some understanding by considering Figure 2.9 (compare Figure 2.8). As can be seen, the greater the bandwidth of the signal, the more faithfully it approximates a digital pulse stream.

Data and Signals

In the foregoing discussion, we have looked at analog signals used to represent analog data and digital signals used to represent digital data. Generally, analog data are a function of time and occupy a limited frequency spectrum; such data can be represented by an electromagnetic signal occupying the same spectrum. Digital data can be represented by digital signals, with a different voltage level for each of the two binary digits.

As Figure 2.13 illustrates, these are not the only possibilities. Digital data can also be represented by analog signals by use of a *modem* (modulator/ demodulator). The modem converts a series of binary (two-valued) voltage pulses into an analog signal by encoding the digital data onto a *carrier frequency*. The resulting signal occupies a certain spectrum of frequency centered about the carrier and may be propagated across a medium suitable for that carrier. The most common modems represent digital data in the voice spectrum and hence allow those data to be propagated over ordinary voice-grade telephone lines. At the other end of the line, the modem demodulates the signal to recover the original data.

In an operation very similar to that performed by a modem, analog data can be represented by digital signals. The device that performs this function for voice data is a *codec* (coder-decoder). In essence, the codec takes an analog signal that directly represents the voice data and approximates that signal by a bit stream. At the receiving end, the bit stream is used to reconstruct the analog data.

Thus Figure 2.13 suggests that data may be encoded into signals in a variety of ways. We will return to this topic in Chapter 3.

Transmission

A final distinction remains to be made. Both analog and digital signals may be transmitted on suitable transmission media. The way these signals are treated is a function of the transmission system. Table 2.2 summarizes the methods of

FIGURE 2.13.   Analog and digital signaling of analog and digital data.

data transmission. *Analog transmission* is a means of transmitting analog signals without regard to their content; the signals may represent analog data (e.g., voice) or digital data (e.g., binary data that pass through a modem). In either case, the analog signal will become weaker (attenuate) after a certain distance. To achieve longer distances, the analog transmission system includes amplifiers that boost the energy in the signal. Unfortunately, the amplifier also boosts the noise components. With amplifiers cascaded to achieve long distances, the signal becomes more and more distorted. For analog data, such as voice, quite a bit of distortion can be tolerated and the data remain intelligible. However, for digital data, cascaded amplifiers will introduce errors.

TABLE 2.2 Analog and Digital Transmission

(a) Data and Signals

	Analog Signal	Digital Signal
Analog Data	Two alternatives: (1) signal occupies the same spectrum as the analog data; (2) analog data are encoded to occupy a different portion of spectrum.	Analog data are encoded using a codec to produce a digital bit stream.
Digital Data	Digital data are encoded using a modem to produce analog signal.	Two alternatives: (1) signal consists of two voltage levels to represent the two binary values; (2) digital data are encoded to produce a digital signal with desired properties.

(b) Treatment of Signals

	Analog Transmission	Digital Transmission
Analog Signal	Is propagated through amplifiers; same treatment whether signal is used to represent analog data or digital data.	Assumes that the analog signal represents digital data. Signal is propagated through repeaters; at each repeater, digital data are recovered from inbound signal and used to generate a new analog outbound signal.
Digital Signal	Not used	Digital signal represents a stream of 1s and 0s, which may represent digital data or may be an encoding of analog data. Signal is propagated through repeaters; at each repeater, stream of 1s and 0s is recovered from inbound signal and used to generate a new digital outbound signal.

Digital transmission, in contrast, is concerned with the content of the signal. A digital signal can be transmitted only a limited distance before attenuation endangers the integrity of the data. To achieve greater distances, repeaters are used. A repeater receives the digital signal, recovers the pattern of 1's and 0's, and retransmits a new signal. Thus the attenuation is overcome.

The same technique may be used with an analog signal if it is assumed that the signal carries digital data. At appropriately spaced points, the transmission system has repeaters rather than amplifiers. The repeater recovers the digital data from the analog signal and generates a new, clean analog signal. Thus noise is not cumulative.

The question naturally arises as to which is the preferred method of transmission. The answer being supplied by the telecommunications industry and its customers is digital, this despite an enormous investment in analog communications facilities. Both long-haul telecommunications facilities and intrabuilding services are gradually being converted to digital transmission and, where possible, digital signaling techniques. The most important reasons:

- *Digital technology:* The advent of large-scale integration (LSI) and very large-scale integration (VLSI) technology has caused a continuing drop in the cost and size of digital circuitry. Analog equipment has not shown a similar drop.
- *Data integrity:* With the use of repeaters rather than amplifiers, the effects of noise and other signal impairments are not cumulative. Thus it is possible to transmit data longer distances and over lesser quality lines by digital means while maintaining the integrity of the data. This is explored in Section 2.3.
- *Capacity utilization:* It has become economical to build transmission links of very high bandwidth, including satellite channels and optical fiber. A high degree of multiplexing is needed to effectively utilize such capacity, and this is more easily and cheaply achieved with digital (time-division) rather than analog (frequency-division) techniques. This is explored in Chapter 6.
- *Security and privacy:* Encryption techniques can be readily applied to digital data and to analog data that have been digitized.
- *Integration:* By treating both analog and digital data digitally, all signals have the same form and can be treated similarly. Thus economies of scale and convenience can be achieved by integrating voice, video, and digital data.

2.3

TRANSMISSION IMPAIRMENTS

With any communications system, it must be recognized that the signal that is received will differ from the signal that is transmitted due to various transmission impairments. For analog signals, these impairments introduce various random modifications that degrade the signal quality. For digital signals, bit errors are introduced: A binary 1 is transformed into a binary 0 and vice versa. In this section, we examine the various impairments and comment on their effect on the information-carrying capacity of a communication link; the next chapter looks at measures that can be taken to compensate for these impairments.

The most significant impairments are

- Attenuation and attenuation distortion.
- Delay distortion.
- Noise.

Attenuation

The strength of a signal falls off with distance over any transmission medium. For guided media, this reduction in strength, or attenuation, is generally logarithmic and thus is typically expressed as a constant number of decibels per unit distance. For unguided media, attenuation is a more complex function of distance and the makeup of the atmosphere. Attenuation introduces three considerations for the transmission engineer. First, a received signal must have sufficient strength so that the electronic circuitry in the receiver can detect and interpret the signal. Second, the signal must maintain a level sufficiently higher than noise to be received without error. Third, attenuation is an increasing function of frequency.

The first and second problems are dealt with by attention to signal strength and the use of amplifiers or repeaters. For a point-to-point link, the signal strength of the transmitter must be strong enough to be received intelligibly, but not so strong as to overload the circuitry of the transmitter, which would cause a distorted signal to be generated. Beyond a certain distance, the attenuation is unacceptably great, and repeaters or amplifiers are used to boost the signal from time to time. These problems are more complex for multipoint lines where the distance from transmitter to receiver is variable.

The third problem is particularly noticeable for analog signals. Because the attenuation varies as a function of frequency, the received signal is distorted, reducing intelligibility. To overcome this problem, techniques are available for equalizing attenuation across a band of frequencies. This is commonly done for voice-grade telephone lines by using loading coils that change the electrical properties of the line; the result is to smooth out attenuation effects. Another approach is to use amplifiers that amplify high frequencies more than lower frequencies.

An example is shown in Figure 2.14a, which shows attenuation as a function of frequency for a typical leased line. In the figure, attenuation is measured relative to the attenuation at 1000 Hz. Positive values on the y axis represent attenuation greater than that at 1000 Hz. A 1000-Hz tone of a given power level is applied to the input, and the power, P_{1000}, is measured at the output. For any other frequency f, the procedure is repeated and the relative attenuation in decibels is

$$N_f = -10 \log_{10} \frac{P_f}{P_{1000}}$$

The solid line in Figure 2.14a shows attenuation without equalization. As can be seen, frequency components at the upper end of the voice band are attenuated much more than those at lower frequencies. It should be clear that this will result in a distortion of the received speech signal. The dashed line shows the effect of equalization. The flattened response curve improves the quality of voice signals. It also allows higher data rates to be used for digital data that are passed through a modem.

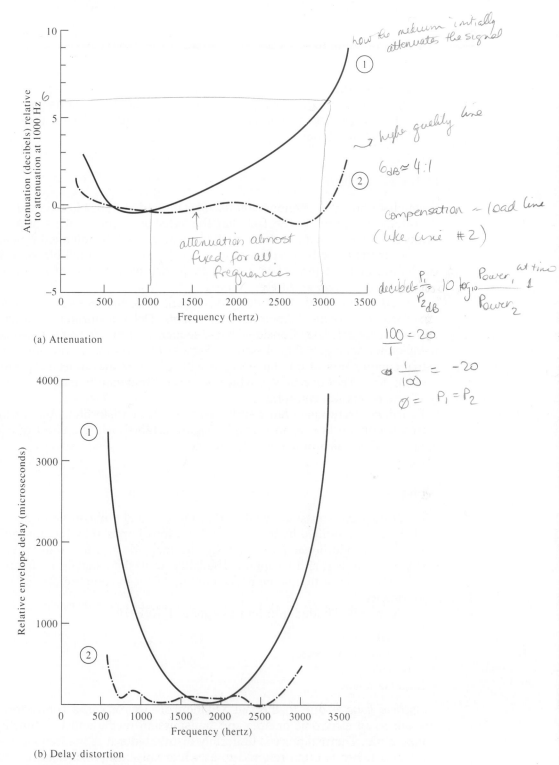

(a) Attenuation

(b) Delay distortion

FIGURE 2.14. Attenuation and delay distortion curves for a voice channel.

Handwritten annotations:

how the medium initially attenuates the signal

→ high quality line

$6_{dB} \approx 4:1$

compensation ~ load line (like line #2)

attenuation almost fixed for all frequencies

$decibel = \frac{P_1}{P_2}_{dB} = 10 \log_{10} \frac{Power, \ at \ time \ 1}{Power_2}$

$\frac{100}{1} = 20$

$\frac{1}{100} = -20$

$\emptyset = P_1 = P_2$

59

Attenuation distortion is much less of a problem with digital signals. As we have seen, the strength of a digital signal falls off rapidly with frequency (Figure 2.6b); most of the content is concentrated near the fundamental frequency or bit rate of the signal.

Delay Distortion

Delay distortion is a phenomenon peculiar to guided transmission media. The distortion is caused by the fact that the velocity of propagation of a signal through a guided medium varies with frequency. For a bandlimited signal, the velocity tends to be highest near the center frequency and fall off toward the two edges of the band. Thus various frequency components of a signal will arrive at the receiver at different times.

This effect is referred to as delay distortion, since the received signal is distorted due to variable delay in its components. Delay distortion is particularly critical for digital data. Consider that a sequence of bits is being transmitted, using either analog or digital signals. Because of delay distortion, some of the signal components of one bit position will spill over into other bit positions, causing *intersymbol interference,* which is a major limitation to maximum bit rate over a transmission control.

Equalizing techniques can also be used for delay distortion. Again using a leased telephone line as an example, Figure 2.14b shows the effect of equalization on delay as a function of frequency.

Noise

For any data transmission event, the received signal will consist of the transmitted signal, modified by the various distortions imposed by the transmission system, plus additional unwanted signals that are inserted somewhere between transmission and reception. The latter, undesired signals are referred to as noise. It is noise that is the major limiting factor in communications system performance.

Noise may be divided into four categories [FREE91]:

- Thermal noise.
- Intermodulation noise.
- Crosstalk.
- Impulse noise.

Thermal noise is due to thermal agitation of electrons in a conductor. It is present in all electronic devices and transmission media and is a function of temperature. Thermal noise is uniformly distributed across the frequency spectrum and hence is often referred to as white noise. Thermal noise cannot be eliminated and therefore places an upper bound on communications system performance. The amount of thermal noise to be found in a bandwidth of 1 Hz in any device or conductor is

$$N_0 = kT$$

where

N_0 = noise power density, watts/hertz
k = Boltzmann's constant = 1.3803×10^{-23} J/°K
T = temperature, degrees Kelvin

The noise is assumed to be independent of frequency. Thus the thermal noise in watts present in a bandwidth of W hertz can be expressed as

$$N = kTW$$

or, in decibel-watts:

$$N = 10 \log k + 10 \log T + 10 \log W$$
$$N = -228.6 \text{ dB W} + 10 \log T + 10 \log W$$

When signals at different frequencies share the same transmission medium, the result may be *intermodulation noise*. The effect of intermodulation noise is to produce signals at a frequency that is the sum or difference of the two original frequencies or multiples of those frequencies. For example, the mixing of signals at frequencies f_1 and f_2 might produce energy at the frequency $f_1 + f_2$. This derived signal could interfere with an intended signal at the frequency $f_1 + f_2$.

Intermodulation noise is produced when there is some *nonlinearity* in the transmitter, receiver, or intervening transmission system. Normally, these components behave as linear systems; that is, the output is equal to the input times a constant. In a nonlinear system, the output is a more complex function of the input. Such nonlinearity can be caused by component malfunction or the use of excessive signal strength. It is under these circumstances that the sum and difference terms occur.

Crosstalk has been experienced by anyone who, while using the telephone, has been able to hear another conversation; it is an unwanted coupling between signal paths. It can occur by electrical coupling between nearby twisted pair or, rarely, coax cable lines carrying multiple signals. Crosstalk can also occur when unwanted signals are picked up by microwave antennas; although highly directional, microwave energy does spread during propagation. Typically, crosstalk is of the same order of magnitude as, or less than, thermal noise.

All of the types of noise discussed so far have reasonably predictable and reasonably constant magnitudes. Thus it is possible to engineer a transmission system to cope with them. *Impulse noise*, however, is noncontinuous, consisting of irregular pulses or noise spikes of short duration and of relatively high amplitude. It is generated from a variety of causes, including external electromagnetic disturbances, such as lightning, and faults and flaws in the communications system.

Impulse noise is generally only a minor annoyance for analog data. For example, voice transmission may be corrupted by short clicks and crackles with no loss of intelligibility. However, impulse noise is the primary source of error in digital data communication. For example, a sharp spike of energy of 0.01 s duration would not destroy any voice data, but would wash out about 50 bits of data being transmitted at 4800 bps. Figure 2.15 is an example of the effect on a digital signal. Here the noise consists of a relatively modest level of thermal noise plus occasional spikes of impulse noise. The digital data are recovered from the signal by sampling the received waveform once per bit time. As can be seen, the noise is occasionally sufficient to change a 1 to a 0 or a 0 to a 1.

FIGURE 2.15.   Effect of noise on a digital signal.

Channel Capacity

We have seen that there are a variety of impairments that distort or corrupt a signal. For digital data, the question that then arises is to what extent these impairments limit the data rate that can be achieved. The rate at which data can be transmitted over a given communication path, or channel, under given conditions, is referred to as the *channel capacity*.

There are four concepts here that we are trying to relate to one another.

- *Data rate:* This is the rate, in bits per second (bps), at which data can be communicated.
- *Bandwidth:* This is the bandwidth of the transmitted signal as constrained by the transmitter and the nature of the transmission medium, expressed in cycles per second, or hertz.
- *Noise:* The average level of noise over the communications path.
- *Error rate:* The rate at which errors occur, where an error is the reception of a 1 when a 0 was transmitted or the reception of a 0 when a 1 was transmitted.

The problem we are addressing is this: Communications facilities are expensive and, in general, the greater the bandwidth of a facility, the greater the cost. Furthermore, all transmission channels of any practical interest are of limited bandwidth. The limitations arise from the physical properties of the transmission medium or from deliberate limitations at the transmitter on the bandwidth to prevent interference from other sources. Accordingly, we would like to make as efficient use as possible of a given bandwidth. For digital data, this means that we would like to get as high a data rate as possible at a particular limit of error rate for a given bandwidth. The main constraint on achieving this efficiency is noise.

To begin, let us consider the case of a channel that is noise-free. In this environment, the limitation on data rate is simply the bandwidth of the signal. A formulation of this limitation, due to Nyquist, states that if the rate of signal transmission is $2W$, then a signal with frequencies no greater than W is sufficient to carry the data rate. The converse is also true: Given a bandwidth of W, the highest signal rate that can be carried is $2W$. This limitation is due to the effect of intersymbol interference [FREE91], such as is produced by delay distortion. The result is useful in the development of digital-to-analog encoding schemes and is derived in Appendix 3A.

Note that in the last paragraph, we referred to signal rate. If the signals to be transmitted are binary (two voltage levels), then the data rate that can be supported by W Hz is $2W$ bps. As an example, consider a voice channel being used, via modem, to transmit digital data. Assume a bandwidth of 3100 Hz. Then the capacity, C, of the channel is $2W = 6200$ bps. However, as we shall see in Chapter 3, signals with more than two levels can be used; that is, each signal element can represent more than one bit. For example, if four possible voltage levels are used as signals, then each signal element can represent two bits. With multilevel signaling, the Nyquist formulation becomes

$$C = 2W \log_2 M$$

where M is the number of discrete signal or voltage levels. Thus, for $M = 8$, a value used with some modems, C becomes 18,600 bps.

So, for a given bandwidth, the data rate can be increased by increasing the number of different signals. However, this places an increased burden on the receiver: Instead of distinguishing one of two possible signals during each signal time, it must distinguish one of M possible signals. Noise and other impairments on the transmission line will limit the practical value of M.

Thus, all other things being equal, doubling the bandwidth doubles the data rate. Now consider the relationship between data rate, noise, and error rate. This can be explained intuitively by again considering Figure 2.15. The presence of noise can corrupt one or more bits. If the data rate is increased, then the bits become "shorter" so that more bits are affected by a given pattern of noise. Thus, at a given noise level, the higher the data rate, the higher the error rate.

All of these concepts can be tied together neatly in a formula developed by the mathematician Claude Shannon. As we have just illustrated, the higher the data rate, the more damage that unwanted noise can do. For a given level of noise, we would expect that a greater signal strength would improve the ability to correctly receive data in the presence of noise. The key parameter involved in this reasoning is the signal-to-noise ratio (S/N), which is the ratio of the power in a signal to the power contained in the noise that is present at a particular point in the transmission. Typically, this ratio is measured at a receiver, since it is at this point that an attempt is made to process the signal and eliminate the unwanted noise. For convenience, this ratio is often reported in decibels:

$$(S/N)_{dB} = 10 \log \frac{\text{signal power}}{\text{noise power}}$$

This expresses the amount, in decibels, that the intended signal exceeds the noise level. A high S/N will mean a high-quality signal and a low number of required intermediate repeaters.

The signal-to-noise ratio is important in the transmission of digital data because it sets the upper bound on the achievable data rate. Shannon's result is that the maximum channel capacity, in bits per second, obeys the equation

$$C = W \log_2 \left(1 + \frac{S}{N}\right)$$

where C is the capacity of the channel in bits per second and W is the bandwidth of the channel in hertz. As an example, consider a voice channel being used, via modem, to transmit digital data. Assume a bandwidth of 3100 Hz. A typical value of S/N for a voice-grade line is 30 dB, or a ratio of 1000:1. Thus

$$C = 3100 \log_2(1 + 1000)$$
$$= 30{,}894 \text{ bps}$$

This represents the theoretical maximum that can be achieved. In practice, however, only much lower rates are achieved. One reason for this is that the formula assumes white noise (thermal noise). Impulse noise is not accounted for, nor are attenuation or delay distortion.

The capacity indicated in the preceding equation is referred to as the error-free capacity. Shannon proved that if the actual information rate on a channel is less than the error-free capacity, then it is theoretically possible to use a suitable signal code to achieve error-free transmission through the channel. Shannon's theorem unfortunately does not suggest a means for finding such codes, but it does provide a yardstick by which the performance of practical communication schemes may be measured.

The measure of efficiency of a digital transmission is the ratio of C/W, which is the bps per hertz that is achieved. Figure 2.16 illustrates the theoretical efficiency of a transmission. It also shows the actual results obtained on a typical voice-grade line.

Several other observations concerning the above equation may be instructive. For a given level of noise, it would appear that the data rate could be increased by increasing either signal strength or bandwidth. However, as the signal strength increases, so do nonlinearities in the system, leading to an in-

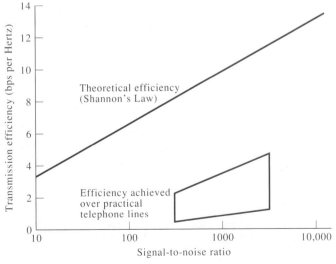

FIGURE 2.16.   Theoretical and actual transmission efficiency.

crease in intermodulation noise. Note also that, since noise is assumed to be white, the wider the bandwidth, the more noise is admitted to the system. Thus, as W increases, S/N decreases.

Finally, we mention a parameter related to S/N that is more convenient for determining digital data rates and error rates. The parameter is the ratio of signal energy per bit to noise power density per hertz, E_b/N_0. Consider a signal, digital or analog, that contains binary digital data transmitted at a certain bit rate R. Recalling that 1 W = 1 J/s, the energy per bit in a signal is given by $E_b = ST_b$, where S is the signal power and T_b is the time required to send one bit. The data rate R is just $R = 1/T_b$. Thus

$$\frac{E_b}{N_0} = \frac{S/R}{N_0} = \frac{S}{kTR}$$

or, in decibel notation,

$$\frac{E_b}{N_0} = S - 10 \log R + 228.6 \text{ dBW} - 10 \log T$$

The ratio E_b/N_0 is important because the bit error rate for digital data is a (decreasing) function of this ratio. Given a value of E_b/N_0 needed to achieve a desired error rate, the parameters in the preceding formula may be selected. Note that as the bit rate R increases, the transmitted signal power, relative to noise, must increase to maintain the required E_b/N_0.

Let us try to grasp this result intuitively by considering again Figure 2.15. The signal here is digital, but the reasoning would be the same for an analog signal. In several instances, the noise is sufficient to alter the value of a bit. Now, if the data rate were doubled, the bits would be more tightly packed together, and the same passage of noise might destroy two bits. Thus, for constant signal and noise strength, an increase in data rate increases the error rate.

Example

For binary phase-shift keying (defined in Chapter 3), $E_b/N_0 = 8.4$ dB is required for a bit error rate of 10^{-4} (probability of error = 10^{-4}). If the effective noise temperature is 290°K (room temperature) and the data rate is 2400 bps, what received signal level is required?

We have

$$8.4 = S(\text{dBW}) - 10 \log 2400 + 228.6 \text{ dBW} - 10 \log 290$$
$$= S(\text{dBW}) - (10)(3.38) + 228.6 - (10)(2.46)$$
$$S = -161.8 \text{ dBW} \qquad \blacksquare$$

2.4

TRANSMISSION MEDIA

The transmission medium is the physical path between transmitter and receiver in a data transmission system. The characteristics and quality of data transmission are determined both by the nature of the signal and the nature of the medium. In the case of guided media, the medium itself is more important in determining the limitations of transmission. Table 2.3 contains typical characteristics for guided media, including the total data rate that the medium can support, the bandwidth the medium can transmit, and the required repeater spacing for digital transmission.

For unguided media, the spectrum or frequency band of the signal produced by the transmitting antenna is more important than the medium in determining transmission characteristics. As we have already mentioned, the higher the center frequency of a signal, the greater the potential bandwidth and hence data rate. Another property of signals transmitted by antenna is *directionality*. In general, at lower frequencies signals are omnidirectional; that is, the signal propagates in all directions from the antenna. At higher frequencies, it is possible to focus the signal into a directional beam.

Two general ranges of frequencies are of interest in this discussion. Microwave frequencies cover a range of about 2 to 40 GHz. At these frequencies, highly directional beams are possible, and microwave is quite suitable for point-to-point transmission. We will refer to signals in the range 30 MHz to 1 GHz as radio waves. Omnidirectional transmission is used and signals at these frequencies are suitable for broadcast applications.

The reader should also be aware of a finer subdivision of the electromagnetic spectrum defined by the International Telecommunications Union and shown in Table 2.4. The table also summarizes key characteristics of each band. Microwave covers part of the UHF and all of the SHF bands, and radio covers the VHF and part of the UHF band. Note that this is a restricted use of the term "radio" that is appropriate for the concerns of this book.

Figure 2.17 depicts the electromagnetic spectrum and indicates the frequencies at which various guided media and unguided transmission techniques operate. In the remainder of this section we examine the three most important

TABLE 2.3   Point-to-Point Transmission Characteristics of Guided Media

Transmission Medium	Total Data Rate	Bandwidth	Repeater Spacing
Twisted pair	4 Mbps	250 kHz	2–10 km
Coaxial cable	500 Mbps	350 MHz	1–10 km
Optical fiber	2 Gbps	2 GHz	10–100 km

TABLE 2.4 Characteristics of Unguided Communications Bands

Frequency Band	Name	Analog Data		Digital Data		Principal Applications
		Modulation	Bandwidth	Modulation	Data Rate	
30 – 300 kHz	LF (low frequency)	Generally not practical		ASK, FSK, MSK	0.1 – 100 bps	Navigation
300 – 3000 kHz	MF (medium frequency)	AM	To 4 kHz	ASK, FSK, MSK	10 – 1000 bps	Commercial AM radio
3 – 30 MHz	HF (high frequency)	AM, SSB	To 4 kHz	ASK, FSK, MSK	10 – 3000 bps	Shortwave radio CB radio
30 – 300 MHz	VHF (very high frequency)	AM, SSB; FM	5 kHz to 5 MHz	FSK, PSK	To 100 kbps	VHF television FM radio
300 – 3000 MHz	UHF (ultra high frequency)	FM, SSB	To 20 MHz	PSK	To 10 Mbps	UHF television Terrestrial microwave
3 – 30 GHz	SHF (super high frequency)	FM	To 500 MHz	PSK	To 100 Mbps	Terrestrial microwave Satellite microwave
30 – 300 GHz	EHF (extremely high frequency)	FM	To 1 GHz	PSK	To 750 Mbps	Experimental short point-to-point

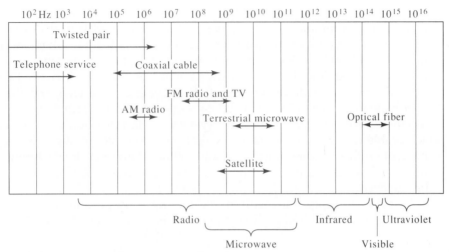

FIGURE 2.17. The electromagnetic spectrum.

guided media—twisted pair, coaxial cable, and optical fiber—as well as the three most important unguided transmission techniques—terrestrial and satellite microwave, and radio. In all cases, we describe the systems physically, then briefly discuss applications, and finally look at transmission characteristics.

Twisted Pair

Physical Description

A twisted pair consists of two insulated copper wires arranged in a regular spiral pattern. A wire pair acts as a single communication link. Typically, a number of these pairs are bundled together into a cable by wrapping them in a tough protective sheath. Over longer distances, cables may contain hundreds of pairs. The twisting of the individual pairs minimizes electromagnetic interference between the pairs. The wires in a pair have thicknesses of from 0.016 to 0.036 in.

Uses

By far the most common transmission medium for both analog and digital data is twisted pair. It is the backbone of the telephone system as well as the workhorse for intrabuilding communications.

In the telephone system, individual telephone sets are connected to the local telephone exchange or "end office" by twisted-pair wire. These are referred to as "local loops." Within an office building, telephone service is often provided by means of a private branch exchange (PBX). The PBX will be discussed in detail in Chapter 8. Essentially, it is an on-premise telephone exchange system that services a number of telephones within a building. It provides for intra-building calls via extension numbers and outside calls by trunk connection to the local end office. Within the building, the telephones are connected to the PBX via twisted pair. For both of the systems just described, twisted pair has primarily been a medium for voice traffic between subscribers and their local telephone exchange office. Digital data traffic can also be carried over moderate distances. For modern digital PBX systems, data rates of about 64 kbps are achievable using digital signaling. Local loop connections typically require a modem, with a maximum data rate of 9600 bps. However, twisted pair is used for long-distance trunking applications and data rates of 4 Mbps or more may be achieved.

Twisted pair is also the medium of choice for a low-cost microcomputer local network within a building. This application is discussed in Chapter 11.

Transmission Characteristics

Wire pairs may be used to transmit both analog and digital signals. For analog signals, amplifiers are required about every 5 to 6 km. For digital signals, repeaters are used every 2 or 3 km.

Compared to other transmission media, twisted pair is limited in distance, bandwidth, and data rate. Figure 2.18 shows that the attenuation for twisted

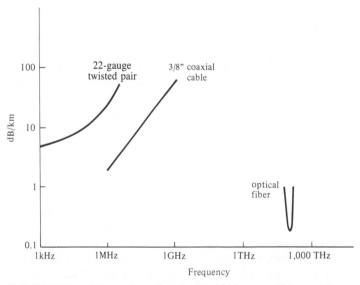

FIGURE 2.18.   Attenuation of typical guided transmission media.

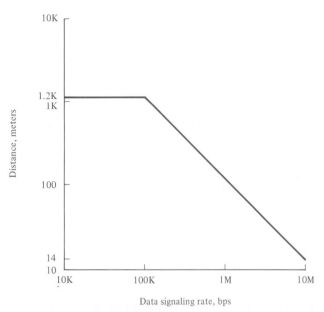

FIGURE 2.19. Twisted-pair cable length vs. data rate for balanced transmission (RS-422).

pair is a very strong function of frequency [FREE91]. Other impairments are also severe for twisted pair. The medium is quite susceptible to interference and noise because of its easy coupling with electromagnetic fields. For example, a wire run parallel to an ac power line will pick up 60-Hz energy. Impulse noise also easily intrudes into twisted pair.

Several measures are taken to reduce impairments. Shielding the wire with metallic braid or sheathing reduces interference. The twisting of the wire reduces low-frequency interference, and the use of different twist lengths in adjacent pairs reduces crosstalk. Another technique is the use of a balanced transmission line. With an unbalanced line, one wire is at ground potential; with balanced transmission, both wires are above ground potential, carrying signals with equal amplitude but opposite phase.

For point-to-point analog signaling, a bandwidth of up to about 250 kHz is possible. For voice transmission, such as the local loop, the attenuation is about 1 dB/km over the voice frequency range. A common standard for telephone lines is a maximum loss of 6 dB; hence a 6-km section of line represents an upper limit on the distance that can be covered. For digital point-to-point lines, data rates of up to a few Mbps are possible. Figure 2.19 shows the achievable data rate versus distance for a common balanced electrical signaling technique, the EIA standard RS-422.

Coaxial Cable

Physical Description

Coaxial cable, like twisted pair, consists of two conductors, but it is constructed differently to permit it to operate over a wider range of frequencies (Figure 2.20). It consists of a hollow outer cylindrical conductor which surrounds a single inner wire conductor. The inner conductor can be either solid or stranded; the outer conductor can be either solid or braided. The inner conductor is held in place by either regularly spaced insulating rings or a solid dielectric material. The outer conductor is covered with a jacket or shield. A single coaxial cable has a diameter of from 0.4 to about 1 in.

Uses

Coaxial cable has been perhaps the most versatile transmission medium and is enjoying increasing utilization in a wide variety of applications. The most important of these are

- Long-distance telephone and television transmission.
- Television distribution.

(a) Insulating beads

(b) Solid dielectric

FIGURE 2.20.   Coaxial cable construction.

- Local area networks.
- Short-run system links.

Coaxial cable has been an important part of the long-distance telephone network, although it is being rapidly supplanted by optical fiber, microwave, and satellite. Using frequency-division multiplexing (FDM, see Chapter 6), a coaxial cable can carry over 10,000 voice channels simultaneously. Cable is also used for long-distance television transmission.

Coaxial cable is also spreading rapidly as a means of distributing TV signals to individual homes—cable TV. From its modest beginnings as Community Antenna Television (CATV), designed to provide service to remote areas, cable TV will eventually reach almost as many homes as the telephone. A CATV system can carry dozens of TV channels at ranges up to a few tens of miles.

An equally explosive growth area for coaxial cable is local area networks (Chapter 11). It is the medium of choice for many local network systems. Coaxial cable can support a large number of devices with a variety of data and traffic types, over distances that encompass a single building or a complex of buildings.

Finally, coaxial cable is commonly used for short-range connections between devices. Using analog signaling, coaxial cable is used to transmit radio or TV signals. With digital signaling, coaxial cable can be used to provide high-speed I/O channels on computer systems.

Transmission Characteristics

Coaxial cable is used to transmit both analog and digital signals. Long-distance systems may be either analog or digital. CATV is analog, and both analog and digital techniques have been used for local networks.

As can be seen from Figure 2.18, coaxial cable has superior frequency characteristics to twisted pair, and can hence be used effectively at higher frequencies and data rates. Because of its shielded, concentric construction, coaxial cable is much less susceptible to interference and crosstalk than twisted pair. The principal constraints on performance are attenuation, thermal noise, and intermodulation noise. The latter is present only when several channels (FDM) or frequency bandwidths are in use on the cable.

Figure 2.21 is an instructive look at the engineering constraints faced in transmission systems. To achieve proper signal quality, a certain signal-to-noise (S/N) ratio must be maintained on the cable. The engineer has two variables to play with: signal power and amplifier spacing. The S/N can be raised by spacing amplifiers closely to boost the signal frequently. However, it is desirable to maximize amplifier spacing to reduce cost and because amplifiers introduce nonlinearities. S/N can be increased, of course, by boosting S. This will work, however, only in a region of operation where the dominant noise source is thermal noise, which is relatively constant independent of the signal. When a number of signals in adjacent bandwidths are being carried on the

(a) Dependence of T1 SNR on signal power and amplifier spacing for systems using 0.375-in cables. The bandwidth occupied by each channel is 1.5 MHz. System length is 20 mi.

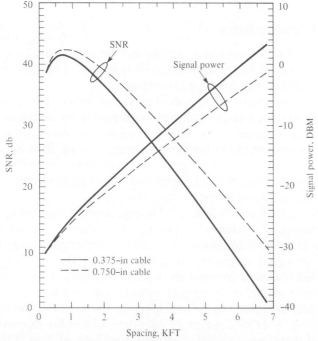

(b) Maximum attainable SNR and the corresponding signal power as a function of spacing. The bandwidth for each channel is 1.5 MHz.

FIGURE 2.21. Dependence of S/N on signal power and amplifier spacing for coaxial cable.

cable, intermodulation noise increases as signal power increases. This phenomenon is seen clearly in Figure 2.21. Figure 2.21b is derived from 2.21a, and shows that, as the spacing between amplifiers increases, the maximum attainable S/N declines and, further, that increasing signal power is required to achieve the maximum.

For long-distance transmission of analog signals, amplifiers are needed every few kilometers, with closer spacing required if higher frequencies are used. The usable spectrum for analog signaling extends to about 400 MHz. For digital signaling, repeaters are needed every kilometer or so, with closer spacing needed for higher data rates. On experimental systems, data rates as high as 800 Mbps have been achieved with a repeater spacing of 1.6 km [KASA83].

Optical Fiber

Physical Description

An optical fiber is a thin (2 to 125 μm), flexible medium capable of conducting an optical ray. Various glasses and plastics can be used to make optical fibers [JORD85]. The lowest losses have been obtained using fibers of ultrapure fused silica. Ultrapure fiber is difficult to manufacture; higher-loss multicomponent glass fibers are more economical and still provide good performance. Plastic fiber is even less costly and can be used for short-haul links, for which moderately high losses are acceptable.

An optical fiber cable has a cylindrical shape and consists of three concentric sections: the core, the cladding, and the jacket. The *core* is the innermost section and consists of one or more very thin strands, or fibers, made of glass or plastic. Each fiber is surrounded by its own *cladding*, a glass or plastic coating that has optical properties different from those of the core. The outermost layer, surrounding one or a bundle of cladded fibers, is the *jacket*. The jacket is composed of plastic and other materials layered to protect against moisture, abrasion, crushing, and other environmental dangers.

Uses

One of the most significant technological breakthroughs in data transmission has been the development of practical fiber optic communications systems. The following characteristics distinguish optical fiber from twisted pair and coaxial cable.

- *Greater bandwidth:* The potential bandwidth, and hence data rate, of a medium increases with frequency. At the immense frequencies of optical fiber, data rates of 2 Gbps over tens of kilometers have been demonstrated. Compare this to the practical maximum of hundreds of Mbps over about 1 km for coaxial cable and just a few Mbps over 1 km for twisted pair.
- *Smaller size and lighter weight:* Optical fibers are considerably thinner than coaxial cable or bundled twisted-pair cable—at least an order of magnitude

thinner for comparable information transmission capacity. For cramped conduits in buildings and underground along public rights-of-way, the advantage of small size is considerable. The corresponding reduction in weight reduces structural support requirements.

- *Lower attenuation:* Attenuation is significantly lower for optical fiber than for coaxial cable or twisted pair (Figure 2.18), and is constant over a wide range.
- *Electromagnetic isolation:* Optical fiber systems are not affected by external electromagnetic fields. Thus the system is not vulnerable to interference, impulse noise, or crosstalk. By the same token, fibers do not radiate energy, causing little interference with other equipment and providing a high degree of security from eavesdropping. In addition, fiber is inherently difficult to tap.
- *Greater repeater spacing:* Fewer repeaters means lower cost and fewer sources of error. The performance of optical fiber systems from this point of view has been steadily improving. For example, Standard Elektrik Lorenz AG in Germany has developed a fiber transmission system that achieves a data rate of 5 Gbps over a distance of 111 km [ANON88] without repeaters. Coaxial and twisted-pair systems generally have repeaters every few kilometers.

Five basic categories of application have become important for optical fiber:

- Long-haul trunks.
- Metropolitan trunks.
- Rural exchange trunks.
- Local loops.
- Local area networks.

Long-haul fiber transmission is becoming increasingly common in the telephone network. Long-haul routes average about 900 miles in length and offer high capacity (typically 20,000 to 60,000 voice channels). These systems compete economically with microwave and have so underpriced coaxial cable in many developed countries that coaxial cable is rapidly being phased out of the telephone network in such countries. US Sprint, one of the major long-distance telephone communications providers, was the first to use optical fiber for 100 percent of its traffic, and the percentage of traffic carried by fiber is increasing steadily for all other U.S carriers.

Metropolitan trunking circuits have an average length of 7.8 miles and may have as many as 100,000 voice channels in a trunk group. Most facilities are installed in underground conduits and are repeaterless, joining telephone exchanges in a metropolitan or city area. Included in this category are routes that link long-haul microwave facilities that terminate at a city perimeter to the main telephone exchange building downtown.

Rural exchange trunks have circuit lengths ranging from 25 to 100 miles and link towns and villages. In the United States, they often connect the exchanges of different telephone companies. Most of these systems have fewer than 5000 voice channels. The technology used in these applications competes with microwave facilities.

Local loop circuits are fibers that run directly from the central exchange to a subscriber. These facilities are beginning to displace twisted pair and coaxial cable links as the telephone networks evolve into full-service networks capable of handling not only voice and data, but also image and video. The initial penetration of optical fiber in this application is for the business subscriber, but fiber transmission into the home will soon begin to appear [SHUM89].

A final important application of optical fiber is for local area networks. Recently, standards have been developed and products introduced for optical fiber networks that have a total capacity of 100 Mbps and can support hundreds or even thousands of stations in a large office building or a complex of buildings [MIER89].

The advantages of optical fiber over twisted pair and coaxial cable become more compelling as the demand for all types of information (voice, data, image, video) increases. By the end of the century, fiber will be the dominant medium for virtually all fixed-location applications [COCH88].

Transmission Characteristics

Optical fiber transmits a signal-encoded beam of light by means of total internal reflection. Total internal reflection can occur in any transparent medium that has a higher index of refraction than the surrounding medium. In effect, the optical fiber acts as a waveguide for frequencies in the range 10^{14} to 10^{15} Hz, which covers the visible spectrum and part of the infrared spectrum.

Figure 2.22a shows the principle of optical fiber transmission. Light from a source enters the cylindrical glass or plastic core. Rays at shallow angles are reflected and propagated along the fiber; other rays are absorbed by the surrounding material. This form of propagation is called multimode, referring to the variety of angles that will reflect. When a fiber core radius is reduced, fewer angles will reflect. By reducing the radius of the core to the order of a wavelength, only a single angle or mode can pass: the axial ray. This single-mode propagation provides superior performance for the following reason. With multimode transmission, multiple propagation paths exist, each with a different path length and hence time to traverse the fiber. This causes signal elements to spread out in time and limits the rate at which data can be accurately received. Since there is a single transmission path with single-mode transmission, such distortion cannot occur. Finally, by varying the index of refraction of the core, a third type of transmission, known as multimode graded index, is possible. This type is intermediate between the other two in characteristics. The variable refraction has the effect of focusing the rays more efficiently than ordinary multimode, also known as multimode step index. Table 2.5 compares the three fiber transmission modes.

Two different types of light source are used in fiber optic systems: the *light-emitting diode* (LED) and the *injection laser diode* (ILD) [WERN86]. Both are semiconductor devices that emit a beam of light when a voltage is applied. The LED is less costly, operates over a greater temperature range, and has a longer operational life. The ILD is more efficient and can sustain greater data rates.

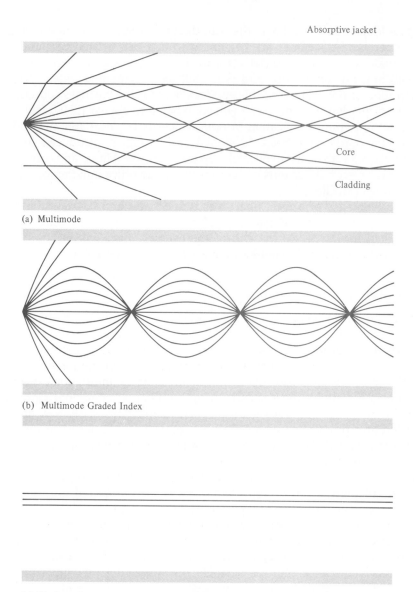

(a) Multimode

(b) Multimode Graded Index

(c) Single mode

FIGURE 2.22.   Optical fiber transmission modes.

The detector used at the receiving end to convert the light into electrical energy is a *photodiode* [FORR86]. Two solid-state devices have been used: the PIN detector and the APD detector. The PIN photodiode has a segment of intrinsic (I) silicon between the P and N layers of a diode. The APD, avalanche photodiode, is similar in appearance but uses a stronger electric field. Both

TABLE 2.5   Comparison of Three Types of Optical Fiber

Light Source	LED or laser	LED or laser	Laser
Bandwidth	20 MHz/km	>1 GHz/km	up to 1000 GHz/km
Splicing	Difficult	Difficult	Difficult
Typical Application	Computer data links, local area networks	Moderate-length telephone lines	Long-distance telecommunication lines
Cost	Least expensive	More expensive	Most expensive
Core Diameter (μm)	>80 μm	50 – 60 μm	1.5 – 5 μm
Cladding Diameter (μm)	>160 μm	100 – 120 μm	15 – 50 μm
Attenuation (dB/km)	0.5 – 2.0	0.5 – 2.0	0.15

Source: [BASC87].

devices are basically photon counters. The PIN is less expensive and less sensitive than the APD.

There is a relationship among the wavelength employed, the type of transmission, and the achievable data rate [MIER86]. Both single mode and multimode can support several different wavelengths of light and can employ laser or LED light sources. In optical fiber, light propagates best in three distinct wavelength "windows," centered on 850, 1300, and 1500 nanometers (nm). These are all in the infrared portion of the frequency spectrum, below the visible-light portion, which is 400 to 700 nm. Most local applications today use 850-nm LED light sources. Although this combination is relatively inexpensive, it is generally limited to data rates under 100 Mbps and distances of a few kilometers. To achieve higher data rates and longer distances, a 1300-nm LED or laser source is needed. The highest data rates and longest distances require 1500-nm laser sources.

The amplitude-shift keying technique is commonly used to transmit digital data over optical fiber; in this context, it is known as *intensity modulation*. For LED transmitters, binary one is represented by a short pulse of light and binary zero by the absence of light. Laser transmitters normally have a fixed "bias" current that causes the device to emit a low light level. This low level represents binary zero, while a higher-amplitude lightwave represents binary one.

Terrestrial Microwave

Physical Description

The most common type of microwave antenna is the parabolic "dish." A typical size is about 10 ft in diameter. The antenna is fixed rigidly and focuses a narrow beam to achieve line-of-sight transmission to the receiving antenna. Microwave antennas are usually located at substantial heights above ground level in order to extend the range between antennas and to be able to transmit over intervening obstacles. With no intervening obstacles, the maximum distance between antennas conforms to

$$d = 7.14 \sqrt{Kh} \tag{2.1}$$

where d is the distance between antennas in kilometers, h is the antenna height in meters, and K is an adjustment factor to account for the fact that microwaves are bent or refracted with the curvature of the earth and will hence propagate farther than the optical line of sight. A good rule of thumb is $K = \frac{4}{3}$ [FREE80]. So, for example, two microwave antennas at a height of 100 m may be as far as $7.14 \times \sqrt{133} = 82$ km apart. To achieve long-distance transmission, a series of microwave relay towers is used, and point-to-point microwave links are strung together over the desired distance.

Uses

The primary use for terrestrial microwave systems is in long-haul telecommunications service, as an alternative to coaxial cable for transmitting television and voice. Like coaxial cable, microwave can support high data rates over long distances. The microwave facility requires far fewer amplifiers or repeaters than coaxial cable for the same distance, but requires line-of-sight transmission. Microwave is commonly used for both voice and television transmission.

Another increasingly common use of microwave is for short point-to-point links between buildings [RUSH82]. This can be used for closed-circuit TV or as a data link between local networks.

Finally, a potential use for terrestrial microwave is for providing digital data transmission in small regions (radius <10 km). This concept has been termed "local data distribution" and would provide an alternative to phone lines for digital networking [ROCH79].

Transmission Characteristics

As Table 2.4 indicates, microwave transmission covers a substantial portion of the spectrum. Common frequencies used for transmission are in the range 2 to 40 GHz. The higher the frequency used, the higher the potential bandwidth and therefore the higher the potential data rate. Table 2.6 indicates bandwidth and data rate for some typical systems.

TABLE 2.6   Typical Digital Microwave Performance

Band (GHz)	Bandwidth (MHz)	Data Rate (Mbps)
2	7	12
6	30	90
11	40	90
18	220	274

Source: [PICK83a].

As with any transmission system, a main source of loss for microwave is attenuation. For microwave (and radio frequency), the loss can be expressed as

$$L = 10 \log \left(\frac{4\pi d}{\lambda}\right)^2 \text{ dB} \tag{2-2}$$

where d is the distance and λ is the wavelength, in the same units. Thus loss varies as the square of the distance. This is in contrast to twisted pair and coaxial cable where the loss varies logarithmically with distance (linear in decibels). Thus repeaters or amplifiers may be placed farther apart for microwave systems—10 to 100 km is typical. Attenuation is increased with rainfall. The effects become noticeable above 10 GHz.

Another source of impairment for microwave is interference. With the growing popularity of microwave, transmission areas overlap and interference is always a danger. Thus the assignment of frequency bands is strictly regulated.

Table 2.7 shows the authorized microwave frequency bands as regulated by the FCC. The most common bands for common carrier long-haul communications are the 4-GHz and 6-GHz bands. With increasing congestion at these frequencies, the 11-GHz band is now coming into use. The 12-GHz band is used as a component of the cable TV system [CUNN80]. Microwave links are used to provide TV signals to local CATV installations; the signals are then distributed to individual subscribers via coaxial cable. The FCC has reserved the 10-GHz band for local data distribution, called the Digital Termination Service. Finally, we mention that higher-frequency microwave is being used for short point-to-point links between buildings [RUSH82]. Typically, the 22-GHz band is used. The higher microwave frequencies are less useful for longer distance because of increased attenuation, but are quite adequate for shorter distances. In addition, at the higher frequencies, antennas are smaller and cheaper.

Satellite Microwave

Physical Description

A communication satellite is, in effect, a microwave relay station. It is used to link two or more ground-based microwave transmitter/receivers, known as earth stations or ground stations. The satellite receives transmissions on one frequency band (uplink), amplifies (analog transmission) or repeats (digital transmission) the signal, and transmits it on another frequency (downlink). A single orbiting satellite will operate on a number of frequency bands, called *transponder channels*, or simply *transponders*.

Figure 2.23 depicts in a general way two common uses of communications satellites. In the first, the satellite is being used to provide a point-to-point link between two distant ground-based antennas. In the second, the satellite provides communication between one ground-based transmitter and a number of ground-based receivers.

TABLE 2.7   Principal Microwave Bands Authorized for Fixed Telecommunications in the United States (1979)

Band Name	Range (GHz)	Maximum Channel Bandwidth (MHz)	Necessary Spectral Efficiency (bits/Hz)	Type of Service
2 GHz	1.71 – 1.85	—		Federal government
2 GHz	1.85 – 1.99	8		Private; local government
2 GHz	2.11 – 2.13	3.5	2	Common carrier (shared)
2 GHz	2.13 – 2.15	0.8/1.6		Private; local government
2 GHz	2.15 – 2.16	10		Private; multipoint
2 GHz	2.16 – 2.18	3.5	2	Common carrier
2 GHz	2.18 – 2.20	0.8/1.6		Private; local government
2 GHz	2.20 – 2.29	—		Federal government
2 GHz	2.45 – 2.50	0.8		Private; local government (shared)
4 GHz	3.70 – 4.20	20	4.5	Common carrier; satellite
6 GHz	5.925 – 6.425	30	3	Common carrier; satellite
6 GHz	6.525 – 6.875	5/10		Private; shared
7–8 GHz	7.125 – 8.40	—		Federal government
10 GHz	10.550 – 10.680	25		Private
11 GHz	10.7 – 11.7	50	2.25	Common carrier
12 GHz	12.2 – 12.7	10/20		Private; local government
13 GHz	13.2 – 13.25	25		Common carrier; private
14 GHz	14.4 – 15.25	—		Federal government
18 GHz	17.7 – 19.7	220		Common carrier; shared
18 GHz	18.36 – 19.04	50/100		Private; local government
22 GHz	21.2 – 23.6	50/100		Private; common carrier
31 GHz	31.0 – 31.2	50/100		Private; common carrier
38 GHz	36.0 – 38.6	—		Federal government
40 GHz	38.6 – 40.0	50		Private; common carrier
	Above 40.0	—		Developmental

For a communication satellite to function effectively, it is generally required that it remain stationary with respect to its position over the earth. Otherwise, it would not be within the line of sight of its earth stations at all times. To remain stationary, the satellite must have a period of rotation equal to the earth's period of rotation. This match occurs at a height of 35,784 km.

Two satellites using the same frequency band, if close enough together, will interfere with each other. To avoid this, current standards require a 4° spacing (angular displacement as measured from the earth) in the 4/6-GHz band, and a 3° spacing at 12/14 GHz. Thus, the number of possible satellites is quite limited.

Uses

The communication satellite is a technological revolution as important as fiber optics [CROC89]. Among the most important applications for satellites are

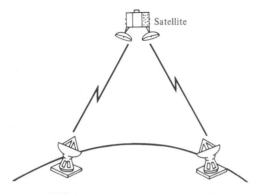

(a) Point–to–point link via satellite microwave

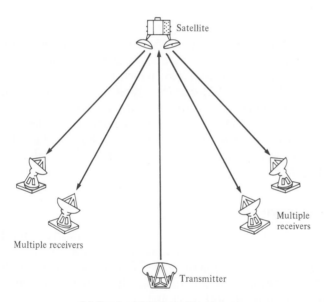

(b) Broadcast link via satellite microwave

FIGURE 2.23.   Satellite communications configurations.

- Television distribution.
- Long-distance telephone transmission.
- Private business networks.

Because of their broadcast nature, satellites are well suited to television distribution and are being used extensively in the United States and throughout the world for this purpose. In its traditional use, a network provides programming from a central location. Programs are transmitted to the satellite and then broadcast down to a number of stations, which then distribute the programs to individual viewers. One network, the Public Broadcasting Service (PBS), distributes its television programming almost exclusively by the use of satellite channels. Other commercial networks also make substantial use of satellite, and cable television systems are receiving an ever-increasing proportion of their programming from satellites. The most recent application of satellite technology to television distribution is direct broadcast satellite (DBS), in which satellite video signals are transmitted directly to the home user. The dropping cost and size of receiving antennas have made DBS economically feasible, and a number of channels are either already in service or in the planning stage.

Satellite transmission is also used for point-to-point trunks between telephone exchange offices in public telephone networks. It is the optimum medium for high-usage international trunks and is competitive with terrestrial systems for many long-distance international links.

Finally, there are a number of business data applications for satellite. The satellite provider can divide the total capacity into a number of channels and lease these channels to individual business users. A user equipped with the antennas at a number of sites can use a satellite channel for a private network. Traditionally, such applications have been quite expensive and limited to larger organizations with high-volume requirements. A recent development is the very small aperture terminal (VSAT) system, which provides a low-cost alternative [FINN89, SHAR89]. Figure 2.24 depicts a typical VSAT configuration. A number of subscriber stations are equipped with low-cost VSAT antennas (about $400 per month per VSAT). Using some discipline, these stations share a satellite transmission capacity for transmission to a hub station. The hub station can exchange messages with each of the subscribers and can relay messages between subscribers.

Transmission Characteristics

The optimum frequency range for satellite transmission is in the range 1 to 10 GHz [SHAR87]. Below 1 GHz, there is significant noise from natural sources, including galactic, solar, and atmospheric noise, and human-made interference from various electronic devices. Above 10 GHz, the signal is severely attenuated by atmospheric absorption and precipitation.

Most satellites providing point-to-point service today use a frequency bandwidth in the range 5.925 to 6.425 GHz for transmission from earth to satellite (uplink) and a bandwidth in the range 3.7 to 4.2 GHz for transmission from satellite to earth (downlink). This combination is referred to as the 4/6 GHz band, or C band. Note that the uplink and downlink frequencies differ. For continuous operation without interference, a satellite cannot transmit and receive on the same frequency. Thus signals received from a ground station on one frequency must be transmitted back on another.

The C band is within the optimum zone of 1 to 10 GHz but has become saturated. Other frequencies in that range are unavailable because of sources of interference operating at those frequencies, usually terrestrial microwave. Therefore, the 12/14 GHz band, or Ku band, has been developed (uplink: 14 to

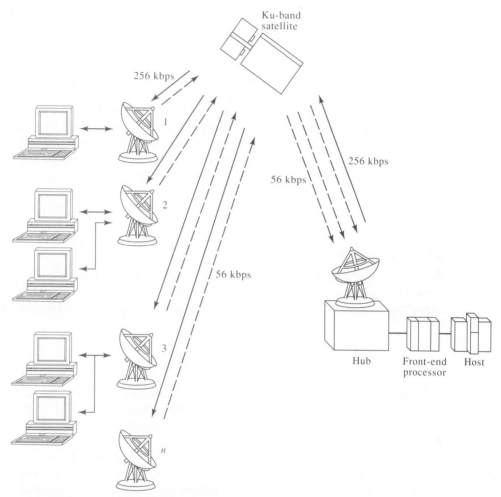

FIGURE 2.24. VSAT configuration.

14.5 GHz; downlink: 11.7 to 12.2 GHz). At this frequency band, attenuation problems must be overcome. Thus, relative to C band, the Ku band systems require higher uplink and downlink radiated power and greater transponder receiver sensitivity. However, smaller and cheaper earth-station receivers can be used. Ku band is particularly well-suited for VSAT applications, although C band is also used for this purpose.

A new development is the use of the satellite for mobile communications. For this purpose, small, low-cost transmitter/receiver devices are used, and transmission is full-duplex directly between the users and the satellite. The service offered is similar to cellular radio, except that the coverage is nationwide. To enable this service, the Federal Communications Commission has recently allocated a portion of the microwave frequency band, known as the L band, for mobile satellite service [CAST88]. The frequencies involved are 1.6465 GHz to 1.66 GHz uplink and 1.545 GHz to 1.5585 GHz downlink.

Several peculiar properties of satellite communications should be noted. First, because of the long distance involved, there is a propagation delay of about 240 to 300 ms from transmission from one earth station to reception by another earth station. This delay is noticeable in ordinary telephone conversations. It also introduces problems in the areas of error control and flow control, which we discuss in later chapters. Second, satellite microwave is inherently a broadcast medium. Many stations can transmit to the satellite, and a transmission from a satellite can be received by many stations.

Radio

Physical Description

The principal difference between radio and microwave is that radio is omnidirectional and microwave is focused. Thus radio does not require dish-shaped antennas, and the antennas need not be rigidly mounted to a precise alignment.

Uses

Radio is a general term sometimes used to encompass all the frequency bands of Table 2.4. We use it in a more restricted sense to cover the VHF and part of the UHF band: 30 MHz to 1 GHz. This range covers FM radio and UHF and VHF television. In addition to these traditional uses, new applications have grown up in this band, and we mention several of these briefly.

A well-known use of radio for digital data communications is packet radio, which is discussed in Chapter 10. A packet radio system uses ground-based antennas to link multiple sites in a data transmission network.

Transmission Characteristics

The range 30 MHz to 1 GHz is a very effective one for broadcast communications. Unlike the case for lower-frequency electromagnetic waves, the ionosphere is transparent to radio waves above 30 MHz. Thus transmission is limited to the line of sight and distant transmitters will not interfere with each other due to reflection from the atmosphere. Unlike the higher frequencies of the microwave region, radio waves are less sensitive to attenuation from rainfall. For digital data communications, the primary drawback of this frequency range is that lower data rates are achievable: in the kilobit rather than the megabit range.

As a line-of-sight propagation technique, radio obeys Equation (2.1); that is, the maximum distance between transmitter and receiver is slightly more than the optical line of sight, or $7.14\sqrt{Kh}$. As with microwave, the amount of atten-

uation due simply to distance obeys Equation (2-2), namely $10 \log \left(\dfrac{4\pi d}{\lambda}\right)^2$ dB.

Because of the longer wavelength, radio waves suffer relatively less attenuation.

A prime source of impairment for radio waves is multipath interference. Reflection from land, water, and natural or human-made objects can create multiple paths between antennas. This effect is frequently evident when TV reception displays multiple images as a plane passes by.

The transmission characteristics of radio used for broadcast communications are straightforward. The first such system was the ALOHA system in Hawaii [ABRA70]. Two frequency bands were used, one at 407.35 MHz for transmitting from users' terminals to a central controller and one at 413.475 MHz for transmission in the opposite direction; the bandwidth on both channels was 100kHz, with the data rate of 9600 bps. Transmission is in the form of short bursts of data called packets. The point-to-point range is about 30 km; repeaters were used to extend the system to a radius of about 500 km. A similar system is in operation in Montreal [ROUL81] using frequencies in the 220-MHz range. A system with mobile stations has been developed by the Printer Terminal Corp. [FORB81] using frequencies between 450 and 510 MHz.

2.5

RECOMMENDED READING

Detailed descriptions of the transmission characteristics of the transmission media discussed in this chapter can be found in [FREE91]. An in-depth treatment is offered in the three-volume [BELL90]. A number of books provide detailed coverage of optical fiber transmission. Two that can be recommended are [GREE93] and [ZANG91]. Mathematical treatments of signal transmission are provided in [COUC90] and [GIBS89].

2.6

PROBLEMS

2.1 **a.** For the multipoint configuration of Figure 2.1, only one device at a time can transmit. Why?

b. There are two methods of enforcing the rule that only one device can transmit. In the centralized method, one station is in control and can either transmit or allow a specified other station to transmit. In the decentralized method, the stations jointly cooperate in taking turns. What do you see as the advantages and disadvantages of the two methods?

2.2 Figure 2.6b shows the frequency domain function for a single square pulse. The single pulse could represent a digital 1 in a communication system. Note that an infinite number of higher frequencies of decreasing magnitudes are needed to represent the single pulse. What implication does that have for a real digital transmission system?

2.3 Suppose that data are stored on 800 kbyte floppy diskettes that weigh 1 oz each. Suppose that a Boeing 747 carries 10 tons of these floppies at a speed of 600 mph over a distance of 3000 miles. What is the data transmission rate in bits per second of this system?

2.4 ASCII is a 7-bit code that allows 128 characters to be defined. In the 1970s, many newspapers received stories from the wire services in a 6-bit code called TTS. This code carried upper and lower case characters as well as many special characters and formatting commands. The typical TTS character set allowed over 100 characters to be defined. How do you think this could be accomplished?

2.5 Figure 2.12 indicates that the vertical blanking pulse has a duration of 830 to 1330 μs. What is the total number of visible lines for each of these two figures?

2.6 For a video signal, what increase in horizontal resolution is possible if a bandwidth of 5 MHz is used? What increase in vertical resolution is possible? Treat the two questions separately; that is, the increased bandwidth is to be used to increase either horizontal or vertical resolution, but not both.

2.7 **a.** Suppose that a digitized TV picture is to be transmitted from a source that uses a matrix of 480×500 picture elements (pixels), where each pixel can take on one of 32 intensity values. Assume that 30 pictures are sent per second. (This digital source is roughly equivalent to broadcast TV standards that have been adopted.) Find the source rate R (bps).

    b. Assume that the TV picture is to be transmitted over a channel with 4.5-MHz bandwidth and a 35-dB signal-to-noise ratio. Find the capacity of the channel (bps).

    c. Discuss how the parameters given in part (a) could be modified to allow transmission of color TV signals without increasing the required value for R.

2.8 Figure 2.5 shows the effect of eliminating higher-harmonic components of a square wave and retaining only a few lower harmonic components. What would the signal look like in the opposite case; that is, retaining all higher harmonics and eliminating a few lower harmonics?

2.9 What is the channel capacity for a teleprinter channel with a 300-Hz bandwidth and a signal-to-noise ratio of 3 dB?

2.10 A digital signaling system is required to operate at 9600 bps.

    a. If a signal element encodes a 4-bit word, what is the minimum required bandwidth of the channel?

    b. Repeat part (a) for the case of 8-bit words.

2.11 What is the thermal noise level of a channel with a bandwidth of 10 kHz carrying 1000 watts of power operating at 50° C?

2.12 Study the works of Shannon and Nyquist on channel capacity. Each places an upper limit on the bit rate of a channel based on two different approaches. How are the two related?

2.13 Given a channel with an intended capacity of 20 Mbps. The bandwidth of the channel is 3 MHz. What signal to noise ratio is required in order to achieve this capacity?

2.14 Explain the logical flaw in the following argument.

According to Table 2.3, a twisted pair can carry a digital data rate of 4 Mbps. Home computers can use a modem with the telephone network to communicate with other computers. The telephone outlet is connected to the central exchange by a local loop, which is a twisted pair. It is very difficult to establish communication by this method at a data rate higher than 9600 bps. This is much lower than 4 Mbps. Therefore, a mistake must have been made in Table 2.3.

2.15 The square wave of Figure 2.8c, with $T = 1$ msec, is passed through a low-pass filter that passes frequencies up to 8 kHz with no attenuation.
a. Find the power in the output waveform.
b. Assuming that at the filter input there is a thermal noise voltage with $N_0 = 0.1$ μWatt/Hz, find the output signal to noise ratio in dB.

2.16 A twisted-pair cable is approximated as a filter with the characteristics shown in the following figure:

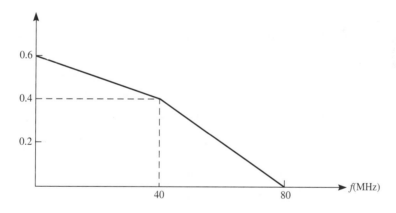

The figure shows the amount of attenuation of the signal as a function of frequency. Assuming that a square wave signal, such as Figure 2.8c with $T = 0.1$ μsec and $A = \pi/4$ is fed to the cable, find the sine wave components, with their magnitudes, that would appear at the output.

2.17 A telephone line with a bandwidth of 100 KHz is known to have a loss of 20 dB. The input signal power is measured as 0.5 watt, and the output signal noise level is measured at 2.5 μwatt. Using this information, calculate the output signal to noise ratio in dB.

$KHz = 10^3 Hz$

$\mu = 10^{-6}$

2.18 A transmitter–receiver pair is connected with a coaxial cable. The signal power measured at the receiver is 0.1 watt. Signal levels change 1000 times per second. Noise energy is 0.05 μJoules for every 1 millisecond. If $E_b/N_0 = 10$ dB is desired, determine how many levels must be accommodated in the signal to encode the bits. What would be the bit rate?

2.19 A 0.375-inch diameter coaxial cable connects a transmitter–receiver pair that is 5000 feet apart. What is the maximum attainable SNR at this distance and what signal power level is needed for this purpose? Assuming a loss of 0.01 dB/foot, what transmitter power is required to achieve the desired SNR?

2.20 Given a 100-watt power source, what is the maximum allowable length for the following transmission media if a signal of 1 watt is to be received?
   a. 22-gauge twisted pair operating at 1 kHz
   b. 22-gauge twisted pair operating at 1 MHz
   c. $\frac{3}{8}''$ coaxial cable operating at 1 MHz
   d. $\frac{3}{8}''$ coaxial cable operating at 1 GHz
   e. optical fiber operating at its optimal frequency

2.21 Coaxial cable is a two-wire transmission system. What is the advantage in connecting the outer conductor to ground?

2.22 The relationship between frequency f and wavelength λ is $\lambda f = c$, where c is the speed of light (3×10^8 m/s). Determine the wavelength ranges for the frequency bands of Table 2.4.

2.23 If an amplifier has a 30-dB gain, what voltage ratio does the gain represent?

2.24 An amplifier has an output of 20 W. What is its output in dBW?

2.25 A periodic bandlimited signal has only three frequency components: dc, 100 Hz, and 200 Hz. In sine-cosine form:

$$x(t) = 12 + 15 \cos 200\pi t + 20 \sin 200\pi t \\ - 5 \cos 400\pi t - 12 \sin 400\pi t$$

Express the signal in amplitude/phase form.

APPENDIX 2A

Fourier Analysis

2A.1 Fourier Series Representation of Periodic Signals

With the aid of a good table of integrals, it is a remarkably simple task to determine the frequency-domain nature of many signals. We begin with periodic signals. Any periodic signal can be represented as a sum of sinusoids, known as a Fourier series:

$$x(t) = \sum_{n=0}^{\infty} a_n \cos(2\pi n f_0 t) + \sum_{n=1}^{\infty} b_n \sin (2\pi n f_0 t)$$

where f_0 is the inverse of the period of the signal ($f_0 = 1/T$). The frequency of f_0 is referred to as the *fundamental frequency*; multiples of f_0 are referred to as *harmonics*. Thus a periodic signal with period T consists of the fundamental frequency $f_0 = 1/T$ plus harmonics of that frequency. If $a_0 \neq 0$, then $x(t)$ has an additional *dc component*.

The values of the coefficients are calculated as follows:

$$a_0 = \frac{1}{T} \int_0^T x(t)dt$$

$$a_n = \frac{2}{T} \int_0^T x(t)\cos(2\pi nf_0t) \, dt$$

$$b_n = \frac{2}{T} \int_0^T x(t)\sin(2\pi nf_0t) \, dt$$

This form of representation, known as the *sine-cosine representation*, is the easiest form to compute, but suffers from the fact that there are two components at each frequency. A more meaningful representation, the *amplitude-phase representation*, takes the form

$$x(t) = c_0 + \sum_{n=1}^{\infty} c_n \cos(2\pi nf_0t + \theta_n)$$

This relates to the earlier representation as follows:

$$c_0 = a_0$$

$$c_n = \sqrt{a_n^2 + b_n^2}$$

$$\theta_n = -\tan^{-1}\left(\frac{b_n}{a_n}\right)$$

Examples of the Fourier series for periodic signals are shown in Figure 2.25.

2A.2   Fourier Transform Representation of Aperiodic Signals

For a periodic signal, we have seen that its spectrum consists of discrete frequency components, at the fundamental frequency and its harmonics. For an aperiodic signal, the spectrum consists of a continuum of frequencies. This spectrum can be defined by the Fourier transform. For a signal $x(t)$ with a spectrum $X(f)$, the following relationships hold:

$$x(t) = \int_{-\infty}^{\infty} X(f)e^{j2\pi ft}df$$

$$X(f) = \int_{-\infty}^{\infty} x(t)e^{-j2\pi ft}dt$$

Figure 2.26 presents some examples of Fourier transform pairs.

Fourier series

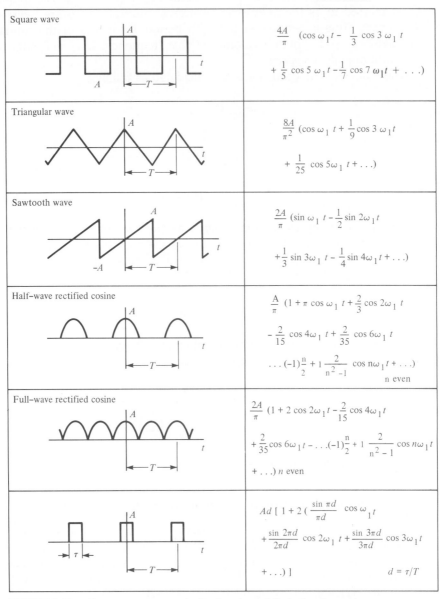

Square wave	$\dfrac{4A}{\pi}$ $(\cos \omega_1 t - \dfrac{1}{3} \cos 3 \omega_1 t$ $+ \dfrac{1}{5} \cos 5 \omega_1 t - \dfrac{1}{7} \cos 7 \omega_1 t + \ldots)$

FIGURE 2.25. Some common periodic signals and their Fourier series.

2A.3 Power Spectral Density and Bandwidth

The absolute bandwidth of any time-limited signal is infinite. In practical terms, however, most of the power in a signal will be concentrated in some finite band, and the effective bandwidth will consist of that portion of the spec-

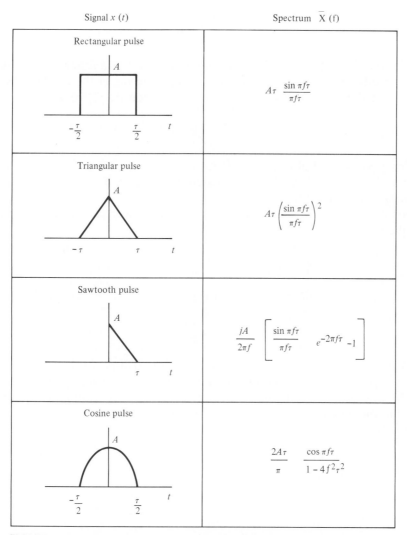

Signal $x(t)$ Spectrum $\bar{X}(f)$

Rectangular pulse

$$A\tau \; \frac{\sin \pi f \tau}{\pi f \tau}$$

Triangular pulse

$$A\tau \left(\frac{\sin \pi f \tau}{\pi f \tau} \right)^2$$

Sawtooth pulse

$$\frac{jA}{2\pi f} \left[\frac{\sin \pi f \tau}{\pi f \tau} \; e^{-2\pi f \tau} - 1 \right]$$

Cosine pulse

$$\frac{2A\tau}{\pi} \; \frac{\cos \pi f \tau}{1 - 4f^2 \tau^2}$$

FIGURE 2.26. Some common signals and their Fourier transforms.

trum that contains most of the power. To make this concept precise, we need to define the power spectral density.

First, we observe the power in the time domain. A function $x(t)$ usually specifies a signal in terms of either voltage or current. In either case, the instantaneous power in the signal is proportional to $|x(t)|^2$. We define the average power of a time-limited signal as

$$P = \frac{1}{t_2 - t_1} \int_{t_1}^{t_2} |x(t)|^2 \, dt$$

For a periodic signal the average power in one period is

$$P = \frac{1}{T} \int_0^T |x(t)|^2 \, dt$$

We would like to know the distribution of power as a function of frequency. For periodic signals, this is easily expressed in terms of the coefficients of the exponential Fourier series. The power spectral density $S(f)$ obeys

$$S(f) = \sum_{n=-\infty}^{\infty} |X_n|^2 \, \delta \, (f - nf_0)$$

The power spectral density $S(f)$ for aperiodic functions is more difficult to define. In essence, it is obtained by defining a "period" T_0 and allowing T_0 to increase without limit.

For a continuous valued function $S(f)$, the power contained in a band of frequencies, $f_1 < f < f_2$, is

$$P = 2 \int_{f_2}^{f_1} S(f) \, df$$

For a periodic waveform, the power through the first j harmonics is

$$P = \tfrac{1}{2} \sum_{n=0}^{2} |C_n|^2$$

With these concepts, we can now define the half-power bandwidth, which is perhaps the most common bandwidth definition. The half-power bandwidth is the interval between frequencies at which $S(f)$ has dropped to half of its maximum value of power, or 3 dB below the peak value.

CHAPTER 3

Data Encoding

In Chapter 2 a distinction was made between analog and digital *data* and analog and digital *signals*. Figure 2.12 suggested that either form of data could be encoded into either form of signal.

Figure 3.1 is another depiction that emphasizes the process involved. For digital signaling, a data source $g(t)$, which may be either digital or analog, is encoded into a digital signal $x(t)$. The actual form of $x(t)$ depends on the encoding technique, and is chosen to optimize use of the transmission medium. For example, the encoding may be chosen to conserve bandwidth or to minimize errors.

The basis for analog signaling is a continuous constant-frequency signal known as the carrier signal. The frequency of the carrier signal is chosen to be compatible with the transmission medium being used. Data may be transmitted using a carrier signal by *modulation*. Modulation is the process of encoding source data onto a *carrier signal* with frequency f_c. All modulation techniques involve operation on one or more of the three fundamental frequency-domain parameters:

- Amplitude.
- Frequency.
- Phase.

The input signal $m(t)$ may be analog or digital and is called the *modulating signal* or *baseband signal*. The result of modulating the carrier signal is called the *modulated signal* $s(t)$. As Figure 3.1b indicates, $s(t)$ is a bandlimited (bandpass) signal. The location of the bandwidth on the spectrum is related to f_c and is often centered on f_c. Again, the actual form of the encoding is chosen to optimize some characteristic of the transmission.

Each of the four possible combinations depicted in Figure 3.1 is in widespread use. The reasons for choosing a particular combination for any given communication task vary. We list here some representative reasons:

- *Digital data, digital signal:* In general, the equipment for encoding digital data into a digital signal is less complex and less expensive than digital-to-analog modulation equipment.

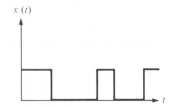

(a) Encoding onto a digital signal

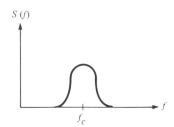

(b) Modulation onto an analog signal

FIGURE 3.1.   Encoding and modulation techniques.

- *Analog data, digital signal:* Conversion of analog data to digital form permits the use of modern digital transmission and switching equipment. The advantages of the digital approach were outlined in Section 2.2.
- *Digital data, analog signal:* Some transmission media, such as optical fiber and the unguided media, will only propagate analog signals.
- *Analog data, analog signal:* Analog data in electrical form can be transmitted as baseband signals easily and cheaply. This is done with voice transmission over voice-grade lines. One common use of modulation is to shift the bandwidth of a baseband signal to another portion of the spectrum. In this way multiple signals, each at a different position on the spectrum, can share the same transmission medium. This is known as frequency-division multiplexing.

We now examine the techniques involved in each of these four combinations.

3.1

DIGITAL DATA, DIGITAL SIGNALS

A digital signal is a sequence of discrete, discontinuous voltage pulses. Each pulse is a *signal element*. Binary data are transmitted by encoding each data bit into signal elements. In the simplest case, there is a one-to-one correspondence between bits and signal elements. An example is shown in Figure 2.15, in which binary 0 is represented by a lower voltage level and binary 1 by a higher voltage level. As we shall see in this section, a variety of other encoding schemes are also used.

First, we define some terms. If the signal elements all have the same algebraic sign, that is, all positive or negative, then the signal is *unipolar*. In *polar* signaling, one logic state is represented by a positive voltage level, and the other by a negative voltage level. The *data signaling rate*, or just *data rate*, of a signal is the rate, in bits per second, that data are transmitted. The *duration* or length of a bit is the amount of time it takes for the transmitter to emit the bit; for a data rate R, the bit duration is $1/R$. The *modulation rate*, in contrast, is the rate at which signal level is changed. This will depend on the nature of the digital encoding, as explained below. The modulation rate is expressed in *bauds*, which means signal elements per second. Finally, the terms *mark* and *space*, for historical reasons, refer to the binary digits 1 and 0, respectively.

The tasks involved in interpreting digital signals at the receiver can be summarized by again referring to Figure 2.15. First, the receiver must know the timing of each bit. That is, the receiver must know with some accuracy when a bit begins and ends. Second, the receiver must determine whether the signal level for each bit position is high (1) or low (0). In Figure 2.15, these tasks are performed by sampling each bit position in the middle of the interval and comparing the value to a threshold. Because of noise and other impairments, there will be errors, as shown.

What factors determine how successful the receiver will be in interpreting the incoming signal? We saw in Chapter 2 that three factors are important: the signal-to-noise ratio (or, better, E_b/N_0), the data rate, and the bandwidth. With other factors held constant, the following statements are true:

- An increase in data rate increases bit error rate (the probability that a bit is received in error).
- An increase in S/N decreases bit error rate.
- An increase in bandwidth allows an increase in data rate.

There is another factor that can be used to improve performance, and that is the encoding scheme. The encoding scheme is simply the mapping from data bits to signal elements. A variety of approaches have been tried. In what follows, we describe some of the more common ones; they are defined in Table 3.1 and depicted in Figure 3.2.

Before describing these techniques, let us consider the ways of evaluating or comparing the various techniques. [LIND73] lists five evaluation factors:

- *Signal spectrum:* Several aspects of the signal spectrum are important. A lack of high-frequency components means that less bandwidth is required for transmission. In addition, lack of a direct-current (dc) component is also desirable. With a dc component to the signal, there must be direct physical attachment of transmission components; with no dc component, ac-coupling

TABLE 3.1   Definition of Digital Signal Encoding Formats

Nonreturn-to-Zero-Level (NRZ-L)   *– not good synch*
  0 = high level
  1 = low level
Nonreturn to Zero Inverted (NRZI)
  0 = no transition at beginning of interval (one bit time)
  1 = transition at beginning of interval
Bipolar-AMI   *Alternate Mark Inversion*
  0 = no line signal
  1 = positive or negative level, alternating for successive ones
Pseudoternary
  0 = positive or negative level, alternating for successive zeros
  1 = no line signal
Manchester
  0 = transition from high to low in middle of interval
  1 = transition from low to high in middle of interval
Differential Manchester
  Always a transition in middle of interval
  0 = transition at beginning of interval
  1 = no transition at beginning of interval
B8ZS
  Same as bipolar AMI, except that any string of eight zeros is replaced by a string with
    two code violations
HDB3
  Same as bipolar AMI, except that any string of four zeros is replaced by a string with
    one code violation

[handwritten margin notes: "differential", "non differential", "LANS", "0=1 (=1)", "at least one transition per bit (synch.)"]

via transformer is possible. This provides excellent electrical isolation, reducing interference. Finally, the magnitude of the effects of signal distortion and interference depend on the spectral properties of the transmitted signal. In practice, it usually happens that the transfer function of a channel is worse near the band edges. Therefore, a good signal design should concentrate the transmitted power in the middle of the transmission bandwidth. In such a case, a smaller distortion should be present in the received signal. To meet this objective, codes can be designed with the aim of shaping the spectrum of the transmitted signal.

- *Clocking:* We mentioned the need to determine the beginning and end of each bit position. This is no easy task. One rather expensive approach is to provide a separate clock lead to synchronize the transmitter and receiver. The alternative is to provide some synchronization mechanism that is based on the transmitted signal. This can be achieved with suitable encoding.
- *Error detection:* We will discuss various error-detection techniques in Chapter 4, and show in Chapter 5 that these are the responsibility of a layer of logic above the signaling level that is known as data link control. However, it is useful to have some error detection capability built into the physical signaling encoding scheme. This permits errors to be detected more quickly.

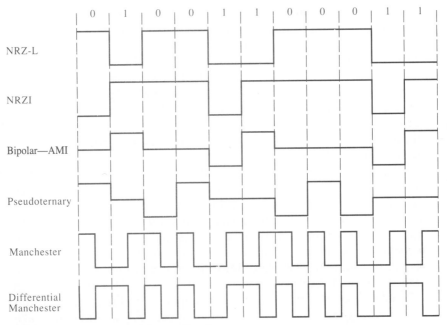

FIGURE 3.2.   Digital signal encoding formats.

- *Signal interference and noise immunity:* Certain codes exhibit superior performance in the presence of noise. This is usually expressed in terms of a bit error rate.
- *Cost and complexity:* Although digital logic continues to drop in price, this factor should not be ignored. In particular, the higher the signaling rate to achieve a given data rate, the greater the cost. We will see that some codes require a signaling rate that is in fact greater than the actual data rate.

We now turn to a discussion of various techniques.

Nonreturn to Zero (NRZ)

The most common, and easiest, way to transmit digital signals is to use two different voltage levels for the two binary digits. Codes that follow this strategy share the property that the voltage level is constant during a bit interval; there is no transition (no return to a zero voltage level). For example, the absence of voltage can be used to represent binary 0, with a constant positive voltage used to represent binary 1. More commonly, a negative voltage is used to represent one binary value and a positive voltage is used to represent the other. This latter code, known as **Nonreturn-to-Zero-Level** (NRZ-L), is illustrated[1] in

---

[1]In this figure, a negative voltage is equated with binary 1 and a positive voltage with binary 0. This is the opposite of the definition used in virtually all other textbooks. However, there is no "standard" definition of NRZ-L, and the definition here conforms to the use of NRZ-L in data communications interfaces and the standards that govern those interfaces.

Figure 3.2. NRZ-L is generally the code used to generate or interpret digital data by terminals and other devices. If a different code is to be used for transmission, it is typically generated from an NRZ-L signal by the transmission system (in terms of Figure 1.1, NRZ-L is $g(t)$ and the encoded signal is $s(t)$).

A variation of NRZ is known as **NRZI** (Nonreturn to Zero, invert on ones). As with NRZ-L, NRZI maintains a constant voltage pulse for the duration of a bit time. The data themselves are encoded as the presence or absence of a signal transition at the beginning of the bit time. A transition (low-to-high or high-to-low) at the beginning of a bit time denotes a binary 1 for that bit time; no transition indicates a binary 0.

NRZI is an example of **differential encoding.** In differential encoding, the signal is decoded by comparing the polarity of adjacent signal elements rather than determining the absolute value of a signal element. One benefit of this scheme is that it may be more reliable to detect a transition in the presence of noise than to compare a value to a threshold. Another benefit is that with a complex transmission layout, it is easy to lose the sense of the polarity of the signal. For example, on a multidrop twisted-pair line, if the leads from an attached device to the twisted pair are accidentally inverted, all 1's and 0's for NRZ-L will be inverted. This cannot happen with differential encoding.

The NRZ codes are the easiest to engineer and, in addition, make efficient use of bandwidth. This latter property is illustrated in Figure 3.3, which compares the spectral density of various encoding schemes. In the figure, fre-

FIGURE 3.3.   Spectral density of various signal encoding schemes.

quency is normalized to the data rate. As can be seen, most of the energy in NRZ and NRZI signals is between dc and half the bit rate. For example, if an NRZ code is used to generate a signal with data rate of 9600 bps, most of the energy in the signal is concentrated between dc and 4800 Hz.

The main limitations of NRZ signals are the presence of a dc component and the lack of synchronization capability. To picture the latter problem, consider that with a long string of 1's or 0's for NRZ-L or a long string of 0's for NRZI, the output is a constant voltage over a long period of time. Under these circumstances, any drift between the timing of transmitter and receiver will result in loss of synchronization between the two.

Because of their simplicity and relatively low frequency response characteristics, NRZ codes are commonly used for digital magnetic recording. However, their limitations make these codes unattractive for signal transmission applications.

Multilevel Binary

A category of encoding techniques known as multilevel binary address some of the deficiencies of the NRZ codes. These codes use more than two signal levels. Two examples of this scheme are illustrated in Figure 3.2, bipolar-AMI (alternate mark inversion) and pseudoternary.[2]

In the case of the **bipolar-AMI** scheme, a binary 0 is represented by no line signal, and a binary 1 is represented by a positive or negative pulse. The binary 1 pulses must alternate in polarity. There are several advantages to this approach. First, there will be no loss of synchronization if a long string of 1's occurs. Each 1 introduces a transition, and the receiver can resynchronize on that transition. A long string of 0's would still be a problem. Second, since the 1 signals alternate in voltage from positive to negative, there is no net dc component. Also, the bandwidth of the resulting signal is considerably less than the bandwidth for NRZ (Figure 3.3). Finally, the pulse alternation property provides a simple means of error detection. Any isolated error, whether it deletes a pulse or adds a pulse, causes a violation of this property.

The comments of the previous paragraph also apply to **pseudoternary.** In this case, it is the binary 1 that is represented by the absence of a line signal, and the binary 0 by alternating positive and negative pulses. There is no particular advantage of one technique versus the other, and each is the basis of some applications.

Although a degree of synchronization is provided with these codes, a long string of 0's in the case of AMI or 1's in the case of pseudoternary still presents a problem. Several techniques have been used to address this deficiency. One approach is to insert additional bits that force transitions. We will see that this

---

[2]These terms are not consistently used in the literature. In some books, these two terms are used for different encoding schemes than those defined here, and a variety of terms have been used for the two schemes illustrated in Figure 3.2. The nomenclature used here corresponds to the usage in various CCITT standards documents.

technique is used in ISDN for relatively low data rate transmission. Of course, at a high data rate, this scheme is expensive, since it results in an increase in an already high signal transmission rate. To deal with this problem at high data rates, a technique that involves scrambling the data is used. We examine two examples of this technique later in this section.

Thus, with suitable modification, multilevel binary schemes overcome the problems of NRZ codes. Of course, as with any engineering design decision, there is a tradeoff. With multilevel binary coding, the line signal may take on one of three levels, but each signal element, which could represent $\log_2 3 = 1.58$ bits of information, bears only one bit of information. Thus multilevel binary is not as efficient as NRZ coding. Another way to state this is that the receiver of multilevel binary signals has to distinguish between three levels ($+A$, $-A$, 0) instead of just two levels in the other signaling formats previously discussed. Because of this, the multilevel binary signal requires approximately 3 dB more signal power than a two-valued signal for the same probability of bit error. This is illustrated in Figure 3.4. Put another way, the bit error rate for NRZ codes, at a given signal-to-noise ratio, is significantly less than that for multilevel binary.

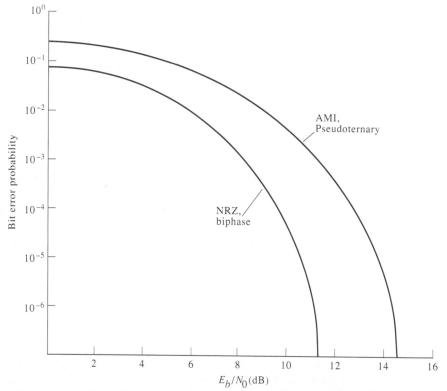

FIGURE 3.4.   Theoretical bit error rate for various digital encoding schemes.

Biphase

There is another set of alternative coding techniques, grouped under the term *biphase*, which overcomes the limitations of NRZ codes. Two of these techniques, Manchester and Differential Manchester, are in common use.

In the **Manchester** code, there is a transition at the middle of each bit period. The mid-bit transition serves as a clocking mechanism and also as data: a low-to-high transition represents a 1, and a high-to-low transition represents a 0[3]. In **Differential Manchester,** the mid-bit transition is used only to provide clocking. The encoding of a 0 is represented by the presence of a transition at the beginning of a bit period, and a 1 is represented by the absence of a transition at the beginning of a bit period. Differential Manchester has the added advantage of employing differential encoding.

All of the biphase techniques require at least one transition per bit time and may have as many as two transitions. Thus, the maximum modulation rate is twice that for NRZ; this means that the bandwidth required is correspondingly greater. To compensate for this, the biphase schemes have several advantages:

- *Synchronization:* Because there is a predictable transition during each bit time, the receiver can synchronize on that transition. For this reason, the biphase codes are known as self-clocking codes.
- *No dc component:* Biphase codes have no dc component, yielding the benefits described earlier.
- *Error detection:* The absence of an expected transition can be used to detect errors. Noise on the line would have to invert both the signal before and after the expected transition to cause an undetected error.

As can be seen from Figure 3.3, the bulk of the energy in biphase codes is between one-half and one times the bit rate. Thus, the bandwidth is reasonably narrow and contains no dc component. However, it is wider than the bandwidth for the multilevel binary codes.

Biphase codes are popular techniques for data transmission. The more common Manchester code has been specified for the IEEE 802.3 standard for baseband coaxial cable and twisted-pair CSMA/CD bus LANs. It has also been used for MIL-STD-1553B, which is a shielded twisted-pair bus LAN designed for high-noise environments. Differential Manchester has been specified for the IEEE 802.5 token ring LAN, using shielded twisted pair.

---

[3]The definition of Manchester presented here conforms to its usage in local area networks. In this definition, a binary 1 corresponds to a low-to-high transition, and a binary 0 to a high-to-low transition. Unfortunately, there is no official standard for Manchester, and a number of respectable textbooks (e.g., [TANE88], [COUC90], [FREE91], [SKLA88], [PEEB87], [BERT92], and the first two editions of this textbook) use the inverse, in which a low-to-high transition defines a binary 0 and a high-to-low transition defines a binary 1. Here, we conform to industry practice and to the definition used in the various LAN standards. For a discussion of this curious discrepancy, see [KESS89].

Modulation Rate

When signal encoding techniques are used, a distinction needs to be made between data rate and modulation rate. The data rate, or bit rate, is $1/t_B$, where t_B = bit duration. However, the modulation rate is the rate at which signal elements are generated. Consider, for example, Manchester encoding. The minimum size signal element is a pulse of one-half the duration of a bit interval. For a string of all binary 0's or all binary 1's, a continuous stream of such pulses is generated. Hence the maximum modulation rate for Manchester is $2/t_B$.

One way of characterizing the modulation rate is to determine the average number of transitions that occur per bit time. In general, this will depend on the exact sequence of bits being transmitted. Table 3.2 compares transition rates for various techniques. It indicates the signal transition rate in the case of a data stream of alternating 1's and 0's, and for the data stream that produces the minimum and maximum modulation rate.

Scrambling Techniques

Although the biphase techniques have achieved widespread use in local-area-network applications at relatively high data rates (up to 10 Mbps), they have not been widely used in long-distance applications. The principal reason for this is that they require a high signaling rate relative to the data rate. This sort of inefficiency is more costly in a long-distance application.

Another approach is to make use of some sort of scrambling scheme. The idea behind this approach is simple: sequences that would result in a constant voltage level on the line are replaced by filling sequences that will provide sufficient transitions for the receiver's clock to maintain synchronization. The filling sequence must be recognized by the receiver and replaced with the original data sequence. The filling sequence is the same length as the original sequence, so there is no data rate increase. The design goals for this approach can be summarized as follows:

• No dc component.
• No long sequences of zero-level line signals.

TABLE 3.2   Normalized Signal Transition Rate of Various Digital Signal Encoding Rates

	Minimum	101010. . .	Maximum
NRZ-L	0 (all 0's or 1's)	1.0	1.0
NRZI	0 (all 0's)	0.5	1.0 (all 1's)
Binary-AMI	0 (all 0's)	1.0	1.0
Pseudoternary	0 (all 1's)	1.0	1.0
Manchester	1.0 (1010 . . .)	1.0	2.0 (all 0's or 1's)
Differential Manchester	1.0 (all 1's)	1.5	2.0 (all 0's)

- No reduction in data rate.
- Error detection capability.

Two techniques are in use in long-distance transmission services; these are illustrated in Figure 3.5.

A coding scheme that is commonly used in North America is known as **bi-polar with 8-zeros substitution (B8ZS)**. The coding scheme is based on a bi-polar-AMI. We have seen that the drawback of the AMI code is that a long string of zeros may result in loss of synchronization. To overcome this problem the encoding is amended with the following rules (Figure 3.5):

- If an octet of all zeros occurs and the last voltage pulse preceding this octet was positive, then the eight zeros of the octet are encoded as **$000 + -0 - +$**.
- If an octet of all zeros occurs and the last voltage pulse preceding this octet was negative, then the eight zeros of the octet are encoded as **$000 - +0 + -$**.

This technique forces two code violations of the AMI code, an event unlikely to be caused by noise or other transmission impairment. The receiver recognizes the pattern and interprets the octet as consisting of all zeros.

A coding scheme that is commonly used in Europe and Japan is known as the **high-density bipolar−3 zeros (HDB3)** code (Table 3.3). As before, it is

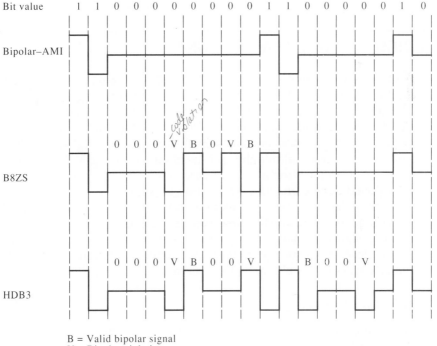

B = Valid bipolar signal
V = Bipolar violation

FIGURE 3.5.   Encoding rules for B8ZS and HDB3.

TABLE 3.3   HDB3 Substitution Rules

Polarity of Preceding Pulse	Number of Bipolar Pulses (Ones) Since Last Substitution	
	Odd	Even
−	000−	+00+
+	000+	−00−

based on the use of AMI encoding. In this case, the scheme replaces strings of four zeros with sequences containing one or two pulses. In each case, the fourth zero is replaced with a code violation. In addition, a rule is needed to ensure that successive violations are of alternate polarity so that no dc component is introduced. Thus, if the last violation was positive, this violation must be negative and vice versa. The table shows that this condition is tested for by knowing whether the number of pulses since the last violation is even or odd and the polarity of the last pulse before the occurrence of the four zeros.

Figure 3.3 shows the spectral properties of these two codes. As can be seen, neither has a dc component. Most of the energy is concentrated in a relatively sharp spectrum around a frequency equal to one-half the data rate. Thus, these codes are well suited to high data rate transmission.

3.2

DIGITAL DATA, ANALOG SIGNALS

We turn now to the case of transmitting digital data using analog signals. The most familiar use of this transformation is for transmitting digital data through the public telephone network. The telephone network was designed to receive, switch, and transmit analog signals in the voice-frequency range of about 300 to 3400 Hz. It is not at present suitable for handling digital signals from the subscriber locations (although this is beginning to change). Thus digital devices are attached to the network via a *modem* (modulator-demodulator), which converts digital data to analog signals, and vice versa.

For the telephone network, modems are used which produce signals in the voice-frequency range. The same basic techniques are used for modems that produce signals at higher frequencies (e.g., microwave). This section introduces these techniques and provides a brief discussion of the performance characteristics of the alternative approaches.

Encoding Techniques

We mentioned that modulation involves operation on one or more of the three characteristics of a carrier signal: amplitude, frequency, and phase. Accordingly, there are three basic encoding or modulation techniques for transforming digital data into analog signals, as illustrated in Figure 3.6.

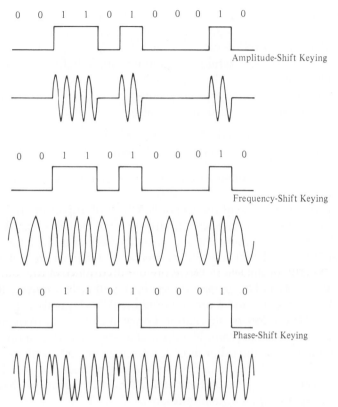

FIGURE 3.6.   Modulation of analog signals for digital data.

- Amplitude-shift keying (ASK).
- Frequency-shift keying (FSK).
- Phase-shift keying (PSK).

In all these cases, the resulting signal occupies a bandwidth centered on the carrier frequency.

In ASK, the two binary values are represented by two different amplitudes of the carrier frequency. Commonly, one of the amplitudes is zero; that is, one binary digit is represented by the presence, at constant amplitude, of the carrier, the other by the absence of the carrier. The resulting signal is

$$s(t) = \begin{cases} A \cos(2\pi f_c t + \theta_c) & \text{binary 1} \\ 0 & \text{binary 0} \end{cases}$$

where the carrier signal is $A \cos(2\pi f_c t + \theta_c)$. ASK is susceptible to sudden gain changes and is a rather inefficient modulation technique. On voice-grade lines, it is typically used only up to 1200 bps.

The ASK technique is used to transmit digital data over optical fiber [WERN86]. For LED transmitters, the equation above is valid. That is, one signal element is represented by a light pulse while the other signal element is represented by the absence of light. Laser transmitters normally have a fixed "bias" current that causes the device to emit a low light level. This low level represents one signal element, while a higher-amplitude lightwave represents another signal element.

In FSK, the two binary values are represented by two different frequencies near the carrier frequency. The resulting signal is

$$s(t) = \begin{cases} A \cos(2\pi f_1 t + \theta_c) & \text{binary 1} \\ A \cos(2\pi f_2 t + \theta_c) & \text{binary 0} \end{cases}$$

where f_1 and f_2 are typically offset from the carrier frequency f_c by equal but opposite amounts.

Figure 3.7 shows an example of the use of FSK for full-duplex operation over a voice-grade line. The figure is a specification for the Bell System 108 series modems. Recall that a voice-grade line will pass frequencies in the approximate range 300 to 3400 Hz, and that full-duplex means that signals are transmitted in both directions at the same time. To achieve full-duplex transmission, this bandwidth is split at 1700 Hz. In one direction (transmit or receive), the frequencies used to represent 1 and 0 are centered on 1170 Hz, with a shift of 100 Hz on either side. The effect of alternating between those two frequencies is to produce a signal whose spectrum is indicated as the shaded area on the left in Figure 3.7. Similarly, for the other direction (receive or transmit) the modem uses frequencies shifted 100 Hz to each side of a center frequency of 2125 Hz. This signal is indicated by the shaded area on the right in Figure 3.7. Note that there is little overlap and thus little interference.

FSK is less susceptible to error than ASK. On voice grade lines, it is typically used up to 1200 bps. It is also commonly used for high-frequency (3 to 30 MHz) radio transmission. It can also be used at even higher frequencies on local networks that use coaxial cable.

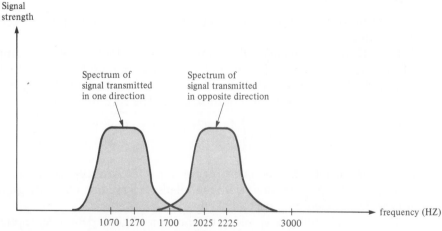

FIGURE 3.7. Full-duplex FSK transmission on a voice-grade line.

In PSK, the phase of the carrier signal is shifted to represent data. The bottom of Figure 3.6 is an example of a two-phase system. In this system, a binary 0 is represented by sending a signal burst of the same phase as the previous signal burst sent. A binary 1 is represented by sending a signal burst of opposite phase to the preceding one. This is known as differential PSK, since the phase shift is with reference to the previous bit transmitted rather than to some constant reference signal. The resulting signal is

$$s(t) = \begin{cases} A \cos(2\pi f_c t + \pi) & \text{binary 1} \\ A \cos(2\pi f_c t) & \text{binary 0} \end{cases}$$

with the phase measured relative to the previous bit interval.

More efficient use of bandwidth can be achieved if each signaling element represents more than one bit. For example, instead of a phase shift of 180°, as allowed in PSK, a common encoding technique, known as *quadrature phase-shift keying* (QPSK) uses phase shifts of multiples of 90°.

$$s(t) = \begin{cases} A \cos(2\pi f_c t + 45°) & 11 \\ A \cos(2\pi f_c t + 135°) & 10 \\ A \cos(2\pi f_c t + 225°) & 00 \\ A \cos(2\pi f_c t + 315°) & 01 \end{cases}$$

Thus each signal element represents two bits rather than one.

This scheme can be extended. It is possible to transmit bits three at a time using eight different phase angles. Further, each angle can have more than one amplitude. For example, a standard 9600 bps modem uses 12 phase angles, four of which have two amplitude values (Figure 3.8). A thorough review of these and other techniques can be found in [OETT79].

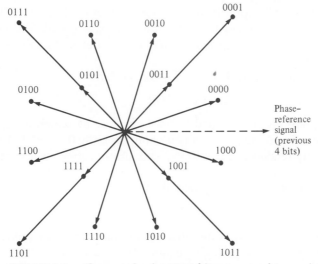

FIGURE 3.8.   Phase angles for 9600 bit-per-second transmission.

This latter example points out very well the difference between the data rate R (in bps) and the modulation rate D (in bauds) of a signal. Let us assume that this scheme is being employed with NRZ-L digital input. The data rate is $R = 1/t_B$ where t_B is the width of each NRZ-L bit. However, the encoded signal contains $l = 4$ bits in each signal element using $L = 16$ different combinations of amplitude and phase. The modulation rate can be seen to be $R/4$, since each change of signal element communicates four bits. Thus the line signaling speed is 2400 bauds, but the data rate is 9600 bps. This is the reason that higher bit rates can be achieved over voice-grade lines by employing more complex modulation schemes.

In general,

$$D = \frac{R}{l} = \frac{R}{\log_2 L}$$

where

D = modulation rate, bauds
R = data rate, bps
L = number of different signal elements
l = number of bits per signal element

The above is complicated when an encoding technique other than NRZ is used. For example, we saw that the maximum modulation rate for RZ signals is $2/t_B$. Thus D for RZ is greater than D for NRZ. This to some extent counteracts the reduction in D achieved by using multilevel signal modulation techniques.

Performance

In looking at the performance of various digital-to-analog modulation schemes, the first parameter of interest is the bandwidth of the modulated signal. This depends on a variety of factors; including the definition of bandwidth used and the filtering technique used to create the bandpass signal. We will use some straightforward results from [COUC87]; a more detailed analysis can be found in [AMOR80].

The transmission bandwidth B_T for ASK is of the form

$$B_T = (1 + r)R$$

where R is the bit rate and r is related to the technique by which the signal is filtered to establish a bandwidth for transmission; typically $0 < r < 1$. Thus the bandwidth is directly related to the bit rate. The formula above is also valid for PSK.

For FSK, the bandwidth can be expressed as

$$B_T = 2\Delta F + (1 + r)R$$

where $\Delta F = f_2 - f_c = f_c - f_1$ is the offset of the modulated frequency from the carrier frequency. When very high frequencies are used, the ΔF term dominates. For example, one of the standards for FSK signaling on a coaxial cable multipoint local network uses $\Delta F = 1.25$ MHz, $f_c = 5$ MHz, and $R = 1$ Mbps. In this case $B_T \approx 2\Delta F = 2.5$ MHz. In the example of the preceding section for the Bell 108 modem, $\Delta F = 100$ Hz, $f_c = 1170$ Hz (in one direction), and $R = 300$ bps. In this case $B_T \approx (1 + r)R$, which is the range 300 to 600 Hz.

With multilevel signaling, significant improvements in bandwidth can be achieved. In general

$$B_T = \left(\frac{1 + r}{l} \right) R = \left(\frac{1 + r}{\log_2 L} \right) R$$

where l is the number of bits encoded per signal element and L is the number of different signal elements.

Table 3.4 shows the ratio of data rate to transmission bandwidth for various schemes. This ratio is also referred to as the bandwidth efficiency. As the name suggests, this parameter measures the efficiency with which bandwidth can be used to transmit data. The advantage of multilevel signaling methods now becomes clear.

Of course, the discussion above refers to the spectrum of the input signal to a communications line. Nothing has yet been said of performance in the presence of noise. Figure 3.9 summarizes some results based on reasonable assumptions concerning the transmission system [COUC87]. Here bit error rate is plotted as a function of the ratio E_b/N_0 defined in Chapter 2. Of course, as that ratio increases, the bit error rate drops. Further, PSK and QPSK are about 3 dB superior to ASK and FSK.

This information can now be related to bandwidth efficiency. Recall that

$$\frac{E_b}{N_0} = \frac{S}{N_0 R}$$

The parameter N_0 is the noise power density in watts/hertz. Hence, the noise in a signal with bandwidth B_T is $N = N_0 B_T$. Substituting, we have

$$\frac{E_b}{N_0} = \frac{S}{N} \frac{B}{R}$$

TABLE 3.4   Data Rate to Transmission Bandwidth Ratio for Various Digital-to-Analog Encoding Schemes

	$r = 0$	$r = 0.5$	$r = 1$
ASK	1.0	0.67	0.5
FSK			
Wideband ($\Delta F \gg R$)	~0	~0	~0
Narrowband ($\Delta F \approx f_c$)	1.0	0.67	0.5
PSK	1.0	0.67	0.5
Multilevel signaling			
$L = 4, l = 2$	2.00	1.33	1.00
$L = 8, l = 3$	3.00	2.00	1.50
$L = 16, l = 4$	4.00	2.67	2.00
$L = 32, l = 5$	5.00	3.33	2.50

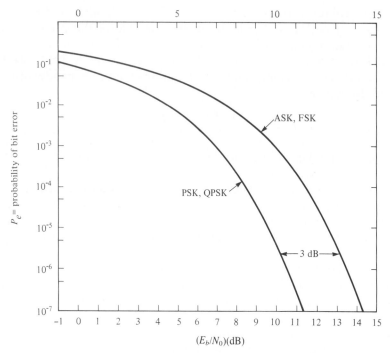

FIGURE 3.9. Bit error rate of various digital-to-analog encoding schemes.

For a given signaling scheme, the bit error rate can be reduced by increasing E_b/N_0, which can be accomplished by increasing the bandwidth or decreasing the data rate: in other words, by reducing bandwidth efficiency.

Example

What is the bandwidth efficiency for FSK, ASK, PSK, and QPSK for a bit error rate of 10^{-7} on a channel with an S/N of 12 dB?
    We have

$$\frac{E_b}{N_0} = 12 \text{ dB} - \left(\frac{R}{B}\right)\text{dB}$$

For FSK and ASK, from Figure 3.8,

$$\frac{E_b}{N_0} = 14.2 \text{ dB}$$

$$\left(\frac{R}{B}\right)\text{dB} = -2.2 \text{ dB}$$

$$\frac{R}{B} = 0.6$$

For PSK, from Figure 3.8

$$\frac{E_b}{N_0} = 11.2 \text{ dB}$$

$$\left(\frac{R}{B}\right)\text{dB} = 0.8 \text{ dB}$$

$$\frac{R}{B} = 1.2$$

The result for QPSK must take into account that the baud rate $D = R/2$. Thus

$$\frac{R}{B} = 2.4 \qquad\qquad\blacksquare$$

As the example above shows, ASK and FSK exhibit the same bandwidth efficiency, PSK is better, and even greater improvement can be achieved with multilevel signaling.

It is worthwhile to compare these bandwidth requirements with those for digital signaling. A good approximation is

$$B_T = 0.5(1 + r)D$$

where D is the modulation rate. For NRZ, $D = R$, and we have

$$\frac{R}{B} = \frac{2}{1+r}$$

Thus digital signaling is in the same ballpark, in terms of bandwidth efficiency, as ASK, FSK, and PSK. Significant advantage for analog signaling is seen with multilevel techniques.

3.3

ANALOG DATA, DIGITAL SIGNALS

In this section we examine the process of transforming analog data into digital signals. Strictly speaking, it might be more correct to refer to this as a process of converting analog data into digital data, which process is known as *digitization*. Once analog data have been converted into digital data, a number of things can happen. The three most common:

1. The digital data can be transmitted using NRZ-L. In this case, we have in fact gone directly from analog data to a digital signal.
2. The digital data can be encoded as a digital signal using a code other than NRZ-L. Thus an extra step is required.
3. The digital data can be converted into an analog signal, using one of the modulation techniques discussed in Section 3.2.

This last, seemingly curious, procedure is illustrated in Figure 3.10, which shows voice data that are digitized and then converted to an analog ASK signal. This allows digital transmission in the sense defined in Chapter 2. The voice data, because they have been digitized, can be treated as digital data, even though transmission requirements (e.g., use of microwave) dictate that an analog signal be used.

The device used for converting analog data into digital form for transmission, and subsequently recovering the original analog data from the digital is known as a *codec* (coder-decoder). In this section we examine the two principal techniques used in codecs, pulse code modulation and delta modulation. The section closes with a discussion of comparative performance.

Pulse Code Modulation

Pulse Code Modulation (PCM) is based on the sampling theorem, which states [JORD85]:

> "If a signal $f(t)$ is sampled at regular intervals of time and at a rate higher than twice the highest significant signal frequency, then the samples contain all the information of the original signal. The function $f(t)$ may be reconstructed from these samples by the use of a low-pass filter."

For the interested reader, a proof is provided in Appendix 3A. If voice data are limited to frequencies below 4000 Hz, a conservative procedure for intelligibility, 8000 samples per second would be sufficient to completely characterize the voice signal. Note, however, that these are analog samples.

This is illustrated in Figure 3.11a and b. The original signal is assumed to be bandlimited with a bandwidth of B. Samples are taken at a rate $2B$, or once every $1/2B$ seconds. These samples are represented as narrow pulses whose amplitude is proportional to the value of the original signal. This process is known as *pulse amplitude modulation* (PAM). By itself, this technique has commercial applicability. It is used, for example, in some of AT&T's Dimension PBX products.

Analog data (voice) → Digitizer → Digital data (NRZ – L) → Modulator → Analog signal (ASK)

FIGURE 3.10. Digitizing analog data.

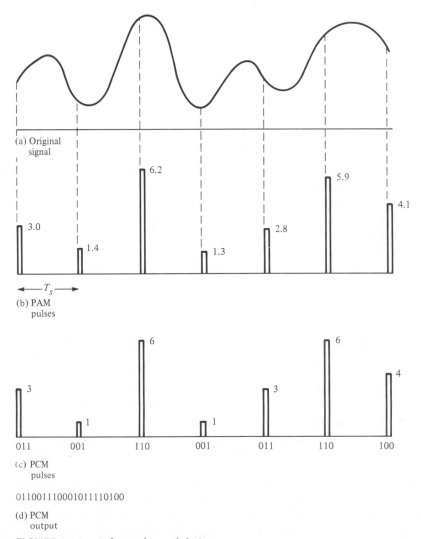

(a) Original
     signal

T_s

(b) PAM
     pulses

(c) PCM
     pulses

011001110001011110100

(d) PCM
     output

FIGURE 3.11.   Pulse-code modulation.

However, the most significant fact about PAM is that it is the first step toward PCM, as depicted in Figure 3.11c. To produce PCM data, the PAM samples are quantized. That is, the amplitude of each PAM pulse is approximated
by an n-bit integer. In the example, $n = 3$. Thus $8 = 2^3$ levels are available for
approximating the PAM pulses.

Figure 3.12 illustrates the process, starting with a continuous-time, continu-
ous-amplitude (analog) signal, in which a digital signal is produced. The digital
signal consists of blocks of n bits, where each n-bit number is the amplitude of

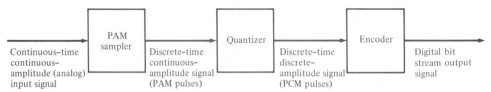

FIGURE 3.12. Analog-to-digital conversion.

a PCM pulse. On reception, the process is reversed to reproduce the analog signal. Notice, however, that this process violates the terms of the sampling theorem. By quantizing the PAM pulse, the original signal is now only approximated and cannot be recovered exactly. This effect is known as *quantizing error* or *quantizing noise*. The signal-to-noise ratio for quantizing noise can be expressed as [JAYA84]:

$$\frac{S}{N} = 6n - a \text{ dB}$$

where a is a constant on the order of 0 to 1.

Thus each additional bit used for quantizing increases S/N by 6 dB.

Typically, the PCM scheme is refined using a technique known as *nonlinear encoding*, which means, in effect, that the quantization levels are not equally spaced. The problem with equal spacing is that the mean absolute error for each sample is the same, regardless of signal level. Consequently, lower-amplitude values are relatively more distorted. By using a greater number of quantizing steps for signals of low amplitude, and a smaller number of quantizing steps for signals of large amplitude, a marked reduction in overall signal distortion is achieved (e.g., see Figure 3.13).

The same effect can be achieved by using uniform quantizing but *companding* (compressing-expanding) the input analog signal. Companding is a process that compresses the intensity range of a signal by imparting more gain to weak signals than to strong signals on input. At output, the reverse operation is performed. Figure 3.14 is a typical companding function.

Nonlinear encoding can significantly improve the PCM S/N ratio. For voice signals, improvements of 24 to 30 dB have been achieved [FREE81].

Delta Modulation (DM)

A variety of techniques have been used to improve the performance of PCM or to reduce its complexity. A discussion of the various approaches that have been taken for voice data can be found in [CROC83]. Here we mention one of the most popular alternatives to PCM: delta modulation (DM).

With delta modulation, an analog input is approximated by a staircase function that moves up or down by one quantization level (δ) at each sampling

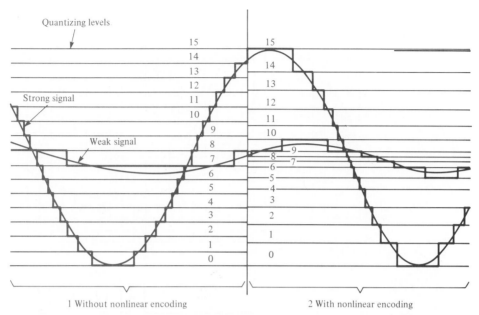

FIGURE 3.13.   Effect of nonlinear coding.

interval (T_s). An example is shown in Figure 3.15, where the staircase function is overlaid on the original analog waveform (the grid is for clarity). The important characteristic of this staircase function is that its behavior is binary: At each sampling time, the function moves up or down a constant amount δ. Thus, the output of the delta modulation process can be represented as a single binary digit for each sample. In essence, a bit stream is produced by approximating the derivative of an analog signal rather than its amplitude: A 1 is generated if the staircase function is to go up during the next interval; a 0 is generated otherwise.

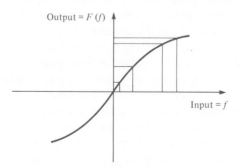

FIGURE 3.14.   Typical companding function.

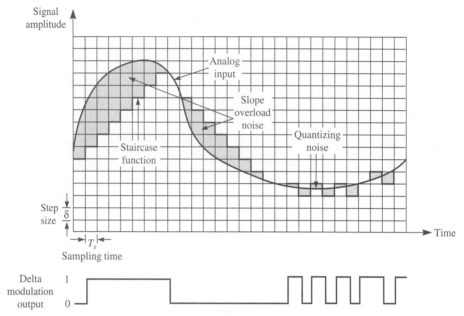

FIGURE 3.15.   Example of delta modulation.

The transition (up or down) that occurs at each sampling interval is chosen so that the staircase function tracks the original analog waveform as closely as possible. Figure 3.16 illustrates the logic of the process, which is essentially a feedback mechanism. For transmission, the following occurs: At each sampling time, the analog input is compared to the most recent value of the approximating staircase function. If the value of the sampled waveform exceeds that of the staircase function, a 1 is generated; otherwise, a 0 is generated. Thus, the staircase is always changed in the direction of the input signal. The output of the DM process is therefore a binary sequence that can be used at the receiver to reconstruct the staircase function. The staircase function can then be smoothed by some type of integration process or by passing it through a low-pass filter to produce an analog approximation of the analog input signal.

There are two important parameters in a DM scheme: the size of the step assigned to each binary digit, δ, and the sampling rate. As Figure 3.15 illustrates, δ must be chosen to produce a balance between two types of errors or noise. When the analog waveform is changing very slowly, there will be *quantizing noise*. This noise increases as δ is increased. On the other hand, when the analog waveform is changing more rapidly than the staircase can follow, there is *slope overload noise*. This noise increases as δ is decreased.

It should be clear that the accuracy of the scheme can be improved by increasing the sampling rate. However, this increases the data rate of the output signal.

(a) Transmission

(b) Reception

FIGURE 3.16. Delta modulation.

The principal advantage of DM over PCM is the simplicity of its implementation. In general, PCM exhibits better *S/N* characteristics at the same data rate [COUC83].

Performance

Good voice reproduction via PCM can be achieved with 128 quantization levels, or 7-bit coding ($2^7 = 128$). A voice signal, conservatively, occupies a bandwidth of 4 kHz. Thus, according to the sampling theorem, samples should be taken at a rate of 8000 samples per second. This implies a data rate of 8000 × 7 = 56 kbps for the PCM-encoded digital data.

Consider what this means from the point of view of bandwidth requirement. An analog voice signal occupies 4 kHz. A 56-kbps digital signal will require on the order of at least 28 kHz! Even more severe differences are seen with higher bandwidth signals. For example, a common PCM scheme for color television uses 10-bit codes, which works out to 92 Mbps for a 4.6-MHz bandwidth signal. In spite of these numbers, digital techniques continue to grow in popularity for transmitting analog data. The principal reasons for this are

- Because repeaters are used instead of amplifiers, there is no additive noise.
- As we shall see, time-division multiplexing (TDM) is used for digital signals instead of the frequency-division multiplexing (FDM) used for analog signals. With TDM, there is no intermodulation noise, whereas we have seen that this is a concern for FDM.
- The conversion to digital signaling allows the use of the more efficient digital switching techniques, discussed in Chapter 8.

Furthermore, techniques are being developed to provide more efficient codes. In the case of voice, a reasonable goal appears to be in the neighborhood of 4 kbps [ROBI86], [JAYA86], [JAYA90]. With video, advantage can be taken of the fact that from frame to frame, most picture elements will not change. Interframe coding techniques should allow the video requirement to be reduced to about 15 Mbps, and for slowly changing scenes, such as found in a video teleconference, down to 1.5 Mbps or less [NETR88], [MURA88], [MURA87].

As a final point, we mention that in many instances, the use of a telecommunications system will result in both digital-to-analog and analog-to-digital processing. The overwhelming majority of local terminations into the telecommunications network is analog, and the network itself uses a mixture of analog and digital techniques. Thus digital data at a user's terminal may be converted to analog by a modem, subsequently digitized by a codec, and perhaps suffer repeated conversions before reaching its destination.

Because of the above, telecommunication facilities handle analog signals that represent both voice and digital data. The characteristics of the waveforms are quite different. Whereas voice signals tend to be skewed to the lower portion of the bandwidth (Figure 2.10), analog encoding of digital signals has a more uniform spectral content over the bandwidth and therefore contains more high-frequency components. Studies have shown that, because of the presence of these higher frequencies, PCM-related techniques are preferable to DM-related techniques for digitizing analog signals that represent digital data [ONEA80].

3.4

ANALOG DATA, ANALOG SIGNALS

Modulation has been defined as the process of combining an input signal $m(t)$ and a carrier at frequency f_c to produce a signal $s(t)$ whose bandwidth is (usually) centered on f_c. For digital data, the motivation for modulation should be clear: When only analog transmission facilities are available, modulation is required to convert the digital data to analog form. The motivation when the data are already analog is less clear. After all, voice signals are transmitted over telephone lines at their original spectrum (referred to as baseband transmission). There are two principal reasons:

- A higher frequency may be needed for effective transmission. For unguided transmission, it is virtually impossible to transmit baseband signals; the required antennas would be many kilometers in diameter.
- Modulation permits frequency-division multiplexing, an important technique explored in Chapter 6.

In this section we look at the principal techniques for modulation using analog data: amplitude modulation (AM), frequency modulation (FM), and phase modulation (PM). As before, the three basic characteristics of a signal are used for modulation.

Amplitude Modulation

Amplitude modulation (AM) is the simplest form of modulation, and is depicted in Figure 3.17. Mathematically, the process can be expressed as

$$s(t) = [1 + n_a x(t)] \cos 2\pi f_c t$$

where $\cos 2\pi f_c t$ is the carrier and $x(t)$ is the input signal (carrying data), both normalized to unity amplitude. The parameter n_a, known as the *modulation index*, is the ratio of the amplitude of the input signal to the carrier. Corresponding to our previous notation, the input signal is $m(t) = n_a x(t)$. The "1" in the preceding equation is a dc component that prevents loss of information, as explained subsequently. This scheme is also known as double sideband transmitted carrier (DSBTC).

Example

Derive an expression for $s(t)$ if $x(t)$ is the amplitude-modulating signal $\cos 2\pi f_m t$.

We have

$$s(t) = [1 + n_a \cos 2\pi f_m t] \cos 2\pi f_c t$$

By trigonometric identity, this may be expanded to

$$s(t) = \cos 2\pi f_c t + \frac{n_a}{2} \cos 2\pi (f_c - f_m)t + \frac{n_a}{2} \cos 2\pi (f_c + f_m)t$$

The resulting signal has a component at the original carrier frequency plus a pair of components each spaced f_m hertz from the carrier. ∎

From the equation above and Figure 3.17, it can be seen that AM involves the multiplication of the input signal by the carrier. The envelope of the resulting signal is $[1 + n_a x(t)]$ and, as long as $n_a < 1$, the envelope is an exact reproduction of the original signal. If $n_a > 1$, the envelope will cross the time axis and information is lost.

(a) Sinusoidal modulating wave

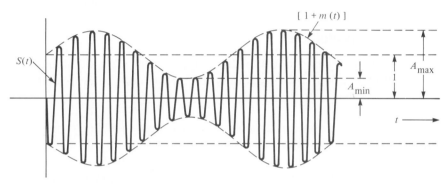

(b) Resulting AM signal

FIGURE 3.17.   Amplitude modulation.

It is instructive to look at the spectrum of the AM signal. An example is shown in Figure 3.18. The spectrum consists of the original carrier plus the spectrum of the input signal translated to f_c. The portion of the spectrum for $|f| > |f_c|$ is the *upper sideband,* and the portion for $|f| < |f_c|$ is the *lower sideband.* Both the upper and lower sidebands are replicas of the original spectrum $M(f)$, with the lower sideband being frequency-reversed. As an example, consider a voice signal with a bandwidth that extends from 300 to 3000 Hz being modulated on a 60-kHz carrier. The resulting signal contains an upper sideband of 60.3 to 63 kHz, a lower sideband of 57 to 59.7 kHz, and the 60-Hz carrier. An important relationship is

$$P_t = P_c \left(1 + \frac{n_a^2}{2} \right)$$

where P_t is the total transmitted power in $s(t)$ and P_c is the transmitted power in the carrier. We would like n_a as large as possible so that most of the signal power is used to actually carry information. However, n_a must remain below 1.

It should be clear that $s(t)$ contains unnecessary components, since each of the sidebands contains the complete spectrum of $m(t)$. A popular variant of

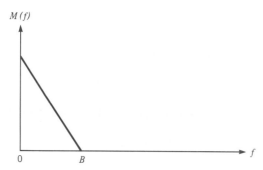

(a) Spectrum of modulating signal

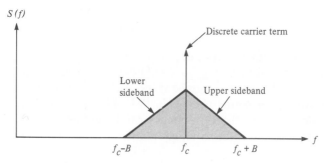

(b) Spectrum of AM signal with carrier at f_c

FIGURE 3.18.   Spectrum of an AM signal.

AM, known as single sideband (SSB), takes advantage of this fact by sending only one of the sidebands, eliminating the other sideband and the carrier. The principal advantages of this approach are

- Only half the bandwidth is required, that is, $B_T = B$, where B is the bandwidth of the original signal. For DSBTC, $B_T = 2B$.
- Less power is required since no power is used to transmit the carrier or the other sideband. Another variant is double sideband suppressed carrier (DSBSC) which filters out the carrier frequency and sends both sidebands. This saves some power but uses as much bandwidth as DSBTC.

The disadvantage of suppressing the carrier is that the carrier can be used for synchronization purposes. For example, suppose that the original analog signal is an ASK waveform encoding digital data. The receiver needs to know the starting point of each bit time to interpret the data correctly. A constant carrier provides a clocking mechanism by which to time the arrival of bits. A compromise approach is vestigial sideband (VSB), which uses one sideband and a reduced-power carrier.

Angle Modulation

Frequency modulation (FM) and *phase modulation* (PM) are special cases of *angle modulation*. The modulated signal is expressed as

$$s(t) = A_c \cos[2\pi f_c t + \phi(t)]$$

For phase modulation, the phase is proportional to the modulating signal:

$$\phi(t) = n_p m(t)$$

where n_p is the phase modulation index.

For frequency modulation, the derivative of the phase is proportional to the modulating signal:

$$\phi'(t) = n_f m(t)$$

where n_f is the frequency modulation index.

The definitions above may be clarified if we consider the following. The phase of $s(t)$ at any instant is just $2\pi f_c t + \phi(t)$. The instantaneous phase deviation from the carrier signal is $\phi(t)$. In PM, this instantaneous phase deviation is proportional to $m(t)$. Since frequency can be defined as the rate of change of phase of a signal, the instantaneous frequency of $s(t)$ is

$$2\pi f_i(t) = \frac{d}{dt} [2\pi f_c t + \phi(t)]$$

$$f_i(t) = f_c + \frac{1}{2\pi} \phi'(t)$$

and the instantaneous frequency deviation from the carrier frequency is $\phi'(t)$, which in FM is proportional to $m(t)$.

Figure 3.19 illustrates amplitude, phase, and frequency modulation by a sine wave. The shapes of the FM and PM signals are very similar. Indeed, it is impossible to tell them apart without knowledge of the modulation function.

Several observations about the FM process are in order. The peak deviation ΔF can be seen to be

$$\Delta F = \frac{1}{2\pi} n_f A_m \quad \text{Hz}$$

where A_m is the maximum value of $m(t)$. Thus an increase in the magnitude of $m(t)$ will increase ΔF, which, intuitively, should increase the transmitted bandwidth B_T. However, as should be apparent from Figure 3.19, this will not increase the average power level of the FM signal, which is $A_c^2/2$. This is distinctly different from AM, where the level of modulation affects the power in the AM signal but does not affect its bandwidth.

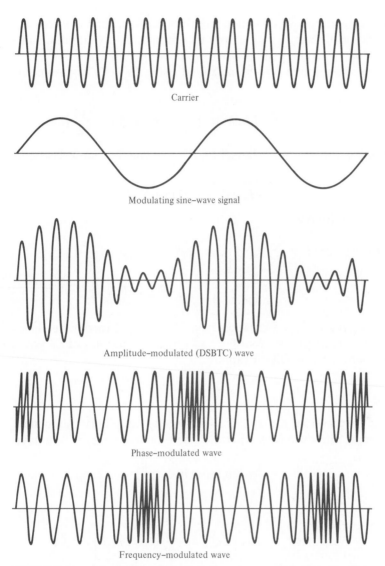

FIGURE 3.19. Amplitude, phase, and frequency modulation of a sine-wave carrier by a sine-wave signal.

Example

Derive an expression for $s(t)$ if $\phi(t)$ is the phase-modulating signal $n_p \cos 2\pi f_m t$. Assume that $A_c = 1$. This can be seen directly to be

$$s(t) = \cos[2\pi f_c t + n_p \cos 2\pi f_m t]$$

The instantaneous phase deviation from the carrier signal is $n_p \cos 2\pi f_m t$. The phase angle of the signal varies from its unmodulated value in a simple sinusoidal fashion, with the peak phase deviation equal to n_p.

The expression above can be expanded using Bessel's trigonometric identities:

$$s(t) = \sum_{n=-\infty}^{\infty} J_n(n_p) \cos\left(2\pi f_c t + 2\pi n f_m t + \frac{n\pi}{2}\right)$$

where $J_n(n_p)$ is the nth order Bessel function of the first kind. Using the property

$$J_{-n}(x) = (-1)^n J_n(x)$$

this can be rewritten as

$$s(t) = J_0(n_p) \cos 2\pi f_c t + \sum_{n=1}^{\infty} J_n(n_p) \left[\cos\left(2\pi(f_c + n f_m)t + \frac{n\pi}{2}\right) \right.$$
$$\left. + \cos\left(2\pi(f_c - n f_m)t + \frac{(n+2)\pi}{2}\right) \right]$$

The resulting signal has a component at the original carrier frequency plus a set of sidebands displaced from f_c by all possible multiples of f_m. For $n_p \ll 1$, the higher-order terms fall off rapidly. ∎

Example

Derive an expression for $s(t)$ if $\phi'(t)$ is the frequency-modulating signal $-n_f \sin 2\pi f_m t$. The form of $\phi'(t)$ was chosen for convenience. We have

$$\phi(t) = -\int n_f \sin 2\pi f_m t \, dt = \frac{n_f}{2\pi f_m} \cos 2\pi f_m t$$

Thus

$$s(t) = \cos\left[2\pi f_c t + \frac{n_f}{2\pi f_m} \cos 2\pi f_m t\right]$$
$$= \cos\left[2\pi f_c t + \frac{\Delta F}{f_m} \cos 2\pi f_m t\right]$$
∎

The instantaneous frequency deviation from the carrier signal is $-n_f \sin 2\pi f_m t$. The frequency of the signal varies from its unmodulated value in a simple sinusoidal fashion, with the peak frequency deviation equal to n_f rad/s.

The equation for the FM signal has the identical form as for the PM signal, with $\Delta F/f_m$ substituted for n_p. Thus the Bessel expansion is the same.

As with AM, both FM and PM result in a signal whose bandwidth is centered at f_c. However, we can now see that the magnitude of that bandwidth is very different. Amplitude modulation is a linear process and produces frequencies that are the sum and difference of the carrier signal and the components of the modulating signal. Hence, for AM:

$$B_T = 2B$$

However, angle modulation includes a term of the form $\cos(\phi(t))$, which is nonlinear and will produce a wide range of frequencies. In essence, for a modulating sinusoid of frequency f_m, $s(t)$ will contain components at $f_c + f_m$, $f_c + 2f_m$, and so on. In the most general case, infinite bandwidth is required to transmit an FM or PM signal. As a practical matter, a very good rule of thumb, known as Carson's rule [COUC83], is

$$B_T = 2(\beta + 1)B$$

where

$$\beta = \begin{cases} n_p A_m & \text{for PM} \\ \dfrac{\Delta F}{B} = \dfrac{n_f A_m}{2\pi B} & \text{for FM} \end{cases}$$

We can rewrite the formula for FM as

$$B_T = 2\Delta F + 2B$$

Thus both FM and PM require greater bandwidth than AM.

3.5

RECOMMENDED READING

A good analysis of digital data and digital signal schemes can be found in [PEEB87]. [BENE87], [SKLA88], and [KAMA86] also provide some insights. The latter is concerned with the use of these codes for magnetic tape recording, but the discussion is valid in the data transmission context. A great deal has been written about analog modulation schemes for digital data. [OETT79] is a good survey. [PEEB87] and [SKLA88] contain lengthy analyses. Other worthwhile sources are [FREE91] and [COUC90].

[MART88] contains a readable introduction to PCM and other techniques for analog-to-digital encoding. More in-depth looks can be found in [COUC90], [JAYA84], [WILL87], and [NETR88]. Three special issues of the *IEEE Journal on Selected Areas in Communications* report on recent developments in voice coding [AOYA88], video coding [HASK87], and both [HUBI92]. Finally, the literature on the various analog modulation schemes for analog data is almost limitless. [BELL90] is a concise overview of the subject.

3.6

PROBLEMS

3.1 Which of the signals of Table 3.1 use differential encoding?

3.2 Develop algorithms for generating each of the codes of Table 3.1 from NRZ-L.

3.3 A modified NRZ code known as *enhanced-NRZ* (E-NRZ) is sometimes used for high density magnetic tape recording. E-NRZ encoding entails separating the NRZ-L data stream into 7-bit words; inverting bits 2, 3, 6, and 7; and adding one parity bit to each word. The parity bit is chosen to make the total number of 1's in the 8-bit word an odd count. What are the advantages of E-NRZ over NRZ-L? Any disadvantages?

3.4 Develop a state diagram (finite state machine) representation of pseudo-ternary coding.

3.5 Consider the following signal encoding technique. Binary data are presented as input, a_m, $m = 1, 2, 3, \ldots$ Two levels of processing occur. First, a new set of binary numbers are produced:

$$b_m = (a_m + b_{m-1}) \bmod 2$$

These are then encoded as

$$c_m = b_m - b_{m-1}$$

On reception, the original data is recovered by

$$a_m = c_m \bmod 2$$

a. Verify that the received values of a_m equal the transmitted values of a_m.
b. What sort of encoding is this?

3.6 For the B8ZS coding scheme to be effective, the probability of occurrences of more than one code violation (two pulses in a row with the same polarity) due to an error must be quite small. What is the probability of the occurrence of more than one code violation in 8 bits for an error rate per bit of 10^{-6}? For an error rate of 10^{-3}?

3.7 For the bit stream 01001110, sketch the waveforms for each of the codes of Table 3.1.

3.8 The following waveform belongs to a Manchester encoded binary data stream. Determine the beginning and end of bit periods (i.e., extract clock information) and give the data sequence.

3.9 A sine wave is to be used for two different signaling schemes: (a) PSK; (b) QPSK. The duration of a signal element is 10^{-5} sec. If the received signal is of the following form:

$$s(t) = 0.005 \sin (2\pi 10^6 t + \theta) \text{ volts}$$

and if the measured noise power at the receiver is 2.5×10^{-8} watts/Hz, determine the E_b/N_0 (in dB) for each case.

3.10 Consider Figure 3.8. Eight of the phases use only a single level of amplitude. The system shown encodes only 4 bits. How many bits could be encoded if the single amplitude phase were made to be double amplitude?

3.11 Consider a channel using PSK designed with a probability of error of 1 part in 1,000,000. If the signal-to-noise ratio is 1000, what is the bandwidth efficiency?

3.12 Derive an expression for baud rate D as a function of bit rate R for QPSK using the digital encoding techniques of Table 3.1.

3.13 What S/N ratio is required to achieve a bandwidth efficiency of 5.0 for ASK, FSK, PSK, and QPSK? Assume that the required bit error rate is 10^{-6}.

3.14 An NRZ-L signal is passed through a filter with $r = 0.5$ and then modulated onto a carrier. The data rate is 2400 bps. Evaluate the bandwidth for ASK and FSK. For FSK assume that the two frequencies used are 50 kHz and 55 kHz.

3.15 Assume that a telephone line channel is equalized to allow bandpass data transmission over a frequency range of 600 to 3000 Hz. The available bandwidth is 2400 Hz with a center frequency of 1800 Hz. For $r = 1$, evaluate the required bandwidth for 2400 bps QPSK and 4800-bps, eight-level multilevel signaling. Is the bandwidth adequate?

3.16 Why should PCM be preferable to DM for encoding analog signals that represent digital data?

3.17 Are the modem and the codec functional inverses (i.e., could an inverted modem function as a codec, or vice versa)?

3.18 The signal of Problem 2.25 is quantized using 10-bit PCM. Find the signal-to-quantization noise ratio.

3.19 Consider an audio signal with spectral components in the range 300 to 3000 Hz. Assume that a sampling rate of 7 kHz will be used to generate a PCM signal.
   a. For $S/N = 30$ dB, what is the number of uniform quantization levels needed?
   b. What data rate is required?

3.20 Find the step size δ required to prevent slope overload noise as a function of the frequency of the highest-frequency component of the signal. Assume that all components have amplitude A.

3.21 A PCM encoder accepts a signal with a full-scale voltage of 10 V and generates 8-bit codes using uniform quantization. The maximum normalized quantized voltage is $1 - 2^{-8}$. Determine: (a) normalized step size, (b) actual step size in volts, (c) actual maximum quantized level in volts, (d) normalized resolution, (e) actual resolution, and (f) percentage resolution.

3.22 The analog waveform shown in the figure is to be delta modulated. The sampling period and the step size are indicated by the grid on the figure.

The first DM output and the staircase function for this period are also shown. Show the rest of the staircase function and give the DM output. Indicate regions where slope overload distortion exists.

DM output

3.23 An analog data waveform is known to range between 0 and 10 volts. This waveform is Pulse Code Modulated using 4-bit samples. The mapping from samples to bits is done by dividing the 0–10 volt range into unequal intervals. Determine the mapping rule (i.e., what voltage ranges must correspond to what bit combinations) so that the maximum possible percentage error committed is the same for each range.

3.24 A carrier with a frequency of 100 kHz is amplitude-modulated with the signal

$$x(t) = 10 \cos 2\pi \times 10^3 t + 8 \cos 4\pi \times 10^3 t + 6 \cos 8\pi \times 10^3 t$$

a. List the frequencies appearing at the output of the modulator.
b. Develop an expression for the DSBTC output $y(t)$. Assume that the carrier has the form $\cos 2\pi \times 10^5 t$.

3.25 An AM broadcast station operates at its maximum allowed total output of 50 kW and 95% modulation ($n_a = 0.95$). How much of its transmitted power conveys information?

3.26 The carrier $c(t) = A_c \sin 2\pi f_c t$ is to be amplitude-modulated by input $m(t) = A_m \sin 2\pi f_m t$. Derive a simplified expression for the modulated signal $s(t)$.

3.27 A modulated RF waveform is given by $s(t) = 500 \cos [2\pi f_c t + 20 \cos 2\pi f_1 t]$, where $f_1 = 1$ kHz and $f_c = 100$ MHz.
a. If the phase modulation index is 100 rad/V, find the expression for the phase modulation voltage $m(t)$. What is its peak value and frequency?

b. If the frequency modulation index is 10^6 rad/V-s, find the frequency modulation voltage $m(t)$. What is its peak value and frequency?

APPENDIX 3A

Proof of The Sampling Theorem

The sampling theorem can be restated as follows. *Given:*

- $x(t)$ is a bandlimited signal with bandwidth f_h.
- $p(t)$ is a sampling signal consisting of pulses at intervals $T_s = 1/f_s$, where f_s is the sampling frequency.
- $x_s(t) = x(t)p(t)$ is the sampled signal.

Then, $x(t)$ can be recovered exactly from $x_s(t)$ if and only if $f_s \geq 2f_h$.

Proof:

Since $p(t)$ consists of a uniform series of pulses, it is a periodic signal and can be represented by a Fourier series:

$$p(t) = \sum_{n=-\infty}^{\infty} P_n e^{j2\pi n f_s t}$$

We have

$$x_s(t) = x(t)p(t)$$

$$= \sum_{n=-\infty}^{\infty} P_n x(t) e^{j2\pi n f_s t}$$

Now consider the Fourier transform of $x_s(t)$:

$$X_s(f) = \int_{-\infty}^{\infty} x_s(t) e^{-j2\pi f t} \, dt$$

Substituting for $x_s(t)$, we have

$$X_s(f) = \int_{-\infty}^{\infty} \sum_{n=-\infty}^{\infty} P_n x(t) e^{j2\pi n f_s t} \, e^{-j2\pi f t} \, dt$$

Rearranging yields

$$X_s(f) = \sum_{n=-\infty}^{\infty} P_n \int_{-\infty}^{\infty} x(t) e^{-j2\pi (f - n f_s) t} \, dt$$

From the definition of the Fourier transform, we can write

$$X(f - n f_s) = \int_{-\infty}^{\infty} x(t) e^{-j2\pi (f - n f_s) t} \, dt$$

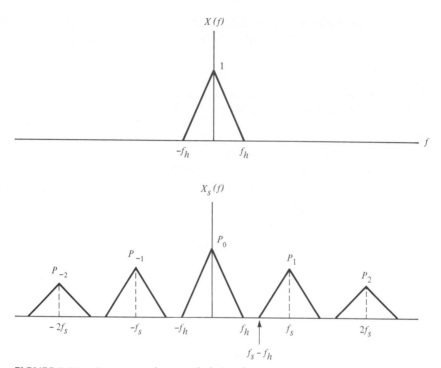

FIGURE 3.20.   Spectrum of a sampled signal.

where $X(f)$ is the Fourier transform of $x(t)$. Substituting this into the preceding equation, we have

$$X_s(f) = \sum_{n=-\infty}^{\infty} P_n X(f - nf_s)$$

This last equation has an interesting interpretation, which is illustrated in Figure 3.20, where we assume without loss of generality that the bandwidth of $x(t)$ is in the range 0 to f_h. The spectrum of $x_s(t)$ is composed of the spectrum of $x(t)$ plus the spectrum of $x(t)$ translated to each harmonic of the sampling frequency. Each of the translated spectra is multiplied by the corresponding coefficient of the Fourier series of $p(t)$. Now, if $f_s > 2f_h$, these various translations do not overlap, and the spectrum of $x(t)$, multiplied by P_0, appears in $X_s(f)$. By passing $X_s(f)$ through a bandpass filter with $f < f_s$, the spectrum of $x(t)$ is recovered. In equation form,

$$X_s(f) = P_0 X(f) \qquad -f_s < f < f_s$$

CHAPTER 4

Digital Data Communication Techniques

In Chapters 2 and 3, we have been concerned primarily with the attributes of data transmission, such as the characteristics of data signals and transmission media, the encoding of signals, and transmission performance. In this chapter we shift our emphasis from data transmission to data communications.

For two devices linked by a transmission medium to exchange data, a high degree of cooperation is required. Typically, data are transmitted one bit at a time over the medium. The timing (rate, duration, spacing) of these bits must be the same for transmitter and receiver. Two common techniques—asynchronous and synchronous—are explored in Section 4.1. Next, we look at the problem of bit errors. As we have seen, data transmission is not an error-free process and some means of accounting for these errors is needed. In Section 4.2 we look at several error-detection techniques. Finally in this chapter, we look at transmission line interfaces. Typically, digital data devices do not attach to and signal across a transmission medium directly. Rather, this process is mediated through a standardized interface.

Another topic relating to these three is that of data link control. This is sufficiently important to warrant a separate chapter, and is explored in Chapter 5.

4.1

ASYNCHRONOUS AND SYNCHRONOUS TRANSMISSION

In this book we are concerned with serial transmission of data; that is, data are transferred over a single communications path rather than a parallel set of lines, as is sometimes done in I/O devices and internal computer signal paths. With serial transmission, signaling elements are sent down the line one at a time. Each signaling element may be

- *Less than one bit:* This is the case, for example, with Manchester coding.
- *One bit:* NRZ-L and FSK are digital and analog examples, respectively.
- *More than one bit:* QPSK is an example.

For simplicity in the following discussion, we assume one bit per signaling element unless otherwise stated. The discussion is not materially affected by this assumption.

It was mentioned in Chapter 1 that synchronization is one of the key tasks of data communications. A transmitter is sending a message one bit at a time through a medium to a receiver. The receiver must recognize the beginning and end of a block of bits. It must also know the duration of each bit so that it can sample the line with the proper timing to read each bit.

Suppose that the sender simply transmits a stream of data bits. The sender has a clock that governs the timing of the transmitted bits. For example, if data are to be transmitted at 10,000 bits per second (bps), then one bit will be transmitted every $1/10,000 = 0.1$ millisecond (ms), as measured by the sender's clock. Typically, the receiver will attempt to sample the medium at the center of each bit time. The receiver will time its samples at intervals of one bit time. In our example, the sampling would occur once every 0.1 ms. If the receiver times its samples based on its own clock, then there will be a problem if the transmitter's and receiver's clocks are not precisely aligned. If there is a drift of 1 percent (the receiver's clock is 1 percent faster or slower than the transmitter's clock), then the first sampling will be 0.01 of a bit time (0.001 ms) away from the center of the bit (center of bit is 0.05 ms from beginning and end of bit). After 50 or more samples, the receiver may be in error because it is sampling in the wrong bit time ($50 \times .001 = .05$ ms). For smaller timing differences, the error would occur later, but eventually the receiver will be out of step with the transmitter if the transmitter sends a sufficiently long stream of bits and if no steps are taken to synchronize the transmitter and receiver.

Asynchronous Transmission

Two approaches are common for achieving the desired synchronization. The first is called, oddly enough, asynchronous transmission. The strategy with this scheme is to avoid the timing problem by not sending long, uninterrupted streams of bits. Instead, data are transmitted one character at a time, where each character is five to eight bits in length. Timing or synchronization must only be maintained within each character; the receiver has the opportunity to resynchronize at the beginning of each new character.

The technique is easily explained with reference to Figure 4.1. When no character is being transmitted, the line between transmitter and receiver is in

(a) Character format

(b) 8-bit asynchronous character stream

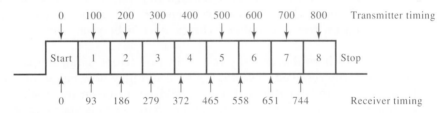

(c) Effect of timing error

FIGURE 4.1. Asynchronous transmission.

an "idle" state. The definition of idle is equivalent to the signaling element for binary 1. For most interface standards, such as EIA-232-D defined later in this chapter, idle corresponds to the presence of a negative voltage on the line. See also the definition of NRZ-L in the preceding chapter. The beginning of a character is signaled by a *start bit* with a value of binary 0. This is followed by the five to eight bits that actually make up the character. The bits of the character are transmitted starting with the least significant bit. For example, for 7-bit ASCII characters, the first bit transmitted is the bit labeled b_1 in Table 2.1. Usually, the character bits are followed by a *parity bit*, which therefore is in the most-significant-bit position. The parity bit is set by the transmitter such that the total number of ones in the character, including the parity bit, is even (even parity) or odd (odd parity), depending on the convention being used. The final element is a *stop*, which is a binary 1. A minimum length for the stop is specified, and this is usually 1, 1.5, or 2 times the duration of an ordinary bit. No maximum value is specified. Since the stop is the same as the idle state, the transmitter will continue to transmit the stop signal until it is ready to send the next character.

If a steady stream of characters is sent, the interval between two characters is uniform and equal to the stop element. For example, if the stop bit has unit length and the ASCII characters ABC are sent (without parity bit), the pattern[1] is 01000001100100001101100001111... The start bit (0) starts the timing sequence for the next eight elements, which are the 7-bit ASCII code and the stop bit. In the idle state, the receiver looks for a transition from 1 to 0 to begin the next character and then samples the input signal at one-bit intervals for seven intervals. It then looks for the next 1-to-0 transition, which will occur no sooner than one bit time.

The timing requirements for this scheme are modest. For example, ASCII characters are typically sent as 8-bit units, including the parity bit. If the receiver is 5 percent slower or faster than the transmitter, the sampling of the eighth information bit will be displaced by 45 percent and still be correctly sampled. Figure 4.1c shows the effects of a timing error of sufficient magnitude to cause an error in reception. In this example we assume a data rate of 10,000 bits per second (10 kbps); therefore, each bit is of 0.1 millisecond (ms), or 100 microseconds' (μs), duration. Assume that the receiver is off by 7 percent, or 7 μs per bit time. Thus, the receiver samples the incoming character every 93 μs (based on the transmitter's clock). As can be seen, the last sample is erroneous.

An error such as this actually results in two errors. First, the last sampled bit is incorrectly received. Second, the bit count may now be out of alignment. If bit 7 is a 1 and bit 8 is a 0, bit 8 could be mistaken for a start bit. This condition is termed a *framing error*, as the character plus start and stop bits is sometimes referred to as a *frame*. A framing error can also occur if some noise condition causes the false appearance of a start bit during the idle state.

Asynchronous communication is simple and cheap but requires an overhead of two to three bits per character. For example, for a 7-bit code, using a 1-bit-long stop bit, two out of every nine bits convey no information but are there merely for synchronization; thus the overhead is 2/9 = 0.22. Of course, the percentage overhead could be reduced by sending larger blocks of bits between the start and stop bits. However, as Figure 4.1c indicates, the larger the block of bits, the greater the cumulative timing error. To use larger blocks of bits successfully, a different form of synchronization, known as synchronous transmission, is used.

Synchronous Transmission

A more efficient means of communication is synchronous transmission. In this mode, blocks of characters or bits are transmitted without start and stop codes, and the exact departure or arrival time of each bit is predictable. To prevent timing drift between transmitter and receiver, their clocks must somehow be synchronized. One possibility is to provide a separate clock line between trans-

---

[1]The bits, reading from left to right, are printed here in order of transmission.

mitter and receiver. Otherwise, the clocking information must be embedded in the data signal. For digital signals, this can be achieved with biphase encoding. For analog signals, a number of techniques can be used; the carrier frequency itself can be used to synchronize the receiver based on the phase of the carrier.

With synchronous transmission, there is another level of synchronization required, to allow the receiver to determine the beginning and end of a block of data. To achieve this, each block begins with a *preamble* bit pattern and generally ends with *postamble* bit pattern. These patterns are control information rather than data. In addition, other control information is included that is used in the data link control procedures discussed in Chapter 5. The data plus control information is called a *frame*. The exact format of the frame depends on whether the transmission scheme is character-oriented or bit-oriented.

With *character-oriented* transmission, the block of data is treated as a sequence of characters (usually 8-bit characters). All control information is in character form. The frame begins with one or more "synchronization characters" (Figure 4.2a). The synchronization character, usually called *SYN*, is a unique bit pattern that signals the receiver that this is the beginning of a block. The postamble is another unique character used in some schemes. The receiver thus is alerted to an incoming block of data by the SYN characters and accepts data until the postamble character is seen. The receiver can then look for the next SYN pattern. Alternatively, another approach is to include frame length as part of the control information. The receiver then looks for a SYN character, determines frame length, reads the indicated number of characters, and then looks for the next SYN character to start the next frame.

With *bit-oriented* transmission, the block of data is treated as a sequence of bits. Neither data nor control information needs to be interpreted in units of 8-bit characters. As with character-oriented schemes, a special bit pattern signals

(a) Character – oriented frame

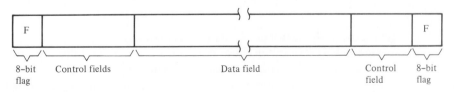

(b) Bit – oriented frame

FIGURE 4.2. Synchronous transmission.

the beginning of a block. In bit-oriented transmission, this preamble is eight bits long and is referred to as a flag. The same flag is also used as a postamble (Figure 4.2b). The receiver looks for the occurrence of the flag pattern to signal start of frame. This is followed by some number of control fields, then a variable-length data field, more control fields, and finally the flag is repeated. The differences between this approach and the character-oriented approach depend on details of the formats and the interpretation of the control information. This subject is explored in Chapter 5.

For sizable blocks of data, synchronous transmission is far more efficient than asynchronous. Asynchronous transmission requires 20% or more overhead. The control information in synchronous transmission is typically less than 100 bits. For example, one of the more common bit-oriented schemes, HDLC, contains 48 bits of control information (including the flags). Thus for a 1000-bit message, the overhead is only $48/1048 \times 100\% = 4.6\%$.

4.2

ERROR DETECTION TECHNIQUES

In earlier chapters we talked about transmission impairments and the effect of data rate and S/N on bit error rate. Regardless of the design of the transmission system, there will be errors. And, while thermal noise errors may be reduced to vanishingly small rates, bursty impulse noise may still result in substantial errors.

When a frame is transmitted, three classes of probabilities can be defined at the receiving end:

- *Class 1 (P_1):* A frame arrives with no bit errors.
- *Class 2 (P_2):* A frame arrives with one or more undetected bit errors.
- *Class 3 (P_3):* A frame arrives with one or more detected bit errors but no undetected bit errors.

First consider the case when no means are taken to detect errors. Then the probability of detected errors (P_3) is zero. To express the remaining probabilities, assume that the probability that any given bit is in error, P_B, is constant and independent of bit position. Then we have

$$P_1 = (1 - P_B)^{N_f}$$
$$P_2 = 1 - P_1$$

where N_f is the number of bits per frame.

Figure 4.3a illustrates these equations and shows how the probability of erroneous frames increases drastically with bit error probability. Consider the rather modest requirement that at most one frame with an undetected bit error should occur per day on a continuously-used 300 bps channel. If the frame length is 16 bits, this requirement means that at most one frame out of 1.62×10^6 has an error ($P_2 = 0.6 \times 10^{-6}$). A typical P_B for a public telephone line

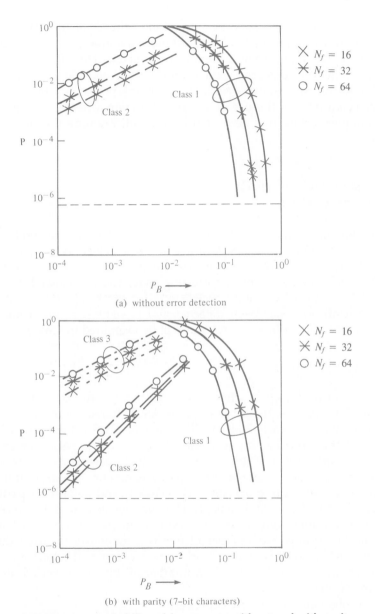

(a) without error detection

(b) with parity (7–bit characters)

FIGURE 4.3.   Probability of frame error without and with parity bits.

using a 300 bps modem is 10^{-4}. The resulting value of P_2 can be seen to be about three orders of magnitude too large to meet our requirement.

This is the kind of result that motivates the use of error-detection techniques. All of these techniques operate on the following principle: For a given frame of bits, additional bits that constitute an *error-detecting code*, are added by the transmitter. This code is calculated as a function of the other transmitted bits. The receiver performs the same calculation and compares the two results. A detected error occurs if and only if there is a mismatch. Thus P_3 is the probability that if a frame contains errors, the error-detection scheme will detect that fact. P_2 is known as the *residual error rate*, and is the probability that an error will be undetected despite the use of an error-detection scheme. A number of specific techniques follow this general rule. We will examine the three most common ones:

* Parity bit.
* Longitudinal redundancy check.
* Cyclic redundancy check.

Of course, the detection of an error does no good unless some action is taken to correct the error. One approach is to use an error-detection technique that generates sufficient information that errors can be corrected by the receiver. This technique is known as an error-correcting code, and is reviewed briefly in this section. A far more common procedure is for the receiver to notify the transmitter that an error has been detected and to request a retransmission. This is an element of data link control and will be examined in Chapter 5.

Parity Checks

The simplest bit error detection scheme is to append a parity bit to the end of each word in the frame. A typical example is ASCII transmission, in which a parity bit is attached to each 7-bit ASCII character. The value of this bit is selected so that the word has an even number of 1's (even parity) or an odd number of 1's (odd parity). Typically even parity is used for asynchronous transmission and odd parity for synchronous transmission. So, for example, if the transmitter is transmitting an ASCII G (1110001) and using odd parity, it will append a 1 and transmit 11100011. The receiver examines the received character and if the total number of 1's is odd, assumes that no error has occurred. If one bit or any odd number of bits is erroneously inverted during transmission (e.g., 11000011), then, clearly, the receiver will detect an error. Note, however, that if two (or any even number of) bits are inverted, an undetected error occurs!

Again the probabilities are easily expressed:

$$P_1 = (1 - P_B)^{N_B N_C}$$

$$P_2 = \sum_{k=1}^{N_C} \binom{N_C}{k} \left[\sum_{j=2,4,\ldots}^{N_B} \binom{N_B}{j} P_B^j (1 - P_B)^{(N_B - j)} \right]^k$$
$$[(1 - P_B)^{N_B}]^{(N_C - k)}$$

$$P_3 = 1 - P_2 - P_1$$

where

N_B = number of bits per character (including the parity bit)
N_C = number of characters per frame

These three probabilities are illustrated in Figure 4.3b ($N_F = N_B \times N_C$). The parity bit dramatically reduces the probability of accepting a frame with undetected errors (P_2), while the probability of receiving a correct frame does not change significantly. For a bit error rate of 10^{-4}, the value of P_2 now approaches the requirements of the preceding example. For longer frames, however, this is still not sufficient.

The problem with the use of the parity bit is that noise impulses are often long enough to destroy more than one bit, particularly at high data rates. Figure 4.4 shows the probability of a second error bit within X bits of a first error bit on a 1200-bps voice-grade line. Thus the formulation used previously for P_2 is too conservative.

A substantial improvement can be achieved by using a second set of parity bits, as illustrated in Figure 4.5. The frame is viewed as a block of characters arranged in two dimensions. To each character is appended a parity bit, as before. In addition, a parity bit is generated for each bit position across all characters. That is, an additional character is generated in which the *I*th bit of the character is a parity bit for the *I*th bit of all other characters in the block. This can be expressed mathematically using the exclusive-or $\oplus$ operation. The exclusive-or of two binary digits is 0 if both digits are 0 or both are 1. If the digits differ, the result is 1. Let us call the parity bit at the end of each character the row parity bit. Then

$$R_j = b_{1j} \oplus b_{2j} \oplus \cdots b_{nj}$$

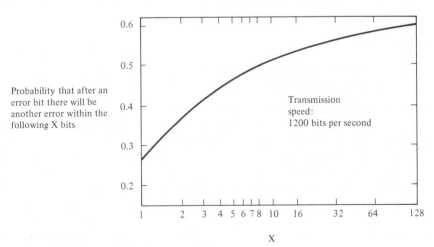

FIGURE 4.4.   **Probability of a second error bit.**

	bit 1	bit 2		bit n	Parity bit
Character 1	b_{11}	b_{21}		bn_1	R_1
Character 2	b_{12}	b_{22}		bn_2	R_2
Character m	b_{1m}	b_{2m}		b_{nm}	R_m
Parity check character	C_1	C_2		C_n	C_{n+1}

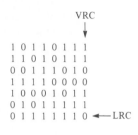

(a) Format   (b) Example

FIGURE 4.5.   Vertical and longitudinal redundancy checks.

where

R_j = parity bit of jth character
b_{ij} = ith bit in jth character
n = number of bits in a character

This equation generates even parity. For the parity check character:

$$C_i = b_{i1} \oplus b_{i2} \oplus \cdots \oplus b_{in}$$

where

C_i = ith bit of parity check character
m = number of characters in a frame

In this format, the parity bits at the end of each character are referred to as the vertical redundancy check (VRC), and the parity check character is referred to as the longitudinal redundancy check (LRC).

Measurements indicate that the use of both VRC and LRC reduces the undetected error rate compared to simple VRC by two to four orders of magnitude [MART88]. However, even this scheme is not foolproof. Consider the case of bits 1 and 3 in character 1 being in error. When the receiver generates the parity bit for character 1, it will match the received parity bit, and no error is detected. However, when it generates the parity check character, bits 1 and 3 will differ from those of the received parity check character, and the error is detected. Now suppose that, in addition, bits 1 and 3 of character 5 are also in error. Not only do the parity bits for characters 1 and 5 fail to detect errors, but the parity check character also fails to detect them. Thus some patterns of even numbers of errors remain undetected.

Cyclic Redundancy Checks

To achieve further improvement, a very powerful but easily implemented technique, known as *cyclic redundancy check* (CRC), can be used. The procedure can be explained as follows. Given a k-bit frame or message, the transmitter generates an n-bit sequence, known as a *frame check sequence* (FCS), so that the resulting frame, consisting of $k + n$ bits, is exactly divisible by some predetermined number. The receiver then divides the incoming frame by the same number and, if there is no remainder, assumes that there was no error.

To clarify the above, we present the procedure in several ways:

- Modulo 2 arithmetic.
- Polynomials.
- Shift registers and exclusive-or gates.

First, we work with binary numbers and modulo 2 arithmetic. Modulo 2 arithmetic uses binary addition with no carries, which is just the exclusive-or operation.

Examples

$$
\begin{array}{r}
1111 \\
+\,1010 \\
\hline
0101
\end{array}
\qquad
\begin{array}{r}
11001 \\
\times\quad 11 \\
\hline
11001 \\
11001 \\
\hline
101011
\end{array}
$$

Now define:

$T = (k + n)$-bit frame to be transmitted, with $n < k$
$M = k$-bit message, the first k bits of T
$F = n$-bit FCS, the last n bits of T
$P = $ pattern of $n + 1$ bits; this is the predetermined divisor mentioned above

We would like T/P to have no remainder. It should be clear that

$$T = 2^n M + F$$

That is, by multiplying M by 2^n, we have in effect shifted it to the left by n bits and padded out the result with 0's. Adding F gives us the concatenation of M and F, which is T. Now we want T to be exactly divisible by P. Suppose that we divided $2^n M$ by P:

$$\frac{2^n M}{P} = Q + \frac{R}{P} \tag{4.1}$$

There is a quotient and a remainder. Since division is binary, the remainder is always one bit less than the divisor. We will use this remainder as our FCS. Then

$$T = 2^n M + R$$

Question: Does this R satisfy our condition? To see that it does, consider

$$\frac{T}{P} = \frac{2^n M + R}{P}$$

Substituting equation (4.1), we have

$$\frac{T}{P} = Q + \frac{R}{P} + \frac{R}{P}$$

However, any binary number added to itself modulo 2 yields zero. Thus

$$\frac{T}{P} = Q + \frac{R + R}{P} = Q$$

There is no remainder, and therefore T is exactly divisible by P. Thus the FCS is easily generated. Simply divide $2^n M$ by P and use the remainder as the FCS. On reception, the receiver will divide T by P and will get no remainder if there have been no errors.

A simple example of the procedure is now presented:

1. Given

$$
\begin{aligned}
\text{Message } M &= 1010001101 \text{ (10 bits)} \\
\text{Pattern } P &= 110101 \text{ (6 bits)} \\
\text{FCS } R &= \text{to be calculated (5 bits)}
\end{aligned}
$$

2. The message is multiplied by 2^5, yielding 101000110100000.
3. This product is divided by P:

```
                              1101010110←Q
       P→110101|101000110100000←2ⁿM
                110101
                111011
                110101
                  111010
                  110101
                    111110
                    110101
                      101100
                      110101
                        110010
                        110101
                          1110←R
```

4. The remainder (R = 01110) is added to $2^n M$ to give T = 10100011010110, ~~type-0~~
   which is transmitted.
5. If there are no errors, the receiver receives T intact. The received frame is
   divided by P:

$$
\begin{array}{r}
1101010110 \\
110101\,\overline{)101000110101110} \\
\underline{110101} \\
111011 \\
\underline{110101} \\
111010 \\
\underline{110101} \\
111110 \\
\underline{110101} \\
101111 \\
\underline{110101} \\
110101 \\
\underline{110101} \\
00
\end{array}
$$

Since there is no remainder, it is assumed that there have been no errors. ∎

The pattern P is chosen to be one bit longer than the desired FCS, and the
exact bit pattern chosen depends on the type of errors expected. At minimum,
both the high- and low-order bits of P must be 1.

The occurrence of an error is easily expressed. An error results in the rever-
sal of a bit. Mathematically, this is equivalent to taking the exclusive-or of the
bit and 1: $0 + 1 = 1$; $1 + 1 = 0$. Thus the errors in an $(n + k)$-bit frame can
be represented by an $(n + k)$-bit field with 1's in each error position. The
resulting frame T_r can be expressed as

$$T_r = T + E$$

where

   T = transmitted frame
   E = error pattern with 1's in positions where errors occur
   T_r = received frame

The receiver will fail to detect an error if and only if T_r is divisible by P, that
is, if and only if E is divisible by P. Intuitively, this seems an unlikely occurrence.

A second way of viewing the CRC process is to express all values as polynomials in a dummy variable X with binary coefficients. The coefficients
correspond to the bits in the binary number. Thus for M = 110011, we have
$M(X) = X^5 + X^4 + X + 1$, and for P = 11001, we have $P(X) = X^4 +
X^3 + 1$. Arithmetic operations are again modulo 2. The CRC process can now
be described as

1. $\dfrac{X^n M(X)}{P(X)} = Q(X) + \dfrac{R(X)}{P(X)}$

2. $T(X) = X^n M(X) + R(X)$

An error $E(X)$ will only be undetectable if it is divisible by $P(X)$. It can be shown [PETE61] that all of the following are not divisible by $P(X)$ and hence are detectable:

1. All single-bit errors.
2. All double-bit errors, as long as $P(X)$ has a factor with at least three terms.
3. Any odd number of errors, as long as $P(X)$ contains a factor $(X + 1)$.
4. Any burst error for which the length of the burst is less than the length of the FCS.
5. Most larger burst errors.

The first assertion is clear. A single-bit error can be represented by $E(X) = X^i$ for some i. We have said that for $P(X)$ both the first and last terms must be nonzero. Thus $P(X)$ has at least two terms and cannot divide the one-term $E(X)$. Similarly, a two-bit error can be represented by $E(X) = X^i + X^j = X^i(1 + X^{j-i})$ for some i and j with $i < j$. Thus $P(X)$ must divide either X^i or $(1 + X^{j-i})$. We have shown that it does not divide X^i, and it can be shown [PETE61] that it does not divide $(1 + X^{j-i})$ except for very large values of $j - i$, beyond the practical frame length. To see the third assertion, assume that $E(X)$ has an odd number of terms and is divisible by $(X + 1)$. Then we can express $E(X)$ as $E(X) = (X + 1)F(X)$. Then $E(1) = (1 + 1)F(1) = 0$ since $1 + 1 = 0$. But $E(1)$ will be 0 if and only if $E(X)$ contains an even number of terms. For the fourth assertion, we define a burst of length j as a string of bits beginning and ending with 1 and containing intervening 1's and 0's. This can be represented as $E(X) = X^i(X^{j-1} + \ldots + 1)$ where i expresses how far the burst is shifted from the right-hand end. We know that $P(X)$ does not divide X^i. For $j < n$, where n is the length of the FCS, $P(X)$ will not divide the second factor, since $P(X)$ is of higher order.

Finally, it can be shown that if all error patterns are considered equally likely, then for a burst of length $r + 1$, the probability that $E(X)$ is divisible by $P(X)$ is $1/2^{r-1}$, and for a longer burst, the probability is $1/2^r$ [PETE61].

Four versions of $P(X)$ are widely used:

$$\begin{aligned}
\text{CRC-12} &= X^{12} + X^{11} + X^3 + X^2 + X + 1 \\
\text{CRC-16} &= X^{16} + X^{15} + X^2 + 1 \\
\text{CRC-CCITT} &= X^{16} + X^{12} + X^5 + 1 \\
\text{CRC-32} &= X^{32} + X^{26} + X^{23} + X^{22} + X^{16} + X^{12} + X^{11} \\
&\quad + X^{10} + X^8 + X^7 + X^5 + X^4 + X^2 + X + 1
\end{aligned}$$

The CRC-12 system is used for transmission of streams of 6-bit characters and generates a 12-bit FCS. Both CRC-16 and CRC-CCITT are popular for 8-bit characters, in the United States and Europe respectively, and both result in a 16-bit FCS. This would seem adequate for most applications, although CRC-32 is specified as an option in some point-to-point synchronous transmission standards. The local network standards committee (IEEE-802), evidently a suspicious lot, has specified the use of CRC-32, which generates a 32-bit FCS. This CRC is also used in some DOD applications.

Finally, the CRC process can be represented by, and indeed implemented as, a dividing circuit consisting of exclusive-or gates and a shift register. The shift register is a string of 1-bit storage devices. Each device has an output line, which indicates the value currently stored, and an input line. At discrete time instants, known as clock times, the value in the storage device is replaced by the value indicated by its input line. The entire register is clocked simultaneously, causing a 1-bit shift along the entire register.

The circuit is implemented as follows:

1. The register contains n bits, equal to the length of the FCS.
2. There are up to n exclusive-or gates.
3. The presence or absence of a gate corresponds to the presence or absence of a term in the divisor polynomial, $P(X)$.

The architecture of this circuit is best explained by first considering an example, which is illustrated in Figure 4.6. In this example, we use

$$\text{Message } M = 1010001101; \quad M(X) = X^9 + X^7 + X^3 + X^2 + 1$$
$$\text{Divisor } P = 110101; \quad P(X) = X^5 + X^4 + X^2 + 1$$

which were used earlier in the discussion.

Part (a) of the figure shows the shift register implementation. The process begins with the shift register cleared (all zeroes). The message, or dividend, is then entered, one bit at a time, starting with the most significant bit. Part (b) is a table that shows the step-by-step operation as the input is applied one bit at a time. Each row of the table shows the values currently stored in the five shift-register elements. In addition, the row shows the values that appear at the outputs of the three exclusive-or circuits. Finally, the row shows the value of the next input bit, which is available for the operation of the next step.

Since no feedback occurs until a 1-dividend bit arrives at the most significant end of the register, the first five operations are simple shifts. Whenever a 1 bit arrives at the left end of the register (c_4), a 1 is subtracted (exclusive-or) from the second (c_3), fourth (c_1), and sixth (input) bits on the next shift. This is identical to the binary long-division process illustrated earlier. The process continues through all the bits of the message, plus five zero bits. These latter bits account for shifting M to the left five positions to accommodate the FCS. After the last bit is processed, the shift register contains the remainder (FCS), which can then be transmitted.

At the receiver, the same logic is used. As each bit of M arrives, it is inserted into the shift register. If there have been no errors, the shift register should contain the bit pattern for R at the conclusion of M. The transmitted bits of R now begin to arrive, and the effect is to zero out the register so that, at the conclusion of reception, the register contains all 0's.

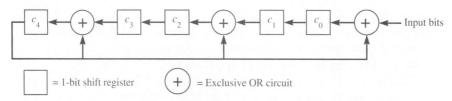

(a) Shift-register implementation

	c_4	c_3	c_2	c_1	c_0	$c_4 \oplus c_3$	$c_4 \oplus c_1$	$c_4 \oplus$ Input	Input	
Initial	0	0	0	0	0	0	0	1	1	
Step 1	0	0	0	0	1	0	0	0	0	
Step 2	0	0	0	1	0	0	1	1	1	
Step 3	0	0	1	0	1	0	0	0	0	
Step 4	0	1	0	1	0	1	1	0	0	
Step 5	1	0	1	0	0	1	1	1	0	Message to be sent
Step 6	1	1	1	0	1	0	1	0	1	
Step 7	0	1	1	1	0	1	1	1	1	
Step 8	1	1	1	0	1	0	1	1	0	
Step 9	0	1	1	1	1	1	1	1	1	
Step 10	1	1	1	1	1	0	0	1	0	
Step 11	0	1	0	1	1	1	1	0	0	
Step 12	1	0	1	1	0	1	0	1	0	Five zeros added
Step 13	1	1	0	0	1	0	1	1	0	
Step 14	0	0	1	1	1	0	1	0	0	
Step 15	0	1	1	1	0	1	1	0	—	

(b) Example with input of 1010001101

FIGURE 4.6. Circuit with shift registers for dividing by the polynomial $(X^5 + X^4 + X^2 + 1)$.

Figure 4.7 indicates the general architecture of the shift register implementation of a CRC for the polynomial $P(X) = \sum_{i=0}^{n} a_i X^i$ where $a_0 = a_n = 1$ and all other a_i equal either 0 or 1.

The shift register implementation makes clear the power of the CRC algorithm. Due to the feedback arrangement, the state of the shift register depends, in a complex way, on the past history of bits presented. Thus it will take an

Input bits

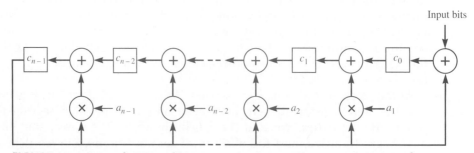

FIGURE 4.7. General CRC architecture to implement divisor $1 + a_1 X + a_2 X^2 + \cdots + a_{n-1} X^{n-1} + X^n$.

extremely rare combination of errors to fool the system. Further, it is evident that the CRC algorithm is easy to implement in hardware.

Forward Error Correction

In addition to error-detecting codes, there are also error-correcting codes. These are rarely used in data transmission, since retransmission schemes (see Chapter 5) are generally more efficient. Error-correcting codes are used in some situations where retransmission is impractical. Examples are broadcast situations in which there are multiple receivers for one transmission and space probes which essentially use simplex transmission. These codes find more use in applications other than data communication, such as computer memory [STAL90b]. Error-correcting codes are referred to as *forward error correction* to indicate that the receiver, on its own, is correcting the error. Retransmission schemes, in contrast, are referred to as *backward error correction,* since the receiver feeds back information to the transmitter, which then retransmits data found to be in error.

As with error-detecting codes, an error-correcting code is calculated from the bits to be transmitted and is then added to the transmission. To achieve acceptable levels of error correction, the length of the code must be about the same as the length of the data, reducing the effective data rate by 50%. With a code of this relative length, a reduction in error rate by a factor of 10^2 to 10^3 is achieved.

The reader interested in such codes is referred to [BHAR83] and [MIER84]. A deeper analysis of both error-detecting and error-correcting codes is found in [GALL68].

4.3

INTERFACING

Most digital data processing devices are possessed of limited data transmission capability. Typically, they generate only digital signals, and these are usually NRZ-L or a variant. The distance across which they can transmit data is also limited. Consequently it is rare for such a device to attach directly to a transmission medium. The more common situation is depicted in Figure 4.8. The devices we are discussing, which include terminals and computers, are generically referred to as *data terminal equipment* (DTE). A DTE makes use of the transmission system through the mediation of *data circuit-terminating equipment* (DCE). An example of the latter is a modem (a good description of a variety of DCEs can be found in [HELD86]).

On one side, the DCE is responsible for transmitting and receiving bits, one at a time, over a transmission medium. On the other side, the DCE must interact with the DTE. In general, this requires both data and control information to be exchanged. This is done over a set of wires referred to as *interchange circuits.* For this scheme to work, a high degree of cooperation is required. The

FIGURE 4.8. Generic interface to transmission medium.

two DCEs must understand each other. That is, the receiver of each must use the same encoding scheme (e.g., Manchester, PSK) as the transmitter of the other. In addition, each DTE-DCE pair must be designed to have complementary interfaces and must be able to interact effectively. To ease the burden on data processing equipment manufacturers and users, standards have been developed that specify the exact nature of the interface between the DTE and the DCE. In contemporary parlance, these standards are known as physical layer protocols, and occupy layer 1 of the OSI model referred to in Chapter 1. In this section we examine the nature and functioning of this interface.

The interface has four important characteristics [BERT80]:

- Mechanical.
- Electrical.
- Functional.
- Procedural.

The *mechanical* characteristics pertain to the actual physical connection of the DTE and DCE. Typically, the signal and control leads are bundled into a cable with a terminator plug, male or female, at each end. The DTE and DCE must each present a plug of opposite gender at one end of the cable, effecting the physical connection. This is analogous to the situation for residential electrical power. Power is provided via a socket or wall outlet, and the device to be attached must have the appropriate plug (two-pronged, two-pronged polarized, three-pronged).

The *electrical* characteristics have to do with the voltage levels and timing of voltage changes. Both DTE and DCE must use the same code (e.g., NRZ-L), must use the same voltage levels to mean the same thing, and must use the same duration of signal elements. These characteristics determine the data rates and distances that can be achieved.

Functional characteristics specify the functions that are performed, by assigning meaning to the various interchange circuits. Functions can be classified into the broad categories of data, control, timing, and ground.

Procedural characteristics specify the sequence of events for transmitting data, based on the functional characteristics of the interface. Examples below should clarify this point.

A variety of standards for interfacing exist. This section presents several of the most important:

- EIA-232-D.
- EIA-530.
- ISDN Physical Interface.

EIA-232-D

By far the most common interface standard in the United States is the 232 standard issued by the Electronic Industries Association. The RS-232 standard was first issued in 1962, and its third revision, RS-232-C, was published in 1969. EIA-232-D was introduced in 1987. It is compatible with RS-232-C. The main differences are: EIA-232-D defines a specific cable connector, whereas RS-232-C allows various connectors to be used; and three additional circuits for test operations have been defined. This interface is used to connect DTE devices to voice-grade modems for use on public analog telecommunications systems. It is also widely used for many other interconnection functions.

The **mechanical specification** for EIA-232-D is illustrated in Figure 4.9. It calls for a 25-pin connector, referred to as the DB-25 connector, with a specific arrangement of leads. Thus, in theory, a 25-wire cable could be used to connect the DTE to the DCE. In practice, fewer interchange circuits are used.

The **electrical specification** defines the signaling between DTE and DCE. Digital signaling is used on all interchange circuits. Depending on the function of the interchange circuit, the electrical values are interpreted either as binary or as control signals. The convention specified is that, with respect to a common ground, a voltage more negative than -3 volts is interpreted as binary 1 and a voltage more positive than $+3$ volts is interpreted as binary 0. The interface is rated at a signal rate of <20 kbps and a distance of <15 m. Greater distances and data rates are possible with good design, but it is reasonable to assume that these limits apply in practice as well as in theory. The same voltage levels apply to control signals: a voltage more negative than -3 volts is interpreted as an OFF condition and a voltage more positive than $+3$ volts is interpreted as an ON condition.

Table 4.1 summarizes the **functional specification** of EIA-232-D. The interchange circuits can be grouped into the categories of data, control, timing, and ground. There is one *data circuit* in each direction, so full-duplex operation is possible. In addition, there are two secondary data circuits that are useful when the device operates in a half-duplex fashion. In the case of half-duplex operation, data exchange between two DTEs (via their DCEs and the intervening communications link) is only possible in one direction at a time. However, there may be a need to send a halt or flow control message to a transmitting device. To accommodate this, the communications link is equipped with a

Dimensions in millimeters

(a) EIA-232-D DTE connector

Dimensions in millimeters

(b) EIA-232-D DCE connector

FIGURE 4.9.   EIA-232-D connector.

152

TABLE 4.1   EIA-232-D Interchange Circuits

Pin/ Circuit Label	Name	Direction to:	Function
Data Signals			
2/BA	Transmitted Data	DCE	Data generated by DTE
3/BB	Received Data	DTE	Data received by DTE
14/SBA	Secondary Transmitted Data	DCE	Data generated by DTE on reverse channel
16/SBB	Secondary Received Data	DTE	Data received by DTE on reverse channel
Control Signals			
4/CA	Request to Send	DCE	DTE wishes to transmit
5/CB	Clear to Send	DTE	DCE is ready to receive; response to Request to Send
6/CC	DCE Ready[1]	DTE	DCE is ready to operate
20/CD	DTE Ready[2]	DCE	DTE is ready to operate
22/CE	Ring Indicator	DTE	Indicates that the DCE is receiving a ringing signal on the communication channel
8/CF	Received Line Signal Detector	DTE	Indicates that the DCE is receiving a carrier signal
21/CG	Signal Quality Detector	DTE	Asserted when there is reason to believe there is an error in the received data
23/CH	Data Signal Rate Select	DCE	Asserted to select the higher of two possible data rates
23/CI	Data Signal Rate Select	DTE	Asserted to select the higher of two possible data rates
19/SCA	Secondary Request to Send	DCE	DTE wishes to transmit on reverse channel
13/SCB	Secondary Clear to Send	DTE	DCE is ready to receive on reverse channel
12/SCF	Secondary Received Line Signal Detector	DTE	Indicates that the DCE is receiving a carrier signal on reverse channel
21/RL	Remote Loopback[3]	DCE	Instructs remote DCE to loop back signals
18/LL	Local Loopback[4]	DCE	Instructs DCE to loop back signals from DTE
25/TM	Test Mode[4]	DTE	Indicates if the local DCE is in a test condition
Timing Signals			
24/DA	Transmitter Signal Element Timing	DCE	Clocking signal; transitions to ON and OFF occur at center of each signal element
15/DB	Transmitter Signal Element Timing	DTE	Clocking signal, as above; both circuits relate to signals on BA
17/DD	Receiver Signal Element Timing	DTE	Clocking signal, as above; for circuit BB
Ground/Shield			
7/AB	Signal Ground/Common Return	N/A	Establishes common ground reference for all circuits
1	Shield[5]	N/A	Used for connection to shield on DTE side to provide shield continuity in cases where several cables are connected end to end

[1]This circuit was Data Set Ready in RS-232-C

[2]This circuit was Data Terminal Ready in RS-232-C

[3]Remote Loopback was not included in RS-232-C; only the CG interpretation

[4]This circuit was unassigned in RS-232-C

[5]This circuit was protective ground in RS-232-C

-153

reverse channel, usually at a much lower data rate than the primary channel, for this purpose. At the DTE–DCE interface, the reverse channel is carried on a separate pair of data circuits.

There are fourteen *control circuits*. The first eight of these listed in Table 4.1 relate to the transmission of data over the primary channel. For asynchronous transmission, six of these circuits are used (CA, CB, CC, CD, CE, CF). The use of these circuits is explained below, in a discussion of procedural specifications. In addition to these six circuits, two other control circuits are used in synchronous transmission. The Signal Quality Detector circuit is turned ON by the DCE to indicate that the quality of the incoming signal over the telephone line has deteriorated beyond some defined threshold. Most high-speed modems support more than one transmission rate so that they can fall back to a lower speed if the telephone line becomes noisy. The Data Signal Rate Selector circuit is used to change speeds. Either the DTE or DCE will have the responsibility of selecting the speed. The next three control circuits (SCZ, SCB, SCF) are used to control the use of the secondary channel.

The last group of control signals relate to loopback testing. These circuits allow the DTE to cause the DCE to perform a loopback test (Figure 4.10). These circuits are only valid if in fact the modem or other DCE supports loopback control; this is now a common modem feature. In the local loopback function, the transmitter output of the modem is connected to the receiver input, disconnecting the modem from the transmission line. A stream of data generated by the user device (e.g., computer) is sent to the modem and looped back to the user device. For remote loopback, the local modem is connected to the transmission facility in the usual fashion, and the receiver output of the remote modem is connected to that modem's transmitter input. During either form of test, the DCE turns ON the Test Mode circuit. Table 4.2 shows the settings for all of the circuits related to loopback testing.

Loopback control is a useful fault isolation tool. For example, suppose that a user at a terminal is communicating with a computer by means of a modem and communication suddenly ceases. Among the possible causes:

1. The terminal's modem has malfunctioned.
2. The communications facility between the two modems has failed.
3. The computer's modem has malfunctioned.
4. The remote computer has malfunctioned.

The loopback tests can help the network manager to isolate the fault. Local loopback checks the functioning of the local interface and the local DCE. Remote loopback tests the operation of the transmission channel and the remote DCE.

There are three *timing circuits* that may be used with synchronous transmission; these provide clock pulses. When the DCE is sending data over circuit BB, it also sends 1-0 and 0-1 transitions on DD, with transitions timed to the middle of each BB signal element. When the DTE is sending data, either the DTE or DCE can provide timing pulses.

(a) Typical configuration for loopback testing

(b) Local loopback testing

(c) Remote loopback testing

FIGURE 4.10. Local and remote loopback with EIA-232-D.

TABLE 4.2   Loopback Circuit Settings for EIA-232-D and EIA-530

Local Loopback		Remote Loopback		
			Local Interface	Remote Interface
Circuit	Condition	Circuit		
DCE Ready	ON	DCE Ready	ON	OFF
Local Loopback	ON	Local Loopback	OFF	OFF
Remote Loopback	OFF	Remote Loopback	ON	OFF
Test Mode	ON	Test Mode	ON	ON

The final set of circuits deal with *grounding and shielding.* The Signal Ground/ Common Return serves as the return circuit for all data leads. Hence, transmission is unbalanced, with only one active wire. The Shield lead is for connection of a shielded cable at the DTE side of the interface. Shielded cables are used to protect against electromagnetic interference.

The **procedural specification** defines the sequence in which the various circuits are used for particular applications. We give a few examples.

The first example is for an asynchronous private line modem, also known as a limited distance modem, used to connect two devises with a point-to-point link. The modem, as a DCE, requires only the following circuits:

- Signal ground (AB).
- Transmitted data (BA).
- Received data (BB).
- Request to send (CA).
- Clear to send (CB).
- DCE ready (CC).
- Received line signal detector (CF).

The first three circuits have been reasonably well explained. When the DTE is ready to send data, it asserts Request to Send. The modem responds, when ready, with Clear to Send, thereby indicating that data may be transmitted over circuit BA. If the arrangement is half-duplex, then Request to Send also inhibits the receive mode. The DCE Ready circuit is asserted by the modem when it is ready to operate. The lead should be asserted before the DTE attempts Request to Send. Finally, Received Line Signal Detector indicates that the remote modem is transmitting. Note that it is not necessary to use timing circuits, since this is asynchronous transmission.

The circuits described so far are sufficient for private line modems used point-to-point, but additional circuits are required when the telephone network is used. Now, the initiator of a connection must call the destination station. Two additional leads are required:

- DTE ready.
- Ring indicator.

With the addition of these two circuits, the DTE-modem system can effectively use the telephone lines in a way analogous to voice telephone usage. Figure 4.11 depicts the steps involved in a dial-up half-duplex operation. In this case, a call is placed from a terminal to a computer. The computer must be available to receive calls, which it indicates to its modem by setting Data

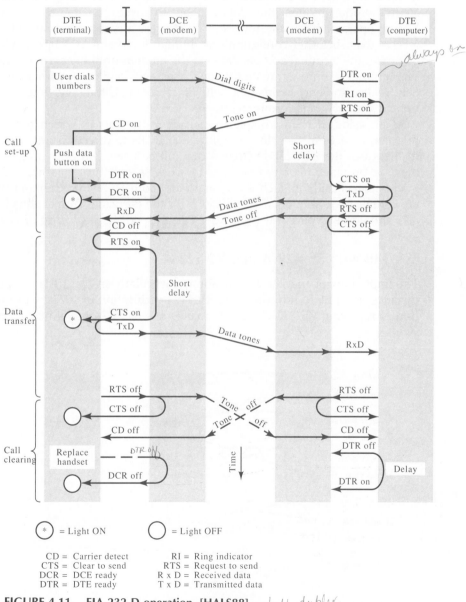

FIGURE 4.11. EIA-232-D operation. [HALS88] *half duplex*

Terminal Ready ON. When the call comes in, indicated to the modem by a ringing tone on the line, the modem alerts the computer with a Ring Indicator. Typically, the computer will respond to an incoming connection request with some sort of prompt message to the terminal. First, the computer sets Request to Send ON to indicate to the modem that it would like to transmit. The modem begins to transmit a carrier frequency on the telephone line and sets Clear to Send to signal the computer that it may begin transmitting. The carrier tone alerts the other modem that data is about to arrive. In some configurations, a human operator hears the tone and must press a data on button to be able to receive data. In other configurations, human intervention is not necessary. In any case, the terminal accepts data via the modem until the carrier is dropped. The terminal can now transmit its own message, beginning with a Request-to-Send, Clear-to-Send handshake with its modem. Ultimately, one side hangs up and the exchange terminates.

As an aside, it is instructive to consider situations in which the distances between devices are so close to allow two DTEs to directly signal each other. In this case, the EIA-232-D circuits can still be used, but now no DCE equipment is provided. For the scheme to work, a *null modem* is needed, which interconnects leads in such a way as to fool both DTEs into thinking that they are connected to modems. The reasons for the particular connections in Figure 4.12 should be apparent if the reader has grasped the preceding discussion.

EIA-530 with RS-422-A and RS-423-A

The limitations of the 232 specification, particularly in the areas of speed and distance, led EIA to introduce the RS-449 specification in 1977, with the intention of replacing RS-232-C. RS-449 makes use of a 37-pin connector, provides

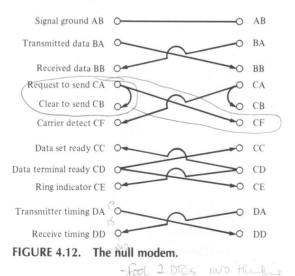

FIGURE 4.12. The null modem.

more functions, and provides an improved speed and distance capability. However, this specification was not embraced by industry and never made a noticeable dent in the 232 base. This is partially due to the tremendous investment in DB-25 hardware. Also, a given product's surface area can hold fewer 37-pin connectors than 25-pin connectors, allowing fewer ports.

Accordingly, in 1987 EIA-530 was introduced. This standard is intended to operate at data rates from 20 kbps to 2 Mbps using the same 25-pin, DB-25 connector used by EIA-232-D and RS-232-C.

The major improvement in EIA-530 over the 232 family is in the electrical characteristics of the new interface. Actually, EIA-530 does not include an electrical specification; rather it refers to two other EIA standards: RS-422-A and RS-423-A. Whereas RS-232 was designed in the era of discrete electronic components, the new standards take advantage of the superior performance possibilities of integrated circuit technology. To understand these standards, we need to define several modes of transmission.

In a conventional telephone system, and indeed in most uses of twisted pair, signals are carried on a *balanced transmission* line consisting of two conductors. Signals are transmitted as a current that travels down one conductor and returns on the other, the two conductors form a complete circuit. For digital signals this technique is known as *differential signaling*, since the binary value depends on the direction of the voltage difference between the two conductors. *Unbalanced transmission* uses a single conductor to carry the signal, with ground providing the return path.

The balanced mode tolerates more, and produces less, noise than the unbalanced. Ideally, interference on a balanced line will act equally on both conductors and not affect the voltage difference. Because unbalanced transmission does not possess these advantages, it is generally limited to use on coaxial cable; when it is used on interchange circuits, such as EIA-232-D, it is limited to very short distances.

RS-423-A specifies unbalanced transmission. As with EIA-232-D, an NRZ-L encoding scheme is used. In this case, a positive voltage of between 2 and 6 volts, with respect to ground, is interpreted as a binary 0, and a negative voltage of between 4 and 6 volts is interpreted as binary 1. RS-423-A achieves the following rated performance: 3 kbps at 1000 m to 300 kbps at 10 m. This is a significant improvement over EIA-232-D, which is a constant limit of 20 kbps up to 15 m. RS-422-A specifies balanced transmission. Again, an NRL-Z scheme is used; in this case a voltage difference between the two circuits in the range 2 to 6 volts is interpreted as a binary digit, with the direction of the difference determining whether it is interpreted as binary 0 or binary 1. The performance with this standard is 100 kbps at 1200 m to 10 Mbps at 12 m; a graph of the rated performance was shown in Figure 2-19. Although the interface is capable of up to 10 Mbps, EIA-232-D specifies a maximum data rate of 2 Mbps.

Most of the EIA-530 circuits use RS-422-A and hence require two pins for balanced transmission; these are referred to as Category I circuits. Only the three loopback circuits use RS-423-A; these are referred to as Category II circuits. Thus, some of the functionality of EIA-232-D must be sacrificed to remain within the 25-pin limit. In particular, the following EIA-232-D circuits are not supported on EIA-530: Ring Indicator, Signal Quality Detector, Data Signal Rate Selector, and the five secondary circuits.

ISDN Physical Connector

The wide variety of functions available with EIA-232D and EIA-530 is provided by the use of a large number of circuits and connections. This is a rather expensive way to achieve results. An alternative would be to provide fewer circuits but to add more logic at the DTE and DCE interfaces. With the dropping costs of logic circuitry, this is an attractive approach. This approach was taken in the X.21 standard for interfacing to public circuit-switched networks, specifying a 15-pin connector. More recently, the trend has been carried further with the specification of an 8-pin physical connector to an Integrated Services Digital Network (ISDN). ISDN, which is an all-digital replacement for existing public telephone and telecommunications networks, is examined in detail in Part IV. In this section, we look at the physical connector defined for ISDN.

In ISDN terminology, a physical connection is made between terminal equipment (TE) and network-terminating equipment (NT). For purposes of our discussion, these terms correspond, rather closely, to DTE and DCE respectively. The physical connection, defined in ISO standard 8877 (ISO 8877), specifies that the NT and TE cables shall terminate in matching plugs that provide for 8 contacts.

Table 4.3 lists the contact assignments for each of the 8 pins on both the NT and TE sides. Two pins each are needed to provide balanced transmission in each direction. These contact points are used to connect twisted-pair leads coming from the NT and TE devices.

TABLE 4.3 Contact Assignments for Plugs and Jacks of ISDN Physical Connector (ISO 8877)

Contact Number	TE	NT
1	Power Source 3	Power Sink 3
2	Power Source 3	Power Sink 3
3	Transmit	Receive
4	Receive	Transmit
5	Receive	Transmit
6	Transmit	Receive
7	Power Sink 2	Power Source 2
8	Power Sink 2	Power Source 2

TE = terminal equipment
NT = network-terminating equipment

Since there are no specific functional circuits, the transmit/receive circuits must be used to carry both data and control signals. The details of this arrangement are deferred until Part IV. For now, suffice it to say that control information is transmitted in the form of messages, and that this information is multiplexed onto the same interface with data using a synchronous TDM technique.

The electrical specification for the interface dictates the use of a pseudoternary coding scheme (Figure 3-2 and Table 3-1). Binary one is represented by the absence of voltage, binary zero is represented by a positive or negative pulse of 750 mV $\pm 10\%$. The data rate is 192 kbps.

4.4

RECOMMENDED READING

An excellent book that covers all of the topics of this chapter is [MCNA88]; the book has somewhat of an electrical engineering orientation but is nevertheless quite approachable and is as thorough as most readers could wish for. [PETE61] is a good presentation of CRC codes; [RAMA88] discusses various CRC software algorithms. [BERT80] discusses various physical-level interfaces. [MCCL83] discusses the physical-level interface from the point of view of its role in an overall communications architecture. [SEYE84] is a detailed presentation of RS-232-C.

4.5

PROBLEMS

4.1 A data source produces 7-bit ASCII characters. Derive an expression for the maximum effective data rate (rate of ASCII data bits) over a B-bps line for the following:
   a. Asynchronous transmission, with a 1.5-unit stop bit and a parity bit.
   b. Bit-synchronous transmission, with a frame consisting of 48 control bits and 128 information bits. The information field contains 8-bit (parity included) ASCII characters.
   c. Same as part (b), except that the information field is 1024 bits.
   d. Character-synchronous transmission, with 9 control characters per frame and 16 or 128 information characters.
   e. Same as part (d), with 12 control characters per frame.

4.2 Demonstrate by example (write down a few dozen arbitrary bit patterns with start and stop bits) that a receiver that suffers a framing error on asynchronous transmission will eventually become realigned.

4.3 Suppose that the sender and receiver agree not to use *any* stop bits. Could this work? If so, explain any necessary conditions.

4.4 Consider a system that is clocked by a master clock running at 8 MHz. This clock has a maximum error of 30 seconds in one month. The system uses asynchronous serial transmission based on characters containing one start bit, seven data bits, one parity bit, and one stop bit. If characters are transmitted in a burst mode, how many characters could be sent before a transmission error caused by the master clock error occurs? Assume that each bit must be sampled within 40% of its center position. Note that the transmission rate is not a factor, since both the bit period and the absolute timing error decrease proportionately at higher transmission rates.

4.5 Many serial terminals have a *break* key. The purpose of this is to allow the receiver to interrupt a sender. There are two ways to implement this break. In the first, a character agreed upon by both sender and receiver is used. This character is reserved and its use always means that the originator of this character wants attention. In the second method the line is held low continuously for a period of time long enough so that the line state is not confused with a character.

   a. For a serial system using 1.5 stop bits, odd parity, and 7 data bits, what is the minimum length of this break sequence?

   b. Under what conditions might a steady stream of ASCII NUL characters accomplish the purpose of a break sequence? Note that a possibility of error must be entertained in order to answer this.

4.6 Suppose that synchronous serial data transmission is clocked by two 8-MHz clocks (one for the sender and one for the receiver) that each have a drift of 1 minute in one year. How long a sequence of bits can be sent before possible clock drift can cause a problem? Assume that a bit waveform will be good if it is sampled within 40% of its center and that the sender and receiver are resynchronized at the beginning of each frame. Consider two cases: (a) 300 bps, and (b) 9600 bps.

4.7 An asynchronous transmission uses 8 data bits, an even parity bit, and 2 stop bits. What percentage of clock inaccuracy can be tolerated at the receiver with respect to the framing error? Assume that the bit samples are taken at the middle of the clock periods. Also assume that at the beginning of the start bit the clock and incoming bits are in phase.

4.8 For a constant P_B, Figure 4.3a shows that the class 2 probability increases with the number of bits per frame and the probability of class 1 errors decreases as the number of bits per frame increases. Would you expect this? Why?

4.9 Would you expect that the inclusion of a parity bit would change the probability of receiving a correct message? Why or why not?

4.10 What is the purpose of using modulo 2 arithmetic in computing an FCS rather than binary arithmetic?

4.11 Using Figure 4.4, work out the probability of an undetected error in 7-bit character with one parity bit, given that at least one error has occurred.

4.12 In the VRC/LRC scheme, is the last bit of the parity check character generated horizontally (from the other bits in the character) or vertically (from the parity bit of all other characters)?

4.13 Consider a frame consisting of two characters of four bits each. Assume that the probability of bit error is 10^{-3} and that it is constant and independent for each bit.
   a. What is P, the probability that the frame is received with no undetected errors?
   b. Now add a parity bit to each character, but assume that parity bits are never in error. What is P?
   c. Now add a parity check character, and again assume parity bits are never in error. What is P?

4.14 Using the CRC-CCITT polynomial, generate the 16-bit CRC code for the message consisting of a 1 followed by 15 0's.

4.15 Explain in words why the shift register implementation of CRC will result in all 0's at the receiver if there are no errors. Demonstrate by example.

4.16 For $P = 110011$ and $M = 11100011$, find the CRC.

4.17 A CRC is constructed to generate a 4-bit FCS for an 11-bit message. The generator polynomial is $X^4 + X^3 + 1$.
   a. Show that the generator polynomial is a valid one.
   b. Draw the shift register circuit that would perform this task (see Figure 4.6).
   c. Encode the data bit sequence 10011011100 (leftmost bit is the least significant bit) using the generator polynomial and give the code word.
   d. Now assume that bit 7 (counting from the LSB) in the codeword is in error and show that the detection algorithm detects the error.

4.18 A modified CRC procedure is commonly used in communications standards. It is defined as follows:

$$\frac{X^{16}\, M(X) + X^k\, L(X)}{P(X)} = Q(X) + \frac{R(X)}{P(X)}$$
$$FCS = L(X) + R(X)$$

where

$$L(X) = X^{15} + X^{14} + X^{13} + \ldots X + 1$$
$$k = \text{number of bits in } M$$

   a. Describe in words the effect of this procedure.
   b. Can you explain the potential benefits?
   c. Show a shift register implementation for $P(X) = X^{16} + X^{12} + X^5 + 1$.

4.19 Draw a timing diagram showing the state of all EIA-232-D leads between two DTE-DCE pairs during the course of a data call on the switched telephone network.

4.20 Explain the operation of each null modem connection in Figure 4.10.

4.21 For the EIA-232-D RL circuit to function properly, what circuits must be logically connected?

4.22 Refer to Figure 4.12. The sender's Request to Send is connected to his own Clear to Send and to the receiver's Carrier Detect. What does this accomplish?

CHAPTER 5

Data Link Control

Our discussion so far has concerned *sending signals over a transmission link*. For effective digital data communications much more is needed to control and manage the exchange. We want to convert the procedure above into one of *sending data over a data communications link*. This is done by adding a layer of control in each communicating device above the physical interfacing discussed in Chapter 4, referred to as *data link control* or *data link protocol*. When a data link control procedure is used, the transmission medium between stations is referred to as a *data link*.

To see the need for data link control, we list some of the requirements and objectives for effective data communication between two directly connected transmitting–receiving stations:

- *Frame synchronization:* Data are sent in blocks called frames. The beginning and end of each frame must be clearly identifiable.
- *Use of a variety of line configurations:* These are defined in Section 5.1.
- *Flow control:* The sending station must not send frames at a rate faster than the receiving station can absorb them.
- *Error control:* The bit errors introduced by the transmission system must be corrected.
- *Addressing:* On a multipoint line, the identity of the two stations involved in a transmission must be known.
- *Control and data on same link:* It is usually not desirable to have a separate communications path for control signals. Accordingly, the receiver must be able to distinguish control information from the data being transmitted.
- *Link management:* The initiation, maintenance, and termination of a sustained data exchange requires a fair amount of coordination and cooperation among stations. Procedures for the management of this exchange are required.

None of these requirements is satisfied by the physical interfacing techniques described in Chapter 4. We shall see in this chapter that a data link protocol that satisfies these requirements is a rather complex affair. To begin, some of the key features of data link control protocols are presented: line configuration control, flow control, and error control. In assessing flow and error control procedures, a novel method of comparing various approaches for various links is presented. This method is based on a parameter *a*, defined as the ratio of propagation delay to frame transmission time. We will have occasion to employ this parameter again in Part II.

Following these preliminaries, a specific data link protocol, HDLC, is discussed in some detail. HDLC is representative of modern data link protocols.

5.1

LINE CONFIGURATIONS

The three characteristics that distinguish various data link configurations are topology, duplexity, and line discipline.

Topology and Duplexity

The *topology* of a data link refers to the physical arrangement of stations on a link. This was discussed in Chapter 2. If there are only two stations, the link is *point-to-point*. If there are more than two stations, then it is a *multipoint* topology. Traditionally, a multipoint link has been used in the case of a computer (primary station) and a set of terminals (secondary stations). More recently, more complex versions of the multipoint topology are found in local networks (Figure 1.4c).

Traditional multipoint lines are made possible when the terminals are only transmitting a fraction of the time. Figure 5.1 illustrates the advantages of the

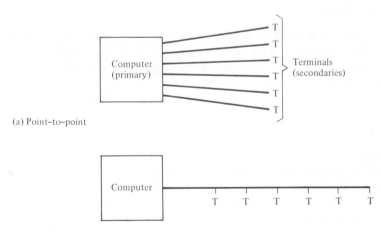

(a) Point-to-point

(b) Multipoint

FIGURE 5.1.   Traditional computer/terminal configurations.

multipoint configuration. If each terminal has a point-to-point link to its computer, then the computer must have one I/O port for each terminal. Also, there is a separate transmission line from the computer to each terminal. In a multipoint configuration, the computer needs only a single I/O port, saving hardware costs. Only a single transmission line is needed, which also saves costs.

The *duplexity* of a link refers to the direction and timing of signal flow. In *simplex* transmission, the signal flow is always in one direction. For example, an input device such as a card reader or remote sensor could be attached to a host so that the device could only transmit, and never receive. An output device such as a printer or actuator could be configured to only receive. Simplex is not in general use since it is not possible to send error or control signals back down the link to the data source. Simplex is similar to a one-lane, one-way bridge.

A *half-duplex* link can transmit and receive, but not simultaneously. This mode is also referred to as "two-way alternate," suggestive of the fact that two stations on a half-duplex link must alternate in transmitting. This is similar to a one-lane, two-way bridge. On a *full-duplex* link, two stations can simultaneously send and receive data from each other. Thus this mode is known as "two-way simultaneous" and may be compared to a two-lane, two-way bridge.

With digital signaling, which requires guided transmission, full-duplex usually requires two separate transmission paths (e.g., two twisted pair), while half-duplex requires only one. For analog signaling, duplicity depends on frequency, whether guided or unguided transmission is used. If a station transmits and receives on the same frequency, it must operate in half-duplex mode (exception: guided transmission using two separate, isolated conductors). If a station transmits on one frequency and receives on another, it may operate in full-duplex mode (Figure 3.7).

Line Discipline

Some discipline is needed in the use of a transmission link. On a half-duplex line, only one station at a time should transmit. On either a half- or full-duplex line, a station should only transmit if it knows that the intended receiver is prepared to receive.

Point-to-Point Links

Line discipline is simple with a point-to-point link. Let us consider first a half-duplex link in which either station may initiate an exchange. An example exchange is depicted in Figure 5.2. If either station wishes to send data to the other, it first performs an enquiry (depicted as enq) of the other station to see if it is prepared to receive. The second station responds with a positive acknowledgment (ack) to indicate that it is ready. The first station then sends some data, which the figure depicts as a frame. In asynchronous communica-

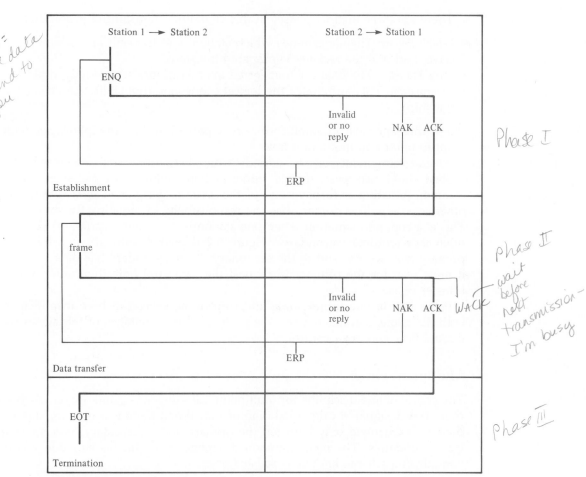

ENQ = I have data to send to you (handwritten)

Phase I (handwritten)

phase II — wait before next transmission — I'm busy (handwritten)

phase III (handwritten)

FIGURE 5.2. Point-to-point link control.

tion, the data would be sent as an asynchronous stream of characters. In any case, after some quantum of data is sent, the first station pauses to await results. The second station acknowledges successful receipt of the data (ack). The first station then sends an end of transmission message (eot) which terminates the exchange and returns the system to its initial state.

Several additional features are added to Figure 5.2 to provide for coping with errors. A negative acknowledgment (nak) is used to indicate that a station is not ready to receive, or that data were received in error. A station may fail to respond or respond with an invalid message. The result of these conditions is indicated by light lines in the figure; the heavy line is the normal sequence of communication events. If an unexpected event occurs, such as a nak or invalid reply, a station may retry its last action or may institute some error recovery procedure (erp).

There are three distinct phases in this communication control procedure:

- *Establishment:* This determines which station is to transmit and which to receive, and that the receiver is prepared to receive.
- *Data Transfer:* The data are transferred in one or more acknowledged blocks.
- *Termination:* This terminates the logical connection (transmitter-receiver relationship).

These three phases, in some form, are a part of all line disciplines for both point-to-point and multipoint links.

Several refinements can be added to our discussion. The relationship described above was peer; that is, either station could initiate transmission. A common situation is to have one of the stations designated *primary* and the other *secondary*. The primary has the responsibility of initiating the exchange. This is a common situation when one station is a computer (primary) and the other is a terminal (secondary). Figure 5.2 depicts a sequence in which the primary has data to send to the secondary. If the secondary has data to send, it must wait for the primary to request the data, and only then enter a data transfer phase.

If the link is full-duplex, data and control messages can be transmitted in both directions simultaneously. We shall see the advantages of this when we discuss flow and error control.

Multipoint Links

The choice of line discipline for multipoint links depends primarily on whether there is a designated primary station or not. When there is a primary station, data are exchanged only between the primary and a secondary, not between two secondaries. The most common disciplines used in this situation are all variants of a scheme known as *poll and select*:

- *Poll:* The primary requests data from a secondary.
- *Select:* The primary has data to send and informs a secondary that data are coming.

Figure 5.3 illustrates these concepts. In Figure 5.3a, the primary polls a secondary by sending a brief polling message. In this case, the secondary has nothing to send and responds with some sort of nak message. The timing for this sequence is indicated. The total time is

$$T_N = t_{\text{prop}} + t_{\text{poll}} + t_{\text{proc}} + t_{\text{nak}} + t_{\text{prop}}$$

where

$$
\begin{aligned}
T_N &= \text{total time to poll terminal with nothing to send} \\
t_{\text{prop}} &= \text{propagation time} = t_1 - t_0 = t_5 - t_4 \\
t_{\text{poll}} &= \text{time to transmit a poll} = t_2 - t_1 \\
t_{\text{proc}} &= \text{time to process poll before acknowledging} = t_3 - t_2 \\
t_{\text{nak}} &= \text{time to transmit a negative acknowledgment} = t_4 - t_3
\end{aligned}
$$

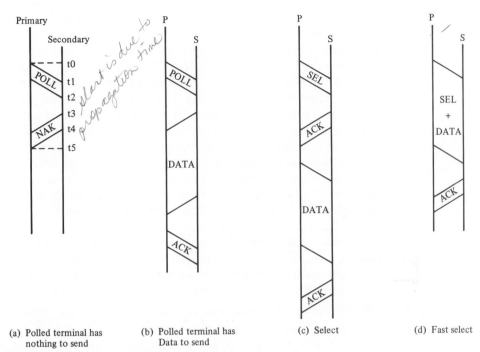

(a) Polled terminal has
    nothing to send

(b) Polled terminal has
    Data to send

(c) Select

(d) Fast select

FIGURE 5.3. Poll and select sequences.

Figure 5.3b depicts the case of a successful poll. The time here is

$$T_P = 3t_{prop} + t_{poll} + t_{ack} + t_{data} + 2t_{proc}$$
$$= T_N + t_{prop} + t_{data} + t_{proc}$$

Here we assume for simplicity that the processing time to respond to any message is a constant.

The most common form of polling is *roll-call polling*, in which the primary selectively polls each secondary in a predetermined sequence. In the simplest case, the primary polls each secondary in a round-robin fashion, $S_1, S_2, \ldots, S_n$, for all n secondaries and then repeats the sequence. The timing can be expressed as

$$T_c = nT_N + kT_D \qquad (5.1)$$

where

T_c = time for one complete polling cycle
T_N = average time to poll a secondary exclusive of data transfer
T_D = time to transfer data = $t_{prop} + t_{data} + t_{proc}$
n = number of secondary stations
k = number of secondary stations with data to send during the cycle

Variants of roll-call polling permit priority handling by, for example, polling some stations more than once per cycle.

The select function is shown in Figure 5.3c. Note that four separate transmissions are required to transfer data from the primary to the secondary. An alternative technique is *fast select*. In this case, the selection message includes the data to be transferred (Figure 5.3d). The first reply from the secondary is an acknowledgment that indicates that the station was prepared to receive and did receive the data successfully. Fast selection is particularly well suited for applications where short messages are frequently transmitted and the transfer time for the message is not appreciably longer than the reply time.

Another form of line discipline is *contention*. In this mode, there is typically no primary but rather a collection of peer stations. A station can transmit if the line is free; otherwise, it must wait. This technique has found widespread use in local networks and satellite systems.

A characteristic of all multipoint line disciplines is the need for addressing. In the case of roll-call polling, transmissions from the primary must indicate the intended secondary; transmissions from a secondary must identify the secondary. In a peer situation, both transmitter and receiver must be identified. Thus there are three cases:

- *Point-to-point:* no address needed.
- *Primary-secondary multipoint:* one address needed, to identify secondary.
- *Peer multipoint:* two addresses needed, to identify transmitter and receiver.

In practice, the first case is subsumed into the second, so that most data link control protocols require one address even for point-to-point transmission. This simplifies the demands on the station by allowing a single protocol to be used in both circumstances. The peer multipoint case is seen in local networks; this chapter will be concerned only with the first two cases, for which traditional data link control protocols were developed.

5.2

FLOW CONTROL

Flow control is a technique for assuring that a transmitting station does not overwhelm a receiving station with data. The receiver will typically allocate a data buffer with some maximum length. When data are received, it must do a certain amount of processing before it can clear the buffer and be prepared to receive more data. In the absence of flow control, the receiver's buffer may overflow while it is processing old data.

In this section, we examine mechanisms for flow control in the absence of errors. The model we will use is depicted in Figure 5.4a, which is a vertical-time sequence diagram. It has the advantages of showing time dependencies and illustrating the correct send-receive relationship. Each arrow represents a single frame transiting a data link between two stations.

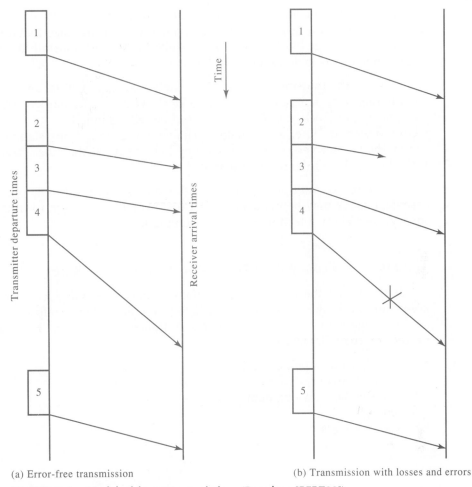

(a) Error-free transmission   (b) Transmission with losses and errors

FIGURE 5.4.   Model of frame transmission. (Based on [BERT92])

As we discussed previously for synchronous transmission, the data are sent in a sequence of frames with each frame containing a portion of the data and some control information. For now, we assume that all frames that are transmitted are successfully received; no frames are lost and none arrive with errors. Furthermore, frames arrive in the same order in which they are sent. However, each transmitted frame suffers an arbitrary and variable amount of delay before reception.

The simplest form of flow control, known as **stop-and-wait flow control,** works as follows. A source entity transmits a frame. After reception, the destination entity indicates its willingness to accept another frame by sending back an acknowledgment to the frame just received. The source must wait until it receives the acknowledgment before sending the next frame. The destination can thus stop the flow of data by simply withholding acknowledgment. This procedure works fine and, indeed, can hardly be improved upon when a message is sent in a few large frames. However, it is often the case that a source will break up a large block of data into smaller blocks and transmit the data in many frames. This is done for the following reasons:

- The longer the transmission, the more likely that there will be an error, necessitating retransmission of the entire block. With smaller blocks, errors are less likely per block, and fewer data need be retransmitted.
- On a multipoint line, it is usually desirable not to permit one station to occupy the line for very long, thus causing long delays at the other stations.
- The buffer size of the receiver may be limited.

With the use of multiple frames for a single message, the simple procedure described above may be inadequate. We first explore the reason for this inadequacy, then show a technique for overcoming it.

The Effect of Propagation Delay and Transmission Rate

Let us determine the maximum potential efficiency of a half-duplex point-to-point line using the stop-and-wait scheme described above. Suppose that a long message is to be sent as a sequence of frames $f_1, f_2, \ldots, f_n$. For a polling procedure, the following events occur:

- Station S_1 sends a poll of station S_2.
- S_2 responds with f_1.
- S_1 sends an acknowledgment.
- S_2 sends f_2.
- S_1 acknowledges.

  .

  .

  .

- S_2 sends f_n.
- S_1 acknowledges.

The total time to send the data is

$$T_D = T_I + nT_F$$

where

T_I = time to initiate sequence = $t_{prop} + t_{poll} + t_{proc}$

T_F = time to send one frame = $t_{prop} + t_{frame} + t_{proc} + t_{prop} + t_{ack} + t_{proc}$

To simplify matters, we ignore a few terms. For a long sequence of frames, T_I is relatively small and can be dropped. Let us assume that the processing time between transmission and reception is negligible, and that the acknowledgment frame is very small. Then we can express T_D as

$$T_D = n(2t_{prop} + t_{frame})$$

Of that time, only $n \times t_{\text{frame}}$ is actually spent transmitting data and the rest is overhead. Thus the utilization or efficiency of the line is

$$U = \frac{n \times t_{\text{frame}}}{n(2t_{\text{prop}} + t_{\text{frame}})}$$

$$U = \frac{t_{\text{frame}}}{2t_{\text{prop}} + t_{\text{frame}}}$$

It is useful to define $a = t_{\text{prop}}/t_{\text{frame}}$. Then

$$U = \frac{1}{1 + 2a} \qquad (5.2)$$

This is the maximum possible utilization of the link. We will see that the frame itself contains overhead bits, so actual utilization is lower. The parameter a is a constant if both t_{frame} and t_{prop} are constants. This is typically the case: Fixed-length frames are often used for all except the last frame in a sequence, and the propagation delay is constant for point-to-point links. An approximation for U can be obtained by using the maximum propagation time on a multipoint link.

To get some insight into Equation (5.2), let us derive a different expression for a. We have

$$a = \frac{\text{Propagation Time}}{\text{Transmission Time}} \qquad (5.3)$$

The propagation time is equal to the distance d of the link divided by the velocity of propagation V. For unguided transmission (except through seawater), V is the speed of light, 3×10^8 m/s. A typical value for guided media is 2×10^8 m/sec. The transmission time is equal to the length of the frame L divided by the data rate R, so

$$a = \frac{d/V}{L/R} = \frac{Rd}{VL}$$

Thus a is proportional to the data rate times the length of the medium. This term, $R \times d$, and hence a, is the single most important parameter determining the performance of a data link. A useful way of looking at a is that it represents the length of the medium in bits ($R \times d/V$) compared to the frame length.

With this interpretation of a in mind, Figure 5.5 validates Equation (5.2). In this figure, transmission time is normalized to 1. Hence the propagation time, by Equation (5.3), is a. First consider the case of $a < 1$; this is the case in which the "bit length" of the link is less than that of the frame. A station begins transmitting a frame at time t_0. At $t_0 + a$, the leading edge of the frame reaches the receiving station, while the sending station is still in the process of transmitting the frame. At $t_0 + 1$, the sending station has completed transmission. At $t_0 + 1 + a$, the receiving station has received the entire frame and immediately transmits a small acknowledgment frame. This acknowledgment arrives

(a) Transmission time = 1; a <| (b) Transmission Time = 1; a >|

FIGURE 5.5.   The effect of *a* on utilization.

back at the sending station at $t_0 + 1 + 2a$. Total elapsed time: $1 + 2a$. Total
transmission time: 1. Hence utilization or efficiency is $1/(1 + 2a)$. The same
result is achieved with $a > 1$, as illustrated in Figure 5.5b.

Let us consider a few examples. At one extreme is a satellite link. The round-
trip propagation time is about 270 ms. A typical digital transmission service is
56 kbps, and a 4000-bit frame is within the typical range. Thus transmission
time equals $4000/56,000 = 71$ ms, and $a = 270/71 = 3.8$. From Equation (5.2)
the maximum utilization is $1/(1 + 7.6) = 0.12$. This is about the smallest value
of a that one might expect for a satellite link. Recent and proposed satellite
services use much shorter transmission times: from 6 ms down to 125μs. For
this range, a is in the range 45 to 2160. Thus for the simple stop-and-wait
acknowledgment protocol described above, efficiency could be as low as
0.0002! At the other extreme, in terms of distance, is the local network. Distances range from 0.1 to 10 km, with data rates of 0.1 to 10 Mbps. Using a
value of $V = 2 \times 10^8$ m/s and a frame size of 500 bits, the value of a is in the
range 10^{-4} to 1. Typical values are 0.01 to 0.1. For the latter range, utilization
is in the range 0.83 to 0.98.

We can see that local networks are inherently quite efficient, whereas satellite links are not. As a final example, let us consider digital data transmission
via modem over a voice-grade line. A practical upper bound on data rate is
9600 bps. We can again use $V = 2 \times 10^8$ m/s. Again, let us consider a 500-bit

frame. Such transmission is used for distances anywhere from a few tens of meters to thousands of kilometers. If we pick, say, as a short distance $d = 100$ m, then $a = (9600 \text{ bps} \times 100 \text{ m})/(2 \times 10^8 \text{ m/s} \times 500 \text{ bits}) = 9.6 \times 10^{-6}$ and utilization is effectively unity. Even in a long-distance case, such as $d = 5000$ km, we have $a = (9600 \times 5 \times 10^6)/(2 \times 10^8 \times 500) = 0.48$ and efficiency equals 0.5.

We can conclude that, in some cases, the simple stop-and-wait acknowledgment procedure provides adequate line utilization. For those cases in which this is not the case, a more elaborate procedure is desirable. Such a procedure, universally accepted, is the sliding-window protocol.

The Sliding Window Protocol

The essence of the problem described so far is that only one frame at a time can be in transit. In situations where the bit length of the link is greater than the frame length ($a > 1$), serious inefficiencies result. The obvious solution is to allow multiple frames to be in transit at one time.

Let us examine how this might work for two stations, A and B, connected via a full-duplex link. Station B allocates buffer space for n frames instead of the one discussed above. Thus B can accept n frames, and A is allowed to send n frames without waiting for an acknowledgment. To keep track of which frames have been acknowledged, each is labeled with a sequence number. B acknowledges a frame by sending an acknowledgment that includes the sequence number of the next frame expected. This acknowledgment also implicitly announces that B is prepared to receive the next n frames beginning with the number specified. This scheme can also be used to acknowledge multiple frames. For example, B could receive frames 2, 3, and 4, but withhold acknowledgment until frame 4 has arrived. By then returning an acknowledgment with sequence number 5, B acknowledges frames 2, 3, and 4 at one time. A maintains a list of sequence numbers that it is allowed to send and B maintains a list of sequence numbers that it is prepared to receive. Each of these lists can be thought of as a *window* of frames. The operation is referred to as **sliding-window flow control.**

An important restriction needs to be noted. Since the sequence number to be used occupies a field in the frame, it is clearly of bounded size. For a k-bit field, the sequence number can range from 0 to $2^k - 1$. Accordingly, frames are numbered modulo 2^k; that is, after sequence number $2^k - 1$, the next number is zero. With this in mind, Figure 5.6 is a useful way of depicting the sliding-window process. It assumes the use of a 3-bit sequence number, so that frames are numbered sequentially from 0 through 7, and then the same numbers are reused for subsequent frames. The shaded rectangle represents the window of frames that may be transmitted. The figure indicates that the sender may transmit 7 frames, beginning with frame 6. Each time a frame is sent, the shaded portion will shrink; each time a new acknowledgment is received, the shaded portion will grow.

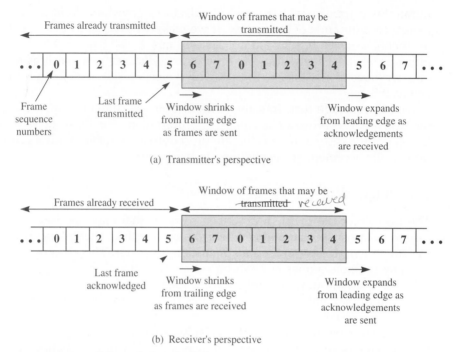

FIGURE 5.6.   Sliding-window depiction.

An example is shown in Figure 5.7. The example assumes a 3-bit sequence number field and a maximum window size of seven. Initially, *A* and *B* have windows indicating that *A* may transmit seven frames, beginning with frame 0 (F0). After transmitting three frames (F0, F1, F2) without acknowledgment, *A* has shrunk its window to four frames. The window indicates that *A* may transmit four frames, beginning with frame number 3. *B* then transmits an ACK 3, which means: "I have received all frames up through frame number 2 and am ready to receive frame number 3; in fact, I am prepared to receive seven frames, beginning with frame number 3." With this acknowledgment, *A* is back up to permission to transmit seven frames, still beginning with frame 3. *A* proceeds to transmit frames 3, 4, 5, and 6. *B* returns an ACK4, which acknowledges frame 3, and allows the transmission of frames 4 through 2. But, by the time that this acknowledgment reaches *A*, it has already transmitted frames 4, 5, and 6. The result is that *A* may only open its window to permit the transmission of 4 frames, beginning with frame 7.

The mechanism so far described does indeed provide a form of flow control: the receiver must only be able to accommodate *n* frames beyond the one it has last acknowledged. To supplement this, most protocols also allow a station to completely cut off the flow of frames from the other side by sending a Receive Not Ready (RNR) message, which acknowledges former frames but forbids transfer of future frames. Thus, RNR 5 means: "I have received all frames up

FIGURE 5.7. Example of a sliding-window protocol.

through number 4 but am unable to accept any more." At some subsequent point, the station must send a normal acknowledgment to reopen the window.

The efficiency of the line now depends on both N, the window size, and a. For convenience, let us again normalize frame transmission time to a value of 1; thus the propagation time is a. Figure 5.8 illustrates the efficiency of a full-duplex point-to-point line. Station A begins to emit a sequence of frames at time t_0. The leading edge of the first frame reaches station B at $t_0 + a$. The first frame is entirely absorbed by $t_0 + a + 1$. Assuming negligible processing time, station B can immediately acknowledge the first frame (ACK1). Let us also assume that the acknowledgment frame is so small that transmission time is negligible. Then the ACK1 reaches station A at $t_0 + 2a + 1$. There are two cases:

- *Case 1:* $N > 2a + 1$. The acknowledgment for frame 1 reaches station A before it has exhausted its window. Thus A can transmit continuously with no pause.
- *Case 2:* $N < 2a + 1$. Station A exhausts its window at $t_0 + N$ and cannot send additional frames until $t_0 + 2a + 1$. Thus the line utilization is N time units out of a period of $(2a + 1)$ time units.

From the above, we can state that

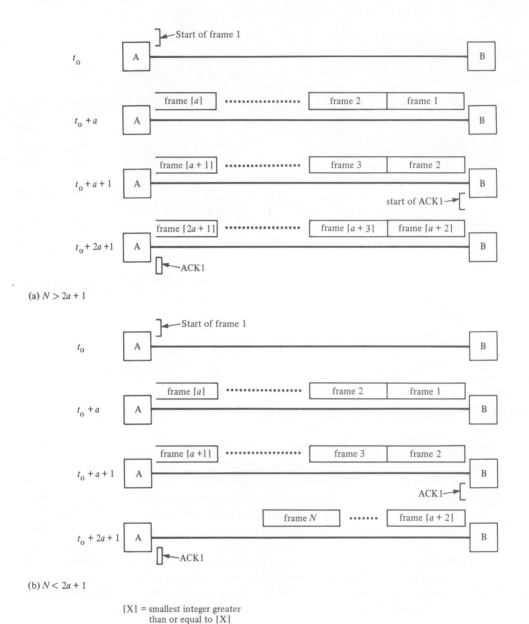

(a) $N > 2a + 1$

(b) $N < 2a + 1$

$\lceil X \rceil$ = smallest integer greater
than or equal to $\lceil X \rceil$

FIGURE 5.8. Timing of a sliding-window protocol.

$$U = \begin{cases} 1 & N > 2a + 1 \\ \dfrac{N}{2a+1} & N < 2a + 1 \end{cases} \qquad (5.4)$$

Typically, the sequence number is provided for in an n-bit field and the maximum window size is $N = 2^n - 1$ (not 2^n; this is explained in Section 5.3). Figure 5.9 shows the maximum efficiency achievable for window sizes of 1, 7, and 127 as a function of a. A window size of one, of course, corresponds to the simple stop-and-wait protocol discussed earlier. A window size of seven (3 bits) should be adequate for most applications. A window size of 127 (7 bits) is adequate for some satellite links.

So far, we have discussed transmission in one direction only. If two stations exchange data, each needs to maintain two windows: one for transmit and one for receive. When this is the case, a technique known as *piggybacking* is often used. If a station has data to send and an acknowledgment to send, it sends both together in one frame, thus saving communications capacity. This technique works with either half-duplex or full-duplex links. For a multipoint link, the primary needs to transmit and receive windows for each secondary.

5.3

ERROR CONTROL

Error control refers to mechanisms to detect and correct errors that occur in the transmission of frames. The model that we will use, which covers the typical case, is illustrated in Figure 5.4b. As before, data are sent as a sequence of

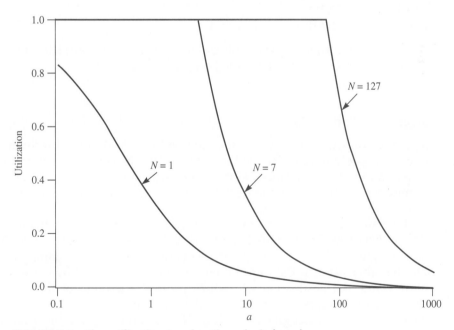

FIGURE 5.9   Line utilization as a function of window size.

frames; frames arrive in the same order in which they are sent; and each transmitted frame suffers an arbitrary and variable amount of delay before reception. In addition, we admit the possibility of two types of errors:

- *Lost frame:* A frame fails to arrive at the other side. A noise burst may damage a frame to the extent that the receiver is not aware that a frame has been transmitted.
- *Damaged frame:* A recognizable frame does arrive but some of the bits are in error (have been altered during transmission).

The most common techniques for error control are based on some or all of the following ingredients:

- *Error Detection:* As discussed in Chapter 4; typically, CRC is used.
- *Positive acknowledgment:* The destination returns a positive acknowledgment to successfully received, error-free frames.
- *Retransmission after timeout:* The source retransmits a frame that has not been acknowledged after a predetermined amount of time.
- *Negative acknowledgment and retransmission:* The destination returns a negative acknowledgment to frames in which an error is detected. The source retransmits such frames.

Collectively, these mechanisms are all referred to as **automatic repeat request** (ARQ). Three versions of ARQ are in common use:

- Stop-and-wait ARQ.
- Go-back-N ARQ.
- Selective-reject ARQ.

All of these forms are based on the use of the flow control techniques described in Section 5.2. We examine each of these in turn.

Stop-and-Wait ARQ

Stop-and-wait ARQ is based on the stop-and-wait flow control technique outlined previously, and is depicted in Figure 5.10. The source station transmits a single frame and then must await an acknowledgment (ACK). No other data frames can be sent until the destination station's reply arrives at the source station.

The frame transmitted by the source could suffer an error. If the error is detected by the destination, it discards the frame and sends a negative acknowledgment (NAK), causing the source to retransmit the damaged frame. On the other hand, if the transmitted frame is so corrupted by noise as not to be received, the destination will not respond. To account for this possibility, the source is equipped with a timer. After a frame is transmitted, the source waits for an acknowledgment (ACK or NAK). If no recognizable acknowledgment is received during the timeout period, then the frame is retransmitted.

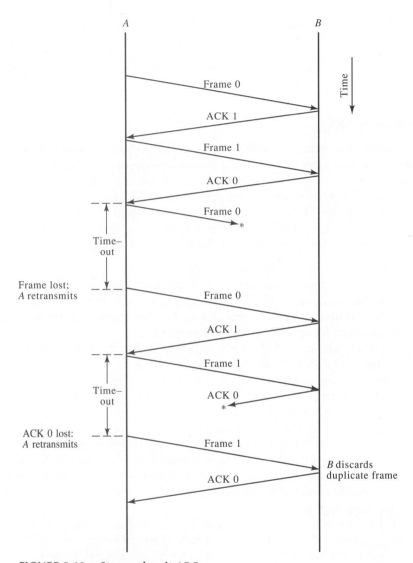

FIGURE 5.10.   Stop-and-wait ARQ.

Note that this system requires that the source maintain a copy of a transmitted frame until an ACK is received for that frame.

One more refinement is needed. If a frame is sent correctly but the acknowledgment is damaged in transit, then the source will time out and retransmit that frame. The destination will now receive and accept two copies of the same frame. To avoid this problem, frames are alternately labeled with 0 or 1 and positive acknowledgments are of the form ACK0 or ACK1: an ACK0 (ACK1) acknowledges receipt of a frame numbered 1 (0) and indicates that the receiver is ready for a frame numbered 0 (1).

The principal advantage of stop-and-wait ARQ is its simplicity. Its principal disadvantage, as discussed in Section 4.3, is that this is an inefficient protocol. The siding-window flow control technique introduced before can be adapted to provide more efficient line use. In this context, it is referred to as **continuous ARQ.**

Go-back-N ARQ

One variant of continuous ARQ is known as go-back-N ARQ. In this technique, a station may send a series of frames determined by window size, using the sliding window flow control technique. While no errors occur, the destination will acknowledge (ACK) incoming frames as usual.

Consider that station A is sending frames to station B. After each transmission, A sets an acknowledgment timer for the frame just transmitted. The go-back-N technique takes into account the following contingencies:

1. Damaged frame. There are three subcases:
    a. A transmits frame i. B detects an error and has previously successfully received frame $(i - 1)$. B sends a NAK i, indicating that frame i is rejected. When A receives this NAK, it must retransmit frame i and all subsequent frames that it has transmitted.
    b. frame i is lost in transit. A subsequently sends frame $(i + 1)$. B receives frame $(i + 1)$ out of order, and sends a NAK i.
    c. frame i is lost in transit and A does not soon send additional frames. B receives nothing and returns neither an ACK or a NAK. A will time out and retransmit frame i.
2. Damaged ACK. There are two subcases:
    a. B receives frame i and sends ACK $(i + 1)$, which is lost in transit. Since ACKs are cumulative (e.g., ACK 6 means that all frames through 5 are acknowledged), it may be that A will receive a subsequent ACK to a subsequent frame that will do the job of the lost ACK before the associated time expires.
    b. If A's timer expires, A retransmits frame i and all subsequent frames.
3. Damaged NAK. If a NAK is lost, A will eventually time out on the associated frame and retransmit that frame and all subsequent frames.

Figure 5.11a shows the frame flow for go-back-N ARQ on a full-duplex line, assuming a 3-bit sequence number.

With go-back-N ARQ, it is not required that each individual frame be acknowledged. For example, station A sends frames 0, 1, 2, and 3. Station B responds with ACK1 after frame 0, but then does not respond to frames 1 and 2. After frame 3 is received, B issues ACK4, indicating that frame 3 and all previous frames are accepted.

We are now in a position to explain why a sequence space of 2^n can support a window size of only $2^n - 1$. It has to do with the interaction of error control and acknowledgment. In most piggyback schemes, a station will send an ac-

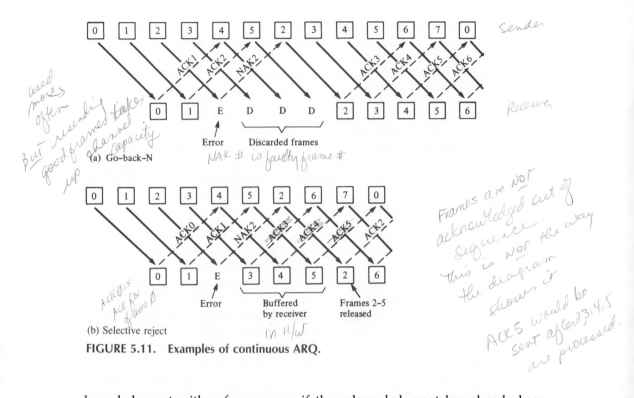

FIGURE 5.11.   Examples of continuous ARQ.

knowledgment with a frame, even if the acknowledgment has already been sent. This is because a fixed-length acknowledgment field of n bits is incorporated into the frame and some number must be put into the frame. This has the side benefit that in case the first ACK gets lost, the second ACK may get through. Now consider a case in which a station transmits frame 0 and gets an ACK1, and then transmits frame 1, 2, 3, 4, 5, 6, 7, 0 and gets another ACK1. This could mean that all eight frames were received correctly. It could also mean that all eight frames were lost in transit, and the receiving station is repeating its previous ACK1.

Selective-reject ARQ

With selective-reject ARQ, the only frames retransmitted are those that receive a NAK or which time out. Figure 5.11b, which exhibits the same error pattern as Figure 5.11a, illustrates selective reject. This would appear to be more efficient than the go-back-N approach, since it minimizes the amount of retransmission. On the other hand, the receiver must contain storage to save post-NAK frames until the frame in error is retransmitted, and contain logic for reinserting that frame in the proper sequence. The transmitter, too, will require more complex logic to be able to send frames out of sequence. Because of such complications, the selective-reject ARQ is rarely implemented.

The window size requirement is more restrictive for selective-reject than for go-back-N. We have seen that for a sequence number space of 2^n, the maximum window size for go-back-N is $2^n - 1$. Now consider the case of a 3-bit sequence number size (sequence space is eight) using selective-reject. Allow a window size of seven, and consider the following scenario [TANE88]:

1. Station A sends frames 0 through 6 to station B.
2. Station B receives and acknowledges all seven frames.
3. Because of a long noise burst, all seven acknowledgments are lost.
4. Station A times out and retransmits frame 0.
5. Station B has already advanced its receive window to accept frames 7, 0, 1, 2, 3, 4, and 5. Thus it assumes that frame 7 has been lost and that this is a new frame 0, which it accepts.

The problem with the foregoing scenario, for selective reject ARQ, is that there is an overlap between the sending and receiving windows. To overcome the problem, the maximum window size should be no more than half the range of sequence numbers. In the scenario above, if only four acknowledged frames may be outstanding, no confusion can result.

Figure 5.11 compares the two approaches, using a window size of seven. In both cases the third frame (frame 2) is transmitted in error. Because of propagation delays, the error is not reported to the sending station until three subsequent frames (frames 3, 4, and 5) have been sent. For the go-back-N algorithm, these three frames are discarded by the destination and must be retransmitted by the source. For the selective-reject algorithm, these frames are stored by the destination. Note that in this latter case, the frames cannot be acknowledged out of sequence, since any acknowledgment implicitly acknowledges all prior frames. Thus, when frame 2 is successfully retransmitted, the destination returns an ACK 6, acknowledging receipt of the new frame 2 and the frames 3, 4, and 5, which had been stored.

Performance

It would appear that both go-back-N and selective-reject are more efficient than stop-and-wait. Let us develop some approximations to determine the degree of improvement to be expected.

First, consider stop-and-wait ARQ. With no errors, the maximum utilization is $1/(1 + 2a)$ as shown in Equation (5.2). Now, we must take into account the fact that some frames are repeated because of errors. To do this, note that the utilization U can be defined as

$$U = \frac{T_f}{T_t}$$

where

T_f = time for transmitter to emit a single frame
T_t = total time that line is engaged in the transmission of a single frame

For error-free operation using stop-and-wait ARQ, we have

$$U = \frac{T_f}{T_f + 2T_p}$$

where T_p is the propagation time. Dividing by T_f and remembering that $a = T_p/T_f$, we again have Equation (5.2). Now, if errors occur, we must modify Equation (5.2) to

$$U = \frac{T_f}{N_r T_t}$$

where N_r is the expected number of transmissions of a frame. Thus for stop-and-wait ARQ we have

$$U = \frac{1}{N_r (1 + 2a)}$$

A simple expression for N_r can be derived by considering the probability P that a single frame is in error. If we assume that ACKs and NAKs are never in error, the probability that it will take exactly i attempts to transmit a frame successfully is $P^{i-1}(1 - P)$. Thus

$$N_r = \sum_{i=1}^{\infty} iP^{i-1}(1 - P) = \frac{1}{1 - P}$$

and

$$Stop\text{-}and\text{-}wait: \quad U = \frac{1 - P}{1 + 2a}$$

For the sliding window protocol, we developed Equation (5-4) for error free operation, which is repeated here:

$$U = \begin{cases} 1 & N > 2a + 1 \\ \dfrac{N}{2a + 1} & N < 2a + 1 \end{cases}$$

For selective-reject ARQ, we can use the same reasoning as applied to stop-and-wait ARQ. That is, the error-free equations must be divided by N_r. Again, $N_r = 1/(1 - P)$. So

Selective-reject:

$$U = \begin{cases} 1 - P & N > 2a + 1 \\ \dfrac{N(1 - P)}{2a + 1} & N < 2a + 1 \end{cases}$$

The same reasoning will still apply for go-back-N ARQ, but we must be more careful in approximating N_r. Each error generates a requirement to retransmit K frames rather than just one frame. Thus

N_r = E[number of transmitted frames to successfully transmit one frame]

$$= \sum_{i=1}^{\infty} f(i)P^{i-1}(1 - P)$$

where $f(i)$ is the total number of frames transmitted if the original frame must be transmitted i times. This can be expressed as

$$f(i) = 1 + (i - 1)K$$
$$= (1 - K) + Ki$$

Substituting yields

$$N_r = (1 - K) \sum_{i=1}^{\infty} P^{i-1}(1 - P) + K \sum_{i=1}^{\infty} iP^{i-1}(1 - P)$$

We can simplify this equation by using the following equalities:

$$\sum_{i=0}^{\infty} r^i = \sum_{i=1}^{\infty} r^{i-1} = \frac{1}{1 - r}; \qquad \sum_{i=1}^{\infty} ir^{i-1} = \frac{1}{(1 - r)^2}$$

Therefore:

$$N_r = 1 - K + \frac{K}{1 - P}$$
$$= \frac{1 - P + KP}{1 - P}$$

By studying Figure 5.8, the reader should conclude that K is approximately equal to $2a + 1$ for $N > (2a + 1)$, and $K = N$ for $N < (2a + 1)$. Thus

Go-back-N:

$$U = \begin{cases} \dfrac{1 - P}{1 + 2aP} & N > 2a + 1 \\[4mm] \dfrac{N(1 - P)}{(2a + 1)(1 - P + NP)} & N < 2a + 1 \end{cases}$$

Note that for $N = 1$, both selective-reject and go-back-N reduce to stop and wait. Figure 5.12[1] compares these three error control techniques for a value of $P = 10^{-3}$. This figure and the equations are only approximations. For example, we have ignored errors in acknowledgment frames and, in the case of go-back-N, errors in retransmitted frames other than the frame initially in error. Nevertheless, the results are very close to those produced by a more careful analysis [MILL81].

---

[1]For $N = 7$, the curves for go-back-N and selective-reject are so close that they appear to be identical in the figure.

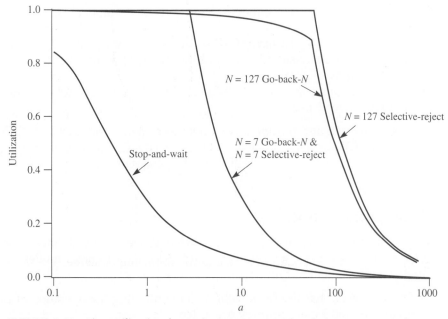

FIGURE 5.12   Line utilization for various error-control techniques ($P = 10^{-3}$).

5.4

DATA LINK CONTROL PROTOCOLS

Bit-oriented protocols are designed to satisfy a wide variety of data link requirements, including

- Point-to-point and multipoint links.
- Half-duplex (two-way alternate) and full-duplex (two-way simultaneous) operation.
- Primary–secondary (e.g., host–terminal) and peer (e.g., computer–computer) interaction.
- Links with large (e.g., satellite) and small (e.g., short-distance direct connect) values of a.

A number of very similar data link control protocols have achieved widespread use:

- *High-level data link control (HDLC):* developed by the International Organization for Standardization (ISO 3309, ISO 4335).
- *Advanced data communication control procedures (ADCCP):* developed by the American National Standards Institute (ANSI X3.66). With very minor exceptions, ADCCP has been adopted by the U.S. National Bureau of Standards (FIPS PUB 71-1) for use on federal government procurements, and by the Federal Telecommunications Standards Committee (FED-STD- 1003A) as

the standard for the national-defense-related National Communications System.

- *Link access procedure, balanced (LAP-B):* adopted by the International Telegraph and Telephone Consultative Committee (CCITT) as part of its X.25 packet-switched network standard.
- *Synchronous data link control (SDLC):* used by IBM. This is not a standard, but is in widespread use.

There are virtually no differences between HDLC and ADCCP. LAP-B is a subset of HDLC. SDLC is also a subset of HDLC, but also includes several minor additional features [BROD83a]. The following discussion is based on HDLC.

Basic Characteristics

To satisfy the variety of requirements listed above, HDLC defines three types of stations, two link configurations, and three data transfer modes of operation. The three station types are

- *Primary station:* has the responsibility for controlling the operation of the link. Frames issued by the primary are called *commands*.
- *Secondary station:* operates under the control of the primary station. Frames issued by the secondary station(s) are called *responses*. The primary maintains a separate logical link with each secondary station on the line.
- *Combined station:* combines the features of primary and secondary stations. A combined station may issue both commands and responses.

The two link configurations are

- *Unbalanced configuration:* used in point-to-point and multipoint operation. This configuration consists of one primary and one or more secondary stations and supports both full-duplex and half-duplex transmission.
- *Balanced configuration:* used only in point-to-point operation. This configuration consists of two combined stations and supports both full-duplex and half-duplex transmission.

The three data transfer modes of operation are

- *Normal response mode (NRM):* This is an unbalanced configuration. The primary may initiate data transfer to a secondary, but a secondary may only transmit data in response to a poll from the primary.
- *Asynchronous balanced mode (ABM):* This is a balanced configuration. Either combined station may initiate transmission without receiving permission from the other combined station.
- *Asynchronous response mode (ARM):* This is an unbalanced configuration. In this mode, the secondary may initiate transmission without explicit permission of the primary (i.e., send a response without waiting for a command). The primary still retains responsibility for the line, including initialization, error recovery, and logical disconnection.

The normal response mode is used on multidrop lines, in which a number of terminals are connected to a computer. The computer polls each terminal for input. NRM is also often used on point-to-point links, particularly if the link connects a terminal or other peripheral to a computer. The asynchronous balanced mode makes more efficient use of a full-duplex point-to-point link, since there is no polling overhead. The asynchronous response mode is rarely used; it is applicable to hub polling and other special situations in which a secondary may need to initiate transmission.

Frame Structure

HDLC uses synchronous transmission. All transmissions are in frames, and a single frame format suffices for all types of data and control exchanges.

Figure 5.13 depicts the structure of the HDLC frame. The frame has the following fields:

- *Flag:* 8 bits.
- *Address:* One or more octets.
- *Control:* 8 or 16 bits.
- *Information*: variable.
- *Frame check sequence (FCS):* 16 or 32 bits.
- *Flag:* 8 bits.

The flag, address, and control fields that precede the data field are known as a *header*. The FCS and flag fields following the data field are referred to as a *trailer*.

Flag Fields

Flag fields delimit the frame at both ends with the unique pattern 01111110. A single flag may be used as the closing flag for one frame and the opening flag for the next. All active stations attached to the link are continuously hunting for the flag sequence to synchronize on the start of a frame. While receiving a frame, a station continues to hunt for that sequence to determine the end of the frame. However, since the HDLC frame allows arbitrary bit patterns, there is no assurance that the pattern 01111110 will not appear somewhere inside the frame, thus destroying frame-level synchronization. To avoid this problem, a procedure known as *bit stuffing* is used. The transmitter will always insert an extra 0 bit after each occurrence of five 1's in the frame (with the exception of the flag fields). After detecting a starting flag, the receiver monitors the bit stream. When a pattern of five 1's appears, the sixth bit is examined. If this bit is 0, it is deleted. If the sixth bit is a 1 and the seventh bit is a 0, the combination is accepted as a flag. If the sixth and seventh bits are both 1, the sending station is signaling an abort condition.

With the use of bit stuffing, arbitrary bit patterns can be inserted into the data field of the frame. This property is known as *data transparency*.

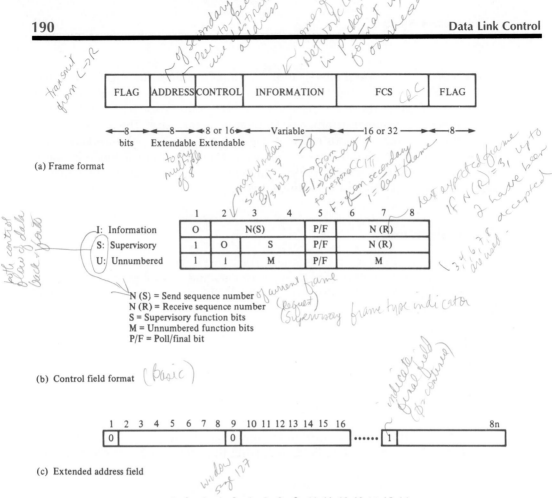

Handwritten annotations throughout the figure:

- transmit from L→R
- of secondary peer
- Peer to peer and destination address
- comes from network layer in packet format w/ overhead
- to any multiple of 8
- max window size is 7 8/3 bits
- 7∅
- F=1 ask for response of CCITT for response primary
- F=∅ from secondary 1 = last frame
- last frame
- last expected
- next expected frame up to N(R) = 31
- 2 have been accepted
- 3,4,6,7,8 are held
- 31 are held accepted
- path control flow of data ack + faults
- N(S) = Send sequence number of current frame (Request)
- (Supervisory frame type indicator)
- (Basic)
- indicates final field (or continue)
- window size 127

(a) Frame format

FLAG | ADDRESS | CONTROL | INFORMATION | FCS | FLAG

←8→ ←8→ ←8 or 16→ ←—Variable—→ ←16 or 32→ ←8→
bits   Extendable Extendable

(b) Control field format

	1	2	3	4	5	6	7	8
I: Information	O		N(S)		P/F		N (R)	
S: Supervisory	1	O		S	P/F		N (R)	
U: Unnumbered	1	1		M	P/F		M	

N (S) = Send sequence number
N (R) = Receive sequence number
S = Supervisory function bits
M = Unnumbered function bits
P/F = Poll/final bit

(c) Extended address field

1	2	3	4	5	6	7	8	9	10	11	12	13	14	15	16		8n
0								0								•••••• 1	

(d) Extended control fields

	1	2	3	4	5	6	7	8	9	10	11	12	13	14	15	16
Information	0			N(S)				P/F			N(R)					
Supervisory	1	0		S	0	0	0	0	P/F			N(R)				

FIGURE 5.13.   HDLC frame structure.

Figure 5.14 shows an example of bit stuffing. Note that in the first two cases, the extra 0 is not strictly necessary for avoiding a flag pattern, but is necessary for the operation of the algorithm. The pitfalls of bit stuffing are also illustrated in this figure. When a flag is used as both an ending and starting flag, a 1-bit error merges two frames into one. Conversely, a 1-bit error inside the frame could split it in two.

Address Field

The address field is used to identify the secondary station that transmitted or is to receive the frame. This field is not needed for point-to-point links, but is

Original pattern

1 1 1 1 1 1 1 1 1 1 1 0 1 1 1 1 1 0 1 1 1 1 1 0

After bit–stuffing

1 1 1 1 0 1 1 1 1 0 1 1 0 1 1 1 1 0 1 0 1 1 1 1 0 1 0

(a) Example

(b) An inverted bit splits a frame in two.

(c) An inverted bit merges two frames.

FIGURE 5.14.   Bit stuffing.

always included for the sake of uniformity. An address is normally eight bits long but, by prior agreement, an extended format may be used in which the address length is a multiple of seven bits. The least significant bit in each octet is 1 or 0 according as it is or is not the last octet of the address field. The remaining seven bits form part of the address. The single octet address of 11111111 is interpreted as the all-stations address in both basic and extended formats. It is used to allow the primary to broadcast a frame for reception by all secondaries.

Control Field

HDLC defines three types of frames, each with a different control field format. *Information frames* (I-frames) carry the data to be transmitted for the station, known as *user data*. Additionally, flow and error control data, using the ARQ mechanism, may be piggybacked on an information frame. *Supervisory frames*

(S-frames) provide the ARQ mechanism when piggybacking is not used, and *unnumbered frames* (U-frames) provide supplemental link control functions. The first one or two bits of the control field serves to identify the frame type. The remaining bit positions are organized into subfields as indicated in Figure 5.13b and d. Their use is explained in the discussion of HDLC operation, below.

Note that the basic control field for S- and I-frames uses 3-bit sequence numbers. With the appropriate set-mode command, an extended control field can be used for S- and I-frames that employs 7-bit sequence numbers.

Information Field

The information field is present only in I-frames and some unnumbered frames. The field can contain any sequence of bits. Its length is undefined in the standard, but is generally limited by each implementation to a specified maximum. Frequently, the length must be a multiple of eight bits.

Frame Check Sequence Field

The frame check sequence is applied to the remaining bits of the frame, exclusive of flags. The normal FCS is the 16-bit CRC-CCITT defined earlier. An optional 32-bit FCS, using CRC-32, may be employed if the frame length or line reliability dictates this choice.

Operation

The operation of HDLC consists of the exchange of I-frames, S-frames, and U-frames between a primary and a secondary or between two primaries. The various commands and responses defined for these frame types are listed in Table 5.1. To describe HDLC operation, we will first discuss these three types of frames, and then give some examples.

Information Frames

The basic operation of HDLC involves the exchange of information frames (I-frames) containing user data. Each I-frame contains the sequence number of the transmitted frame as well as a piggybacked positive acknowledgment. The acknowledgment is the sequence number of the *next* frame expected. A maximum window size of 7 or 127 is allowed.

The I-frame also contains a poll/final (P/F) bit. The bit is a poll bit for commands (from primary) and a final bit (from secondary) for responses. In normal response mode (NRM), the primary issues a poll giving permission to send by setting the poll bit to 1, and the secondary sets the final bit to 1 on the last I-frame of its response. In asynchronous response mode (ARM) and asynchronous balanced mode (ABM), the P/F bit is sometimes used to coordinate the exchange of S- and U-frames.

TABLE 5.1   HDLC Commands and Responses

Name	Function	Description
Information (I)	C/R	Exchange user data
Supervisory (S)		
Receive Ready (RR)	C/R	Positive acknowledgment; ready to receive I-frame
Receive Not Ready (RNR)	C/R	Positive acknowledgment; not ready to receive
Reject (REJ)	C/R	Negative acknowledgment; go back N
Selective Reject (SREJ)	C/R	Negative acknowledgment; selective reject
Unnumbered (U)		
Set Normal Response/ Extended Mode (SNRM/SNRME)	C	Set mode; extended = two-octet control field
Set Asynchronous Response/ Extended Mode (SARM/SARME)	C	Set mode; extended = two-octet control field
Set Asynchronous Balanced/ Extended Mode (SABM/SABME)	C	Set mode; extended = two-octet control field
Set Initialization Mode (SIM)	C	Initialize link control functions in addressed station
Disconnect (DISC)	C	Terminate logical link connection
Unnumbered Acknowledgment (UA)	R	Acknowledges acceptance of one of the above set-mode commands
Disconnected Mode (DM)	R	Secondary is logically disconnected
Request Disconnect (RD)	R	Request for DISC command
Request Initialization Mode (RIM)	R	Initialization needed; request for SIM command
Unnumbered Information (UI)	C/R	Used to exchange control information
Unnumbered Poll (UP)	C	Used to solicit control information
Reset (RSET)	C	Used for recovery; resets N(R), N(S)
Exchange Identification (XID)	C/R	Used to request/report identity and status
Test (TEST)	C/R	Exchange identical information fields for testing
Frame Reject (FRMR)	R	Reports receipt of unacceptable frame

Supervisory Frames

The supervisory frame (S-frame) is used for flow and error control. Both go-back-N ARQ (REJ) and selective-reject ARQ (SREJ) are allowed. The latter is rarely implemented because of the buffering requirements. A frame may be positively acknowledged with a receive ready (RR) when an I-frame is not available for piggybacking. In addition, a receive not ready (RNR) is used to accept a frame but request that no more I-frames be sent until a subsequent RR is used. For the RR, RNR, and REJ frames, N(R) indicates the sequence number of the next expected I-frame. For SREJ, N(R) is the sequence number of the rejected frame.

The P/F bit on a supervisory frame may be employed as follows. The primary may set the P bit in an RR frame to poll the secondary. This is done when the primary has no I-frame upon which to piggyback the poll. The secondary responds with an I-frame if it has one; otherwise, it sends an RR with the F bit set to indicate that it has no data to send. The primary (combined station) may set the P bit in the RNR command to solicit the receive status of a secondary/combined station. The response will be an RR with the F bit set if the station can receive I-frames, and an RNR with the F bit set if the station is busy.

Unnumbered Frames

Unnumbered frames are used for a variety of control functions. As the name indicates, these frames do not carry sequence numbers and do not alter the sequencing or flow of numbered I-frames. We can group these frames into the following categories:

- Mode-setting commands and responses.
- Information transfer commands and responses.
- Recovery commands and responses.
- Miscellaneous commands and responses.

Mode-setting commands are transmitted by the primary/combined station to initialize or change the mode of the secondary/combined station. The secondary/combined station acknowledges acceptance by responding with an unnumbered acknowledgment (UA) frame; the UA has the F bit set to the same value as the received P bit. Once established, a mode remains in effect at a secondary station until the next mode-setting command is accepted, and at a combined station until the next mode-setting command is either accepted or transmitted and acknowledged.

The commands SNRM, SNRME, SARM, SARME, SABM, and SABME are self-explanatory. Upon acceptance of the command, the I-frame sequence numbers in both directions are set to 0. The set initialization mode (SIM) command is used to cause the addressed secondary/combined station to initiate a station-specified procedure to initialize its data link control functions (e.g., accept a new program or update operational parameters). While in initialization mode, the required information is sent using unnumbered information (UI) frames. The disconnect command (DISC) is used to inform the addressed station that the transmitting station is suspending operation.

In addition to UA, there are several other responses related to mode setting. The disconnected mode (DM) response is sent in response to all commands to indicate that the responding station is logically disconnected. When sent in response to a mode-setting command, DM is a refusal to set the requested mode. The request initialization mode (RIM) response is used in response to a mode-setting command when the station is not ready and wishes to initialize. The request disconnect (RD) response is used to request a disconnect of the logical link.

Information transfer commands and responses are used to exchange information between stations. This is done primarily through the unnumbered information (UI) command/response. Examples of UI frame information are higher-level status, operational interruption, time of day, and link initialization parameters. The unnumbered poll (UP) command is used to solicit an unnumbered response, as a way of establishing the status of the addressed station.

Recovery commands and responses are used when the normal ARQ mechanism does not apply or will not work. The frame reject (FRMR) response is used to report an error in a received frame, such as

- Invalid control field.
- Data field too long.
- Data field not allowed with received frame type.
- Invalid receive count (i.e., a frame is acknowledged that has not yet been sent).

The reset (RSET) command is used to clear the FRMR condition. RSET announces that the sending station is resetting its send sequence number, and the addressed station should reset its receive sequence number.

Finally, there are two *miscellaneous* command/responses that fit into no neat category. The exchange identification (XID) command/response is used for two stations to exchange station identification and the characteristics of the two stations. The actual information exchanged is implementation dependent. A recently added frame type is the test (TEST) command/response. A test command must be echoed with a test response at the earliest opportunity. This is a simple means of testing that the link and the addressed station are still functioning.

Examples of Operation

In order to better understand HDLC operation, several examples are presented in Figure 5.15. In the example diagrams, each arrow includes a legend that specifies the frame name, the setting of the P/F bit, and, where appropriate, the values of N(R) and N(S). The setting of the P or F bit is 1 if the designation is present and 0 if it is absent.

Figure 5.15a shows the frames involved in link setup and disconnect. The HDLC entity for one side issues an SABM command to the other side and starts a timer. The other side, upon receiving the SABM, returns a UA response and sets local variables and counters to their initial values. The initiating entity receives a UA response, sets its variables and counters, and stops the timer. The logical connection is now active, and both sides may begin transmitting frames. Should the timer expire without a response, the originator will repeat the SABM, as illustrated. This would be repeated until a UA or DM is received or until, after a given number of tries, the entity attempting initiation gives up and reports failure to a management entity. In such a case, higher-layer intervention is necessary. The same figure (Figure 5.15a) shows the disconnect procedure. One side issues a DISC command, and the other responds with a UA response.

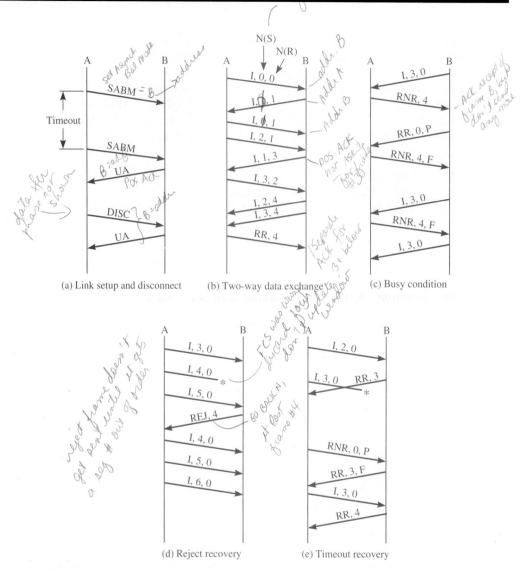

FIGURE 5.15. Examples of HDLC operation.

Figure 5.15b illustrates the full-duplex exchange of I-frames. When an entity sends a number of I-frames in a row with no incoming data, then the receive sequence number is simply repeated (e.g., I,1,1;I,2.1 in the A-to-B direction). When an entity receives a number of I-frames in a row with no outgoing frames, then the receive sequence number in the next outgoing frame must reflect the cumulative activity (e.g., I,1,3 in the B-to-A direction). Note that, in addition to I-frames, data exchange may involve supervisory frames.

Figure 5.15c shows an operation involving a busy condition. Such a condition may arise because an HDLC entity is not able to process I-frames as fast as they are arriving, or the intended user is not able to accept data as fast as they arrive in I-frames. In either case, the entity's receive buffer fills up, and it must halt the incoming flow of I-frames using an RNR command. In this example, the station issues an RNR, which requires the other side to halt transmission of I-frames. The station receiving the RNR will usually poll the busy station at some periodic interval by sending an RR with the P bit set. This requires the other side to respond with either an RR or an RNR. When the busy condition has cleared, B returns an RR, and I-frame transmission from NT can resume.

An example of error recovery using the REJ command is shown in Figure 5.15d. In this example, A transmits I-frames numbered 3, 4, and 5. Number 4 suffers an error. B detects the error and discards the frame. When B receives I-frame number 5, it discards this frame because it is out of order and sends an REJ with an N(R) of 4. This causes A to initiate retransmission of all I-frames sent, beginning with frame 4. It may continue to send additional frames after the retransmitted frames.

An example of error recovery using a timeout is shown in Figure 5.15e. In this example, A transmits I-frame number 3 as the last in a sequence of I-frames. The frame suffers an error. B detects the error and discards it. However, B cannot send an REJ. This is because there is no way to know if this was an I-frame. If an error is detected in a frame, all of this bits of that frame are suspect, and the receiver has no way to act upon it. A, however, started a timer as the frame was transmitted. This timer has a duration long enough to span the expected response time. When the timer expires, A initiates recovery action. This is usually done by polling the other side with an RR command with the P bit set, to determine the status of the other side. Since the poll demands a response, the entity will receive a frame containing an N(R) field and be able to proceed. In this case, the response indicates that frame 3 was lost, which A retransmits.

These examples are not exhaustive. However, they should give the reader a good feel for the behavior of HDLC.

5.5

RECOMMENDED READING

Detailed discussions of data link control protocols are contained in [MART88], [CYPS78], and [MCNA88]. An excellent and very detailed treatment of flow control and error control is to be found in [BERT92].

5.6

PROBLEMS

5.1 Draw a diagram similar to Figure 5.3 for the case in which the primary requests data from the secondary.

5.2 Derive an equation similar to Equation (5.1) for roll-call polling on a multi-point line. Assume that t_0 is constant for all stations and that the primary does not send a poll until it is assured that the response of that poll will not arrive prior to the end of a transmission.

5.3 In Figure 5.2, it would appear that efficiency could be improved by station 1 sending its EOT with the last data frame. Comment on this procedure.

5.4 A computer with many terminals will usually be set up to poll the terminals to see if they have information to send. A computer with only a few terminals will allow the terminals to interrupt it. What are the trade-offs between the two methods of operation?

5.5 Consider a half-duplex point-to-point line using the stop and wait scheme defined in Section 5.2. In the derivation of the total time required to send data (T_D), the assumption is made that the time to initiate the sequence, the processing times, and the acknowledgment times are small compared to the propagation time and the frame time. Check the validity of this assumption for the following case:

$$t_{prop} = t_{frame}$$
$$t_{proc} = t_{poll} = t_{ack} = 0.1\, t_{prop}$$
$$n = 100$$

What percent error does this assumption introduce for this case?

5.6 Consider a half-duplex point-to-point line using a stop and wait scheme.
   a. What is the effect on line utilization of increasing the message size so that fewer messages will be required? Other factors remain constant.
   b. What is the effect on line utilization of increasing the number of frames for a constant message size?
   c. What is the effect on line utilization of increasing frame size?

5.7 A channel has a data rate of 4 kbps and a propagation delay of 20 ms. For what range of frame sizes does stop-and-wait give an efficiency of at least 50%?

5.8 Suppose that a selective-reject ARQ is used where $N = 4$. Show, by example, that a 3-bit sequence number is needed.

5.9 Why is it not necessary to have NAK0 and NAK1 for stop-and-wait ARQ?

5.10 Consider the use of 1000-bit frames on a 1-Mbps satellite channel. What is the maximum link utilization for
   a. Stop-and-wait ARQ?
   b. Continuous ARQ with a window size of 7?
   c. Continuous ARQ with a window size of 127?
   d. Continuous ARQ with a window size of 255?

5.11 Consider the following multipoint architecture, which consists of one primary and N equally spaced secondaries.

Let a = (propagation time)/(transmission time), where the propagation time is from the primary to the farthest secondary.

a. Assume roll call polling. Also assume that the transmission time for the poll and that primary and secondary processing times are negligible. If every secondary is always ready to transmit, show that the line utilization is

$$U = \frac{1}{1 + a}$$

If only one station is ready to transmit during any polling cycle show that

$$U = \frac{1}{1 + aN}$$

b. Now consider the same architecture for hub polling. Show that if every secondary is always ready to transmit, the utilization can be approximated by

$$U = \frac{1}{1 + a/2 + a/N}$$

[Hint: Ignore the first station to be polled (from P) and derive the total time it takes for a typical secondary to be polled and transmit.] Now show that if only one station is ready to transmit in each cycle,

$$U = \frac{1}{1 + 2.5a}$$

5.12 Using the same assumptions that are used for Figure 5.12, plot line utilization as a function of P, the probability that a single frame is in error, for the following error-control techniques:

a. Stop-and-wait.
b. Go-back-N with N = 7.
c. Go-back-N with N = 127.
d. Selective reject with N = 7.
e. Selective reject with N = 127.

Do all of the preceding for the following values of a: 0.1, 1, 10, 100. Draw conclusions about which technique is appropriate for various ranges of a.

5.13 In the following figure, frames generated by node A are sent to node C through node B. Determine the minimum transmission rate required between nodes B and C so that the buffers of node B are not flooded, based on the following:

- The data rate between A and B is 100 kbps.
- The propagation delay is 10 μsec/mile for both lines.
- There are full duplex lines between the nodes.
- All data frames are 1000 bits long; ACK frames are separate frames of negligible length.
- Between A and B, a sliding-window protocol with window size of 3 is used.
- Between B and C, stop-and-wait protocol is used.
- There are no errors.

Hint: In order not to flood the buffers of B, the average number of frames entering and leaving B must be the same over a long interval.

5.14 A channel has a data rate of R bps and a propagation delay of t seconds per kilometer. The distance between the sending and receiving nodes is L kilometers. Nodes exchange fixed-size frames of B bits. Find a formula that gives the minimum sequence field size of the frames as a function of R, t, B and L (considering maximum utilization). Assume that ACK packets are negligible in size and the processing at the nodes is instantaneous.

5.15 Two neighboring nodes (A and B) are a sliding-window protocol with a 3-bit sequence number. As the ARQ mechanism, Go-back-N is used with a window size of 4. Assuming A is transmitting and B is receiving, show the window positions for the following succession of events:
a. Before A sends any frames.
b. After A sends frames 0, 1, 2 and B acknowledges 0, 1 and the ACKs are received by A.
c. After A sends 3, 4, 5 and B acknowledges 4.

5.16 It was stated in Section 5.3 that out-of-sequence acknowledgment could not be used for selective-reject ARQ. That is, if frame i is rejected by station X, all subsequent I-frames and RR frames sent by X must have $N(R) = i$, until frame i is successively received, even if other frames with $N(S) > i$ are successfully received in the meantime. One possible refinement is the following: $N(R) = j$ in an I-frame or an RR frame is interpreted to mean that frame $j-1$ and all preceding frames are accepted except for those that have been explicitly rejected using an SREJ frame. Comment on any possible drawback to this scheme.

5.17 The ISO standard for HDLC procedures (ISO 4335) includes the following definitions: (1) an REJ condition is considered cleared upon the receipt of an I-frame with an N(S) equal to the N(R) of the REJ frame; and (2) a SREJ condition is considered cleared upon the receipt of an I-frame with an N(S) equal to the N(R) of the SREJ frame. The standard includes rules concerning the relationship between REJ and SREJ frames. These rules indicate what is allowable (in terms of transmitting REJ and SREJ frames) if an REJ frame has not yet been cleared and what is allowable if an SREJ frame has not yet been cleared. Deduce the rules and justify your answer.

5.18 Two stations communicate via a 1-Mbps satellite link. The satellite serves merely to retransmit data received from one station to another, with negligible switching delay. The up-and-down propagation delay for a synchronous orbit is 270 ms. Using HDLC frames of length 1024 bits, what is the maximum possible data throughput (not counting overhead bits)?

5.19 It is clear that bit stuffing is needed for the address, data, and FCS fields of an HDLC frame. Is it needed for the control field?

5.20 Suggest improvements to the bit-stuffing algorithm to overcome the problems of a single-bit error.

5.21 Using the example bit string of Figure 5.14, show the signal pattern on the line using NRZ-L coding. Does this suggest a side benefit of bit stuffing?

5.22 Assume that the primary HDLC station in NRM has sent six I-frames to a secondary. The primary's N(S) count was three (011 binary) prior to sending the six frames. If the poll bit is on in the sixth frame, what will be the N(R) count back from the secondary after the last frame? (Assume error-free operation.)

5.23 Consider that several physical links connect two stations. We would like to use a "multilink HDLC" that makes efficient use of these links by sending frames on a FIFO basis on the next available link. What enhancements to HDLC are required?

CHAPTER 6

Multiplexing

In Chapter 5, we spent a lot of time trying to devise efficient techniques for utilizing a data link under heavy load. Specifically, with two devices connected by a point-to-point link, it was felt to be desirable to have multiple frames outstanding so that the data link not become a bottleneck between the stations. Now consider the opposite problem. Transmission facilities are, by and large, expensive. It is often the case that two communicating stations will not utilize the full capacity of a data link. For efficiency, it should be possible to share that capacity. The generic term for such sharing is multiplexing.

A simple example of multiplexing is the multidrop line. Here, a number of secondary devices (e.g., terminals) and a primary (e.g., host computer) share the same line. This has several advantages:

- The host computer needs only one I/O port for multiple terminals.
- Only one transmission line is needed.

These types of benefits are applicable in other contexts. In long-haul communications, a number of high-capacity fiber, coaxial, terrestrial microwave, and satellite facilities have been built. These facilities can carry large numbers of voice and data transmissions simultaneously using multiplexing.

This chapter concentrates on three types of multiplexing techniques. The first, frequency-division multiplexing (FDM), is the most widespread and is familiar to anyone who has ever used a radio or television set. The second is a particular case of time-division multiplexing (TDM) often known as synchronous TDM. This is commonly used for multiplexing digitized voice streams. The third type seeks to improve on the efficiency of synchronous TDM by adding complexity to the multiplexer. It is known by a variety of names, including:

- Statistical TDM.
- Asynchronous TDM.
- Intelligent TDM.

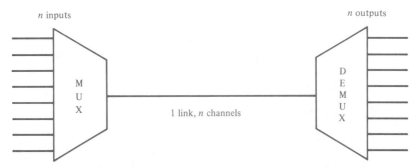

FIGURE 6.1.   Multiplexing.

We shall refer to it as statistical TDM, since this label points out one of its chief properties.

Figure 6.1 depicts the multiplexing function generically. There are *n* inputs to a multiplexer. The multiplexer is connected by a single data link to a de-multiplexer. The link is able to carry *n* separate *channels* of data. The multiplexer combines (multiplexes) data from the *n* input lines and transmits over a higher-capacity data link. The demultiplexer accepts the multiplexed data stream, separates (demultiplexes) the data according to channel, and delivers them to the appropriate output lines.

In addition to the three types of multiplexing listed above, there are other multiplexing techniques more properly termed medium access control techniques. A poll-and-select multipoint line is one example. Other examples are explored in Part II.

6.1

FREQUENCY-DIVISION MULTIPLEXING

Characteristics

Frequency-division multiplexing (FDM) is possible when the useful bandwidth of the medium exceeds the required bandwidth of signals to be transmitted. A number of signals can be carried simultaneously if each signal is modulated onto a different carrier frequency, and the carrier frequencies are sufficiently separated that the bandwidths of the signals do not overlap. A general case of FDM is shown in Figure 6.2a. Six signal sources are fed into a multiplexer, which modulates each signal onto a different frequency ($f_1, \ldots, f_6$). Each modulated signal requires a certain bandwidth centered around its carrier frequency, referred to as a *channel*. To prevent interference, the channels are separated by guard bands, which are unused portions of the spectrum.

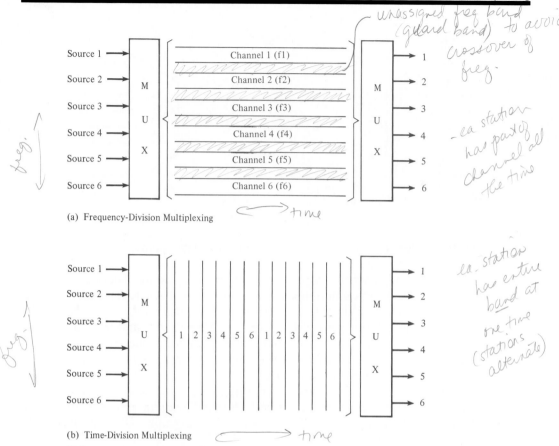

(handwritten annotations:) unassigned freq band (guard band) to avoid crossover of freq.

(handwritten annotations:) — ea. station has part of channel all the time

(handwritten, left margin:) freq.

(handwritten, beneath (a):) time

(a) Frequency-Division Multiplexing

(handwritten annotations:) ea. station has entire band at one time (stations alternate)

(handwritten, left margin:) freq.

(handwritten, beneath (b):) time

(b) Time-Division Multiplexing

FIGURE 6.2. FDM and TDM.

The composite signal transmitted across the medium is analog. Note, however, that the input signals may be either digital or analog. In the case of digital input, the techniques of Section 3.2 would be used to produce an analog signal centered at the desired frequency. In the case of analog input, such as voice, the techniques of Section 3.4 apply.

Figure 3.7, which shows full-duplex FSK transmission, is a simple example of FDM. Two signals are carried on the medium, one centered at 1170 Hz, the other at 2125 Hz. In this case, the signals propagate in opposite directions. More typically, FDM is used to refer to a situation in which multiple signals are carried in the same direction.

A familiar example of FDM is broadcast and cable television. The television signal discussed in Chapter 2 fits comfortably into a 6-MHz bandwidth. Figure 6.3 depicts the transmitted TV signal and its bandwidth. The black-and-white video signal is AM modulated on a carrier signal f_{cv}. Since the baseband video signal has a bandwidth of 4 MHz, we would expect the modulated signal to have a bandwidth of 8 MHz centered on f_{cv}. To conserve bandwidth, the signal

(a) Amplitude modulation with video signal

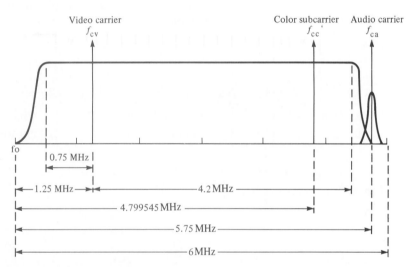

(b) Magnitude spectrum of RF video signal

FIGURE 6.3.   Transmitted TV signal.

is passed through a sideband filter so that most of the lower sideband is suppressed. The resulting signal extends from about $f_{cv} - 0.75$ MHz to $f_{cv} + 4.2$ MHz. A separate color subcarrier, f_{cc}, is used to transmit color information. This is spaced far enough from f_{cv} that there is essentially no interference. Finally, the audio portion of the signal is modulated on f_{ca}, outside the effective bandwidth of the other two signals. A bandwidth of 50 kHz is allocated for the audio signal. The composite signal fits into a 6-MHz bandwidth with the video, color, and audio signal carriers at 1.25 MHz, 4.799545 MHz, and 5.75 MHz above the lower edge of the band, respectively. Thus multiple TV signals can be frequency-division multiplexed on a CATV cable, each with a bandwidth of

6 MHz. Given the enormous bandwidth of coaxial cable (as much as 500 MHz), dozens of TV signals can be simultaneously carried using FDM. Of course, using radio-frequency propagation through the atmosphere is also a form of FDM; Table 6.1 shows the frequency allocation in the United States for broadcast television.

A generic depiction of an FDM system is shown in Figure 6.4. A number of analog or digital signals $[m_i(t), i = 1, N]$ are to be multiplexed onto the same transmission medium. Each signal $m_i(t)$ is modulated onto a carrier f_{sci}; since multiple carriers are to be used, each is referred to as a *subcarrier*. Any type of modulation may be used. The resulting analog, modulated signals are then summed to produce a composite signal $m_c(t)$. Figure 6.4b shows the result. The spectrum of signal $m_i(t)$ is shifted to be centered on f_{sci}. For this scheme to work, f_{sci} must be chosen so that the bandwidths of the various signals do not overlap. Otherwise, it will be impossible to recover the original signals.

The composite signal may then be shifted as a whole to another carrier frequency by an additional modulation step. We will see examples of this below.

TABLE 6.1 Broadcast Television Channel Frequency Allocation

Channel Number	Band (MHz)	Channel Number	Band (MHz)	Channel Number	Band (MHz)
2	54–60	25	536–542	48	674–680
3	60–66	26	542–548	49	680–686
4	66–72	27	548–554	50	686–692
5	76–82	28	554–560	51	692–698
6	82–88	29	560–566	52	698–704
7	174–180	30	566–572	53	704–710
8	180–186	31	572–578	54	710–716
9	186–192	32	578–584	55	716–722
10	192–198	33	584–590	56	722–728
11	198–204	34	590–596	57	728–734
12	204–210	35	596–602	58	734–740
13	210–216	36	602–608	59	740–746
14	470–476	37	608–614	60	746–752
15	476–482	38	614–620	61	752–758
16	482–488	39	620–626	62	758–764
17	488–494	40	626–632	63	764–770
18	494–500	41	632–638	64	770–776
19	500–506	42	638–644	65	776–782
20	506–512	43	644–650	66	782–788
21	512–518	44	650–656	67	788–794
22	518–524	45	656–662	68	794–800
23	524–530	46	662–668	69	800–806
24	530–536	47	668–674		

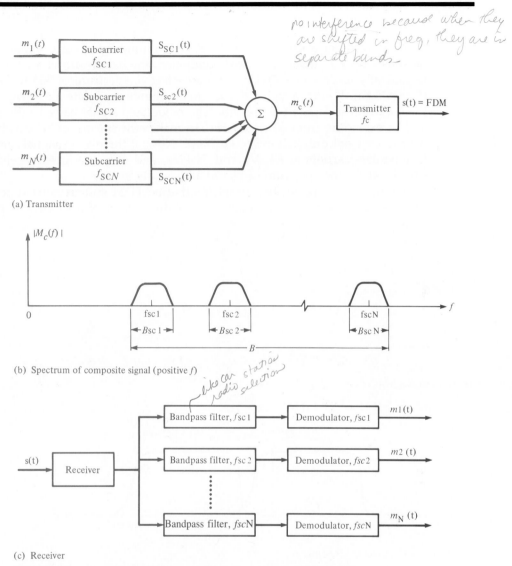

no interference because when they are shifted in freq, they are in separate bands

(a) Transmitter

(b) Spectrum of composite signal (positive *f*)

like car station radio selection

(c) Receiver

FIGURE 6.4. Frequency division multiplexing. Source: [COUC87]

This second modulation step need not use the same modulation technique as the first.

The composite signal has a total bandwidth B, where $B > \sum_{i=1}^{N} B_{sci}$. This analog signal may be transmitted over a suitable medium. At the receiving end, the composite signal is passed through N bandpass filters, each filter centered on f_{sci} and having a bandwidth B_{sci}, for $1 < i < N$. In this way, the signal is again split into its component parts. Each component is then demodulated to recover the original signal.

Let us consider a simple example of transmitting three voice signals simultaneously over a medium. As was mentioned, the bandwidth of a voice signal is generally taken to be 4 kHz, with an effective spectrum of 300 to 3400 Hz (Figure 6.5a). If such a signal is used to amplitude-modulate a 64-kHz carrier, the spectrum of Figure 6.5b results. The modulated signal has a bandwidth of 8 kHz, extending from 60 to 68 kHz. To make efficient use of bandwidth, we elect to transmit only the lower sideband. Now, if three voice signals are used to modulate carriers at 64, 68, and 72 kHz, and only the lower sideband of each is taken, the spectrum of Figure 6.5c results.

This figure points out two problems that an FDM system must cope with. The first is crosstalk, which may occur if the spectra of adjacent component

(a) Spectrum of $m_i(t)$, positive f

(b) Spectrum of $s_{SC1}(t)$ for f_{SC1} = 64 kHz

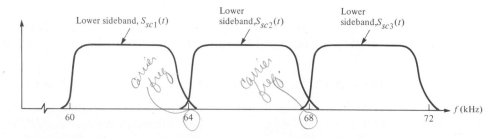

(c) Spectrum of composite signal using subcarriers at
64 kHz, 68kHz, and 72 kHz

FIGURE 6.5. FDM of three voiceband signals.

signals overlap significantly. In the case of voice signals, with an effective bandwidth of only 3100 Hz (300 to 3400), a 4 kHz bandwidth is adequate. The spectra of signals produced by modems for voiceband transmission also fit well in this bandwidth. Another potential problem is intermodulation noise, which was discussed in Chapter 2. On a long link, the nonlinear effects of amplifiers on a signal in one channel could produce frequency components in other channels.

Carrier Systems

The long-distance carrier system provided in the United States and throughout the world is designed to transmit voiceband signals over high-capacity transmission links, such as coaxial cable and microwave systems. The earliest, and still most common, technique for utilizing high-capacity links is FDM. In the United States, AT&T has designated a hierarchy of FDM schemes to accommodate transmission systems of various capacities. A similar, but unfortunately not identical, system has been adopted internationally under the auspices of CCITT (Table 6.2).

Figure 6.6 shows the first three levels of the AT&T-defined hierarchy. At the first level, 12 voice channels are combined to produce a *group* signal with a bandwidth of 12 $\times$ 4 kHz = 48 kHz, in the range 60 to 108 kHz. The signals are produced in a fashion similar to that described above, using subcarrier frequencies of from 64 to 108 kHz in increments of 4 kHz. The next basic building block is the 60-channel *supergroup*, which is formed by frequency-division multiplexing five group signals. At this step, each group is treated as a single signal with a 48 kHz bandwidth and is modulated by a subcarrier. The subcarriers have frequencies from 420 to 612 kHz in increments of 48 kHz. The resulting signal occupies 312 to 552 kHz.

TABLE 6.2 North American and International FDM Carrier Standards

Number of Voice Channels	Bandwidth	Spectrum	AT&T	CCITT
12	48 kHz	60–108 kHz	Group	Group
60	240 kHz	312–552 kHz	Supergroup	Supergroup
300	1.232 MHz	812–2044 kHz		Mastergroup
600	2.52 MHz	564–3084 kHz	Mastergroup	
900	3.872 MHz	8.516–12.388 MHz		Supermaster group
N × 600			Mastergroup multiplex	
3,600	16.984 MHz	0.564–17.548 MHz	Jumbogroup	
10,800	57.442 MHz	3.124–60.566 MHz	Jumbogroup multiplex	

FIGURE 6.6. AT&T FDM hierarchy (first three levels).

Note: f_{sc} is in KHz

Master group output
600 VF channels
2.52 MHz Bandwidth

Mastergroup
Multiplexer

$f_{SC} = 3396$	3048 2844
$f_{SC} = 3148$	2836 2596
$f_{SC} = 2900$	2588 2348
$f_{SC} = 2652$	2340 2100
$f_{SC} = 2356$	2044 1804
$f_{SC} = 2108$	1796 1556
$f_{SC} = 1860$	1548 1308
$f_{SC} = 1612$	1300 1060
$f_{SC} = 1364$	1052 812
$f_{SC} = 1116$	804 564

10 supergroup inputs

Supergroup output
60 VF channels,
240 kHz Bandwidth

5 × 48

$f_{SC} = 612$	552 504
$f_{SC} = 564$	504
$f_{SC} = 516$	456
$f_{SC} = 468$	408
$f_{SC} = 420$	360 312

Supergroup multiplexer

Identical channels @ 108
60 → ? @

5 group inputs

Group output
12 VF channels
48 kHz Bandwidth

Bandwidth Boundaries

$f_{SC} = 108$	108 104
$f_{SC} = 104$	104 100
$f_{SC} = 100$	100 96
$f_{SC} = 96$	96 92
$f_{SC} = 92$	92 88
$f_{SC} = 88$	88 84
$f_{SC} = 84$	84 80
$f_{SC} = 80$	80 76
$f_{SC} = 76$	76 72
$f_{SC} = 72$	72 68
$f_{SC} = 68$	68 64
$f_{SC} = 64$	64 60

12 Voice frequency channel Input (0 – 4 kHz)

Group multiplexer

won't work for video — need at least 6 MHz

→ LPF → modulator → BPF →

f_{sc}

f_{sc}

210

TABLE 6.3   North American and International TDM Carrier Standards

(a) North American			(b) International (CCITT)		
Digital Signal Number	Number of Voice Channels	Data Rate (Mbps)	Level Number	Number of Voice Channels	Data Rate (Mbps)
DS-1	24	1.544	1	30	2.048
DS-1C	48	3.152	2	120	8.448
DS-2	96	6.312	3	480	34.368
DS-3	672	44.736	4	1920	139.264
DS-4	4032	274.176	5	7680	565.148

There are several variations to supergroup formation. Each of the five inputs to the supergroup multiplexer may be a group channel containing 12 multiplexed voice signals. In addition, any signal up to 48 kHz wide whose bandwidth is contained within 60 to 108 kHz may be used as input to the supergroup multiplexer. As another variation, it is possible to directly combine 60 voiceband channels into a supergroup. This may reduce multiplex costs where an interface with existing group multiplex is not required.

The next level of the hierarchy is the *mastergroup* which combines 10 supergroup inputs. Again, any signal with a bandwidth of 240 kHz in the range 312 to 552 kHz can serve as input to the mastergroup multiplexer. The mastergroup has a bandwidth of 2.52 MHz and can support 600 voice frequency (VF) channels. Higher-level multiplexing is defined above the mastergroup, as shown in Table 6.2.

Note that the original voice or data signal may be modulated many times. For example, a data signal may be encoded using QPSK to form an analog voice signal. This signal could then be used to modulate a 76 kHz carrier to form a component of a group signal. This group signal could then be used to modulate a 516 kHz carrier to form a component of a supergroup signal. Each stage can distort the original data; this is so, for example, if the modulator/multiplexer contains nonlinearities or introduces noise.

6.2

SYNCHRONOUS TIME-DIVISION MULTIPLEXING

Characteristics

Synchronous time-division multiplexing is possible when the achievable data rate (sometimes, unfortunately, called bandwidth) of the medium exceeds the data rate of digital signals to be transmitted. Multiple digital signals (or analog signals carrying digital data) can be carried on a single transmission path by interleaving portions of each signal in time. The interleaving can be at the bit level or in blocks of bytes or larger quantities. For example, the multiplexer in Figure 6.2b has six inputs which might each be, say, 9.6 kbps. A single line with a capacity of at least 57.6 kbps (plus overhead capacity) could accommodate all six sources.

A generic depiction of a synchronous TDM system is provided in Figure 6.7. A number of signals $[m_i(t), i = 1, N]$ are to be multiplexed onto the same

(a) Transmitter

(b) TDM frames

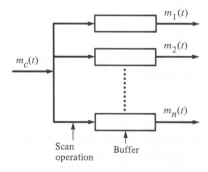

(c) Receiver

FIGURE 6.7.   Synchronous time-division multiplexing.

transmission medium. The signals carry digital data and are generally digital signals. The incoming data from each source are briefly buffered. Each buffer is typically one bit or one character in length. The buffers are scanned sequentially to form a composite digital data stream $m_c(t)$. The scan operation is sufficiently rapid so that each buffer is emptied before more data can arrive. Thus the data rate of $m_c(t)$ must at least equal the sum of the data rates of the $m_i(t)$. The digital signal $m_c(t)$ may be transmitted directly, or passed through a modem so that an analog signal is transmitted. In either case, transmission is typically synchronous.

The transmitted data may have a format something like Figure 6.7b. The data are organized into frames. Each frame contains a cycle of time slots. In each frame, one or more slots is dedicated to each data source. The sequence of slots dedicated to one source, from frame to frame, is called a channel. The slot length equals the transmitter buffer length, typically a bit or a character.

The *character-interleaving* technique is used with asynchronous sources. Each time slot contains one character of data. Typically, the start and stop bits of each character are eliminated before transmission and reinserted by the receiver, thus improving efficiency. The *bit-interleaving* technique is used with synchronous sources and may also be used with asynchronous sources. Each time slot contains just one bit.

At the receiver, the interleaved data are demultiplexed and routed to the appropriate destination buffer. For each input source $m_i(t)$, there is an identical output source which will receive the input data at the same rate at which it was generated.

Synchronous TDM is called synchronous not because synchronous transmission is used, but because the time slots are preassigned to sources and fixed. The time slots for each source are transmitted whether or not the source has data to send. This is, of course, also the case with FDM. In both cases, capacity is wasted to achieve simplicity of implementation. Even when fixed assignment is used, however, it is possible for a synchronous TDM device to handle sources of different data rates. For example, the slowest input device could be assigned one slot per cycle, while faster devices are assigned multiple slots per cycle.

TDM Link Control

The reader will note that the transmitted data stream depicted in Figure 6.7 does not contain the headers and trailers that we have come to associate with synchronous transmission. The reason is that the control mechanisms provided by a data link protocol are not needed. It is instructive to ponder this point, and we do so by considering two key data link control mechanisms: flow control and error control. It should be clear that, as far as the multiplexer and demultiplexer (Figure 6.1) are concerned, flow control is not needed. The data rate on the multiplexed line is fixed, and the multiplexer and demultiplexer are designed to operate at that rate. But suppose that one of the individual output lines attaches to a device that is temporarily unable to accept data? Should the transmission of TDM frames cease? Clearly not, since the remaining output lines are expecting to receive data at predetermined times. The solution is for the saturated output device to cause the flow of data from the corresponding input device to cease. Thus, for a while, the channel in question will carry empty slots, but the frames as a whole will maintain the same transmission rate.

The reasoning for error control is the same. It would not do to request retransmission of an entire TDM frame because an error occurs on one channel. The devices using the other channels do not want a retransmission nor would they know that a retransmission had been requested by some other device on another channel. Again, the solution is to apply error control on a per-channel basis.

How are flow control, error control, and other good things to be provided on a per-channel basis? The answer is simple: Use a data link control protocol such as HDLC on a per-channel basis. A simplified example is shown in Figure 6.8. We assume two data sources, each using HDLC. One is transmitting a stream of HDLC frames containing three octets of data, the other is transmitting HDLC frames containing four octets of data. For clarity, we assume that character-interleaved multiplexing is used, although bit interleaving is more typical. Notice what is happening. The octets of the HDLC frames from the two sources are shuffled together for transmission over the multiplexed line. The reader may initially be uncomfortable with this diagram, since the HDLC frames have lost their integrity in some sense. For example, each frame check sequence (FCS) on the line applies to a disjointed set of bits. Even the FCS is not in one piece! However, the pieces are reassembled correctly before they are seen by the device on the other end of the HDLC protocol. In this sense, the multiplexing/demultiplexing operation is transparent to the attached stations; to each communicating pair of stations, it appears that they have a dedicated link.

One refinement is needed in Figure 6.8. Both ends of the line need to be a combination multiplexer/demultiplexer with a full-duplex line in between.

(a) Configuration

(b) Input data stream

(c) Multiplexed data stream

FIGURE 6.8.   Use of data link control on TDM channels.

Then each channel consists of two sets of slots, one traveling in each direction. The individual devices attached at each end can, in pairs, use HDLC to control their own channel. The multiplexer/demultiplexers need not be concerned with these matters.

Framing

So we have seen that a link control protocol is not needed to manage the overall TDM link. There is, however, a basic requirement for framing. Since we are not providing flag or SYNC characters to bracket TDM frames, some means is needed to assure frame synchronization. It is clearly important to maintain framing synchronization since, if the source and destination are out of step, data on all channels are lost.

Perhaps the most common mechanism for framing is known as *added-digit framing*. In this scheme, typically, one control bit is added to each TDM frame. An identifiable pattern of bits, from frame to frame, is used on this "control channel." A typical example is the alternating bit pattern, 101010. . . This is a pattern unlikely to be sustained on a data channel. Thus to synchronize, a receiver compares the incoming bits of one frame position to the expected pattern. If the pattern does not match, successive bit positions are searched until the pattern persists over multiple frames. Once framing synchronization is established, the receiver continues to monitor the framing bit channel. If the pattern breaks down, the receiver must again enter a framing search mode.

Pulse Stuffing

Perhaps the most difficult problem in the design of a synchronous time-division multiplexer is that of synchronizing the various data sources. If each source has a separate clock, any variation among clocks could cause loss of synchronization. Also, in some cases the data rates of the input data streams are not related by a simple rational number. For both these problems, a technique known as *pulse stuffing* is an effective remedy. With pulse stuffing, the outgoing data rate of the multiplexer, excluding framing bits, is higher than the sum of the maximum instantaneous incoming rates. The extra capacity is used by stuffing extra dummy bits or pulses into each incoming signal until its rate is raised to that of a locally generated clock signal. The stuffed pulses are inserted at fixed locations in the multiplexer frame format so that they may be identified and removed at the demultiplexer.

Example

An example, from [COUC83], illustrates the use of synchronous TDM to multiplex digital and analog sources. Consider that there are 11 sources to be multiplexed on a single link:

- *Source 1:* Analog, 2-kHz bandwidth.
- *Source 2:* Analog, 4-kHz bandwidth.

- *Source 3:* Analog, 2-kHz bandwidth.
- *Sources 4–11:* Digital, 7200 bps synchronous.

As a first step, the analog sources are converted to digital using PCM. Recall from Chapter 4 that PCM is based on the sampling theorem, which dictates that a signal be sampled at a rate equal to twice its bandwidth. Thus the required sampling rate is 4000 samples per second for sources 1 and 3, and 8000 samples per second for source 2. These samples, which are analog (PAM), must then be quantized or digitized. Let us assume that 4 bits are used for each analog sample. For convenience, these three sources will be multiplexed first, as a unit. At a scan rate of 4 kHz, one PAM sample each is taken from sources 1 and 3, and two PAM samples are taken from source 2 per scan. These four samples are interleaved and converted to 4-bit PCM samples. Thus a total of 16 bits is generated at a rate of 4000 times per second, for a composite bit rate of 64 kbps.

For the digital sources, pulse stuffing is used to raise each source to a rate of 8 kbps, for an aggregate data rate of 64 kbps. A frame can consist of multiple cycles of 32 bits, each containing 16 PCM bits and two bits from each of the eight digital sources. Figure 6.9 depicts the result.

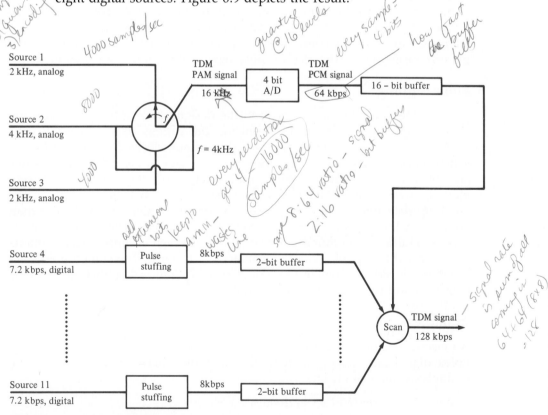

FIGURE 6.9.   TDM of analog and digital sources.

Carrier Systems

As with FDM, synchronous TDM is used as part of the long-haul telecommunications system, and a hierarchy of TDM carriers has been developed. Table 6.3 shows the scheme used in North America (also used in Japan) plus the international (CCITT) standard.

The basis of the TDM hierarchy is the DS-1 transmission format (Figure 6.10) which multiplexes 24 channels. Each frame contains eight bits per channel plus a framing bit for $24 \times 8 + 1 = 193$ bits. For voice transmission, the following rules apply. Each channel contains one PCM word. As described earlier, PCM for voice assumes a 4-kHz bandwidth. Therefore, 8000 samples per second are taken. Therefore, each channel slot and hence each frame must repeat 8000 times per second. With a frame length of 193 bits, we have a data rate of 8000 $\times$ 193 = 1.544 Mbps. For five of every six frames, 8-bit PCM is used. For every sixth frame, each channel contains a 7-bit PCM word plus a signaling bit. The eighth bits form a stream for each voice channel which contains network control and routing information, for example, to establish a connection or terminate a call.

The same overall DS-1 format is used to provide digital data service. For compatibility with voice, the same 1.544-Mbps data rate is used. In this case 23 channels of data are provided. The twenty-fourth channel position is reserved for a special sync byte which allows faster and more reliable reframing following a framing error. Within each channel, seven bits per frame are used for data, with the eighth bit used to indicate whether the channel, for that frame, contains user data or system control data. With seven bits per channel, and since each frame is repeated 8000 times per second, a data rate of 56 kbps can be provided per channel. Lower data rates are provided using a technique

Notes:
1. Bit 193 is a framing bit, used for synchronization.
2. Voice channels:
   . 8-bit PCM used on five of six frames.
   . 7-bit PCM used on every sixth frame, bit 8 of each channel is a signalling bit.
3. Data channels:
   . Channel 24 used for signaling only in some schemes.
   . Bit 8 is a control bit.
   . Bits 1 – 7 used for 56 kbps service.
   . Bits 2 – 7 used for 9.6 kbps, 4.8 kbps, and 2.4 kbps service.

FIGURE 6.10. DS-1 transmission format.

known as subrate multiplexing. For this technique, an additional bit is robbed from each channel to indicate which subrate multiplexing speed is being provided. This leaves a total capacity per channel of $6 \times 8000 = 48$ kbps. This capacity is used to multiplex five 9.6-kbps channels, ten 4.8-kbps channels, or twenty 2.4-kbps channels. For example, if channel 2 is used to provide 9.6-kps service, then up to five data subchannels share this channel. The data for each subchannel appears as six bits in channel 2 in every fifth frame.

Finally, the DS-1 format can be used to carry a mixture of voice and data channels. In this case all 24 channels are utilized; no sync byte is provided.

Above this basic data rate of 1.544 Mbps, higher-level multiplexing is achieved by interleaving bits from DS-1 inputs. For example, the DS-2 transmission system combines four DS-1 inputs into a 6.312 Mbps stream. Data from the four sources are interleaved 12 bits at a time. Note that $1.544 \times 4 = 6.176$ Mbps. The remaining capacity is used for framing and control bits, and pulse stuffing. The reader interested in the details of this and other digital carrier TDM formats should consult [BELL90].

As with FDM, a higher level of the TDM hierarchy is formed by multiplexing signals from the next lower level or by combination of those signals plus input at the appropriate data rate from other sources. Figure 6.11 illustrates this hierarchy. First, the DS-1 transmission rate is used to provide both a voice and data service. The data service is known as the Dataphone Digital Service (DDS). The DDS provides digital transmission service between customer data devices at data rates of from 2.4 to 56 kbps [SLAN81], [ERIK86]. The service is available at customer premises over two twisted-pair lines. The advantage of this service is that it eliminates the need for modems.

Various standardized multiplexers are employed to create higher-capacity transmission facilities. The most commonly-used ones are shown in Figure 6.11. The designations, DS1, DS1C, and so on refer to the multiplexing scheme used for carrying information. AT&T and other carriers supply transmission facilities that support these various multiplexed signals, referred to as carrier systems. These are designated with a "T" label. Thus, the T-1 carrier provides a data rate of 1.544 Mbps and is thus capable of supporting the DS-1 multiplex format, and so on for higher data rates.

Table 6.4 lists some of these TDM facilities for various transmission media. Comparable FDM facilities are also provided. These facilities provide high-capacity transmission for today's long-haul telecommunications systems. Each facility is given a designation that indicates the capacity provided. Thus the *T1 carrier* provides a 1.544-Mbps service, using the DS-1 transmission format. The column labeled transmission denotes whether an analog or digital transmission service is provided. As was mentioned in Chapter 2, analog service implies analog signaling, but a digital transmission service can be provided with either analog or digital service. For example, the T4 service uses digital signaling over coaxial cable, but the FT3 and 11-GHz digital services use analog signaling.

FIGURE 6.11. North American (AT&T) digital TDM hierarchy.

TABLE 6.4   Capacity of Some Communication Carriers

Transmission Medium	Designation	Transmission	Number of Voice Channels	Operating Frequency (MHz)	Data Rate (Mbps)
Twisted pair	N3	Analog	24	0.172–0.268	1.544
	T1	Digital	24		
	T2	Digital	96		6.312
Coaxial cable	L1	Analog	600	0.006–2.79	
	L4	Analog	3600	0.564–17.55	
	L5	Analog	10,800	3.12–60.5	
	T4	Digital	4032		274.176
Optical fiber	FT3	Digital	672		44.736
Microwave	TD3	Analog	1200	3700–4200	
	TH1	Analog	1800	5925–6425	
	TN1	Analog	1800	10,700–11,700	
	11-GHz	Digital	672		44.736
	18-GHz	Digital	4032		274.176
Satellite	Intelsat V	Analog	~24,000	6/4 -GHz band and 14/11-GHz band	

6.3

STATISTICAL TIME-DIVISION MULTIPLEXING

Characteristics

In a synchronous time-division multiplexer, it is generally the case that many of the time slots in a frame are wasted. A typical application of a synchronous TDM involves linking a number of terminals to a shared computer port. Even if all terminals are actively in use, most of the time there is no data transfer at any particular terminal.

An alternative to synchronous TDM is *statistical TDM*, also known as asynchronous TDM and intelligent TDM. The statistical multiplexer exploits this common property of data transmission by dynamically allocating time slots on demand. As with a synchronous TDM, the statistical multiplexer has a number of I/O lines on one side and a higher speed multiplexed line on the other. Each I/O line has a buffer associated with it. In the case of the statistical multiplexer, there are n I/O lines, but only k, where $k < n$, time slots available on the TDM frame. For input, the function of the multiplexer is to scan the input buffers, collecting data until a frame is filled, and then send the frame. On output, the multiplexer receives a frame and distributes the slots of data to the appropriate output buffers.

Because statistical TDM takes advantage of the fact that the attached devices are not all transmitting all of the time, the data rate on the multiplexed line is less than the sum of the data rates of the attached devices. Thus, a statistical multiplexer can use a lower data rate to support as many devices as a synchronous multiplexer. Alternatively, if a statistical multiplexer and a synchronous multiplexer both use a link of the same data rate, the statistical multiplexer can support more devices.

Figure 6.12 contrasts statistical and synchronous TDM. The figure depicts four data sources and shows the data produced in four time epochs (t_0, t_1, t_2, t_3). In the case of the synchronous multiplexer, the multiplexer has an effective output rate of four times the data rate of any of the input devices. During each epoch, data are collected from all four sources and sent out. For example, in the first epoch, sources C and D produce no data. Thus two of the four time slots transmitted by the multiplexer are empty.

In contrast, the statistical multiplexer does not send empty slots if there are data to send. Thus, during the first epoch, only slots for A and B are sent. However, the positional significance of the slots is lost in this scheme. It is not known ahead of time which source's data will be in any particular slot. Since data arrive from and are distributed to I/O lines unpredictably, address information is required to assure proper delivery. Thus there is more overhead per slot for statistical TDM since each slot carries an address as well as data.

The frame structure used by a statistical multiplexer has an impact on performance. Clearly, it is desirable to minimize overhead bits to improve throughput. Generally, a statistical TDM system will use a synchronous protocol such as HDLC. Within the HDLC frame, the data frame must contain control bits for the multiplexing operation. Figure 6.13 shows two possible formats [BACH83]. In the first case, only one source of data is included per frame.

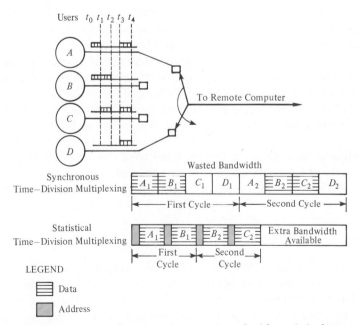

FIGURE 6.12.   Synchronous TDM contrasted with statistical TDM.

FLAG	Address	Control	Statistical TDM Sub frame	FCS	Flag

(a) Overall frame

Address	Data

(b) One source per frame

Address	Length	Data	••••••	Address	Length	Data

(c) Multiple sources per frame

FIGURE 6.13.   Statistical TDM frame formats.

That source is identified by an address. The length of the data field is variable, and its end is marked by the end of the overall frame. This scheme can work well under light load, but is quite inefficient under heavy load.

A way to improve efficiency is to allow multiple data sources to be packaged in a single frame. Now, however, some means is needed to specify the length of data for each source. Thus the statistical TDM subframe consists of a sequence of data fields, each labeled with an address and a length. Several techniques can be used to make this approach even more efficient. The address field can be reduced by using relative addressing. That is, each address specifies the number of the current source relative to the previous source, modulo the total number of sources. So, for example, instead of an 8-bit address field, a 4-bit field might suffice.

Another refinement is to use a two-bit label with the length field [SEID78]. A value of 00, 01, or 10 corresponds to a data field of one, two, or three bytes; no length field is necessary. A value of 11 indicates that a length field is included.

Performance

We have said that the data rate of the output of a statistical multiplexer is less than the sum of the data rates of the inputs. This is allowable because it is anticipated that the average amount of input is less than the capacity of the multiplexed line. The difficulty with this approach is that, while the average aggregate input may be less than the multiplexed line capacity, there may be peak periods when the input exceeds capacity.

TABLE 6.5 Example of Statistical Multiplexer Performance

Input[a]	Capacity = 5000 bps		Capacity = 7000 bps	
	Output	Backlog	Output	Backlog
6	5	1	6	0
9	5	5	7	2
3	5	3	5	0
7	5	5	7	0
2	5	2	2	0
2	4	0	2	0
2	2	0	2	0
3	3	0	3	0
4	4	0	4	0
6	5	1	6	0
1	2	0	1	0
10	5	5	7	3
7	5	7	7	3
5	5	7	7	1
8	5	10	7	2
3	5	8	5	0
6	5	9	6	0
2	5	6	2	0
9	5	10	7	2
5	5	10	7	0

[a]Input = 10 sources, 1000 bps/source; average input rate = 50% of maximum.

The solution to this problem is to include a buffer in the multiplexer to hold temporary excess input. Table 6.5 gives an example of the behavior of such systems. We assume 10 sources, each capable of 1000 bps, and we assume that the average input per source is 50% of its maximum. Thus, on average, the input load is 5000 bps. Two cases are shown: multiplexers of output capacity 5000 bps and 7000 bps. The entries of the table show the number of bits input from the 10 devices each millisecond and the output from the multiplexer. When the input exceeds the output, backlog develops that must be buffered.

There is a trade-off between the size of the buffer used and the data rate of the line. We would like to use the smallest possible buffer and the smallest possible data rate, but a reduction in one requires an increase in the other. Note that we are not so much concerned with the cost of the buffer—memory is cheap—as we are with the fact that the more buffering there is, the longer the delay. Thus the trade-off is really one between system response time and the speed of the multiplexed line. In this section, we present some approximate measures that examine this trade-off. These are sufficient for most purposes. A more careful analysis can be found in [CHU73].

Let us define the following parameters for a statistical time-division multiplexer:

N = number of input sources
R = data rate of each source, bps
M = effective capacity of multiplexed line, bps
α = mean fraction of time each source is transmitting,
   $0 < \alpha < 1$
$K = \dfrac{M}{NR}$ = ratio of multiplexed line capacity to total maximum input

In the above, we have defined M taking into account the overhead bits introduced by the multiplexer. That is, M represents the maximum rate at which data bits can be transmitted.

The parameter K is a measure of the compression achieved by the multiplexer. For example, for a given data rate M, if $K = 0.25$, there are four times as many devices being handled as by a synchronous time-division multiplexer using the same link capacity. The value of K can be bounded:

$$\alpha \leq K \leq 1$$

A value of $K = 1$ corresponds to a synchronous time-division multiplexer, since the system has the capacity to service all input devices at the same time. If $K < \alpha$, the input will exceed the multiplexer's capacity.

Some results can be obtained by viewing the multiplexer as a single-server queue. A queueing situation arises when a "customer" arrives at a service facility and, finding it busy, is forced to wait. The delay incurred by a customer is the time spent waiting in the queue plus the time for the service. The delay depends on the pattern of arriving traffic and the characteristics of the server. Table A-3c in the Appendix to this book summarizes results for the case of random (Poisson) arrivals and constant service time. This model is easily related to the statistical multiplexer:

$$\lambda = \alpha\, NR$$
$$S = \frac{1}{M}$$

The average arrival rate λ, in bps, is the total potential input (NR) times the fraction of time α that each source is transmitting. The service time S, in seconds, is the time it takes to transmit one bit, which is $1/M$. Note that

$$\rho = \lambda\, S = \alpha\, NR/M = \frac{\alpha}{K} = \frac{\lambda}{M}$$

The parameter ρ is the utilization or fraction of total link capacity being used. For example, if the capacity M is 50 kbps and $\rho = 0.5$, the load on the system is 25 kbps. The parameter q is a measure of the amount of buffer space being used in the multiplexer. Finally, t_q is a measure of the average delay encountered by an input source.

Figure 6.14 gives some insight into the nature of the trade-off between system response time and the speed of the multiplexed line. It assumes that data

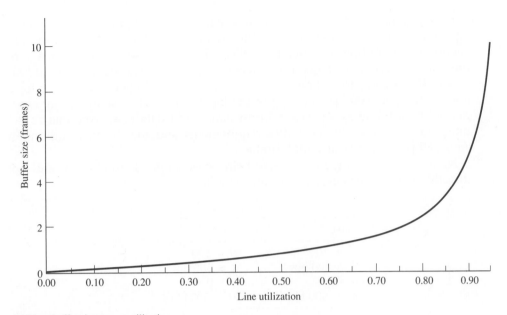

(a) Mean buffer size versus utilization

(b) Mean delay versus utilization

FIGURE 6.14.   Buffer size and delay for a statistical multiplexer.

are being transmitted in 1000-bit frames. Part (a) of the figure shows the average number of frames that must be buffered as a function of the average utilization of the multiplexed line. The utilization is expressed as a percentage of the total line capacity. Thus, if the average input load is 5000 bps, the utilization is 100 percent for a line capacity of 5000 bps and about 71 percent for a line capacity of 7000 bps. Part (b) of the figure shows the average delay experienced by a frame as a function of utilization and data rate. Note that as the utilization rises, so do the buffer requirements and the delay. A utilization above 80 percent is clearly undesirable.

Note that the average buffer size being used depends only on ρ, and not directly on M. For example, consider the following two cases:

Case I	Case II
$N = 10$	$N = 100$
$R = 100$ bps	$R = 100$ bps
$\alpha = 0.4$	$\alpha = 0.4$
$M = 500$ bps	$M = 5000$ bps

In both cases, the value of ρ is 0.8 and the mean buffer size is 2.4. Thus, proportionately, a smaller amount of buffer space per source is needed for multiplexers that handle a larger number of sources. Figure 6.14b also shows that the average delay will be smaller as the link capacity increases, for constant utilization.

So far, we have been considering average queue length, and hence the average amount of buffer capacity needed. Of course, there will be some fixed upper bound on the buffer size available. The variance of the queue size grows with utilization. Thus, at a higher level of utilization, a larger buffer is needed to hold the backlog. Even so, there is always a finite probability that the buffer will overflow. Figure 6.15, based on [CHU73], shows the strong dependence of overflow probability on utilization. This figure, plus Figure 6.14, suggest that utilization above about 0.8 is undesirable.

6.4

RECOMMENDED READING

A discussion of FDM and TDM carrier systems can be found in [BELL90] and [FREE89]. More detailed description and analysis of TDM carrier systems is provided by [POWE90] and [DAYT89]. [CHU73] provides a definitive mathematical analysis of statistical TDM.

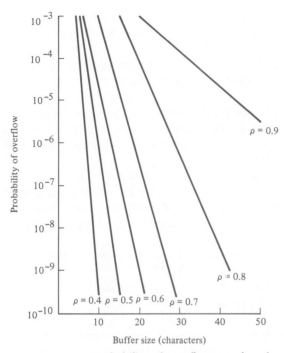

FIGURE 6.15. Probability of overflow as a function of buffer size.

6.5

PROBLEMS

6.1 In Figure 6.6, why is it that the frequency of the carrier, f_{sc}, is not within the boundaries of the bandwidth of the modulated signal for group and supergroup inputs?

6.2 The information in four analog signals is to be multiplexed and transmitted over a telephone channel which has a 400- to 3100-Hz bandpass. Each of the analog baseband signals is bandlimited to 500 Hz. Design a communication system (block diagram) that will allow the transmission of these four sources over the telephone channel using

   a. Frequency-division multiplexing with SSB subcarriers.

   b. Time-division multiplexing using PCM.

Show the block diagrams of the complete system, including the transmission, channel, and reception portions. Include the bandwidths of the signals at the various points in the systems.

6.3 Draw the spectrum of the group signal of Figure 6.6.

6.4 To paraphrase Lincoln: . . . all of the channel some of the time, some of the channel all of the time. . . . Refer to Figure 6.2 and relate the preceding to the figure.

6.5 Consider a transmission system using frequency-division multiplexing. What cost factors are involved in adding one more pair of stations to the system?

6.6 Ten analog signals that are bandlimited to frequencies below 16 kHz are sampled at the Nyquist rate. The digitizing error is to be held below 0.2%. The signals are to travel on a synchronous TDM channel. What is the data rate required for the channel?

6.7 In Synchronous TDM, it is possible to interleave bits, one bit from each channel participating in a cycle. If the channel is using a self-clocking code in order to assist synchronization, would not this bit interleaving introduce problems, since there is not a continuous stream of bits from one source?

6.8 Why is it that the start and stop bits can be eliminated when character interleaving is used in synchronous TDM?

6.9 Explain in terms of data link control and physical layer concepts how error and flow control are accomplished in synchronous time-division multiplexing.

6.10 Bit 193 in the DS-1 transmission format is used for frame synchronization. Explain its use.

6.11 In the DS-1 format, what is the control signal data rate for each voice channel?

6.12 Twenty-four voice signals are to be multiplexed and transmitted over twisted pair. What is the bandwidth required for FDM? Assuming a bandwidth efficiency of 1 bps/Hz, what is the bandwidth required for TDM using PCM?

6.13 Draw a block diagram similar to Figure 6.9 for a TDM PCM system that will accommodate four 300-bps, synchronous, digital inputs and one analog input with a bandwidth of 500 Hz. Assume that the analog samples will be encoded into 4-bit PCM words.

6.14 A character-interleaved time-division multiplexer is used to combine the data streams of a number of 110-bps asynchronous terminals for data transmission over a 2400-bps digital line. Each terminal sends characters consisting of 7 data bits, 1 parity bit, 1 start bit, and 2 stop bits. Assume that one synchronization character is sent every 19 data characters and, in addition, at least 3% of the line capacity is reserved for pulse stuffing to accommodate speed variations from the various terminals.
  a. Determine the number of bits per character.
  b. Determine the number of terminals that can be accommodated by the multiplexer.
  c. Sketch a possible framing pattern for the multiplexer.

6.15 Assume that two 600-bps terminals, five 300-bps terminals, and a number of 150-bps terminals are to be time-multiplexed in a character-interleaved format over a 4800-bps digital line. The terminals send 10 bits/character and one synchronization character is inserted for every 99 data characters. All the terminals are asynchronous and 3% of the line capacity is allocated for pulse stuffing to accommodate variations in the terminal clock rates.

a. Determine the number of 150-bps terminals that can be accommodated.

b. Sketch a possible framing pattern for the multiplexer.

6.16 Find the number of the following devices that could be accommodated by a T1-type TDM line if 1% of the line capacity is reserved for synchronization purposes.

a. 110-bps teleprinter terminals.

b. 300-bps computer terminals.

c. 1200-bps computer terminals.

d. 9600-bps computer output ports.

e. 64-kbps PCM voice-frequency lines.

How would these numbers change if each of the sources were operational an average of 10% of the time?

6.17 Ten 9600-bps lines are to be multiplexed using TDM. Ignoring overhead bits, what is the total capacity required for synchronous TDM? Assuming that we wish to limit average line utilization of 0.8, and assuming that each line is busy 50% of the time, what is the capacity required for statistical TDM? $M/D/1$ model

6.18 For a statistical time-division multiplexer, define the following parameters

$$F = \text{frame length, bits}$$
$$OH = \text{overhead in a frame, bits}$$
$$L = \text{load of data in the frame, bps}$$
$$C = \text{capacity of link, bps}$$

a. Express F as a function of the other parameters. Explain why F can be viewed as a variable rather than a constant.

b. Plot F versus L for $c = 9.6$ kbps and values of $OH = 40, 80, 120$. Comment on the results and compare to Figure 6.14.

c. Plot F versus L for $OH = 40$ and values of $C = 9.6$ kbps and 7.2 kbps. Comment on the results and compare to Figure 6.14.

6.19 The Clambake Zipper Company has two locations. The international headquarters is located at Cut and Shoot, Texas, while the factory is at Conroe, about 25 miles away. The factory has four 300-bps terminals that communicate with the central computer facilities at headquarters over leased voice grade lines. The company is considering installing time division multiplexing equipment so that only one line will be needed. What cost factors should be considered in the decision?

6.20 In statistical TDM, there may be a length field. What alternative could there be to the inclusion of a length field? What problem might this solution cause and how could it be solved?

6.21 In synchronous TDM, the I/O lines serviced by the two multiplexers may be either synchronous or asynchronous although the channel between the two multiplexers must be synchronous. Is there any inconsistency in this? Why or why not?

6.22 Assume that you are to design a TDM carrier, say T-489, to support 30 voice channels using 6 bit samples and a structure similar to T-1. Determine the required bit rate.

PART II

DATA COMMUNICATION NETWORKING

Part I dealt with the transfer of data between devices that are directly connected, generally by a point-to-point link. Often, however, this arrangement is impractical, and a data communication network is required to transmit data between devices.

Communication networks can be categorized as follows:

- Switched networks
  - Circuit-switched networks
  - Packet-switched networks
- Broadcast networks
  - Local area networks
  - Metropolitan area networks (MANs)

Each of these network types is presented and discussed in Part II.

CHAPTER 7

Circuit Switching

Circuit switching is the dominant technology for voice communications today and will remain so well into the ISDN era. This chapter begins with an introduction to the concept of a switched communications network and then looks at the key characteristics of a circuit-switched network.

Any treatment of the technology and architecture of circuit-switched networks must of necessity focus on the internal operation of a single switch. This is in contrast to packet-switched networks, which are best explained by the collective behavior of the set of switches that make up a network. Therefore, the next section in this chapter summarizes the functionality of a single circuit-switching node. Next, the digital private branch exchange is examined. Finally, the topic of control signaling is introduced.

7.1

SWITCHING NETWORKS

In its simplest form, information communication takes place between two devices that are directly connected by some form of transmission medium. Often, however, it is impractical for two devices to be directly connected. This is so in one (or both) of the following arrangements:

- The devices are very far apart. It would be inordinately expensive, for example, to string a dedicated link between two devices thousands of miles apart.
- There is a set of devices, each of which may require a link to many of the others at various times. Examples are all of the telephones in the world and all of the terminals and computers owned by a single organization. Except for the case of a very few devices, it is impractical to provide a dedicated wire between each pair of devices.

The problem with the second arrangement listed above is illustrated in Figure 7.1. Each device has a point-to-point link with each other device. This is

(a) 2 Stations

(b) 3 Stations

(c) 4 Stations

(d) 5 Stations

FIGURE 7.1.   The problem with fully connected or mesh topology.

referred to as a fully connected, or mesh topology. If there are N devices, then $N(N - 1)/2$ full-duplex links are required, and each device requires $(N - 1)$ input/output (I/O) ports. Thus, the cost of the system, in terms of cable instal-lation and I/O hardware, grows with the square of the number of devices.

The solution to these problems is to attach each device to a *communication network*. The network can be designed to minimize transmission costs and to provide full connectivity among the attached devices. Figure 7.2 illustrates this

Communication network node

Network station

FIGURE 7.2.   Interconnection via a communication
network.

concept in a general way. There is a collection of devices that need to communicate; we will refer to them generically as *stations*. The stations may be computers, terminals, telephones, or other communicating devices. Each station attaches to a network *node*. The set of nodes to which stations attach is the boundary of the communication network, which is capable of transferring data between pairs of attached stations. The communication network is not concerned with the content of the data exchanged between stations; its purpose is simply to move those data from source to destination.

The types of networks that are discussed in this and the next chapter are referred to as *switched communication networks*. Such a network consists of an interconnected collection of nodes, in which data are transmitted from source station to destination station by being routed through the network of nodes. Figure 7.3 is a simplified illustration of the concept. The nodes are connected by transmission paths. Data entering the network from a station are routed to the destination by being switched from node to node. For example, data from station A intended for station F are sent to node 4. They may then be routed via nodes 5 and 6 or nodes 7 and 6 to the destination. Several observations are in order:

1. Some nodes connect only to other nodes (e.g., 5 and 7). Their sole task is the internal (to the network) switching of data. Other nodes have one or more stations attached as well; in addition to their switching functions, such nodes accept data from and deliver data to the attached stations.

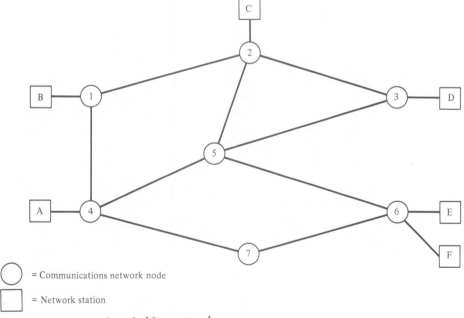

FIGURE 7.3.   Generic switching network.

2. Node–node links are usually multiplexed links, using either frequency-division multiplexing (FDM) or time-division multiplexing (TDM).
3. Usually, the network is not fully connected; that is, there is not a direct link between every possible pair of nodes. However, it is always desirable to have more than one possible path through the network for each pair of stations. This enhances the reliability of the network.

Two quite different technologies are used in wide-area switched networks: circuit switching and packet switching. These two technologies differ in the way the nodes switch information from one link to another on the way from source to destination. In this chapter, we look at the details of circuit switching; packet switching is pursued in Chapter 8.

7.2

CIRCUIT SWITCHING

Communication via circuit switching implies that there is a dedicated communication path between two stations. That path is a connected sequence of links between network nodes. On each physical link, a channel is dedicated to the connection. The most common example of circuit switching is the telephone network.

Communication via circuit switching involves three phases, which can be explained with reference to Figure 7.3.

1. *Circuit establishment.* Before any signals can be transmitted, an end-to-end (station-to-station) circuit must be established. For example, station *A* sends a request to node 4 requesting a connection to station *E*. Typically, the link from *A* to 4 is a dedicated line, so that part of the connection already exists. Node 4 must find the next leg in a route leading to node 6. Based on routing information and measures of availability and perhaps cost, node 4 selects the link to node 5, allocates a free channel (using frequency-division multiplexing, FDM, or time-division multiplexing, TDM) on that link and sends a message requesting connection to *E*. So far, a dedicated path has been established from *A* through 4 to 5. Since a number of stations may attach to 4, it must be able to establish internal paths from multiple stations to multiple nodes. How this is done is discussed later in this chapter. The remainder of the process proceeds similarly. Node 5 dedicates a channel to node 6 and internally ties that channel to the channel from node 4. Node 6 completes the connection to *E*. In completing the connection, a test is made to determine if *E* is busy or is prepared to accept the connection.
2. *Data transfer.* Information can now be transmitted from *A* through the network to *E*. The data may be analog or digital, depending on the nature of the network. As the carriers evolve to fully integrated digital networks, the use of digital (binary) transmission for both voice and data is becoming the

dominant method. The path is : A–4 link, internal switching through 4, 4–5 channel, internal switching through 5, 5–6 channel, internal switching through 6, 6–E link. Generally, the connection is full duplex.

3. *Circuit disconnect*. After some period of data transfer, the connection is terminated, usually by the action of one of the two stations. Signals must be propagated to nodes 4, 5, and 6 to deallocate the dedicated resources.

Note that the connection path is established before data transmission begins. Thus channel capacity must be reserved between each pair of nodes in the path and each node must have available internal switching capacity to handle the requested connection. The switches must have the intelligence to make these allocations and to devise a route through the network.

Circuit switching can be rather inefficient. Channel capacity is dedicated for the duration of a connection, even if no data are being transferred. For a voice connection, utilization may be rather high, but it still does not approach 100 percent. For a terminal-to-computer connection, the capacity may be idle during most of the time of the connection. In terms of performance, there is a delay prior to signal transfer for call establishment. However, once the circuit is established, the network is effectively transparent to the users. Information is transmitted at a fixed data rate with no delay other than the propagation delay through the transmission links. The delay at each node is negligible.

7.3

SINGLE-NODE NETWORKS

A network built around a single circuit-switching node consists of a collection of stations attached to a central switching unit. The central switch establishes a dedicated path between any two devices that wish to communicate. Figure 7.4 depicts the major elements of such a one-node network.

The heart of a modern system is a **digital switch.** The function of the digital switch is to provide a transparent signal path between any pair of attached devices. The path is transparent in the sense that it appears to the attached pair of devices that there is a direct connection between them. Typically, the connection must allow full-duplex transmission. Figure 7.5 illustrates a switch with 15 attached lines. The dotted lines inside the switch symbolize the connections that are currently active.

The **network interface** element represents the functions and hardware needed to connect digital devices, such as data processing devices and digital telephones, to the network. Analog telephones can also be attached if the network interface contains the logic for converting to and from digital signals. Trunks to other digital switches carry TDM signals and provide the links for constructing multiple-node networks.

The **control unit** performs three general tasks. First. it establishes connections. This is generally done on demand, that is, at the request of an attached

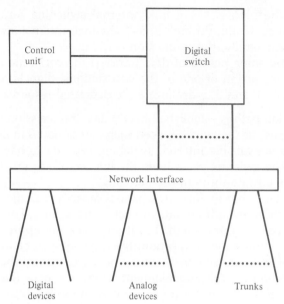

FIGURE 7.4.   Elements of a one-node circuit switch.

FIGURE 7.5.   Abstract representation of circuits.

device. To establish a connection, the control unit must handle and acknowl-edge the request, determine if the intended destination is free, and construct a path through the switch. Second, the control unit must maintain the connec-tion. Since the digital switch uses time-division principles, this may require ongoing manipulation of the switching elements. However, the bits of the communication are transferred transparently (from the point of view of the attached devices). Third, the control unit must tear down the connection, ei-ther in response to a request from one of the parties or for its own reasons.

An important characteristic of a circuit-switching device is whether it is blocking or nonblocking. Blocking occurs when the network is unable to con-nect two stations because all possible paths between them are already in use. A **blocking network** is one in which such blocking is possible. Hence a **non-blocking network** permits all stations to be connected (in pairs) at once and grants all possible connection requests as long as the called party is free. When a network is supporting only voice traffic, a blocking configuration is generally acceptable, since it is expected that most phone calls are of short duration and that therefore only a fraction of the telephones will be engaged at any time. However, when data processing devices are involved, these assumptions may be invalid. For example, for a data entry application, a terminal may be contin-uously connected to a computer for hours at a time. [BHUS85] reports that typical voice connections on a private branch exchange (PBX) have a duration of 120 to 180 seconds, whereas data calls have a range of from 8 seconds to 15 hours. Hence, for data applications, there is a requirement for a nonblocking or "nearly nonblocking" (very low probability of blocking) configuration.

7.4

DIGITAL SWITCHING CONCEPTS

This section looks at the concepts underlying contemporary digital switching. We begin with a look at space-division switching, which was originally devel-oped for the analog environment and has been carried over into digital tech-nology. Then the various forms of time-division switching, which were devel-oped specifically to be used in digital switches, are examined.

Space-Division Switching

Space-division switching was originally developed for the analog environment and has been carried over into the digital realm. The fundamental principles are the same, whether the switch is used to carry analog or digital signals. As its name implies, a space-division switch is one in which the signal paths that are set up are physically separate from one another (divided in space). Each connection requires the establishment of a physical path through the switch that is dedicated solely to the transfer of signals between the two endpoints.

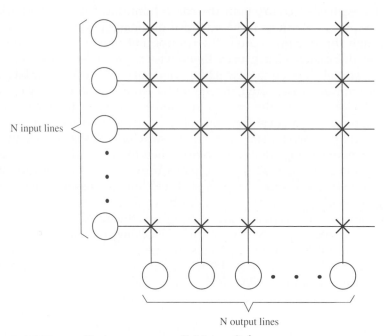

FIGURE 7.6 Single-stage space-division switch.

The basic building block of the switch is a metallic crosspoint or semiconductor gate that can be enabled and disabled by a control unit.

Figure 7.6 shows a simple crossbar matrix with N full-duplex I/O lines. The matrix has N inputs and N outputs; each station attaches to the matrix via one input and one output line. Interconnection is possible between any two lines by enabling the appropriate crosspoint. Note that a total of N^2 crosspoints is required. The crossbar switch has a number of limitations:

- The number of crosspoints grows with the square of the number of attached stations. This is costly for a large switch.
- The loss of a crosspoint prevents connection between the two devices whose lines intersect at that crossspoint.
- The crosspoints are inefficiently utilized (at most N out of N^2).

To overcome these limitations, multiple-stage switches are employed. N input lines are broken up into N/n groups of n lines. Each group of lines goes into a first-stage matrix. The outputs of the first-stage matrices become inputs to a group of second-stage matrices, and so on. The last stage has N outputs; thus, each device attaches its input line to the first stage and its output line to the last stage. Figure 7.7 depicts a three-stage network of switches that is symmetric; that is, the number of inputs to the first stage equals the number of outputs from the last stage. There are k second-stage matrices, each with N/n inputs and N/n outputs. Each first-stage matrix has k outlets so that it connects

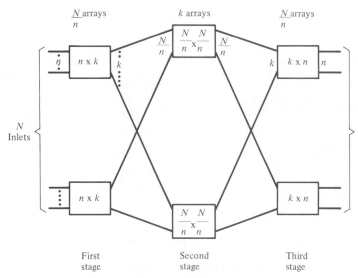

FIGURE 7.7.   Three-stage space-division switch.

to all second-stage matrices. Each second-stage matrix has N/n outputs so that it connects to all third-stage matrices.

This type of arrangement has several advantages over the simple crossbar switch:

- The number of crosspoints is reduced (see below), increasing crossbar utilization.
- There is more than one path through the network to connect two endpoints, increasing reliability.

Of course, a multistage network requires a more complex control scheme. To establish a path in a single-stage network, it is only necessary to open a single gate. In a multistage network, a free path through the stages must be determined and the appropriate gates opened.

A consideration with a multistage space-division switch is that it may be blocking. It should be clear from Figure 7.6 that a crossbar matrix is nonblocking; that is, a path is always available to connect an input to an output. That this is not always the case with a multiple-stage switch can be seen in Figure 7.8. The figure shows a three-stage switch with $N = 9$, $n = 3$, and $k = 3$. The heavier lines indicate lines that are already in use. In this state, input line 9 cannot be connected to either output line 4 or 6, even though both of these output lines are available.

It should be clear that by increasing the value of k (the number of outlets from each first-stage switch and the number of second stage switches), the probability of blocking is reduced. What value of k is required for a nonblocking three-stage switch? The answer is depicted in Figure 7.9. Consider that

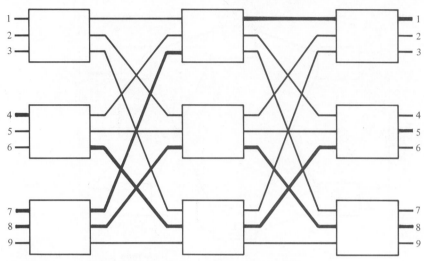

FIGURE 7.8.   Example of blocking in a three-stage switch.

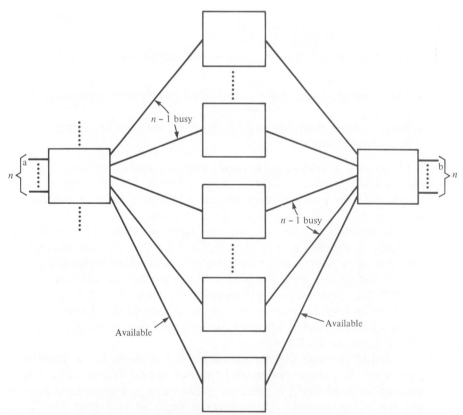

FIGURE 7.9.   Nonblocking three-stage switch.

TABLE 7.1   Number of Crosspoints in a Nonblocking Switch

Number of Lines	Number of Crosspoints for Three-Stage Switch	Number of Crosspoints for Single-Stage Switch
128	7,680	16,384
512	63,488	262,144
3,048	516,096	4.2×10^6
8,192	4.2×10^6	6.7×10^7
32,768	3.3×10^7	1×10^9
131,072	2.6×10^8	1.7×10^{10}

we wish to establish a path from input line a to output line b. The worst-case situation for blocking occurs if all of the remaining $n - 1$ input lines and $n - 1$ output lines are busy and are connected to different center-stage switches. Thus a total of $(n - 1) + (n - 1) = 2n - 2$ center switches are unavailable for creating a path from a to b. However, if one more center-stage switch exists, the appropriate links must be available for the connection. Thus, a three-stage network will be nonblocking if

$$k = 2n - 1 \tag{7.1}$$

We now return to our claim that a multiple-stage switch requires fewer crosspoints than a single-stage switch. From Figure 7.7, the total number of crosspoints N_x in a three-stage switch is

$$N_x = 2Nk + k\left(\frac{N}{n}\right)^2 \tag{7.2}$$

Substituting Equation (7.1) into (7.2),

$$N_x = 2N(2n - 1) + (2n - 1)\left(\frac{N}{n}\right)^2 \tag{7.3}$$

for a nonblocking switch. The actual value as a function of N depends on the number of switches (N/n) in the first and third stages. To optimize, differentiate N_x with respect to n and set the result to 0. For large N, the result converges to $n = (N/2)^{1/2}$. Substituting into (7.3),

$$N_x = 4N(\sqrt{2N} - 1)$$

Table 7.1 compares this value with the number of crosspoints in a single-stage switch. As can be seen, there is a savings that grows with the number of lines.

Time-Division Switching

In contrast to space-division switching, in which dedicated paths are used, *time-division switching* involves the partitioning of a lower-speed data stream into pieces that share a higher-speed data stream with other data pieces. The individual pieces or slots are manipulated by the control logic to route data from input to output. Three concepts comprise the technique of time-division switching:

- TDM bus switching.
- Time-slot interchange (TSI).
- Time-multiplex switching (TMS).

TDM Bus Switching

As discussed in Chapter 6, TDM is a technique that allows multiple signals to share a single transmission line by separating them in time. In this chapter, we are concerned primarily with synchronous TDM, that is, a situation in which time slots are preassigned so that few or no overhead bits are required. We will see that this technique permits multiple channels of data to be handled efficiently within switching systems as well as on transmission systems.

Let us briefly review synchronous TDM. As shown in Figure 7.10a, synchronous TDM was designed to permit multiple low-speed streams to share a high-speed line. A set of inputs is sampled in turn. The samples are organized

(a) Synchronous Time Division Multiplexing

(b) A Simple Time-Division Switch   (c) A Simple Folded Time-Division Switch

FIGURE 7.10. TDM bus switching.

serially into slots (channels) to form a recurring frame of n slots. A slot may be a bit, a byte, or some longer block. An important point to note is that with synchronous TDM, the source and destination of the data in each time slot are known. Hence there is no need for address bits in each slot.

The mechanism for synchronous TDM may be quite simple. For example, each input line deposits data in a buffer; the multiplexer scans these buffers sequentially, taking fixed size chunks of data from each buffer and sending them out on the line. One complete scan produces one frame of data. For output to the lines, the reverse operation is performed, with the multiplexer filling the output line buffers one by one.

The I/O lines attached to the multiplexer may be synchronous or asynchronous; the multiplexed line between the two multiplexers is synchronous and must have a data rate equal to the sum of the data rates of the attached lines. Actually, the multiplexed line must have a slightly higher data rate, since each frame will include some overhead bits (headers and trailers) for synchronization.

The time slots in a frame are assigned to the I/O lines on a fixed, predetermined basis. If a device has no data to send, the multiplexer must send empty slots. Thus the actual data transfer rate may be less than the capacity of the system.

Figure 7.10b shows a simple way in which this technique can be adapted to achieve switching. A set of buffered input and output lines are connected through controlled gates to a high-speed digital bus. Each input line is assigned a time slot. During that time, that line's gate is enabled, allowing a small burst of data onto the bus. For that same time slot, one of the output line gates is also enabled. Since the enabling and disabling of gates is controlled, the sequence of input and output line activations need not be in the same order. Hence a form of switching is possible. Curiously, this technique has no specific name; we shall refer to it as TDM bus switching.

Of course, such a scheme need not be two-sided. As shown in Figure 7.10c, a "folded" switch can be devised by attaching n I/O pairs to the bus. Any attached device achieves full duplex operation by transmitting during one assigned time slot and receiving during another. The other end of the connection is an I/O pair for which these time slots have the opposite meanings.

The TDM bus switch has an advantage over a crossbar switch in terms of efficient use of gates. For N devices, the TDM bus switch requires $2N$ gates or switch points, whereas the most efficient multistage crossbar network requires on the order of $N \sqrt{N}$ switch points.

Let us look at the timing involved a bit more closely. First, consider a nonblocking implementation of Figure 7.10c. There must be N repetitively occurring time slots, each one assigned to an input and an output line. We will refer to one iteration for all time slots as a frame. The input assignment may be fixed; the output assignments vary to allow various connections. When a time slot begins, the designated input line may insert a burst of data onto the line, where it will propagate to both ends past all other lines. The designated ouput line will, during that time, copy the data if any as they go by. The time slot, then, must equal the transmission time of the input line plus the propagation delay between input and output lines. In order to keep the successive time slots uniform, time slot length should be defined as transmission time plus the end-to-end bus propagation delay. For efficiency, the propagation delay should be much less than the transmission time, and in practice this is so. Note that only one time slot or burst of data may be on the bus at a time.

To keep up with the input lines, the slots must recur sufficiently frequently. For example, consider a system connecting full-duplex lines at 19.2 kbps. Input data on each line are buffered at the gate. The buffer must be cleared, by enabling the gate, fast enough to avoid overrun. So if there are 100 lines, the capacity of the bus must be at least 1.92 Mbps. Actually, it must be higher than that to account for the wasted time due to propagation delay.

These considerations determine the traffic-carrying capacity of a blocking switch as well. For a blocking switch, there is no fixed assignment of input lines to time slots; they are allocated on demand. The data rate on the bus dictates how many connections can be made at a time. For a system with 200 devices at 19.2 kbps and a bus at 2 Mbps, about half of the devices can be connected at any one time.

The TDM bus switching scheme can accommodate lines of varying data rates. For example, if a 9600-bps line gets one slot per frame, a 19.2-kbps line would get two slots per frame. Of course, only lines of the same data rate can be connected.

Figure 7.11 is an example that suggests how the control for a TDM bus switch could be implemented. Let us assume that propagation time on the bus is zero. Time on the bus is organized into 30-μs frames of six 5-μs slots each. A control memory indicates which gates are to be enabled during each time slot. In this example, 6 words of memory are needed. A controller cycles through the memory at a rate of one cycle every 30 μs. During the first time slot of each cycle, the input gate from device 1 and the output gate to device 3 are enabled, allowing data to pass from device 1 to device 3 over the bus. The remaining words are accessed in succeeding time slots and treated accordingly. As long as the control memory contains the contents depicted in Figure 7.11, connections are maintained between 1 and 3, 2 and 5, and 4 and 6.

Several questions may occur to you. For one, is this circuit switching? Circuit switching, recall, was defined as a technique in which a dedicated communications path is established between devices. This is indeed the case in Figure 7.10b and c. To establish a connection between an input and output line, the controller dedicates a certain number of time slots per frame to that connection. The appropriate input and output gates are enabled during those time slots to allow data to pass. Although the bus is shared by other connections, it is nevertheless used to create a dedicated path between input and output. Another question: Is this synchronous TDM? Synchronous TDM is generally associated with creating permanent dedicated time slots for each input line. The scheme depicted in Figure 7.10b and c can assume a dynamic character, with

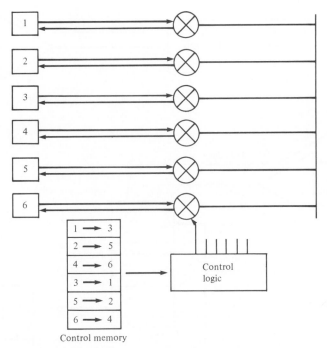

FIGURE 7.11.   Control of a TDM bus switch.

the controller allocating available time slots among connections. Nevertheless, at steady state (a period when no connections are made or broken) a fixed number of slots is dedicated per channel and the system behaves in a manner similar to a synchronous time-division multiplexer.

The control logic for the system described above requires the enabling of two gates to achieve a connection. This logic can be simplified if the input burst into a time slot contains destination address information. All output devices can then always connect to the bus and copy the data from time slots with their address. This scheme blurs the distinction between circuit switching and packet switching.

Time-Slot Interchange

The basic building block of many time-division switches is the *time-slot interchange* (TSI) mechanism. A TSI unit operates on a synchronous TDM stream of time slots, or channels, by interchanging pairs of slots to achieve full-duplex operation. Figure 7.12a shows how the input line of device I is connected to the output line of device J, and vice versa. In this figure, the input lines of N devices are passed through a synchronous multiplexer to produce a TDM stream with N slots. To achieve interconnection, the slots corresponding to two

(a) TSI operation

(b) TSI mechanism

FIGURE 7.12.   Time-slot interchange (TSI).

inputs are interchanged. This results in a full-duplex connection between two lines.

Figure 7.12b depicts a mechanism for TSI. Individual I/O lines are multiplexed and demultiplexed. These functions can be integrated as part of the switch itself, or they may be implemented remotely, as a device clustering mechanism. A random-access data store whose width equals one time slot of data and whose length equals the number of slots in a frame is used. An incoming TDM frame is written sequentially, slot by slot, into the data store. An outgoing TDM frame is created by reading slots from memory in an order dictated by an address store that reflects the existing connections. In the figure, the data in channels I and J are interchanged, creating a full-duplex connection between the corresponding stations.

We can see that, to allow the interchange of any two slots, the incoming data in a slot must be stored until they can be sent out on the right channel in the next frame cycle. Hence the TSI introduces a delay and produces output

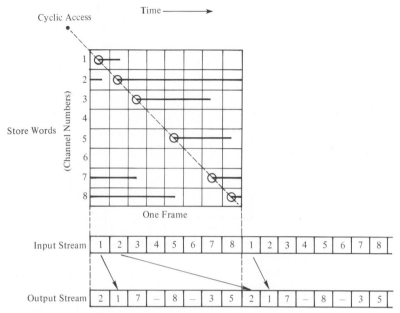

FIGURE 7.13. Operation of TSI store.

slots in the desired order. These are then demultiplexed and routed to the appropriate output line. Since each channel is provided a time slot in the frame, whether or not it transmits data, the size of the TSI unit must be chosen for the capacity of the TDM line, not the actual data transfer rate.

Let us look more closely at the operation of the data store; in particular, we need to view it as a function of time. As an example [DAVI73], consider a system with eight input/output lines, in which the following connections exist: 1–2, 3–7, and 5–8. The other two stations are not in use. Figure 7.13 depicts the contents of the data store over the course of one frame (eight slots). During the first time slot, data are stored in location 1 and read from location 2. During the second time slot, data are stored in location 2 and read from location 1. And so on.

As can be seen, the write accesses to the data store are cyclic, that is, accessing successive locations in sequential order, whereas the read accesses are acyclic, requiring the use of an address store. The figure also depicts two frames of the input and output sequences and indicates the transfer of data between channels 1 and 2. Note that in half the cases, data slots move into the next frame.

As with the TDM bus switch, the TSI unit can handle inputs of varying data rates. Figure 7.14 suggests a way in which this may be done. Instead of presenting the input lines to a synchronous multiplexer, they are presented to a selector device. This device will select an input line based on a channel assignment provided from a store controlled by the time slot counter. Hence, instead

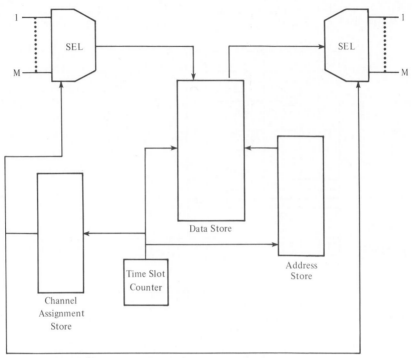

FIGURE 7.14.   TSI operation with variable-rate input.

of sampling equally from each input, it may gather more slots from some channels than others.

Time-Multiplexed Switching

TSI is a simple, effective way of switching TDM data. However, the size of such a switch, in terms of number of connections, is limited by the memory access speed. It is clear that, in order to keep pace with the input, data must be read into and out of memory as fast as they arrive. So, for example, if we have 24 sources operating at 64 kbps each, and a slot size of 8 bits, we would have an arrival rate of 192,000 slots per second (this is like the structure of the PCM T1 carrier). For each time slot, both a read and a write are required. Thus memory access time would need to be $1/(192,000 \times 2)$, or about 2.6 µs.

We can see, then, that a TSI unit can support only a limited number of connections. Further, as the size of the unit grows, for a fixed access speed, the delay at the TSI grows. To overcome both of these problems, multiple TSI units are used. Now, to connect two channels entering a single TSI unit, their time slots can be interchanged. However, to connect a channel on one TDM stream (going into one TSI) to a channel on another TDM stream (going into another TSI), some form of space division multiplexing is needed. Naturally, we do not wish to switch all of the time slots from one stream to another; we would like to do it one slot at a time. This technique is known as *time-multiplexed switching* (TMS).

Multiple-stage networks can be built up by concatenating TMS and TSI stages. TMS stages, which move slots from one stream to another, are referred to as S, and TSI stages are referred to as T. Systems are generally described by an enumeration of their stages from input to output, using the symbols T and S. Figure 7.15 is an example of a two-stage TS network. Such a network is blocking. For example, if one channel on input stream 1 is to be switched to the third channel in output stream 1, and another channel on input stream 1 is to be switched to the third channel on output stream 2, one of the connections is blocked.

To avoid blocking, three or more stages are used. Some of the more common structures used in commercially available systems are [SKAP79]:

- TST.
- TSSST.
- STS.
- SSTSS.
- TSTST.

The requirements on the TMS unit are stringent. The unit must provide space-division connections between its input and output lines, and these connections must be reconfigured for each time slot. This requires, in effect, a control store whose width is sufficient to handle the number of ingoing and outgoing lines and whose length equals the number of time slots in a frame.

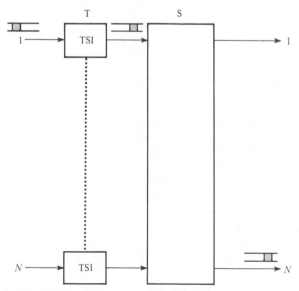

FIGURE 7.15.   Two-stage digital switch.

One means of implementing the TMS stage is the crossbar switch discussed earlier. This requires that the crosspoints be manipulated at each time slot. More commonly, the TMS stage is implemented by digital selectors (SEL) which select only one input at a time on a time-slot basis. These SEL devices are the same as those described in the preceding section, except that here each of their inputs is a TDM stream rather than a single line. Figure 7.16 shows STS and TST networks implemented with the SEL units.

In an STS network, the path between an incoming and outgoing channel has multiple possible physical routes equal to the number of TSI units but only one time route. For a fully nonblocking network, the number of TSI units must be double the number of incoming and outgoing TDM streams. On the other

(a) Space-Time-Space Network

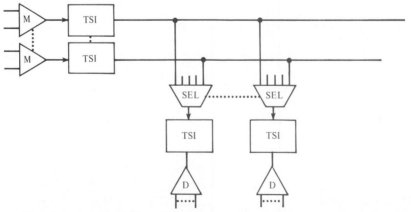

(b) Time-Space-Time Network

FIGURE 7.16. Three-stage TDM switches.

hand, the multiple routes between two channels in a TST network are all in the time domain; there is only one physical path possible. Here, too, blocking is a possibility. One way to avoid blocking is by expanding the number of time slots in the space stage. In all multistage networks, whether space- or time-division, a path-search algorithm is needed to determine the route from input to output.

It is interesting to compare the TDM bus switch with TSI and TMS. It does not exactly fit into either category. Compare it to a space switch. The TDM bus switch does connect any input with any output, as in a crossbar or SEL switch. The space switch operates simultaneously on all inputs, whereas the TDM bus switch operates on the inputs sequentially. However, because the frame time on the bus is less than the slot time of any input, the switching is effectively simultaneous. On the other hand, a comparison of Figures 7.12 and 7.10b reveals the similarity between TSI and TDM bus switching.

7.5

THE DIGITAL PRIVATE BRANCH EXCHANGE

Evolution of the Digital PBX

The digital PBX is a marriage of two technologies: digital switching and telephone exchange systems. The forerunner of the digital PBX is the private branch exchange (PBX). A PBX is an on-premise facility, owned or leased by an organization, which interconnects the telephones within the facility and provides access to the public telephone system. Typically, a telephone user on the premises dials a three- or four-digit number to call another telephone on the premises, and dials one digit (usually 8 or 9) to get a dial tone for an "outside line," which allows the caller to dial a number in the same fashion as a residential user.

The original private exchanges were manual, with one or more operators at a switchboard required to make all connections. Back in the 1920s, these began to be replaced by automatic systems, called *private automatic branch exchanges* (PABXs), which did not require attendant intervention to place a call. These "first-generation" systems used electromechanical technology and analog signaling. Data connections could be made via modems. That is, a user with a terminal, a telephone, and a modem or acoustic coupler in the office could dial up an on-site or remote number that reached another modem and exchange data.

The "second-generation" PBXs were introduced in the middle 1970s. These systems use electronic rather than electromagnetic technology and the internal switching is digital. Such a system is referred to as digital PBX, or computerized branch exchange (CBX). These systems were designed primarily to handle analog voice traffic, with the codec function built into the switch so that digital switching could be used internally. The systems were also capable of handling digital data connections without the need of a modem.

The "third-generation" systems are touted as "integrated voice/data" systems, although the differences between third generation and upgraded second generation are rather blurred. Perhaps a better term is "improved digital PBX." Some of the characteristics of these systems that differ from those of earlier systems include

- *The use of digital phones:* This permits integrated voice/data workstations.
- *Distributed architecture:* Multiple switches in a hierarchical or meshed configuration with distributed intelligence provides enhanced reliability.
- *Nonblocking configuration:* Typically, dedicated port assignments are used for all attached phones and devices.

As new features and technologies are employed, incremental improvements make difficult the continuing classification of PBXs into generations. Nevertheless, it is worth noting recent advances in PBX products that, together, might be considered to constitute a fourth generation:

- *Integrated LAN link:* This capability provides a direct high-speed link to a local area network. This allows an optimum distribution of lower-speed devices (terminals) on the PBX and higher-speed devices (computers) on the LAN in a fashion that is fully transparent to the user.
- *Dynamic bandwidth allocation:* Typically, a PBX offers one or only a small number of different data rate services. The increased sophistication of capacity allocation within the PBX allows it to offer virtually any data rate to an attached device. This allows the system to grow as user requirements grow. For example, full-motion color video at 448 kbps or advanced codecs at 32 kbps could be accommodated.
- *Integrated packet channel:* This allows the PBX to provide access to an X.25 packet-switched network.

It is worthwhile to summarize the main reasons why the evolution described above has taken place. To the untrained eye, analog and digital PBXs would seem to offer about the same level of convenience. The analog PBX can handle telephone sets directly and uses modems to accommodate digital data devices; the digital PBX can handle digital data devices directly and uses codecs to accommodate telephone sets. Some of the advantages of the digital approach are

- *Digital technology:* By handling all internal signals digitally, the digital PBX can take advantage of low-cost LSI and VLSI components. Digital technology also lends itself more readily to software and firmware control.
- *Time-division multiplexing:* Digital signals lend themselves readily to TDM techniques, which provide efficient use of internal data paths, access to public TDM carriers, and TDM switching techniques, which are more cost effective than older, crossbar techniques.

- *Digital control signals:* Control signals are inherently digital and can easily be integrated into a digital transmission path via TDM. The signaling equipment is independent of the transmission medium.
- *Encryption:* This is more easily accommodated with digital signals.

Telephone Call Processing Requirements

The characteristic that distinguishes the digital PBX from a digital data switch is its ability to handle telephone connections. Freeman [FREE89] lists eight functions required for telephone call processing:

- Interconnection.
- Control.
- Attending.
- Busy testing.
- Alerting.
- Information receiving.
- Information transmitting.
- Supervisory.

The interconnection function encompasses three contingencies. The first contingency is a call originated by a station bound for another station on the digital PBX. The switching technologies that we have discussed are used in this context. The second contingency is a call originated by a digital PBX station bound for an external recipient. For this, the PBX must not only have access to an external trunk, but must perform internal switching to route the call from the user station to the trunk interface. The PBX also performs a line to trunk concentration function to avoid the expense of one external line per station. The third contingency is a call originated externally bound for a PBX station. Referred to as *direct inward dialing*, this allows an external caller to use the unique phone number of a PBX station to establish a call without going through an operator. This requires trunk-to-line expansion plus internal switching.

The control function includes, of course, the logic for setting up and tearing down a connection path. In addition, the control function serves to activate and control all other functions and to provide various management and utility services, such as logging, accounting, and configuration control.

The PBX must recognize a request for a connection; this is the attending function. The PBX then determines if the called party is available (busy testing) and, if so, alerts that party (alerting). The process of setting up the connection involves an exchange of information between the PBX and the called and calling parties.

Finally, a supervisory function is needed to determine when a call is completed and the connection may be released, freeing the switching capacity and the two parties for future connections.

Let us look more closely at the sequence of events required to complete a call successfully. First, consider an internal call from extension 226 to extension 280. The following steps occur:

1. 226 goes off-hook (picks up the receiver). The control unit recognizes this condition.
2. The control unit finds an available digit receiver and sets up a circuit from 226 to the digit receiver. The control unit also sets up a circuit from a dial-tone generator to 226.
3. When the first digit is dialed, the dial-tone connection is released. The digit receiver accumulates dialed digits (280).
4. After the last digit is dialed, the connection to the digit receiver is released. The control unit examines the number for legitimacy. If it is not, the caller is informed by some means, such as connection to a rapid busy signal generator. Otherwise, the control unit then determines if 280 is busy. If so, 226 is connected to a busy-signal generator.
5. If 280 is free, the control unit sets up a connection between 226 and a ring-back-tone generator and a connection between 280 and a ringer. A connection path between 226 and 280 is reserved.
6. When 280 answers by going off-hook, the ringing and ring-back connections are dropped and a connection is set up between 226 and 280.
7. When either 280 and 226 goes on-hook, the connection between them is dropped.

For outgoing calls, the following steps are required:

1–3. As above. In this case the caller will be dialing an access code number (e.g., the single digit 9) to request access to an outgoing trunk.
4. The control unit releases the connection to the digit receiver and finds a free trunk group and sends out an off-hook signal.
5. When a dial tone is returned from the central office, the control unit repeats steps 2 and 3.
6. The control unit releases the connection to the digit receiver and sends the number out to the trunk and makes a connection from the caller to the trunk.
7. When either the caller or the trunk signals on-hook, the connection between them is dropped.

There are variations on the foregoing sequence. For example, if the PBX performs least-cost routing, it will wait until the number is dialed and then select the appropriate trunk.

Finally, incoming calls, when direct inward dialing is supported, proceed as follows.

1. The control unit detects a trunk seizure signal from the central office, sets up a path from the trunk to a digit receiver, and sends a start-dialing signal out on that trunk.

2. The control unit releases the receiver path and examines the dialed number and checks the called station for busy, in which case a busy signal is returned.
3. If the called number is free, the control unit sets up a ringing connection to the called number and a ring-back connection to the trunk. It monitors the called station for answer and the trunk for abandon.
4. When the called station goes off-hook, the ringing and ring-back connections are dropped and a connection is set up between the trunk and the called station.
5. When either the trunk or called station signals on-hook, the connection between them is dropped.

Data Switching Requirements

For any circuit-switching system used to connect digital data transmitting devices, certain generic requirements can be defined. These requirements apply both to pure digital data switching devices and to digital PBX systems.

The devices attached to a data switch will use either asynchronous or synchronous transmission. Asynchronous transmission, recall, is character-at-a-time. Each character consists of a start bit, 5 to 8 data bits, a parity bit, and a stop signal, which may be 1, 1.5, or 2 bit times in length. Logic is available which can automatically determine character length, parity, and even bit rate. Hence it is a relatively easy matter for a data switch to handle asynchronous transmission. On input, data are accumulated a character at a time, and transmitted internally using synchronous transmission. At the other end of the connection, they are buffered and transmitted a character at a time to the output line. This applies to any switch using time-division switching techniques. Of course, a pure space-division switch need not concern itself with such matters: A dedicated physical path is set up and bits are transmitted transparently.

Synchronous transmission represents a greater challenge. Synchronous communication requires either a separate clock lead from the transmission point to the reception point or the use of a self-clock encoding scheme, such as Manchester. The latter technique is typical. With synchronous communication, the data rate must be known ahead of time, as well as the synchronization pattern (bits or characters used to signal the beginning of a frame). Thus there can be no universal synchronous interface (until a universal synchronous transmission technique is standardized).

Of course, for either synchronous or asynchronous transmission, full duplex operation is required. Typically, this requires two twisted pairs (known as a twin pair) between a device and the switch, one for transmission in each direction. This is in contrast to the case with analog signaling where a single twisted-pair suffices (see Figure 3.6). Recently, however, some vendors have begun to offer full-duplex digital signaling on a single twisted pair, using a *ping-pong protocol*. In essence, data are buffered at each end and sent across the line at double the data rate with the two ends taking turn. So, for example, two devices may communicate, full duplex, at 56 kbps if they are attached to a 112-kbps line and the line drivers at each end buffer the device data and transmit, alternately, at 112 kbps. In fact, an even higher data rate is required to account for propagation delay and control signals.

Digital PBX Architecture

A variety of architectures have been developed by digital PBX manufacturers. Since these are proprietary, the details are not generally known in most cases. In this section we attempt to present the general architectural features common to all PBX systems.

Digital PBX Components

Figure 7.17 presents a generic PBX architecture. You should find it quite similar to the data switching architecture that we have discussed. Indeed, since the requirements for the PBX are a superset of those for the data switch, a similar architecture is not surprising.

As always, the heart of the system is some kind of digital switching network. The switch is responsible for the manipulation and switching of time multi-

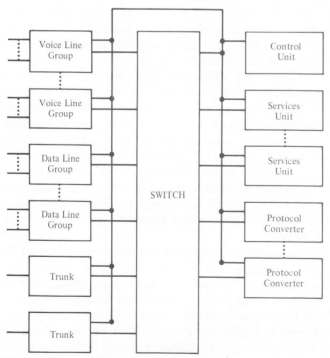

FIGURE 7.17.   Generic digital PBX architecture.

plexed digital signal streams, using the techniques described in Section 7.3. The digital switching network consists of some number of space and time switching stages. Many of the PBXs are not sufficiently large, in terms of lines or capacity, to require complex switching networks. Indeed, some have no network as such, but simply use a TDM bus switch.

Attached to the switch are a set of interface units, which provide access to/from the outside world. Typically, an interface unit will perform a synchronous time-division multiplexing function in order to accommodate multiple incoming lines. On the other side, the unit requires two lines into the switch for full duplex operation.

It is important to understand that the interface unit is performing synchronous and not statistical TDM, even though connections are dynamically changing. On the input side, the unit performs a multiplex operation. Each incoming line is sampled at a specified rate. For n incoming lines each of data rate x, the unit must achieve an input rate of nx. The incoming data are buffered and organized into chunks of time-slot size. Then, according to the timing dictated by the control unit, individual chunks are sent out into the switch at the internal PBX data rate, which may be in the range 50 to 100 Mbps. In a nonblocking switch, n time slots are dedicated to the interface unit for transmission, whether or not they are used. In a blocking switch, time slots are assigned for the duration of a connection. In either case, the time-slot assignment is fixed for the duration of the connection, and synchronous TDM techniques may be used.

On the output side, the interface unit accepts data from the switch during designated time slots. In a nonblocking switch these may be dedicated (requiring more than a simple TDM bus switch), but are in any case fixed for the duration of the connection. Incoming data are demultiplexed, buffered, and presented to the appropriate output port at its data rate.

Several types of interface unit are used. A data line group unit handles data devices. An analog voice line group handles voice input/output over a number of twisted-pair phone lines. The interface unit must include codecs for digital-to-analog (input) and analog-to-digital (output) conversion. A separate type of unit may be used for integrated digital voice/data workstation, which present digitized voice at 64 kbps and data at the same or a lower rate. The range of lines accommodated by interface units is typically 8 to 24.

In addition to multiplexing interface units that accommodate multiple lines, trunk interface units are used to connect to off-site locations. These may be analog voice trunks or digital trunks, which may carry either data or PCM voice. Whereas a line interface unit must multiplex incoming lines to place on the switch, and demultiplex switch traffic to send to the lines, the trunk unit may have to demultiplex and multiplex in both directions (see Figure 7.18). Consider an incoming digital line with n channels of time-multiplexed data (the argument is the same for an analog trunk, which presents n channels of frequency-multiplexed voice). These data must be demultiplexed and stored in a buffer of length n units. Individual units of the buffer are then transmitted out

FIGURE 7.18.   Operation of trunk interface unit.

to the switch at the designated time slots. Question: Why not pass the TDM stream directly from input to the bus, filling n contiguous time slots? Actually, in a nonblocking dedicated port system, this is possible. But for a system with dynamic time-slot assignment, the incoming data must be buffered and sent out on time slots that vary as connections are made and broken.

The other boxes in Figure 7.17 can be explained briefly. The control unit operates the digital switch and exchanges control signals with attached devices. For this purpose, a separate bus or other data path may be used or the control signals may propagate through the switch itself. As part of this or a separate unit, network administration and control functions are implemented. Service units would include such things as tone and busy-signal generators and dialed-digit registers. Some PBX systems provide protocol convertors for connecting dissimilar lines. A connection is made from each line to the protocol convertor.

It should be noted that this generic architecture lends itself to a high degree of reliability. The failure of any interface unit means the loss of only a small number of lines. Key elements such as the control unit can be made redundant.

Distributed Architecture

For reasons of efficiency and reliability, many PBX manufacturers offer distributed architectures for their larger systems. The PBX is organized into a central switch and one or more distributed modules, with twisted pair, coaxial cable, or fiber optic cable between the central switch and the modules, in a two-level hierarchical star topology.

The distributed modules off-load at least some of the central-switch processor's real-time work load (such as off-hook detection). The degree to which control intelligence is off-loaded varies. At one extreme, the modules may be

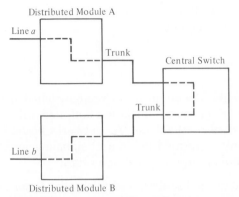

FIGURE 7.19.   Circuit establishment in a distributed digital PBX.

replicas of the central switch, in which case they function almost autonomously with the exception of certain overall management and accounting functions. At the other extreme, the modules are as limited as possible.

A distributed architecture means that it will often be necessary to concatenate several connections to achieve a connection between two devices. Consider Figure 7.19. A connection is desired between lines *a* and *b*. In module *A*, a connection is established between line *a* and one channel on a TDM trunk to the central switch. In the central switch, that channel is connected to a channel on a TDM trunk to module *B*. In module *B*, that channel is connected to line *b*.

There are several advantages to a distributed architecture:

- It permits growth beyond the practical size of a single digital switch.
- It provides better performance by off-loading of functions.
- It provides higher reliability: the loss of a single module need not disable the entire system.
- It reduces twisted-pair wiring distances.

7.6

CONTROL SIGNALING

In a circuit-switched network, control signals are the means by which the network is managed and by which calls are established, maintained, and terminated. Both call management and overall network management require that information be exchanged between subscriber and switch, among switches, and between switch and network management center. For a large public telecommunications network, a relatively complex control signaling scheme is required. In this section, we provide a brief overview of control signal functionality and then look at the technique that is the basis of modern integrated digital networks, common channel signaling.

Signaling Functions

Control signals are necessary for the operation of a circuit-switched network, and involve every aspect of network behavior, including both network services visible to the subscriber and internal mechanisms. As networks become more complex, the number of functions performed by control signaling necessarily grows. The following functions are among the most important:

1. Audible communication with the subscriber, including dial tone, ringing tone, busy signal, and so on.
2. Transmission of the number dialed to switching offices that will attempt to complete a connection.
3. Transmission of information between switches indicating that a call cannot be completed.
4. Transmission of information between switches indicating that a call has ended and that the path can be disconnected.
5. A signal to make a telephone ring.
6. Transmission of information used for billing purposes.
7. Transmission of information giving the status of equipment or trunks in the network. This information may be used for routing and maintenance purposes.
8. Transmission of information used in diagnosing and isolating system failures.
9. Control of special equipment such as satellite channel equipment.

An example of the use of control signaling is shown in Figure 7.20 [REY83], which illustrates a typical telephone connection sequence from one line to another in the same central office. The steps involved appear as circled numbers in the figure:

1. Prior to the call, both telephones are not in use (on-hook). The call begins when one subscriber lifts the receiver (off-hook), which is automatically signaled to switch.
2. The switch responds with an audible dial tone, signaling the subscriber that the number may be dialed.
3. The caller dials the number, which is communicated as a destination address to the switch.
4. If the called subscriber is not busy, the switch alerts the subscriber to an incoming call by sending a ringing signal, which causes the telephone to ring.
5. Feedback is provided to the calling subscriber by the switch:
   a. If the called subscriber is not busy, the switch returns an audible ringing tone to the caller while the ringing signal is being sent to the called subscriber.

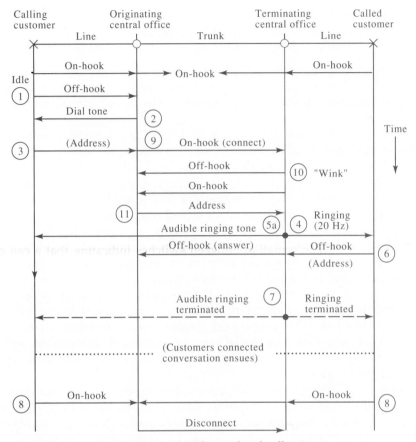

FIGURE 7.20. Signaling on a typical completed call [REY83].

    b. If the called subscriber is busy, the switch sends an audible busy signal to the caller (not shown in the figure).

    c. If the call cannot be completed through the switch, the switch sends an audible "reorder" message to the caller (not shown in the figure).

6. The called party accepts the call by lifting the receiver (off-hook), which is automatically signaled to the switch.

7. The switch terminates the ringing signal and the audible ringing tone, and establishes a connection between the two subscribers.

8. The connection is released when either subscriber hangs up.

    When the called subscriber is attached to a different switch than the calling subscriber, the following switch-to-switch trunk signaling functions are required:

9. The originating switch seizes an idle interswitch trunk, sends an off-hook indication on the trunk, and requests a digit register at the far end, so that the address may be communicated.

10. The terminating switch sends an off-hook followed by an on-hook signal, known as a "wink." This indicates a register-ready status.
11. The originating switch sends the address digits to the terminating switch.

This example gives some idea of the functions that are performed using control signals. The functions performed by control signals can be roughly grouped into the category of supervisory, address, call information, and network management.

The term *supervisory* is generally used to refer to control functions that have a binary character (true/false; on/off), such as request for service, answer, alerting, and return to idle. They deal with the availability of the called subscriber and of the needed network resources. Supervisory control signals are used to determine if a needed resource is available and, if so, to seize it. They are also used to communicate the status of requested resources.

Address signals identify a subscriber. Initially, an address signal is generated by a calling subscriber when dialing a telephone number. The resulting address may be propagated through the network to support the routing function and to locate and ring the called subscriber's phone.

The term *call information* refers to those signals that provide information to the subscriber about the status of a call. This is in contrast to internal control signals between switches used in call establishment and termination. Such internal signals are analog or digital electrical messages. In contrast, call information signals are audible tones that can be heard by the caller or an operator with the proper phone set.

Supervisory, address, and call information control signals are directly involved in the establishment and termination of a call. In contrast, *network management* signals are used for the maintenance, troubleshooting, and overall operation of the network. Such signals may be in the form of messages, such as a list of preplanned routes being sent to a station to update its routing tables. These signals cover a broad scope and it is this category that will expand most with the increasing complexity of switched networks.

Location of Signaling

Control signaling needs to be considered in two contexts: signaling between a subscriber and the network and signaling within the network. Typically, signaling operates differently within these two contexts.

The signaling between a telephone or other subscriber device and the switching office to which it attaches is, to a large extent, determined by the characteristics of the subscriber device and the needs of the human user. Signals within the network are entirely computer-to-computer. The internal signaling is concerned not only with the management of subscriber calls but with the management of the network itself. Thus, for this internal signaling, a more complex repertoire of commands, responses, and set of parameters is needed.

Because two different signaling techniques are used, and local switching office to which the subscriber is attached must provide a mapping between the relatively less complex signaling technique used by the subscriber and the more complex technique used within the network. In Part IV, we will see a specific example of each technique as part of ISDN, namely I.451 for subscriber-to-network signaling and Signaling System No. 7 for internal network signaling.

Common Channel Signaling

Traditional control signaling in circuit-switched networks has been on a per-trunk or inchannel basis. With *inchannel signaling*, the same channel is used to carry control signals as is used to carry the call to which the control signals relate. Such signaling begins at the originating subscriber and follows the same path as the call itself. This has the merit that no additional transmission facilities are needed for signaling; the facilities for voice trnsmission are shared with control signaling.

Two forms of inchannel signaling are in use: inband and out-of-band. *Inband signaling* uses not only the same physical path as the call it serves, it also uses the same frequency band as the voice signals that are carried. This form of signaling has several advantages. Because the control signals have the same electromagnetic properties as the voice signals, they can go anywhere that the voice signals go. Thus there are no limits on the use of inband signaling anywhere in the network, including places where analog-to-digital or digital-to-analog conversion takes place. In addition, it is impossible to set up a call on a faulty speech path, since the control signals that are used to set up that path would have to follow the same path.

Out-of-band signaling takes advantage of the fact that voice signals do not use the full 4 kHz bandwidth allotted to them. A separate narrow signaling band, within the 4 kHz, is used to send control signals. The major advantage of this approach is that the control signals can be sent whether or not voice signals are on the line, thus allowing continuous supervision and control of a call. However, an out-of-band scheme needs extra electronics to handle the signaling band, and the signaling rates are slower because the signal has been confined to a narrow bandwidth.

The information transfer rate is quite limited with inchannel signaling. With inband signals, the voice channel being used is only available for control signals when there are no voice signals on the circuit. With out-of-band signals, a very narrow bandwidth is available. With such limits, it is difficult to accommodate, in a timely fashion, any but the simplest form of control messages. However, to take advantage of the potential services and to cope with the increasing complexity of evolving network technology, a richer and more powerful control signal repertoire is needed.

A second drawback of inchannel signaling is the amount of delay from the time a subscriber enters an address (dials a number) and the connection is established. The requirement to reduce this delay is becoming more important as the network is used in new ways. For example, computer-controlled calls,

TABLE 7.2   Signaling Techniques for Circuit-Switched Networks

Technique	Description	Comment
Inchannel		
Inband	Transmit control signals in the same band of frequencies used by the voice signals.	The simplest technique. It is necessary for call information signals, and may be used for other control signals. Inband can be used over any type of line plant.
Out-of-band	Transmit control signals using the same facilities as the voice signal but a different part of the frequency band.	In contrast to inband, provides continuous supervision during the life of a connection.
Common Channel	Transmit control signals over signaling links that are dedicated to control signals and are common to a number of voice channels.	Reduces call setup time compared to inchannel methods. It is also more adaptable to evolving functional needs.

such as with transaction processing, use relatively short messages; therefore, the call setup time represents an appreciable part of the total transaction time.

Both of these problems can be addressed with *common channel signaling*, in which control signals are carried over paths completely independent of the voice channels (Table 7.2). One independent control signal path can carry the signals for a number of subscriber channels, and hence is a common control channel for these subscriber channels.

The principle of common channel signaling is illustrated and contrasted with inchannel signaling in Figure 7.21. As can be seen, the signal path for common channel signaling is physically separate from the path for voice or other subscriber signals. The common channel can be configured with the bandwidth required to carry control signals for a rich variety of functions. Thus, both the signaling protocol and the network architecture to support that protocol are more complex than inchannel signaling. However, the continuing drop in computer hardware costs makes common channel signaling increasingly attractive. The control signals are messages that are passed between switches and between a switch and the network management center. Thus, the control signaling portion of the network is in effect a distributed computer network carrying short messages.

Two modes of operation are used in common channel signaling (Figure 7.22). In the *associated mode*, the common channel closely tracks along its entire length the interswitch trunk groups that are served between endpoints. The control signals are on different channels from the subscriber signals, and inside the switch, the control signals are routed directly to a control signal processor. A more complex, but more powerful, mode is the *nonassociated mode*. With this mode, the network is augmented by additional nodes, known as signal transfer points. There is now no close or simple assignment of control

(a) Inchannel

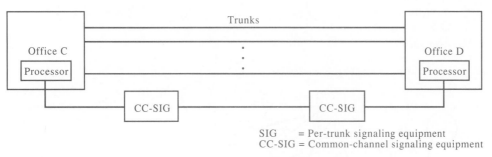

SIG   = Per-trunk signaling equipment
CC-SIG = Common-channel signaling equipment

(b) Common channel

FIGURE 7.21.   Inchannel and common channel signaling.

channels to trunk groups. In effect, there are now two separate networks, with links between them so that the control portion of the network can exercise control over the switching nodes that are servicing the subscriber calls. Network management is more easily exerted in the nonassociated mode since control channels can be assigned to tasks in a more flexible manner. The nonassociated mode is likely to be the mode used in ISDN (see Part IV).

With inchannel signaling, control signals from one switch are originated by a control processor and switched onto the outgoing channel. On the receiving end, the control signals must be switched from the voice channel into the control processor. With common channel signaling, the control signals are transferred directly from one control processor to another, without being tied to a voice signal. This is a simpler procedure, and one that is less susceptible to accidental or intentional interference between subscriber and control signals. This is one of the main motivations for common channel signaling. Another key motivation for common channel signaling is that call setup time is reduced. Consider the sequence of events for call setup with inchannel signaling when

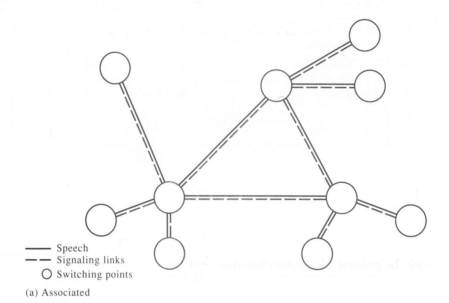

— Speech
– – Signaling links
○ Switching points

(a) Associated

— Speech network
– – Signaling network
○ Switching points (speech)
□ Switching points (signal
  transfer points)

(b) Nonassociated

FIGURE 7.22.   Common channel signaling modes.

more than one switch is involved. A control signal will be sent from one switch
to the next in the intended path. At each switch, the control signal cannot be
transferred through the switch to the next leg of the route until the associated
circuit is established through that switch. With common channel signaling, forwarding of control information can overlap the circuit-setup process.

With nonassociated signaling, a further advantage emerges: One or more central control points can be established. All control information can be routed to a network center where requests are processed and from which control signals are sent to switches that handle subscriber traffic. In this way, requests can be processed with a more global view of network conditions.

Of course, there are disadvantages to common channel signaling. These primarily have to do with the complexity of the technique. However, the dropping cost of digital hardware and the increasingly digital nature of telecommunication networks make common channel signaling the appropriate technology.

All of the discussion in this section has dealt with the use of common channel signaling inside the network, that is, to control switches. Even in a network that is completely controlled by common channel signaling, inchannel signaling is needed for at least some of the communication with the subscriber. For example, dial tone, ringback, and busy signals must be inchannel to reach the user. In general, the subscriber does not have access to the common channel signaling portion of the network and does not employ the common channel signaling protocol.

7.7

RECOMMENDED READING

As befits its age, circuit switching has inspired a voluminous literature. Two good books on the subject are [BELL91] and [KEIS85]. The first of these is particularly lucid and comprehensive. Worthwhile accounts may also be found in [MART90] and [DAVI73]. [BROO83] discusses alternative internal organizations for a switch. [COOV89] contains a collection of articles on the digital PBX.

Discussions of control signaling can be found in [FREE89], [REY83], and [KEIS85].

7.8

PROBLEMS

7.1 Demonstrate why there is a high probability of blocking in a two-stage switch such as Figure 7.15.

7.2 What is the magnitude of delay through a TSI stage?

7.3 Assume that the velocity of propagation on a TDM bus is $0.7c$, its length is 10 m, and the data rate is 500 Mbps. How many bits should be transmitted in a time slot to achieve a bus efficiency of 99%?

7.4 Demonstrate that in a TSI data store, at most, only half of the memory is usefully occupied at any one time. Devise a means of reducing the TSI memory requirement while maintaining its nonblocking property.

7.5 Consider the use of a 500-ns memory in a TSI device. How many full-duplex voice channels can be supported, if the voice is encoded using PCM?

7.6 Determine the number of crosspoints and the total number of memory bits required for a TST switch defined as follows:

- Number of lines = 32.
- Single stage space switch.
- Number of channels per frame = 30.
- Time expansion = 2.

7.7 How many bits of memory are needed in a TSI unit for a 60-channel signal with nine bits per time slot?

7.8 Consider a 3-stage crossbar switch system with 1000 input and 1000 output lines. It is non-blocking. For an optimum design, what is the total number of crosspoints required? How many arrays are needed for each stage and how many input and output lines are there per stage?

7.9 Repeat Problem 7.8 using 2048 as the number of input and output lines.

7.10 Consider the configuration of Figure 7.10b. Suppose that the maximum length of the bus is 1 meter. What is the maximum delay that could occur end-to-end on the bus (assume electricity travels in a copper wire at a rate of 0.8 times the speed of light)?

7.11 For the system of Problem 7.8, how many switch points would be needed if a TDM bus were used?

7.12 Consider a simple non-blocking implementation of Figure 7.10c. Suppose that the bus is 1500 meters long and that 2048 bits of data are to be input in each time slot. The data rate of the bus is 100 Mbps. The maximum number of stations attached to the bus is limited so that a station is guaranteed a slot every 10 milliseconds. Assume that electricity travels in copper wire at 0.8 times the speed of light.
   a. What is the guaranteed data rate for a station?
   b. What is the maximum sustained data rate of the system?
   c. What is the maximum number of stations that can be serviced by this system?

7.13 Consider a simple time-slot interchange switching system. Assume a memory of 50-nsec cycle time. The memory is organized into 16-bit words. Frames are 1024 bits. What is the maximum data rate per channel? What is the data rate of the trunk lines to and from the switch?

7.14 Section 7.5 contains the following sentence: "The PBX may support a voice/data workstation with one twisted pair for the phone and two pairs for the terminal." Why is there one for the phone and two for the terminal? Is not the phone operating with communications both ways also?

7.15 Explain why it is necessary that the interface units for Figure 7.18 perform synchronous TDM rather than statistical TDM.

7.16 Consider a simple telephone network consisting of two end offices and one toll center with a 1-MHz full-duplex trunk between each end office and the toll center. The average telephone is used to make four calls per 8-hour workday, with a mean call duration of six minutes. Ten percent of the calls are long distance. What is the maximum number of telephones an end office can support?

7.17 If one examines the rate structures of the long-distance telephone services, it would appear that distance, while important, is not the major factor in determining cost. Speculate on the reason for this.

CHAPTER 8

Packet Switching

Around 1970, research began on a new form of architecture for long-distance digital data communications: packet switching. Although the technology of packet switching has evolved substantially since that time, it is remarkable that (1) the basic technology of packet switching is fundamentally the same today as it was in the early-1970s networks, and (2) packet switching remains one of the few effective technologies for long-distance data communications.

This chapter provides an overview of packet-switching technology. We will see that many of the advantages of packet switching (flexibility, resource sharing, robustness, responsiveness) come with a cost. The packet-switched network is a distributed collection of packet-switched nodes. In the ideal, all packet-switched nodes would always know the state of the entire network. Unfortunately, because the nodes are distributed, there is always a time delay between a change in status in one portion of the network and the knowledge of that change elsewhere. Furthermore, there is overhead involved in communicating status information. As a result, a packet-switched network can never perform "perfectly," and elaborate algorithms are used to cope with the time delay and overhead penalties of network operation.

The chapter begins with an introduction to packet-switched network principles. Next, we look at the internal operation of these networks, introducing the concepts of virtual circuits and datagrams. Following this, the key technologies of routing and flow control are examined. The chapter concludes with an introduction to X.25, which is the standard interface between an end system and a packet-switched network.

8.1

PACKET-SWITCHING PRINCIPLES

The long-haul circuit-switched telecommunications network was originally designed to handle voice traffic, and the majority of traffic on these networks continues to be voice. A key characteristic of circuit-switched networks is that resources within the network are dedicated to a particular call. For voice connections, the resulting circuit will enjoy a high percentage of utilization since, most of the time, one party or the other is talking. However, as the circuit-switched network began to be used increasingly for data connections, two shortcomings became apparent:

- In a typical terminal-to-host data connection, much of the time the line is idle. Thus, with data connections, a circuit-switched approach is inefficient.
- In a circuit-switched network, the connection provides for transmission at constant data rate. Thus each of the two devices that are connected must transmit and receive at the same data rate as the other. This limits the utility of the network in interconnecting a variety of host computers and terminals.

To understand how packet switching addresses these problems, let us briefly summarize packet-switching operation. Data are transmitted in short packets. A typical upper bound on packet length is 1000 octets (bytes). If a source has a longer message to send, the message is broken up into a series of packets (Figure 8.1). Each packet contains a portion (or all for a short message) of the user's data plus some control information. The control information, at a minimum, includes the information that the network requires in order to be able to route the packet through the network and deliver it to the intended destination. At each node en route, the packet is received, stored briefly, and passed on to the next node.

Let us return to Figure 7.3, but now consider that this is a simple packet-switched network. Consider a packet to be sent from station A to station E. The packet will include control information that indicates that the intended destination is E. The packet is sent from A to node 4. Node 4 stores the packet, determines the next leg of the route (say 5), and queues the packet to go out on that link (the 4–5 link). When the link is available, the packet is transmitted

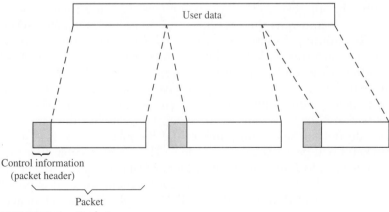

Control information
(packet header)

Packet

FIGURE 8.1. Packets.

to node 5, which will forward the packet to node 6, and finally to E. This approach has a number of advantages over circuit switching:

- Line efficiency is greater, since a single node-to-node link can be dynamically shared by many packets over time. The packets are queued up and transmitted as rapidly as possible over the link. By contrast, with circuit switching, time on a node-to-node link is preallocated using synchronous time-division multiplexing. Much of the time, such a link may be idle because a portion of its time is dedicated to a connection that is idle.
- A packet-switched network can carry out data-rate conversion. Two stations of different data rates can exchange packets, since each connects to its node at its proper data rate.
- When traffic becomes heavy on a circuit-switched network, some calls are blocked; that is, the network refuses to accept additional connection requests until the load on the network decreases. On a packet-switched network, packets are still accepted, but delivery delay increases.
- Priorities can be used. Thus, if a node has a number of packets queued for transmission, it can transmit the higher-priority packets first. These packets will therefore experience less delay than lower-priority packets.

Switching Technique

A station has a message to send through a packet-switched network that is of length greater than the maximum packet size. It therefore breaks the message up into packets and sends these packets, one at a time, to the network. A question arises as to how the network will handle this stream of packets as it attempts to route them through the network and deliver them to the intended destination. There are two approaches that are used in contemporary networks: datagram and virtual circuit.

In the **datagram** approach, each packet is treated independently, with no reference to packets that have gone before. Let us consider the implication of this approach. Suppose that station A in Figure 7.3 has a three-packet message to send to E. It transmits the packets, 1-2-3, to node 4. On *each* packet, node 4 must make a routing decision. Packet 1 arrives for delivery to E. Node 4 could plausibly forward this packet to either node 5 or node 7 as the next step in the route. In this case, node 4 determines that its queue of packets for node 5 is shorter than for node 7, so it queues the packet for node 5. Ditto for packet 2. But for packet 3, node 4 finds that its queue for node 7 is now shorter and so queues packet 3 for that node. So the packets, each with the same destination address, do not all follow the same route. Because of this, it is just possible that packet 3 will beat packet 2 to node 6. Thus it is possible that the packets will be delivered to E in a different sequence from the one in which they were sent. It is up to E to figure out how to reorder them. Also, it is possible for a packet to be destroyed in the network. For example, if a packet-switched node crashes momentarily, all of its queued packets may be lost. If this were to happen to one of the packets in our example, node 6 has no way of knowing that one of the packets in the sequence of packets has been lost. Again, it is up to E to detect the loss of a packet and figure out how to recover it. In this technique, each packet, treated independently, is referred to as a datagram.

In the **virtual circuit** approach, a preplanned route is established before any packets are sent. For example, suppose that A has one or more messages to send to E. It first sends a special control packet, referred to as a Call Request packet, to 4, requesting a logical connection to E. Node 4 decides to route the request *and* all subsequent packets to 5, which decides to route the requests and all subsequent packets to 6, which finally delivers the Call Request packet to E. If E is prepared to accept the connection, it sends a Call Accept packet to 6. This packet is passed back through nodes 5 and 4 to A. Stations A and E may now exchange data over the route that has been established. Because the route is fixed for the duration of the logical connection, it is somewhat similar to a circuit in a circuit-switching network and is referred to as a virtual circuit. Each packet now contains a virtual circuit identifier as well as data. Each node on the preestablished route knows where to direct such packets; no routing decisions are required. Thus every data packet from A intended for E traverses nodes 4, 5, and 6; every data packet from E intended for A traverses nodes 6, 5, and 4. Eventually, one of the stations terminates the connection with a Clear Request packet. At any time, each station can have more than one virtual circuit to any other station and can have virtual circuits to more than one station.

So the main characteristic of the virtual-circuit technique is that a route between stations is set up prior to data transfer. Note that this does not mean that this is a dedicated path, as in circuit switching. A packet is still buffered at each node and queued for output over a line. The difference from the datagram approach is that, with virtual circuits, the node need not make a routing decision for each packet. It is made only once for all packets using that virtual circuit.

If two stations wish to exchange data over an extended period of time, there are certain advantages to virtual circuits. First, the network may provide services related to the virtual circuit, including sequencing and error control. Sequencing refers to the fact that, since all packets follow the same route, they arrive in the original order. Error control is a service that assures not only that packets arrive in proper sequence, but that all packets arrive correctly. For example, if a packet in a sequence from node 4 to node 6 fails to arrive at node 6, or arrives with an error, node 6 can request a retransmission of that packet from node 4. Another advantage is that packets should transit the network more rapidly with a virtual circuit; it is not necessary to make a routing decision for each packet at each node.

One advantage of the datagram approach is that the call setup phase is avoided. Thus, if a station wishes to send only one or a few packets, datagram delivery will be quicker. Another advantage of the datagram service is that, because it is more primitive, it is more flexible. For example, if congestion develops in one part of the network, incoming datagrams can be routed away from the congestion. With the use of virtual circuits, packets follow a predefined route, and thus it is more difficult for the network to adapt to congestion. A third advantage is that datagram delivery is inherently more reliable. With the use of virtual circuits, if a node fails, all virtual circuits that pass through that node are lost. With datagram delivery, if a node fails, subsequent packets may find an alternate route that bypasses that node.

Packet Size

One important design issue is the packet size to be used in the network. There is a significant relationship between packet size and transmission time, as illustrated in Figure 8.2. In this example, it is assumed that there is a virtual circuit from station X through nodes a and b to station Y. The message to be sent comprises 30 octets, and each packet contains 3 octets of control information, which is placed at the beginning of each packet and is referred to as a *header*. If the entire message is sent as a single packet of 33 octets (3 octets of header plus 30 octets of data), then the packet is first transmitted from station X to node a (Figure 8.2a). When the entire packet is received, it can then be transmitted from a to b. When the entire packet is received at node b, it is then transferred to station Y. The total transmission time at the nodes is 99 octet-times (33 octets × 3 packet transmissions).

Suppose now that we break the message up into two packets, each containing 15 octets of the message and, of course, 3 octets each of header or control information. In this case, node a can begin transmitting the first packet as soon as it has arrived from X, without waiting for the second packet. Because of this overlap in transmission, the total transmission time drops to 72 octet-times. By breaking the message up into 5 packets, each intermediate node can begin transmission even sooner and the savings in time is greater, with a total of 63 octet-times. However, this process of using more and smaller packets eventually results in increased, rather than reduced delay, as illustrated in Figure 8.2d. This is because each packet contains a fixed amount of header, and more packets mean more of these headers. Furthermore, the example does not show the processing and queueing delays at each node. These delays are also greater when more packets are handled for a single message. Thus, packet-switched network designers must consider these factors in attempting to find an optimum packet size.

Comparison of Circuit Switching and Packet Switching

Having looked at the internal operation of packet switching, we can now return to a comparison of this technique with circuit switching. We first look at the important issue of performance and then examine other characteristics.

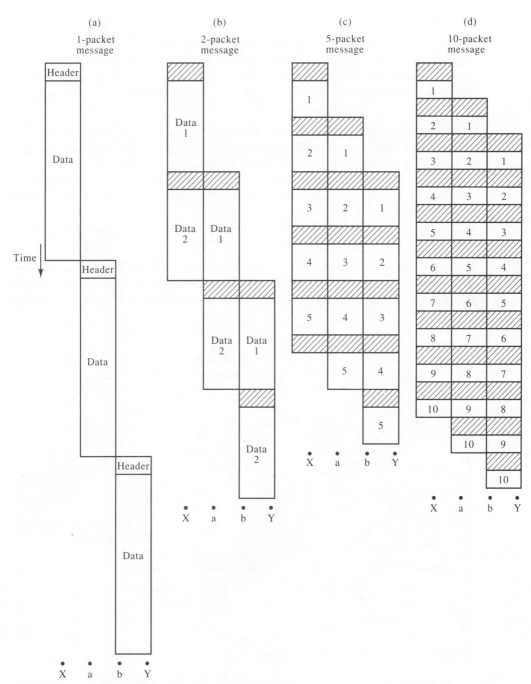

FIGURE 8.2.   Effect of packet size on transmission time.

Performance

A simple comparison of circuit switching and the two forms of packet switching is provided in Figure 8.3. The figure depicts the transmission of a message across four nodes, from a source station attached to node 1 to a destination station attached to node 4. In this figure, we are concerned with three types of delay:

- *Propagation delay:* the time it takes a signal to propagate from one node to the next. This time is generally negligible. The speed of electromagnetic signals through a wire medium, for example, is typically 2×10^8 m/s.
- *Transmission time:* the time it takes for a transmitter to send out a block of data. For example, it takes 1 s to transmit a 10,000-bit block of data onto a 10-kbps line.
- *Node delay:* the time it takes for a node to perform the necessary processing as it switches data.

For circuit switching, there is a certain amount of delay before the message can be sent. First, a call request signal is sent through the network, to set up a connection to the destination. If the destination station is not busy, a call ac-

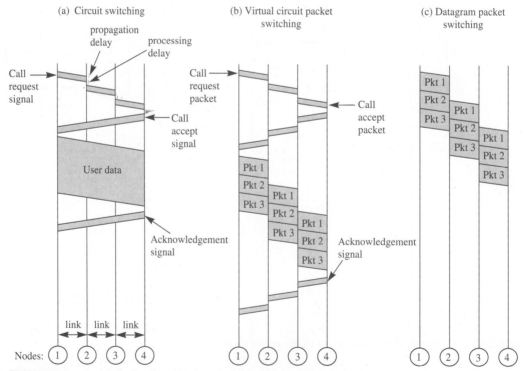

FIGURE 8.3.   Event timing for circuit switching and packet switching.

cepted signal returns. Note that a processing delay is incurred at each node during the call request; this time is spent at each node setting up the route of the connection. On the return, this processing is not needed, since the connection is already set up. After the connection is set up, the message is sent as a single block, with no noticeable delay at the switching nodes.

Virtual-circuit packet switching appears quite similar to circuit switching. A virtual circuit is requested using a call request packet, which incurs a delay at each node. The virtual circuit is accepted with a call accept packet. In contrast to the circuit-switching case, the call acceptance also experiences node delays, even though the virtual circuit route is now established. The reason is that this packet is queued at each node and must wait its turn for transmission. Once the virtual circuit is established, the message is transmitted in packets. It should be clear that this phase of the operation can be no faster than circuit switching, for comparable networks. This is because circuit switching is an essentially transparent process, providing a constant data rate across the network. Packet switching requires some node delay at each node in the path. Worse, this delay is variable and will increase with increased load.

Datagram packet switching does not require a call setup. Thus, for short messages, it will be faster than virtual-circuit packet switching and perhaps circuit switching. However, since each individual datagram is routed independently, the processing for each datagram at each node may be longer than for virtual-circuit packets. Thus, for long messages, the virtual-circuit technique may be superior.

Figure 8.3 is intended only to suggest what the relative performance of the techniques might be; however, actual performance depends on a host of factors, including the size of the network, its topology, the pattern of load, and the characteristics of typical exchanges. The interested reader may pursue these topics in [KLEI76], [KUMM80], and [STUC85].

Other Characteristics

Besides performance, there are a number of other characteristics that may be considered in comparing the techniques we have been discussing. Table 8.1 summarizes the most important of these. Most of these characteristics have already been discussed. A few additional comments follow.

As was mentioned, circuit switching is essentially a transparent service. Once a connection is established, a constant data rate is provided to the connected stations. This is not the case with packet switching, which typically introduces variable delay, so that data arrive in a choppy manner. Indeed, with datagram packet switching, data may arrive in a different order than the one in which they were transmitted.

An additional consequence of transparency is that there is no overhead required to accommodate circuit switching. Once a connection is established, the analog or digital data are passed through, as is, from source to destination. For packet switching, analog data must be converted to digital before transmis-

TABLE 8.1   Comparison of Communication Switching Techniques

Circuit Switching	Datagram Packet Switching	Virtual-Circuit Packet Switching
Dedicated transmission path	No dedicated path	No dedicated path
Continuous transmission of data	Transmission of packets	Transmission of packets
Fast enough for interactive	Fast enough for interactive	Fast enough for interactive
Messages are not stored	Packets may be stored until delivered	Packets stored until delivered
The path is established for entire conversation	Route established for each packet	Route established for entire conversation
Call setup delay; negligible transmission delay	Packet transmission delay	Call setup delay; packet transmission delay
Busy signal if called party busy	Sender may be notified if packet not delivered	Sender notified of connection denial
Overload may block call setup; no delay for established calls	Overload increases packet delay	Overload may block call setup; increases packet delay
Electromechanical or computerized switching nodes	Small switching nodes	Small switching nodes
User responsible for message loss protection	Network may be responsible for individual packets	Network may be responsible for packet sequences
Usually no speed or code conversion	Speed and code conversion	Speed and code conversion
Fixed bandwidth transmission	Dynamic use of bandwidth	Dynamic use of bandwidth
No overhead bits after call setup	Overhead bits in each message	Overhead bits in each packet

sion; in addition, each packet includes overhead bits, such as the destination address.

8.2

EXAMPLE SYSTEMS

Perhaps the clearest way to present the concepts and techniques of packet switching is by example. In this section we present an overview of four quite different packet-switched systems. The two best-documented communications networks are ARPANET/DDN and TYMNET. In addition, we present one commercially available computer network package: IBM's SNA. SNA is not merely a communications network, but it is the most widely used approach for constructing user-controlled packet-switched networks.

ARPANET/DDN

The ARPA computer network (ARPANET) began under the sponsorship of the Advanced Research Projects Agency (ARPA) to study and demonstrate computer resource sharing. By 1975, this network had many operational users and was no longer an experimental network, so responsibility for its operation transferred to the Defense Communications Agency. ARPANET has since been transformed into the Defense Data Network (DDN). The DDN is designed to meet DOD needs for both a secure command and control communications network and for ordinary unclassified communications.

TYMNET

TYMNET was originally developed to provide cost-effective connection of terminals to central time-sharing computers [TYME71]. Both access and internode speeds were rather limited. As the system grew, higher data rates were provided and the system evolved into TYMNET II [KOPF77]. TYMNET II, although still terminal-oriented, provides a general-purpose packet-switched service for terminal-host and host-host transfers.

SNA

Both ARPANET and TYMNET originally became operational in 1969. Both are, in our terminology, communication networks that are independent of the attached hosts. As the technology of packet switching evolved, computer vendors realized that they could provide not only the endpoint computer functions, but the switching functions as well. The era of computer vendor-based network architectures began with the announcement in 1974 by IBM of its systems network architecture (SNA).

SNA was developed by IBM to protect its customer base and allow its customers to take advantage of new IBM offerings. The problem was that there was a proliferation of communications protocols and user access methods on IBM machines. Customers developed complex applications and were unable to easily incorporate new computers into their operation. Many of the communications techniques were inefficient and a flourishing business in front-end processors developed among minicomputer and communications vendors. These factors led to the development of a network architecture that would provide efficient user access to a network of computers. We will return to SNA in the context of computer network architecture in Part III. For now, we are only concerned with its packet-switching capability.

8.3

VIRTUAL CIRCUITS AND DATAGRAMS

External and Internal Operation

One of the most important characteristics of a packet-switched network is whether it uses datagrams or virtual circuits. Actually, there are two levels or dimensions of this characteristic, as illustrated in Figure 8.4. At the interface

(a) External virtual circuit. A logical connection is set up between two stations.
    Packets are labeled with a virtual circuit number and a sequence number.
    Packets arrive in sequence.

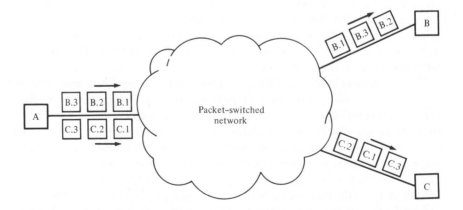

(b) External datagram. Each packet is transmitted independently. Packets are
    labeled with a destination address and may arrive out of sequence.

FIGURE 8.4.   External and internal virtual circuits and datagrams.

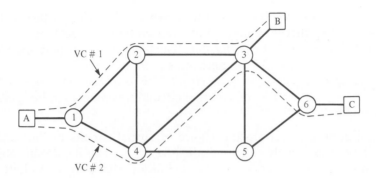

(c) Internal virtual circuit. A route for packets between two stations is defined and labeled. All packets for that virtual circuit follow the same route and arrive in sequence.

(d) Internal datagram. Each packet is treated independently by the network. Packets are labeled with a destination address and may arrive at the destination node out of sequence.

FIGURE 8.4. (continued)

between station and network node, a network may provide either a virtual circuit or datagram service. With a virtual-circuit interface, the user performs a call request to set up a virtual circuit and uses sequence numbers to exercise flow control and error control. The network attempts to deliver the packets in sequence. With datagram service, the network only agrees to handle packets independently. Internally, the network may actually construct a dedicated path between endpoints (virtual circuit) or not. These internal and external design decisions need not coincide:

- *External virtual circuit, internal virtual circuit:* When the user requests a virtual circuit, a dedicated route through the network is constructed. All packets will follow that same route.
- *External virtual circuit, internal datagram:* The network handles each packet separately. Thus different packets for the same virtual circuit may take different routes. However, the network endeavors to deliver packets to the des-

tination in sequence. Typically, the network will buffer packets at the destination node so that they may be ordered properly for delivery.

- *External datagram, internal datagram:* Each packet is treated independently from both the user's and the network's point of view.
- *External datagram, internal virtual circuit:* This combination makes little sense, since one incurs the cost of a virtual circuit implementation but gets none of the benefits.

The question arises as to the choice of virtual circuits or datagrams, both internally and externally. This will depend on the specific design objective of the communication network and the cost factors that prevail. So here we offer only a few general comments.

First, consider internal datagram and virtual circuit mechanisms. A major advantage of a datagram mechanism is its robustness and flexibility. If nodes or links in the network are unavailable, datagrams can be routed around the affected area. On the other hand the loss of a node or link could destroy some virtual circuits. Similarly, the datagram mechanism can react more quickly to congestion by making routing decisions on a per-packet basis. With virtual circuits, routing decisions are usually made only at setup time. Of course, virtual circuit routes can be changed dynamically at the cost of processing overhead. An advantage of the virtual circuit mechanism is that it minimizes perpacket overhead; routing decisions need only be made once per virtual circuit. Also, internal virtual circuits provide sequenced delivery, which is an asset if the external service is virtual circuit.

With respect to the external service, the following observations apply. The datagram service allows for efficient use of the network: no call setup or disconnection, and no need to hold up packets while a packet in error is retransmitted. This latter feature is desirable in some real-time applications. The virtual circuit service can provide end-to-end sequencing, flow control, and error control. However, in many cases, these services are provided by a higher-layer protocol and need not be duplicated by the network service.

Again, depending on circumstances, any of the three combinations listed above may be the most appropriate and all have been used. Table 8.2 compares the four example networks in terms of these combinations.

Example Systems

ARPANET

Externally, ARPANET offers both datagram and virtual circuit service. When datagram service is used, the attached station (called a host) may transmit packets containing up to 991 bits of data to its local node (called an interface message processor or IMP). The node routes this packet through the network to its destination with no guarantee of delivery or of maintaining sequencing. Using the virtual circuit service, a host may establish a connection with another

TABLE 8.2 Virtual Circuit and Datagram Implementations

| | | Internal Operation | |
		Datagram	Virtual Circuit
External Service	Datagram	ARPANET (packet)	—
	Virtual Circuit	ARPANET (message, packet)	TYMNET (packet multiplexing) SNA (virtual and explicit routes)

host and then send a sequence of messages, each containing up to 8063 bits of data. ARPANET guarantees that it will deliver all messages and that they will be delivered in sequence.

Internally, ARPANET functions as a datagram network with an unusual two-level structure. For the datagram service, the network simply treats each incoming datagram independently. For the virtual circuit service, when a message is received by a node for transmission, the message is broken up into as many as eight packets, each containing a maximum of 1008 user data bits. These packets are treated internally as datagrams and are routed independently to the node of the destination station. At the destination node, the packets are buffered until all of the packets of a single message arrive. They are then reassembled into a message and delivered to the destination host. This seemingly curious technique facilitates an effective form of traffic control, as explained below.

TYMNET

TYMNET uses virtual circuits both internally and externally, based on a technique that might be called *packet multiplexing* [RIND79a]. In essence, TYMNET views each station as a source of a character stream rather than a packet stream. As data come in from a station to a local node, they are buffered and then sent along a fixed route to the destination. The amount of data that is packetized for node-to-node hops is variable. Thus an initial burst of data may become spread out across several nodes in transit. Alternatively, characters that are transmitted later by a station may catch up with earlier characters in the network and end up exiting as a block at the destination. Furthermore, a single packet transmitted between two nodes may contain data for more than one virtual circuit.

To support virtual circuits, each node is equipped with a buffer pool and a number of index vectors, two for each link to an adjacent node. Each of these links supports a fixed number of channels, using a statistical TDM protocol. We use the following notation:

$$R_n(l,c) = \text{read vector of node } n \text{ for channel } c \text{ of link } l$$
$$W_n(l,c) = \text{write vector of node } n \text{ for channel } c \text{ of link } l$$

Figure 8.5 illustrates the use of these vectors to construct a virtual circuit between a terminal attached to node 1000 and a host attached to node 5. When the virtual circuit is constructed, buffer space is allocated in each node along the route and a channel between each pair of these nodes is dedicated to that circuit. Figure 8.5 illustrates the buffers and the write vectors. Data from the terminal are stored in buffer 4 of node 1000. The node has $R_{1000}(112,2)$ set to 4. Thus the node will read data from buffer 4 to transmit on channel 2 to node 112. At node 112, $W_{112}(1000,2) = 200$. This instructs the node to store data on channel 2 from node 1000 in buffer 200. These data are subsequently transmitted to node 5 on channel 1. Finally, the data are directed to buffer 8 of node 5, which is dedicated to output to the attached host.

The assignment of buffers and channels to a virtual circuit is done by a central node, the supervisor. Details are provided below. Note that in this scheme, it is not necessary for the nodes to have knowledge of the overall virtual circuit. They merely need to keep track of local buffer/channel assignments.

Data are transmitted between links in frames, using the format of Figure 8.6. Transmission is done via a character-oriented synchronous protocol, using 3-bit sequence numbers and acknowledgments. Each frame contains one or more packets of data, and each packet contains data for one channel. Note the similarity between Figures 8.6 and 6.13; the internode communication is clearly a form of statistical TDM. Each physical record is formed by picking up data

FIGURE 8.5.   A virtual circuit in TYMNET.

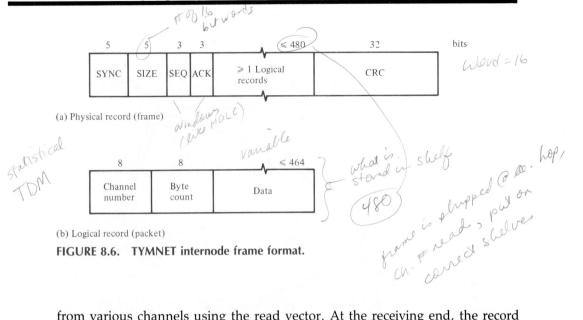

(a) Physical record (frame)

(b) Logical record (packet)

FIGURE 8.6. TYMNET internode frame format.

from various channels using the read vector. At the receiving end, the record is unpacked and data are stored in buffers as dictated by the write vector. Note that these data, all of which came in on one link, may now fan out to various links based on the virtual circuit routing. This technique is very similar to that of the switching statistical multiplexer discussed in the preceding chapter. The strength of this technique, in terms of routing and traffic control, will become evident in due course.

SNA

Initially, SNA was structured with a host-centered, host-controlled philosophy, but it is gradually evolving toward a more flexible approach tailored to true distributed systems [GURU87]. Figure 8.7 presents those aspects of SNA relevant to the present discussion. The communication network is formed by *subarea nodes*, each of which may be a host or a communications controller. *Peripheral nodes*, such as terminals and terminal concentrators, attach to subarea nodes. The link between adjacent subarea nodes consists of one or more transmission groups. A *transmission group* is either a single physical link or multiple links used for parallel transmission. SNA provides a virtual-circuit service using a two-level internal virtual-circuit implementation. Between each pair of subarea nodes, a number of *explicit routes* are predefined. Each route consists of a sequence of transmission groups forming a path between the two nodes. A *virtual route* is simply a source-destination node pair assigned dynamically to an explicit route. The details are provided below, in the discussion of routing.

Note that in Figure 8.7, the identities of nodes and stations have merged. Each subarea node is a communications node capable of performing switching. It may also be a network station that supports users or applications that use the network.

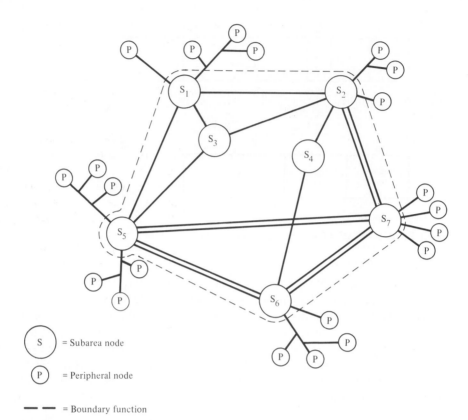

S = Subarea node

P = Peripheral node

— — = Boundary function

FIGURE 8.7.   An example SNA network configuration.

ROUTING

One of the most complex and crucial aspects of packet switched network design is routing. This section provides an overview. We begin with a survey of
key characteristics that can be used to classify routing strategies. Next, the
underlying route-calculation algorithms are examined. This is followed by a
discussion of routing strategies and a look at some examples.

Characteristics

The primary function of a packet-switched network is to accept packets from a
source station and deliver them to a destination station. To accomplish this, a
path or route through the network must be selected; generally, more than one
route is possible. Thus a routing function must be performed. [TANE88] sug-

gests a number of desirable attributes of the routing function: correctness, simplicity, robustness, stability, fairness, and optimality. To this one might also add efficiency.

The first two items on the list are self-explanatory. Robustness has to do with the ability of the network to deliver packets via some route in the face of localized failures and overloads. Ideally, the network can react to such contingencies without loss of packets or the breaking of virtual circuits. The designer who seeks robustness must cope with the competing claims for stability. Techniques that react to changing conditions have an unfortunate tendency to either react too slowly to events or to experience unstable swings from one extreme to another. For example, the network may react to congestion in one area by shifting most of the load to a second area. Now the second area is overloaded and the first is underutilized, causing a second shift. During these shifts, packets may travel in loops through the network.

A trade-off also exists between fairness and optimality. Some performance criteria may favor the exchange of packets between nearby stations and discourage the exchange between distant stations. This policy will appear unfair to the station which primarily needs to communicate with distant stations. Finally, any routing technique involves some processing overhead at each node and often a transmission overhead as well. The penalty of such overhead needs to be less than the benefit accrued based on some reasonable metric, such as increased robustness or fairness.

With these attributes in mind, we turn to the techniques of routing that can be employed. Table 8.3 lists the elements or dimensions of the routing task. These elements are not completely orthogonal and may not even encompass all aspects of this complex problem. Nevertheless, they serve to clarify and

TABLE 8.3 Elements of Routing Techniques

Performance criterion	Network information source
Number of hops	None
Cost	Local
Delay	Adjacent nodes
Throughput	Nodes along route
Decision time	All nodes
Packet (datagram)	Routing strategy
Session (virtual circuit)	Fixed
Decision place	Flooding
Each node (distributed)	Random
Central node (centralized)	Adaptive
Originating node	Adaptive routing update time
	Continuous
	Periodic
	Major load change
	Topology change

organize routing concepts. First, we comment briefly on each of these dimensions; several are then explored in detail.

The selection of a route is generally based on some *performance criterion*. The simplest criterion is to choose the "shortest" route (one that passes through the least number of nodes) through the network. This results in the least number of hops per packet (one hop = traversal of one node-to-node link). A generalization of the shortest-route criterion is least-cost routing. In this case, a cost is associated with each link, and the route through the network that accumulates the least cost is sought. For example, Figure 8.8 illustrates a network in which two arrowed lines between a pair of nodes represent a link between those nodes; the numbers on the lines represent the current link cost in each direction. The shortest path from node 1 to node 6 is 1-3-6, but the least cost path is 1-4-5-6. The cost assignment is intended to support one or more design objectives. For example, the cost could be related to the capacity of the link (i.e., the higher the capacity, the lower the cost), or the current queueing delay to use the link. In the first case, the least-cost route should provide the highest throughput. In the second case, the least-cost route should minimize delay.

So, to deliver a packet from one station to another, a routing decision is made based on some performance criterion. Key characteristics of this decision are the time and place of the decision. The *decision time* is either at the packet or virtual-circuit level. When the internal operation of the network is datagram, a routing decision is made individually for each packet. For internal virtual-circuit operation, a routing decision is made at the time that the circuit is established. All subsequent packets using that virtual circuit follow the same route. Note that we are here talking about an internal virtual circuit. For some networks, the routing strategy permits the route of individual packets of an external virtual circuit to vary. This is the case when the network uses datagrams internally but provides an external virtual circuit.

The *decision place* also varies among networks. In some networks, each node has the responsibility of selecting an output link for routing packets as they arrive (distributed routing). The principal alternative is for the routing decision to be made by a central node, such as a network control center (centralized routing). The danger of the latter approach is that the loss of the network control center may block the operation of the network. The distributed approach is perhaps more complex, but is also more robust. An infrequently used alternative is for the originating node to select the route (source node routing). Observe that the decision time and decision place are independent. Again referring to Figure 8.8, suppose that the decision place is each node and that the values depicted are the costs at a given instant in time; the costs may change. If a packet is to be delivered from node 1 to node 6, it might follow the route 1-4-5-6, with each leg of the route determined locally by the transmitting node. Now suppose that the values change such that 1-4-5-6 is no longer the optimum route. In a datagram network, the next packet may follow a different route, again determined by each node along the way. In a virtual circuit net-

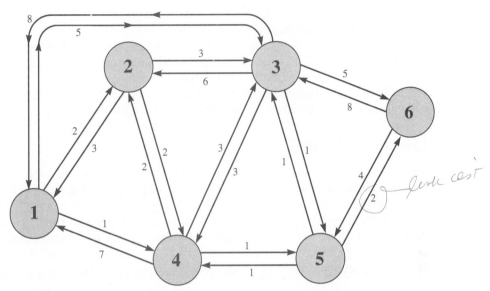

FIGURE 8.8. Example packet-switched network.

work, each node will remember the routing decision that was made when the virtual circuit was established, and simply pass on the packets without making a new decision.

The next element of routing, *network information source*, depends on the performance criterion, decision place, and routing strategy. It is nevertheless worth calling out separately. The information referred to is information about the topology of the network, traffic load, and cost. Surprisingly, some strategies use no information at all and yet manage to get packets through; flooding and some random strategies (discussed below) are in this category. With distributed routing (decision place = each node), the individual node may make use of only local information, such as the cost of each outgoing link or the queue size for each outgoing link. The node might also collect information from adjacent nodes. Finally, there are algorithms that allow the node to gain information from all nodes on any potential route of interest. Examples of all these are provided below. With centralized routing, the central node may use information obtained from all nodes. As you might expect, the more information used, the more likely the network is to make good routing decisions. On the other hand, the transmission of that information consumes network resources.

A related concept is that of information update time, which is a function of both the information source and the routing strategy. Clearly, if no information is used, there is no update. If the only information used is local, the update is essentially continuous. That is, the local node always knows the current local conditions. For all other information source categories (adjacent nodes, nodes along route, all nodes), the update time is a function of the routing strategy.

For a fixed strategy, the information is never updated, except when there is a topology change. For an adaptive strategy, information update time is expressed as an *adaptive routing update time*, as described below. Again, you should expect that increased frequency of update improves the routing decision at the expense of increased overhead.

Finally, a large number of *routing strategies* have evolved. These are discussed below, after an explanation of least-cost routing algorithms.

Least-Cost Algorithms

Virtually all packet-switched networks base their routing decision on some form of least-cost criterion. If the criterion is to minimize the number of hops, each link has a value of 1. More typically, the link value is inversely proportional to the link capacity, proportional to the current load on the link, or some combination. In any case, the assignment of value is of no concern to the *least-cost routing algorithm*, which can be simply stated as:

> Given a network of nodes connected by bidirectional links, where each link has a cost associated with it in each direction, define the cost of a path between two nodes as the sum of the costs of the links traversed. For each pair of nodes find the path with least cost.

Note that the cost of a link may differ in the two directions. This would be true, for example, if the cost of the link equaled the length of the queue of packets awaiting transmission from each of the two nodes on the link. In what follows, we assume for simplicity that the cost of a link is the same in each direction.

Most least-cost routing algorithms in use in packet-switched networks are variations of one of two common algorithms, known as Dijkstra's algorithm and the Bellman–Ford algorithm. These algorithms are defined in this section, using notation similar to that in [BERT92] and an example adapted from [SCHW80]. Later sections will show their application in a variety of routing strategies.

Dijkstra's algorithm [DIJK59] can be stated as: Find the shortest paths from a given source node to all other nodes by developing the paths in order of increasing path length. The algorithm proceeds in stages. By the kth stage, the shortest paths to the k nodes closest to (least cost away from) the source node have been determined; these nodes are in a set M. At the $(k + 1)$st stage, that node not in M that has the shortest path from the source node is added to M. As each node is added to M, its path from the source is defined. The algorithm can be formally described as follows. Define:

N = set of nodes in the network
s = source node
M = set of nodes so far incorporated by the algorithm
d_{ij} = link cost from node i to node j; $d_{ii} = 0$, and $d_{ij} = \infty$ if the two nodes are not directly connected; $d_{ij} \geq 0$ if the two nodes are directly connected

D_n = cost of the least-cost path from node s to node n that is currently known to the algorithm

The algorithm has three steps; steps 2 and 3 are repeated until $M = N$. That is, steps 2 and 3 are repeated until final paths have been assigned to all nodes in the network:

1. Initialize:
   $M = \{s\}$ i.e., set of nodes incorporated is only the source node.
   $D_n = d_{sn}$ for $n \neq s$ i.e., initial path costs to neighboring nodes are simply the link costs.
2. Find the neighboring node not in M that has the least-cost path from node s and incorporate that node into M:
   Find $w \notin M$ such that $D_w = \min_{j \notin M} D_j$
   Add w to M
3. Update least-cost paths:
   $D_n = \min[D_n, D_w + d_{wn}]$ for all $n \notin M$
   If the latter term is the minimum, the path from s to n is now the path from s to w concatenated with the link from w to n.

One iteration of steps 2 and 3 adds one new node to M and defines the least-cost path from s to that node. That path passes only through nodes that are in M. To see this, consider the following line of reasoning. After k iterations, there are k nodes in M, and the least-cost path from s to each of these nodes has been defined. Now consider all possible paths from s to nodes not in M. Among those paths, there is one of least cost that passes exclusively through nodes in M (see Problem 8.7), ending with a direct link from some node in M to a node not in M. This node is added to M and the associated path is defined as the least-cost path for that node.

Table 8.4a shows the result of applying this algorithm to Figure 8.8, using $s = 1$. Note that at each step the path to each node plus the total cost of that path is generated. After the final iteration, the least-cost path to each node and the cost of that path have been developed. The same procedure can be used with node 2 as source node, and so on.

The **Bellman–Ford algorithm** [FORD62] can be stated as: Find the shortest paths from a given source node subject to the constraint that the paths contain at most one link; then find the shortest paths with a constraint of paths of at most two links, and so on. This algorithm also proceeds in stages. The algorithm can be formally described as follows. Define:

s = source node
d_{ij} = link cost from node i to node j; $d_{ii} = 0$; $d_{ij} = \infty$ if the two nodes are not directly connected; $d_{ij} \geq 0$ if the two nodes are directly connected
h = maximum number of links in a path at the current stage of the algorithm

TABLE 8.4 Example of Least-Cost Routing Algorithms (using Figure 8.8)

(a) Dijkstra's Algorithm ($s = 1$)

Iteration	M	D_2	Path	D_3	Path	D_4	Path	D_5	Path	D_6	Path
1	{1}	2	1-2	5	1-3	1	1-4	∞	—	∞	—
2	{1, 4}	2	1-2	4	1-4-3	1	1-4	2	1-4-5	∞	—
3	{1, 2, 4}	2	1-2	4	1-4-3	1	1-4	2	1-4-5	∞	—
4	{1, 2, 4, 5}	2	1-2	3	1-4-5-3	1	1-4	2	1-4-5	4	1-4-5-6
5	{1, 2, 3, 4, 5}	2	1-2	3	1-4-5-3	1	1-4	2	1-4-5	4	1-4-5-6
6	{1, 2, 3, 4, 5, 6}	2	1-2	3	1-4-5-3	1	1-4	2	1-4-5	4	1-4-5-6

(b) Bellman–Ford Algorithm ($s = 1$)

h	$D_2^{(h)}$	Path	$D_3^{(h)}$	Path	$D_4^{(h)}$	Path	$D_5^{(h)}$	Path	$D_6^{(h)}$	Path
0	∞	—	∞	—	∞	—	∞	—	∞	—
1	2	1-2	5	1-3	1	1-4	∞	—	∞	—
2	2	1-2	4	1-4-3	1	1-4	2	1-4-5	10	1-3-6
3	2	1-2	3	1-4-5-3	1	1-4	2	1-4-5	4	1-4-5-6
4	2	1-2	3	1-4-5-3	1	1-4	2	1-4-5	4	1-4-5-6

$D_n^{(h)}$ = cost of the least-cost path from node s to node n under the constraint of no more than h links

The algorithm has the following steps; step 2 is repeated until none of the costs change:

1. Initialize:
   $D_n^{(0)} = ∞$, for all $n \neq s$
   $D_s^{(h)} = 0$, for all h
2. For each successive $h \geq 0$:

$$D_n^{(h + 1)} = \frac{\min}{j} [D_j^{(h)} + d_{jn}]$$

The path from s to i terminates with the link from j to i.

For the iteration of step 2 with $h = K$, and for each destination node n, the algorithm compares potential paths from s to n of length $K + 1$ with the path that existed at the end of the previous iteration. If the previous, shorter path has less cost, then that path is retained. Otherwise, a new path with length $K + 1$ is defined from s to n; this path consists of a path of length K from s to some node j, plus a direct hop from node j to node n. In this case, the path from s to j that is used is the K-hop path for j defined in the previous iteration (see Problem 8.8).

Table 8.4b shows the result of applying this algorithm to Figure 8.8, using $s = 1$. At each step, the least cost paths with a maximum number of links equal to h are found. After the final iteration, the least-cost path to each node and the cost of that path has been developed. The same procedure can be used with node 2 as source node, and so on. Note that the results agree with those obtained using Dijkstra's algorithm. Figure 8.9 illustrates the results of Table 8.4.

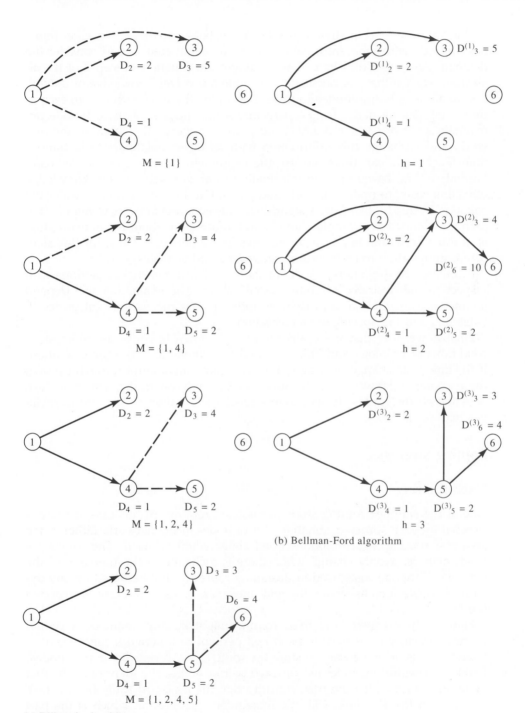

(b) Bellman-Ford algorithm

(a) Dijkstra's algorithm

FIGURE 8.9. Example of least-cost routing algorithm (based on Table 8.4).

One interesting comparison can be made between these two algorithms, having to do with what information needs to be gathered. Let us consider the Bellman–Ford algorithm first. If we examine the equation in step 2 of the algorithm, we see that the calculation for node n involves knowledge of the link cost to all neighboring nodes to node n (d_{jn}) plus the total path cost to each of those neighboring nodes from a particular source node s ($D_j^{(h)}$). Each node can maintain a set of costs and associated paths for every other node in the network, and exchange this information with its direct neighbors from time to time. Each node can therefore use the expression in step 2 of the Bellman–Ford algorithm, based only on information from its neighbors and knowledge of its link costs, to update its costs and paths. On the other hand, consider the equation in step 3 of Dijkstra's algorithm. This equation appears to require that each node must have complete topological information about the network; that is, it must know the link costs of all links in the network. Thus, for this algorithm, information must be exchanged with all other nodes.

Evaluation of the relative merits of the two algorithms should be done with respect to the desirable attributes listed earlier. The evaluation will depend on the implementation approach, as indicated by the various categories in Table 8.2, and the specific implementation.

Finally, we note that these algorithms are known to converge under static conditions of topology and link costs and will converge to the same solution. If the link costs change over time, the algorithm will attempt to catch up with these changes. However, if the link cost depends on traffic, which in turn depends on the routes chosen, then a feedback situation exists, and instabilities may result.

Routing Strategies

Fixed Routing

One of the simplest routing strategies is fixed routing. In this case, a route is selected for each source-destination pair of nodes in the network. Either of the least-cost routing algorithms described above could be used. The routes are fixed, or at least only change when there is a change in the topology of the network. Thus the costs used in designing routes cannot be based on any dynamic variable such as traffic. It could, however, be based on cost or expected traffic.

Figure 8.10 suggests how fixed routing might be implemented. A central routing directory is created, to be stored perhaps at a network control center. Note that it is not necessary to store the route for each possible pair of nodes. Rather, it is sufficient to know, for each pair of nodes, the identity of the first node on the route. To see this, consider that the least-cost route from X to Y begins with the X-A link. Call the remainder of the route, which is the part from A to Y, R_1. Call the least-cost route for A to Y, R_2. Now, if the cost of R_1 is greater than R_2, then the X-Y route can be improved by using R_2 instead. If

CENTRAL ROUTING DIRECTORY

To Node

		1	2	3	4	5	6
	1	–	2	4	4	4	4
	2	1	–	3	4	4	4
From Node	3	5	2	–	5	5	5
	4	1	2	5	–	5	5
	5	4	4	3	4	–	6
	6	5	5	5	5	5	–

Node 1 Directory		Node 2 Directory		Node 3 Directory	
Destination	Next node	Destination	Next node	Destination	Next node
2	2	1	1	1	5
3	4	3	3	2	2
4	4	4	4	4	5
5	4	5	4	5	5
6	4	6	4	6	5

Node 4 Directory		Node 5 Directory		Node 6 Directory	
Destination	Next node	Destination	Next node	Destination	Next node
1	1	1	4	1	5
2	2	2	4	2	5
3	5	3	3	3	5
5	5	4	4	4	5
6	5	6	6	5	5

FIGURE 8.10. Fixed routing (using Fig. 8.8).

the cost of R_1 is less than R_2, then R_2 is not the least-cost route from A to Y. Thus, at each point along a route, it is only necessary to know the identity of the next node, not the entire route. Because of this, each node need only store a single row of the routing directory. The node's directory shows the next node to take for each destination.

With fixed routing, there is no difference between routing for datagrams and virtual circuits. All packets from a given source to a given destination follow the same route. The advantage of fixed routing is its simplicity, and it should work well in a reliable network with a steady load. Its disadvantage is its lack of flexibility. It does not react to network congestion or failures.

A refinement to fixed routing that would accommodate link and node outages would be to supply the nodes with an alternate next node for each direction. For example, the alternate next nodes in the node 1 directory might be 4,
3, 2, 3, 3.

Flooding

Another simple routing technique is flooding. This technique requires no network information whatsoever, and works as follows. A packet is sent by a
source node to every one of its neighbors. At each node, an incoming packet
is retransmitted on all outgoing links except for the link that it arrived from.
Again as an example, consider Figure 8.8. If node 1 has a packet to send to
node 6, it sends a copy of that packet to nodes 2, 3, and 4. Node 2 will send a
copy to nodes 3 and 4. Node 4 will send a copy to nodes 2, 3, and 5. And so
it goes. Eventually, a number of copies of the packet will arrive at node 6. The
packet must have some unique identifier (e.g. source node, sequence number;
or virtual circuit number, sequence number) so that node 6 knows to discard
all but the first copy.

It is clear that unless something is done to stop the incessant retransmission
of packets, the number of packets in circulation just from a single source packet
grows without bound. One way to prevent this is for each node to remember
the identity of those packets it has already retransmitted. When duplicate copies of the packet arrive, they are discarded. A simpler technique is to include
a hop count field with each packet. The count can be originally set to some
maximum value, such as the "diameter" of the network. Each time a node
passes on a packet, it decrements the count by one. When the count reaches
zero, the packet is discarded.

An example of this latter tactic is shown in Figure 8.11. Again, assume that
a packet is to be sent from node 1 to node 6. On the first hop, three copies of
the packet are created. For the second hop of all these copies, a total of nine
copies are created. One of these copies reaches node 6, which absorbs it and
does not retransmit. However, the other nodes generate a total of 22 new copies for their third and final hop. Note that if a node is not keeping track of
packet identifiers, it may generate multiple copies at this third stage. After the
third hop is completed, all packets are destroyed. Node 6 has received four
additional copies of the packet.

The flooding technique has two remarkable properties:

- All possible routes between source and destination are tried. Thus, no matter
  what link or node outages have occurred, a packet will always get through
  as long as at least one path between source and destination exists.
- Because all routes are tried, at least one copy of the packet to arrive at the
  destination will have used a minimum-hop route.

Because of the first property, the flooding technique is highly robust and
could be used to send high-priority messages. An example application is a

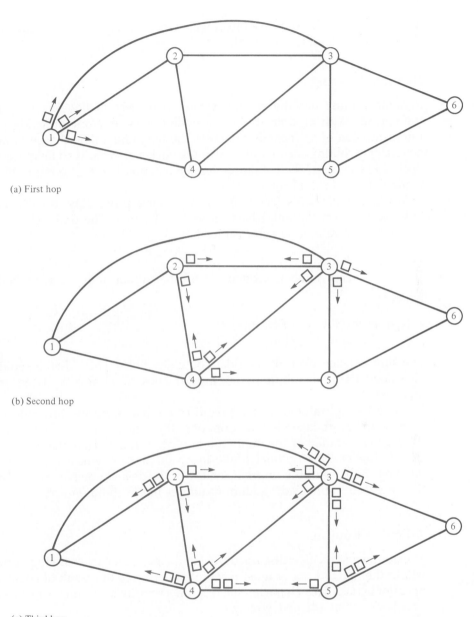

(a) First hop

(b) Second hop

(c) Third hop

FIGURE 8.11.   Flooding example (hop count = 3).

military network that is subject to extensive damage. Because of the second property, flooding might be used to initially set up the route for a virtual circuit. On the other hand, the principal disadvantage of flooding is the total traffic load that it generates, which is directly proportional to the connectivity of the network. This increased load will increase delay for all subsequent traffic if the network load is nontrivial.

Random Routing

Random routing has the simplicity and robustness of flooding with far less traffic load. With random routing, a node selects only one outgoing path for retransmission of an incoming packet. The outgoing link is chosen at random, generally excluding the link on which the packet arrived. If all links are equally likely to be chosen, then a simple implementation is for a node to utilize outgoing links in a round-robin fashion.

A refinement of this technique is to assign a probability to each outgoing link and to select the link based on that probability. The probability could be based on data rate, in which case we have

$$P_i = \frac{R_i}{\Sigma_j R_j}$$

where

P_i = probability of selecting i
R_j = data rate on link j

The sum is taken over all candidate outgoing links. This scheme should provide good traffic distribution. The probabilities could also be based on fixed link costs.

Like flooding, random routing requires the use of no network information. Because the route taken is a random one, the actual route will typically not be the least-cost route nor the minimum hop-count route. Thus the network must carry a higher than optimal traffic load, although not nearly as high as for flooding. Because of the unpredictability of the delay in delivering packets and the increased traffic load, random routing is not in common use.

Adaptive Routing

The routing strategies discussed so far do not react to changing conditions within the network, or at most react infrequently as the result of some system operator action. This characteristic is not necessarily a bad one. Consider these drawbacks of an adaptive strategy:

- The routing decision is more complex; therefore, the processing burden on the network increases.
- In most cases, adaptive strategies depend on status information that is collected at one place but used at another; therefore, the traffic burden on the network increases.
- An adaptive strategy may react too quickly, causing congestion-producing oscillation, or too slowly, being irrelevant.

Despite these real dangers, adaptive routing strategies are by far the most prevalent, for two reasons:

- An adaptive routing strategy can improve performance as seen by the network user.
- An adaptive strategy can aid in traffic control, discussed later.

These benefits may or may not be realized, depending on the soundness of design and the nature of the load. By and large, it is an extraordinarily complex task to perform properly. Proof of this is seen in the fact that our two example communication networks, ARPANET and TYMNET, have both endured major overhauls of their routing strategy. In the former case the change was largely made to correct design flaws; in the latter it was to adapt to a changing traffic mix.

Adaptive routing strategies can be characterized by the fact that they adapt to measurable changing conditions and by the other elements listed in Table 8.3. Those elements that serve most directly to differentiate the various strategies are the decision place and the network information source. Based on those two parameters, virtually all strategies are in one or a hybrid combination of the following categories:

- *Isolated adaptive:* local information, distributed control.
- *Distributed adaptive:* information from adjacent nodes, distributed control.
- *Centralized adaptive:* information from all nodes, centralized control.

A simple isolated adaptive scheme is for a node to route each packet to the outgoing link with the shortest queue length, Q. This would have the effect of balancing the load on outgoing links. However, outgoing paths may not be headed in the correct general direction. An improvement can be obtained by also taking into account preferred directions, much as with random routing. In this case, each link emanating from the node would have a bias B_i for each destination i. For each incoming packet headed for node i, the node would choose the outgoing link that minimizes $Q + B_i$. Thus a node would tend to send packets in the right direction, with a concession made to current traffic delays.

As an example, Figure 8.12 shows the status of node 4 of Figure 8.8 at a certain point in time. Node 4 has links to four other nodes. A fair number of packets have been arriving and a backlog has built up, with a queue of packets waiting for each of the outgoing links. A packet arrives from node 1 destined for node 6. Question: To which outgoing link should the packet be routed? Based on current queue lengths and the values of bias (B_6) for each outgoing link, the minimum value of $Q + B_6$ is four, on the link to node 3. Thus the packet is routed through node 3.

Isolated adaptive schemes are not in general use since they make little use of available information. The other two adaptive strategies are commonly found. Both take advantage of the information that each node has about the delays and outages that it experiences. In the distributed adaptive case, each

FIGURE 8.12. Example of isolated adaptive routing.

node exchanges this delay information with other nodes. Based on this incoming information, a node tries to estimate the delay situation throughout the network, and applies one of the routing algorithms discussed earlier. In the case of a centralized adaptive algorithm, each node reports its information to a central node, which designs routes based on this incoming information and sends the routing information back to the nodes. In the next section we examine several examples of each approach.

Example Systems

Let us now examine the routing techniques used in the four example networks introduced earlier. Table 8.5 summarizes key characteristics of each approach.

ARPANET

The ARPANET routing algorithm is in its third generation. It is instructive to describe these algorithms. The original routing algorithm, designed in 1969, was a distributed adaptive algorithm using estimated delay as the performance criterion and a version of the Bellman–Ford algorithm. For this algorithm, each node maintains two vectors:

$$
D_i = \begin{bmatrix} d_{i1} \\ \vdots \\ d_{iN} \end{bmatrix}
\qquad\qquad
S_i = \begin{bmatrix} s_{i1} \\ \vdots \\ s_{iN} \end{bmatrix}
$$

TABLE 8.5 Routing Techniques for Some Networks

	Original ARPANET	Revised ARPANET	TYMNET I	TYMNET II	SNA
Performance criterion	Delay	Delay	Delay rate, overload	Data rate, load, link and traffic types	User-defined
Decision time	Packet	Packet	Session	Session	Session
Decision place	Each node	Each node	Central node	Central node	Originating node
Information source	Adjacent nodes	All nodes	All nodes	All nodes	User-defined
Routing strategy	Adaptive	Adaptive	Adaptive	Adaptive	User-defined
Update time	Periodic	Periodic	Load change	Load change	Topology change
Routing algorithm	Backward-search	Forward-search	Backward-search	Forward-search	User-defined

where

D_i = delay vector for node i
d_{ij} = current estimate of minimum delay from node i to node j ($d_{ii} = 0$)
N = number of nodes in the network
S_i = successor node vector for node i
s_{ij} = the next node in the current minimum-delay route from i to j

Periodically (every 128 ms), each node exchanges its delay vector with all of its neighbors. On the basis of all incoming delay vectors, a node k updates both of its vectors as follows:

$$d_{kj} = \min_{i \in A} [d_{ij} + l_{ki}]$$

$$s_{kj} = i \quad \text{using } i \text{ that minimizes the expression above}$$

where

A = set of neighbor nodes for k
l_{ki} = current estimate of delay from k to i

Figure 8.13 provides an example of the original ARPANET algorithm, using the network of Figure 8.14. This is the same network as that of Figure 8.8, with some of the link costs having different values (and assuming the same cost in both directions). Figure 8.13a shows the routing table for node 1 at an instant in time that reflects the link costs of Figure 8.14. For each destination, a delay is specified, and the next node on the route that produces that delay. At some point, the link costs change to those of Figure 8.8. Assume that node 1's neigh-

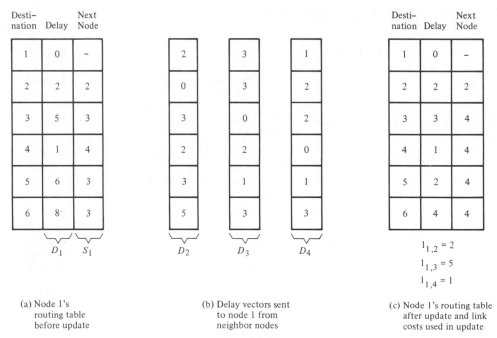

Destination	Delay	Next Node
1	0	–
2	2	2
3	5	3
4	1	4
5	6	3
6	8	3

D_1 S_1

D_2	D_3	D_4
2	3	1
0	3	2
3	0	2
2	2	0
3	1	1
5	3	3

Destination	Delay	Next Node
1	0	–
2	2	2
3	3	4
4	1	4
5	2	4
6	4	4

$l_{1,2} = 2$
$l_{1,3} = 5$
$l_{1,4} = 1$

(a) Node 1's
routing table
before update

(b) Delay vectors sent
to node 1 from
neighbor nodes

(c) Node 1's routing table
after update and link
costs used in update

FIGURE 8.13.   Original ARPANET routing algorithm.

bors (node 2, 3, and 4) learn of the change before node 1. Each of these nodes updates its delay vector and sends a copy to all of its neighbors, including node 1 (Figure 8.13b). Node 1 discards its current routing table and builds a new one, based solely on the incoming delay vector and its own estimate of link delay to each of its neighbors. The result is shown in Figure 8.13c.

The estimated link delay is simply the queue length for that link. Thus in building a new routing table, the node will tend to favor outgoing links with shorter queues. This tends to balance the load on outgoing links. However, because queue lengths vary rapidly with time, the distributed perception of the shortest route could change while a packet is en route. This could lead to

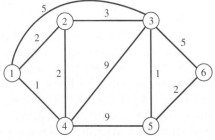

FIGURE 8.14.   Network for example of Figure 8.13a.

a thrashing situation in which a packet continues to seek out areas of low congestion rather than aiming at the destination.

After some years of experience and several minor modifications, the original routing algorithm was replaced by a quite different one in 1979 [MCQU80]. The major shortcomings of the old algorithm were these:

- The algorithm did not consider line speed, merely queue length. Thus higher-capacity links were not given the favored status they deserved.
- Queue length is, in any case, an artificial measure of delay, since some variable amount of processing time elapses between the arrival of a packet at a node and its placement in an outbound queue.
- The algorithm was not very accurate. In particular, it responded slowly to congestion and delay increases.

The new algorithm is also a distributed adaptive one, using delay as the performance criterion, but the differences are significant. Rather than using queue length as a surrogate for delay, the delay is measured directly. At a node, each incoming packet is timestamped with an arrival time. A departure time is recorded when the packet is transmitted. If a positive acknowledgment is returned, the delay for that packet is recorded as the departure time minus the arrival time plus transmission time and propagation delay. The node must therefore know link data rate and propagation time. If a negative acknowledgment comes back, the departure time is updated and the node tries again, until a measure of successful transmission delay is obtained.

Every 10 s, the node computes the average delay on each outgoing link. If there are any significant changes in delay, the information is sent to all other nodes using flooding. Each node maintains an estimate of delay on every network link. When new information arrives, it recomputes its routing table using Dijkstra's algorithm.

Experience with this new strategy indicated that it was more responsive and stable than the old one. The overhead induced by flooding was moderate since each node does this at most once every 10 seconds. However, as the load on the network grew, a shortcoming in the new strategy began to appear, and the strategy was revised in 1987 [KHAN89].

The problem with the second strategy is the assumption that the measured packet delay on a link is a good predictor of the link delay encountered after all nodes re-route their traffic based on this reported delay. Thus, it is an effective routing mechanism only if there is some correlation between the reported values and those actually experienced after re-routing. This correlation tends to be rather high under light and moderate traffic loads. However, under heavy loads, there is little correlation. Therefore, immediately after all nodes have made routing updates, the routing tables are obsolete!

As an example, consider a network that consists of two regions with only two links, A and B, connecting the two regions (Figure 8.15). Each route between two nodes in different regions must pass through one of these links. Assume that a situation develops in which most of the traffic is on link A. This

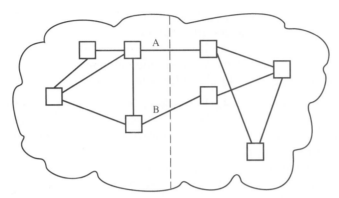

FIGURE 8.15. Packet-switching network subject to oscillations.

will cause the link delay on A to be significant, and at the next opportunity, this delay value will be reported to all other nodes. These updates will arrive at all nodes at about the same time, and all will update their routing tables immediately. It is likely that this new delay value for link A will be high enough to make link B the preferred choice for most, if not all, inter-region routes. Because all nodes adjust their routes at the same time, most or all inter-region traffic shifts at the same time to link B. Now the link delay value on B will become high, and there will be a subsequent shift to link A. This oscillation will continue until the traffic volume subsides.

There are a number of reasons why this oscillation is undesirable:

1. A significant portion of available capacity is unused at just the time when it is needed most: under heavy traffic load.
2. The over-utilization of some links can lead to the spread of congestion within the network (this will be seen in the discussion of Figure 8.19).
3. The large swings in measured delay values result in the need for more frequent routing update messages. This increases the load on the network at just the time when the network is already stressed.

The ARPANET designers concluded that the essence of the problem was that every node was trying to obtain the best route for all destinations, and that these efforts conflicted. It was concluded that under heavy loads, the goal of routing should be to give the *average* route a good path instead of attempting to give *all* routes the best path.

The designers decided that it was unnecessary to change the overall routing algorithm. Rather, it was sufficient to change the function that calculates link costs. This was done in such a way as to damp routing oscillations and reduce routing overhead. The calculation begins with measuring the average delay over the last 10 seconds. This value is then transformed with the following steps:

1. Using a simple *M/M/1* queueing model (see Appendix A), the measured delay is transformed into an estimate of link utilization. From queueing theory, utilization can be expressed as a function of delay as follows:

$$\rho = \frac{2(s - t)}{s - 2t}, \text{ where}$$

ρ = link utilization
t = measured delay
s = service time

The service time was set at the network-wide average packet size (600 bits) divided by the data rate of the link.

2. The result is then smoothed by averaging it with the previous estimate of utilization:

$U(n + 1) = 0.5 \times \rho(n + 1) + 0.5 \times U(n)$, where
$U(n)$ = average utilization calculated at sampling time n
$\rho(n)$ = link utilization measured at sampling time n

Averaging increases the period of routing oscillations, thus reducing routing overhead.

3. The link cost is then set as a function of average utilization that is designed to provide a reasonable estimate of cost while avoiding oscillation. Figure 8.16 indicates the way in which the estimate of utilization is converted into a cost value. The final cost value is, in effect, a transformed value of delay. In the figure, delay is normalized to the value achieved on an idle line, which is just propagation delay plus transmission time. One curve on the

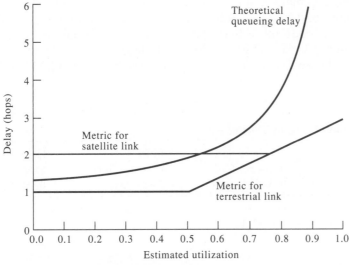

FIGURE 8.16.   ARPANET delay metrics.

figure indicates the way in which the actual delay rises as a function of utilization; the increase in delay is due to queueing delay at the node. For the revised algorithm, the cost value is kept at the minimum value until a given level of utilization is reached. This feature has the effect of reducing routing overhead at low traffic levels. Above a certain level of utilization, the cost level is allowed to rise to a maximum value that is equal to three times the minimum value. The effect of this maximum value is to dictate that traffic should not be routed around a heavily utilized line by more than two additional hops.

Note that the minimum threshold is set higher for satellite links. This encourages the use of terrestrial links under conditions of light traffic, since the terrestrial links have much lower propagation delay. Note also that the actual delay curve is much steeper than the transformation curves at high utilization levels. It is this steep rise in link cost which forces all of the traffic on a link to be shed, which in turn causes routing oscillations.

In summary, the revised cost function is keyed to utilization rather than delay. The function acts similar to a delay-based metric under light loads and to a capacity-based metric under heavy loads.

TYMNET Routing

As with ARPANET, the TYMNET routing algorithm has gone through two major versions. The first version [RIND77, RAJA78], used with TYMNET I, made use of a simple cost allocation based on link capacity and load. The cost table is depicted in Table 8.6. With each link, a fixed cost is associated that is a decreasing function of the data rate of the link. If the link is overloaded in one direction, a penalty cost of 16 is added; if it is overloaded in both directions, a penalty cost of 32 is added. An overload is defined as a condition in which it takes a node more than 0.5 s to service a virtual circuit; this is, in effect, a queueing delay. The last row of the table refers to a composite node made up of individual nodes connected with very high speed DMA links. Such

TABLE 8.6   Link Costs in TYMNET

Line Type	Line Not Overloaded	Line Overloaded One Way	Line Overloaded Both Ways
9600 bps	10	26	42
7200 bps	11	27	43
4800 bps	12	28	44
2400 bps	16	32	48
Memory shuffler	1	17	33

composite nodes are required where large numbers of transmission lines converge.

TYMNET is a centralized network with a central node known as the supervisor responsible for routing. The supervisor knows the fixed cost of each link. When an overload condition exists, this is reported by the affected node to the supervisor which increases the assigned cost to the appropriate link. The cost is decreased when the node reports that the overload condition no longer exists. Thus, with only minor delay, the supervisor has a global picture of network status.

The supervisor performs routing on a virtual-circuit basis. When a virtual circuit is requested, the supervisor determines the least cost route between source and destination using a version of the Bellman-Ford algorithm. The supervisor then passes the necessary routing information for this virtual circuit to each node on the route. When the virtual circuit terminates, the supervisor informs each node on the route. During the life of the virtual circuit, the route is fixed. If an outage occurs, the source and destination stations are required to construct a new virtual circuit. If the supervisor fails, one of three backup nodes assumes responsibility.

The TYMNET I technique had several useful features. Under light loading, the highest-capacity links are preferred. As the load increases, the algorithm tends to spread out the traffic nicely. Also, the processing burden on each node is minimal.

As the network grew, the TYMNET designers upgraded the routing function to improve efficiency and handle a wider variety of traffic [TYME81]. Whereas TYMNET I handled primarily interactive traffic over low-speed (up to 9600 bps) lines, TYMNET II also handles computer-to-computer traffic and has higher-speed links, including satellite links. In TYMNET II, link cost is based on data rate, load factor, satellite versus land-based link, and traffic type. For example, if the station is a low-speed interactive terminal, a 9600-bps land link is assigned a lower cost than a 56-kbps satellite link because of the added delay of the satellite. If the virtual circuit is to be used for host-to-host file transfer, the satellite link has the lower cost; throughput is more important than response time.

As before, virtual circuit routes are established by the supervisor, which now uses a version of Dijkstra's algorithm, deemed more efficient. Now, instead of transmitting routing information to each node, the supervisor sends a "needle" to the source node, containing the route as an ordered list of nodes. The needle threads its way along the designated route, depositing routing information as it goes. If an outage is encountered, the needle retraces to the origin and the supervisor is informed. This overcomes a problem in TYMNET I in which proper operation depended on each node successfully receiving routing information from the supervisor.

The recovery procedure is also improved. If an outage destroys a route, the supervisor finds another route for the virtual circuit. Lost packets must be recovered by an end-to-end protocol, but the virtual circuit is not lost.

SNA Routing

The routing function in SNA is to some extent left up to the user. What SNA provides is a foundation upon which a routing technique can be built [ATK180, GURU87, MART87]. To understand SNA routing, four concepts need to be distinguished:

- *Transmission group:* A set of one or more direct links with similar transmission characteristics between adjacent nodes. There may be more than one transmission group between any pair of nodes.
- *Explicit route:* A predefined fixed path between two nodes in an SNA network. The explicit route is defined in terms of the sequence of nodes and transmission groups that constitute the path. This concept corresponds to that of internal vitual circuit, described in Section 8.3.
- *Virtual route:* A logical connection between two nodes, defined by identifying the two nodes. The concept corresponds, roughly, to that of external virtual circuit, described in Section 8.3.
- *Session:* A logical relationship between two network endpoints that supports a user or network application. This concept corresponds roughly to that of a transport connection, which is described in Chapter 12; in essence, a session is a mechanism for providing the reliable exchange of data between endpoint applications.

A transmission group forms a single logical link that has higher capacity than each of the individual links in the group. Load leveling is used so that all of the links in the group share the demand. A group provides enhanced availability: if one of the individual links fails, traffic continues to pass on the remaining links, with no disruption of the network.

Explicit routes must be set up by the network manager. Up to eight explicit routes can be defined between any pair of nodes in the network. The use of multiple explicit routes allows for the balancing of transmission workload: the traffic between any two nodes can be divided up among a number of different explicit routes. In addition, different explicit routes may offer different transmission characteristics, in terms of throughput, response time, and level of security.

Whereas explicit routes have to do with the internal operation of the network, virtual routes are visible to the end systems, and map into explicit routes in a predetermined way. Virtual routes are characterized in two ways. First, a virtual route is assigned one of three priority levels (high, medium, low). Second, a virtual route has one of 48 classes of service. The class of service corresponds to various requirements, such as level or response time, security, or reliability that is desired. When a virtual route is created and assigned to an explicit route, the network administrator associates a particular class of service with the virtual route, based on the administrator's judgment that that particular virtual route will provide that particular class of service.

Finally, a session provides the logical relationship between two user or network applications. A session, when it is created, is assigned to a particular virtual route and therefore to a particular explicit route. Multiple sessions may be assigned to a single virtual route. When initiating a session, a network user can request a particular class of service for that session. Examples of service class are interactive, remote job entry, file transfer, secure, and real time. These are user-visible labels. These are mapped by SNA into particular service class numbers, and each virtual route is associated with a specific service class number.

When a source user requests a session with a destination user, the local node will attempt to assign the session to a virtual route between the corresponding source and destination nodes. The node attempts to match the requested class of service with a virtual route of that service class. Opportunity for load leveling exists by considering the current load (number of sessions) on each eligible virtual route. If an outage occurs during a session, cutting an explicit route and therefore disabling all of the virtual routes on that explicit route, the opportunity exists to reestablish the session by assigning it to a different route within the class.

The distinction between virtual routes and explicit routes provides for flexibility as well as simplicity. Explicit routes are fixed allowing the use of simple, static routing tables. The ability to assign a virtual route to any available explicit route and to assign multiple virtual routes to a single explicit route provides the flexibility needed to react to changing network conditions and to specific user requirements.

Figure 8.17 is an example of a routing table in SNA. Included in the header of each SNA packet (referred to as a path information unit), is the destination address (referred to as the destination subarea) and an explicit route number. This information is used by each intermediate node to look up the address of the next node in the route and the transmission group to be used to get to that

Destination subarea	Explicit route number	Transmission group number	Next number
3	5	1	7
3	8	2	7
3	12	1	2
4	6	4	5
4	7	1	7
6	15	3	2
.	.	.	.
.	.	.	.
.	.	.	.

FIGURE 8.17. SNA routing table [MART87].

next node. Using the routing table in this example, if a packet were destined for node 3 using explicit route 8, it would be sent next to node 7 using transmission group 2. If transmission group 2 includes more than one physical link, the next available link will be used.

The packet (path information unit) header also includes the virtual route number and its priority. When several packets are waiting to be transmitted from one node to another, across the same transmission group, their respective priorities determine the order in which they are transmitted. Thus, even if two virtual routes share the same explicit route, preferential treatment can be given to the session on one of those routes based on priority. The virtual route is also the fundamental element of traffic control, as discussed in Section 8.5.

The SNA approach has some similarity with the TYMNET II approach. In both cases, different types of traffic can be provided with different routes based on link properties. In the case of TYMNET, the supervisor may construct a new route in response to an outage. In SNA, this task is performed by the source node.

8.5

TRAFFIC CONTROL

As with routing, the concept of traffic control in a packet-switched network is complex, and a wide variety of approaches have been proposed. Following the pattern of Section 8.4, we present the major elements of traffic control, provide a brief description of the most important strategies, and present examples. The interested reader may pursue the topic in several survey articles [GERL80, POUZ81, HSIE84c].

Two related topics should be mentioned. Traffic control, as we use it here, deals with the control of the number of packets entering and using the network. It is concerned with preventing the network from becoming a bottleneck and in using it efficiently. It does not directly serve the end user (i.e., the stations attached to the network). The end users are in need of end-to-end flow control; this is provided at a higher level, and is discussed in Part III. Second, note that many of the adaptive routing techniques attempt to balance traffic throughout the network. This is not traffic control per se and cannot substitute for traffic control. At most, adaptive routing can smooth out temporary problems and defer an overload condition [THAK86].

Table 8.7 summarizes the key elements or characteristics of traffic control in a packet-switched network. We discuss each of these categories, and then look at the approaches taken in our example networks.

Types of Traffic Control

Traffic control mechanisms are of three general types, each with different objectives; flow control, congestion control, and deadlock avoidance.

TABLE 8.7 Elements of Traffic Control Techniques

Type	Scope	Level
Flow control	Packet (datagram)	Hop
Congestion control	Stream (virtual circuit)	Network access
Deadlock avoidance		Entry-to-exit

Flow Control

Flow control is concerned with the regulation of the rate of data transmission between two points. The basic purpose of flow control is to enable the receiver to control the rate at which it receives data, so that it is not overwhelmed. Typically, flow control is exercised with some sort of sliding-window technique, such as is illustrated in Figure 5.7.

We have seen examples of flow control in Chapter 5 for the case of two devices that are directly connected. Flow control can also be used between devices that are indirectly connected, such as two nodes in a packet-switched network that are the endpoints of an internal virtual circuit. It can also be used on a logical connection between two host systems attached to a network. We will see several examples of this latter use in Part III (specifically, in transport protocols).

In considering the internal mechanisms of a packet-switching network, as we are in this chapter, flow control is not so much an end in itself as it is a tool for implementing other types of traffic control policies, as we shall see.

Congestion Control

A quite different type of traffic control is referred to as congestion control. The objective here is to maintain the number of packets within the network below the level at which performance falls off dramatically.

To understand the issue involved in congestion control, we need to look at some results from queueing theory. In essence, a packet-switching network is a network of queues. At each node, there is a queue of packets for each outgoing channel. If the rate at which packets arrive and queue up exceeds the rate at which packets can be transmitted, the queue size grows without bound and the delay experienced by a packet goes to infinity. Even if the packet arrival rate is less than the packet transmission rate, queue length will grow dramatically as the arrival rate approaches the transmission rate. We saw this kind of behavior in Figure 6.14. As a rule of thumb, when the line for which packets are queueing becomes more than 80% utilized, the queue length grows at an alarming rate [MART72].

Consider the queueing situation at a single packet-switching node, such as is illustrated in Figure 8.18. Any given node has a number of transmission links

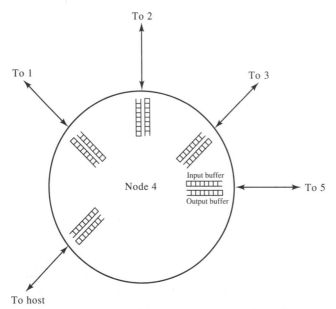

FIGURE 8.18.   Input and output queues at node 4 of Figure 8.8.

attached to it: one or more to other packet-switching nodes, and zero or more to host systems. On each link, packets arrive and depart. We can consider that there are two buffers at each link, one to accept arriving packets, and one to hold packets that are waiting to depart. In practice, there might be two fixed-size buffers associated with each link, or there might be a pool of memory available for all buffering activities. In the latter case, we can think of each link having two variable-size buffers associated with it, subject to the constraint that the sum of all buffer sizes is a constant.

In any case, as packets arrive, they are stored in the input buffer of the corresponding link. The node examines each incoming packet to make a routing decision, and then moves the packet to the appropriate output buffer. Packets queued up for output are transmitted as rapidly as possible; this is in effect statistical time-division multiplexing. Now, if packets arrive too fast for the node to process them (make routing decisions) or faster than packets can be cleared from the outgoing buffers, then eventually packets will arrive for which no memory is available.

When such a saturation point is reached, one of two general strategies can be adopted. The first such strategy is to simply discard any incoming packet for which there is no available buffer space. The alternative is for the node that is experiencing these problems to exercise some sort of flow control over its neighbors so that the traffic flow remains manageable. But, as Figure 8.19 illustrates, each of a nodes neighbors is also managing a number of queues. If node 6 restrains the flow of packets from node 5, this causes the output buffer

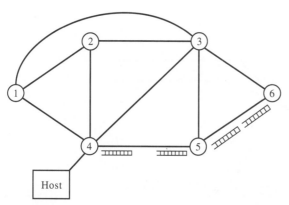

FIGURE 8.19. The interaction of queues in a packet-switching network.

in node 5 for the link to node 6 to fill up. Thus, congestion at one point in the network can quickly propagate throughout a region or all of the network. While flow control is indeed a powerful tool, we need to use it in such a way as to manage the traffic on the entire network.

Figure 8.20 shows the effect of congestion in general terms. Figure 8.20a plots the throughput of a network (number of packets delivered to destination stations) versus the offered load (number of packets transmitted by source stations). Both axes are normalized to the maximum capacity of the network, which can be expressed as the rate at which the network is theoretically capable of handling packets. In the ideal case, throughput and hence network utilization increases to accommodate an offered load up to the maximum capacity of the network. Utilization then remains at 100%. The ideal case, of course, requires that all stations somehow know the timing and rate of packets that can be presented to the network, which is impossible. If no congestion control is exercised, we have the curve labeled "uncontrolled." As the load increases, utilization increases for a while. Then as the queue lengths at the various nodes begin to grow, throughput actually drops. The reason for this is that the buffers at each node are of finite size. When a node's buffers are full, it must discard packets. Thus the source stations must retransmit the discarded packets in addition to the new packets. This only exacerbates the situation: As more and more packets are retransmitted, the load on the system grows, and more buffers become saturated. While the system is trying desperately to clear the backlog, stations are pumping old and new packets into the system. Even successfully delivered packets may be retransmitted because it takes so long to acknowledge them: The sender assumes that the packet did not go through. Under these circumstances, the effective capacity of the system is virtually zero.

It is clear that these catastrophic events must be avoided, which is the task of congestion control. The object of all congestion control techniques is to limit

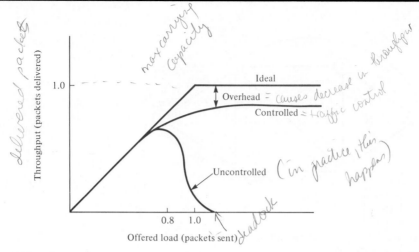

(a) Throughput

Handwritten annotations: delivered packets; max carrying capacity; Overhead = causes decrease in throughput; Controlled = traffic control; (in practice, this happens); deadlock

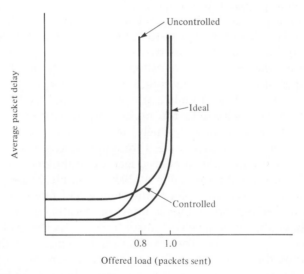

(b) Delay

FIGURE 8.20.　The effects of congestion.

queue lengths at the nodes so as to avoid throughput collapse. This control involves some unavoidable overhead. Thus a congestion control technique cannot perform as well as the theoretical ideal. However, a good congestion control strategy will avoid throughput collapse and maintain a throughput that differs from the ideal by an amount roughly equal to the overhead of the control.

Figure 8.20b points out that no matter what technique is used, the average delay experienced by packets grows without bound as the load approaches the capacity of the system. Note that initially the uncontrolled policy results in less delay than a controlled policy, because of its lack of overhead. However, the uncontrolled policy will saturate at lower load.

A number of control mechanisms for congestion control have been suggested and tried. [JAIN88] lists the following:

1. Send a control packet from a congested node to some or all source nodes. This *choke packet* will have the effect of stopping or slowing the rate of transmission from sources and hence limit the total number of packets in the network. This approach requires additional traffic on the network during a period of congestion.
2. Rely on routing information. Routing algorithms, such as ARPANET's provide link delay information to other nodes, which influences routing decisions. This information could also be used to influence the rate at which new packets are produced. Because these delays are being influenced by the routing decision, they may vary too rapidly to be used effectively for congestion control.
3. Make use of an end-to-end probe packet. Such a packet could be timestamped to measure the delay between two particular endpoints. This has the disadvantage of adding overhead to the network.
4. Allow packet switching nodes to add congestion information to packets as they go by. There are two possible approaches here. A node could add such information to packets going in the direction opposite of the congestion. This information quickly reaches the source node, which can reduce the flow of packets into the network. Alternatively, a node could add such information to packets going in the same direction as the congestion. The destination either asks the source to adjust the load or returns the signal back to the source in the packets (or acknowledgements) going in the reverse direction. A combination of these two approaches is used in SNA, as discussed below.

Deadlock Avoidance

A problem equally serious to that of congestion is deadlock, a condition in which a set of nodes are unable to forward packets because no buffers are available. This condition can occur even without a heavy load. *Deadlock avoidance* techniques are used to design the network in such a way that deadlock cannot occur. We briefly describe three types of deadlock to which a packet-switched network may be prone.

The simplest form of deadlock is *direct store-and-forward deadlock* and can occur if a node uses a common buffer pool from which buffers are assigned to packets on demand. Figure 8.21a shows a situation in which all of the buffer space in node *A* is occupied with packets destined for B. The reverse is true at

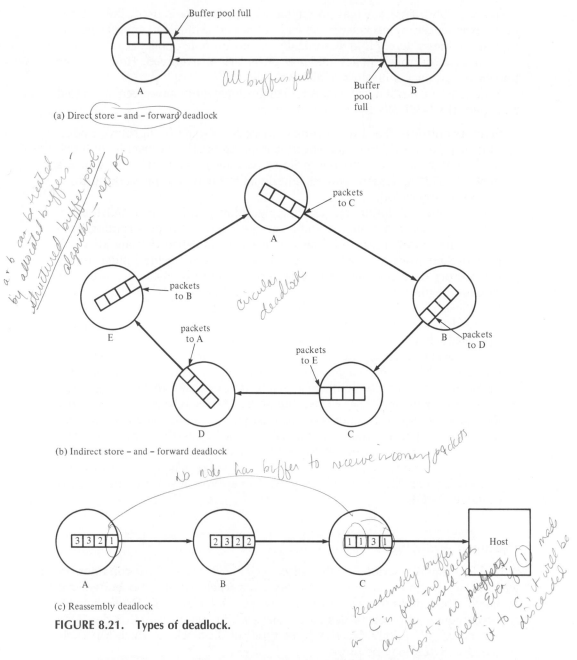

(a) Direct store – and – forward deadlock

[handwritten annotations: "All buffers full"]

[handwritten margin note: "a & b can be treated by allocated buffers / structured buffer pool algorithm - next pg"]

[handwritten: "circular deadlock"]

(b) Indirect store – and – forward deadlock

[handwritten annotation: "No node has buffer to receive incoming packets"]

(c) Reassembly deadlock

[handwritten annotations: "reassembly buffer at C is full - no packet can be passed to host & no buffers freed. Every 1 made it to C, it will be discarded"]

FIGURE 8.21. Types of deadlock.

B. Neither node can accept any more packets since their buffers are full. Thus neither node can transmit or receive on any link.

Direct store-and-forward deadlock can be avoided by not allowing all buffers to end up dedicated to a single link. Using separate fixed-size buffers, such as

FIGURE 8.22.   Structured buffer pool for deadlock avoidance.

illustrated in Figure 8.19, will achieve this prevention. Even if a common buffer pool is used, deadlock is avoided if no single link is allowed to acquire all of the buffer space.

A more subtle form of deadlock, *indirect store-and-forward deadlock*, is illustrated in Figure 8.21b. For each node, the queue to the adjacent node in one direction is full with packets destined for the next node beyond. One simple way to prevent this type of deadlock is to employ a structured buffer pool (Figure 8.22). The buffers are organized in a hierarchical fashion. The pool of memory at level 0 is unrestricted; any incoming packet can be stored there. From level 1 to level N (where N is the maximum number of hops on any network path), buffers are reserved in the following way: Buffers at level k are reserved for packets that have traveled at least k hops so far. Thus, in heavy load conditions, buffers fill up progressively from level 0 to level N. If all buffers up through level k are filled, arriving packets that have covered k or less hops are discarded. It can be shown [GOPA85] that this strategy eliminates direct and indirect store-and-forward deadlocks.

Finally, there is reassembly deadlock, which is peculiar to ARPANET and similar networks. Figure 8.21c shows a situation in which node C has three of four packets from message 1 and one from message 3. All of its buffers are full, so it can accept no more packets. Yet, because it has no complete message,

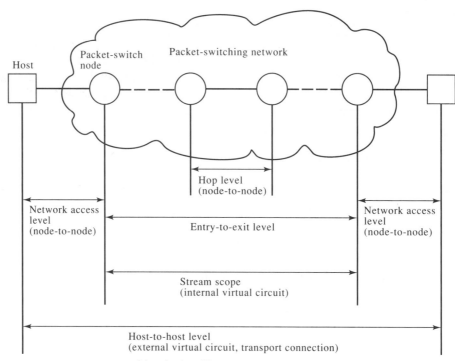

FIGURE 8.23.   Scope and level of traffic control.

it cannot reassemble packets and deliver them to the host. We will examine a solution to this problem in our discussion of ARPANET, below.

Scope and Level of Traffic Control

Traffic control techniques can be categorized by their scope of application. Packet techniques are concerned with controlling the flow of individual packets. This is all that is possible in a datagram network, and is sometimes used in virtual circuit networks. Stream techniques have to do with controlling the stream of packets flowing through a virtual circuit.

A third dimension of traffic control is the level, or extent, of application. This is illustrated in Figure 8.23. The hop level is concerned with controls exerted between adjacent nodes. These typically have to do with congestion control or deadlock avoidance. Network access control limits the number of new packets entering the network. These typically are used in congestion control. Finally, entry-to-exit controls are concerned with the flow of packets between two endpoints.

Table 8.8 summarizes the traffic control techniques of our example networks; these are described below. For more detail on traffic control techniques in general, the reader is referred to the references listed above.

TABLE 8.8 Traffic Control Techniques for Some Networks

Scope	Hop	Network Access	Entry-to-Exit
Packet	———	———	———
Stream	TYMNET (quota) SNA (pacing)	TYMNET (quota) ARPANET (RFNM)	ARPANET (window, reassembly buffer allocation) SNA (pacing)

Example Systems

ARPANET

For its virtual-circuit service, ARPANET provides two levels of traffic control [BBN81]. One is an entry-to-exit technique. Recall that a virtual circuit is used to send a sequence of numbered messages between hosts. ARPANET enforces a limit of eight messages in transit between any pair of hosts. This window mechanism with window size of eight is used to prevent any host from flooding the network.

Of more serious concern is a situation of reassembly deadlock, as described earlier. ARPANET's solution is to require that a source node reserve space for each message in advance with a "request for buffer space" packet. When a destination node receives this request, and has available eight buffers for the eight packets that the message might contain, it returns an "allocation" packet. After the entire message is received and reassembled, the receiving node sends back an acknowledgment known as *ready for next message* (RFNM). If the node has buffer space for an additional message, it piggybacks an allocation packet with the RFNM. Thus, during stream transmission, the source node need not send request packets. A time may come when the source has no messages to send but has collected one or more allocation permits. The source node is then obligated to send a "give back" packet to free up buffer space at the destination.

For datagram service, no positive flow control is enforced. Rather, a destination node will discard datagrams for which it has no free buffer space. It is up to the source station to determine from the destination station if the datagram did not get through and to resend it if necessary.

TYMNET

It is in the area of traffic control that the real strength of the TYMNET approach is seen. The TYMNET traffic control mechanism has the following positive features.

- It is simple.
- It requires very little overhead.
- Deadlocks cannot occur and therefore no mechanisms are needed to avoid it.

- Under conditions of heavy load, virtual circuits with low data rate require-ments get all the capacity they need; circuits with high data rate require-ments get at least some of what they need. Thus no active circuit is denied service.

Traffic control in TYMNET is on a virtual-circuit basis and includes both net-work access and hop-level mechanisms [RIND79b, TYME81]. The network ac-cess flow control is based on the establishment of the virtual circuit. When the supervisor sets up a virtual circuit, it assigns a quota of buffer space for each channel used along the circuit. The quota is based on throughput class. A node can only transmit data on a particular channel until the quota is exhausted. It must then wait for the next node to refresh its quota. Every half-second, each node sends a "backpressure vector" to each adjacent node. The vector contains one bit for each channel on the link. If a bit is set to 1, the sending node may reset the quota for the corresponding buffer. Otherwise, the sending node con-tinues to decrement the quota for a particular channel for each character that is transmitted. The result is a backpressure mechanism that eventually works its way back to the sending host.

For example, in Figure 8.5, suppose that the terminal connected to node 1000 is 10 characters per second (cps) and the host is connected to node 5 over a 30-cps virtual-circuit link. As characters arrive from the host they start to flow through the virtual circuit. The characters arrive at node 1000 at 30 cps but can leave at only 10 cps. After the number of characters buffered in node 1000 exceeds the quota of 30, the bit for channel 2 in the backpressure vector is set to zero. Thus node 1000 will have at most 60 characters buffered for this circuit. Now node 112 will go through the same process resulting in at most 60 char-acters in its buffer. Now the buffer in node 5 begins to grow and, when it reaches 30, the host will be requested to stop transmitting. This request may be in the form of an HDLC RNR (receiver not ready) packet. When the number of characters in node 1000's buffer drops below 30, data again begin to flow from 112 to 1000, from 5 to 112, and finally from the host.

Two refinements help to reduce congestion further. A situation may arise when a station wishes to abort a transmission; for example, a terminal user realizes that what is printing on the screen is of no interest and wishes to stop it with an abort command. To clear out the characters in transit, the host can send a *character gobbler*. This is a PACman-like device that ignores backpressure and goes through the circuit at full speed, gobbling all characters in front of it. A second refinement: When a virtual circuit is terminated, a *circuit zapper* is sent which not only gobbles characters, but releases the buffer pairs and clears the table entries to free up these resources for new circuits.

We have discussed how flow control is performed at the virtual circuit level using a backpressure mechanism. Since TYMNET uses a statistical TDM tech-nique at the hop level (Figure 8.6), there remains the question of how capacity is allocated to the active channels on a link. Frames are constructed using a round-robin technique among all active channels. A node sends frames as fast as possible over each link. Each frame contains one or more packets, each corresponding to a different channel. To construct a frame, a node cycles through all channels, picking up packets, until it has a total of 480 bits of data or until it has completed a full cycle. The frame is then sent and a new frame constructed. For each channel visited, the amount of data collected is

$$MIN(Q, D, F)$$

where

Q = quota for that channel
D = amount of data in the read buffer of that channel
F = amount of data space remaining in the frame

Thus, when bandwidth is oversubscribed, channels that only need little get what they want with little or no queueing delay, whereas channels that want all they can get share the remaining bandwidth fairly.

The TYMNET approach is a powerful one that possesses the positive characteristics listed above. The only disadvantage is the packets are torn down and reconstructed at each node, which increases processing requirements.

SNA

Traffic control in SNA [ATKI80], [GEOR82] is an interesting hybrid. The control is exercised on a virtual circuit (virtual route) basis. This control may be triggered by either the destination node, to avoid overflow, or by an intermediate node to reduce congestion. In the case of the endpoint, control is selectively exercised on a particular virtual circuit. In the case of an intermediate node, the node will exercise control on all virtual circuits that pass through a congested link.

The technique is known as pacing, and is a complex version of the sliding-window technique, operating at the virtual-route level. We provide a brief overview here. More detail can be found in [GURU87] and [MEIJ87].

The key elements of the SNA pacing algorithm are listed in Table 8.9. When a virtual route is established, a maximum (WS-MAX) and minimum (WS-MIN) window size are defined. WS-MIN is equal to the hop count of the explicit route selected for this virtual route. This number is based on flow control studies [DEAT79] indicating that this is the minimum window size that provides reasonable throughput. WS-MAX is set at three times WS-MIN. Each sender maintains a window size WS and a pacing count PC, which is the number of additional packets it may send; both are initialized to WS-MIN. Thus, when a virtual route is created, each side is automatically provided with a permission to send WS-MIN.

Each side is responsible for providing the other with permission to send blocks of packets equal to the current window size. The key to the pacing algorithm is the management of the size and rate of arrival of these window permissions.

TABLE 8.9   Elements for SNA Virtual Route Pacing Algorithm

Pacing count (PC)
  Number of additional packets that a node may send on a virtual route, before a virtual route pacing response is required.
Window size (WS)
  Amount by which pacing count is increased with each virtual route pacing response.
Minimum pacing window size (WS-MIN)
  Minimum value that WS may take on. WS is initialized to WS-MIN when a virtual route is created.
Maximum pacing window size (WS-MAX)
  Maximum value that WS may take on.
Virtual route pacing count indicator (VRPCI)
  Sent with last packet in window to indicate that an additional window is needed.
Virtual route pacing request (VRPRQ)
  Sent with first packet in window, to request an additional window.
Virtual route pacing response (VRPRS)
  Packet sent from destination back to source, allowing the source to increment its PC by WS.
Virtual route change window reply indicator (CWRI)
  Sent by destination back to source to cause WS to be decremented by one.
Virtual route reset window indicator (RWI)
  Sent by destination or intermediate system back to source to cause WS to be set to the WS-MIN.
Virtual route change window indicator (CWI)
  Sent by intermediate system to destination system to cause the destination system to issue a CWRI back to the source.

First consider the use of pacing for entry-to-exit flow control. The sending node sets a virtual route pacing request (VRPRQ) bit in the first packet of a window (i.e., when PC = WS). When the receiving node gets the request, and when it has buffer space, it returns a virtual route pacing response (VRPRS) packet, which allows the sender to increment PC by WS. Since the sender decrements PC by 1 with each packet sent, the maximum value of PC is 2WS-1. Thus the receiving node can exercise flow control by simply withholding the VRPRS. If a node gets to the point that PC = 1, then it sets the virtual route pacing count indicator (VRPCI) bit in the last packet that it can send. This is a signal to the other side to provide an additional window as soon as possible.

To improve throughput, the sending node is allowed to increment its window size by 1, up to WS-MAX, if its pacing count has gone to 0 by the time it receives VRPRS. The assumption is that the receiving node could handle packets at a faster rate. Unfortunately, the opposite may be true: The receiving node is withholding its VRPRS because it is getting too many packets! To account for this contingency, the receiver may set a change window reply indicator (CWRI) bit or a reset window indicator (RWI) bit on its next VRPRS. The former requests that the sender decrement WS by 1 (down to a minimum of WS-MIN). The latter requests that WS be reset to WS-MIN.

These techniques are also used to relieve congestion in the network. If a node suffers minor congestion on an outgoing link (i.e., queue length is beginning to grow), it sets the change window indicator (CWI) bit on all packets on all virtual routes going out that link. When the receiver gets a packet with CWI set, it sets CRWI on its next VRPRS. Thus, all sending nodes whose virtual routes go through the complaining node will decrement their window size and relieve the congestion. If severe congestion occurs (i.e., buffer saturation), the intermediate node takes more drastic action to relieve the problem. Instead of acting on packets going out the congested link, it sets the RWI bit on all packets coming in on that link. Thus all sending nodes will quickly reset their window sizes to their minimum value.

Each sending node dynamically adjusts its window size based on pacing controls set both in data packets and VRPRS packets. Figures 8.24 through

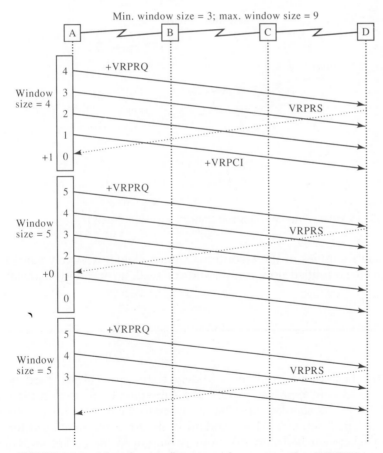

FIGURE 8.24.   Virtual route flow control: no congestion [MEIJ87].

FIGURE 8.25. Virtual route flow control: minor congestion [MEIJ87].

8.26 provide examples of the algorithm. Thus a single, relatively simple technique provides a unified flow control and congestion control mechanism.

8.6

X.25

Perhaps the best-known and most widely used protocol standard is X.25, which was originally approved in 1976 and subsequently revised in 1980, 1984, 1988, and 1992. The standard specifies an interface between a host system and a packet-switched network. This standard is almost universally used for interfacing to packet-switched networks and is employed for packet switching in ISDN. In this section, a brief overview of the standard is provided.

FIGURE 8.26. Virtual route flow control: severe congestion [MEIJ87].

The standard specifically calls out three layers of functionality (Figure 8.27):

- Physical layer.
- Link layer.
- Packet layer.

These three layers correspond to the lowest three layers of the OSI model (see Figure 1.10). The physical layer deals with the physical interface between an attached station (computer, terminal) and the link that attaches that station to the packet-switching node. It makes use of the physical-layer specification in a standard known as X.21, but in many cases other standards, such as EIA-232, are substituted. The link layer provides for the reliable transfer of data across the physical link by transmitting the data as a sequence of frames. The link layer standard is referred to as LAP-B (Link Access Protocol—Balanced).

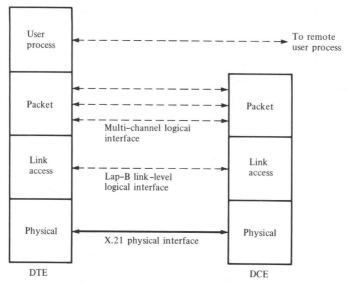

FIGURE 8.27.   X.25 interface.

LAP-B is a subset of HDLC, described in Chapter 5. The packet layer provides an external virtual-circuit service and is described in this section.

Figure 8.28 illustrates the relationship between the levels of X.25. User data are passed down to X.25 level 3, which appends control information as a header, creating a *packet*. This control information is used in the operation of the protocol, as we shall see. The entire X.25 packet is then passed down to the LAP-B entity, which appends control information at the front and back of the packet, forming a LAP-B *frame*. Again, the control information in the frame is needed for the operation of the LAP-B protocol.

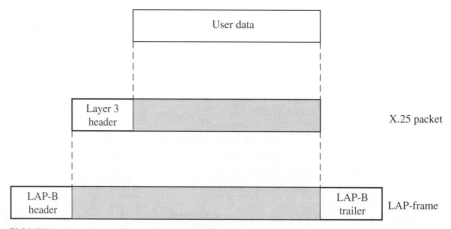

FIGURE 8.28.   User data and X.25 protocol control information.

Virtual-Circuit Service

With the X.25 packet layer, data are transmitted in packets over external virtual circuits. The virtual-circuit service of X.25 provides for two types of virtual circuit: virtual call and permanent virtual circuit. A *virtual call* is a dynamically established virtual circuit using a call setup and call clearing procedure, explained below. A *permanent virtual circuit* is a fixed, network-assigned virtual circuit. Data transfer occurs as with virtual calls, but no call setup or clearing is required.

Figure 8.29 shows a typical sequence of events in a virtual call. The left-hand part of the figure shows the packets exchanged between user machine A and the packet-switching node to which is attaches; the right-hand part shows the packets exchanged between user machine B and its node. The routing of packets inside the network is not visible to the user. The standard refers to user machines as data terminal equipment (DTE) and to a packet-switching node to which a DTE is attached as data circuit-terminating equipment (DCE).

The sequence of events is as follows:

1. A requests a virtual circuit to B by sending a Call Request packet to A's DCE. The packet includes the source and destination addresses, as well as the virtual circuit number to be used for this new virtual circuit. Future incoming and outgoing transfers will be identified by this virtual-circuit number.
2. The network routes this call request to B's DCE.
3. B's DCE receives the call request and sends an Incoming Call packet to B. This packet has the same format as the Call Request packet but a different virtual-circuit number, selected by B's DCE from the set of locally unused numbers.
4. B indicates acceptance of the call by sending a Call Accepted packet specifying the same virtual-circuit number as that of the Incoming Call packet.
5. A receives a Call Connected packet with the same virtual-circuit number as that of the Call Request packet.
6. A and B send data and control packets to each other using their respective virtual-circuit numbers.
7. A (or B) sends a Clear Request packet to terminate the virtual circuit and receives a Clear Confirmation packet.
8. B (or A) receives a Clear indication packet and transmits a Clear Confirmation packet.

Packet Format

A variety of packet types are used (Table 8.10), all using the same basic format, with variations (Figure 8.30). For user data, the data are broken up into blocks of some maximum size, and a 24-bit or 32-bit header is appended to each block to form a **data packet.** The header includes a 12-bit virtual-circuit number (expressed as a 4-bit group number and an 8-bit channel number). The P(S) and

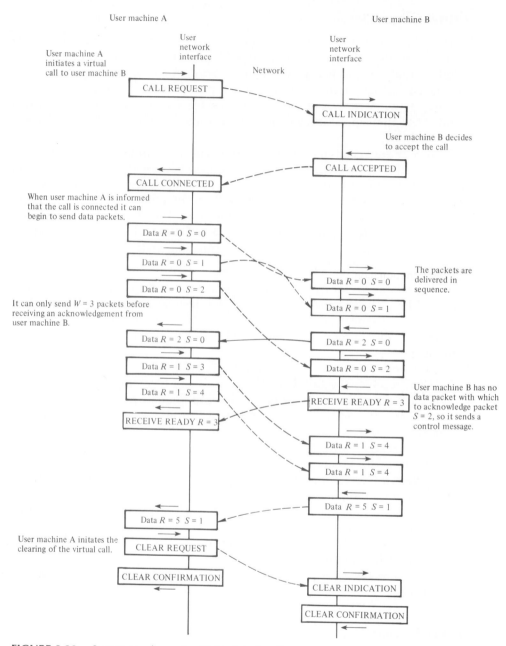

FIGURE 8.29.   Sequence of events—X.25 virtual call.

P(R) fields support the functions of flow control and error control on a virtual circuit basis, as explained below. The M and D bits are described below. The Q bit is not defined in the standard, but allows the user to distinguish two types of data.

TABLE 8.10 X.25 Packet Types

Packet Type		Service	
From DCE to DTE	From DTE to DCE	VC	PVC
Call Setup and Clearing			
Incoming call	Call request	X	
Call connected	Call accepted	X	
Clear indication	Clear request	X	
DCE clear confirmation	DTE clear confirmation	X	
Data and Interrupt			
DCE data	DTE data	X	X
DCE interrupt	DTE interrupt	X	X
DCE interrupt confirmation	DTE interrupt confirmation	X	X
Flow Control and Reset			
DCE RR	DTE RR	X	X
DCE RNR	DTE RNR	X	X
	DTE REJ	X	X
Reset indication	Reset request	X	X
DCE reset confirmation	DTE reset confirmation	X	X
Restart			
Restart indication	Restart request	X	X
DCE restart confirmation	DTE restart confirmation	X	X
Diagnostic			
Diagnostic		X	X
Registration			
Registration confirmation	Registration request	X	X

(a) Data packet with 3-bit sequence numbers

(b) Data packet with 7-bit sequence numbers

(c) Control packet

(d) RR, RNR, and REJ packets with 3-bit sequence numbers

(e) RR, RNR, and REJ, packets with 7-bit sequence numbers

FIGURE 8.30. X.25 packet formats.

331

In addition to transmitting user data, X.25 must transmit control information related to the establishment, maintenance, and termination of virtual circuits. Control information is transmitted in a **control packet.** Each control packet includes the virtual-circuit number; the packet type, which identifies the particular control function; and additional control information related to that function. For example, a Call Request packet includes the following additional fields:

- Calling DTE address length (4 bits): Length of the corresponding address field in 4-bit units.
- Called DTE address length (4 bits): Length of the corresponding address field in 4-bit units.
- DTE addresses (variable): The calling and called DTE addresses.
- Facility length: Length of the facility field in octets.
- Facilities: A sequence of facility specifications. Each specification consists of an 8-bit facility code and zero or more parameter codes. An example of a facility is reverse charging.

Table 8.10 lists all of the X.25 control packets. Most of these have already been discussed. A brief description of the remainder follows.

A DTE may send an Interrupt packet that bypasses the flow control procedures for data packets. The interrupt packet is to be delivered to the destination DTE by the network at a higher priority than data packets in transit. An example of the use of this capability is the transmission of a terminal break character.

The Reset packets provide a facility for recovering from an error by reinitializing a virtual circuit. This means that the sequence numbers on both ends are set to 0. Any data or interrupt packets in transit are lost. A reset can be triggered by a number of error conditions, including loss of a packet, sequence number error, congestion, or loss of the network's internal logical connection. In the latter case, the two DCEs must rebuild the internal logical connection to support the still-existing X.25 DTE–DTE virtual circuit.

A more serious error condition is dealt with by a Restart, which terminates all active virtual calls. An example of a condition warranting restart is temporary loss of access to the network.

The Diagnostic packet provides a means to signal certain error conditions that do not warrant reinitialization. The Registration packets are used to invoke and confirm X.25 facilities.

Multiplexing

Perhaps the most important service provided by X.25 is multiplexing. A DTE is allowed to establish up to 4095 simultaneous virtual circuits with other DTEs over a single physical DTE–DCE link. The DTE can internally assign these circuits in any way it pleases. Individual virtual circuits could correspond to applications, processes, or terminals, for example. The DTE–DCE link provides full-duplex multiplexing. That is, at any time, a packet associated with a given virtual circuit can be transmitted in either direction.

To sort out which packets belong to which virtual circuits, each packet contains a 12-bit virtual-circuit number (expressed as a 4-bit logical group number plus an 8-bit logical channel number). The assignment of virtual-circuit numbers follows the convention depicted in Figure 8.31. Number zero is always

Reserved for net control messages

X-25 is full duplex

pVC

minimize Collision between diff types

Virtual Calls

LIC = Lowest incoming channel
HIC = Highest incoming channel
LTC = Lowest two-way channel
HTC = Highest two-way channel
LOC = Lowest outgoing channel
HOC = Highest outgoing channel

Virtual circuit
number = logical group
number & logical channel
number

FIGURE 8.31. Virtual-circuit number assignment.

reserved for diagnostic packets common to all virtual circuits. Then, contiguous ranges of numbers are allocated for four categories of virtual circuits. Permanent virtual circuits are assigned numbers beginning with 1. The next category is one-way incoming virtual calls. This means that only incoming calls from the network can be assigned these numbers; the virtual circuit, however, is two-way (full duplex). When a call request comes in, the DCE selects an unused number from this category.

One-way outgoing calls are those initiated by the DTE. In this case, the DTE selects an unused number from among those allocated for these calls. This separation of categories is intended to avoid the simultaneous selection of the same number for two different virtual circuits by the DTE and DCE.

The two-way virtual call category provides an overflow for allocation shared by DTE and DCE. This allows for peak differences in traffic flow.

Flow and Error Control

Flow control and error control at the X.25 packet layer are virtually identical in format and procedure to flow control used for HDLC, as described in Chapter 5. A sliding-window protocol is used. Each data packet includes a send sequence number, $P(S)$, and a receive sequence number, $P(R)$. As a default, 3-bit sequence numbers are used. Optionally, a DTE may request, via the user facility mechanism, the use of extended 7-bit sequence numbers. As Figure 8.30 indicates, for 3-bit sequence numbers, the third and fourth bits of all data and control packets are 01; for 7-bit sequence numbers, the bits are 10.

$P(S)$ is assigned by the DTE on outgoing packets on a virtual-circuit basis; that is, the $P(S)$ of each new outgoing data packet on a virtual circuit is one more than that of the preceding packet, modulo 8 or modulo 128. $P(R)$ contains the number of the next packet expected from the other side of a virtual circuit; this provides for piggybacked acknowledgment. If one side has no data to send, it may acknowledge incoming packets with the Receive Ready (RR) and Receive Not Ready (RNR) control packets, with the same meaning as for HDLC. The default window size is 2, but it may be set as high as 7 for 3-bit sequence numbers and as high as 127 for 7-bit sequence numbers.

Acknowledgment (in the form of the $P(R)$ field in the data, RR, or RNR packet), and hence flow control, may have either local or end-to-end significance, based on the setting of the D bit. When $D = 0$, (the usual case), acknowledgment is exercised between the DTE and the network. This is used by the local DCE and/or the network to acknowledge receipt of packets and control the flow from the DTE into the network. When $D = 1$, acknowledgements come from the remote DTE.

The basic form of **error control** is go-back-N ARQ. Negative acknowledgment is in the form of a Reject (REJ) control packet. If a node receives a negative acknowledgment, it will retransmit the specified packet and all subsequent packets.

Packet Sequences

X.25 provides the capability to identify a contiguous sequence of data packets, which is called a **complete packet sequence.** This feature has several uses. One important use is by internetworking protocols (described in Chapter 12), to allow longer blocks of data to be sent across a network with a smaller packet size restriction without losing the integrity of the block.

To specify this mechanism, X.25 defines two types of packets: A packets and B packets. An **A packet** is one in which the M bit is set to 1, the D bit is set to 0, and the packet is full (equal to the maximum allowable packet length). A **B packet** is any packet that is not an A packet. A complete packet sequence consists of zero or more A packets followed by a B packet. The network may combine this sequence to make one larger packet. The network may also segment a B packet into smaller packets to produce a complete packet sequence.

The way in which the B packet is handled depends on the setting of the M and D bits. If D = 1, and end-to-end acknowledgment is sent by the receiving DTE to the sending DTE. This is in effect an acknowledgment of the entire complete packet sequence. If M = 1, there are additional complete packet sequences to follow. This enables the formation of subsequences as part of a larger sequence, so that end-to-end acknowledgment can occur before the end of the larger sequence.

Figure 8.32 shows examples of these concepts. It is the responsibility of the DCEs to reconcile the changes in sequence numbering that segmentation and reassembly cause.

EXAMPLE PACKET SEQUENCES

Original seq.   Combined seq.

Pkt type	M	D	Pkt type	M	D
A	1	0			
A	1	0	A	1	0
A	1	0			
A	1	0	A	1	0
A	1	0			
B	0	1	B	0	1

Segmented seq

| B | 0 | 0 | A | 1 | 0 |
| | | | B | 0 | 0 |

EXAMPLE PACKET SEQUENCE
WITH INTERMEDIATE E-E ACK

Pkt type	M	D	
A	1	0	
A	1	0	
A	1	0	*
B	1	1	
A	1	0	
A	1	0	*
B	1	1	
A	1	0	
A	1	0	
A	1	0	*
B	0	1	

end of sequence

* Groups of packets that can be combined

FIGURE 8.32.   X.25 packet sequences.

8.7

RECOMMENDED READING

The literature on packet switching is enormous. Only a few of the worth-while references are mentioned here. A number of survey articles were written in the early days of packet switching; among the most interesting are [KIMB75], [GREE77], and [KLEI78]. Surveys of specific networks include [WOOD85], [ROBE78], and [QUAR86]. Books with good treatments of this subject include [BERT92], [SPRA91], and [STUC85]. There is also a large body of literature on performance; good summaries are to be found in [KLEI76] and [SCHW77]. [BELL86] and [HSIE84 a and b] compare the routing algorithms of ARPANET, TYMENET, and SNA.

There is a large literature on X.25; [DHAS86] and [SIRB85] are recommended.

8.8

PROBLEMS

8.1 Explain the flaw in the following logic:
   Packet switching requires control and address bits to be added to each packet. This causes considerable overhead in packet switching. In circuit switching, a transparent circuit is established. No extra bits are needed.

   a. Therefore, there is no overhead in circuit switching.
   b. Since there is no overhead in circuit switching, line utilization must be more efficient than in packet switching.

8.2 Define the following parameters for a switching network:

   - N: number of hops between two given stations.
   - L: message length in bits.
   - B: data rate, in bps, on all links.
   - P: packet size in bits.
   - H: overhead (header) bits per packet.
   - S: call setup time (circuit-switched or virtual circuit) in seconds.
   - D: propagation delay per hop, in seconds.

   a. For $N = 4$, $L = 3200$, $B = 9600$, $P = 1024$, $H = 16$, $S = 0.2$, $D = 0.001$, compute the end-to-end delay for circuit switching, virtual-circuit packet switching, and datagram packet switching. Assume that there is no node delay.
   b. Derive general expressions for the three techniques, taken two at a time (six expressions in all) showing the conditions under which delays are equal.

8.3 What value of P, as a function of N, B, and H, results in minimum end-to-end delay in a datagram network? Assume that L is much larger than P, and that D is zero.

8.4 Consider a packet-switched network of N nodes, connected by the following topologies:

   a. Star: one central node with no attached station; all other nodes attach to the central node.

   b. Loop: each node connects to two other nodes to form a closed loop.

   c. Fully connected: each node is directly connected to all other nodes.

   For each case, give the average number of hops between stations.

8.5 Consider a binary tree topology for a packet-switched network. The root node connects to two other nodes. All intermediate nodes connect to one node in the direction toward the root, and two in the direction away from the root. At the bottom are nodes with just one link back toward the root. If there are $2^N - 1$ nodes, derive an expression for the mean number of hops per packet for large N, assuming that trips between all node pairs are equally likely.

8.6 Dijkstra's algorithm can be expressed in the following program:

```
for n: = 1 to N do
   begin
       D[n]: = ∞; final[n]: = false; {all nodes are temporarily labeled with ∞}
       pred[n]: = -1
   end;
D[s]: = 0; final[s]: = true;    {node s is permanently labeled with 0}
recent: = s;      {the most recent node to be permanently labeled is s}
path: = true;
{initialization over }

1for n: = 1 to N do      {find new label}
   if (d[recent, n] <∞) AND (NOT final[n]) then
   {for every immediate successor of recent that is not permanently labeled, do }
       begin {update temporary labels}
           newlabel: = D[recent] + d[recent,n];
           if newlabel <D[n] then
               begin  D[n]: = newlabel;   pred[n]: = recent   end
               {relabel n if there is a shorter path via node recent and make
                   recent the predecessor of n on the shortest path from s}
       end;
       temp: = ∞;
       for x: = 1 to N do   {find node with smallest temporary label}
           if (NOT final[x]) AND (D[x] < temp) then
               begin y: = x; temp: = D[x]   end;
   if temp < ∞ then   {there is a path}
       begin final[y]: = true; recent: = y end
       {y, the next closest node to s gets permanently labeled}
```

In this program, each node is assigned a temporary label initially. As a final path to a node is determined, it is assigned a permanent label equal to the cost of the path from s. Write a similar program for the Bellman–Ford algorithm. Hint: The Bellman–Ford algorithm is often called a *label-correcting method*, in contrast to Dijkstra's *label-setting method*.

8.7 In the discussion of Dijkstra's algorithm in Section 8.4, it is asserted that at each iteration, a new node is added to M and that the least-cost path for that new node passes only through nodes already in M. Demonstrate that this is true. Hint: Begin at the beginning. Show that the first node added to M must have a direct link to the source node. Then show that the second node to M must either have a direct link to the source node or a direct link to the first node added to M, and so on. Remember that all link costs are assumed nonnegative.

8.8 In the discussion of the Bellman–Ford algorithm in Section 8.4, it is asserted that at the iteration for which $h = K$, if any path of length $K + 1$ is defined, the first K hops of that path form a path defined in the previous iteration. Demonstrate that this is true.

8.9 In step 3 of Dijkstra's algorithm, the least-cost path values are only updated for nodes not yet in M. Is it not possible that a shorter path could be found to a node already in M? If so, demonstrate by example. If not, provide reasoning as to why not.

8.10 Using Dijkstra's algorithm, generate a least-cost route to all other nodes for nodes 2 through 6 of Figure 8.8. Display the results as in Table 8.4a. Do the same for the Bellman–Ford algorithm.

8.11 Apply Dijkstra's routing algorithm to the networks in Figure 8.33. Provide a table similar to Table 8.4 and a figure similar to Figure 8.9.

8.12 Repeat Problem 8.11 using the Bellman–Ford algorithm.

8.13 Will Dijkstra's algorithm and the Bellman–Ford algorithm always yield the same solutions? Why or why not?

8.14 Both Dijkstra's algorithm and the Bellman–Ford algorithm find the least-cost paths from one node to all other nodes. The Floyd–Warshall algorithm finds the least-cost paths between all pairs of nodes together. Define:

N = set of nodes in the network

d_{ij} = link cost from node i to node j; $d_{ii} = 0$, and $d_{ij} = \infty$ if the nodes are not directly connected

$D_{ij}^{(n)}$ = cost of the least-cost path from node i to node j with the constraint that only nodes $1, 2, \ldots, n$ can be used as intermediate nodes on paths

The algorithm has the following steps:
1. Initialize:

$$D_{ij}^{(0)} = d_{ij}, \text{ for all } i, j, i \neq j$$

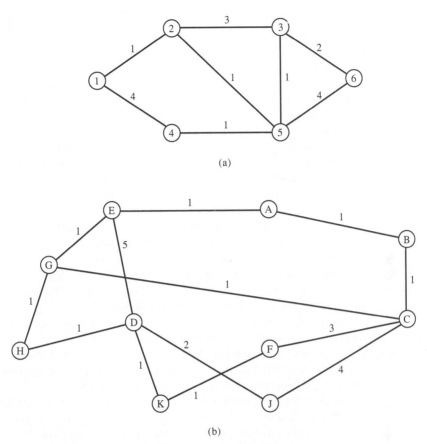

FIGURE 8.33. Packet-switching networks with link costs.

2. For $n = 0, 1, \ldots, N - 1$

$$D_{ij}^{(n+1)} = \min [D_{ij}^{(n)}, D_{i(n+1)}^{(n)} + D_{(n+1)j}^{(n)}] \text{ for all } i \neq j$$

Explain the algorithm in words. Use induction to demonstrate that the algorithm works.

8.15 In Figure 8.8, node 1 sends a packet to node 6 using flooding. Counting the transmission of one packet across one link as a load of one, what is the total load generated if:

a. Each node discards duplicate incoming packets?

b. A hop count field is used and is initially set to 3? 4

8.16 It was shown that flooding can be used to determine the minimum-hop route. Can it be used to determine the minimum delay route?

8.17 With random routing, only one copy of the packet is in existence at a time. Nevertheless, it would be wise to utilize a hop count field. Why?

8.18 Another adaptive routing scheme is known as *backward learning*. As a packet is routed through the network, it carries not only the destination address, but the source address plus a running hop count that is incremented for each hop. Each node builds a routing table that gives the next node and hop count for each destination. How is the packet information used to build the table? What are the advantages and disadvantages of this technique?

8.19 Build a centralized routing directory for the networks of Problem 8.11.

8.20 Consider a system using flooding with a hop counter. Suppose that the hop counter is originally set to the "diameter" of the network. When the hop count reaches zero, the packet is discarded except at its destination. Does this always ensure that a packet will reach its destination if there exists at least one operable path? Why or why not?

8.21 Prove that the deadlock avoidance strategy illustrated in Figure 8.22 works. Hint: Show by induction, starting with $k = N$, that at each node the buffers of class k cannot fill up permanently.

8.22 Suggest an alternative solution to reassembly deadlock.

8.23 What effect does the ARPANET limit of eight messages between hosts have on channel capacity and buffer capacity?

8.24 Suggest a technique for avoiding indirect store-and-forward deadlock.

8.25 Explain why deadlock cannot occur in TYMNET.

8.26 A proposed traffic control measure is known as *isarithmic* control. In this method, the total number of packets in transit is fixed by inserting a fixed number of permits into the network. These permits circulate through the network at random. Whenever a node wants to send a packet just given to it by a station, it must first capture and destroy a permit. When the packet reaches the destination node, that node reissues the permit.
  a. What type of traffic control is this?
  b. List three potential problems with this technique.

8.27 What is the maximum number of packets that may be in transit at any one time on an ARPANET virtual circuit?

8.28 Consider the following network of nodes of Figure 8.34: C is the capacity of a link in packets per second. Node A presents a constant load of 0.8 packet per second destined for A'. Node B presents a load λ destined for B'. Node S has a common pool of buffers that it uses for traffic to both A' and B'. When the buffer is full, packets are discarded, and are later retransmitted by the host. Plot the total throughput (i.e., the sum of $A - A'$ and $B - B'$ delivered traffic) as a function of λ. What fraction of the throughput is $A - A'$ traffic for $\lambda > 1$?

8.29 Assuming no malfunction in any of the stations or nodes of a network, is it possible for a packet to be delivered to the wrong destination?

8.30 Flow-control mechanisms are used at both levels 2 and 3 of X.25. Are both necessary or is this redundant? Explain.

8.31 There is no error-detection mechanism (frame check sequence) in X.25. Isn't this needed to assure that all of the packets are delivered properly?

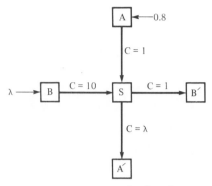

FIGURE 8.34. Network of nodes.

8.32 When an X.25 DTE and the DCE to which it attaches both decide to put a call through at the same time, a call collision occurs and the incoming call is canceled. When both sides try to clear the same virtual circuit simultaneously, the clear collision is resolved without canceling either request; the virtual circuit in question is cleared. Do you think that simultaneous resets are handled like call collisions or clear collisions? Why?

8.33 In X.25, why is the virtual-circuit number used by one station of two communicating stations different from the virtual-circuit number used by the other station? After all, it is the same full-duplex virtual circuit.

CHAPTER 9

Local and Metropolitan Area Networks

In this chapter, we examine local area networks (LANs) and metropolitan area networks (MANs). These networks share the characteristic of being packet broadcasting networks. With a broadcast communications network, each station is attached to a transmission medium shared by other stations. In its simplest form, a transmission from any one station is broadcast to and received by all other stations. As with packet-switched networks, transmission on a packet broadcasting network is in the form of packets. Table 9.1 provides useful definitions of LANs and MANs, taken from one of the IEEE 802 standards documents.

The nature of a LAN or MAN is determined primarily by three factors: transmission medium, topology, and medium access control protocol. The bulk of this chapter is devoted to these topics, together with a look at LAN/MAN performance. Throughout, reference is made to standards developed for LANs and MANs; these are described briefly in the appendix to this chapter.

9.1

LAN/MAN TECHNOLOGY

The principal technology alternatives that determine the nature of a LAN or MAN are the topology and transmission medium of the network. Together, they in large measure determine the type of data that may be transmitted, the speed and efficiency of communications, and even the kinds of applications that a network may support.

This section surveys the topologies and transmission media that, within the state of the art, are appropriate for LANs and MANs. The discussion in this

TABLE 9.1   Definitions of LANs and MANs [IEEE90a]

The LANs described herein are distinguished from other types of data networks in that they are optimized for a moderate-size geographic area such as a single office building, a warehouse, or a campus. The IEEE 802 LAN is a shared medium peer-to-peer communications network that broadcasts information for all stations to receive. As a consequence, it does not inherently provide privacy. The LAN enables stations to communicate directly using a common physical medium on a point-to-point basis without any intermediate switching node being required. There is always need for an access sublayer in order to arbitrate the access to the shared medium. The network is generally owned, used, and operated by a single organization. This is in contrast to Wide Area Networks (WANs) that interconnect communication facilities in different parts of a country or are used as a public utility. These LANs are also different from networks, such as backplane buses, that are optimized for the interconnection of devices on a desk top or components within a single piece of equipment.

A MAN is optimized for a larger geographical area than a LAN, ranging from several blocks of buildings to entire cities. As with local networks, MANs can also depend on communications channels of moderate-to-high data rates. Error rates and delay may be slightly higher than might be obtained on a LAN. A MAN might be owned and operated by a single organization but usually will be used by many individuals and organizations. MANs might also be owned and operated as public utilities. They will often provide means for internetworking of local networks. Although not a requirement for all LANs, the capability to perform local networking of integrated voice and data (IVD) devices is considered an optional function for a LAN. Likewise, such capabilities in a network covering a metropolitan area are optional functions of a MAN.

section is organized around the common topologies used for LANs and MANs: ring, bus, tree, and star (Figure 9.1).

Ring Topology

In the ring topology, the network consists of a set of repeaters joined by point-to-point links in a closed loop. Hence each repeater participates in two links on the ring. The repeater is a comparatively simple device, capable of receiving data on one link and transmitting it, bit by bit, on the other link as fast as it is received, with no buffering at the repeater. The links are unidirectional; that is, data are transmitted in one direction only, and all oriented in same way. Thus data circulate around the ring in one direction (clockwise or counter-clockwise).

Each station attaches to the network at a repeater. Data are transmitted in packets inserted onto the ring by the stations. The packet contains source and destination address fields as well as other control information and user data. As a packet circulates, the destination station copies the data into a local buffer. Typically, the packet continues to circulate until it returns to the source station, where it is absorbed, removing it from the ring.

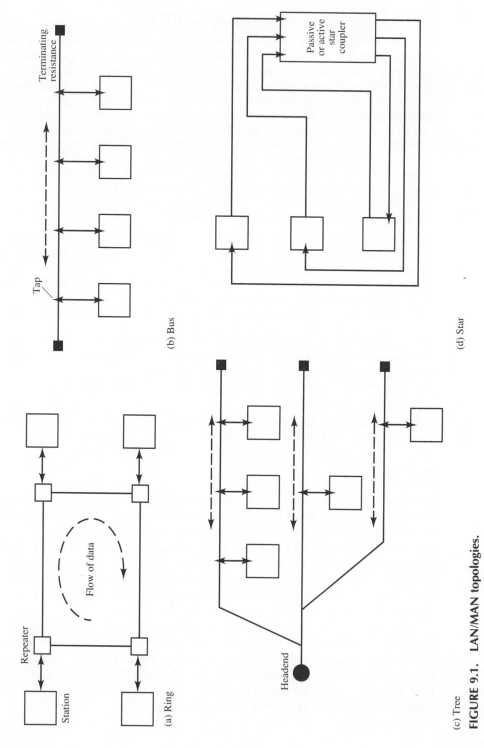

FIGURE 9.1. LAN/MAN topologies.

(a) Ring

(b) Bus

(c) Tree

(d) Star

Terminating resistance

Tap

Repeater

Station

Flow of data

Headend

Passive or active star coupler

Since multiple devices share the ring, some form of medium access logic is needed to control the order and timing of packet transmissions. This topic is explored later in this chapter.

Because the ring is constructed as a series of point-to-point links, almost any transmission medium can be used. Twisted pair, because of its low cost, is common. Coaxial cable provides greater capacity. Optical fiber is used to achieve very high data transfer rates. Table 9.2 summarizes representative parameters for transmission media for commercially-available ring local area networks.

Bus and Tree Topologies

Both bus and tree topologies are characterized by the use of a multipoint medium. With the bus topology, all stations attach, through appropriate interfacing hardware, directly to a linear transmission medium, or bus. A transmission from any station propagates the length of the medium in both directions and can be received by all other stations.

The tree topology is a generalization of the bus topology. The transmission medium is a branching cable with no closed loops. The tree layout begins at a point known as the headend. One or more cables start at the headend, and each of these may have branches. The branches in turn may have additional branches to allow quite complex layouts. Again, a transmission from any station propagates throughout the medium, can be received by all other stations, and is absorbed at the endpoints.

As with the ring, transmission is in the form of packets containing addresses and user data. Each station monitors the medium and copies packets addressed to itself. Because all stations share a common transmission link, only one station can successfully transmit at a time, and some form of medium access control technique is needed to regulate access.

One of the most common communications transmission media, and one that is certainly applicable to bus/tree local networks, is twisted pair wiring. Although typically used for low speed transmission, data rates of up to a few Mbps can be achieved. Twisted pair is relatively low cost and is typically preinstalled in office buildings. It is the most cost-effective choice for single-building, low-traffic requirements.

TABLE 9.2   Transmission Media for Local Networks: Ring

Transmission Medium	Data Rate (Mbps)	Distance Between Repeaters (km)	Number of Repeaters
Unshielded twisted pair	4	0.1	72
Shielded twisted pair	16	0.3	250
Baseband coaxial cable	16	1.0	250
Optical fiber	100	2.0	240

Higher performance requirements can be met by coaxial cable, which provides higher throughput, can support a larger number of devices, and can span greater distances than twisted pair. Two transmission methods, baseband and broadband, can be employed on a coax cable; these are explained below. Baseband systems are typically from 1 to 10 Mbps and are generally limited to a single building. However, by limiting the distance covered and the number of devices attached, data rates of 50 Mbps can be achieved. Broadband systems are also typically in the range of 1 to 10 Mbps for a single data path, with 20 Mbps representing a practical upper limit. However, as explained below, broadband can support multiple data paths in contrast to the single data path of baseband. Broadband systems use CATV (Community Antenna Television) cable, which is suitable for outdoor as well as indoor environments. Hence interbuilding and even intracity networks can be supported.

Optical fiber has even greater capacity than coaxial cable and is a promising candidate for future bus MAN installations. It has been little used so far due to cost and technical limitations. As the cost of optical fiber transmission components drops, this configuration will become practical.

Table 9.3 summarizes representative parameters for transmission media for commercially available bus/tree LANs and MANs. Comparing with Table 9.2, one can see that the performance of a given medium is lower for multipoint versus point-to-point configurations. This is because the presence of multiple taps on the multipoint configurations results in higher signal attenuation.

Star Topology

In the star topology, each station is directly connected to a common central switch. One example of the use of this topology is the case in which the central switch uses circuit-switching technology. The digital data switch and digital private branch exchange are examples of this approach.

The star topology is also employed for implementing a packet-broadcasting LAN or MAN. In this case, each station attaches to a central node, referred to as the star coupler, via two point-to-point links, one for transmission in each direction. A transmission from any one station enters the central node and is retransmitted on all of the outgoing links. Thus, although the arrangement is physically a star, it is logically a bus: a transmission from any station is received by all other stations, and only one station at a time may successfully

TABLE 9.3   Transmission Media for Local Networks: Bus/Tree

Transmission Medium	Data Rate (Mbps)	Range (km)	Number of Taps
Twisted pair	1–10	<2	10's
Baseband coaxial cable	10; 50 with limitations	<3	100's
Broadband coaxial cable	500; 20 per channel	<30	1000's
Optical fiber	45	<150	500's

TABLE 9.4 Transmission Media for Local Networks: Passive or Active Star

Transmission Medium	Data Rate (Mbps)	Distance from Station to Central Switch (km)	Number of Stations
Unshielded twisted pair	1–10	0.5 (1 Mbps)– 0.1 (10 Mbps)	10's
Baseband coaxial cable	70	<1	10's
Optical fiber	10 –20	<1	10's

transmit. Thus, the medium access control techniques used for the packet star topology are the same as for bus and tree.

There are two ways of implementing the star coupler. In the case of the passive star coupler, there is an electromagnetic linkage in the coupler so that any incoming transmission is physically passed to all of the outgoing links. In the case of optical fiber, this coupling is achieved by fusing together a number of fibers, so that incoming light is automatically split among all of the outgoing fibers. In the case of coaxial cable or twisted pair, transformer coupling is used to split the incoming signal.

The other type of star coupler is the active star coupler. In this case, there is digital logic in the central node that acts as a repeater. As bits arrive on any input line, they are automatically regenerated and repeated on all outgoing lines. If multiple input signals arrive simultaneously, a collision signal is transmitted on all outgoing lines.

Any form of guided transmission medium can be used with either the passive or active star coupler. In terms of commercially-available products, the passive star coupler has been used with both baseband coaxial cable and optical fiber products. In both cases, high data rates have been achieved with limited distance and a limited number of devices. Active star couplers have been used in unshielded twisted-pair implementations. Table 9.4 summarizes representative parameters.

9.2

BUS/TREE AND STAR TOPOLOGIES USING METALLIC MEDIA

Characteristics of Bus/Tree LANs and MANs

The bus/tree topology is a multipoint configuration. That is, there are more than two devices connected to the medium and capable of transmitting on the medium. Because multiple devices share a single data path, only one may transmit at a time. A station usually transmits data in the form of a packet containing the address of the destination. The packet propagates throughout the medium and is received by all other stations. The addressed station copies the packet as it goes by.

Two transmission techniques are in use for bus/tree LANs and MANs: baseband and broadband. Baseband, using digital signaling, can be employed on

TABLE 9.5 Bus/Tree Transmission Techniques

Baseband	Broadband
Digital signaling	Analog signaling (requires RF modem)
Entire bandwidth consumed by signal—no FDM	FDM possible—multiple data channels, video, audio
Bidirectional	Unidirectional
Bus topology	Bus or tree topology
Distance: up to a few kilometers	Distance: up to tens of kilometers

twisted pair or coaxial cable. Broadband, using analog signaling in the RF range, employs coaxial cable. Some of the differences are highlighted in Table 9.5, and the following two subsections explore the two methods in some detail. There is also a variant known as carrierband that has the signaling characteristics of broadband but some of the restrictions of baseband; this is also covered below.

The multipoint nature of the bus/tree topology gives rise to several rather stiff problems. First is the problem of determining which station on the medium may transmit at any point in time. With point-to-point links (only two stations on the medium), this is a fairly simple task. If the line is full-duplex, both stations may transmit at the same time. If the line is half-duplex, then a rather simple mechanism is needed to ensure that the two stations take turns. Historically, the most common shared access scheme has been the multidrop line, in which access is determined by polling from a controlling station (discussed in Chapter 5). The controlling station may send data to any other station, or it may issue a poll to a specific station, asking for an immediate response. This method, however, negates some of the advantages of a distributed system and also is awkward for communication between two non-controller stations. A variety of distributed strategies, referred to as medium access control protocols, have now been developed for bus and tree topologies. These are discussed in Section 9.5.

A second problem has to do with signal balancing. When two devices exchange data over a link, the signal strength of the transmitter must be adjusted to be within certain limits. The signal must be strong enough so that, after attenuation across the medium, it meets the receiver's minimum signal strength requirements. It must also be strong enough to maintain an adequate signal to noise ratio. On the other hand, the signal must not be so strong as to overload the circuitry of the transmitter, which creates harmonics and other spurious signals. Though easily done for a point-to-point link, signal balancing is no easy task for a multipoint line. If any device can transmit to any other device, the signal balancing must be performed for all permutations of stations taken two at a time. For n stations that works out to $n \times (n - 1)$ permutations. So, for a 200-station network (not a particularly large system), 39,800 signal strength constraints must be satisfied simultaneously. With interdevice distances ranging from tens to thousands of meters, this is an impossible task for any but small networks. In systems that use radio-frequency (RF) signals, the problem is compounded because of the possibility of RF signal interference across frequencies. The solution is to divide the medium into segments within which pairwise balancing is possible, using amplifiers or repeaters between segments.

Baseband Systems

A baseband LAN or MAN is defined as one that uses digital signaling. Digital signals are inserted on the line as voltage pulses. The entire frequency spectrum of the medium is used to form the signal; hence frequency-division multiplexing (FDM) cannot be used. Transmission is bidirectional. That is, a signal inserted at any point on the medium propagates in both directions to the ends, where it is absorbed (Figure 9.2a). The digital signaling requires a bus topology; unlike analog signals, digital signals can not easily be propagated through the splitters and joiners required for a tree topology. Baseband systems can extend only a limited distance, about a kilometer at most. This is because the attenuation of the signal, which is most pronounced at higher frequencies, causes a blurring of the pulses and a weakening of the signal to the extent that communication over larger distances is impractical.

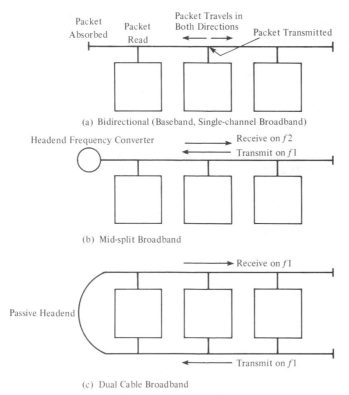

(a) Bidirectional (Baseband, Single-channel Broadband)

(b) Mid-split Broadband

(c) Dual Cable Broadband

FIGURE 9.2.   Baseband and broadband transmission techniques.

Baseband Coax

The most popular form of baseband bus LAN uses coaxial cable. Unless otherwise indicated, this discussion is based on the IEEE standard [IEEE90b] and the almost-identical Ethernet system [METC76], [SHOC82].

Most baseband coax systems use a special 50-ohm cable rather than the standard CATV 75-ohm cable. This is because, for digital signals, the 50-ohm cable suffers less intense reflections from the insertion capacitance of the taps, and provides better immunity against low-frequency electromagnetic noise.

As with any transmission system, there are engineering trade-offs involving data rate, cable length, number of taps, and the electrical characteristics of the transmit and receive components for a baseband coaxial system. For example, the lower the data rate, the longer the cable can be. That latter statement is true for the following reason: when a signal propagates along a transmission medium, the integrity of the signal suffers due to attenuation, noise, and other impairments. The longer the propagation, the greater the effect, increasing the probability of error. However, at a lower data rate, the individual pulses of a digital signal last longer and can be recovered in the presence of impairments more easily than higher-rate, shorter pulses.

With the above in mind, we give one example that illustrates some of the trade-offs. The Ethernet specification and the original IEEE 802.3 standard specified the use of 50-ohm cable with a 0.4-inch diameter, and a data rate of 10 Mbps. With these parameters, the maximum length of the cable is set at 500 meters. Stations attach to the cable by means of a tap, with the distance between any two taps being a multiple of 2.5 m; this is to ensure that reflections from adjacent taps do not add in phase [YEN83]. A maximum of 100 taps is allowed. In IEEE jargon, this system is referred to as 10BASE5 (10 Mbps, baseband, 500-m segment length). The first two digits give the data rate in megabits per second; the four letters are an abbreviation for the medium (baseband); and the final digit is the maximum cable length in hundreds of meters.

To provide a lower-cost system for personal computer local networks, IEEE later added a 10BASE2 specification. Table 9.6 compares this scheme, dubbed Cheapernet, with the 10BASE5 specification. The key difference is the use of a

TABLE 9.6   IEEE Specification for 10-Mbps Baseband Coaxial Bus Local Area Networks

Parameter	10BASE5	10BASE2
Data rate	10 Mbps	10 Mbps
Maximum segment length	500 m	200 m
Network span	2500 m	1000 m
Nodes per segment	100	30
Node spacing	2.5 m	0.5 m
Cable diameter	0.4 in	0.25 in

thinner (0.25 in) cable, which is employed in products such as public address systems. The thinner cable is more flexible; thus it is easier to bend around corners and bring to a workstation rather than installing the cable in the wall and having to provide a drop cable with transmitters and receivers between the main cable and the workstation. The cable is easier to install and requires cheaper electronics than the thicker cable. On the other hand, the thinner cable suffers greater attenuation and lower noise resistance than the thicker cable. Thus it supports fewer taps over a shorter distance.

To extend the length of the network, a repeater may be used. It consists, in essence, of two transceivers joined together and connected to two different segments of coax cable. The repeater passes digital signals in both directions between the two segments, amplifying and regenerating the signals as they pass through. A repeater is transparent to the rest of the system; since it does no buffering, it in no sense isolates one segment from another. So, for example, if two stations on different segments attempt to transmit at the same time, their packets will interfere with each other (collide). To avoid multipath interference, only one path of segments and repeaters is allowed between any two stations. A maximum of four repeaters is allowed in the path between any two stations, extending the effective cable length to 2.5 km. Figure 9.3 is an example of a baseband system with three segments and two repeaters.

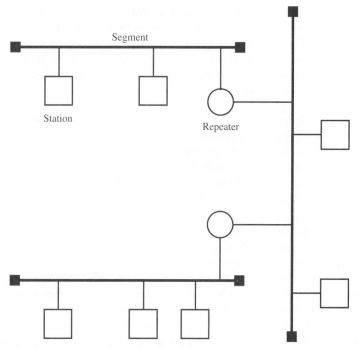

FIGURE 9.3.   Baseband configuration.

Unshielded Twisted Pair Baseband

In recent years, there has been increasing interest in the use of twisted pair as a transmission medium for LANs. From the earliest days of commercial LAN availability, twisted-pair bus LANs have been popular. However, such LANs suffer in comparison with a coaxial cable LAN. First of all, the apparent cost advantage of twisted pair is not as great as it might seem, when a linear bus layout is used. True, twisted-pair cable is less expensive than coaxial cable. On the other hand, much of the cost of LAN wiring is the labor cost of installing the cable, which is no greater for coaxial cable than for twisted pair. Second, coaxial cable provides superior signal quality, and therefore can support more devices over longer distances at higher data rates than twisted pair.

The renewed interest in twisted pair, at least in the context of LANs, is in the use of unshielded twisted pair in a star topology arrangement. The reason for the interest is that unshielded twisted pair is simply telephone wire, and virtually all office buildings are equipped with spare twisted pairs running from wiring closets to each office. This yields several benefits when deploying a LAN:

1. There is essentially no installation cost with unshielded twisted pair, since the wire is already there. Coaxial cable has to be pulled. In older buildings, this may be difficult since existing conduits may be crowded.
2. In most office building, it is impossible to anticipate all the locations where network access will be needed. Since it is extravagantly expensive to run coaxial cable to every office, a coaxial-cable based LAN will typically only cover a portion of a building. If equipment subsequently has to be moved to an office not covered by the LAN, a significant expense is involved in extending the LAN coverage. With telephone wire, this problem does not arise, since all offices are covered.

The most popular approach to the use of unshielded twisted pair for a LAN is therefore a star-topology approach. The products on the market use a scheme suggested by Figure 9.4, in which central element of the star is an active element, referred to as the **hub.** Each station is connected to the hub by two twisted pairs (transmit and receive). The hub acts as a repeater: When a single station transmits, the hub repeats the signal, on the outgoing line to each station.

Note that although this scheme is physically a star, it is logically a bus: A transmission from any one station is received by all other stations, and if two stations transmit at the same time there will be a collision.

Multiple levels of hubs can be cascaded in a hierarchical configuration. Figure 9.5 illustrates a two-level configuration. There is one **header hub** (HHUB) and one or more **intermediate hubs** (IHUB). Each hub may have a mixture of stations and other hubs attached to it from below. This layout fits well with building wiring practices. Typically, there is a wiring closet on each floor of an

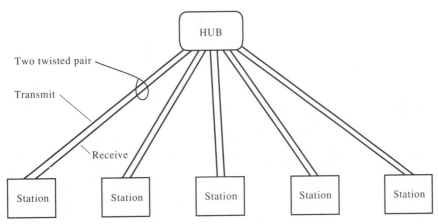

FIGURE 9.4. Twisted-pair, star-wiring, logical-bus arrangement.

office building, and a hub can be placed in each one. Each hub could service the stations on its floor.

Figure 9.6 shows an abstract representation of the intermediate and header hubs. The header hub performs all the functions described previously for a single-hub configuration. In the case of an intermediate hub, any incoming signal from below is repeated upward to the next higher level. Any signal from above is repeated on all lower-level outgoing lines. Thus, the logical bus char-

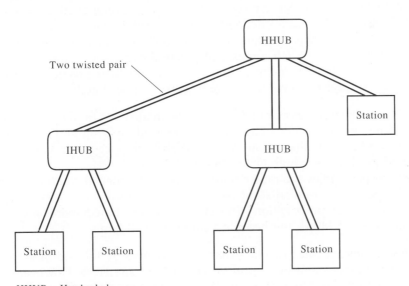

HHUB = Header hub
IHUB = Intermediate hub

FIGURE 9.5. Two-level hierarchy.

(a) Intermediate hub   (b) Header hub

FIGURE 9.6.   Intermediate and header hubs.

acteristic is retained: A transmission from any one station is received by all other stations, and if two stations transmit at the same time there will be a collision.

The initial version of the above scheme employed a data rate of 1 Mbps, and was dubbed StarLAN. More recently, products operating at 10 Mbps have begun to appear. These are intended to be compatible with the 10-Mbps baseband coaxial cable bus systems, requiring only a change of transceiver. Although there is now a fair amount of practical experience with these higher-speed systems, there remains a controversy about their practicality [CLAI88, ORLO88]. Several reasons for this controversy can be stated:

- Existing telephone wire in buildings can be inadequate for data transmission. Problems include twisted pair that isn't twisted, splicing and other connections, and other faults that are not noticeable for voice transmission but that would produce very high error rates at 10 Mbps.
- Twisted-pair cables are rather tightly packed together in conduits. The mutual capacitance from adjacent pairs adversely affects attenuation, crosstalk, and velocity of propagation. The effects on data transmission may not be noticeable at 1 Mbps, but become a problem at 10 Mbps.

These problems can to some extent be overcome by the use of signal processing techniques and by careful design of the transceiver. However, just as we saw with the 10-Mbps coaxial cable bus, there are trade-offs to be made. In this case, IEEE recommends a maximum distance between station and hub of 250 meters at 1 Mbps and 100 meters at 10 Mbps.

Broadband Systems

FDM Broadband LAN/MAN

In the context of local networks, broadband refers to the use of analog signaling. Thus frequency-division multiplexing (FDM) is possible: The frequency spectrum of the cable can be divided into channels or sections of bandwidth. Separate channels can support data traffic, TV, or radio signals. Broadband components allow splitting and joining operations; hence both bus and tree topologies are possible. Much greater distances—tens of kilometers—are possible with broadband compared to baseband. This is because the analog signals that carry the digital data can propagate greater distances before the noise and attenuation damage the data.

As with baseband, stations attach to the cable by means of a tap. Unlike baseband, however, broadband is inherently a unidirectional medium; signals inserted onto the medium can propagate in only one direction. The primary reason for this is that it is infeasible to build amplifiers that will pass signals of one frequency in both directions. This unidirectional property means that only those stations "downstream" from a transmitting station can receive its signals. How, then, can full connectivity be achieved?

Clearly, two data paths are needed. These paths are joined at a point on the network known as the headend. For bus topology, the headend is simply one end of the bus. For tree topology, the headend is the root of the branching tree. All stations transmit on one path toward the headend (inbound). Signals received at the headend are then propagated along a second data path away from the headend (outbound). All stations receive on the outbound path.

Physically, two different configurations are used to implement the inbound, outbound paths (Figure 9.2b and c). On a dual-cable configuration, the inbound and outbound paths are separate cables, with the headend simply a passive connector between the two. Stations send and receive on the same frequency.

By contrast, on the split configuration, the inbound and outbound paths are different frequency bands on the same cable. Bidirectional amplifiers pass lower frequencies inbound, and higher frequencies outbound. The headend contains a device, known as a frequency converter, for translating inbound frequencies to outbound frequencies. The frequency converter at the headend can be either an analog or digital device. The analog device simply translates signals to a new frequency and retransmits them. The digital device recovers the digital data from the headend and then retransmits the cleaned-up data on the new frequency.

Split systems are categorized by the frequency allocation of the two paths, as shown in Table 9.7. Subsplit, commonly used by the cable television industry was designed for metropolitan area television distribution, with limited subscriber-to-central office communication. It provides the easiest way to upgrade existing one-way cable systems to two-way operation. Subsplit has lim-

TABLE 9.7   Common Broadband Cable Frequency Splits

Format	Inbound Frequency Band	Outbound Frequency Band	Maximum Two-way Bandwidth
Subsplit	5 to 30 MHz	54 to 400 MHz	25 MHz
Midsplit	5 to 116 MHz	168 to 400 MHz	111 MHz
Highsplit	5 to 174 MHz	232 to 400 MHz	168 MHz
Dual Cable	40 to 400 MHz	40 to 400 MHz	360 MHz

ited usefulness for local area networking because a bandwidth of only 25 MHz is available for two-way communication. Midsplit is more suitable for LANs, since it provides a more equitable distribution of bandwidth. However, midsplit was developed at a time when the practical spectrum of a cable-TV cable was 300 MHz, whereas a spectrum of 400 to 450 MHz is now available. Accordingly, a highsplit specification has been developed to provide greater two-way bandwidth for a split cable system.

The differences between split and dual are minor. The midsplit system is useful when a single cable plant is already installed in a building. Also, the installed system is about 10–15% cheaper than a dual cable system [HOPK79]. On the other hand, a dual cable has over twice the capacity of midsplit. It does not require the frequency translator at the headend, which may need to be redundant for reliability.

Broadband systems use standard, off-the-shelf CATV components, including 75-ohm coaxial cable. All endpoints are terminated with a 75-ohm terminator to absorb signals. Broadband is suitable for tens of kilometers' radius from the headend and hundreds or even thousands of devices. For all but very short distances, amplifiers are required.

The broadband LAN can be used to carry multiple channels, some used for analog signals, such as video and voice, and some for digital. Digital channels can generally carry a data rate of somewhere between 0.25 and 1 bps/Hz.

Carrierband

An abridged form of broadband, known as single-channel broadband or carrierband, is one in which the entire spectrum of the cable is devoted to a single transmission path for analog signals. In general, a single-channel broadband LAN has the following characteristics [KLEI86, RELC87]. Bidirectional transmission, using a bus topology, is employed. Hence there can be no amplifiers, and there is no need for a headend. Some form of FSK is used, generally at a low frequency (a few megahertz). This is an advantage since attenuation is less at lower frequencies.

Because the cable is dedicated to a single task, it is not necessary to take care that the modem output is confined to a narrow bandwidth. Energy can spread over the cable's spectrum. As a result, the electronics are simple and inexpensive. This scheme would appear to give comparable performance, at a comparable price, to baseband.

Baseband Versus Broadband

Baseband has the advantage over broadband of simplicity, and, in principle, lower cost. The layout of a baseband cable plant is simple: There are just five rules for trunk layout in the Ethernet specification. A relatively inexperienced local network engineer should be able to cope.

The potential disadvantages of baseband include the limitations in capacity and distance—only disadvantages if your requirements exceed those limitations. Another concern has to do with grounding. Because dc signal components are on the cable, it can be grounded in only one place. Care must be taken to avoid potential shock hazards and antenna effects.

Broadband's strength is its tremendous capacity; it can carry a wide variety of traffic on a number of channels. With the use of active amplifiers, broadband can achieve very wide area coverage. Also, the system is based on a mature CATV technology. Components are reliable and readily available.

Broadband systems are more complex than baseband to install and maintain. The layout design must include cable type selection, and placement and setting of all amplifiers and taps. Maintenance involves periodic testing and alignment of all network parameters. These are jobs for experienced RF engineers. Finally, the average propagation delay between stations for broadband is twice that for a comparable baseband system. This reduces the efficiency and performance of the system.

9.3

OPTICAL FIBER BUS

In recent years, there has been increasing research and development activity in the area of the optical fiber bus topology. Several approaches can be taken in the design of a fiber bus topology LAN or MAN [MUKH91]. The differences have to do with the nature of the taps into the bus and the detailed topology.

Optical Fiber Taps

With an optical fiber bus, either an active or passive tap can be used. In the case of an active tap (Figure 9.7a), the following steps occur:

1. Optical signal energy enters the tap from the bus.
2. Clocking information is recovered from the signal and the signal is converted to an electrical signal.

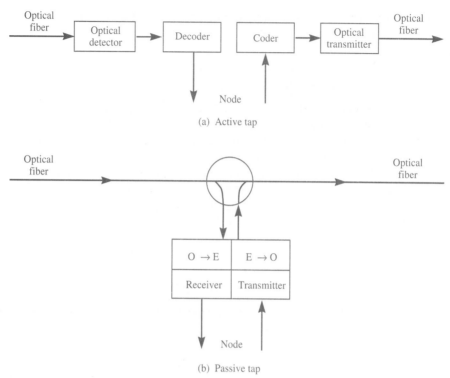

FIGURE 9.7.   Optical fiber bus taps.

3. The converted signal is presented to the node and perhaps modified by the latter.
4. The optical output (a light beam) is modulated according to the electrical signal and launched into the bus.

In effect, the bus consists of a chain of point-to-point links, and each node acts as a repeater. Each tap actually consists of two of these active couplers and requires two fibers. This is because of the inherently unidirectional nature of the device of Figure 9.7a.

In the case of a passive tap (Figure 9.7b), the tap extracts a portion of the optical energy from the bus for reception and it injects optical energy directly into the medium for transmission. Thus, there is a single run of cable rather than a chain of point-to-point links. This passive approach is equivalent to the type of taps typically used for twisted pair and coaxial cable. Each tap must connect to the bus twice, once for transmit and once for receive.

The electronic complexity and interface cost are drawbacks for the implementation of the active tap. Also, each tap will add some increment of delay, just as in the case of a ring. For passive taps, the lossy nature of pure optical taps limits the number of devices and the length of the medium. However, the performance of such taps has improved sufficiently in recent years to make fiber bus networks practical [ZANG91].

Optical Fiber Bus Configurations

A variety of configurations for the optical fiber bus have been proposed. All of these fall into two categories: those that use a single bus and those that use two buses.

Figure 9.8a shows a typical single-bus configuration, referred to as a loop bus. The operation of this bus is essentially the same as that of the dual-bus broadband coaxial system described earlier. Each station transmits on the bus in the direction toward the headend and receives on the bus in the direction away from the headend. In addition to the two connections shown, some medium-access control protocols require that each station have an additional *sense tap* on the inbound (toward the headend) portion of the bus. The sense

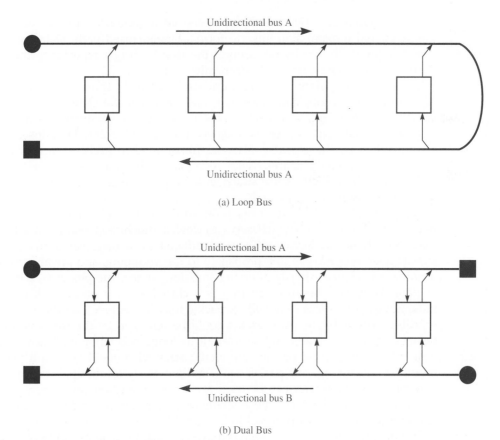

(a) Loop Bus

(b) Dual Bus

FIGURE 9.8.   Optical fiber bus configurations.

tap is able to sense the presence or absence of light on the fiber but is not able to recover data.

Figure 9.8b shows the two-bus configuration. Each station attaches to both buses and has both transmit and receive taps on both buses. On each bus, a station may transmit only to those stations downstream from it. By using both buses, a station may transmit to and receive from all other stations. A given node, however, must know which bus to use to transmit to another node; if not, all data would have to be sent out on both buses. This is the configuration used in the IEEE 802.6 MAN and is described later in this chapter.

9.4

THE RING TOPOLOGY

Characteristics of Ring LANs

A ring consists of a number of repeaters, each connected to two others by unidirectional transmission links to form a single closed path. Data are transferred sequentially, bit by bit, around the ring from one repeater to the next. Each repeater regenerates and retransmits each bit.

For a ring to operate as a communication network, three functions are required: data insertion, data reception, and data removal. These functions are provided by the repeaters. Each repeater, in addition to serving as an active element on the ring, serves as a device attachment point. Data insertion is accomplished by the repeater. Data are transmitted in packets, each of which contains a destination address field. As a packet circulates past a repeater, the address field is copied. If the attached station recognizes the address, the remainder of the packet is copied.

Repeaters perform the data insertion and reception functions in a manner not unlike that of taps, which serve as device attachment points on a bus or tree. Data removal, however, is more difficult on a ring. For a bus or tree, signals inserted onto the line propagate to the endpoints and are absorbed by terminators. Hence, shortly after transmission ceases, the bus or tree is clean of data. However, because the ring is a closed loop, a packet will circulate indefinitely unless it is removed. A packet may by removed by the addressed repeater. Alternatively, each packet could be removed by the transmitting repeater after it has made one trip around the loop. This latter approach is more desirable because (1) it permits automatic acknowledgment and (2) it permits multicast addressing: one packet sent simultaneously to multiple stations.

A variety of strategies can be used for determining how and when packets are inserted onto the ring. These strategies are, in effect, medium access control protocols, and are discussed in Section 9.5.

The repeater, then, can be seen to have two main purposes: (1) to contribute to the proper functioning of the ring by passing on all the data that come its

way, and (2) to provide an access point for attached stations to send and receive data. Corresponding to these two purposes are two states (Figure 9.9):
the listen state and the transmit state.

In the listen state, each received bit is retransmitted with a small delay, required to allow the repeater to perform required functions. Ideally, the delay
should be on the order of one bit time (the time it takes for a repeater to
transmit one complete bit onto the outgoing line). These functions are:

- Scan passing bit stream for pertinent patterns. Chief among these is the address or addresses of attached stations. Another pattern, used in the token
  control strategy explained later, indicates permission to transmit. Note that
  to perform the scanning function, the repeater must have some knowledge
  of packet format.
- Copy each incoming bit and send it to the attached station, while continuing
  to retransmit each bit. This will be done for each bit of each packet addressed
  to this station.
- Modify a bit as it passes by. In certain control strategies, bits may be modified to, for example, indicate that the packet has been copied. This would
  serve as an acknowledgment.

FIGURE 9.9. Ring repeater states.

When a repeater's station has data to send and when the repeater, based on the control strategy, has permission to send, the repeater enters the transmit state. In this state, the repeater receives bits from the station and retransmits them on its outgoing link. During the period of transmission, bits may appear on the incoming ring link. There are two possibilities, and they are treated differently:

- The bits could be from the same packet that the repeater is still in the process of sending. This will occur if the "bit length" of the ring is shorter than the packet. In this case, the repeater passes the bits back to the station, which can check them as a form of acknowledgment.
- For some control strategies, more than one packet could be on the ring at the same time. If the repeater, while transmitting, receives bits from a packet it did not originate, it must buffer them to be transmitted later.

These two states, listen and transmit, are sufficient for proper ring operation. A third state, the bypass state, is also useful. In this state, a bypass relay can be activated, so that signals propagate past the repeater with no delay other than medium propagation. The bypass relay affords two benefits: (1) it provides a partial solution to the reliability problem, discussed later, and (2) it improves performance by eliminating repeater delay for those stations that are not active on the network.

Twisted pair, baseband coax, and fiber optic cable can all be used to provide the repeater-to-repeater links. Broadband coax, however, could not easily be used. Each repeater would have to be capable, asynchronously, of receiving and transmitting data on multiple channels.

Timing Jitter

On a ring transmission medium, some form of clocking is included with the signal, as for example with the use of Differential Manchester encoding (Section 3.1). As data circulate around the ring, each repeater receives the data, and recovers the clocking for two purposes: first, to know when to sample the incoming signal to recover the bits of data, and second, to use the clocking for transmitting the signal to the next repeater. This clock recovery will deviate in a random fashion from the mid-bit transitions of the received signal for several reasons, including noise during transmission and imperfections in the receiver circuitry. The predominant reason, however, is delay distortion (described in Section 2.3). The deviation of clock recovery is known as timing jitter.

As each repeater receives incoming data, it issues a clean signal with no distortion. However, the timing error is not eliminated. Thus the digital pulse width will expand and contract in a random fashion as the signal travels around the ring, and the timing jitter accumulates. The cumulative effect of the jitter is to cause the bit latency or "bit length" of the ring to vary. However, unless the latency of the ring remains constant, bits will be dropped (not retransmitted) as the latency of the ring decreases, or added as the latency increases.

This timing jitter places a limitation on the number of repeaters in a ring. Although this limitation cannot be entirely overcome, several measures can be taken to improve matters [KELL83], [HONG86]. In essence, two approaches are used in combination. First, each repeater can include a phase-lock loop. This is a device that uses feedback to minimize the deviation from one bit time to the next. Second, a buffer can be used at one or more repeaters. The buffer is initialized to hold a certain number of bits, and expands and contracts to keep the bit length of the ring constant. The combination of phase-locked loops and a buffer significantly increase maximum feasible ring size. The values in Table 9.2 assume the use of these measures.

Potential Ring Problems

There are a number of potential problems with the ring topology. A break in any link or the failure of a repeater disables the entire network. Installation of a new repeater to support new devices requires the identification of two nearby, topologically adjacent repeaters. Timing jitter must be dealt with. Finally, because the ring is closed, a means is needed to remove circulating packets, with backup techniques to guard against error.

The last problem is a protocol issue, discussed later. The remaining problems can be handled by a refinement of the ring topology, discussed next.

The Star-Ring Architecture

Two observations can be made about the basic ring architecture described above. First, there is a practical limit to the number of repeaters on a ring. This limit is suggested by the jitter, reliability, and maintenance problems just cited and by the accumulating delay of a large number of repeaters. A limit of a few hundred repeaters seems reasonable. Second, the functioning of the ring does not depend on the actual routing of the cables that link the repeaters.

These observations have led to the development of a refined ring architecture, the star-ring, which overcomes some of the problems of the ring and allows the construction of larger local networks.

As a first step, consider the rearrangement of a ring into a star. This is achieved by having the interrepeater links all thread through a single site. This *ring wiring concentrator* has a number of advantages. Because there is centralized access to the signal on every link, it is a simple matter to isolate a fault. A message can be launched into the ring and tracked to see how far it gets without mishap. A faulty segment can be disconnected and repaired at a later time. New repeaters can easily be added to the ring: simply run two cables from the new repeater to the site of ring wiring concentration and splice into the ring.

The bypass relay associated with each repeater can be moved into the ring wiring concentrator. The relay can automatically bypass its repeater and two links for any malfunction. A nice effect of this feature is that the transmission path from one working repeater to the next is approximately constant; thus the range of signal levels to which the transmission system must automatically adapt is much smaller.

The ring wiring concentrator permits rapid recovery from a cable or repeater failure. Nevertheless, a single failure could, at least temporarily, disable the entire network. Furthermore, throughput and jitter considerations still place a practical upper limit on the number of stations in a ring, since each repeater adds an increment of delay. Finally, in a spread-out network, a single wire concentration site dictates a lot of cable.

To attack these remaining problems, consider a local network consisting of multiple rings (Figure 9.10). Each ring consists of a connected sequence of wir-

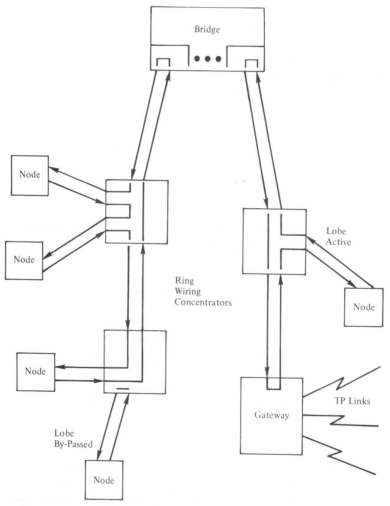

FIGURE 9.10.   Ring bridge.

ing concentrators; the set of rings is connected by a *bridge*. The bridge routes data packets from one ring subnetwork to another based on addressing information in the packet so routed. From a physical point of view, each ring operates independently of the other rings attached to the bridge. From a logical point of view, the bridge provides transparent routing between the two rings.

The bridge must perform five functions:

- *Input filtering*: For each ring, the bridge monitors the traffic on the ring and copies all packets addressed to other rings on the bridge. This function can be performed by a repeater programmed to recognize a family of addresses rather than a single address.
- *Input buffering:* Received packets may need to be buffered, either because the interring traffic is peaking, or because the target output buffer is temporarily full.
- *Switching:* Each packet must be routed through the bridge to its appropriate destination ring.
- *Output buffering:* A packet may need to be buffered at the threshold of the destination ring, waiting for an opportunity to be inserted.
- *Output transmission:* This function can be performed by an ordinary repeater.

Two principal advantages accrue from the use of a bridge. First, the failure of a ring, for whatever reason, will disable only a portion of the network, and failure of the bridge does not prevent intraring traffic. (This assumes that the bridge is a station attached to a repeater; therefore, the bridge can fail but its repeater remain operational.) Second, multiple rings may be employed to obtain a satisfactory level of performance when the throughput capability of a single ring is exceeded.

There are several pitfalls to be noted. First, the automatic acknowledgment feature of the ring is lost; higher level protocols must provide acknowledgment. Second, performance may not significantly improve if there is a high percentage of interring traffic. If it is possible to do so, network devices should be judiciously allocated to rings to minimize interring traffic.

Bus Versus Ring

For the user with a large number of devices and high capacity requirements, the bus or tree broadband LAN seems the best suited to the requirements. For more moderate requirements, however, the choice between a baseband bus LAN and a ring LAN is not at all clear cut.

The baseband bus is the simpler system. Passive taps rather than active repeaters are used. There is no need for the complexity of bridges and ring wiring concentrators.

The most important benefit or strength of the ring is that it uses point-to-point communication links. There are a number of implications of this fact. First, because the transmitted signal is regenerated at each node, transmission errors are minimized and greater distances can be covered than with baseband bus. Broadband bus/tree can cover a similar range, but cascaded amplifiers can result in loss of data integrity at high data rates. Second, the ring can accommodate optical fiber links, which provide very high data rates and excellent electromagnetic interference (EMI) characteristics. Finally, the electronics and maintenance of point-to-point lines are simpler than for multipoint lines.

9.5

MEDIUM ACCESS CONTROL PROTOCOLS

All LANs and MANs consist of collections of devices that must share the network's transmission capacity. Some means of controlling access to the transmission medium is needed to provide for an orderly and efficient use of that capacity. This is the function of a medium access control (MAC) protocol. We begin this section with an overview of medium access control techniques, then examine the most important MAC protocols.

Medium Access Control Techniques

The key parameters in any medium access control technique are where and how. *Where* refers to whether control is exercised in a centralized or distributed fashion. In a centralized scheme, a controller is designated that has the authority to grant access to the network. A station wishing to transmit must wait until it receives permission from the controller. In a decentralized network, the stations collectively perform a medium access control function to dynamically determine the order in which stations transmit. A centralized scheme has certain advantages, including

- It may afford greater control over access for providing such things as priorities, overrides, and guaranteed capacity.
- It enables the use of relatively simple access logic at each station.
- It avoids problems of coordination.

    The principal disadvantages of a centralized scheme are

- It creates a single point of failure.
- It may act as a bottleneck, reducing performance.

    The pros and cons of distributed schemes are mirror images of the points made above.

    The second parameter, *how,* is constrained by the topology and is a tradeoff among competing factors, including cost, performance, and complexity. In general, we can categorize access control techniques as being either synchronous or asynchronous. With synchronous techniques, a specific capacity is dedicated to a connection. This is the same approach used in circuit switching, frequency-division multiplexing (FDM), and synchronous time-division multiplexing (TDM). Such techniques are generally not optimal in LANs and MANs because the needs of the stations are unpredictable. It is preferable to be able to allocate capacity in an asynchronous (dynamic) fashion, more or less in response to immediate demand. The asynchronous approach can be further subdivided into three categories: round robin, reservation, and contention.

Round Robin

With round robin, each station in turn is given the opportunity to transmit. During that opportunity, the station may decline to transmit or may transmit subject to a specified upper bound, usually expressed as a maximum amount of data transmitted or time for this opportunity. In any case, the station, when it is finished, relinquishes its turn, and the right to transmit passes to the next station in logical sequence. Control of sequence may be centralized or distributed. Polling is an example of a centralized technique.

When many stations have data to transmit over an extended period of time, round robin techniques can be very efficient. If only a few stations have data to transmit over an extended period of time, then there is a considerable overhead in passing the turn from station to station, since most of the stations will not transmit but simply pass their turns. Under such circumstances other techniques may be preferable, largely depending on whether the data traffic has a stream or bursty characteristic. Stream traffic is characterized by lengthy and fairly continuous transmissions; examples are voice communication, telemetry, and bulk file transfer. Bursty traffic is characterized by short, sporadic transmissions; interactive terminal–host traffic fits this description.

Reservation

For stream traffic, reservation techniques are well suited. In general, for these techniques, time on the medium is divided into slots, much as with synchronous TDM. A station wishing to transmit reserves future slots for its use. Again, reservations may be made in a centralized or distributed fashion.

Contention

For bursty traffic, contention techniques are usually appropriate. With these techniques, no control is exercised to determine whose turn it is; all stations contend for time in a way that can be, as we shall see, rather rough and tumble. These techniques are of necessity distributed in nature. Their principal advantage is that they are simple to implement and, under light to moderate load, efficient. For some of these techniques, however, performance tends to collapse under heavy load.

The discussion above has been somewhat abstract and should become clearer as specific techniques are discussed in this section. For future reference,

TABLE 9.8   Standardized Medium Access Control Techniques

	Bus Topology	Ring Topology
Round Robin	Token Bus (IEEE 802.4)	Token Ring (IEEE 802.5; FDDI)
Reservation	DQDB (IEEE 802.6)	
Contention	CSMA/CD (IEEE 802.3)	

Note: The DQDB and FDDI protocols for circuit-switched traffic are not fully specified in the standards and may be either distributed or centralized. All other standardized MAC protocols are distributed.

Table 9.8 places the techniques that will be discussed into the classification just outlined.

Carrier Sense Multiple Access with Collision Detection (CSMA/CD)

The most commonly used medium access control technique for bus/tree and star topologies is CSMA/CD. The original baseband version of this technique was developed and patented by Xerox [METC77] as part of its Ethernet LAN [METC76]. The original broadband version was developed and patented by MITRE [HOPK80] as part of its MITREnet LAN. All of this work formed the basis for the IEEE 802.3 standard for CSMA/CD [IEEE90b].

Before examining this technique, we look at some earlier schemes from which CSMA/CD evolved.

Precursors

CSMA/CD and its precursors can be termed random access, or contention, techniques. They are random access in the sense that there is no predictable or scheduled time for any station to transmit; station transmissions are ordered randomly. They are contention in the sense that stations contend for time on the medium.

The earliest of these techniques, known as ALOHA, was developed for packet radio networks [ABRA70]. However, it is applicable to any shared transmission medium. ALOHA, or pure ALOHA, as it is sometimes called, is a true free-for-all. Whenever a station has a frame[1] to send, it does so. The station then listens for an amount of time equal to the maximum possible round-trip propagation delay on the network (twice the time it takes to send a frame between the two most widely separated stations) plus a small fixed time increment. If the station hears an acknowledgment during that time, fine; otherwise, it resends the frame. If the station fails to receive an acknowledgment after repeated transmissions, it gives up. A receiving station determines

---

[1]Packets transmitted using a MAC protocol are generally referred to as MAC frames, rather than packets.

the correctness of an incoming frame by examining a frame-check-sequence field, as in HDLC. If the frame is valid and if the destination address in the frame header matches the receiver's address, the station immediately sends an acknowledgment. The frame may be invalid due to noise on the channel or because another station transmitted a frame at about the same time. In the latter case, the two frames may interfere with each other at the receiver so that neither gets through; this is known as a *collision*. If a receiving station determines that a frame is invalid, it simply ignores the frame.

ALOHA is as simple as can be and pays a penalty for it. Because the number of collisions rises rapidly with increased load, the maximum utilization of the channel is only about 18% (see [STAL93b]).

To improve efficiency, a modification of ALOHA, known as slotted ALOHA [ROBE75], was developed. In this scheme, time on the channel is organized into uniform slots whose size equals the frame transmission time. Some central clock or other technique is needed to synchronize all stations. Transmission is permitted to begin only at a slot boundary. Thus, frames that do overlap will do so totally. This increases the maximum utilization of the system to about 37%.

Both ALOHA and slotted ALOHA exhibit poor utilization. Both fail to take advantage of one of the key properties of both packet radio and LANs, which is that propagation delay between stations is usually very small compared to frame transmission time. Consider the following observations. If the station-to-station propagation time is large compared to the frame transmission time, then, after a station launches a frame, it will be a long time before other stations know about it. During that time, one of the other stations may transmit a frame; the two frames may interfere with each other and neither gets through. Indeed, if the distances are great enough, many stations may begin transmitting, one after the other, and none of their frames get through unscathed. Suppose, however, that the propagation time is small compared to frame transmission time. In that case, when a station launches a frame, all the other stations know it almost immediately. So, if they had any sense, they would not try transmitting until the first station was done. Collisions would be rare since they would occur only when two stations began to transmit almost simultaneously. Another way to look at it is that a short delay time provides the stations with better feedback about the state of the network; this information can be used to improve efficiency.

The foregoing observations led to the development of carrier sense multiple access (CSMA). With CSMA, a station wishing to transmit first listens to the medium to determine if another transmission is in progress (carrier sense). If the medium is in use, the station must wait. If the medium is idle, the station may transmit. It may happen that two or more stations attempt to transmit at about the same time. If this happens, there will be a collision; the data from both transmissions will be garbled and not received successfully. To account for this, a station waits a reasonable amount of time after transmitting for an acknowledgment, taking into account the maximum round-trip propagation delay and the fact that the acknowledging station must also contend for the channel in order to respond. If there is no acknowledgment, the station assumes that a collision has occurred and retransmits.

One can see how this strategy would be effective for networks in which the average frame transmission time is much longer than the propagation time. Collisions can occur only when more than one user begins transmitting within a short time (the period of the propagation delay). If a station begins to transmit a frame and there are no collisions during the time it takes for the leading edge of the packet to propagate to the farthest station, then there will be no collision for this frame since all other stations are now aware of the transmission.

The maximum utilization achievable using CSMA can far exceed that of ALOHA or slotted ALOHA. The maximum utilization depends on the length of the frame and on the propagation time; the longer the frames or the shorter the propagation time, the higher the utilization. This subject is explored in Section 9.6.

With CSMA, an algorithm is needed to specify what a station should do if the medium is found busy. Three approaches are depicted in Figure 9.11. One algorithm is *nonpersistent CSMA*. A station wishing to transmit listens to the medium and obeys the following rules:

1. If the medium is idle, transmit; otherwise, go to step 2.
2. If the medium is busy, wait an amount of time drawn from a probability distribution (the retransmission delay) and repeat step 1.

The use of random delays reduces the probability of collisions. To see this, consider that two stations become ready to transmit at about the same time while another transmission is in progress; if both stations delay the same amount of time before trying again, they will both attempt to transmit at about

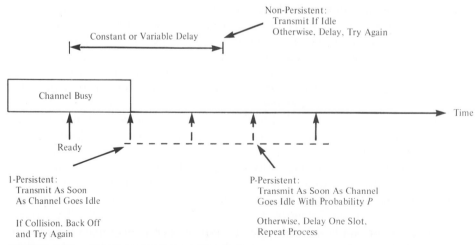

FIGURE 9.11.   CSMA persistence and backoff.

the same time. A problem with this approach is that capacity is wasted because the medium will generally remain idle following the end of a transmission even if there are one or more stations waiting to transmit.

To avoid idle channel time, the *1-persistent protocol* can be used. A station wishing to transmit listens to the medium and obeys the following rules:

1. If the medium is idle, transmit; otherwise, go to step 2.
2. If the medium is busy, continue to listen until the channel is sensed idle; then transmit immediately.

Whereas nonpersistent stations are deferential, 1-persistent stations are selfish. If two or more stations are waiting to transmit, a collision is guaranteed. Things get sorted out only after the collision.

A compromise that attempts to reduce collisions, like nonpersistent, and reduce idle time, like 1-persistent, is *p-persistent*. The rules are

1. If the medium is idle, transmit with probability p, and delay one time unit with probability $(1 - p)$. The time unit is typically equal to the maximum propagation delay.
2. If the medium is busy, continue to listen until the channel is idle and repeat step 1.
3. If transmission is delayed one time unit, repeat step 1.

The question arises as to what is an effective value of p. The main problem to avoid is one of instability under heavy load. Consider the case in which n stations have frames to send while a transmission is taking place. At the end of the transmission, the expected number of stations that will attempt to transmit is equal to the number of stations ready to transmit times the probability of transmitting, or np. If np is greater than 1, on average, multiple stations will attempt to transmit and there will be a collision. What is more, as soon as all these stations realize that their transmission suffered a collision, they will be back again, almost guaranteeing more collisions. Worse yet, these retries will compete with new transmissions from other stations, further increasing the probability of collision. Eventually, all stations will be trying to send, causing continuous collisions, with throughput dropping to zero. To avoid this catastrophe, np must be less than one for the expected peaks of n; therefore, if a heavy load is expected to occur with some regularity, p must be small. However, as p is made smaller, stations must wait longer to attempt transmission. At low loads, this can result in very long delays. For example, if only a single station desires to transmit, the expected number of iterations of step 1, above, is $1/p$ (see Problem 9.8). Thus, if $p = 0.1$, at low load, a station will wait an average of 9 time units before transmitting on an idle line!

Description of CSMA/CD

CSMA, although more efficient than ALOHA or slotted ALOHA, still has one glaring inefficiency. When two frames collide, the medium remains unusable for the duration of transmission of both damaged frames. For long frames, compared to propagation time, the amount of wasted capacity can be considerable. This waste can be reduced if a station continues to listen to the medium while transmitting. This leads to the following rules for CSMA/CD:

1. If the medium is idle, transmit; otherwise, go to step 2.
2. If the medium is busy, continue to listen until the channel is idle, then transmit immediately.
3. If a collision is detected during transmission, transmit a brief jamming signal to assure that all stations know that there has been a collision and then cease transmission.
4. After transmitting the jamming signal, wait a random amount of time, then attempt to transmit again (repeat from step 1).

Figure 9.12 illustrates the technique for a baseband bus. At time t_0, station A begins transmitting a packet addressed to D. At t_1, both B and C are ready to

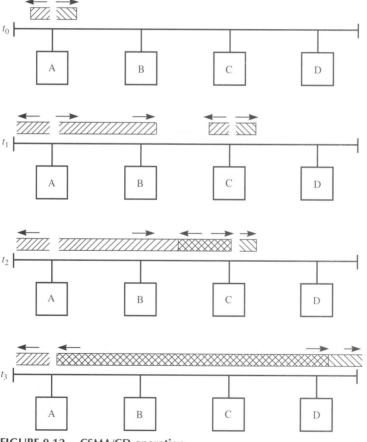

FIGURE 9.12. CSMA/CD operation.

transmit. B senses a transmission and so defers. C, however, is still unaware of A's transmission and begins its own transmission. When A's transmission reaches C, at t_2, C detects the collision and ceases transmission. The effect of the collision propagates back to A, where it is detected some time later, t_3, at which time A ceases transmission.

With CSMA/CD, the amount of wasted capacity is reduced to the time it takes to detect a collision. Question: How long does that take? Let us consider first the case of a baseband bus and consider two stations as far apart as possible. For example, in Figure 9.12, suppose that station A begins a transmission and that just before that transmission reaches D, D is ready to transmit. Since D is not yet aware of A's transmission, it begins to transmit. A collision occurs almost immediately and is recognized by D. However, the collision must propagate all the way back to A before A is aware of the collision. By this line of reasoning, we conclude that the amount of time that it takes to detect a collision is no greater than twice the end-to-end propagation delay. For a broadband bus, the delay is even longer. Figure 9.13 shows a dual-cable system. This time, the worst case occurs for two stations as close together as possible and as far as possible from the headend. In this case, the maximum time to detect a collision is four times the propagation delay from an end of the cable to the headend.

An important rule followed in most CSMA/CD systems, including the IEEE standard, is that frames should be long enough to allow collision detection prior to the end of transmission. If shorter frames are used, then collision detection does not occur, and CSMA/CD exhibits the same performance as the less efficient CSMA protocol.

As with CSMA, CSMA/CD employs one of the three persistence algorithms. You may be surprised to learn that the most common choice is 1-persistent. It is used by both Ethernet and MITREnet, and is in the IEEE 802 standard. As was mentioned, the problem with the nonpersistent scheme is the wasted idle time. Though more efficient, p-persistent may still result in considerable waste. With the l-persistent scheme, that waste is eliminated at the cost of wasted collision time.

What saves the day is that the wasted time due to collisions is mercifully short (if the packets are long relative to propagation delay, i.e., a $<<$ 1). And with random backoff, the two stations involved in a collision are unlikely to collide on their next tries. To ensure that this backoff maintains stability, a technique known as binary exponential backoff is used. A station will attempt to transmit repeatedly in the face of repeated collisions, but, after each collision, the mean value of the random delay is doubled.

Although the implementation of CSMA/CD is substantially the same for baseband and broadband, there are differences. One is the means for performing carrier sense. For baseband systems, this is done by detecting a voltage pulse train. For broadband, the RF carrier is detected.

Collision detection also differs for the two systems. For baseband, a collision should produce substantially higher voltage swings than those produced by a single transmitter. Accordingly, the IEEE standard dictates that the transmitter

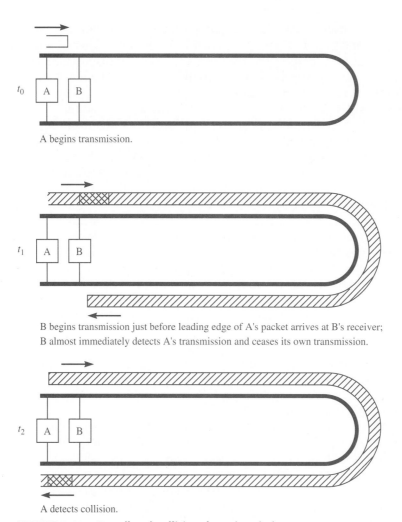

FIGURE 9.13.   Broadband collision detection timing.

will detect a collision if the signal on the cable at the transmitter tap point exceeds the maximum that could be produced by the transmitter alone. Because a transmitted signal attenuates as it propagates, there is a potential problem: If two stations far apart are transmitting, each station will receive a greatly attenuated signal from the other. The signal strength could be so small that when it is added to the transmitted signal at the transmitter tap point, the combined signal does not exceed the CD threshold. For this reason, among others, the IEEE standard restricts the maximum length of coaxial cable to 500 m for 10BASE5 and 200 m for 10BASE2.

A much simpler collision detection scheme is possible with the twisted-pair star-topology approach (Figure 9.1d). In this case, collision detection is based

(a) A transmitting

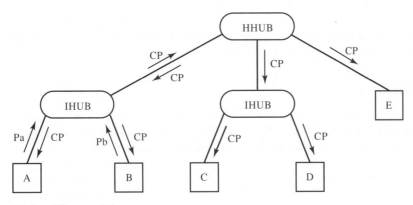

(b) A and B transmitting

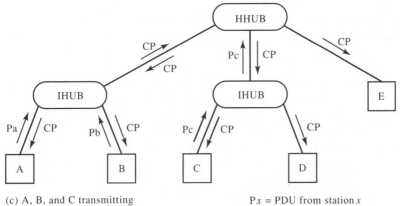

(c) A, B, and C transmitting

Px = PDU from station x
CP = Collision presence signal

FIGURE 9.14.   Operation of a two-level star-wired CSMA/CD configuration.

on logic rather than sensing voltage magnitudes. For any hub, if there is activity (signal) on more than one input, a collision is assumed. A special signal called the *collision presence* signal is generated. This signal is generated and sent out as long as activity is sensed on any of the input lines. This signal is interpreted by every node as an occurrence of collision. Figure 9.14 gives examples of the operation of a star-wired system with and without collisions. In the first example, a frame transmitted from station A propagates up to HHUB and is eventually received by all stations in the network. In the second example, a collision is detected by A's IHUB. The collision presence signal propagates up to HHUB and is rebroadcast down to all hubs and stations. The third example shows the result of a three-way collision.

There are several possible approaches to collision detection in broadband systems. The most common of these is to perform a bit-by-bit comparison between transmitted and received data. When a station transmits on the inbound channel, it begins to receive its own transmission on the outbound channel after a propagation delay to the headend and back. Note the similarity to a satellite link. Another approach, for split systems, is for the headend to perform detection based on garbled data.

Token Bus

Token bus is a technique in which the stations on the bus or tree form a logical ring; that is, the stations are assigned positions in an ordered sequence, with the last member of the sequence followed by the first. Each station knows the identity of the stations preceding and following it (Figure 9.15).

A control packet known as the token regulates the right of access. When a station receives the token, it is granted control of the medium for a specified time. The station may transmit one or more packets and may poll stations and

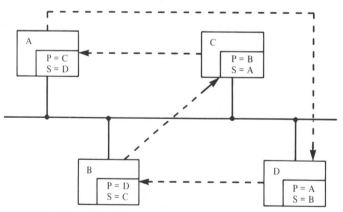

FIGURE 9.15.   Token bus.

receive responses. When the station is done, or time has expired, it passes the token on to the next station in logical sequence. This station now has permission to transmit. Hence steady-state operation consists of alternating data transfer and token transfer phases.

Note that non-token-using stations are allowed on the bus. These stations can only respond to polls or requests for acknowledgment. It should also be pointed out that the physical ordering of the stations on the bus is irrelevant and independent of the logical ordering.

This scheme requires considerable maintenance. The following functions, at a minimum, must be performed by one or more stations on the bus:

- *Ring initialization:* When the network is started up, or after the logical ring has broken down, it must be reinitialized. Some cooperative, decentralized algorithm is needed to sort out who goes first, who goes second, and so on.
- *Addition to ring:* Periodically, nonparticipating stations must be granted the opportunity to insert themselves in the ring.
- *Deletion from ring:* A station can voluntarily remove itself from the ring by splicing together its predecessor and successor.
- *Fault management:* A number of errors can occur. These include duplicate address (two stations think it's their turn) and broken ring (no station thinks that it is its turn).

The remainder of this subsection briefly describes the approach taken for these functions in the IEEE 802 standard. To accomplish *addition to ring*, each node in the logical ring has the responsibility of periodically granting an opportunity for new nodes to enter the ring. While holding the token, the node issues a *solicit-successor* packet, inviting nodes with an address between itself and the next node in logical sequence to demand entrance. The transmitting node then waits for one response window or slot time (equal to twice the end-to-end propagation delay of the medium). If there is no response, the node passes the token to its successor as usual. If there is one response, the token holder sets its successor node to be the requesting node and transmits the token to it; the requestor sets its linkages accordingly and proceeds. If more than one node demands to enter the ring, the token holder will detect a garbled response.

The conflict is resolved by an address-based contention scheme. The token holder transmits a *resolve-contention* packet and waits four response windows. Each demander can respond in one of these windows based on the first two bits of its address. If a demander hears anything before its window comes up, it refrains from demanding. If the token holder receives a valid response, it is in business. Otherwise, it tries again, and only those nodes that responded the first time are allowed to respond this time, based on the second pair of bits in their address. This process continues until a valid response is received, no response is received, or a maximum retry count is reached. In the latter two cases, the token holder gives up and passes the token.

Deletion from ring is a much simpler process. If a node wishes to drop out, it waits until it receives the token, then sends a *set-successor* packet to its predecessor, instructing it to splice to its successor.

Fault management by the token holder covers a number of contingencies. First, while holding the token, a node may hear a packet indicating that another node has the token. If so, it immediately drops the token by reverting to listener mode. In this way, the number of token holders drops immediately to 1 or 0. A second problem may arise when, upon completion of its turn, the token holder issues a token packet to its successor. The successor should immediately issue a data or token packet. Therefore, after sending a token, the token issuer will listen for one slot time to make sure that its successor is active. This precipitates a sequence of events:

1. If the successor node is active, the token issuer will hear a valid packet and revert to listener mode.
2. If the issuer does not hear a valid packet, it reissues the token to the same successor one more time.
3. After two failures, the issuer assumes that its successor has failed and issues a *who-follows* packet, asking for the identity of the node that follows the failed node. The issuer should get back a set-successor packet from the second node down the line. If so, the issuer adjusts its linkage and issues a token (back to step 1).
4. If the issuing node gets no response to its who-follows packet, it tries again.
5. If the who-follows tactic fails, the node issues a solicit-successor packet with the full address range (i.e., every node is invited to respond). If this process works, a two-node ring is established and life goes on.
6. If two attempts of step 5 fail, the node assumes that a catastrophe has occurred; perhaps the node's receiver has failed. In any case, the node ceases activity and listens to the bus.

Logical *ring initialization* occurs when one or more stations detect a lack of bus activity of duration longer than a timeout value: The token has been lost. This can be due to a number of causes, such as the network has just been powered up, or a token-holding station fails. Once its timeout expires, a node will issue a *claim-token* packet. Contending claimants are resolved in a manner similar to the response-window process.

As an option, a token bus system can include classes of service that provide a mechanism of prioritizing access to the bus. Four classes of service are defined, in descending order of priority: 6, 4, 2, 0. Any station may have data in one or more of these classes to send. The object is to allocate network capacity to the higher-priority frames and only send lower-priority frames when there is sufficient capacity. To explain, let us define the following variables:

THT = token holding time. The maximum time that a station can hold the token to transmit class 6 data.

TRT_i = token rotation time for class i (i = 4,2,0). The maximum time that a token can take to circulate and still permit class i transmission.

When a station receives the token, it can transmit classes of data according to the following rules (Figure 9.16): First, the station may transmit class 6 data for a time THT. Hence, for an n-station ring, during one circulation of the token, the maximum amount of time available for class 6 transmission is

FIGURE 9.16.   Token bus priority scheme.

$n \times$ THT. Next, after transmitting class 6 data, or if there were no class 6 data to transmit, it may transmit class 4 data only if the amount of time for the last circulation of the token (including any class 6 data just sent) is less than TRT4. Class 2 and class 0 data are then handled in the same way as class 4.

This scheme, within limits, gives preference to packets of higher priority. More specifically, it guarantees that class 6 data may have a certain portion of the capacity. Two cases are possible. If $n \times$ THT is greater than MAX[TRT4, TRT2, TRT0], the maximum possible token circulation time is $n \times$ THT, and class 6 data may occupy the entire cycle to the exclusion of the other classes. If $n \times$ THT is less than MAX[TRT4, TRT2, TRT0], the maximum circulation time is MAX[TRT4, TRT2, TRT0], and class 6 data are guaranteed $n \times$ THT amount of that time.

Figure 9.17, which is adapted from one in [JAYA87], illustrates the average behavior of the IEEE token bus capacity-allocation scheme. That is, the plots ignore temporary load fluctuations, instead depicting the steady-state performance. For convenience, we assume that TRT4 > TRT2 > TRT0 and that the load generated in each class of data is the same.

Figure 9.17a depicts the first case ($n \times$ THT > TRT4). At very low loads, the token circulation time is very short, and all of the data offered in all four classes are transmitted. As the load increases, the average token circulation time reaches TRT0. There is then a range, as indicated in the figure, in which the load continues to increase but the token circulation time remains at TRT0. In this range, the other classes of data increase their throughput at the expense of Class 0 data, whose throughput declines. At some point, the load is such that the token circulation time equals TRT0, but the amount of transmission in Classes 2, 4, and 6 uses up all of that time and no Class 0 data can be transmitted. Further increase in offered load results in renewed increase in the token circulation time. The same pattern repeats for Class 2 and Class 4 data. There is a period when the load increases at a constant token circulation time of TRT2, and during that period, Class 2 data is gradually crowded out. Class 4 data is similarly crowded out at a higher level of load. Finally, a situation is reached in which only Class 6 data is being transmitted, and the token circulation time stabilizes at $n \times$ THT.

For the second case just mentioned ($n \times$ THT < TRT4), we need to examine two subcases. Figure 9.17b shows the case in which $\dfrac{\text{TRT4}}{2} < (n \times \text{THT})$ < TRT4. As before, with increasing load, Class 0 and Class 2 traffic are eliminated and the token circulation time increases. At some point, the increasing load drives the token circulation time to TRT4. Using our simple example, when this point is reached, approximately half of the load is Class 4 data and the other half is Class 6. But, since $n \times \text{THT} > \dfrac{\text{TRT4}}{2}$, if the load on the network continues to increase, the portion of the load that is Class 6 traffic will also increase. This will cause a corresponding decrease in Class 4 traffic.

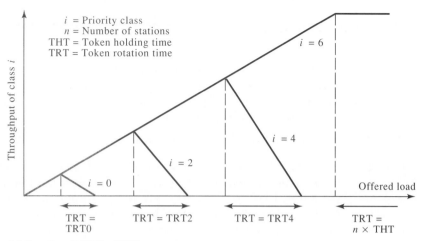

(a) Case I: $n \times$ THT > TRT4

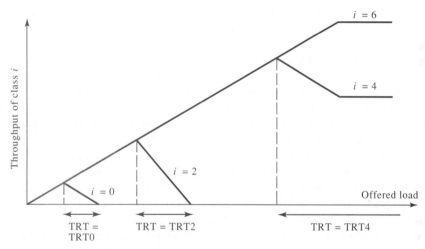

(b) Case IIa: (TRT4/2)< $n \times$ THT < TRT4

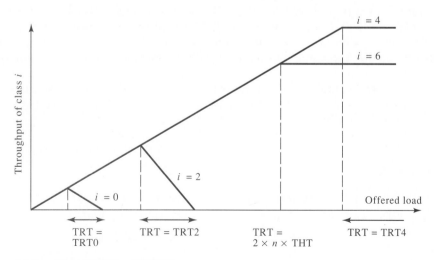

(c) Case IIb: $n \times$ THT < (TRT4/2)

FIGURE 9.17. Throughput of token bus priority classes.

Eventually, a point is reached at which all of the allowable Class 6 traffic is being handled during each token circulation. This will take an amount of time $n \times$ THT and still leave some time left over for Class 4 data. Thereafter, the total token circulation time remains stable at TRT4.

Finally, Figure 9.17c shows the case in which $n \times$ THT $< \dfrac{\text{TRT4}}{2}$. As before, increasing load eliminates Class 0 and Class 2 traffic. A point is reached at which the token circulation time is $2 \times n \times$ THT, with half of the traffic being Class 4 and half being Class 6. This is a maximum throughput-per-token-circulation for Class 6. However, the amount of Class 4 data can continue to increase until the token circulation time is TRT4.

It should be obvious that the principal disadvantage of token bus is its complexity. The logic at each station far exceeds that required for CSMA/CD. A second disadvantage is the overhead involved. Under lightly loaded conditions, a station may have to wait through many fruitless token passes for a turn.

Indeed, at first glance it would seem difficult to make a case for this technique. Such a case can be made [MILL82], [STIE81] and it includes the following elements. First, it is possible to regulate the traffic in a number of ways. Multiple priority levels can be used, and different stations can be allowed to hold the token different amounts of time. This type of discrimination is difficult to achieve with CSMA/CD. Second, unlike with CSMA/CD, there is no minimum packet-length requirement with token bus. Third, the necessity for listening while talking imposes physical and electrical constraints on CSMA/CD system; these do not apply to token systems where no station need listen and talk at the same time. Finally, under heavy loads, where it counts, token bus exhibits significantly superior performance to CSMA/CD, as discussed below.

Another advertised advantage of token bus is that it is "deterministic"; that is, there is a known upper bound to the amount of time any station must wait before transmitting. This upper bound is known because each station in the logical ring can only hold the token for a specified time. In contrast, with CSMA/CD, the delay time can only be expressed statistically. Furthermore, since every attempt to transmit under CSMA/CD can in principle produce a collision, there is a possibility that a station could be shut out indefinitely. For process-control and other real-time applications, this "nondeterministic" behavior is undesirable. Alas, in the real world, there is always a finite possibility of transmission error, which can cause a lost token. This adds a statistical component to token bus.

Token Ring

In this section, we introduce the most widely used protocol for the ring topology, token ring, and examine its application in two standards.

Token Ring Operation

This is probably the oldest ring control technique, originally proposed in 1969 [FARM69] and referred to as the Newhall ring. This has become the most popular ring access technique in the United States. This technique is the one ring access method selected for standardization by the IEEE 802 Local Network Standards Committee.

The token ring technique is based on the use of a small token packet that circulates around the ring. When all stations are idle, the token packet is labeled as a "free" token. A station wishing to transmit must wait until it detects a token passing by. It then changes the token from "free token" to "busy token" by altering the bit pattern. The station then transmits a packet immediately following the busy token (Figure 9.18).

There is now no free token on the ring, so other stations wishing to transmit must wait. The packet on the ring will make a round trip and be purged by the transmitting station. The transmitting station will insert a new free token on the ring when both of the following conditions have been met:

- The station has completed transmission of its packet.
- The busy token has returned to the station.

If the bit length of the ring is less than the packet length, the first condition implies the second. If not, a station could release a free token after it has finished transmitting but before it receives its own busy token; the second condition is not strictly necessary. However, this might complicate error recovery, since several packets will be on the ring at the same time. In any case, the use of a token guarantees that only one station at a time may transmit.

When a transmitting station releases a new free token, the next station downstream with data to send will be able to seize the token and transmit.

As with token bus, token ring requires fault management techniques. The key error conditions are no token circulating and persistent busy token. To address these problems, one station is designated as active token monitor. The monitor detects the lost-token condition by using a timeout greater than the time required for the longest frame to traverse the ring completely. If no token is seen during this time, it is assumed to be lost. To recover, the monitor purges the ring of any residual data and issues a free token. To detect a circulating busy token, the monitor sets a monitor bit to 1 on any passing busy token. If it sees a busy token with a bit already set, it knows that the transmitting station failed to purge its packet. The monitor changes the busy token to a free token. Other stations on the ring have the role of passive monitor. Their primary job is to detect failure of the active monitor and assume that role. A contention-resolution algorithm is used to determine which station takes over.

The token ring technique shares many of the advantages of token bus. Perhaps its principal advantage is that traffic can be regulated, either by allowing stations to transmit differing amounts of data when they receive the token, or

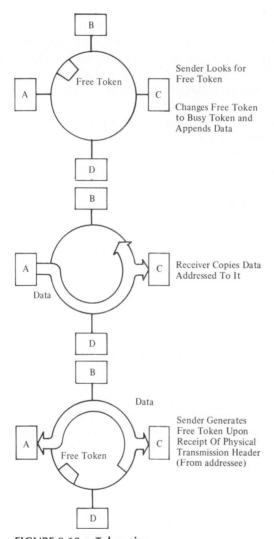

Sender Looks for Free Token

Changes Free Token to Busy Token and Appends Data

Receiver Copies Data Addressed To It

Sender Generates Free Token Upon Receipt Of Physical Transmission Header (From addressee)

FIGURE 9.18.   Token ring.

by setting priorities so that higher-priority stations have first claim on a circulating token.

The principal disadvantage of token ring is the requirement for token maintenance. Loss of the free token prevents further utilization of the ring. Duplication of the token can also disrupt ring operation. One station must be elected monitor to assure that exactly one token is on the ring and to reinsert a free token if necessary.

IEEE 802 Ring Standard

The IEEE 802 token ring standard follows the general scheme outlined above. The major addition is a scheme for capacity allocation using priorities. The 802 specification provides for eight levels of priority. It does this by providing two three-bit fields in each packet and token: a priority field and a reservation field. For clarity, let us define three variables: P_m = priority of message to be transmitted by a station; P_r = received priority; and R_r = received reservation. The scheme works as follows:

1. A station wishing to transmit must wait for a free token with $P_r \leq P_m$.
2. While waiting, a station may reserve a future token at its priority level (P_m). If a packet goes by, it may set the reservation field to its priority ($R_r \leftarrow P_m$) if the reservation field is less than its priority ($R_r < P_m$). If a free token goes by, it sets the reservation field to its priority ($R_r \leftarrow P_m$) if $R_r < P_m$ and $P_m < P_r$. This has the effect of preempting any lower-priority reservations.
3. When a station seizes a token, it sets the reservation field to 0 and leaves the priority field unchanged.
4. Following transmission, a station issues a new token with the priority set to the maximum of P_r, R_r, and P_m, and a reservation set to the maximum of R_r and P_m.

The effect of the above steps is to sort out competing claims and allow the waiting transmission of highest priority to seize the token as soon as possible. A station having a higher priority than the current busy token can reserve the next free token for its priority level as the busy token passes by. When the current transmitting station is finished, it issues a free token at that higher priority. Stations of lower priority cannot seize the token, so it passes to the requesting station of equal or higher priority with data to send.

A moment's reflection reveals that, as is, the algorithm has a ratchet effect on priority, driving it to the highest used level and keeping it there. To avoid this, the station that upgraded the priority level is responsible for downgrading it to its former level when all higher-priority stations are finished. When that station sees a free token at the higher priority, it can assume that there is no more higher-priority traffic waiting, and it downgrades the token before passing it on. Figure 9.19 is an example of the operation of the priority mechanism.

FDDI Ring Standard

The Fiber Distributed Data Interface (FDDI) is a standard for a high-speed ring LAN [ROSS89]. Like the IEEE 802 standard, FDDI employs the token ring algorithm. There are, however, several differences that are intended to allow FDDI to take advantage of the high speed (100 Mbps) of its ring and maximize efficiency.

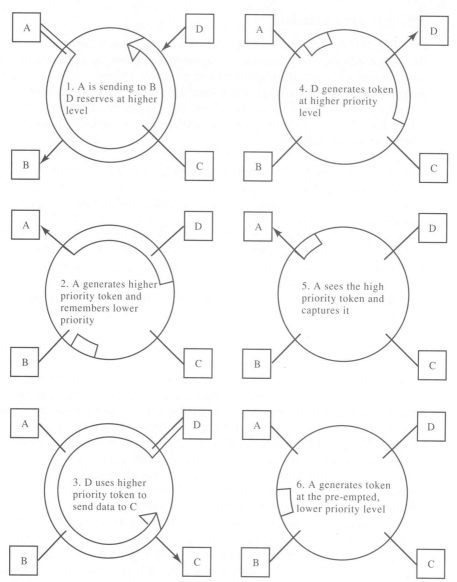

FIGURE 9.19.   IEEE token ring priority scheme.

Figure 9.20 gives an example of ring operation. After station A has seized the token, it transmits frame F1 and immediately transmits a new token. F1 is addressed to station C, which copies it as it circulates past. The frame eventually returns to A, which absorbs it. Meanwhile, B seizes the token issued by A and transmits F2 followed by a token. This action could be repeated any number of times, so that at any one time, there may be multiple frames circulating

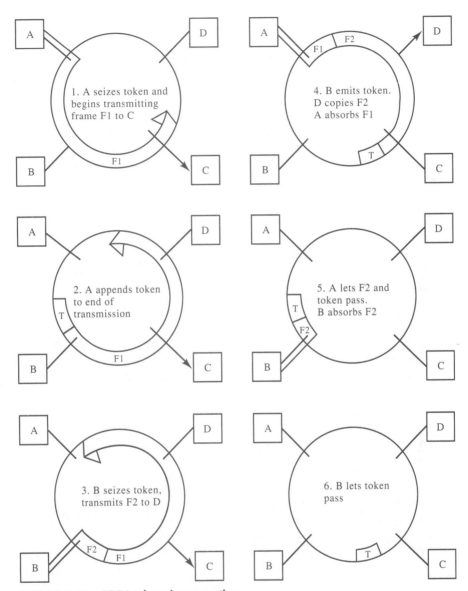

FIGURE 9.20. FDDI token ring operation.

the ring. Each station is responsible for absorbing its own frames based on the source address field.

Note that in FDDI, a station emits a new token immediately following the frame, where as in IEEE token ring, a station emits a new token only after the leading edge of its transmitted frame returns. The FDDI scheme is thus more efficient, especially in large rings.

Another difference between the IEEE token ring algorithm and that of FDDI is in the area of capacity allocation. The FDDI scheme is designed to be efficient and flexible in meeting a wide range of high-speed requirements. Specifically, FDDI provides support for a mixture of stream and bursty traffic, which is a requirement that was discussed in the context of satellite protocols in Chapter 10.

To accommodate this requirement, FDDI defines two types of traffic: synchronous and asynchronous. The scheme works as follows. A target token rotation time (TTRT) is defined; each station stores the same value for TTRT. Some or all stations may be provided a synchronous allocation (SA_i), which may vary among stations. The allocations must be such that:

$$DMax + FMax + TokenTime + \Sigma \, SA_i \leq TTRT$$

where

$$SA_i = \text{allocation for station } i$$
$$DMax = \text{propagation time for one complete circuit of the ring}$$
$$FMAX = \text{time required to transmit a maximum-length packet (4500 octets)}$$
$$TokenTime = \text{time required to transmit a token}$$

Thus all stations have the same value of TTRT and a separately assigned value of SA_i. In addition, several variables that are required for the operation of the capacity-allocation algorithm are maintained at each station:

- Token-rotation timer (TRT).
- Token-holding timer (THT).
- Late counter (LC).

Each station's TRT is initialized to TTRT; when it is enabled, it counts down until it expires at TRT = 0. It is then reset to TTRT and enabled again. LC is initialized at zero and is incremented when TRT expires. Thus LC records the number of times, if any, that TRT has expired since the token was last received at that station. The token is considered to arrive early if TRT has not expired since the station received the token, that is, if LC = 0.

When a station receives the token, its actions will depend on whether the token is early or late. If the token is early, the station saves the remaining time in TRT in THT; resets TRT, and enables TRT:

THT ⟵ TRT
TRT ⟵ TTRT
enable TRT

The station can then transmit according to the following rules:

1. It may transmit synchronous frames for a time SA_i.
2. After transmitting synchronous frames, or if there were no synchronous frames to transmit, THT is enabled. The station may transmit asynchronous frames only so long as THT > 0.

If a station receives a token and the token is late, then LC is set to zero, and TRT continues to run. The station can then transmit synchronous frames for a time SA_i. The station may not transmit any asynchronous frames.

This scheme is designed to assure that the time between successive sighting of a token is on the order of TTRT or less. Of this time, a given amount is always available for synchronous traffic and any excess capacity is available for asynchronous traffic. Because of random fluctuations in traffic, the actual token circulation time may exceed TTRT [JOHN87, SEVC87], as demonstrated below.

The FDDI algorithm is similar to the 802.4 algorithm with only two classes of data, 6 and 4. Synchronous data corresponds to Class 6, and the value of SA_i in FDDI corresponds to the token holding time in 802.4. Finally, TTRT corresponds to TRT4. Since the sum of the SA_i (all the synchronous allocations) must be less than or equal to TTRT, the FDDI restrictions correspond to Case IIa in Figure 9.17.

Figure 9.21 provides a simplified example of a 4-station ring. The following assumptions are made:

- Traffic consists of fixed-length frames.
- TTRT = 100 frame times.
- SA_i = 20 frame times for each station.
- Each station is always prepared to send its full synchronous allocation and as many asynchronous frames as possible.

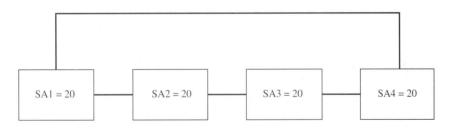

Arrival Time	TRT	Sync	Async	Arrival Time	TRT	Sync	Async	Arrival Time	TRT	Sync	Async	Arrival Time	TRT	Sync	Async
0	100	0	0	1	100	0	0	2	100	0	0	3	100	0	0
4	96	20	96	121	80*	20	0	142	60*	20	0	163	40*	20	0
184	20*	20	0	205	96	20	0	226	76*	20	0	247	56*	20	0
268	36*	20	0	289	16	20	16	326	76*	20	0	347	56*	20	0
368	36*	20	0	389	0	20	0	410	92*	20	0	431	72*	20	0
452	52*	20	0	473	16	20	16	510	92*	20	0	531	72*	20	0
552	52*	20	0	573	0	20	0	594	8	20	8	623	80*	20	0
644	60*	20	0	665	8	20	8	694	0	20	0	715	88*	20	0
736	68*	20	0	757	8	20	8	786	8	20	8	815	88*	20	0
836	68*	20	0	857	0	20	0	878	8	20	8	907	96*	20	0
928	76*	20	0	949	8	20	8	978	0	20	0	999	4	20	4
1024	80*	20	0	1045	4	20	4	1070	8	20	8	1099	0	20	0

*LC = 1

FIGURE 9.21.   Operation of FDDI capacity allocation scheme.

• The total overhead during one complete token circulation is 4 frame times (one frame time per station).

One row of the table corresponds to one circulation of the token. For each station, the token arrival time is shown, followed by the value of TRT at the time of arrival, followed by the number of synchronous and asynchronous frames transmitted while the station holds the token.

The example begins after a period during which no data frames have been sent, so that the token has been circulating as rapidly as possible (4 frame times). Thus, when Station 1 receives the token at time 4, it measures a circulation time of 4 (its TRT = 96). It is therefore able to send not only its 20 synchronous frames but also 96 asynchronous frames; recall that THT is not enabled until after the station has sent its synchronous frames. Station 2 experiences a circulation time of 120 (20 frames + 96 frames + 4 overhead frames) but is nevertheless entitled to transmit its 20 synchronous frames. Note that if each station continues to transmit its maximum allowable synchronous frames, then the circulation time surges to 180 (at time 184) but soon stabilizes at approximately 100. With a total synchronous utilization of 80 and an overhead of 4 frame times, there is an average capacity of 16 frame times available for asynchronous transmission. Note that if all stations always have a full backlog of asynchronous traffic, the opportunity to transmit asynchronous frames is distributed among them.

Distributed-Queue, Dual Bus (DQDB)

The DQDB MAC protocol has been standardized by the IEEE 802.6 committee as part of its MAN standard. The DQDB protocol is intended for use with a dual-bus configuration (see Figure 9.8b). For clarity in our discussion, we use the following terminology (not part of the 802.6 standard): upstream(A) refers to upstream on bus A; downstream(A) refers to downstream on bus A. The node that is upstream(A) of all other nodes is designated head of bus A, or head(A). The terms upstream(B), downstream(B), and head(B) have the obvious corresponding meanings.

Synchronization and Timing

Transmission on each bus consists of a steady stream of fixed-size slots with a length of 53 octets. Nodes read and copy data from the slots; they also gain access to the medium by writing to the slots. Head(A) is responsible for generating the slots on bus A, while head(B) is responsible for generating the slots on bus B. The slot-generation function is indicated by a solid circle in Figure 9.8b; the bus termination function is indicated by a solid square.

Operation of the subnetwork is controlled by a 125-μsec clock. The slot generators in head(A) and head(B) transmit multiple slots to the shared medium every 125 μsec; the number of slots generated per clock cycle depends on the physical data rate.

All slots on the bus are 53 octets in length, consisting of a 1-octet access control field and a 52-octet segment. The two types of slots generated on the network are queue arbitrated (QA) and pre-arbitrated (PA) slots. QA slots are used to carry packet-switched type data and PA slots are used to carry circuit-switched type data. For PA slots, some arbitration function must be used to allocate a dedicated stream of slots for each circuit-switched stream of data. This function has not yet been standardized. The remainder of this section is concerned with the allocation of QA slots.

Description of the DQDB Protocol

Access to QA slots on the DQDB medium is provided by the distributed queue access protocol. Although the basic mechanism of this protocol at any one node is straightforward, the resulting distributed activity is complex. In discussing the distributed queue protocol, we need to remember that there are actually two media: bus A and bus B. Since the access control mechanisms are exactly the same with respect to bus A and bus B, we will generally confine ourselves to a discussion of access control of bus A unless otherwise noted.

The distributed queue access protocol is a distributed reservation scheme. This scheme must take into account the nature of the topology. The essence of the protocol can be summarized as follows. Node X wishes to transmit a block of data to node Y. X must choose the bus on which Y is downstream from X. Let us assume that the bus is A; that is, Y is downstream(A) from X. For X to transmit a block of data in a slot to Y, it must use an available block coming from upstream(A). If the upstream(A) stations monopolize the medium, X is prevented from transmitting. Therefore, X's reservation request must be made to its upstream(A) peers. This requires the use of bus B, since those stations upstream(A) from X are also downstream(B) from X and capable of receiving a reservation request from X on bus B.

The protocol requires that each station defer its own need to transmit to the needs of its downstream peers. As long as one or more downstream peers have outstanding reservation requests, a station will refrain from transmitting, allowing unused slots to continue downstream. The key requirement for the protocol, then, is a mechanism by which each station can keep track of the requests of all of its downstream peers.

The actual behavior of a node will depend on its position on the bus. The four positions of significance (with respect to bus A) are illustrated in Figure 9.22, which shows a DQDB subnetwork with N nodes. Consider first **node (N-1)**, which is head(B). This node has no downstream(A) nodes, and therefore does not transmit data on bus A and does not need to make reservations on bus B. The only data transfer activity for node (N-1) on bus A is reception. The node reads all passing slots. Any QA slot with a destination address matching node (N-1) is copied.

Now consider the node closest to head(B), which in this case is labeled **node (N-2)**. Whenever this node needs to transmit a segment of data, it issues a request on bus B for an available slot on bus A. This actually done by setting

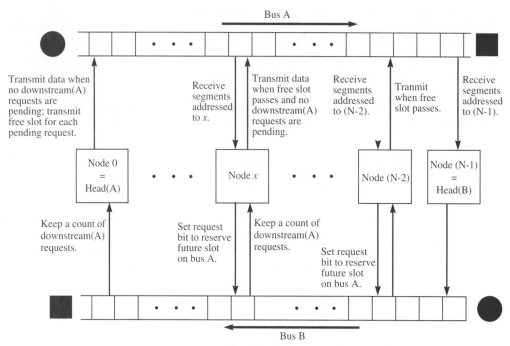

FIGURE 9.22. Basic operation of the distributed queue protocol (data transmission on bus A).

a request bit in a passing slot. Although node (N-2) makes reservations on bus B, it never receives any reservation requests on bus B: Its only upstream(B) peer is node (N-1), which does not issue requests on bus B. On bus A, node (N-2) receives segments of data addressed to it. In addition, when node (N-2) has data to send on bus A and has issued a request on bus B, it may transmit its segment of data in the first free slot on bus A that passes. One bit in the slot indicates whether the slot is free or busy.

A third node whose position is important is head(A), which is labeled **node 0** in the figure. As the head of bus A, this node is responsible for generating the stream of slots on bus A. Thus there will be no QA slots on bus A with data addressed to this node, and all QA slots originate as free slots. When this node has data to send to any other node, it can simply insert that data in the next QA slot that it generates. Because there are no upstream(B) peers of node 0, it has no need to issue requests.

However, it is responsible for seeing that outstanding requests plus its own needs are satisfied in a round-robin, or first-come-first-served basis. To do this, node 0 must keep a running count of how many requests have arrived on bus B that have not yet been satisfied. Table 9.9a summarizes the required behavior. Head(A) keeps track of the number of outstanding requests, which is simply the difference between incoming QA slots with a request and outgoing QA

TABLE 9.9   Behavior of Nodes in Figure 9.22

(a) Behavior of Head(A)

At instant of time when it is ready to issue the next QA slot on bus A

	No preceding requests outstanding	One or more preceding requests outstanding
Head(A) has no data to send	Issue a free QA slot (busy bit set to zero).	Issue a free QA slot and reduce by one the count of preceding requests.
Head(A) has a segment of QA data to send	Issue a QA slot containing the data (busy bit set to one; destination address and data inserted); following requests, if any, now become preceding requests.	Issue a free QA slot and reduce by one the count of preceding requests.

At instant of time when it receives the next QA slot on bus B

	Incoming slot contains a request	Incoming slot does not contain a request
Head(A) has no data to send	Add 1 to count of preceding requests	—
Head(A) has a segment of QA data to send	Add 1 to count of following requests	—

(b) Behavior of Node *x*

At instant of time when it observes a free QA slot on bus A

	No preceding requests outstanding	One or more preceding requests outstanding
Node x has no data to send	Let free slot pass.	Let free slot pass and reduce by one the count of preceding requests.
Node has a segment of QA data to send and has previously issued a request on bus B	Set the busy bit to one on the passing slot and insert data; following requests, if any, now become preceding requests.	Let fee slot pass and reduce by one the count of preceding requests.

TABLE 9.9   *continued*

At instant of time when it observes a QA slot on bus B

	Incoming slot contains a request	Incoming slot does not contain a request
Node x *does not have an outstanding request*	Add 1 to count of preceding requests	—
Node x *has a segment of QA data to send and has already issued a request for that segment*	Add 1 to count of following requests	—
Node x *has a segment of QA data to send and has not yet issued a request for that segment*	Add 1 to count of preceding requests	Insert request into passing slot (set request bit to 1)

slots that are free. If head(A) has a segment of data to send at time T, it must wait until it has satisfied all of the requests outstanding at that time by issuing free QA slots. Once it has satisfied all those requests, it may transmit its own segment. Meanwhile, head(A) must keep track of additional requests that arrive after time T. To distinguish between requests that arrive before and after time T, they are referred to as preceding and following requests, respectively, in Table 9.9.

One way to visualize this operation is to think of it in terms of tickets. Each time that a request arrives, head(A) generates a ticket. Each time that head(A) issues a free QA slot, it discards the oldest ticket. When the node has its own data to send, it generates a ticket on its behalf and places it on the bottom of the stack. As additional tickets are generated by arriving requests, these are placed on the bottom of the stack. When head(A)'s ticket reaches the top of the stack, head(A) can issue a busy QA slot containing its data.

Finally, Figure 9.22 also depicts the behavior of a node other than the three already discussed, labeled **node x.** Like node (N-2), whenever node x needs to transmit a segment of data, it issues a request on bus B for an available slot on bus A. In addition, like node 0, node x must keep a count of requests that pass by on bus B so that its own requests are handled fairly. On bus A, node x receives segments of data addressed to it. In order to enforce a round-robin discipline, node x must keep track of incoming requests that precede and follow its own request, in a manner similar to the behavior of node 0. When node x has data to send and has issued a request, it may transmit its segment of data in a passing free slot only after all preceding requests have been satisfied. Table 9.9b, which is quite similar to Table 9.9a, summarizes the rules of behavior for node x.

Counter Mechanism

The DQDB protocol can be described in terms of a distributed collection of FIFO queues. At each node, a queue is formed for each bus. For each request read in a passing slot, the node inserts one item in the queue. When the node itself issues a request, it adds an item to the queue for itself. When its own item is at the top of the queue, the node may transmit in the next free QA slot. A node may only have one item for itself in each queue (one for each bus) at any time.

This queueing mechanism can be simply implemented with a pair of counters for each queue. When the node is not ready to send, it keeps track of requests on bus B from its downstream(A) neighbors in a request count (RQ). Each time a request is observed (request bit is set), RQ is increased by 1; each time that a free slot passes on bus A, RQ is decremented by 1 to a minimum count of 0.

At any time, the value of RQ represents the unmet need for free QA slots by the node's downstream(A) peers. The node is obligated to let this number of free slots pass before itself using a QA slot to transmit. Therefore, when the node does have data to transmit on bus, it issues a request on bus B as soon as possible. The earliest opportunity will be the first slot to pass in which the request bit has not yet been set. Of course, while waiting for the opportunity to set the request bit, the node must continue to count passing requests in RQ. When the node does set the request bit on a passing slot on bus B, it immediately transfers the current value of RQ to a countdown count (CD) and resets RQ to 0. The node then decrements CD until it reaches 0, at which time the node may transmit on bus A in the next free QA slot. Meanwhile, the node counts new requests on bus B in RQ. The effect of the above is to maintain a single FIFO queue into which the node may insert its own request.

Note that the queue formation is such that a slot is never wasted on the subnetwork if there is a segment queued for it. This is so since the CD count in the queued nodes represents the number of segments queued ahead. Since at any point in time one segment must have queued first, then at least one node is guaranteed to have a CD count of zero. It is that node that will access the next passing free QA slot.

This is a remarkably effective protocol. Under conditions of light load, the value of CD will be small or 0 and free QA slots will be frequent. Thus, with a light load, delay is negligible, a property shared by CSMA/CD protocols. Under heavy loads, virtually every free QA slot will be utilized by one of the waiting nodes. Thus, with a heavy load, efficiency approaches 100 percent, a property shared by token bus and token ring protocols. This combination of quick access under light load and predictable queueing under heavy load makes the protocol suitable for a MAN of high data rate that will carry a mix of bursty traffic (e.g., interactive use) and more sustained stream-like traffic (e.g., file transfers).

A Simple Example

Figure 9.23, adapted from an example in 802.6 document, provides a simple example of the operation of the basic protocol. The example is limited to transmission of data on bus A; none of the nodes is a head-of-bus node.

The example starts at a point when there are no outstanding requests. At that point, all nodes have an RQ value of 0. Then, the following events occur:

1. Node E issues a request on bus B by changing the busy bit in a passing slot from 0 to 1. Each downstream(B) node (nodes A–D) increments its RQ counter. At the same time, node E transfers its RQ count to its CD count. In this case, the count is 0, so node E can transmit on bus A as soon as it sees a free QA slot.
2. Node B issues a request on bus B. The node transfers the value of RQ, which is 1, to CD and sets RQ to 0. This node will have to wait until 1 free QA slot passes on bus A before gaining access. Node A sees the request bit that has been set and increments its RQ value to 2.
3. Node C issues a request on bus B. C sets its CD value to 1 and its RQ value to 0. Node B increments its RQ value to 1. Note that B's CD value is unchanged; the arrival of new requests after B has issued its own request does not affect the timing of B's access to bus A. Node A increments its RQ to 3.
4. A free QA slot passes down bus A. Nodes A and D decrement their RQ counts. Nodes B and C decrement their CD counts. Node E has a CD of 0 and so can seize the free slot by changing the busy bit from 0 to 1 and inserting a QA segment.
5. Another free QA slot passes down bus A. Node A decrements its RQ count. Both nodes B and C are eligible to seize the free slot. However, the free slot passes node B first, which uses it to transmit a QA segment.
6. Node C uses the next passing free slot to transmit. The system returns to its original state, in which all nodes have an RQ value of 0.

Note that the three requests are satisfied in the order issued. Thus, the behavior of the network as a whole is that of a FIFO queue.

9.6

MAC PERFORMANCE

The choice of a LAN or MAN architecture is based on many factors, but one of the most important is performance. Of particular concern is the behavior (throughput, response time) of the network under heavy load. In this section,

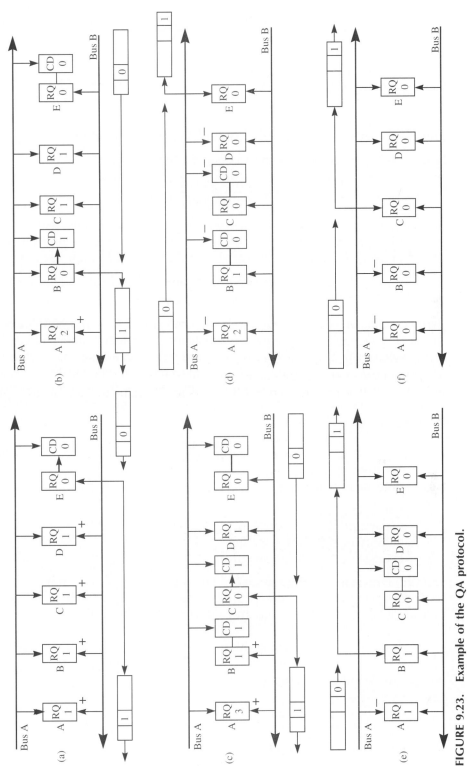

FIGURE 9.23. Example of the QA protocol.

we provide an introduction to this topic. A more detailed discussion can be found in [STAL93b].

The Effect of Propagation Delay and Transmission Rate

In Chapter 5, we introduced the parameter a, defined as

$$a = \frac{\text{Propagation time}}{\text{Transmission time}}$$

In that context, we were concerned with a point-to-point link, with a given propagation time between the two endpoints and a transmission time for either a fixed or average frame size. It was shown that a could be expressed as

$$a = \frac{\text{Length of data link in bits}}{\text{Length of frame in bits}}$$

This parameter is also important in the context of LANs and MANs and in fact determines an upper bound on utilization. Consider a perfectly efficient access mechanism that allows only one transmission at a time. As soon as one transmission is over, another station begins transmitting. Furthermore, the transmission is pure data, no overhead bits. What is the maximum possible utilization of the network? It can be expressed as the ratio of total throughput of the network to its capacity:

$$U = \frac{\text{Throughput}}{\text{Capacity}} \tag{9.1}$$

Now define, as in Chapter 5:

R = data rate of the channel
d = maximum distance between any two stations
V = velocity of signal propagation
L = average or fixed frame length

The throughput is just the number of bits transmitted per unit time. A frame contains L bits, and the amount of time devoted to that frame is the actual transmission time (L/R) plus the propagation delay (d/V). Thus

$$\text{Throughput} = \frac{L}{d/V + L/R} \tag{9.2}$$

But by our definition of a, above:

$$a = \frac{d/V}{L/R} = \frac{Rd}{LV} \tag{9.3}$$

Substituting (9.2) and (9.3) into (9.1):

$$U = \frac{1}{1 + a} \tag{9.4}$$

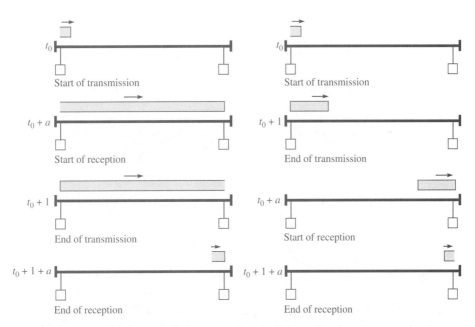

(a) Transmission time = 1; propagation time = $a < 1$ (b) Transmission time = 1; propagation time = $a > 1$

FIGURE 9.24.   The effect of a on utilization: baseband bus.

Note that this differs from Equation (5.2). This is because the latter assumed a half-duplex protocol (no piggybacked acknowledgments).

So utilization varies with a. This can be grasped intuitively by studying Figure 9.24, which shows a baseband bus with two stations as far apart as possible (worst case) that take turns sending frames. If we normalize time such that frame transmission time = 1, then the propagation time = a. For $a < 1$, the sequence of events is as follows:

1. A station begins transmitting at t_0.
2. Reception begins at $t_0 + a$.
3. Transmission is completed at $t_0 + 1$.
4. Reception ends at $t_0 + 1 + a$.
5. The other station begins transmitting.

For $a > 1$, events 2 and 3 are interchanged. In both cases, the total time for one "turn" is $1 + a$, but the transmission time is only 1, for a utilization of $1/(1 + a)$.

The same effect can be seen to apply to a ring network in Figure 9.25. Here we assume that one station transmits and then waits to receive its own transmission before any other station transmits. The identical sequence of events outlined above applies.

Typical values of a range from about 0.01 to 0.1 for LANs and 0.1 to well over 1.0 for MANs. Table 9.10 gives some representative values for a bus to-

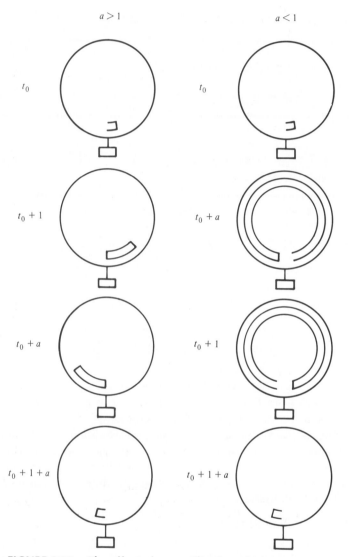

FIGURE 9.25. The effect of a on utilization: ring.

pology. As can be seen, for larger and/or higher-speed networks, utilization suffers. For this reason, the restriction of only one frame at a time is lifted for LANs such as FDDI and DQDB. For both these protocols, multiple frames may be in transit at a time, raising utilization.

Finally, the analysis above assumes a "perfect" protocol, for which a new frame can be transmitted as soon as an old frame is received. In practice, the MAC protocol adds overhead that makes utilization worse. This is demonstrated in the next subsection for token-passing and CSMA/CD.

TABLE 9.10 Representative Values of a

Data rate (Mbps)	Frame size (bits)	Network length (km)	a	$\dfrac{1}{1 + a}$
1	100	1	0.05	0.95
1	1,000	10	0.05	0.95
1	100	10	0.5	0.67
10	100	1	0.5	0.67
10	1,000	1	0.05	0.95
10	1,000	10	0.5	0.67
10	10,000	10	0.05	0.95
100	35,000	200	2.8	0.26
100	1,000	50	25	0.04

Simple Performance Models of Token Passing and CSMA/CD

The purpose of this section is to give the reader some insight into the relative performance of the most important LAN protocols: CSMA/CD, token bus, and token ring, by developing two simple performance models. It is hoped that this exercise will aid in understanding the results of more rigorous analyses.

For these models we assume a local network with N active stations, and a maximum normalized propagation delay of a. To simplify the analysis, we assume that each station is always prepared to transmit a packet. This allows us to develop an expression for maximum achievable utilization (U). Although this should not be construed to be the sole figure of merit for a local network, it is the single most analyzed figure of merit, and does permit useful performance comparisons.

First, let us consider token ring. Time on the ring will alternate between data packet transmission and token passing. Refer to a single instance of a data packet followed by a token as a cycle and define:

$$C = \text{average time for one cycle}$$
$$T_1 = \text{average time to transmit a data packet}$$
$$T_2 = \text{average time to pass a token}$$

It should be clear that the average cycle rate is just $1/C = 1/(T_1 + T_2)$. Intuitively,

$$U = \frac{T_1}{T_1 + T_2} \tag{9.5}$$

That is, the throughput, normalized to system capacity, is just the fraction of time that is spent transmitting data.

Refer now to Figure 9.25; time is normalized such that packet transmission time equals 1 and propagation time equals a. Note that the propagation time must include repeater delays. For the case of $a < 1$, a station transmits a packet at time t_0, receives the leading edge of its own packet at $t_0 + a$, and completes transmission at $t_0 + 1$. The station then emits a token, which takes an average time a/N to reach the next station. Thus one cycle takes $1 + a/N$ and the transmission time is 1. So $S = 1/(1 + a/N)$.

For $a > 1$, the reasoning is slightly different. A station transmits at t_0, completes transmission at $t_0 + 1$, and receives the leading edge of its frame at $t_0 + a$. At that point, it is free to emit a token, which takes an average time a/N to reach the next station. The cycle time is therefore $a + a/N$ and $U = 1/(a (1 + 1/N))$.

Summarizing,

$$
Token\ U = \begin{cases} \dfrac{1}{1 + a/N} & a < 1 \\[2ex] \dfrac{1}{a (1 + 1/N)} & a > 1 \end{cases} \tag{9.6}
$$

The reasoning above applies equally well to token bus, where we assume that the logical ordering is the same as the physical ordering and that token-passing time is therefore a/N.

For CSMA/CD, we base our approach on a derivation in [METC76]. Consider time on the medium to be organized into slots whose length is twice the end-to-end propagation delay. This is a convenient way to view the activity on the medium; the slot time is the maximum time, from the start of transmission, required to detect a collision. Again, assume that there are N active stations. Clearly, if each station always has a packet to transmit, and does so, there will be nothing but collisions on the line. So we assume that each station restrains itself to transmitting during an available slot with probability P.

Time on the medium consists of two types of intervals. First is a transmission interval, which lasts $1/2a$ slots. Second is a contention interval, which is a sequence of slots with either a collision or no transmission in each slot. The throughput is just the proportion of time spent in transmission intervals [similar to the reasoning for Equation (9.5)].

To determine the average length of a contention interval, we begin by computing A, the probability that exactly one station attempts a transmission in a slot and therefore acquires the medium. This is just the binomial probability that any one station attempts to transmit and the others do not:

$$
A = \binom{N}{1} P^1 (1 - P)^{N-1}
$$

$$
A = NP(1 - P)^{N-1}
$$

This function takes on a maximum over P when $P = 1/N$:

$$
A = (1 - 1/N)^{N-1}
$$

Why are we interested in the maximum? Well, we want to calculate the maximum throughput of the medium. It should be clear that this will be achieved if we maximize the probability of successful seizure of the medium. This says that the following rule should be enforced: During periods of heavy usage, a station should restrain its offered load to $1/N$. (This assumes that each station knows the value of N. In order to derive an expression for maximum possible throughput, we live with this assumption.) On the other hand, during periods of light usage, maximum utilization cannot be achieved because G is too low; this region is not of interest here.

Now we can estimate the mean length of a contention interval, w, in slots:

$$E[w] = \sum_{i=1}^{\infty} i \Pr[i \text{ slots in a row with a collision or no transmission followed by a slot with one transmission}]$$

$$= \sum_{i=1}^{\infty} i(1 - A)^i A$$

The summation converges to

derived from # of stations

$$E[w] = \frac{1 - A}{A}$$

We can now determine the maximum utilization, which is just the length of a transmission interval as a proportion of a cycle consisting of a transmission and a contention interval:

ratio — *prop* = *d/v*
t frame (*entire bus*)/R

$$\text{CSMA/CD: } U = \frac{1/2a}{1/2a + (1 - A)/A} = \frac{1}{1 + 2a(1 - A)/A} \tag{9.7}$$

Figure 9.26 shows normalized throughput as a function of a for various values of N and for both token passing and CSMA/CD. For both protocols, throughput declines as a increases. This is to be expected. But the dramatic difference between the two protocols is seen in Figure 9.27, which shows throughput as a function of N. Token-passing performance actually improves as a function of N, because less time is spent in token passing. Conversely, the performance of CSMA/CD decreases because of the increased likelihood of collision or no transmission.

It is interesting to note the asymptotic value of U as N increases. For token:

$$\text{Token: } \lim_{N \to \infty} U = \begin{cases} 1 & a < 1 \\ \dfrac{1}{a} & a > 1 \end{cases} \tag{9.8}$$

For CSMA/CD, we need to know that $\lim (1 - 1/N)^{N-1} = 1/e$. Then CSMA/CD:

$$\lim_{N \to \infty} U = \frac{1}{1 + 3.44a} \tag{9.9}$$

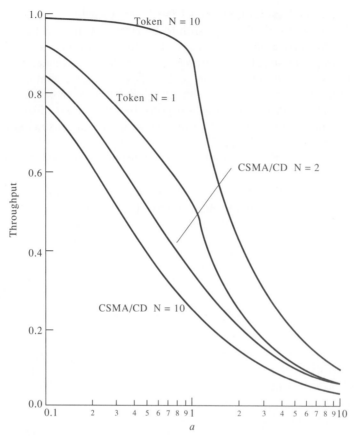

FIGURE 9.26. Throughput as a function of *a* for token passing and CSMA/CD.

LAN/MAN STANDARDS

In recent years, the market for LAN and MAN products has come to be dominated by those that conform to standards. The reasons for this are compelling:

1. The published standards are the product of a broad-based effort involving highly knowledgeable individuals from a wide spectrum of vendor and customer organizations. Thus, the specified combinations chosen for standardization reflect a consensus as to which combinations meet typical requirements.

2. The LAN standards have achieved widespread and rapid acceptance both by vendors and customers. Thus, the customer benefits from the cost savings of mass production and has a broad range of compatible products to choose from.

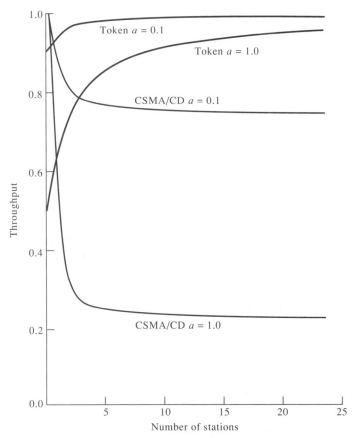

FIGURE 9.27. Throughput as a function of N for token passing and CSMA/CD.

The standards that have been issued are illustrated in Figure 9.28. Most of the standards were developed by a committee known as IEEE 802, sponsored by the Institute for Electrical and Electronics Engineers; one of the standards was developed by the American National Standards Institute (ANSI). All of these standards have subsequently been adopted as international standards by the International Organization for Standardization (ISO).

The standards are organized as a three-layer protocol hierarchy. Logical link control (LLC) is responsible for addressing and data link control. It is independent of the topology, transmission medium, and medium access control technique chosen and was issued as a separate standard. Below logical link control are the medium access control (MAC) and physical layers. Because of the interdependence between medium access control, medium, and topology, these layers were organized into standards based on the medium access control algorithm, with the physical layer specified as part of the medium access control standard.

Logical link control (LLC)		IEEE 802.2 • Unacknowledged connectionless service • Connection-mode service • Acknowledged connectionless service				
Medium access control (MAC)		CSMA/CD	Token bus	Token ring	Token ring	DQDB
Physical	IEEE 802.3	Baseband coaxial: 10 Mbps (2 versions) Unshielded twisted pair: 1,10 Mbps Broadband coaxial: 10 Mbps	IEEE 802.4 Broadband coaxial: 1, 5, 10 Mbps Carrierband: 1, 5, 10 Mbps Optical fiber: 5, 10, 20 Mbps	IEEE 802.5 Shielded twisted pair: 4, 16 Mbps Unshielded twisted pair: 4 Mbps	FDDI Optical fiber: 100 Mbps	IEEE 802.6 Optical fiber or coaxial: 44.736 Mbps

bus/tree/star topologies   ring topology   dual bus topology

FIGURE 9.28.   LAN/MAN standards.

Figure 9.29 relates the LAN standards to the OSI architecture (first introduced in Figure 1.10). The work on LAN standards has resulted, in effect, in a communications architecture for LAN communication. Fortunately, this architecture was designed to be a subset of the OSI architecture. This makes it easy to see that any set of higher-layer protocols, such as TCP/IP, SNA, or the OSI-related standards, can be used in conjunction with the various LAN protocols.

Figure 9.30 illustrates the relationship between the levels of the architecture (compare Figure 8.28). User data are passed down to LLC, which appends control information as a header, creating an *LLC protocol data unit (PDU).* This control information is used in the operation of the LLC protocol. The entire LLC PDU is then passed down to the MAC layer, which appends control information at the front and back of the packet, forming a *MAC frame.* Again, the control information in the frame is needed for the operation of the MAC protocol. Figure 9.31 shows the format of the LLC PDU and MAC frames.[2]

Logical Link Control (IEEE 802.2)

LLC provides a layer of functionality above the MAC layer. Essentially, LLC provides most of the functions of a traditional data link control protocol such

[2]The 802.6 format, which is quite complex, is not shown. See [STAL93a] or [STAL93b] for a detailed description.

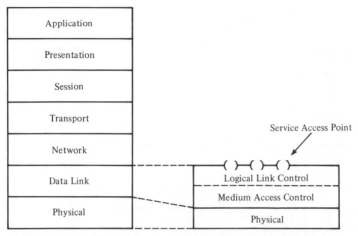

FIGURE 9.29.   IEEE 802 reference model relationship to OSI model.

as HDLC. We look first at the services that LLC provides to a higher-level user, then at the LLC protocol.

LLC Services

LLC specifies the mechanisms for addressing stations across the medium and for controlling the exchange of data between two users. The operation and format of this standard is based on HDLC. Three services are provided as alternatives for attached devices using LLC:

• *Unacknowledged connectionless service:* This service is a datagram-style service. It is a very simple service that does not involve any of the flow- and error-

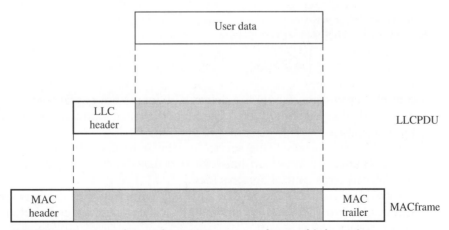

FIGURE 9.30.   User data and LAN/MAN protocol control information.

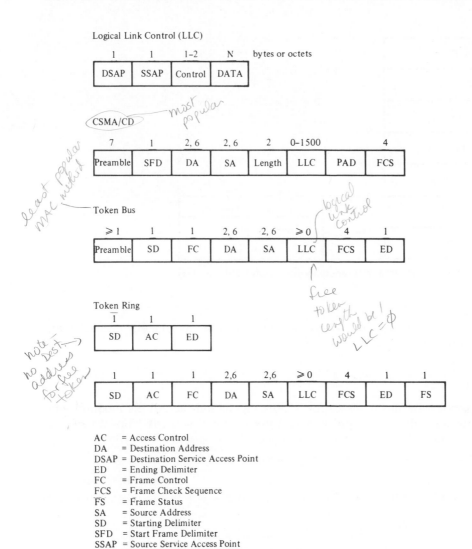

Logical Link Control (LLC)

1	1	1–2	N	bytes or octets
DSAP	SSAP	Control	DATA	

CSMA/CD — *most popular*

7	1	2, 6	2, 6	2	0–1500		4
Preamble	SFD	DA	SA	Length	LLC	PAD	FCS

least popular MAC method

Token Bus

logical link control

≥ 1	1	1	2, 6	2, 6	≥ 0	4	1
Preamble	SD	FC	DA	SA	LLC	FCS	ED

free token length would be / LLC = ∅

Token Ring

1	1	1
SD	AC	ED

note — no Dest. address for free token

1	1	1	2,6	2,6	≥ 0	4	1	1
SD	AC	FC	DA	SA	LLC	FCS	ED	FS

AC   = Access Control
DA   = Destination Address
DSAP = Destination Service Access Point
ED   = Ending Delimiter
FC   = Frame Control
FCS = Frame Check Sequence
FS   = Frame Status
SA   = Source Address
SD   = Starting Delimiter
SFD = Start Frame Delimiter
SSAP = Source Service Access Point

FIGURE 9.31.   LAN standard formats.

control mechanisms. Thus, the delivery of data is not guaranteed. However, in most devices, there will be some higher layer of software that deals with reliability issues.

- *Connection-mode service:* This service is similar to that offered by HDLC. A logical connection is set up between two users exchanging data, and flow control and error control are provided.
- *Acknowledged connectionless service:* This is a cross between the previous two services. It provides that datagrams are to be acknowledged, but no prior logical connection is set up.

Typically, a vendor will provide these services as options that the customer can select when purchasing the equipment. Alternatively, the customer can purchase equipment that provides two or all three services and select a specific service based on application.

The **unacknowledged connectionless service** requires minimum logic and is useful in two contexts. First, it will often be the case that higher layers of software will provide the necessary reliability and flow-control mechanism, and it is efficient to avoid duplicating them. For example, either TCP or the ISO transport protocol standard would provide the mechanisms needed to ensure that data are delivered reliably. Second, there are instances in which the overhead of connection establishment and maintenance is unjustified or even counterproductive, for example, data collection activities that involve the periodic sampling of data sources, such as sensors and automatic self-test reports from security equipment or network components. In a monitoring application, the loss of an occasional data unit would not cause distress, as the next report should arrive shortly. Thus, in most cases, the unacknowledged connectionless service is the preferred option.

The **connection-mode service** could be used in very simple devices, such as terminal controllers, that have little software operating above this level. In these cases, it would provide the flow control and reliability mechanisms normally implemented at higher layers of the communications software.

The **acknowledged connectionless service** is useful in several contexts. With the connection-mode service, the logical link control software must maintain some sort of table for each active connection, to keep track of the status of that connection. If the user needs guaranteed delivery, but there are a large number of destinations for data, then the connection-mode service may be impractical because of the large number of tables required. An example is a process control or automated factory environment where a central site may need to communicate with a large number of processors and programmable controllers. Another example is the handling of important and time-critical alarm or emergency control signals in a factory. Because of their importance, an acknowledgment is needed so that the sender can be assured that the signal got through. Because of the urgency of the signal, the user might not want to take the time to first establish a logical connection and then send the data.

LLC Protocol

The basic LLC protocol is modeled after HDLC and has similar functions and formats. The differences between the two protocols can be summarized as follows:

1. LLC makes use of the asynchronous balanced mode of operation of HDLC, to support connection-mode LLC service; this is referred to as type 2 operation. The other HDLC modes are not employed.
2. LLC supports a connectionless service using the unnumbered information PDU; this is known as type 1 operation.

3. LLC supports an acknowledged connectionless service by using two new unnumbered PDUs; this is known as type 3 operation.
4. LLC permits multiplexing by the use of LLC service access points (LSAPs).

All three LLC protocols employ the same PDU format (top of Figure 9.31), which consists of four fields. The DSAP and SSAP fields each contain 7-bit addresses, which specify the destination and source users of LLC. One bit of the DSAP indicates whether this is an individual or group address. One bit of the SSAP indicates whether it is a command or response PDU. The format of the LLC control field is identical to that of HDLC (Figure 5.13), using extended (7-bit) sequence numbers.

For **type 1 operation,** which supports the unacknowledged connectionless service, the unnumbered information (UI) PDU is used to transfer user data. There is no acknowledgment, flow control, or error control. However, there are error detection and discard at the MAC level.

Two other PDUs are used to support management functions associated with all three types of operation. Both PDUs are used in the following fashion. An LLC entity may issue a command (C/R bit = 0) XID or TEST. The receiving LLC entity issues a corresponding XID or TEST in response. The XID PDU is used to exchange two types of information: types of operation supported and window size. The TEST PDU is used to conduct a loop-back test of the transmission path between two LLC entities. Upon receipt of a TEST command PDU, the addressed LLC entity issues a TEST response PDU as soon as possible.

With **type 2 operation,** a data link connection is established between two LLC SAPs prior to data exchange. Connection establishment is attempted by the type 2 protocol in response to a request from a user. The LLC entity issues a SABME PDU[3] to request a logical connection with the other LLC entity. If the connection is accepted by the LLC user designated by the DSAP, then the destination LLC entity returns an unnumbered acknowledgment (UA) PDU. The connection is henceforth uniquely identified by the pair of user SAPs. If the destination LLC user rejects the connection request, its LLC entity returns a disconnected mode (DM) PDU.

Once the connection is established, data are exchanged using information PDUs, as in HDLC. The information PDUs include send and receive sequence numbers, for sequencing and flow control. The supervisory PDUs are used, as in HDLC, for flow control and error control. Either LLC entity can terminate a logical LLC connection by issuing a disconnect (DISC) PDU.

With **type 3 operation,** each transmitted PDU is acknowledged. A new (not found in HDLC) unnumbered PDU, the Acknowledged Connectionless (AC) Information PDU, is defined. User data are sent in AC command PDUs and must be acknowledged using an AC response PDU. To guard against lost

---

[3]This stands for Set Asynchronous Balanced Mode Extended. It is used in HDLC to choose ABM and to select extended sequence numbers of seven bits. Both ABM and 7-bit sequence numbers are mandatory in type 2 operation.

PDUs, a 1-bit sequence number is used. The sender alternates the use of 0 and 1 in its AC command PDU, and the receiver responds with an AC PDU with the opposite sequence number of the corresponding command. Only one PDU in each direction may be outstanding at any time.

CSMA/CD (IEEE 802.3)

Medium Access Control

The 802.3 medium access control technique is CSMA/CD, as described in this chapter. In order to implement the CSMA/CD algorithm, data are transmitted in the form of packets, referred to as MAC frames, which contain user information and the control information needed for the algorithm. Figure 9.31 shows the format of the IEEE 802.3 MAC frame. The preamble is a special 7-octet pattern used by each receiver to establish bit synchronization. This is followed by a start frame delimiter which is a special pattern that signals the beginning of the frame proper. The destination and source addresses specify the transmitting station and the intended receiving station respectively. The length field specifies the number of data octets that follow. The pad field is inserted by the transmitter if needed to assure that the frame is long enough for proper CD operation. Finally, the frame check sequence is a 32-bit cyclic redundancy check for error detection.

Medium Options

Table 9.11a summarizes the options defined for the IEEE 802.3 medium. The **original 802.3 standard (10BASE5)** specified a 10-Mbps baseband coaxial cable LAN using standard baseband coaxial cable. The maximum length of a segment of cable is 500 meters, with a maximum of 100 taps per segment allowed. The length of the network can be extended using repeaters. The standard allows a maximum of four repeaters in the path between any two stations, extending the effective length of the network to 2.5 km.

This original version, issued in 1985, was soon followed by a new option, sometimes called **Cheapernet (10BASE2).** This provides for the use of a thinner coaxial cable at the same data rate. The thinner cable results in significantly cheaper electronics, at the penalty of fewer stations and shorter length. Segment length is reduced to 185 meters with a maximum of 30 taps per segment. It is targeted to lower-cost devices, such as UNIX workstations and personal computers.

Another option, known as **StarLAN (1BASE5),** specifies an unshielded twisted-pair version operating at 1 Mbps, using a passive star topology. This option is substantially lower in cost than either of the coaxial cable options and is targeted specifically at personal computer installations that do not require high capacity. This option could be appropriate for a departmental-level LAN. The most recent addition to the standard is the **10BASE-T** option which is also

TABLE 9.11 Physical Layer Specifications for LAN and MAN Standards

(a) IEEE 802.3 (CSMA/CD)

	Transmission Medium	Signaling Technique	Data Rate (Mbps)	Maximum Segment Length (m)
10BASE5	Coaxial Cable (50 ohm)	Baseband (Manchester)	10	500
10BASE2	Coaxial Cable (50 ohm)	Baseband (Manchester)	10	185
1BASE5	Unshielded Twisted Pair	Baseband (Manchester)	1	250
10BASE-T	Unshielded Twisted Pair	Baseband (Manchester)	10	100
10BROAD36	Coaxial Cable (75 ohm)	Broadband (DPSK)	10	3600

(b) IEEE 802.4 (Token Bus)

	Transmission Medium	Signaling Technique	Data Rate (Mbps)	Maximum Segment Length (m)
Broadband	Coaxial Cable (75 ohm)	Broadband (AM/PSK)	1, 5, 10	Not specified
Carrierband	Coaxial Cable (75 ohm)	Broadband (FSK)	1, 5, 10	7600
Optical Fiber	Optical Fiber	ASK-Manchester	5, 10, 20	Not specified

(c) IEEE 802.5 (Token Ring)

Transmission Medium	Signaling Technique	Data Rate (Mbps)	Maximum Number of Repeaters	Maximum Distance Between Repeaters (m)
Shielded Twisted Pair	Differential Manchester	4, 16	250	Not specified
Unshielded Twisted Pair	Differential Manchester	4	250	Not specified

TABLE 9.11 *continued*

(d) Fiber Distributed Data Interface (FDDI)

Transmission Medium	Signaling Technique	Data Rate (Mbps)	Maximum Number of Repeaters	Maximum Distance Between Repeaters (m)
Optical Fiber	ASK-NRZI	100	1000	2000

(e) IEEE 802.6 (DQDB)

Transmission Medium	Signaling Technique	Data Rate (Mbps)	Maximum segment Length (m)
Optical Fiber or Coaxial Cable	Not specified	44.736	160,000

a passive-star-topology LAN using unshielded twisted pair, but operating at 10 Mbps.

A 10-Mbps **broadband (10BROAD36)** option has also been added. This provides for the support of more stations over greater distances than the baseband versions, at greater cost.

Token Bus (IEEE 802.4)

Medium Access Control

The 802.4 medium access control technique is the token bus algorithm. Figure 9.31 shows the MAC frame format. The only new field, compared to 802.3, is the frame control field. This field contains information needed for the proper operation of the algorithm. One bit indicates whether this frame carries user data or is a control frame. In the latter case, the remaining bits specify which control frame (e.g., token, who-follows).

Medium Options

The token bus standard specifies three physical layer options (Table 9.11b). The first is a **broadband** system, which supports data channels at 1, 5, and 10 Mbps with bandwidths of 1.5, 6, and 12 MHz, respectively. The standard recommends the use of a single-cable split system with a headend frequency translator. The dual cable configuration is also allowed.

The second is a scheme known as **carrierband,** or single-channel broadband. Because carrierband is dedicated to a single data channel, it is not necessary to take care that the modem output be confined to a narrow bandwidth. Energy can spread over the cable's spectrum. As a result, the electronics are simple and inexpensive compared with those for broadband. Carrierband data rates of 1, 5, and 10 Mbps are specified.

The most recent option is one using optical fiber at data rates of 5, 10, and 20 Mbps. Either a passive or active star topology can be used.

Token Ring (IEEE 802.5)

Medium Access Control

The 802.5 medium access control technique is token passing on a ring topology. Figure 9.31 shows the frame format. The access control field includes a token bit to indicate whether this is a frame or not. In the former case, the remainder of the frame simply consists of the ending delimiter. The access control field also includes a 3-bit priority and a 3-bit reservation, used in the capacity allocation algorithm. The frame control field serves the same function as in the 802.4 MAC frame. The frame status field contains bits that may be set by the receiver to indicate that it has recognized its address and copied the frame; these bits can then be read by the source station when it absorbs the frame.

Medium Option

The IEEE 802.5 standard specifies **shielded twisted pair** at 4 and 16 Mbps or **unshielded twisted pair** at 4 Mbps (Table 9.11c).

This standard is supported by IBM, and there is a large number of other vendors with 802.5 products on the market.

Fiber Distributed Data Interface (FDDI)

Medium Access Control

The FDDI medium access control technique is also a token-passing ring technique. As explained in the discussion earlier in this chapter, FDDI does not use the priority/reservation scheme of 802.5 for reasons of efficiency. Accordingly, the FDDI MAC frame (Figure 9.31) is the same as that of 802.5 except that there is no access control field in the FDDI frame.

Medium Option

The medium specified is 100-Mbps optical fiber (Table 9.11d). The medium specifications specifically incorporate measures designed to ensure high availability.

DQDB (IEEE 802.6)

The 802.6 medium access control technique is the distributed-queue dual-bus (DQDB) protocol. The DQDB layer is independent of the physical layer. Therefore, a variety of DQDB networks can be implemented using the same access layer but operating at different data rates over different transmission systems. Three transmission systems are referenced in the standard:

- ANSI DS3: Transmits at 44.736 Mbps over coaxial cable or optical fiber.
- ANSI SONET (CCITT SDH): Transmits data at 155.52 Mbps and above over single-mode optical fiber.
- CCITT G.703: Transmits data at 34.368 Mbps and 139.264 Mbps over a metallic medium.

For each transmission system, a physical layer convergence protocol is used to provide a consistent physical-layer service to the DQDB layer. The only physical-layer convergence function defined in the current standard is for DS3.

9.8

RECOMMENDED READING

The literature on LANs and MANs is vast. The material in this chapter is covered in much more depth in [STAL93b]. [STAL93e] contains reprints of key articles on LANs and MANs, as well as an annotated bibliography.

[SLON91], [MART89], and [NAUG91] are good book-length treatments of LANs. [KESS92] covers MANs.

Books with rigorous treatments of LAN/MAN performance include [STUC85], [HAMM86], [SPAR91], and [BERT92].

[STAL90] is a treatment oriented toward managers and end users.

9.9

PROBLEMS

9.1 An alternative to a local network for meeting local requirements for data processing and computer applications is a centralized time-sharing system plus a large number of terminals dispersed throughout the local area. What are the major benefits and pitfalls of this approach compared to a local network?

9.2 Could HDLC be used as a data link control protocol for a local network? If not, what is missing?

9.3 An asynchronous device, such as a teletype, transmits characters one at a time with unpredictable delays between characters. What problems, if any, do you foresee if such a device is connected to a local network and allowed to transmit at will (subject to gaining access to the medium)? How might such problems be resolved?

9.4 Consider the transfer of a file containing one million characters from one station to another. What is the total elapsed time and effective throughput for the following cases:

a. A circuit-switched, star topology local network. Call setup time is negligible, and the data rate on the medium is 64 kbps.

b. A bus topology local network with two stations a distance D apart, a data rate of B bps, and a packet size P with 80 bits of overhead. Each packet is acknowledged with an 88-bit packet before the next is sent. The propagation speed on the bus is 200 m/μs. Solve for:

(1) $D = 1$ km, $B = 1$ Mbps, $P = 256$ bits
(2) $D = 1$ km, $B = 10$ Mbps, $P = 256$ bits
(3) $D = 10$ km, $B = 1$ Mbps, $P = 256$ bits
(4) $D = 1$ km, $B = 50$ Mbps, $P = 10,000$ bits

c. A ring topology with a total circular length of $2D$, with the two stations a distance D apart. Acknowledgment is achieved by allowing a packet to circulate past the destination station, back to the source station. There are N repeaters on the ring, each of which introduces a delay of one bit time. Repeat the calculation for each of b_1 through b_4 for $N = 10$; 100; 1000.

9.5 A tree-topology local network is to be provided that spans two buildings. If permission can be obtained to string cable between the two buildings, one continuous tree layout will be used. Otherwise, each building will have an independent tree topology network and a point-to-point link will connect a special communications station on one network with a communications station on the other network. What functions must the communications stations perform? Repeat for ring and star.

9.6 System A consists of a single ring with 300 stations, one per repeater. System B consists of three 100-station rings linked by a bridge. If the probability of a link failure is P_1, a repeater failure is P_r, and a bridge failure is P_b, derive an expression for parts (a) through (d):

a. Probability of failure of system A.

b. Probability of complete failure of system B.

c. Probability that a particular station will find the network unavailable, for systems A and B.

d. Probability that any two stations, selected at random, will be unable to communicate, for systems A and B.

e. Compute values for parts (a) through (d) for $P_1 = P_b = P_r = 10^{-2}$.

9.7 The binary exponential backoff algorithm is defined by IEEE 802 thus: "The delay is an integral multiple of slot time. The number of slot times to delay before the nth retransmission attempt is chosen as a uniformly distributed random integer r in the range $0 < r < 2**K$, where $K = \min(n,10)$." Slot time is, roughly, twice the round-trip propagation delay. Assume that two stations always have a frame to send. After a collision, what is the mean number of retransmission attempts before one station successfully transmits? What is the answer if three stations always have frames to send?

9.8 For the p-persistent protocol (Figure 9.11), consider the following situation. A station is ready to transmit and is listening to the current transmission. No other station is ready to transmit and there will be no other transmissions for an indefinite period. If the time unit used in the protocol is T, show that the average number of iterations of step 1 of the protocol is $1/p$ and that therefore the expected time that the station will have to wait after the current transmission is over is $T\left(\dfrac{1}{p} - 1\right)$. Hint: Use the equality $\displaystyle\sum_{i=1}^{\infty} iX^{i-1} = \dfrac{1}{(1 - X)^2}$.

9.9 Another medium access control technique for rings is the slotted ring. A number of fixed-length slots circulate continuously on the ring. Each slot contains a leading bit to designate the slot as empty or full. A station wishing to transmit waits until an empty slot arrives, marks the slot full, and inserts a packet of data as the slot goes by. The full slot makes a complete round trip, to be marked empty again by the station that marked it full. In what sense are the slotted ring and token ring protocols the complement of each other?

9.10 For a token ring system, suppose that the destination station removes the data frame and immediately sends a short acknowledgment frame to the sender, rather than letting the original frame return to sender. How will this affect performance?

9.11 Consider a slotted ring of length 10 km with a data rate of 10 Mbps and 500 repeaters, each of which introduces a 1-bit delay. Each slot contains room for one source address byte, one destination address byte, two data bytes, and five control bits for a total length of 37 bits. How many slots are on the ring?

9.12 Compare the capacity allocation schemes for token bus, IEEE 802 token ring, and FDDI. What are the relative pros and cons?

9.13 Compare equations (9.4), (9.6), and (9.7). Under what circumstances does the throughput for the latter two equations exceed the theoretical maximum of (9.4)? Explain.

9.14 Equations (9.6) and (9.8) are valid for token ring and for token baseband bus. What are equivalent equations for broadband bus?

9.15 The maximum distance for a 10-Mbps baseband bus LAN without repeaters is about 500 m. If stations are located at the end of such a system, what is the delay from one station to the other? Does this present a problem? Why or why not?

9.16 Refer to Figure 9.16. Is it possible that class 0 data might experience starvation (never get a chance to transmit)? Consider two cases:

a. A node that has class 0 and class 6 data to send

b. A node that only has class 0 data to send

9.17 A motivation for using a different capacity allocation scheme for FDDI compared to the IEEE token ring scheme is that the FDDI scheme is more flexible and efficient in allocating capacity for stream and bursty traffic. But it is also the case that the IEEE scheme *cannot* be used on FDDI. Why?

9.18 Rework the example of Figure 9.21 using a TTRT of 12 packets and assume that no station ever has more than 8 asynchronous packets to send.

9.19 Consider a token ring LAN with 12 stations equally spaced around the ring. Assume that each station is always prepared to send a packet. Calculate the throughput normalized to system capacity for the following cases:

a. $a = 3$

b. $a = 0.35$

9.20 Repeat Problem 9.19 substituting a ring version of CSMA/CD for token passing. Assume that each station transmits with a probability 1/N.

9.21 How many slots are spread out on the DQDB bus in each direction for a 30-km bus running at 150 Mbps?

9.22 A disadvantage of the contention approach for broadcast networks is the capacity wasted due to multiple stations attempting to access the channel at the same time. Suppose that time is divided into discrete slots with each of N stations attempting to transmit with probability p during each slot. What fraction of the slots are wasted due to multiple transmission attempts?

PART III

COMPUTER COMMUNICATIONS ARCHITECTURE

We have dealt, so far, with the technologies and techniques used to exchange data between two devices. Part I dealt with the case in which the two devices share a dedicated transmission link. Part II was concerned with the case in which a *communication network* provides a shared transmission capacity for multiple attached stations.

For voice communication, the above is adequate. However, for communication among data processing devices (computers, terminals), much more is needed. The data processing devices must implement a set of communications functions that will allow them to cooperatively perform some task. This set of functions is organized into a *communications architecture*. With these functions implemented, the network of stations and communications nodes is referred to as a *computer network*.

We begin this part with a detailed but generic look at the elements of a communications architecture (Chapter 10). The open systems interconnection (OSI) model is introduced as a model architecture and a framework for standards. Chapters 11 through 15 examine various aspects of a communications architecture, organized into five broad levels of functionality.

Protocols and Architecture

The purpose of this chapter is to serve as an overview and necessary background to the detailed material that follows in the remainder of Part III. It will also serve to show how the concepts of Parts I and II fit into the broader area of computer networks and computer communications.

We begin with an exposition of the concept of a communications protocol. It is shown that protocols are fundamental to all data communications. Next, we look at a way of systematically describing and implementing the communications function by viewing the communications task in terms of a column of layers, each of which contains protocols. This is the view of the now-famous open systems interconnection (OSI) model.

Although the OSI model is almost universally accepted as the framework for discourse in this area, there is another point of view which grows out of the extensive research and practical experience of ARPANET. This viewpoint, which is characterized by a hierarchy of protocols, is also presented.

Both of the viewpoints above describe the communications function in terms of an architecture, which specifies protocols and their interrelationships. To lend concreteness to the discussion, a commercial architecture is presented: IBM's SNA.

Finally, the standards being developed by various organizations involved in protocol standardization are described briefly in Appendix 10A.

10.1

PROTOCOLS

Characteristics

The concepts of distributed processing and computer networking imply that entities in different systems need to communicate. We use the terms "entity" and "system" in a very general sense. Examples of entities are user application programs, file transfer packages, data base management systems, electronic mail facilities, and terminals. Examples of systems are computers, terminals, and remote sensors. Note that in some cases the entity and the system in which it resides are coextensive (e.g., terminals). In general, an *entity* is anything capable of sending or receiving information, and a *system* is a physically distinct object that contains one or more entities.

For two entities to successfully communicate, they must "speak the same language." What is communicated, how it is communicated, and when it is communicated must conform to some mutually acceptable set of conventions between the entities involved. The set of conventions is referred to as a *protocol*, which may be defined as a set of rules governing the exchange of data between two entities. The key elements of a protocol are

- *Syntax:* includes such things as data format, coding, and signal levels.
- *Semantics:* includes control information for coordination and error handling.
- *Timing:* includes speed matching and sequencing.

HDLC is an example of a protocol. The data to be exchanged must be sent in frames of a specific format (syntax). The control field provides a variety of regulatory functions such as setting a mode and establishing a connection (semantics). Provisions are also included for flow control (timing). Most of Part III will be devoted to discussing other examples of protocols.

Some important characteristics of a protocol are

- Direct/indirect.
- Monolithic/structured.
- Symmetric/asymmetric.
- Standard/nonstandard.

Communication between two entities may be *direct or indirect*. Figure 10.1 depicts the possible situations. If two systems share a point-to-point link, the entities in these systems may communicate directly; that is, data and control information pass directly between entities with no intervening active agent. The same may be said of a multipoint configuration, although here the entities must be concerned with the issue of access control, making the protocol more complex. If systems connect through a switched communication network, a direct protocol is no longer possible. The two entities must depend on the functioning of other entities to exchange data. A more extreme case is a situation in which two entities do not even share the same switched network, but are indirectly connected through two or more networks. A set of such interconnected networks is termed an *internet*.

An important protocol design consideration is raised by the latter two configurations (Figure 10.1c and d), namely, the extent to which the entities and hence their protocol must be aware of the characteristics of intervening systems. Ideally, the intervening systems would be transparent and the protocol between the two entities would be the same as for a point-to-point link. We shall see that this ideal cannot be met.

(a) Point-to-point

(b) Multipoint/broadcast network

(c) Switched network

(d) Internet

FIGURE 10.1.   Means of connection of communicating systems.

Another characteristic of a protocol is whether it is *monolithic or structured*. It should become clear as Part III proceeds that the task of communication between entities on different systems is too complex to be handled as a unit. For example, consider an electronic mail package running on two computers connected by a synchronous HDLC link. To be truly monolithic, the package would need to include all of the HDLC logic. If the connection were over a packet-switched network, the package would still need the HDLC logic (or some equivalent) to attach to the network. It would also need logic for breaking up mail into packet-sized chunks, logic for requesting a virtual circuit, and so forth. Mail should only be sent when the destination system and entity are active and ready to receive. Logic is needed for that kind of coordination. And, as we shall see, the list goes on. A change in any aspect means that this huge package must be modified, with the risk of introducing difficult-to-find bugs.

An alternative is to use structured design and implementation techniques. Instead of a single protocol, there is a set of protocols that exhibit a hierarchical or layered structure. Lower-level, more primitive functions are implemented in lower-level entities that provide services to higher-level entities. For example, there could be an HDLC module (entity) that is invoked by an electronic mail facility when needed. Note that this is just another form of indirection: Higher-level entities rely on lower level entities to exchange data. See the discussion in Section 1.5 for an introduction to the concept of a communications architecture.

When structured protocol design is used, we refer to the hardware and software used to implement the communications function as a *communications architecture*. The remainder of this chapter, after this section, is devoted to this concept.

A protocol may be either *symmetric or asymmetric*. Most of the protocols that we shall study are symmetric. That is, they involve communication between peer entities. Asymmetry may be dictated by the logic of an exchange (e.g., a "user" and a "server" process), or by the desire to keep one of the entities or systems as simple as possible. An example of the latter is the normal response mode of HDLC. Typically, this involves a computer which polls and selects a number of terminals. The logic on the terminal end is quite straightforward.

Finally, a protocol may be either *standard or nonstandard*. A nonstandard protocol is one built for a specific communications situation or, at most, a particular model of a computer. Thus, if K different kinds of information sources have to communicate with L types of information receivers, $K \times L$ different protocols are needed without standards and a total of $2 \times K \times L$ implementations are required (Figure 10.2a). If all systems shared a common protocol, only $K + L$ implementations would be needed (Figure 10.2b). The increasing use of distributed processing and the decreasing inclination of customers to

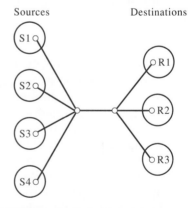

(a) Without standards: 12 different protocols, 24 protocol implementations

(b) With standards: 1 protocol, 7 implementations

FIGURE 10.2.   The use of standard protocols.

remain locked in to a single vendor dictate that all vendors implement protocols that conform to an agreed-upon standard. Appendix 10A lists the key organizations involved in standards development and outlines the current status of standards development.

Functions

Before turning to a discussion of communications architecture and the various levels of protocols, let us consider a rather small set of functions that form the basis of all protocols. Not all protocols have all functions; this would involve a significant duplication of effort. There are, nevertheless, many instances of the same type of function being present in protocols at different levels.

This discussion will, of necessity, be rather abstract. It does provide an integrated overview of the characteristics and functions of communications protocols. The concept of protocol is fundamental to all of the remainder of Part III, and as we proceed, specific examples of all these functions will be seen.

We can group protocol functions into the following categories:

- Segmentation and reassembly.
- Encapsulation.
- Connection control.
- Ordered delivery.
- Flow control.
- Error control.
- Synchronization.
- Addressing.
- Multiplexing.
- Transmission services.

Segmentation and Reassembly

A protocol is concerned with exchanging streams of data between two entities. Usually, the transfer can be characterized as consisting of a sequence of blocks of data of some bounded size. At the application level, we refer to a logical unit of data transfer as a *message*. Now, whether the application entity sends data in messages or in a continuous stream, lower level protocols may need to break the data up into blocks of some smaller bounded size. This process is called *segmentation,* or *fragmentation*. For convenience, we shall refer to a block of data exchanged between two entities via a protocol as a *protocol data unit* (PDU).

There are a number of motivations for segmentation, depending on the context. Among the typical reasons for segmentation:

- The communications network may only accept blocks of data up to a certain size. DDN, for example, limits messages to 8063 bytes in length.

- Error control may be more efficient with a smaller PDU size. For example, fewer bits need to be retransmitted using smaller blocks with the selective repeat technique.
- More equitable access to shared transmission facilities, with shorter delay, can be provided. For example, without a maximum block size, one station could monopolize a multipoint medium.
- A smaller PDU size may mean that receiving entities can allocate smaller buffers (e.g., the ARPANET entry-to-exit protocol).
- An entity may require that data transfer comes to some sort of "closure" from time to time, for checkpoint and restart/recovery operations.

There are several disadvantages to segmentation that argue for making blocks as large as possible:

- Each PDU, as we shall see, contains a fixed amount of control information. Hence the smaller the block, the greater the percentage overhead.
- PDU arrival may generate an interrupt that must be serviced. Smaller blocks result in more interrupts.
- More time is spent processing smaller, more numerous PDUs.

All of these factors must be taken into account by the protocol designer in determining minimum and maximum PDU size.

The counterpart of segmentation is *reassembly*. Eventually, the fragmented data must be reassembled into messages appropriate to the application level. If PDUs arrive out of order, the task is complicated.

The process of segmentation was illustrated in Figure 1.8.

Encapsulation

Each PDU contains not only data but control information. Indeed, some PDUs consist solely of control information and no data. The control information falls into three general categories:

- *Address:* The address of the sender and/or receiver may be indicated.
- *Error-detecting code:* Some sort of frame check sequence is often included for error detection.
- *Protocol control:* Additional information is included to implement the protocol functions listed in the remainder of this section.

The addition of control information to data is referred to as *encapsulation*. Data are accepted or generated by an entity and encapsulated into a PDU containing that data plus control information (See Figures 1.8 and 1.9). An example of this is the HDLC frame (Figure 5.13).

Connection Control

An entity may transmit data to another entity in an unplanned fashion and without prior coordination. This is known as *connectionless data transfer*; an ex-

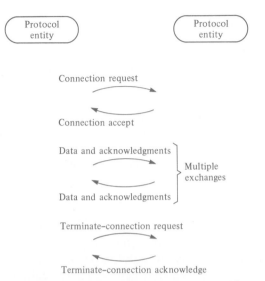

FIGURE 10.3. The phases of a connection-oriented data transfer.

ample is the use of the datagram. While this mode can be useful, it is less common than *connection-oriented data transfer*, of which the virtual circuit is an example [CHAP83].

Connection-oriented data transfer is to be preferred (even required) if stations anticipate a lengthy exchange of data and/or certain details of their protocol must be worked out dynamically. A logical association, or *connection*, is established between the entities. Three phases occur (Figure 10.3):

- Connection establishment.
- Data transfer.
- Connection termination.

With more sophisticated protocols, there may also be connection interrupt and recovery phases to cope with errors and other sorts of interruptions.

During the connection establishment phase, two entities agree to exchange data. Typically, one station will issue a connection request (in connectionless fashion!) to the other. A central authority may or may not be involved. In simpler protocols, the receiving entity either accepts or rejects the request and, in the former case, away they go. In more complex proposals, this phase includes a negotiation concerning the syntax, semantics, and timing of the protocol. Both entities must, of course, be using the same protocol. But the protocol may allow certain optional features and these must be agreed upon by means of negotiation. For example, the protocol may specify a PDU size of *up to* 8000 bytes; one station may wish to restrict this to 1000 bytes.

Following connection establishment, the data transfer phase is entered. During this phase both data and control information (e.g., flow control, error control) is exchanged. Finally, one side or the other wishes to terminate the connection and does so by sending a termination request. Alternatively, a central authority might forcibly terminate a connection.

The key characteristic of connection-oriented data transfer is that sequencing is used. Each side sequentially numbers the PDUs that it sends to the other side. Because each side remembers that it is engaged in a logical connection, it can keep track of both outgoing numbers, which it generates, and incoming numbers, which are generated by the other side. Indeed, one can essentially define a connection-oriented data transfer as one in which both sides number PDUs and keep track of both incoming and outgoing numbers. Sequencing supports three main functions: ordered deliver, flow control, and error control.

Ordered Delivery

If two communicating entities are in different hosts connected by a network, there is a risk that PDUs will not arrive in the order in which they were sent, because they may traverse different paths through the network. In connection-oriented protocols, it is generally required that PDU order be maintained. For example, if a file is transferred between two systems, we would like to be assured that the records of the received file are in the same order as those of the transmitted file, and not shuffled. If each PDU is given a unique number, and numbers are assigned sequentially, then it is a logically simple task for the receiving entity to reorder received PDUs on the basis of sequence number. The only hitch in this scheme is that, with a finite sequence number field, sequence numbers repeat (modulo some maximum number). Evidently, the maximum sequence number must be greater than the maximum number of PDUs that could be outstanding at any time. In fact the maximum number may need to be *twice* the maximum number of PDUs that could be outstanding (e.g., selective-repeat ARQ; see Chapter 5).

Flow Control

Flow control was introduced in Chapter 5 and seen again in Chapter 8. In essence, flow control is a function performed by a receiving entity to limit the amount or rate of data that is sent by a transmitting entity.

The simplest form of flow control is a stop-and-wait procedure, in which each PDU must be acknowledged before the next can be sent. More efficient protocols involve some form of credit provided to the transmitter, which is the amount of data that can be sent without an acknowledgment. The sliding-window technique is an example of this mechanism. Closely related are SNA's pacing algorithm and ARPANET's ready-for-next-message command.

Flow control is a good example of a function that must be implemented in several protocols. Consider again Figure 1.5. Network A will need to exercise flow control over station 1's network services module via the network access protocol, in order to enforce network traffic control. At the same time, station 2's network services module has only limited buffer space and needs to exercise flow control over station 1's network services module via the process-to-process protocol. Finally, even though station 2's network service module can control its data flow, station 2's application may be vulnerable to overflow. For example, the application could be hung up waiting for disk access. Thus flow control is also needed over the application-oriented protocol.

Error Control

Another previously introduced function is error control. Techniques are needed to guard against loss or damage of data and control information. Most techniques involve error detection, based on a frame check sequence, and PDU retransmission. Retransmission is often activated by a timer. If a sending entity fails to receive an acknowledgment to a PDU within a specified period of time, it will retransmit.

As with flow control, error control is a function that must be performed at various levels of protocol. Consider again Figure 1.5. The network access protocol should include error control to assure that data are successfully exchanged between station and network. However, a packet of data may be lost inside the network, and the process-to-process protocol should be able to recover from this loss.

Synchronization

It should be apparent from the discussion so far that a protocol entity needs to remember a certain number of parameters (e.g., window size, connection phase, timer value). These parameters can be viewed as state variables and their collection defines the state of the entity. It is occasionally important that two communicating protocol entities be simultaneously in a well-defined state, for example at initialization, checkpointing, and termination. This is termed synchronization.

The difficulty with achieving synchronization is that one entity has knowledge of the state of the other only by virtue of received PDUs. These PDUs do not arrive instantly. They take some time, perhaps a variable amount of time, to traverse from sender to receiver. Furthermore, a PDU may be lost in transit.

An example from [POUZ78] illustrates the problem. Consider two entities, A and B, performing mutual data base updating. Neither should terminate until both are finished updating and the two data bases are synchronized. Question: How can the two entities be sure that both have terminated?

Figure 10.4a shows a state diagram for A. State 1 indicates that A has finished its work. When A has finished, it sends a DONE message to B. When it receives a DONE message back, A is free to terminate and disappear. However, B may finish first. To cover this contingency, let us refine the state diagram as shown in Figure 10.4b. When each station has sent and received a DONE message, in either order, it terminates.

(a) Partial synchronization

(b) Simple synchronization

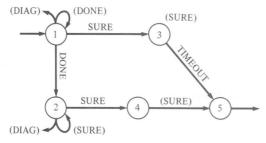

(c) Safe synchronization

(DONE): message sent   DONE: message received

FIGURE 10.4.   Synchronization example.

Figure 10.4b will only work if no messages are lost. Consider: *A* arrives in state 3 and waits for the DONE message from *B*. *B* sends such a message but it is lost in transit. After waiting a reasonable amount of time, what should *A* do? Going to state 4 and terminating is risky: the two data bases may not agree; *B* may not yet have reached state 1 and may need *A*'s cooperation to complete its task. On the other hand, going back to state 1 could hang *A* up, since *B* may already have gone to state 4 and vanished.

The diagram of Figure 10.4c takes errors into account. When *A* has both transmitted and received a DONE, it issues a SURE message, indicating that it knows that *B* is done. Neither entity can terminate until the other has reached state 2. In case one entity gets hung up in state 2, it at least knows that the other has reached state 1, and possibly state 5. If either entity gets hung up in state 1 or 2, it initializes a diagnostic procedure to resolve the deadlock.

This example is not meant to indicate a generally applicable solution for the synchronization problem. Rather, it serves to illustrate its complexity.

Addressing

For two entities to communicate, other than over a point-to-point link, they must somehow be able to identify each other. For example, on a broadcast network each station looks for packets that contain its identifier. On a switched network, the network needs to know the identity of the destination station in order to properly route data or set up a connection.

A distinction is generally made among names, addresses, and routes [SHOC78]. A name specifies what an object is; an address specifies where it is; and a route indicates how to get there. For our purposes, it is more useful to draw a distinction suggested in [POUZ78]:

- *Local name:* the name by which an entity is identified within its own system.
- *Global name:* the name by which an entity is known outside its own system.

There are several points of importance here. First, it is desirable to distinguish between local names and global names. Communication may involve a variety of systems of different types and from different vendors. Each system likes to have its own naming convention, and it seems hopeless to attempt to enforce uniform local naming rules. On the other hand, no entity or system can be expected to deal with a variety of name lengths, formats, and global conventions. Thus both local and global names are needed. Second, an address is a form of global name. However, and third, there may not be a unique global name for an entity. If the entity is mobile, its address changes. If it attaches directly to more than one network, each may have its own address for the entity.

The problem of naming and addressing of entities admits of no unique solution. In the remainder of this subsection, we outline some approaches and considerations. During the discussion, we refer to the entities in Figure 10.5.

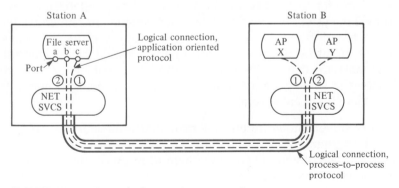

FIGURE 10.5. Example for naming conventions.

The following topics are considered:

- Name structure.
- Name knowledge.
- Connection names.
- Port names.
- Group names.

The *name structure* used for global names can be either hierarchical or flat. A hierarchical name would have the structure SYSTEM.ENTITY, or in the case of multiple networks, NETWORK.SYSTEM.ENTITY. The fields SYSTEM and NETWORK contain global identifiers of some fixed format. ENTITY must presumably be a name of some fixed maximum length. The name could have global significance, in which case the system containing that entity would have to contain a mapping from global entity identifiers to local entity identifiers. Alternatively, if all systems could live with a particular field length, local and global entity identifiers could be the same. As an example, application X in station B is identified as B.X.

A flat name structure is one in which each entity has a global name that is unique throughout the domain of communication. Names could be assigned by preallocation; that is, each system is given a set of global names, which it then assigns to its local entities. Alternatively, a mapping or directory function could be used which globally assigns names to entities.

The hierarchical structure has several advantages. It is easier to add new names to the universe of names with a hierarchical scheme, since entity names need only be unique within a system. With flat names, it must be determined that any new name added to the system is not the same as any previous name. Second, a hierarchical name is an aid to routing since it identifies the system containing the entity. Thus a hierarchical name has more the flavor of an address than does a flat name.

Regardless of name structure, there is a requirement for *name knowledge*. An entity can only send data to or request a connection with an entity whose name it knows. Consider that entity 1 in system A wishes to establish a connection with entity 2 in system B. The possibilities for naming are numerous; we mention only a few. System A could maintain a directory of global names of all entities that might be of interest. Each of these would have some identifier understandable to station A's entities. Another possibility is that entity 1 wishes access to some generic service, such as transaction processing (TP) on system B. Here there are several subpossibilities:

- A network server known to entity 1 maintains a directory mapping generic services by system onto global names.
- There is a "well-known entity" on system B. Entity 1 queries this entity for the global name of system B's TP.
- The well-known entity on system B is a log-on facility. Entity 1 logs on to system B and is then allowed access to TP.

At bottom, the problem is this: Entity 1 must know the name of entity 2 to exchange data with it, but how can it get that name unless it already knows it? The preceding should give some feel for the various approaches that can be taken.

For connectionless data transfer, a global name is used with each data transmission. For connection-oriented transfer, it is sometimes desirable to use only a *connection name* during the data transfer phase. The scenario is this: Entity 1 on system *A* requests a connection to entity 2 on system *B*, perhaps using the global address B.2. When B.2 accepts the connection, a connection name (usually a number) is provided and is used by both entities for future transmissions. As an example, two connections between applications, labeled "1" and "2," are shown in Figure 10.5. The use of a connection name has several advantages:

- *Reduced overhead:* Connection names are generally shorter than global names. For example, in the X.25 protocol (discussed in Chapter 13) used over packet-switched networks, connection request packets contain both source and destination address fields, each with a system-defined length that may be a number of bytes. After a virtual circuit is established, data packets contain just a 12-bit virtual circuit number.
- *Routing:* In setting up a connection, a fixed route may be defined (e.g. SNA and TYMNET, but not ARPANET). The connection name serves to identify the route for handling future PDUs.
- *Multiplexing:* We address this function in more general terms below. Here we note that an entity may wish to enjoy more than one connection simultaneously. Thus incoming PDUs must be identified by connection name.

Another concept often found with protocols is that of *port name*. A port name is a global entity name. If each entity has a single port name, there is not much point to the concept. However, it is often the case that multiple port names are associated with an entity. This can be used to provide multiplexing, as with connection names. For example, a file server module may be able to service a number of users simultaneously. Also, port names can indicate different entry points within an entity. For example, a file server might have a different entry point for users authorized to read and update and for users authorized only to read. In many systems, port names are unique within the system across all entities and entity names are not needed. So, for a hierarchical structure, the form NETWORK.SYSTEM.PORT would be used. For example, the three ports depicted in Figure 10.5 are designated A.a, A.b, and A.c.

Finally, we mention the concept of *group name*, which is a name that refers to more than one entity or port. This term has been used to mean a number of things. One usage is to identify a contention group, as discussed in Chapter 8. A more meaningful use, in the present context, is that a group name identifies multiple simultaneous recipients for data. For example, a user might wish to send a memo to a number of individuals. The network control center may wish to notify all users that the network is going down. A group name may

TABLE 10.1   Multicasting and Broadcasting

Destination	Network Address	System Address	Entity/Port Address
Specific	Specific	Specific	Specific
Multicast	Specific	Specific	Group
	Specific	All	Group
	All	All	Group
Broadcast	Specific	Specific	All
	Specific	All	All
	All	All	All

be *broadcast*, intended for all entities within a domain, or *multicast*, intended for a specific subset of entities. Table 10.1 illustrates the possibilities.

Multiplexing

We have already seen one type of multiplexing that is used with protocols: the multiplexing of data transfers into an entity. This can be accomplished using connection names, which permits multiple simultaneous connection. It can also be accomplished via port names, which also permit multiple simultaneous connections. The latter is shown in Figure 10.5, where the file server in A has two connections active at the same time. Port names also accommodate multiple connectionless transfers from different sources to the same destination. With the use of different port names, interference is avoided.

Multiplexing is used in another context as well, namely the mapping of connections from one level to another. Consider again Figure 1.5. Network *A* might provide a virtual circuit service. For each process-to-process connection established at the network services level, a virtual circuit could be created at the network access level. This is a one-to-one relationship, but need not be so. Multiplexing can be used in one of two directions (Figure 10.6). *Upward multiplexing* occurs when multiple higher-level connections are multiplexed on, or share, a single lower-level connection. This may be needed to make more efficient use of the lower-level service or to provide several higher-level connections in an environment where only a single lower-level connection exists. Figure 10.5 shows an example of upward multiplexing. *Downward multiplexing,* or *splitting,* means that a single higher-level connection is built on top of multiple lower-level connections, the traffic on the higher connection being divided among the various lower connections. This technique may be used to provide reliability, performance, or efficiency.

Transmission Services

A protocol may provide a variety of additional services to the entities that use it. We mention here three common examples:

- *Priority:* Certain messages, such as control messages, may need to get through to the destination entity with minimum delay. An example would be a close connection request. Thus priority could be assigned on a message basis. Additionally, priority could be assigned on a connection basis.
- *Grade of service:* Certain classes of data may require a minimum throughput or a maximum delay threshold.
- *Security:* Security mechanisms, restricting access, may be invoked.

(a) One–to–one

(b) Upward multiplexing

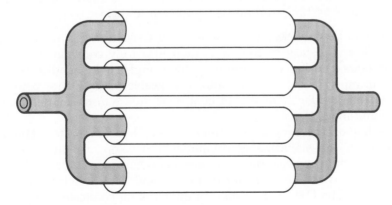

(c) Downward multiplexing

FIGURE 10.6.   Multiplexing and protocol connections.

All of these services depend on the underlying transmission system and any intervening lower-level entities. If it is possible for these services to be provided from below, the protocol can be used by the two entities to exercise those services.

10.2

THE OSI MODEL

Motivation

When work is done that involves more than one computer, additional elements must be added to the system: the hardware and software to support the communication between or among the systems. Communications hardware is reasonably standard and generally presents few problems. However, when communication is desired among heterogeneous (different vendors, different models of same vendor) machines, the software development effort can be a nightmare. Different vendors use different data formats and data exchange conventions. Even within one vendor's product line, different model computers may communicate in unique ways.

As the use of computer communications and computer networking proliferates, a one-at-a-time special-purpose approach to communications software development is too costly to be acceptable. The only alternative is for computer vendors to adopt and implement a common set of conventions. For this to happen, a set of international or at least national standards must be promulgated by appropriate organizations. Such standards have two effects:

- Vendors feel encouraged to implement the standards because of an expectation that, because of wide usage of the standards, their products would be less marketable without them.
- Customers are in a position to require that the standards be implemented by any vendor wishing to propose equipment to them.

It should become clear from the ensuing discussion that no single standard will suffice. The task of communication in a truly cooperative way between applications on different computers is too complex to be handled as a unit. The problem must be decomposed into manageable parts. Hence before one can develop standards, there should be a structure or *architecture* that defines the communications tasks.

This line of reasoning led the International Organization for Standardization (ISO) in 1977 to establish a subcommittee to develop such an architecture. The result was the *Open Systems Interconnection* (OSI) reference model, adopted in 1983, which is a framework for defining standards for linking heterogeneous computers. The OSI model provides the basis for connecting "open" systems for distributed applications processing. The term "open" denotes the ability of

TABLE 10.2   Purpose of the OSI Model

The purpose of this International Standard Reference Model of Open Systems Interconnection is to provide a common basis for the coordination of standards development for the purpose of systems interconnection, while allowing existing standards to be placed into perspective within the overall Reference Model.

The term Open Systems Interconnection (OSI) qualifies standards for the exchange of information among systems that are "open" to one another for this purpose by virtue of their mutual use of the applicable standards.

The fact that a system is open does not imply any particular systems implementation, technology or means of interconneciton, but refers to the mutual recognition and support of the applicable standards.

It is also the purpose of this International Standard to identify areas for developing or improving standards, and to provide a common reference for maintaining consistency of all related standards. It is not the intent of this International Standard either to serve as an implementation specification, or to be a basis for appraising the conformance of actual implementations, or to provide a sufficient level of detail to define precisely the services and protocols of the interconnection architecture. Rather, this International Standard provides a conceptual and functional framework which allows international teams of experts to work productively and independently on the development of standards for each layer of the Reference Model of OSI.

any two systems conforming to the reference model and the associated standards to connect.

Table 10.2, extracted from the basic OSI document [ISO84] summarizes the purpose of the model.

Concepts

A widely accepted structuring technique, and the one chosen by ISO, is *layering*. The communications functions are partitioned into a vertical set of layers. Each layer performs a related subset of the functions required to communicate with another system. It relies on the next lower layer to perform more primitive functions and to conceal the details of those functions. It provides services to the next higher layer. Ideally, the layers should be defined so that changes in one layer do not require changes in the other layers. Thus we have decomposed one problem into a number of more manageable subproblems.

The task of the ISO subcommittee was to define a set of layers and the services performed by each layer. The partitioning should group functions logically, should have enough layers to make each layer manageably small, but should not have so many layers that the processing overhead imposed by the collection of layers is burdensome. The principles by which ISO went about its task are summarized in Table 10.3. The resulting OSI reference model has seven layers, which are listed with a brief definition in Table 10.4. Table 10.5 provides ISO's justification for the selection of these layers.

TABLE 10.3   Principles Used in Defining the OSI Layers

1. Do not create so many layers as to make the system engineering task of describing and integrating the layers more difficult than necessary.
2. Create a boundary at a point where the description of services can be small and the number of interactions across the boundary are minimized.
3. Create separate layers to handle functions that are manifestly different in the process performed or the technology involved.
4. Collect similar functions into the same layer.
5. Select boundaries at a point which past experience has demonstrated to be successful.
6. Create a layer of easily localized functions so that the layer could be totally redesigned and its protocols changed in a major way to take advantage of new advances in architectural, hardware or software technology without changing the services expected from and provided to the adjacent layers.
7. Create a boundary where it may be useful at some point in time to have the corresponding interface standardized.
8. Create a layer where there is a need for a different level of abstraction in the handling of data (e.g., morphology, syntax, semantics).
9. Allow changes of functions or protocols to be made within a layer without affecting other layers.
10. Create for each layer boundaries with its upper and lower layer only.

Similar principles have been applied to sublayering:

11. Create further subgrouping and organization or functions to form sublayers within a layer in cases where distinct communication services need it.
12. Create, where needed, two or more sublayers with a common, and therefore minimal functionality to allow interface operation with adjacent layers.
13. Allow bypassing of sublayers.

TABLE 10.4   The OSI Layers

1. Physical	Concerned with transmission of unstructured bit stream over physical medium; deals with the mechanical, electrical, functional, and procedural characteristics to access the physical medium
2. Data link	Provides for the reliable transfer of information across the physical link; sends blocks of data (frames) with the necessary synchronization, error control, and flow control
3. Network	Provides upper layers with independence from the data transmission and switching technologies used to connect systems; responsible for establishing, maintaining, and terminating connections
4. Transport	Provides reliable, transparent transfer of data between end points; provides end-to-end error recovery and flow control
5. Session	Provides the control structure for communication between applications; establishes, manages, and terminates connections (sessions) between cooperating applications
6. Presentation	Provides independence to the application processes from differences in data representation (syntax)
7. Application	Provides access to the OSI environment for users and also provides distributed information services

TABLE 10.5   Justification of the OSI Layers

a.   It is essential that the architecture permit usage of a realistic variety of physical media for interconnection with different control procedures (e.g., V.24, V.25, X.21, etc.). Application of principles 3, 5, and 8 [Table 10.3] leads to indentification of a *Physical Layer* as the lowest layer in the architecture.

b.   Some physical communication media (e.g., telephone line) require specific techniques to be used in order to transmit data between systems despite a relatively high error rate (i.e., an error rate not acceptable for the great majority of applications). These specific techniques are used in data-link control procedures which have been studied and standardized for a number of years. It must also be recognized that new physical communication media (e.g., fiber optics) will require different data-link control procedures. Application of principles 3, 5, and 8 leads to identification of a *Data Link Layer* on top of the Physical Layer in the architecture.

c.   In the open systems architecture, some systems will act as the final destination of data. Some systems may act only as intermediate nodes (forwarding data to other systems). Application of principles 3, 5, and 7 leads to identification of a *Network Layer* on top of the Data Link Layer. Network oriented protocols such as routing, for example, will be grouped in this layer. Thus, the Network Layer will provide a connection path (network-connection) between a pair of transport-entities, including the case where intermediate nodes are involved.

d.   Control of data transportation from source end-system to destination end-system (which is not performed in intermediate nodes) is the last function to be performed in order to provide the totality of the transport-service. Thus, the upper layer in the transport-service part of the architecture is the *Transport Layer*, on top of the Network Layer. This Transport Layer relieves higher layer entities from any concern with the transportation of data between them.

e.   There is a need to organize and synchronize dialogue, and to manage the exchange of data. Application of principles 3 and 4 leads to the identification of a *Session Layer* on top of the Transport Layer.

f.   The remaining set of general interest functions are those related to representation and manipulation of structured data for the benefit of application programs. Application of principles 3 and 4 leads to identification of a *Presentation Layer* on top of the Session Layer.

g.   Finally, there are applications consisting of application processes which perform information processing. An aspect of these application processes and the protocols by which they communicate comprise the *Application Layer* as the highest layer of the architecture.

Table 10.4 defines, in general terms, the functions that must be performed in a system for it to communicate. Of course, it takes two to communicate, so the same set of layered functions must exist in two systems. Communication is achieved by having corresponding ("peer") entities in the same layer in two different systems communicate via a protocol.

Figure 10.7 illustrates the OSI model. Each system contains the seven layers. Communication is between applications in the systems, labeled application X and application Y in the figure. If application X wishes to send a message to

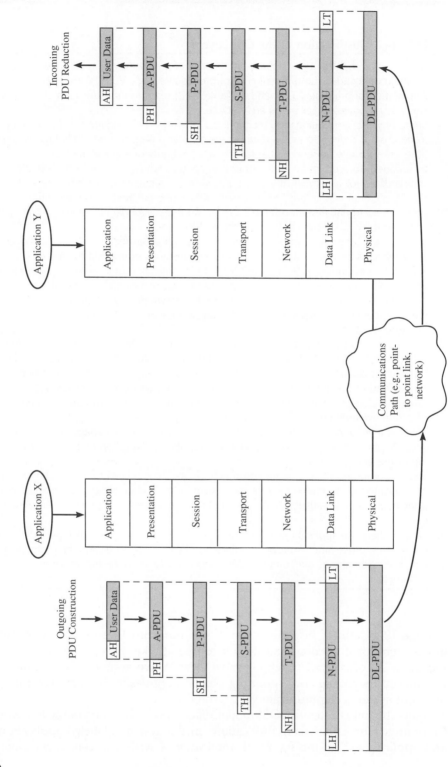

FIGURE 10.7. The OSI environment.

application Y, it invokes the application layer (layer 7). Layer 7 establishes a peer relationship with layer 7 of the target machine, using a layer 7 protocol. This protocol requires services from layer 6, so the two layer 6 entities use a protocol of their own, and so on down to the physical layer, which actually passes the bits through a transmission medium.

Note that there is no direct communication between peer layers except at the physical layer. That is, above the physical layer, each protocol entity sends data *down* to the next lower layer in order to get the data *across* to its peer entity. Even at the physical layer, the OSI model does not stipulate that two systems be directly connected. For example, a packet-switched or circuit-switched network may be used to provide the communications link. This point should become clearer below, when we discuss the network layer.

The attractiveness of the OSI approach is that it promises to solve the heterogeneous computer communications problem. Two systems, no matter how different, can communicate effectively if they have the following in common:

- They implement the same set of communications functions.
- These functions are organized into the same set of layers. Peer layers must provide the same functions, but note that it is not necessary that they provide them in the same way.
- Peer layers must share a common protocol.

To assure the above, standards are needed. Standards must define the functions and services to be provided by a layer (but not how it is to be done—that may differ from system to system). Standards must also define the protocols between peer layers (each protocol must be identical for the two peer layers). The OSI model, by defining a seven-layer architecture, provides a framework for defining these standards.

Some useful OSI terminology is illustrated in Figure 10.8. For simplicity, any layer is referred to as the *(N) layer,* and names of constructs associated with that layer are also preceded by (N). Within a system, there are one or more active entities in each layer. An *(N) entity* implements functions of the (N) layer and also the protocol for communicating with (N) entities in other systems. An example of an entity is a process in a multiprocessing system. Or it could simply be a subroutine. There might be multiple identical (N) entities, if this is convenient or efficient for a given system. There might also be differing (N) entities, corresponding to different protocol standards at that level.

Each entity communicates with entities in the layers above and below it across an *interface.* The interface is realized as one or more *service access points* (SAPs), which function in the manner of ports, discussed earlier. The (N − 1) entity provides *services* to an (N) entity via the invocation of *primitives.* A primitive specifies the function to be performed and is used to pass data and control information. The actual form of a primitive is implementation-dependent. An example is a subroutine call.

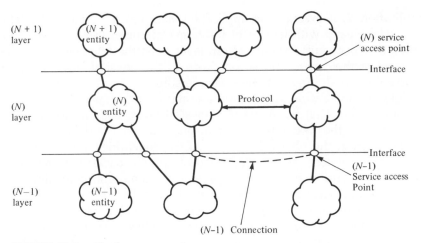

FIGURE 10.8.   The layer concept.

The OSI model is connection-oriented. Two (N) entities communicate, using a protocol, by means of an (N − 1) connection. This logical connection is provided by (N − 1) entities between (N − 1) SAPs. ISO is currently at work on a connectionless mode, but this is not yet reflected in the model.

Figure 10.7 illustrates the OSI principles in operation. First, consider the most common way in which protocols are realized. When application X has a message to send to application Y, it transfers those data to an application entity in the application layer. A *header* is appended to the data that contains the required information for the peer layer 7 protocol (encapsulation). The original data, plus the header, is now passed as a unit to layer 6. The presentation entity treats the whole unit as data, and appends its own header (a second encapsulation). This process continues down through layer 2, which generally adds both a header and a trailer (e.g., HDLC). This layer 2 unit, called a *frame*, is then passed by the physical layer onto the transmission medium. When the frame is received by the target system, the reverse process occurs. As the data ascend, each layer strips off the outermost header, acts on the protocol information contained therein, and passes the remainder up to the next layer.

At each stage of the process, a layer may fragment the data unit it receives from the next higher layer into several parts, to accommodate its own requirements. These data units must then be reassembled by the corresponding peer layer before being passed up.

When two peer entities wish to exchange data, this may be done with or without a prior connection. We have seen an example of this in the use of virtual circuits or datagrams. A connection can exist at any layer of the hierarchy. In the abstract, a connection is established between two (N) entities by identifying an (N − 1) SAP for each (N) entity.

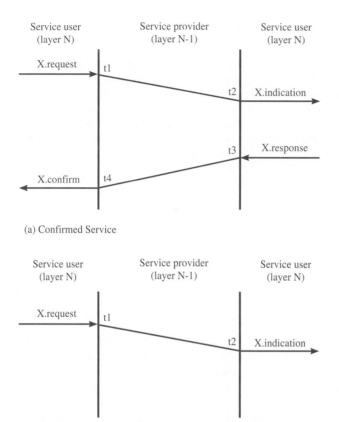

(a) Confirmed Service

(b) Nonconfirmed Service

FIGURE 10.9.   Time sequence diagrams for service primitives.

Service Primitives and Parameters

In a communications architecture, such as the OSI model, each layer is defined in two parts: the protocol between peer (at the same layer) entities in different systems and the services provided by one layer to the next higher layer in the same system.

We have seen a number of examples of protocols (e.g., HDLC, X.25 packet layer), which are defined in terms of the formats of protocol data units (PDUs) that are exchanged and the rules governing the use of those PDUs. The services between adjacent layers are expressed in terms of primitives and parameters. A primitive specifies the function to be performed, and the parameters are used to pass data and control information. The actual form of a primitive is implementation dependent. For example, a primitive could be implemented as a procedure call or a process invocation.

TABLE 10.6   Service Primitive Types

REQUEST	A primitive issued by a service user to invoke some service and to pass the parameters needed to fully specify the requested service.

INDICATION	A primitive issued by a service provider to either
	   1. Indicate that a procedure has been invoked by the peer service user on the connection and to provide the associated parameters, or
	   2. Notify the service user of a provider-initiated action.

RESPONSE	A primitive issued by a service user to acknowledge or complete some procedure previously invoked by an indication to that user.
CONFIRM	A primitive issued by a service provider to acknowledge or complete some procedure previously invoked by a request by the service user.

Four types of primitives are used in standards to define the interaction between adjacent layers in the architecture. These are defined in Table 10.6. The layout of Figure 10.9a suggests the time ordering of these events. For example, consider the transfer of data from an (N) entity to a peer (N) entity in another system. The following steps occur:

1. The source (N) entity invokes its (N − 1) entity with a DATA.request primitive. Associated with the primitive are the parameters needed, such as the data to be transmitted and the destination address.
2. The source (N − 1) entity prepares an (N − 1) PDU to be sent to its peer (N − 1) entity.
3. The destination (N − 1) entity delivers the data to the appropriate destination (N) entity via a DATA.indication, which includes the data and source address as parameters.
4. If an acknowledgment is called for, the destination (N) entity issues a DATA.response to its (N − 1) entity.
5. The (N − 1) entity conveys the acknowledgment in an (N − 1) PDU.
6. The acknowledgment is delivered to the (N) entity as a DATA.confirm.

This sequence of events is referred to as a **confirmed service,** as the initiator receives confirmation that the requested service has had the desired effect at the other end. If only request and indication primitives are involved (corresponding to steps 1 through 3), then the service dialogue is a **nonconfirmed service;** the initiator receives no confirmation that the requested action has taken place (Figure 10.9b).

Layers

In this section we discuss briefly each of the layers and, where appropriate, give examples of standards for protocols at those layers.

Physical Layer

The *physical layer* covers the physical interface between devices and the rules by which bits are passed from one to another. The physical layer has four important characteristics [BERT80, MCCL83]:

- Mechanical.
- Electrical.
- Functional.
- Procedural.

We have already covered physical layer protocols in some detail in Section 4.3. Examples of standards at this layer are EIA-232-D, EIA-530, and portions of ISDN and LAN/MAN standards.

Data Link Layer

While the physical layer provides only a raw bit stream service, the *data link layer* attempts to make the physical link reliable and provides the means to activate, maintain, and deactivate the link. The principal service provided by the link layer to the higher layers is that of error detection and control. Thus, with a fully functional data link layer protocol, the next higher layer may assume virtually error-free transmission over the link. However, if communication is between two systems that are not directly connected, the connection will comprise a number of data links in tandem, each functioning independently. Thus the higher layers are not relieved of an error control responsibility.

Chapter 5 was devoted to data link protocols. Examples of standards at this layer are HDLC, ADCCP, and LAP-B.

Network Layer

The network layer provides for the transfer of information between end systems across some sort of communications network. It relieves higher layers of the need to know anything about the underlying data transmission and switching technologies used to connect systems. At this layer, the computer system engages in a dialogue with the network to specify the destination address and to request certain network facilities, such as priority.

Communications across a network between processes in separate systems can be thought of as involving two kinds of entities:

- The end systems, which contain the processes and implement some sort of communications architecture, such as the seven-layer OSI architecture.
- The nodes, or switching systems, of the network, which manage communication across the network.

In most cases, an end system attaches to a communications device that is considered, from an architectural point of view, to be part of the network. CCITT refers to an end system and the communications device to which it attaches as data terminal equipment (DTE) and data circuit-terminating equipment (DCE), respectively.

To understand the protocol implications of the requirement for network attachment, we need to look at the various possible cases. Figure 10.10a depicts the case in which an end system (DTE) attaches to a packet-switching node (DCE) that is part of a packet-switched network. As an example, the packet layer of the X.25 standard is a network layer standard for this situation. The lower three layers are concerned with attaching to and communicating with the network. The packets that are created by the end system pass through one or more network nodes, which act as relays between the two end systems. Note that, in addition to a layer 3 protocol, a data link layer protocol (layer 2) over a physical link (layer 1) between the DTE and DCE is needed. Hence, the DTE–DCE interaction consists of protocols at layers 1, 2, and 3. The local DCE uses a different set of protocols to route data units through the network to the destination DCE, which in turn has a layer 1–3 set of protocols with the destination DTE. The internal operation of the network is transparent to the user, and the internal protocol structure in the network is of no concern to the end systems.

A quite different circumstance is illustrated in Figure 10.10b, which shows two DTEs connected by a point-to-point link. Typically, this configuration also involves the use of DCEs. There is a standardized physical-level interface, such as EIA–232–D, between the end system and a DCE (e.g., a modem), and the two DCEs communicate using some other physical protocol across a transmission line (see Figure 4.8). In this case, the DCE operates purely at layer 1 and simply relays the bits from the DTE onto the transmission line and vice versa. Thus, layers 2 and 3, as well as layer 4, are end to end, or DTE to DTE. In this configuration, the layer 3 protocol has very little work to do. There are no network facilities to request, and there is no need for address information to support routing.

A similar situation exists in the case of a circuit-switched network (Figure 10.10c). Once a circuit has been set up between two DTEs across the network, it appears to the two stations that they have a direct point-to-point link. The nodes of the network act simply as layer 1 relays of the bits being transmitted. Again, very little is needed at layer 3.

The architecture of a LAN or MAN is depicted in Figure 10.10d. The layer 2 protocols are end to end between attached devices. So, once again, the LAN acts simply as a layer 1 facility for moving bits between two DTEs. In this case, there is no readily identifiable DCE; the DTEs connect directly to the shared network medium. As in the preceding two cases, there is not a great deal for a layer 3 protocol to do.

In a more complex configuration, two end systems might wish to communicate but are not even connected to the same network. Rather, they are

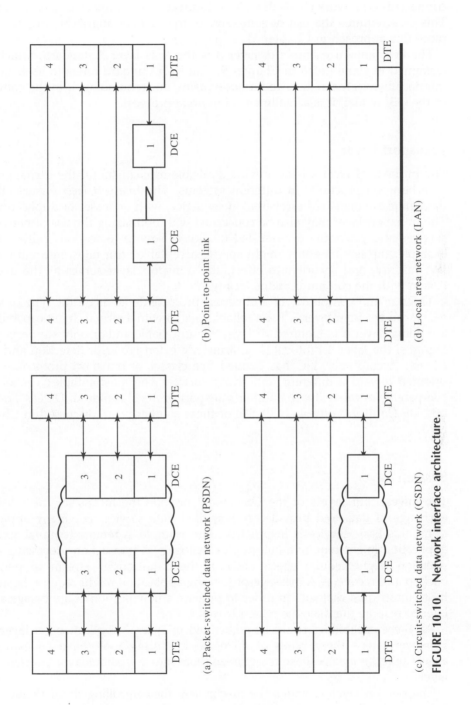

(a) Packet-switched data network (PSDN)

(b) Point-to-point link

(c) Circuit-switched data network (CSDN)

(d) Local area network (LAN)

FIGURE 10.10. Network interface architecture.

447

connected to networks that, directly or indirectly, are connected to each other. This case requires the use of some sort of internetworking technique; we explore this approach in Chapter 11.

The best known example of layer 3 is the X.25 layer 3 standard, which is examined in some detail in Chapter 9. The X.25 standard refers to itself as an interface between a station and a node (using our terminology). In the context of the OSI model, it is actually a station-node protocol.

Transport Layer

The purpose of layer 4 is to provide a reliable mechanism for the exchange of data between processes in different systems. The *transport layer* ensures that data units are delivered error-free, in sequence, with no losses or duplications. The transport layer may also be concerned with optimizing the use of network services and providing a requested quality of service to session entities. For example, the session entity might specify acceptable error rates, maximum delay, priority, and security. In effect, the transport layer serves as the user's liaison with the communications facility.

The size and complexity of a transport protocol depends on the type of service it can get from layer 3. For a reliable layer 3 with a virtual circuit capability, a minimal layer 4 is required. If layer 3 is unreliable and/or only supports datagrams, the layer 4 protocol should include extensive error detection and recovery. Accordingly, ISO has defined five classes of transport protocol, each oriented toward a different underlying service. The most complex version is comparable in capability to another transport protocol standard. DOD's Transmission Control Protocol (TCP). All of these standards are discussed in Chapter 12.

Session Layer

The lowest four layers of the OSI model provide the means for the reliable exchange of data and provide an expedited data service. For many applications, this basic service is insufficient. For example, a remote terminal access application might require a half-duplex dialogue. A transaction-processing application might require checkpoints in the data-transfer stream to permit backup and recovery. A message-processing application might require the ability to interrupt a dialogue in order to prepare a new portion of a message and later to resume the dialogue where is was left off.

All these capabilities could be embedded in specific applications at layer 7. However, since these types of dialogue-structuring tools have widespread applicability, it makes sense to organize them into a separate layer: the session layer.

The session layer provides the mechanism for controlling the dialogue between applications in end systems. In may cases, there will be little or no need for session-layer services, but for some applications, such services are used. The key services provided by the session layer include

- *Dialogue discipline:* This can be two-way simultaneous (full duplex) or two-way alternate (half duplex).
- *Grouping:* The flow of data can be marked to define groups of data. For example, if a retail store is transmitting sales data to a regional office, the data can be marked to indicate the end of the sales data for each department. This would signal the host computer to finalize running totals for that department and start new running counts for the next department.
- *Recovery:* The session layer can provide a checkpointing mechanism, so that if a failure of some sort occurs between checkpoints, the session entity can retransmit all data since the last checkpoint.

ISO has issued a standard for the session layer that includes as options services such as those just described.

A discussion of the principles of session protocols and the ISO standard is presented in Chapter 13.

Presentation Layer

The *presentation layer* is concerned with the syntax of the data exchanged between application entities. Its purpose is to resolve differences in format and data representation. The presentation layer defines the syntax used between application entities and provides for the selection and subsequent modification of the representation to be used.

Examples of presentation protocols are encryption and virtual terminal protocol. A virtual terminal protocol converts between specific terminal characteristics and a generic or virtual model used by application programs. The presentation layer is discussed in Chapter 14.

Application Layer

The *application layer* provides a means for application processes to access the OSI environment. This layer contains management functions and generally useful mechanisms to support distributed applications. Examples of protocols at this level are file transfer and electronic mail. The application layer is discussed in Chapter 15.

Summary

Figure 10.11 provides a useful perspective on the OSI architecture. The annotation along the right side suggests viewing the seven layers in three parts, corresponding to the simple 3-layer architecture introduced in Chapter 1. The lower three layers contain the logic for a computer to interact with a network. The host is attached physically to the network, uses a data link protocol to

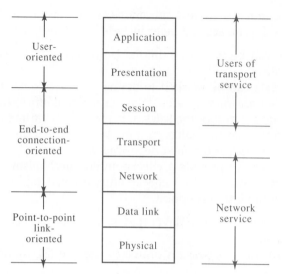

FIGURE 10.11.   Perspectives on the OSI architecture.

reliably communicate with the network, and uses a network protocol to request data exchange with another device on the network and to request network services (e.g., priority). The X.25 standard for packet-switching networks encompasses these three layers. Continuing from this perspective, the transport layer provides a reliable end-to-end service regardless of the intervening network facility; in effect, it is the user's liaison to the communications facility. Finally, the upper three layers, taken together, are involved in the exchange of data between end users, making use of a transport service for reliable data transfer.

Another perspective is suggested by the annotation on the left. Again, consider host systems attached to a common network. The lower two layers deal with the link between the host and the network. The next three layers are all involved in transferring data from one host to another: The network layer makes use of the communication network facilities to transfer data from one host to another; the transport layer assures that the transfer is reliable; and the session layer manages the flow of data over the logical connection. Finally, the upper two layers are oriented to the user's concerns, including considerations of the application to be performed and any formatting issues.

10.3

THE TCP/IP PROTOCOL SUITE

In recent years, much of the discussion and development work on communications protocols reported in the open literature has used the terminology and frame of reference of the OSI model. Remarkably, little attention has been given to a communications architecture that predates the OSI model and for which there is far more implementation and practical experience. This architecture is an outgrowth of the development of ARPANET [ROBE70] and the Defense Data Network (DDN) [ELSA86]. Whereas the OSI architecture is intended to guide the future development of protocols, it is the experience already gained in the development and use of protocols within ARPANET that has led to the communications architecture we are about to describe. This architecture has only recently been articulated as such and has no universally accepted name. We refer to it as the TCP/IP protocol suite.

Both OSI and the TCP/IP protocol suite deal with communications among heterogeneous computers. Both are based on the concept of protocol and have many similarities. However, there are philosophical and practical differences between the OSI model and the TCP/IP protocol suite, and the serious student of communications architecture needs to understand both.

In this section we provide an overview of the TCP/IP protocol suite. More detail is provided as various specific topics are pursued in the course of Part III.

Characteristics

The U.S. Department of Defense (DOD) has issued standards for a set of communications protocols [STAL90c]. Its motivations are much the same as those of the ISO and any computer system customer. DOD needs to have efficient, cost-effective communications among heterogeneous computers. That DOD has chosen to develop its own protocols and architecture rather than adopt the developing international standards is for three reasons [ENNI82]:

1. The DOD protocols were specified and have enjoyed extensive use prior to ISO standardization of alternative protocols. Because DOD's need was immediate, it was deemed impractical to wait for the ISO protocols to evolve and to stabilize.
2. DOD-specific communications requirements have a major impact on the design of protocols and an architecture. These concerns have not been uppermost in the minds of the ISO developers, and predictably are not reflected in the OSI model.
3. There are philosophic differences concerning the appropriate nature of a communications architecture and its protocols.

The first reason is self-explanatory. The second reason need not concern us in this context. The specific DOD requirements, many of which are also relevant in other contexts, include availability, survivability, security, network interoperability, and the ability to handle surge traffic. The interested reader is referred to [CERF83a].

The third reason is best explained by examining the differences between the

TCP/IP protocol suite and the OSI model. There are four fundamental differences [ENNI83]:

- The concept of hierarchy versus layering.
- The importance of internetworking.
- The utility of connectionless services.
- The approach to management functions.

Hierarchy Versus Layering

The TCP/IP protocol suite recognizes that the task of communications is too complex and too diverse to be accomplished by a single unit. Accordingly, the task is broken up into modules or entities that may communicate with peer entities in another system. One entity within a system provides services to other entities and, in turn, uses the services of other entities. Good software design practice dictates that these entities be arranged hierarchically (i.e., no entity uses its own services, directly or indirectly).

The OSI model is based on the same reasoning, but takes it one step further. The next step is the recognition that, in many respects, protocols at the same level of the hierarchy have certain features in common. This yields the concept of rows or layers, and the attempt to describe in an abstract fashion what features are held in common by the protocols within a given row.

Now, as an explanatory tool, a layered model has significant value and, indeed, the OSI model is used for precisely that purpose in the remainder of this book. The objection sometimes raised by the designers of the TCP/IP protocol suite and its protocols is that the OSI model is prescriptive rather than descriptive. It dictates that protocols within a given layer perform certain functions. This may not be always desirable. It is possible to define more than one protocol at a given layer, and the functionality of those protocols may not be the same or even similar. Rather, what is common about a set of protocols at the same layer is that they share the same set of support protocols at the next lower layer.

Furthermore, there is the implication in the OSI model that, because interfaces between layers are well defined, a new protocol can be substituted for an old one at a given layer with no impact on adjacent layers (see principle 6, Table 10.3). This is not always desirable or even possible. For example, a local network lends itself easily to multicast and broadcast addressing at the link level. If the IEEE 802 link level were inserted below a network protocol entity that did not support multicasting and broadcasting, that service would be denied to upper layers of the hierarchy. To get around some of these problems, OSI proponents talk of null layers and sublayers (we will see examples). It sometimes seems that these artifacts save the model at the expense of good protocol design.

To make the points above specific, consider the following prescriptions, commonly agreed to be part of the OSI model:

- (N) entities must exchange data using services provided by (N − 1) entities. Another way of saying this is that (N − 1) entities must be involved in every data transfer between (N) entities.
- (N − 1) entities provide their service by exchanging data units which contain (N − 1) control information and data from (N) entities.
- (N) control information is passed to the remote side as (N − 1) data.

The TCP/IP protocol suite is intended not to be so restrictive. As examples, the following techniques would be allowed:

- An entity may directly use the services of a hierarchically lower entity, even if it is not in an adjacent layer.
- Escape characters can be used to allow the placement of control characters within a data stream (e.g., TELNET, see Chapter 14). This situation is not correctly described by the concept of data units containing both control and higher-level data.
- Separate control and data connections may be used, in which higher-level data and control information do not share a data unit. This is useful, since one might wish to provide different services (priority, reliability) for the different types of connections.
- Lower-level control information can be used to accomplish higher-level control. For example, the closing of a lower-level connection can implicitly close an isomorphic higher-level connection, without requiring the higher-level entity to pass control information.
- Multiple entity cooperation is allowed. For example, an application-level protocol may dictate that the services of a name server entity be employed at the start of a sequence of data transfers, but the latter entity need not be involved after transfer begins.

It may, of course, be possible to provide all of these features within the OSI model, although neither the OSI document [ISO84] nor any of the developing protocols shows any evidence of them. The argument of the TCP/IP protocol suite proponents is not that certain things can be done in the TCP/IP protocol suite that cannot be done in the OSI model. Rather, the argument is that the TCP/IP protocol suite, by simply mandating that protocols be modular and hierarchical, give the designer more freedom to develop efficient, cost-effective, and rich protocols.

Whether the philosophical difference between hierarchy and layering results in any practical difference remains to be seen as more protocols are developed and used.

Internetworking

An historical difference between the TCP/IP protocol suite and the ISO model is the importance that the former places on internetworking. Internetworking occurs when two communicating systems do not attach to the same network.

Thus transferred data must traverse at least two networks. Further, these networks may be quite dissimilar.

The requirement for internetworking has led to the development of an Internet Protocol, discussed in Chapter 11. Such a protocol was not originally given a place within the OSI model. The current OSI document makes brief reference to the possibility of networks in tandem, and an internet protocol has emerged as a sublayer of the network layer (layer 3). This is not a clean solution, but it is the only one possible within the seven-layer architecture.

Connectionless Service

A connectionless service, as the name implies, is one in which data are transferred from one entity to another without the prior mutual construction of a connection (e.g., datagrams). The TCP/IP protocol suite places equal importance on connectionless and connection-oriented services, whereas the OSI model is couched solely in terms of connection-oriented service. It is expected, however, that future versions of the OSI model will incorporate connectionless service [CHAP83].

A primary use of the connectionless service within the TCP/IP protocol suite is in internetworking. Since it is not safe to assume that all intermediate networks are reliable, a connectionless internet protocol is used, with end-to-end connectivity provided at a higher level. A name-address directory server is another example where connectionless service might be desirable.

Management Functions

A final difference between the TCP/IP protocol suite and the OSI model is the way in which various management-related functions are treated. Examples of such functions are the naming (identification) of resources, the control of access to resources, and the accounting for resource and network usage.

The concept of management functions seems not to meld well with the OSI model, partly because these are mostly connectionless services, and partly because there's no "place" for them. It would appear that such functions must be classified according to layer and embedded as management entities within each layer. The TCP/IP protocol suite does not preclude this approach but goes further. Within this architecture, a uniform approach is taken to many of these functions and they are provided by protocols that can best be described as "session layer" protocols. This description reflects the fact that these protocols make use of transport services. This concept of session will be explored in Chapter 13.

TCP/IP Protocol Architecture

The TCP/IP protocol suite architecture is based on a view of communication that involves three agents: processes, hosts, and networks. *Processes* are the fundamental entities that communicate. Processes execute on *hosts* (stations), which can often support multiple simultaneous processes. Communication between processes takes place across *networks* to which the hosts are attached.

These three concepts yield a fundamental principle of the TCP/IP protocol suite: the transfer of information to a process can be accomplished by first getting it to the host in which the process resides and then getting it to the process within the host. These two levels of demultiplexing can be handled independently. Therefore, a network need only be concerned with routing data between hosts, as long as the hosts agree how to direct data to processes.

With the concepts above in mind, it is natural to organize protocols into four layers. We emphasize here that the important fact is the hierarchical ordering of protocols. The designation of layers is purely for explanatory purposes. An entity in a layer may use the services of another entity in the same layer, or directly use the services of an entity in a lower but not adjacent layer. With that caveat in mind, the DPA organizes protocols into four layers (as suggested by Figure 10.2):

- Network access layer.
- Internet layer.
- Host–host layer.
- Process/application layer.

The *network access layer* contains those protocols that provide access to a communication network. Protocols at this layer are between a communications node and an attached host or its logical equivalent. A function of all these protocols is to route data between hosts attached to the same network. Other services that may be provided are flow control and error control between hosts, and various quality of service features. Examples of the latter are priority and security. A network layer entity is typically invoked by an entity in either the internet or host–host layer, but may be invoked by a process/application layer entity.

The *internet layer* consists of the procedures required to allow data to traverse multiple networks between hosts. Thus it must provide a routing function. This protocol is usually implemented within hosts and gateways. A gateway is a processor connecting two networks whose primary function is to relay data between networks using an internetwork protocol.

The *host–host layer* contains protocol entities with the ability to deliver data between two processes on different host computers. A protocol entity at this level may (or may not) provide a logical connection between higher-level entities. Indeed, it is at this level that explicit connections make the most sense, with a logical connection being one used to exchange data between the ultimate endpoints (processes). Other possible services include error and flow control and the ability to deal with control signals not associated with a logical data connection. Four general types of protocols seem to be needed at this level [MCFA79]: a reliable connection-oriented data protocol, a datagram protocol, a speech protocol, and a real-time data protocol. Each has different services requirements:

- A reliable connection-oriented data protocol is characterized by the need for reliable, sequenced delivery of data. Many data processing applications would use such a service.
- A datagram protocol is a low-overhead, minimum functionality protocol that may be appropriate for some traffic, particularly applications that prefer to implement their own connection-oriented functionality.
- A speech protocol is characterized by the need for handling a steady stream of data with minimum delay variance.
- A real-time data protocol has the demanding characteristics of both a reliable connection-oriented protocol and a speech protocol.

The *process/application layer* contains protocols for resource sharing (e.g., computer-to-computer) and remote access (e.g., terminal-to-computer).

Within this architecture, DOD has issued the following protocol standards:

- Internet layer: IP (MIL-STD-1777)
- Host-to-host layer: TCP (MIL-STD-1778)
- Process/application layer: FTP (MIL-STD-1780); SMTP (MIL-STD-1781; TELNET (MIL-STD-1782)

These protocol standards are defined briefly in Table 10.7. Note that these standards fit into the upper three layers of the architecture. At the network access layer, systems may be interfaced to a variety of networks. By and large,

TABLE 10.7   DOD Military Standard Protocols

MIL-STD-1777 Internet Protocol (IP)

Provides a connectionless service for end systems to communicate across one or more networks. Does not assume the networks to be reliable.

MIL-STD-1778 Transmission Control Protocol (TCP)

A reliable end-to-end data transfer service. Equivalent to the ISO Class 4 transport protocol.

MIL-STD-1780 File Transfer Protocol (FTP)

A simple application for transfer of ASCII, EBCDIC, and binary files.

MIL-STD-1781 Simple Mail Transfer Protocol (SMTP)

A simple electronic mail facility.

MIL-STD-1782 Telnet Protocol

Provides a simple asynchronous terminal capability.

DOD will rely on national and international standards at this layer, such as X.25 for long-haul packet-switched networks and IEEE 802 for local networks.

Operation of TCP and IP

Figure 10.12 indicates how these protocols are configured for communications. To make clear that the total communications facility may consist of multiple networks, the constituent networks are usually referred to as *subnetworks*. Some sort of network access protocol, such as token ring, is used to connect a computer to a subnetwork. This protocol enables the host to send data across the subnetwork to another host or, in the case of a host on another subnetwork, to a router. IP is implemented in all of the end systems and the routers. It acts as a relay to move a block of data from one host, through one or more routers, to another host. TCP is implemented only in the end systems; it keeps track of the blocks of data to assure that all are delivered reliably to the appropriate application.

For successful communication, every entity in the overall system must have a unique address. Actually, two levels of addressing are needed. Each host on a subnetwork must have a unique global internet address; this allows the data to be delivered to the proper host. Each process with a host must have an address that is unique within the host; this allows the host-to-host protocol (TCP) to deliver data to the proper process. These latter addresses are known as ports.

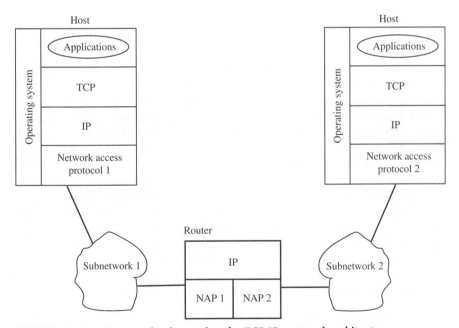

FIGURE 10.12.   Communications using the TCP/IP protocol architecture.

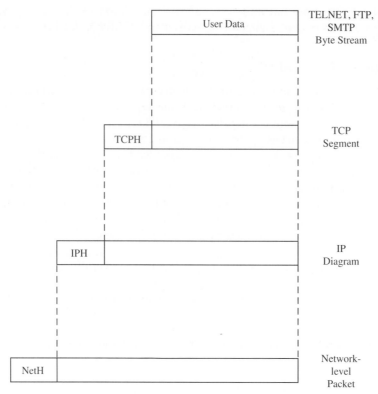

FIGURE 10.13.   Protocol data units in the TCP/IP architecture.

Let us trace a simple operation. Suppose that a process, associated with port 1 at host A, wishes to send a message to another process, associated with port 2 at host B. The process at A hands the message down to TCP with instructions to send it to host B, port 2. TCP hands the message down to IP with instructions to send it to host B. Note that IP need not be told the identity of the destination port. All that it needs to know is that the data are intended for host B. Next, IP hands the message down to the network access layer (e.g., Ethernet logic) with instructions to send it to router X (the first hop on the way to B).

To control this operation, control information as well as user data must be transmitted, as suggested in Figure 10.13. Let us say that the sending process generates a block of data and passes this to TCP. TCP may break this block into smaller pieces to make it more manageable. To each of these pieces, TCP appends control information known as the TCP header, forming a *TCP segment*. The control information is to be used by the peer TCP protocol entity at host B. Examples of items that are included in this header are

• *Destination port:* When the TCP entity at B receives the segment, it must know to whom the data are to be delivered.

- *Sequence number:* TCP numbers the segments that it sends to a particular destination port sequentially, so that if they arrive out of order, the TCP entity at B can reorder them.
- *Checksum:* The sending TCP includes a code that is a function of the contents of the remainder of the segment. The receiving TCP performs the same calculation and compares the result with the incoming code. A discrepancy results if there has been some error in transmission.

Next, TCP hands each segment over to IP, with instructions to transmit it to B. These segments must be transmitted across one or more subnetworks and relayed through one or more intermediate routers. This operation, too, requires the use of control information. Thus IP appends a header of control information to each segment to form an *IP datagram.* An example of an item stored in the IP header is the destination host address (in this example, B).

Finally, each IP datagram is presented to the network access layer for transmission across the first subnetwork in its journey to the destination. The network access layer appends its own header, creating a packet, or frame. The packet is transmitted across the subnetwork to router X. The packet header contains the information that the subnetwork needs to transfer the data across the subnetwork. Examples of items that may be contained in this header include

- *Destination subnetwork address:* The subnetwork must know to which attached device the packet is to be delivered.
- *Facilities requests:* The network access protocol might request the use of certain subnetwork facilities, such as priority.

At router X, the packet header is stripped off and the IP header examined. On the basis of the destination address information in the IP header, the IP module in the router directs the datagram out across subnetwork 2 to B. To do this, the datagram is again augmented with a network access header.

When the data are received at B, the reverse process occurs. At each layer, the corresponding header is removed, and the remainder is passed on to the next higher layer until the original user data are delivered to the destination process.

Protocol Interfaces

Each layer in the TCP/IP protocol suite interacts with its immediate adjacent layers. At the source, the process layer makes use of the services of the host-to-host layer and provides data down to that layer. A similar relationship exists at the interface of the host-to-host and internet layers and at the interface of the internet and network access layers. At the destination, each layer delivers data up to the next higher layer.

This use of each individual layer is not required by the architecture. As Figure 10.14 suggests, it is possible to develop applications that directly invoke

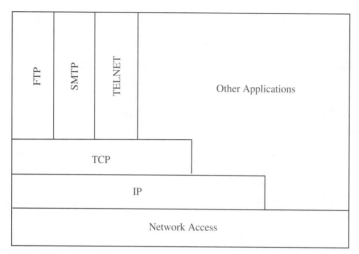

FIGURE 10.14.   TCP/IP protocol suite: interfaces.

the services of any one of the layers. Most applications require a reliable end-to-end protocol and thus make use of TCP. Some special-purpose applications do not need the services of TCP. Some of these applications, such as the simple network management protocol (SNMP), use an alternative host-to-host protocol known as the user datagram protocol (UDP); others may make use of IP directly. Applications that do not involve internetworking and that do not need TCP have been developed to invoke the network access layer directly.

It is important to note that TCP/IP protocol suite is not limited to the five military standard protocols. Rather, a variety of applications and other processes may make use of this architecture. Figure 10.15 shows the position of some of the key protocols commonly implemented as part of the TCP/IP protocol suite.

The Applications

The **simple mail transfer protocol (SMTP)** provides a basic electronic mail facility. It provides a mechanism for transferring messages among separate hosts. Features of SMTP include mailing lists, return receipts, and forwarding. The SMTP protocol does not specify the way in which messages are to be created; some local editing or native electronic mail facility is required. Once a message is created, SMTP accepts the message and makes use of TCP to send it to an SMTP module on another host. The target SMTP module will make use of a local electronic mail package to store the incoming message in a user's mailbox.

The **file transfer protocol (FTP)** is used to send files from one system to another under user command. Both text and binary files are accommodated,

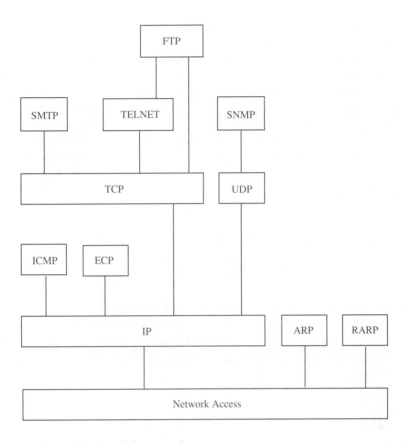

ARP   = address resolution protocol
EG   = external gateway protocol
FTP   = file transfer protocol
ICMP = internet control message protocol
IP   = internet protocol
RARP = reverse address resolution protocol
SMTP = simple mail transfer protocol
SNMP = simple network management protocol
TCP   = transport control protocol
UDP   = user datagram protocol

FIGURE 10.15.   Protocol dependencies.

and the protocol provides features for controlling user access. When a user requests a file transfer, FTP sets up a TCP connection to the target system for the exchange of control messages. These allow user ID and password to be transmitted and allow the user to specify the file and file actions desired. Once a file transfer is approved, a second TCP connection is set up for the data transfer. The file is transferred over the data connection, without the overhead of any headers or control information at the application level. When the transfer is complete, the control connection is used to signal the completion and to accept new file transfer commands.

TELNET provides a remote logon capability, which enables a user at a terminal or personal computer to logon to a remote computer and function as if directly connected to that computer. The protocol was designed to work with simple scroll-mode terminals. TELNET is actually implemented in two modules: User TELNET interacts with the terminal I/O module to communicate with a local terminal. It converts the characteristics of real terminals to the network standard and vice versa. Server TELNET interacts with an application, acting as a surrogate terminal handler so that remote terminals appear as local to the application. Terminal traffic between User and Server TELNET is carried on a TCP connection.

10.4

SYSTEMS NETWORK ARCHITECTURE

It is instructive to compare the standardized approaches with a proprietary communications architecture. For this purpose, we return to an architecture introduced in Chapter 8, IBM's system network architecture (SNA). Figure 10.16 compares SNA with OSI and the TCP/IP protocol suite.

SNA consists of seven layers:

- Physical control.
- Data link control.
- Path control.
- Transmission control.
- Data flow control.
- Presentation services.
- Transaction services.

Physical Control

The physical control layer corresponds to OSI layer 1. It specifies the physical interface between nodes. Two types of interface are specified: those for serial communications links and those for parallel links. The interfaces for serial communications links are of the kind discussed in Chapter 4, and are used for most node-to-node connections. SNA networks can also include high-speed parallel links between a mainframe and a front-end communication processor.

Data Link Control

The data link control layer corresponds to OSI layer 2. This layer provides for the reliable transfer of data across a physical link. The protocol specified for serial communications links is SDLC. SDLC is basically a subset of HDLC,

OSI		TCP/IP Protocol Suite		SNA	
7	Applications	7	Process/ application	7	Transaction services
6	Presentations	6		6	Presentation services
5	Session	5	Host-Host	5	Data flow control
4	Transport	4		4	Transmission control
3	Network	3	Internet	3	Path control
2	Data link	2	Network access	2	Data link control
1	Physical	1		1	Physical control

FIGURE 10.16. A comparison of communications architectures.

which was covered in Chapter 5. The protocol for high-speed parallel links is the S/370 data channel protocol, which is described in [STAL93c].

Path Control

The *path control* layer [ATKI80] creates logical channels between endpoints, referred to as network addressable units (NAUs). An NAU is an application-level entity capable of being addressed and of exchanging data with other entities. Thus key functions of the path control layer are routing and flow control.

Path control is based on the concepts of transmission group, explicit route, and virtual route, introduced in Chapter 8. To recall, a *transmission group* is a set of one or more physical links between adjacent nodes in the network. An *explicit route* is a path between endpoints, defined as an ordered sequence of transmission groups. A *virtual route* is a logical connection between endpoints that is dynamically assigned to an explicit route. Corresponding to these three concepts are three sublayers of the path control layer.

The primary function of the transmission group control sublayer is to make the set of links in a transmission group appear to higher layers as a single physical link. The main advantages of this are increased reliability and capacity for transmission between adjacent nodes. The protocol at this sublayer accepts data units and places them in a FIFO queue. Each data unit is sent out in turn over the next available physical link, using SDLC. Because of errors or differences in propagation delay, units may arrive out of order at the other end of the transmission group. Sequence numbers are used so that the receiving protocol entity can reorder the units. Another function performed at this sublayer is blocking. When a transmission group consists of a single link, the protocol entity may block incoming data units into a larger unit before transmission. This can increase efficiency, for example, by reducing the number of channel I/O operations that data link control needs to execute. The function of this sublayer is unusual and seems to fit best as part of layer 2 of the OSI model.

The explicit route control sublayer is primarily responsible for routing. Explicit routes are predefined in SNA and each node maintains routing information in the form of (explicit route number, next node). Thus, any incoming data must contain an explicit route number. On the basis of that number, the protocol entity selects the next node and passes the data to the transmission group control sublayer.

The virtual route control sublayer provides a logical connection on which traffic from sessions is multiplexed and on which flow control mechanisms are applied. Both entry-to-exit flow control and congestion control are exercised using the pacing algorithm described in Chapter 9. In addition, this sublayer has the ability to segment data units from higher layers to improve efficiency. Segmented data units must be reassembled at the other end. This sublayer and the explicit route control sublayer more or less encompass the functions of OSI's layer 3.

Transmission Control

The next higher layer of SNA is *transmission control*, which corresponds roughly to layer 4 of the OSI model. The transmission control layer is responsible for establishing, maintaining, and terminating SNA sessions. A *session*, which corresponds to OSI's transport connection is a logical relation between endpoints (NAUs). The transmission control layer can establish a session in response to a request from the next higher layer (data flow control), from an application process, or for its own control purposes.

The layer is composed of two modules: the connection point manager (CPMGR), which handles individual data transfers, and session control, which handles session-level matters. The *CPMGR* performs the following functions:

- *Routing:* This is essentially a demultiplexing function. Incoming data units are routed to the appropriate entity, which may be at the same or some higher layer.
- *Encapsulation:* Outgoing messages are encapsulated in a data unit; the header, which is appended to the data, contains control information for expedited delivery, pacing, encryption, and other control functions.

- *Pacing:* This is the same mechanism as is used on virtual routes. In this case, it is used only by the endpoints, to control the flow of data units. A fixed window size is used.

Session control is invoked to activate or deactivate a session. It is also invoked when CPMGR detects a session error, such as a missing sequence number.

Data Flow Control

Within SNA logical connections, called sessions, may be established between applications. SNA has chosen to divide the management of sessions into two layers. The transmission control layer is transmission oriented and, as we have said, corresponds nicely of OSI's layer 4. The *data flow control* layer is end-user oriented and corresponds equally nicely to OSI's layer 5. This layer is responsible for providing session-related services that are visible and of interest to end-user processes and terminals. The principal functions are in the following categories.

- *Send/receive mode:* Three modes may be specified: full duplex, half-duplex flip-flop, and half-duplex contention. The distinction between the latter two roughly corresponds to the distinction between HDLC's normal response mode and asynchronous balanced mode.
- *Chaining:* Chaining is a mechanism to delineate transmission sequences for the purpose of recovery (as discussed under the OSI session layer, above).
- *Bracketing:* Whereas chaining deals with a sequence of data units transmitted in one direction, bracketing deals with a sequence of exchanges. This concept may be used to define and control transaction sequences.
- *Response options:* Three response modes may be specified. For each data unit, (1) do not send a response, (2) send a response only in case of an exception, and (3) always send a response.
- *Quiesce/shutdown:* A temporary or permanent halt to the flow of data may be requested.

Presentation Services

The top two layers of SNA were, until recently, considered as a single layer referred to as the function management data (FMD) services layer [HOBE80]. The FMD services layer comprised a set of functions and services provided to the end user. That layer corresponded to OSI layers 6 and 7. Now, the functions are split into two layers, presentation services and transaction services.
The presentation services layer includes the following services:

- *Format translation:* This service allows each endpoint to have a different view of the exchanged data. For example, it can be used to allow one application to handle multiple terminal types.

- *Compression and compaction:* Data can be compressed at the bit or byte level using specified procedures, to reduce transmission volume.
- *Transaction program support:* This service controls conversation-level communication between transaction programs by (1) loading and invoking transaction programs, (2) maintaining send and receive mode protocols, and (3) enforcing correct verb parameter usage and sequencing restrictions.

Most of these services correspond to OSI layer 6, although some of the transaction program support functions are more in the nature of layer 7.

Transaction Services

This layer is primarily intended to provide network management services. Since these services are directly used by an end user, such as a system manager or network operator, they best fit in OSI's layer 7. The following are included:

- *Configuration services:* allow an operator to start up or reconfigure a network by activating and deactivating links.
- *Network operator services:* include such nonconfiguration operator functions as the collection and display of network statistics, and the communication of data from users and processes to the network operator.
- *Session services:* support the activation of a session on the behalf of end users and applications. In effect, this is the user interface to the transmission control layer.
- *Maintenance and management services:* provide for the testing of network facilities and assist in fault isolation and identification.

SNA Encapsulation

Unlike the apparent OSI policy, SNA does not require the use of a header at each layer of the hierarchy. Figure 10.17 depicts the overall SNA encapsulation strategy. The most basic piece of data in SNA is the *request/response unit* (RU), which contains either user data or network control information. A services manager creates RUs from user data. The FMD services layer may perform certain transformations on the data to accommodate presentation services or may add control information relating to chains of RUs. The latter are contained in a *FMD header.* This header is optional and, if used, may only appear occasionally (at the start of a chain or bracket); thus it is not shown in the figure.

The transmission control layer then adds a request/response header (RH), containing control information both for itself and the data flow control layer. Rather than create a separate header, the data flow control layer is content to pass parameters to the transmission control layer to include in the header that it constructs. This seems more efficient than the OSI approach, but implies a tighter coupling between layers.

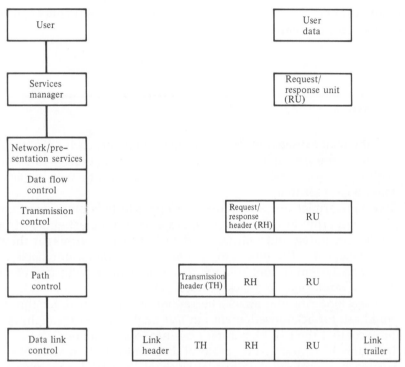

FIGURE 10.17.   SNA data encapsulation. Source: [METZ83]

The next two layers add their own headers for their own requirements. Data link control also adds a trailer; this corresponds to the trailer for HDLC, described in Chapter 5.

10.5

RECOMMENDED READING

[STAL93a] is a detailed description of the OSI model and of the standards at each layer of the model. The material is also covered in [TANE88], which averages about one chapter per layer. [HENS90] and [TANG92] cover various OSI-related standards, with emphasis on the upper layers. [COLE90] discusses OSI from the point of view of the practical implementation issues. [STAL92] contains reprints of key articles covering OSI and standards at each layer.

A detailed description of the TCP/IP protocol suite and of the individual standards is contained in [STAL90b]. Two other detailed treatments are [COME91] and [FEIT93].

Two excellent treatments of SNA are [MART87] and [MEIJ87]. Both are detailed, complete, and clearly written. [TILL90] provides an interesting analysis of the interconnection of SNA and OSI systems. [CYPS91] covers all three of the architectures presented in this chapter.

10.6

PROBLEMS

10.1 List the major disadvantages with the layered approach to protocols.

10.2 Based on the principles enunciated in Table 10.3, design an architecture with eight layers and make a case for it. Design one with six layers and make a case for that.

10.3 Two blue armies are each poised on opposite hills preparing to attack a single red army in the valley. The red army can defeat either of the blue armies separately but will fail to defeat both blue armies if they attack simultaneously. The blue armies communicate via an unreliable communications system (a foot soldier). The commander, with one of the blue armies, would like to attack at noon. His problem is this: If he sends a message ordering the attack, he cannot be sure it will get through. He could ask for acknowledgment but *that* might not get through. Is there a protocol that the two blue armies can use to avoid defeat?

10.4 In Figure 10.7, exactly one protocol data unit (PDU) in layer N is encapsulated in a protocol data unit at layer (N-1). It is also possible to break one N-level PDU into multiple (N-1)-level PDUs (segmentation) or to group multiple N-level PDUs into one (N-1)-level PDU (blocking). (a) In the case of segmentation, is it necessary that each (N-1)-level segment contain a copy of the N-level header? (b) In the case of blocking, is it necessary that each N-level PDU retain its own header, or can the data be consolidated into a single N-level PDU with a single N-level header?

10.5 Discuss the need or lack of need for a network layer (OSI layer 3) in a broadcast network.

10.6 Compare SNA to the OSI and TCP/IP frameworks. To which is it closest philosophically? Discuss similarities and differences.

10.7 What must be added to the OSI model to reconcile the differences with TCP/IP?

APPENDIX 10A

Standards

Section 1.6 described the most important standard-making organizations and Figure 10.18 shows the relationship to the OSI model of some of the most important standards. Remember that the OSI layers are not standards; they merely provide a framework for standards.

OSI	ISO	CCITT	DOD	IEEE 802	ASC X3T9.5
7. Application	FTAM	X.400	FTP SMTP		
6. Presentation	VTP		TELNET		
5. Session	ISO Session		TCP		
4. Transport	ISO Transport				
3. Network	ISO IP	ISDN	IP		
2. Data Link		X.25		Logical link control	
1. Physical		X.21		Medium access control Physical	

FIGURE 10.18.   Some well-known protocol standards.

ISO, of course, continues to play the key role in the evolution of the OSI model. Their interest in individual standards has focused on layer 3 and above. ISO has issued standards for layers 4 and 5 and is in the process of issuing a variety of standards that cover layers 6 and 7. ISO has also developed a sublayer of layer 3 that deals with internetworking, which involves communication across multiple networks.

CCITT has been concerned with defining access protocols to public communication networks. It has developed standards for connecting *data terminal equipment* (DTE) to a packet-switched network that provides *data circuit-terminating equipment* (DCE). These terms correspond to the stations and nodes of Figure 7.2. The standard, X.25, specifically addresses layer 3 and subsumes standards for layers 2 and 1. Layer 2 is referred to as LAP-B (Link Access Protocol—Balanced) and is almost identical with ISO's HDLC (High-Level Data Link Control) and ANSI's ADCCP (Advanced Data Communication Control Procedures). A corresponding standard, X.21, has been developed for circuit-switched networks. CCITT is the controlling organization for developing ISDN standards. CCITT is also concerned with the area known as *telematics,* which covers user-oriented information transmission services. Teletex (communication among office word processing systems), videotex (interactive information retrieval), and facsimile (imagery transmission) are included under this term.

DCA is the issuing agency for communications standards for DOD. They have promulgated the Transmission Control Protocol (TCP) as a transport protocol standard and the Internet Protocol (IP) for internetworking. In addition they have issued standards at higher layers. All of these protocols, unfortunately, differ from planned and issued standards from ISO and NBS.

For the type of local network that we refer to as a *local area network* (LAN), the Institute of Electrical and Electronics Engineers (IEEE), through its 802 committee, has developed a three-layer architecture that corresponds to layers 1 and 2 of the OSI model. A number of standards have been developed by the committee for these layers. Similarly, a subcommittee responsible to the American National Standards Institute (ANSI), known as ANS X3T9.5, has developed standards for the type of local network we refer to as a *high speed local network* (HSLN). These standards, one per layer, correspond nicely to layers 1 and 2 of the OSI model.

This variety may be disheartening, given the alleged benefit of standards, which is to put everyone on the same road. The picture, however, is far from bleak. Tremendous progress has been made toward the development and issuance of standards. Most organizations are cooperating to reduce the incidence of duplicate, competing standards. And while vendors and customers are faced in some areas with multiple standards, the customer at least is far better off than in the 1970s, when virtually no standards existed above layer 1, and those that did were frequently ignored.

An interesting discussion of standards and standards-making organizations is [CERN84].

CHAPTER 11

Internetworking

Packet-switched and packet broadcasting networks grew out of a need to allow the computer user to have access to resources beyond that available in a single system. In a similar fashion, the resources of a single network are often inadequate to meet users' needs. Because the networks that might be of interest exhibit so many differences, it is impractical to consider merging them into a single network. Rather, what is needed is the ability to interconnect various networks so that any two stations on any of the constituent networks can communicate.

Table 11.1 lists some commonly used terms relating to the interconnection of networks, or internetworking. An interconnected set of networks, from a user's point of view, may appear simply as a larger network. However, if each of the constituent networks retains its identity and special mechanisms are needed for communicating across multiple networks, then the entire configuration is often referred to as an **internet,** and each of the constituent networks as a **subnetwork.**

Each constituent subnetwork in an internet supports communication among the devices attached to that subnetwork. In addition, subnetworks are connected by devices referred to in the ISO documents as **intermediate systems** (ISs).[1] ISs provide a communications path and perform the necessary relaying and routing functions so that data can be exchanged between devices attached to different subnetworks in the internet.

Two types of ISs of particular interest are bridges and routers. The differences between them have to do with the types of protocols used for the internetworking logic. In essence, a bridge operates at layer 2 of the open systems interconnection (OSI) 7-layer architecture and acts as a relay of frames between like networks. A router operates at layer 3 of the OSI architecture and routes packets between potentially different networks. Both the bridge and the router assume that the same upper-layer protocols are in use.

---

[1]The term *gateway* is sometimes used to refer to an IS or to a particular kind of IS. Because of the lack of consistency in the use of this term, we will avoid it.

TABLE 11.1   Internetworking Terms

Communication Network

A facility that provides a data transfer service among stations attached to the network.

Internet

A collection of communication networks interconnected by bridges and/or routers.

Subnetwork

Refers to a constituent network of an internet. This avoids ambiguity since the entire internet, from a user's point of view, is a single network.

Intermediate System (IS)

A device used to connect two subnetworks and permit communication between end systems attached to different subnetworks.

Bridge

An IS used to connect two LANs that use identical LAN protocols. The bridge acts as an address filter, picking up packets from one LAN that are intended for a destination on another LAN and passing those packets on. The bridge does not modify the contents of the packets and does not add anything to the packet. The bridge operates at layer 2 of the OSI model.

Router

An IS used to connect two networks that may or may not be similar. The router employs an internet protocol present in each router and each host of the network. The router operates at layer 3 of the OSI model.

We begin our examination with a discussion of the principles underlying various approaches to internetworking. We then examine the three principal architectural approaches to internetworking: bridge, connectionless layer 3 routers, and connection-oriented routers. These three approaches are explored in some detail.

11.1

PRINCIPLES OF INTERNETWORKING

Requirements

Although a variety of approaches have been taken to provide internetwork service, the overall requirements on the internetworking facility can be stated in general. These include

1. Provide a link between networks. At minimum, a physical and link control connection is needed.
2. Provide for the routing and delivery of data between processes on different networks.
3. Provide an accounting service that keeps track of the use of the various networks and gateways and maintains status information.

4. Provide the services listed above in such a way as not to require modifications to the networking architecture of any of the constituent networks. This means that the internetworking facility must accommodate a number of differences among networks. These include:
   a. *Different addressing schemes:* The networks may use different endpoint names and addresses and directory maintenance schemes. Some form of global network addressing must be provided, as well as a directory service.
   b. *Different maximum packet size:* Packets from one network may have to be broken up into smaller pieces for another. This process is referred to as segmentation.
   c. *Different network access mechanisms:* The network access mechanism between station and network may be different for stations on different networks.
   d. *Different timeouts:* Typically, a connection-oriented transport service will await an acknowledgment until a timeout expires, at which time it will retransmit its block of data. In general, longer times are required for successful delivery across multiple networks. Internetwork timing procedures must allow successful transmission that avoids unnecessary retransmissions.
   e. *Error recovery:* Intranetwork procedures may provide anything from no error recovery up to reliable end-to-end (within the network) service. The internetwork service should not depend on nor be interfered with by the nature of the individual network's error recovery capability.
   f. *Status reporting:* Different networks report status and performance differently. Yet it must be possible for the internetworking facility to provide such information on internetworking activity to interested and authorized processes.
   g. *Routing techniques:* Intranetwork routing may depend on fault detection and congestion control techniques peculiar to each network. The internetworking facility must be able to coordinate these to adaptively route data between stations on different networks.
   h. *User access control:* Each network will have its own user access control technique (authorization for use of the network). These must be invoked by the internetwork facility as needed. Further, a separate internetwork access control technique may be required.
   i. *Connection, connectionless:* Individual networks may provide connection-oriented (e.g., virtual circuit) or connectionless (datagram) service. It may be desirable for the internetwork service not to depend on the nature of the connection service of the individual networks.

These points are worthy of further comment but are best pursued in the context of specific architectural approaches. We outline these approaches next, and then turn to a more detailed discussion of each approach.

Architectural Approaches

In describing the interworking function, two dimensions are important:

- The mode of operation (connection-mode or connectionless).
- The protocol architecture.

The mode of operation determines the protocol architecture. ISO has standardized two general approaches, as depicted in Figure 11.1.

Connection-Mode Operation

In the connection-mode operation, it is assumed that each subnetwork provides a connection-mode form of service. That is, it is possible to establish a logical network connection (e.g., virtual circuit) between any two DTEs attached to the same subnetwork. With this in mind, we can summarize the connection-mode approach as follows:

1. ISs are used to connect two or more subnetworks; each IS appears as a DTE to each of the subnetworks to which it is attached.
2. When DTE A wishes to exchange data with DTE B, a logical connection is set up between them. This logical connection consists of the concatenation of a sequence of logical connections across subnetworks. The sequence is such that it forms a path from DTE A to DTE B.
3. The individual subnetwork logical connections are spliced together by ISs. For example, there is a logical connection from DTE A to IS I across subnetwork 1 and another logical connection from IS I to IS M across subnetwork 2. Any traffic arriving at IS I on the first logical connection is retransmitted on the second logical connection and vice versa.

Several additional points can be made about this form of operation. First, this approach is suited to providing support for a connection-mode network service. From the point of view of network users in DTEs A and B, a logical network connection is established between them that provides all of the features of a logical connection across a single network.

The second point to be made is that this approach assumes that there is a connection-mode service available from each subnet and that these services are equivalent. Clearly, this may not always be the case. For example, an IEEE 802 or FDDI local area network provides a service defined by the logical link control (LLC). Two of the options with LLC provide only connectionless service. Therefore, in this case, the subnetwork service must be enhanced. An example of how this would be done is for the ISs to implement X.25 on top of LLC across the LAN.

Figure 11.2a illustrates the protocol architecture for connection-mode operation. Access to all subnetworks, either inherently or by enhancement, is by means of the same network layer protocol. The interworking units operate at

(a) Connection-mode operation

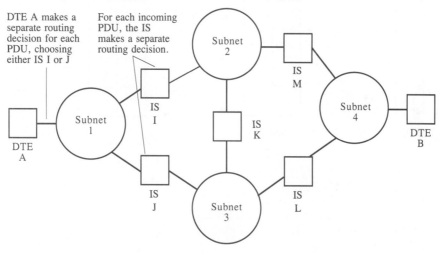

(b) Connectionless-mode operation

FIGURE 11.1.   Internetworking approaches.

layer 3. As was mentioned, layer 3 ISs are commonly referred to as routers. A connection-oriented router performs the following key functions:

- *Relaying:* Data units arriving from one subnetwork via the network layer protocol are relayed (retransmitted) on another subnetwork. Traffic is over logical connections that are spliced together at the routers.

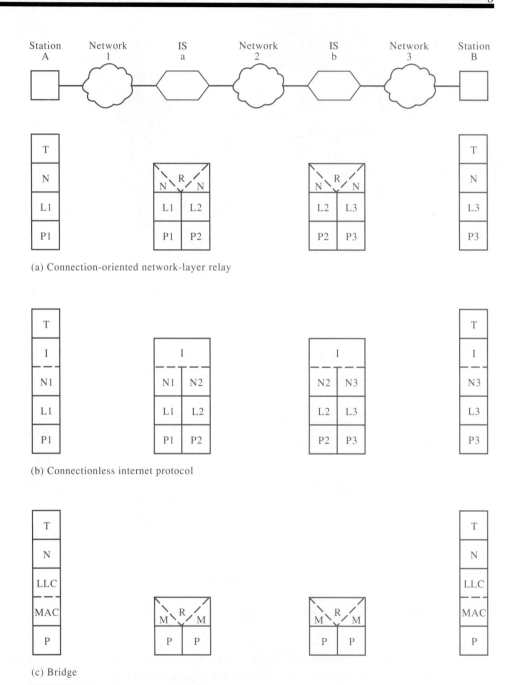

(a) Connection-oriented network-layer relay

(b) Connectionless internet protocol

(c) Bridge

FIGURE 11.2.   Internetwork architectures.

- *Routing:* When an end-to-end logical connection, consisting of a sequence of logical connections, is to be set up, each router in the sequence must make a routing decision which determines the next hop in the sequence.

Thus, at layer 3, a relaying operation is performed. It is assumed that all of the end systems share common protocols at layer 4 (transport) and above for successful end-to-end communication.

We examine the connection-oriented approach in Section 11.3.

Connectionless-Mode Operation

Figure 11.2b illustrates the connectionless mode of operation. Whereas connection-mode operation corresponds to the virtual circuit mechanism of a packet-switching network (Figure 8.4c), connectionless-mode operation corresponds to the datagram mechanism of a packet-switching network (Figure 8.4d). Each network protocol data unit is treated independently and routed from source DTE to destination DTE through a series of routers and networks. For each data unit transmitted by A, A makes a decision as to which router should receive the data unit. The data unit hops across the internet from one router to the next until it reaches the destination subnetwork. At each router, a routing decision is made (independently for each data unit) concerning the next hop. Thus, different data units may travel different routes between source and destination DTE.

Figure 11.2b illustrates the protocol architecture for connectionless-mode operation. All DTEs and all routers share a common network layer protocol known generically as the internet protocol (IP). An internet protocol was initially developed for the DARPA internet project, and has been standardized by the U.S. Department of Defense. The ISO standard, ISO 8473, provides similar functionality. Below this internet protocol, there is needed a protocol to access the particular subnetwork. Thus, there are typically two protocols operating in each DTE and router at the network layer: an upper sublayer that provides the internetworking function, and a lower sublayer that provides subnetwork access.

We examine the connectionless internet protocol approach in Section 11.4.

Bridge Approach

A third approach that is quite common is the use of a bridge. The bridge, also known as a MAC-level relay uses a connectionless mode of operation (Figure 11.1b), but does so at a lower level than a router.

The protocol architecture for a bridge is illustrated in Figure 11.2c. In this case, the end systems share common transport and network protocols. In addition, it is assumed that all of the networks use the same protocols at the link layer. In the case of IEEE 802 and FDDI LANs, this means that all of the LANs share a common LLC protocol and a common MAC protocol. For example, all of the LANs are IEEE 802.3 using the unacknowledged connectionless form of LLC. In this case, MAC frames are relayed through bridges between the LANs. We examine the bridge approach in Section 11.2.

Addressing

In order to transfer data from one DTE to another DTE, there must be some way of uniquely identifying the destination DTE. Thus, with each DTE, we must be able to associate a unique identifier, or address. This address will allow DTEs and ISs to perform the routing function properly.

In the OSI environment, this unique address is equated to a network service access point (NSAP). An NSAP uniquely identifies a DTE within the internet. A DTE may have more than one NSAP, but each is unique to that particular system. We can refer to such an address as a **global internet address**. Frequently, this address is in the form of (*network, host*), where the parameter *network* identifies a particular subnetwork and the parameter *host* identifies a particular DTE attached to that subnetwork.

Figure 11.3 suggests that another level of addressing may be needed. Each subnetwork must maintain a unique address for each DTE attached to that subnetwork. This allows the subnetwork to route data units through the subnetwork and deliver them to the intended DTE. We can refer to such an address as a **subnetwork attachment point address.**

It would appear convenient for the *host* parameter in the global address to be identical to the subnetwork attachment point address for that DTE. Unfortunately, this may not always be practical. Different networks use different addressing formats and different address lengths. Furthermore, a station may enjoy more than one attachment point into the same network. Accordingly, we must assume that the *host* parameter has global significance and the sub-

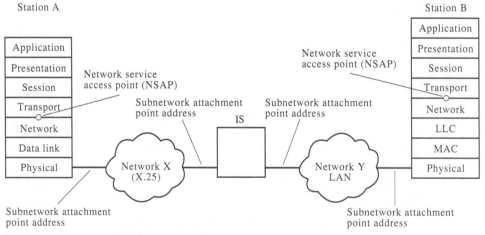

FIGURE 11.3.   Network-layer addressing.

network attachment point address has significance only within a particular subnetwork. In this case, the internetworking facility must translate from the global address to the locally significant address to route data units.

11.2

THE BRIDGE

Functions of a Bridge

The simplest of the internetworking devices is the bridge. This device is designed for use between local area networks (LANs) that use identical protocols for the physical and medium access layers (e.g., all conforming to IEEE 802.3 or all conforming to FDDI). Because the devices all use the same protocols, the amount of processing required at the bridge is minimal. The concept of a bridge was introduced in Chapter 9 as a means of linking multiple rings.

Figure 11.4 illustrates the operation of a bridge between two LANs, A and B. The bridge performs the following functions:

- Read all frames transmitted on A, and accept those addressed to stations on B.

FIGURE 11.4.   Bridge operation.

- Using the medium access control protocol for B, retransmit the frames onto B.
- Do the same for B-to-A traffic.

In addition to these basic functions, there are some interesting design considerations:

1. The bridge makes no modifications to the content or format of the frames it receives.
2. The bridge should contain enough buffer space to meet peak demands. Over a short period of time, frames may arrive faster than they can be retransmitted.
3. The bridge must contain addressing and routing intelligence. At a minimum, the bridges must know which addresses are on each network in order to know which frames to forward. Further, there may be more than two networks in a sort of cascade configuration. The bridge must be able to pass along frames intended for networks further on. The subject of routing is explored later in this section.

In summary, the bridge provides an extension to the LAN that requires no modification to the communications software in the stations attached to the LANs. It appears to all stations on the two (or more) LANs that there is a single LAN on which each station has a unique address. The station uses that unique address and need not explicitly discriminate between stations on the same LAN and stations on other LANs; the bridge takes care of that.

Since the bridge is used in a situation in which all of the LANs have the same characteristics, the reader may ask why not simply have one large LAN. Depending on circumstance, there are several reasons for the use of multiple LANs connected by bridges:

- *Reliability:* The danger in connecting all data processing devices in an organization to one network is that a fault on the network may disable communication for all devices. By using bridges, the network can be partitioned into self-contained units.
- *Performance:* In general, performance on a LAN declines with an increase in the number of devices or the length of the medium. A number of smaller LANs will often give improved performance if devices can be clustered so that *intra*-network traffic significantly exceeds *inter*-network traffic.
- *Security*: The establishment of multiple LANs may improve security of communications. It is desirable to keep different types of traffic (e.g., accounting, personnel, strategic planning) that have different security needs on physically separate media. At the same time, the different types of users with different level of security need to communicate through controlled and monitored mechanisms.
- *Geography:* Clearly, two separate LANs are needed to support devices clustered in two geographically distant locations. Even in the case of two buildings separated by a highway, it may be far easier to use a microwave bridge

link than to attempt to string coaxial cable between the two buildings. In the case of widely separated networks, two "half bridges" are needed (see Figures 11.6 and 11.7, below).

The description above has applied to the simplest sort of bridge. More sophisticated bridges can be used in more complex collections of LANs. These would include additional functions, such as:

- Each bridge can maintain status information on other bridges, together with the cost and number of bridge-to-bridge hops required to reach each network. This information may be updated by periodic exchanges of information among bridges. This allows the bridges to perform a dynamic routing function.
- A control mechanism can manage frame buffers in each bridge to overcome congestion. Under saturation conditions, the bridge can give precedence to en-route packets over new packets just entering the internet from an attached LAN, thus preserving the investment in line bandwidth and processing time already made in the enroute frame.

Bridge Protocol Architecture

The IEEE 802 committee has produced two specifications for bridges [IEEE90d, IEEE91c]. In both cases, the devices are referred to as MAC-level relays. In addition, all of the MAC standards suggest formats for a globally administered set of MAC station addresses across multiple homogeneous LANs. In this subsection, we examine the protocol architecture of these bridges.

Within the 802 architecture, the endpoint or station address is designated at the MAC level. At the LLC level, only an SAP address is specified. Thus, it is at the MAC level that a bridge can function. Figure 11.5 shows the simplest case, which consists of two LANs connected by a single bridge. The LANs employ the same MAC and LLC protocols. The bridge operates as previously described. A MAC frame whose destination is not on the immediate LAN is captured by the bridge, buffered briefly, and then transmitted on the other LAN. As far as the LLC layer is concerned, there is a dialogue between peer LLC entities in the two endpoint stations. The bridge need not contain an LLC layer since it is merely serving to relay the MAC frames.

Figure 11.5b indicates the way in which data is encapsulated using a bridge. Data is provided by some user to LLC. The LLC entity appends a header and passes the resulting data unit to the MAC entity, which appends a header and a trailer to form a MAC frame. On the basis of the destination MAC address in the frame, it is captured by the bridge. The bridge does not strip off the MAC fields; its function is to relay the MAC frame intact to the destination LAN. Thus the frame is deposited on the destination LAN and captured by the destination station.

The concept of a MAC relay bridge is not limited to the use of a single bridge to connect two nearby LANs. If the LANs are some distance apart, then they

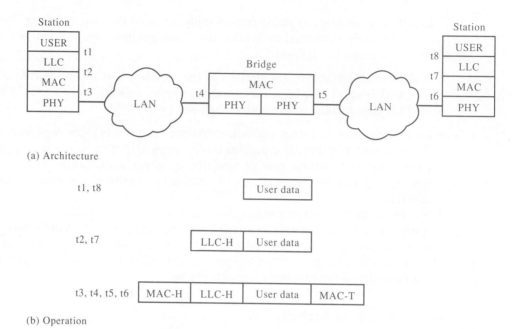

(a) Architecture

t1, t8 | User data |

t2, t7 | LLC-H | User data |

t3, t4, t5, t6 | MAC-H | LLC-H | User data | MAC-T |

(b) Operation

FIGURE 11.5.   Connection of two LANs by a bridge.

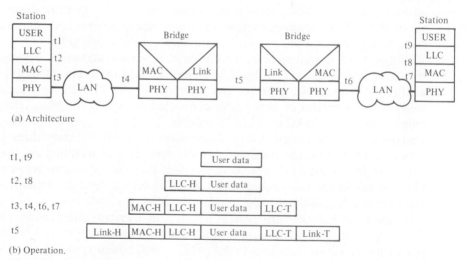

(a) Architecture

t1, t9 | User data |

t2, t8 | LLC-H | User data |

t3, t4, t6, t7 | MAC-H | LLC-H | User data | LLC-T |

t5 | Link-H | MAC-H | LLC-H | User data | LLC-T | Link-T |

(b) Operation.

FIGURE 11.6.   Bridge over a point-to-point link.

can be connected by two bridges that are in turn connected by a communications facility. For example, Figure 11.6 shows the case of two bridges connected by a point-to-point link. In this case, when a bridge captures a MAC frame, it appends a link layer (e.g., HDLC) header and trailer to transmit the MAC frame across the link to the other bridge. The target bridge strips off these link fields and transmits the original, unmodified MAC frame to the destination station.

The intervening communications facility can even be a network, such as a wide-area packet-switching network, as illustrated in Figure 11.7. In this case, the bridge is somewhat more complicated although it performs the same function of relaying MAC frames. The connection between bridges is via an X.25 virtual circuit. Again, the two LLC entities in the end systems have a direct logical relationship with no intervening LLC entities. Thus, in this situation, the X.25 packet layer is operating below an 802 LLC layer. As before, a MAC frame is passed intact between the endpoints. When the bridge on the source LAN receives the frame, it appends an X.25 packet layer header and an X.25 link-layer header and trailer and sends the data to the DCE (packet-switching node) to which it attaches. The DCE strips off the link layer fields and sends the X.25 packet through the network to another DCE. The target DCE appends the link layer field and sends this to the target bridge. The target bridge strips off all the X.25 fields and transmits the original unmodified MAC frame to the destination endpoint.

11.3

ROUTING WITH BRIDGES

In the configuration of Figure 11.4, the bridge makes the decision to relay a frame on the basis of destination MAC address. In a more complex configuration, the bridge must also make a routing decision. Consider the configuration of Figure 11.8. Suppose that station 1 transmits a frame on LAN A intended for station 5. The frame will be read by both bridge 101 and bridge 102. For each bridge, the addressed station is not on a LAN to which the bridge is attached. Therefore, each bridge must make a decision of whether or not to retransmit the frame on its other LAN, in order to move it closer to its intended destination. In this case, bridge 101 should repeat the frame on LAN B, whereas bridge 102 should refrain from retransmitting the frame. Once the frame has been transmitted on LAN B, it will be picked up by both bridges 103 and 104. Again, each must decide whether or not to forward the frame. In this case, bridge 104 should retransmit the frame on LAN E, where it will be received by the destination, station 5.

Thus we see that, in the general case, the bridge must be equipped with a routing capability. When a bridge receives a frame, it must decide whether or not to forward it. If the bridge is attached to more than two networks, then it must decide whether or not to forward the frame and, if so, on which LAN the frame should be transmitted.

The routing decision may not always be a simple one. In Figure 11.9, bridge 107 is added to the previous configuration, directly linking LAN A and LAN E. Such an addition may be made to provide for higher overall internet avail-

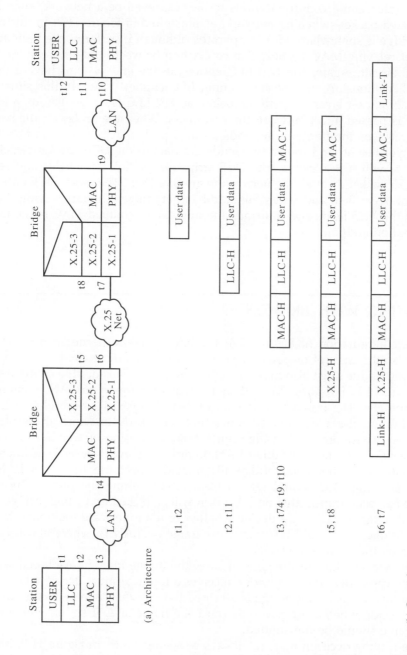

(a) Architecture

(b) Operation

FIGURE 11.7. Bridge over an X.25 network.

FIGURE 11.8.   Internet configuration of bridges and LANs.

FIGURE 11.9.   Internet configuration of bridges and LANs, with alternate routes.

ability. In this case, if Station 1 transmits a frame on LAN A intended for station 5 on LAN E, then either bridge 101 or bridge 107 could forward the frame. It would appear preferable for bridge 107 to forward the frame, since it will involve only one "hop," whereas if the frame travels through bridge 101, it must suffer two hops. Another consideration is that there may be changes in the configuration. For example, bridge 107 may fail, in which case subsequent frames from station 1 to station 5 go through bridge 101. So we can say that the routing capability must take into account the topology of the internet configuration and may need to be dynamically altered.

One final point: Figure 11.9 suggests that a bridge knows the identity of each station on each LAN. In a large configuration, such an arrangement is unwieldy. Furthermore, as stations are added to and dropped from LANs, all directories of station location must be updated. It would facilitate the development of a routing capability if all MAC-level addresses were in the form of a network part and a station part. For example, the IEEE 802.5 standard suggests that 16-bit MAC addresses consist of a 7-bit LAN number and an 8-bit station number, and that 48-bit addresses consist of a 14-bit LAN number and a 32-bit station number.[2] In the remainder of this discussion, we assume that all MAC addresses include a LAN number and that routing is based on the use of that portion of the address only.

A variety of routing strategies have been proposed and implemented in recent years. The simplest, and most common strategy, is **fixed routing.** This strategy is suitable for small internets and for internets that are relatively stable. More recently, two groups within the IEEE 802 committee have developed specifications for routing strategies. The IEEE 802.1 group has issued a standard for routing based on the use of a **spanning tree** algorithm. The token ring committee, IEEE 802.5, has issued its own specification, referred to as **source routing.** We examine these three strategies in turn.

Fixed Routing

For fixed routing, a route is selected for each source-destination pair of LANs in the internet. If alternate routes are available between two LANs, then typically the route with the least number of hops is selected. The routes are fixed, or at least only change when there is a change in the topology of the internet.

Figure 11.10 suggests how fixed routing might be implemented. A central routing matrix is created, to be stored perhaps at a network control center. The matrix shows, for each source–destination pair of LANs, the identity of the first bridge on the route. So for example, the route from LAN E to LAN F begins by going through bridge 107 to LAN A. Again consulting the matrix,

---

[2]The remaining bit in the 16-bit format is used to indicate whether this is a group or individual address. Of the two remaining bits in the 48-bit format, one is used to indicate whether this is a group or individual address, and the other is used to indicate whether this is a locally-administered or globally administered address.

Central Routing Matrix

Destination LAN

Source LAN \ Destination LAN	A	B	C	D	E	F	G
A	–	101	102	101	107	102	102
B	101	–	101	103	104	101	101
C	102	102	–	102	102	105	106
D	103	103	103	–	103	103	103
E	107	104	107	104	–	107	107
F	105	105	105	105	105	–	105
G	106	106	106	106	106	106	–

Bridge 101 table

from LAN A		from LAN B	
Dest	Next	Dest	Next
B	B	A	A
C	–	C	A
D	B	D	–
E	–	E	–
F	–	F	A
G	–	G	A

Bridge 102 table

from LAN A		from LAN C	
Dest	Next	Dest	Next
B	–	A	A
C	C	B	A
D	–	D	A
E	–	E	A
F	C	F	–
G	C	G	–

Bridge 103 table

from LAN B		from LAN D	
Dest	Next	Dest	Next
A	–	A	B
C	–	B	B
D	D	C	B
E	–	E	B
F	–	F	B
G	–	G	B

Bridge 104 table

from LAN B		from LAN E	
Dest	Next	Dest	Next
A	–	A	–
C	–	B	B
D	–	C	–
E	E	D	B
F	–	F	–
G	–	G	–

Bridge 105 table

from LAN C		from LAN F	
Dest	Next	Dest	Next
A	–	A	C
B	–	B	C
D	–	C	C
E	–	D	C
F	F	E	C
G	–	G	C

Bridge 106 table

from LAN C		from LAN G	
Dest	Next	Dest	Next
A	–	A	C
B	–	B	C
D	–	C	C
E	–	D	C
F	–	E	C
G	G	F	C

Bridge 107 table

from LAN A		from LAN E	
Dest	Next	Dest	Next
B	–	A	A
C	–	B	–
D	–	C	A
E	E	D	–
F	–	F	A
G	–	G	A

FIGURE 11.10.   Fixed routing (using Figure 11.9).

the route from LAN A to LAN F goes through bridge 102 to LAN C. Finally, the route from LAN C to LAN F is directly through bridge 105. Thus the complete route from LAN E to LAN F is bridge 107, LAN A, bridge 102, LAN C, bridge 105.

From this overall matrix, routing tables can be developed and stored at each bridge. Each bridge needs one table for each LAN to which it attaches. The information for each table is derived from a single row of the matrix. For example, bridge 105 has two tables, one for frames arriving from LAN C and one for frames arriving from LAN F. The table shows, for each possible destination MAC address, the identity of the LAN to which the bridge should forward the frame. The table labeled "from LAN C" is derived from the row labeled C in the routing matrix. Every entry in that row that contains bridge number 105 results in an entry in the corresponding table in bridge 105.

Once the directories have been established, routing is a simple matter. A bridge copies each incoming frame on each of its LANs. If the destination MAC address corresponds to an entry in its routing table, the frame is retransmitted on the appropriate LAN.

The fixed routing strategy is widely used in commercially-available products. It has the advantage of simplicity and minimal processing requirements. However, in a complex internet, in which bridges may be dynamically added and in which failures must be allowed for, this strategy is too limited. We now turn to two more powerful alternatives.

The Spanning Tree Approach

The spanning tree approach is a mechanism in which bridges automatically develop a routing table and update that table in response to changing topology [BACK88, HART88, IEEE88b, PERL84]. The algorithm consists of three mechanisms: frame forwarding, address learning, and loop resolution.

Frame Forwarding

In this scheme, a bridge maintains a **forwarding database** for each port attached to a LAN. The database indicates the station addresses for which frames should be forwarded through that port. We can interpret this in the following fashion. For each port, a list of stations is maintained. A station is on the list if it is on the "same side" of the bridge as the port. For example, for bridge 102 of Figure 11.8, stations on LANs C, F, and G are on the same side of the bridge as the LAN C port, and stations on LANs A, B, D, and E are on the same side of the bridge as the LAN A port. When a frame is received on any port, the bridge must decide whether that frame is to be forwarded through the bridge and out through one of the bridge's other ports. Suppose that a bridge receives a MAC frame on port x. The following rules are applied (Figure 11.11):

1. Search the forwarding database to determine if the MAC address is listed for any port except port x.
2. If the destination MAC address is not found, discard the frame.
3. If the destination address is in the forwarding database for some port y, then determine whether port y is in a blocking or forwarding state. For reasons explained below, a port may sometimes be blocked, which prevents it from receiving or transmitting frames.

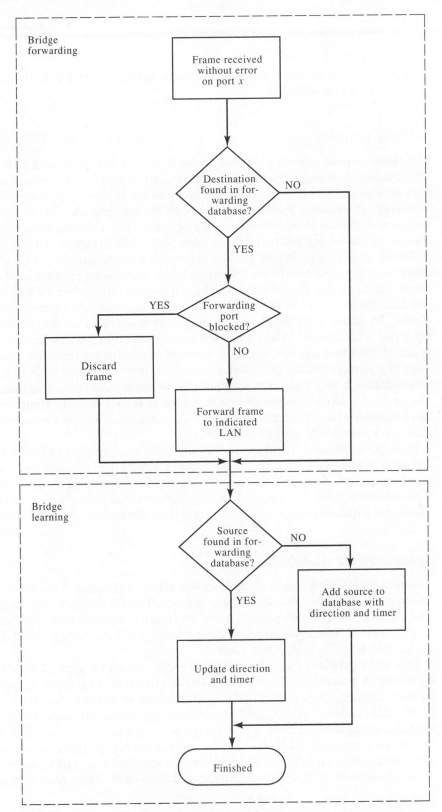

FIGURE 11.11. Bridge forwarding and learning.

4. If port y is not blocked, transmit the frame through port y onto the LAN to which that port attaches.

Address Learning

The above scheme assumes that the bridge is already equipped with a forwarding database that indicates the direction, from the bridge, of each destination station. This information can be preloaded into the bridge, as in static routing. However, an effective automatic mechanism for learning the direction of each station is desirable. A simple scheme for acquiring this information is based on the use of the source address field in each MAC frame (Figure 11.11).

The strategy is this. When a frame arrives on a particular port, it clearly has come from the direction of the incoming LAN. The source address field of the frame indicates the source station. Thus, a bridge can update its forwarding database for that port on the basis of the source address field of each incoming frame. To allow for changes in topology, each element in the database is equipped with a timer. When a new element is added to the database, its timer is set. If the timer expires, then the element is eliminated from the database, since the corresponding direction information may no longer be valid. Each time a frame is received, its source address is checked against the database. If the element is already in the database, the entry is updated (the direction may have changed) and the timer is reset. If the element is not in the database, a new entry is created, with its own timer.

The above discussion indicated that the individual entries in the database are station addresses. If a two-level address structure (LAN number, station number) is used, then only LAN addresses need to be entered in the database. Both schemes work the same. The only difference is that the use of station addresses requires a much larger database than the use of LAN addresses.

Spanning Tree Algorithm

The address learning mechanism described above is effective if the topology of the internet is a tree; that is, if there are no alternate routes in the network. The existence of alternate routes means that there is a closed loop. For example in Figure 11.9, the following is a closed loop: LAN A, bridge 101, LAN B, bridge 104, LAN E, bridge 107, LAN A.

To see the problem created by a closed loop, consider Figure 11.12. At time t_0, station A transmits a frame addressed to station B. The frame is captured by both bridges. Each bridge updates its database to indicate that station A is in the direction of LAN X, and retransmits the frame on LAN Y. Say that bridge α retransmits at time t_1 and bridge β a short time later, t_2. Thus B will receive two copies of the frame. Furthermore, each bridge will receive the other's transmission on LAN Y. Note that each transmission is a MAC frame with a source address of A and a destination address of B. Thus each bridge will

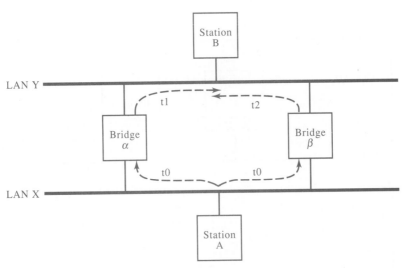

FIGURE 11.12.   Loop of bridges.

update its database to indicate that station A is in the direction of LAN Y. Neither bridge is now capable of forwarding a frame addressed to station A.

To overcome this problem, a simple result from graph theory is used: For any connected graph, consisting of nodes and edges connecting pairs of nodes, there is a spanning tree of edges that maintains the connectivity of the graph but contains no closed loops. In terms of internets, each LAN corresponds to a graph node, and each bridge corresponds to a graph edge. Thus, in Figure 11.9, the removal of one (and only one) of bridges 107, 101, and 104, results in a spanning tree. What is desired is to develop a simple algorithm by which the bridges of the internet can exchange sufficient information to automatically (without user intervention) derive a spanning tree. The algorithm must be dynamic. That is, when a topology change occurs, the bridges must be able to discover this fact and automatically derive a new spanning tree.

The algorithm is based on the use of the following:

1. Each bridge is assigned a unique identifier; in essence, the identifier consists of a MAC address for the bridge plus a priority level.
2. There is a special group MAC address that means "all bridges on this LAN." When a MAC frame is transmitted with the group address in the destination address field, all of the bridges on the LAN will capture that frame and interpret it as a frame addressed to itself.
3. Each port of a bridge is uniquely identified within the bridge, with a "port identifier."

With this information established, the bridges are able to exchange routing information in order to determine a spanning tree of the internet. We will explain the operation of the algorithm using Figures 11.13 and 11.14 as an

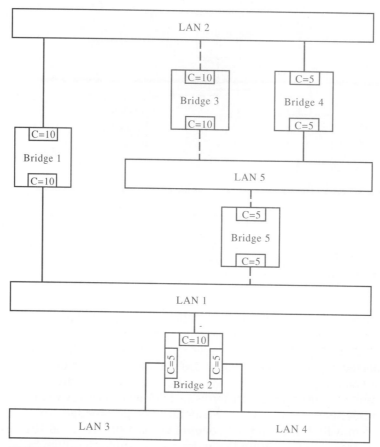

FIGURE 11.13. Example configuration for spanning tree algorithm.

example. The following concepts are needed in the creation of the spanning tree:

- *Root bridge:* The bridge with the lowest value of bridge identifier is chosen to be the root of the spanning tree.
- *Path cost:* Associated with each port on each bridge is a path cost, which is the cost of transmitting a frame onto a LAN through that port. A path between two stations will pass through zero or more bridges. At each bridge, the cost of transmission is added to give a total cost for a particular path. In the simplest case, all path costs would be assigned a value of 1; thus the cost of a path would simply be a count of the number of bridges along the path. Alternatively, costs could be assigned in inverse proportion to the data rate of the corresponding LAN, or any other criterion chosen by the network manager.

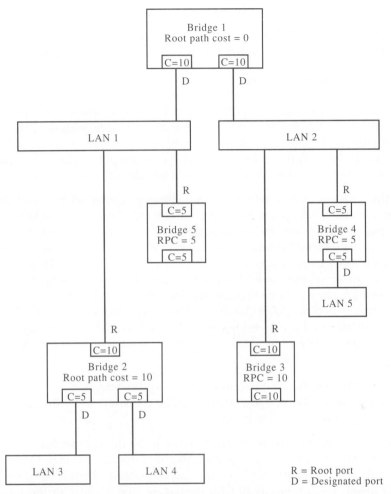

FIGURE 11.14.   Spanning tree for configuration of Figure 11.13.

- *Root port:* Each bridge discovers the first hop on the minimum-cost path to the root bridge. The port used for that hop is labeled the root port.
- *Root path cost:* For each bridge, the cost of the path to the root bridge with minimum cost (the path that starts at the root port) is the root path cost for that bridge.
- *Designated bridge, designated port:* On each LAN, one bridge is chosen to be the designated bridge. This is the bridge on that LAN that provides the minimum cost path to the root bridge. This is the only bridge allowed to forward frames to and from the LAN for which it is the designated bridge. The port of the designated bridge that attaches the bridge to the LAN is the designated port. For all LANs to which the root bridge is attached, the root bridge

is the designated bridge. All internet traffic to and from the LAN passes through the designated port.

In general terms, the spanning tree is constructed in the following fashion:

1. Determine the root bridge.
2. Determine the root port on all other bridges.
3. Determine the designated port on each LAN. This will be the port with the minimum root path cost. In the case of two or more bridges with the same root path cost, then the highest-priority bridge is chosen as the designated bridge. If the designated bridge has two or more ports attached to this LAN, then the port with the lowest value of port identifier is chosen.

By this process, when two LANs are directly connected by more than one bridge, all of the bridges but one are eliminated. This cuts any loops that involve two LANs. It can be demonstrated that this process also eliminates all loops involving more than two LANs and that connectivity is preserved. Thus, this process discovers a spanning tree for the given internet. In our example, the solid lines indicate the bridge ports that participate in the spanning tree.

The steps outlined above require that the bridges exchange information. The information is exchanged in the form of bridge protocol data units (BPDUs). A BPDU transmitted by one bridge is addressed to and received by all of the other bridges on the same LAN. Each BPDU contains the following information:

• The identifier of this bridge and the port on this bridge.
• The identifier of the bridge that this bridge considers to be the root.
• The root path cost for this bridge.

To begin, all bridges consider themselves to be the root bridge. Each bridge will broadcast a BPDU on each of its LANs that asserts this fact. On any given LAN, only one claimant will have the lowest-valued identifier and will maintain its belief. Over time, as BPDUs propagate, the identity of the lowest-valued bridge identifier throughout the internet will be known to all bridges. The root bridge will regularly broadcast the fact that it is the root bridge on all of the LANs to which it is attached. This allows the bridges on those LANs to determine their root port and the fact that they are directly connected to the root bridge. Each of these bridges in turn broadcasts a BPDU on the other LANs to which it is attached (all LANs except the one on its root port), indicating that it is one hop away from the root bridge. This activity is propagated throughout the internet. Every time that a bridge receives a BPDU, it transmits BPDUs indicating the identity of the root bridge and the number of hops to reach the root bridge. On any LAN, the bridge claiming to be the one that is closest to the root becomes the designated bridge.

We can trace some of this activity with the configuration of Figure 11.13. At startup time, Bridges 1, 3, and 4 all transmit BPDUs on LAN 2 claiming to be the root bridge. When bridge 3 receives the transmission from bridge 1, it recognizes a superior claimant and defers. Bridge 3 has also received a claiming BPDU from bridge 5 via LAN 5. Bridge 3 recognizes that Bridge 1 has a superior claim to be the root bridge; it therefore assigns its LAN 2 port to be its root port, and sets the root path cost to 10. By similar actions, bridge 4 ends up with a root path cost of 5 via LAN 2; bridge 5 has a root path cost of 5 via LAN 1; and bridge 2 has a root path cost of 20 via LAN 1.

Now consider the assignment of designated bridges. On LAN 5, all three bridges transmit BPDUs attempting to assert a claim to be designated bridge. Bridge 3 defers because it receives BPDUs from the other bridges that have a lower root path cost. Bridges 4 and 5 have the same root path cost, but bridge 4 has the higher priority and therefore becomes the designated bridge.

The results of all this activity are shown in Figure 11.14. Only the designated bridge on each LAN is allowed to forward frames. All of the ports on all of the other bridges are placed in a blocking state. After the spanning tree is established, bridges continue to periodically exchange BPDUs to be able to react to any change in topology, cost assignments, or priority assignment. Any time that a bridge receives a BPDU on a port it makes two assessments:

1. If the BPDU arrives on a port that is considered the designated port, does the transmitting port have a better claim to be designated port?
2. Should this port be my root port?

Source Routing

The source routing approach is a mechanism in which the sending station determines the route that the frame will follow and includes the routing information with the frame; bridges read the routing information to determine if they should forward the frame [DIXO88, HAMN88, PITT87, BEDE86, PITT85, IEEE88c].

Basic Operation

The basic operation of the algorithm can be described with reference to the configuration of Figure 11.15a. A frame from station X can reach station Y by either of the following routes:

• LAN 1, bridge B1, LAN 3, bridge B3, LAN 2
• LAN 1, bridge B2, LAN 4, bridge B4, LAN 2

Station X may choose one of these two routes and place the information, in the form of a sequence of LAN and bridge identifiers, in the frame to be transmitted. When a bridge receives a frame, it will forward that frame if the bridge is on the designated route; all other frames are discarded. In this case, if the first route above is specified, bridges B1 and B3 will forward the frame; if the second route is specified, bridges B2 and B4 will forward the frame.

Note that with this scheme, bridges need not maintain routing tables. The bridge makes the decision whether or not to forward a frame solely on the basis of the routing information contained in the frame. All that is required is that the bridge know its own unique identifier and the identifier of each LAN to which it is attached. The responsibility for designing the route falls to the source station.

For this scheme to work, there must be a mechanism by which a station can determine a route to any destination station. Before dealing with this issue, we need to discuss different types of routing directives.

Routing Directives and Addressing Modes

The source routing scheme developed by the IEEE 802.5 committee includes four different types of routing directives. Each frame that is transmitted includes an indicator of the type of routing desired. The four directive types are:

- *Null:* No routing is desired. In this case, the frame can only be delivered to stations on the same LAN as the source station.
- *Nonbroadcast:* The frame includes a route, consisting of a sequence of LAN numbers and bridge numbers that defines a unique route from the source station to the destination station. Only bridges on that route forward the frame, and only a single copy of the frame is delivered to the destination station.
- *All-routes broadcast:* The frame will reach each LAN of the internet by all possible routes. Thus each bridge will forward each frame once to each of its ports in a direction away from the source node and multiple copies of the frame may appear on a LAN. The destination station will receive one copy of the frame for each possible route through the network.
- *Single-route broadcast:* Regardless of the destination address of the frame, the frame will appear once, and only once, on each LAN in the internet. For this effect to be achieved, the frame is forwarded by all bridges that are on a spanning tree (with the source node as the root) of the internet. The destination station receives a single copy of the frame.

Let us examine the potential application of each of these four types of routing, and then examine the mechanisms that may be employed to achieve them. First, consider null routing. In this case the bridges that share the LAN with the source station are told not to forward the frame. This will be done if the intended destination is on the same LAN as the source station. Nonbroadcast routing is used when the two stations are not on the same LAN and the source station knows a route that can be used to reach the destination station. Only the bridges on that route will forward the frame.

The remaining two types of routing can be used by the source to discover a route to the destination. For example, the source station can use all-routes broadcasting to send a request frame to the intended destination. The destination returns a response frame, using nonbroadcast routing, on each of the routes followed by the incoming request frame. The source station can pick one of these routes and send future frames on that route. Alternatively, the source station could use single-route broadcasting to send a single request to the destination station. The destination station could send its response frame via all-routes broadcasting. The incoming frames would reveal all of the possible routes to the destination station, and the source station could pick one of these for future transmissions. Finally, single-route broadcasting could be used for group addressing, as discussed below.

Now consider the mechanisms for implementing these various routing directives. Each frame must include an indicator of which of the four types of routing is required. For null routing, the frame is ignored by the bridge. For nonbroadcast routing, the frame includes an ordered list of LAN numbers and bridge numbers. When a bridge receives a nonbroadcast frame, it forwards the frame only if the routing information contains the sequence LAN i, Bridge x, LAN j, where

> LAN i = LAN from which the frame arrived
> Bridge x = this bridge
> LAN j = another LAN to which this bridge is attached

For all-routes broadcasting, the source station marks the frame for this type of routing, but includes no routing information. Each bridge that forwards the frame will add its bridge number and the outgoing LAN number to the frame's routing information field. Thus, when the frame reaches its destination, it will include a sequenced list of all LANs and bridges visited. To prevent the endless repetition and looping of frames, a bridge obeys the following rule: When an all-routes broadcast frame is received, the bridge examines the routing information field. If the field contains the number of a LAN to which the bridge is attached, the bridge will refrain from forwarding the frame on that LAN. Put the other way, the bridge will only forward the frame to a LAN that the frame has not already visited.

Finally, for single-route broadcasting, a spanning tree of the internet must be developed. This can either be done automatically, as in the 802.1 specification, or manually. In either case, as with the 802.1 strategy, one bridge on each LAN is the designated bridge for that LAN, and is the only one that forwards single-route frames.

It is worth noting the relationship between addressing mode and routing directive. There are three types of MAC addresses:

- *Individual:* the address specifies a unique destination station.
- *Group:* the address specifies a group of destination addresses; this is also referred to as *multicast*.
- *All-stations:* the address specifies all stations that are capable of receiving this frame; this is also referred to as *broadcast*. We will refrain from using this latter term since it is also used in the source routing terminology.

TABLE 11.2 Effects of Various Combinations of Addressing and Source Routing

Addressing Mode	Routing Specification			
	No Routing	Nonbroadcast	All-Routes	Single-Route
Individual	Received by station if it is on the same LAN	Received by station if it is on one of the LANs on the route	Received by station if it is on any LAN	Received by station if it is on any LAN
Group	Received by all group members on the same LAN	Received by all group members on all LANs visited on this route	Received by all group members on all LANs	Received by all group members on all LANs
All-Stations	Received by all stations on the same LAN	Received by all stations on all LANs visited on this route	Received by all stations on all LANs	Received by all stations on all LANs

In the case of a single, isolated LAN, group and all-stations addresses refer to stations on the same LAN as the source station. In an internet, it may be desirable to transmit a frame to multiple stations on multiple LANs. Indeed, since a set of LANs interconnected by bridges should appear to the user as a single LAN, the ability to do group and all-stations addressing across the entire internet is mandatory.

Table 11.2 summarizes the relationship between routing specification and addressing mode. If no routing is specified, then all addresses refer only to the immediate LAN. If nonbroadcast routing is specified, then addresses may refer to any station on any LAN visited on the nonbroadcast route. From an addressing point of view, this combination is not generally useful for group and all-stations addressing. If either the all-routes or single-route specification is included in a frame, then all stations on the internet can be addressed. Thus, the total internet acts as a single network from the point of view of MAC addresses. Since less traffic is generated by the single-route specification, this is to be preferred for group and all-stations addressing. Note also that the single-route mechanism in source routing is equivalent to the 802.1 spanning tree approach. Thus, the latter supports both group and all-stations addressing.

Route Discovery and Selection

With source routing, bridges are relieved of the burden of storing and using routing information. Thus the burden falls on the stations that wish to transmit frames. Clearly, some mechanism is needed by which the source stations can know the route to each destination for which frames are to be sent. Three strategies suggest themselves.

1. Manually load the information into each station. This is simple and effective but has several drawbacks. First, any time that the configuration changes, the routing information at all stations must be updated. Secondly, this approach does not provide for automatic adjustment in the face of the failure of a bridge or LAN.
2. One station on a LAN can query other stations on the same LAN for routing information about distant stations. This approach may reduce the overall amount of routing messages that must be transmitted, compared to option 3, below. However, at least one station on each LAN must have the needed routing information, so this is not a complete solution.
3. When a station needs to learn the route to a destination station, it engages in a dynamic route discovery procedure.

Option 3 is the most flexible and the one that is specified by IEEE 802.5. As was mentioned earlier, two approaches are possible. The source station can transmit an all-routes request frame to the destination. Thus, all possible routes to the destination are discovered. The destination station can send back a non-broadcast response on each of the discovered routes, allowing the source to choose which route to follow in subsequently transmitting the frame. This approach generates quite a bit of both forward and backward traffic, and requires the destination station to receive and transmit a number of frames. An alternative is for the source station to transmit a single-route request frame. Only one copy of this frame will reach the destination. The destination responds with an all-routes response frame, which generates all possible routes back to the source. Again, the source can choose among these alternative routes.

Figure 11.15 illustrates the latter approach. Assume that the spanning tree that has been chosen for this internet consists of bridges B1, B3, and B4. In this example, station X wishes to discover a route to station Z. Station X issues a single-route request frame. Bridge B2 is not on the spanning tree and so does not forward the frame. The other bridges do forward the frame and it reaches station Z. Note that bridge B4 forwards the frame to LAN 4, although this is not necessary; it is simply an effect of the spanning-tree mechanism. When Z receives this frame, it responds with an all-routes frame. Two messages reach X: one on the path LAN 2, B3, LAN 3, B1, LAN 1, and the other on the path LAN 2, B4, LAN 4, B2, LAN 1. Note that the frame that arrived by the latter route is received by bridge B1 and forwarded onto LAN 3. However, when bridge B3 receives this frame, it sees in the routing information field that the frame has already visited LAN 2; therefore it does not forward the frame. A similar fate occurs for the frame that follows the first route and is forwarded by bridge B2.

Once a collection of routes have been discovered, the source station needs to select one of the routes. The obvious criterion would be to select the mini-

(a) Configuration

(b) Single-route broadcast request

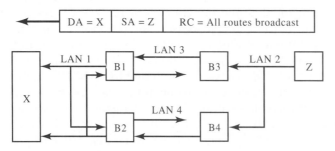

(c) All-routes broadcast response

FIGURE 11.15.   Route discovery example [DIX088].

mum-hop route. Alternatively, a minimum-cost route could be selected, where the cost of a network is inversely proportional to its data rate. In either case, if two or more routes are equivalent by the chosen criterion, then there are several alternatives:

Choose the route corresponding to the response message that arrives first. One may assume that that particular route is less congested than the others since the frame on that route arrived earliest.

Choose randomly. This should have the effect, over time, of leveling the load among the various bridges.

Another point to consider is how often to update a route. Routes should certainly be changed in response to network failures and perhaps should be changed in response to network congestion. If connection-oriented logical link control is used (see Chapter 9), then one possibility is to rediscover the route with each new connection. Another alternative, which works with either connection-oriented or connectionless service, is to associate a timer with each selected route, and rediscover the route when its time expires.

11.4

CONNECTIONLESS INTERNETWORKING

The internet protocol (IP) was developed as part of the DARPA internet project. Somewhat later, when the international standards community recognized the need for a connectionless approach to internetworking, the connectionless network protocol (CLNP) was standardized. The functionality of IP and CLNP is very similar; they differ in the formats used and in some minor functional features. In this section, we examine the essential functions of an internetworking protocol, which apply to both CLNP and IP. For convenience, we refer to IP, but it should be understood that the narrative in this section applies to both IP and CLNP. The two protocols are described in Section 11.5.

Operation of a Connectionless Internetworking Scheme

IP provides a connectionless, or datagram, service between end systems. There are a number of advantages to this connectionless approach:

- A connectionless internet facility is flexible. It can deal with a variety of networks, some of which are themselves connectionless. In essence, IP requires very little of the constituent networks.
- A connectionless internet service can be made highly robust. This is basically the same argument made for a datagram network service versus a virtual circuit service. For a further discussion, the reader is referred to Section 8.2.
- A connectionless internet service is best for connectionless transport protocols.

As an example, Figure 11.16 depicts the operation of IP for data exchange between host A on a packet-switching network and host B on a LAN, connected by a router. The data to be sent by A are encapsulated in an internet protocol data unit, referred to as a **datagram,** with an IP header specifying the global internet address of B. This datagram is then encapsulated in the X.25 packet and link fields and transmitted to the router. The router strips off the X.25 fields to expose the IP datagram. This is then wrapped in the IEEE 802 protocol fields and sent to B.

With this example in mind, we describe briefly the sequence of steps involved in sending a datagram between two stations on different networks. The process starts in the sending station. The station wants to send an IP datagram to a station in another network. The IP module in the station constructs the datagram with a global network address and recognizes that the destination is on another network. So the first step is to send the datagram to a router (example: station *A* to the router in Figure 11.16). To do this, the IP module appends to the IP datagram a header appropriate to the network that contains the address of the router. For example, for an X.25 network, a layer 3 packet encapsulates the IP datagram to be sent to the router.

Next, the packet travels through the network to the router, which receives it via a DCE–DTE protocol. The router unwraps the packet to recover the original datagram. The router analyzes the IP header to determine whether this datagram contains control information intended for the router, or data intended for a station farther on. In the latter instance, the router must make a routing decision. There are four possibilities:

1. The destination station is attached directly to one of the networks to which the router is attached. This is referred to as "directly connected." For example, in Figure 11.17, all stations labeled S0 are directly connected to the router G1.
2. The destination station is on a network that has a router that directly connects to this router. This is known as a "neighbor router." In Figure 11.17, G2 is a neighbor router of G1, and all stations labeled S1 are one "hop" from G1.
3. To reach the destination station, more than one additional router must be traversed. This is known as a "multiple-hop" situation. In Figure 11.17, all stations labeled S2 are in this category.
4. The router does not know the destination address.

In case 4, the router returns an error message to the source of the datagram. For cases 1 through 3, the router must select the appropriate route for the data, and insert them into the appropriate network with the appropriate address. For case 1, the address is the destination station address. For cases 2 and 3, the address is a router address. Remember, we are speaking here of a lower layer address, usually a layer 3 address or, in the case of local networks, a layer 2 address.

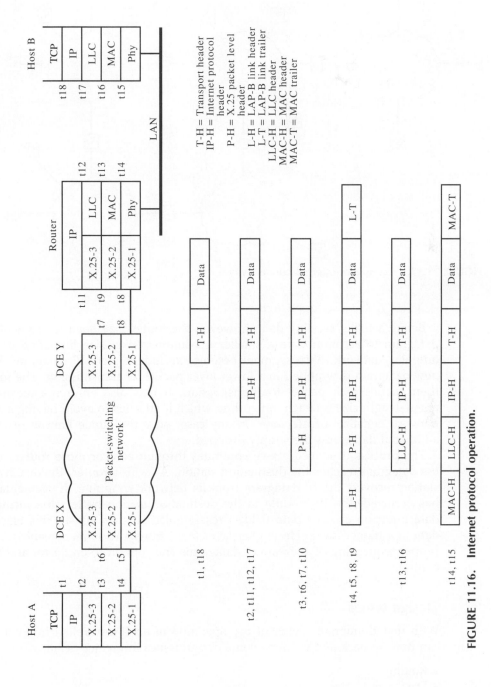

FIGURE 11.16. Internet protocol operation.

503

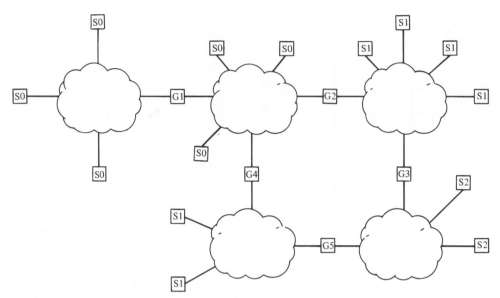

FIGURE 11.17. Example of internet connectivity.

Before actually sending data, however, the router may need to segment the datagram to accommodate a smaller maximum packet size limitation on the outgoing network. Each segment becomes an independent IP datagram. Each new datagram is wrapped in a lower layer packet for transmission. The router then queues each packet for transmission. It may also enforce a maximum queue-length size for each network to which it attaches to avoid having a slow network penalize a faster one. In any case, once the queue limit is reached, additional datagrams are simply dropped.

The process described above continues through zero or more routers until the datagram reaches the destination station. As with a router, the destination station recovers the IP datagram from its network wrapping. If segmentation has occurred, the IP module in the destination station buffers the incoming data until the original data field is reassembled. It then passes this block of data to a higher layer. The higher layer (e.g., transport) is responsible for the proper sequencing of a stream of datagrams and for end-to-end error and flow control.

Design Issues

With that thumbnail sketch of the operation of an IP-controlled internet, we can now go back and examine some design issues in greater detail:

- Routing.
- Datagram lifetime

- Segmentation and reassembly.
- Error control.
- Flow control.

As we proceed with this discussion, the reader will note many similarities with the design issues and techniques relevant to packet-switched networks. To see the reason for this, consider Figure 11.18 [HIND83], which compares an internet architecture with a packet-switched network architecture. The routers (G1, G2, G3) in the internet correspond to the packet-switched nodes (P1, P2, P3) in the network, and the networks (N1, N2, N3) in the internet correspond to the transmission links (T1, T2, T3) in the networks. The routers perform essentially the same functions as packet-switched nodes, and use the intervening networks in a manner analogous to transmission links.

Routing

Routing is generally accomplished by maintaining a routing table in each station and router that gives, for each possible destination network, the next router to which the IP datagram should be sent.

Table 11.3 shows the routing table for the BBN router, which is part of the DARPA internet. If a network is directly connected, it is so indicated. Otherwise, the datagram must be directed through one or more routers (one or more hops). The table indicates the identity of the next router on the route (which must share a common network with this router or host) and the number of hops to the destination.

The routing table may be static or dynamic. A static table, however, could contain alternate routes if a router is unavailable. A dynamic table is more flexible in responding both to error and congestion situations. In the DARPA internet, for example, when a router goes down, all of its neighbors will send out a status report, allowing other routers and hosts to update their routing tables. A similar scheme can be used to control congestion. This latter is particularly important because of the mismatch in capacity between local and long-haul networks. The interested reader may consult [DARP81], which specifies a variety of internet control messages used to facilitate routing.

Routing tables may also be used to support other internet services, such as security and priority. For example, individual networks might be classified to handle data up to a given security classification. The routing mechanism must assure that data of a given security level is not allowed to pass through networks not cleared to handle such data.

Another routing technique is source routing. The source station specifies the route by including a sequential list of routers in the datagram. This, again, could be useful for security or priority requirements.

Finally, we mention a service related to routing: route recording. To record a route, each router appends its address to a list of addresses in the datagram. This feature is useful for testing and debugging purposes.

(a) Packet–switched network architecture

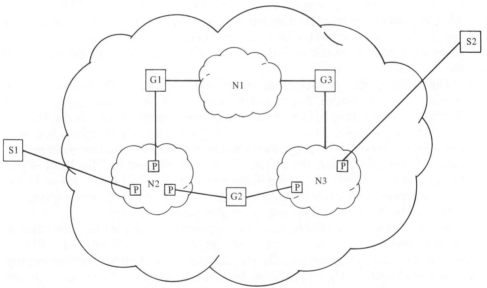

(b) Internet architecture

FIGURE 11.18.   The internet as a network. From [HIND83]

TABLE 11.3 Internet Routing Table[a]

Network Name	Net Address	Route[b]
SATNET	4	Directly connected
ARPANET	10	Directly connected
BBN-NET	3	1 hop via RCC 10.3.0.72 (ARPANET 3/72)
Purdue-Computer Science	192.5.1	2 hops via Purdue 10.2.0.37 (ARPANET 2/37)
INTELPOST	43	2 hops via Mills 10.3.0.17 (ARPANET 3/17)
DECNET-TEST	38	3 hops via Mills 10.3.0.17 (ARPANET 3/17)
Wideband	28	3 hops via RCC 10.3.0.72 (ARPANET 3/72)
BBN-Packet Radio	1	2 hops via RCC 10.3.0.72 (ARPANET 3/72)
DCN-COMSAT	29	1 hop via Mills 10.3.0.17 (ARPANET 3/17)
FIBERNET	24	3 hops via RCC 10.3.0.72 (ARPANET 3/72)
Bragg-Packet Radio	9	1 hop via Bragg 10.0.0.38 (ARPANET 0/38)
Clark Net	8	2 hops via Mills 10.3.0.17 (ARPANET 3/17)
LCSNET	18	1 hop via MIT LCS 10.0.0.77 (ARPANET 0/77)
BBN-Terminal Concentrator	192.1.2	3 hops via RCC 10.3.0.72 (ARPANET 3/72)
BBN-Jericho	192.1.3	3 hops via RCC 10.3.0.72 (ARPANET 3/72)
UCLNET	11	1 hop via UCL 4.0.0.60 (SATNET 60)
RSRE-NULL	35	1 hop via UCL 4.0.0.60 (SATNET 60)
RSRE-PPSN	25	2 hops via UCL 4.0.0.60 (SATNET 60)
San Francisco-Packet Radio-2	6	1 hop via C3PO 10.1.0.51 (ARPANET 1/51)

[a] Network table for BBN router.
[b] Names and acronyms identify routers in the INTERNET system.
Source: [SHEL82].

Datagram Lifetime

If dynamic or alternate routing is used, the potential exists for a datagram to loop indefinitely through the internet. This is undesirable for two reasons. First, an endlessly circulating datagram consumes resources. Second, we will see in Chapter 12 that a transport protocol may depend on there being an upper bound on datagram lifetime. To avoid these problems, each datagram can be marked with a lifetime. Once the lifetime expires, the datagram is discarded.

A simple way to implement lifetime is to use a hop count. Each time that a datagram passes through a router, the count is decremented. Alternatively, the lifetime could be a true measure of time. This requires that the routers must somehow know how long it has been since the datagram or segment last crossed a router, in order to know by how much to decrement the lifetime field. This would seem to require some global clocking mechanism.

The advantage of using a true time measure is that it can be used in the reassembly algorithm, described next.

Segmentation and Reassembly

Individual networks within an internet will generally be diverse and, in particular, specify different maximum (and sometimes minimum) packet sizes. It would be inefficient and unwieldy to try to dictate uniform packet size across networks. Thus routers may need to segment incoming datagrams into smaller pieces before transmitting on to the next network.

If datagrams can be segmented (perhaps more than once) in the course of their travels, the question arises as to where they should be reassembled. The easiest solution is to have reassembly performed at the destination only. The principal disadvantage of this approach is the packets can only get smaller as data move through the internet. This may seriously impair the efficiency of some networks (e.g., CSMA/CD LANs). On the other hand, if intermediate router reassembly is allowed, the following disadvantages result:

1. Large buffers are required at routers, and there is a potential for reassembly deadlock.
2. All segments of a datagram must pass through the same router. This inhibits the use of dynamic routing.

Both DOD and ISO IP specify an efficient technique for segmentation. The technique requires the following fields in the datagram header:

- ID.
- Data Length.
- Offset.
- More flag.

The *ID* is some means of uniquely identifying a station-originated datagram. In DOD IP, it consists of the source and destination addresses, an identifier of the protocol layer that generated the data, and a sequence number supplied by that protocol layer. The *Data Length* is the length of the data field in octets, and the *Offset* is the position of a segment in the original datagram in multiples of 64 bits.

The source station IP layer creates a datagram with Data Length equal to the entire length of the data field, with Offset 0, and a More Flag set to False. To segment a long packet, an IP module in a router performs the following tasks:

1. Create two new datagrams and copy the header fields of the incoming datagram into both.
2. Divide the data into two approximately equal portions along a 64-bit boundary, placing one portion in each new datagram. The first portion must be a multiple of 64 bits.
3. Set the Data Length field of the first datagram to the length of the inserted data, and set the More Flag to True. The Offset field is unchanged.
4. Set the Data Length field of the second datagram to the length of the inserted data, and add the length of the first data portion divided by eight to the Offset field. The More Flag remains the same.

TABLE 11.4   Segmentation Example

Original datagram	
Data Length	= 472
Offset	= 0
More Flag	= 0
First segment	
Data Length	= 240
Offset	= 0
More Flag	= 1
Second segment	
Data Length	= 232
Offset	= 30
More Flag	= 0

Table 11.4 gives an example. The procedure can be generalized to an *n*-way split.

To reassemble a datagram, there must be sufficient buffer space at the reassembly point. As segments with the same ID arrive, their data fields are inserted in the proper position in the buffer until the entire datagram is reassembled, which is achieved when a contiguous set of data exists starting with an *Offset* of zero and ending with data from a segment with a false *More Flag*.

One eventuality that must be dealt with is that one or more of the segments may not get through; the IP connectionless service does not guarantee delivery. Some means is needed to decide to abandon a reassembly effort in order to free up buffer space. The ISO IP standard suggests two possibilities. First, assign a reassembly lifetime to the first segment to arrive. This is a local, real time which is assigned by the reassembly function and decremented while some, but not all segments of the PDU are being buffered. If the timer expires, all received segments are discarded. The second possibility is that the destination IP entity can make use of the datagram lifetime, which is part of the incoming PDU. The lifetime field continues to be decremented by the reassembly function as if the PDU were still in transit (in a sense, it still is).

Error Control

The internetwork facility does not guarantee successful delivery of every datagram. When a datagram is discarded by a router, the router should attempt to return some information to the source, if possible. The source internet protocol entity may use this information to modify its transmission strategy and may notify higher layers. To report that a specific datagram has been discarded, some means of datagram identification is needed.

Datagrams may be discarded for a number of reasons, including lifetime expiration, congestion, and FCS error. In the latter case, notification is not possible since the source address field may have been damaged.

Flow Control

Internet flow control allows routers and/or receiving stations to limit the rate at which they receive data. For the connectionless type of service we are describing, flow control mechanisms are limited. The best approach would seem to be to send flow control packets, requesting reduced data flow, to other routers and source stations.

11.5

CONNECTIONLESS INTERNETWORK PROTOCOL STANDARDS

ISO Internetwork Protocol Standard

In this subsection, we look at the CLNP standard developed by ISO. As with any protocol, IP can be described in two parts:

- The interface with a higher layer (e.g., ISO TP), specifying the services that IP provides.
- The IP protocol, specifying protocol data unit format and station–router and router–router interaction.

CLNP Services

CLNP provides a connectionless data transfer service to CLNP users (e.g., ISO TP) in stations attached to networks of the internet. Two primitives are defined at the user-CLNP interface. The CLNP user requests transmission of a unit of data with N-UNITDATA.request. N-UNITDATA.indication is used by CLNP to notify a user of the arrival of a data unit. For both primitives, the following parameters are used:

- *Source address:* internetwork address of sending CLNP entity.
- *Destination address:* internetwork address of CLNP entity that is to receive the data.
- *Quality of service:* options requested by the CLNP user.
- *NS-user-data:* user data to be transmitted.

The quality of service feature allows the user to specify additional services (beyond simple data transfer). The CLNP entity will endeavor, within the limitations of the network services available to it, to provide these additional services:

- *Transit delay:* the elapsed time between an N-UNITDATA.request at the source and the corresponding N-UNITDATA.indication at the destination.
- *Protection from unauthorized access:* prevention of unauthorized monitoring or manipulation of the user-originated information.
- *Cost determinants:* specification of cost considerations for the CLNP entity to use in selection of a route for the data.
- *Residual error probability:* the likelihood that a particular unit of data will be lost, duplicated, or delivered incorrectly.
- *Priority:* relative priority of user data.
- *Source routing:* Sequenced list of router addresses that specifies the route.

CLNP Protocol

The CLNP protocol is designed to provide the CLNP services described above. It is best explained by describing the CLNP data unit format (Figure 11.19).

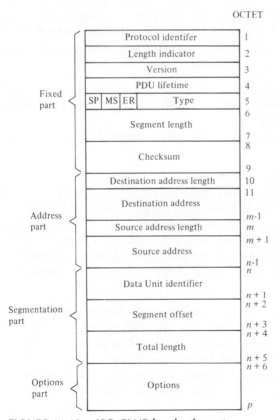

FIGURE 11.19.   ISO CLNP header format.

The header consists of four parts. The fixed part is always present and is of fixed length. It contains the following fields:

- *Protocol identifier:* When the source and destination stations are connected to the same network, an internet protocol is not needed. In that case, the internet layer is null and the header consists of this single field of 8 bits.
- *Length indicator:* length of the header in octets.
- *Version:* included to allow evolution of the protocol. Either header format or semantics might change.
- *PDU Lifetime:* Expressed as a multiple of 500 ms. It is determined and set by the source station. Each router that the CLNP data unit visits decrements this field by 1 for each 500 ms of estimated delay for that hop (transmit time to this router plus processing time).
- *Flags:* The SP flag indicates whether segmentation is permitted. The MS flag is the more flag described earlier. The ER flag indicates whether an error report is desired by the source station if a CLNP data unit is discarded.
- *Type:* Indicates whether this is a Data (contains user data) or Error (contains error report) PDU.
- *PDU Segment Length:* total data unit length, including header, in octets.
- *PDU checksum:* result of a checksum algorithm (defined in the appendix to this chapter, page 535) computed on the entire header. Since some header fields may change (e.g., time to live, segmentation-related fields), this is reverified and recomputed at each router.

The address part of the header is variable length and is always present. Since addresses may be of variable length, an address length field precedes both the source and destination addresses.

If the SP flag is set to one, then the header includes a segmentation part, with the following fields:

- *Data unit identifier:* intended to uniquely identify the PDU. Thus, the station CLNP entity must assign values that are unique for the PDU's destination and for the maximum time that the PDU may remain in the internet.
- *Segment offset:* indicates where in the initial PDU this segment belongs, measured in 64-bit units. This implies that segments other than the last one must contain user data fields that are a multiple of 64 bits in length.
- *Total length:* specifies the total length of the original PDU, including header and data.

Finally, an optional part may be included in the header, and is used to convey optional parameters. Each option is encoded in three fields: parameter code, parameter length, and parameter value. The parameters that may be specified include: Security, defined by the user; Source Routing, which list the routers to be visited; Recording of Route, which traces the route the PDU has taken so far; Quality of service, which specifies reliability and delay values; and Priority.

Internet Protocol (IP)

IP Services

Two primitives are defined at the user–IP interface. The Send primitive is used to request transmission of a data unit. The Deliver primitive is used by IP to notify a user of the arrival of a data unit. Although not part of the standard, IP is expected to use some sort of Error primitive to notify a user of failure in providing the requested service. This service is not assumed to be reliable; that is, there is no guarantee that errors will be reported.

The Send primitive includes the following parameters:

- *Source address:* internetwork address of sending IP entity.
- *Destination address:* internetwork address of IP entity to receive data.
- *Protocol:* identifies the recipient protocol entity (an IP user).
- *Type of service indicators:* used to specify the treatment of the data unit in its transmission through component networks. The indicators are precedence (eight levels), reliability (two levels), delay (two levels), and throughput (two levels). *Precedence* attempts preferential treatment for high importance datagrams. *Reliability* attempts to minimize data loss and error rate. *Delay* and *throughput* attempt to minimize delay or maximize throughput, respectively. To the extent possible, these parameters are passed on to the individual networks for their use. Of course, if a particular network supports only a single grade of service, this parameter has no effect for that leg of the journey.
- *Identifier:* is used, along with the source and destination addresses and user protocol, to identify the data unit uniquely. This parameter is needed for reassembly and error reporting.
- *Don't fragment identifier:* indicates whether IP can segment (called fragment in this standard) data to accomplish delivery.
- *Time to live:* measured in network hops.
- *Data length:* length of data being transmitted.
- *Option data:* options requested by the IP user.
- *Data:* user data to be transmitted.

The *options* feature allows for future extensibility and for inclusion of parameters that are not present with every data unit. The currently defined options are:

- *Security:* The security parameter allows each data unit to be labeled with a security label (e.g., SECRET, CONFIDENTIAL). Compartments are used to specify user groups authorized to access information (i.e., have a "need to know").
- *Source routing:* A sequenced list of router addresses specifies the route. Routing may be strict (only identified routers may be visited) or loose (other intermediate routers may also be visited).

- *Record routing:* A field is allocated to record the route of the datagram through a sequence of routers. The field should be large enough to prevent overflow.
- *Stream identification:* Reserved resources used for stream service are named. This service provides special handling for volatile periodic traffic (e.g., voice). IP must endeavor to maintain a constant delay per datagram.
- *Timestamp:* The source internet protocol entity and some or all intermediate routers add a timestamp (accurate to milliseconds) to the data unit as it goes by.

The Deliver primitive includes the following parameters:

- Source address.
- Destination address.
- Protocol.
- Type of service indicators.
- Data length.
- Option data.
- Data.

IP Protocol

The protocol between IP entities is best described by defining the IP datagram format, which is shown in Figure 11.20a. The fields are:

(a) IP protocol data unit

(b) ICMP protocol data unit

FIGURE 11.20.   DOD internet protocol formats.

- *Version (4 bits):* version number, included to allow evolution of the protocol. Either header format or semantics might change.
- *Internet header length (IHL) (4 bits):* length of header in 32-bit words. The minimum value is five. Thus a header is at least 20 octets long.
- *Type of service (8 bits):* specifies reliability, precedence, delay, and throughput parameters.
- *Total length (16 bits):* total data unit length, including header, in octets.
- *Identifier (16 bits):* together with source address, destination address, and user protocol, intended to uniquely identify a datagram. Thus the identifier must be unique for the datagram's source, destination, and user protocol for the time during which the datagram will remain in the catenet.
- *Flags (3 bits):* one bit, the More flag, used for fragmentation (segmentation) and reassembly. Another bit, if set, prohibits fragmentation. This facility may be useful if it is known that the destination does not have the capability to reassemble fragments. An example is to down-line load a small microprocessor. However, if this bit is set, the datagram may be discarded if it exceeds the maximum size of an en route network. When the bit is set, it may be advisable to use source routing to avoid networks with small maximum packet sizes. The third bit is currently not used.
- *Fragment offset (13 bits):* indicates where in the datagram this fragment belongs. It is measured in 64-bit units. This implies that fragments (other than the last fragment) must contain a data field that is a multiple of 64 bits long.
- *Time to live (8 bits):* measured in router hops.
- *Protocol (8 bits):* indicates the next level protocol which is to receive the data field at the destination.
- *Header checksum (16 bits):* frame check sequence on the header only. Since some header fields may change (e.g., time to live, fragmentation-related fields), this is reverified and recomputed at each router. The checksum field is the 16-bit one's complement addition of all 16 bit words in the header. For purposes of computation, the checksum field itself is considered to have a value of zero.
- *Source address (32 bits):* coded to allow a variable allocation of bits to specify the network and the station within the specified network (7 and 24, 14 and 16, or 21 and 8).
- *Destination address (32 bits):* as above.
- *Options (variable):* encodes the options requested by the sender.
- *Padding (variable):* used to ensure that the internet header ends on a 32-bit boundary.
- *Data (variable):* the data field must be a multiple of eight bits in length. Total length of data field plus header is a maximum of 65,535 octets.

It should be easy to see how the services specified above map into the fields of the IP data units.

Internet Control Message Protocol

DOD has defined an *internet control message protocol* (ICMP) which is a required companion to IP. Basically, ICMP provides feedback about problems in the communication environment. Examples of its use are: When a datagram cannot reach its destination, when the router does not have the buffering capacity to forward a datagram, and when the router can direct the station to send traffic on a shorter route.

Although ICMP is, in effect, at the same level as IP, it is a user of IP. An ICMP message is constructed and then passed on to IP, which encapsulates the message with an IP header and then transmits it to the destination gateway or station. Figure 11.20b shows the general format of ICMP messages. The fields are

- *Type (8 bits):* specifies the type of ICMP message.
- *Code (8 bits):* used to specify parameters of the message that can be encoded in one or a few bits.
- *Checksum (16 bits):* checksum of the entire ICMP message.
- *Parameters (32 bits):* used to specify more lengthy parameters.
- *Information (variable):* provides additional information related to the message.

In those cases in which the ICMP message refers to a prior datagram, the information field includes the entire IP header plus the first 64 bits of the data field of the original datagram. This enables the source host to match the incoming ICMP message with the prior datagram. The reason for including the first 64 bits of the data field is that this will enable the IP module in the host to determine which upper-level protocol or protocols were involved. In particular, the first 64 bits would include the TCP header or other transport-level header.

Eleven types of messages have been defined:

- Destination unreachable.
- Time exceeded.
- Parameter problem.
- Source quench.
- Redirect.
- Echo.
- Echo reply.
- Timestamp.
- Timestamp reply.
- Information request.
- Information reply.

The **destination unreachable** message covers a number of contingencies. A router may return this message if it does not know how to reach the destination network. In some networks, an attached router may be able to determine if a particular host is unreachable, and return the message. The destination host itself may return this message if the user protocol or some higher-level service access point is unreachable. This could happen if the corresponding field in the IP header was set incorrectly. If the datagram specifies a source route that is unusable, a message is returned. Finally, if a router must fragment a datagram but the Don't Fragment flag is set, a message is returned.

A router will return a **time exceeded** message if the lifetime of the datagram expires. A host will send this message if it cannot complete reassembly within a time limit.

A syntactic or semantic error in an IP header will cause a **parameter problem** message to be returned by a router or host. For example, an incorrect argument may be provided with an option. The parameter field contains a pointer to the octet in the original header where the error was detected.

The **source quench** message provides a rudimentary form of flow control. Either a router or a destination host may send this message to a source host, requesting that it reduce the rate at which it is sending traffic to the internet destination. On receipt of a source quench message, the source host should cut back the rate at which it is sending traffic to the specified destination until it no longer receives source quench messages. The source quench message can be used by a router or host which must discard datagrams because of a full buffer. In that case, the router or host will issue a source quench message for every datagram that it discards. In addition, a system may anticipate congestion and issue source quench messages when its buffers approach capacity. In that case, the datagram referred to in the source quench message may well be delivered. Thus, receipt of a source quench message does not imply delivery or nondelivery of the corresponding datagram.

A router sends a **redirect** message to a host on a directly connected router to advise the host of a better route to a particular destination. The following is an example of its use. A router, R1, receives a datagram from a host on a network to which the router is attached. The router, R1, checks its routing table and obtains the address for the next router, R2, on the route to the datagram's internet destination network, X. If R2 and the host identified by the internet source address of the datagram are on the same network, a redirect message is sent to the host. The redirect message advises the host to send its traffic for network X directly to router R2, as this is a shorter path to the destination. The router forwards the original datagram to its internet destination (via R2). The address of R2 is contained in the parameter field of the redirect message.

The **echo** and **echo reply** messages provide a mechanism for testing that communication is possible between entities. The recipient of an echo message is obligated to return the message in an echo reply message. An identifier and sequence number are associated with the echo message to be matched in the echo reply message. The identifier might be used like a serviced access point to identify a particular session and the sequence number might be incremented on each echo request sent.

The **timestamp** and **timestamp reply** messages provide a mechanism for sampling the delay characteristics of the internet. The sender of a timestamp message may include an identifier and sequence number in the parameters field and include the time that the message is sent (originate timestamp). The receiver records the time it received the message and the time that it transmits the reply message in the timestamp reply message. If the timestamp message is sent using strict source routing, then the delay characteristics of a particular route can be measured.

The **information request** and **information reply** messages can be used by a host to discover the address of the network to which it is attached, in the following way. The host sends an information request message with the network portion of the source address field of the IP header set to 0. The use of 0 is interpreted as "this network." The replying IP module should send the reply with the addresses fully specified.

11.6

ROUTER-LEVEL PROTOCOLS

The routers in an internet perform much the same function as packet-switching nodes (PSNs) in a packet-switching network (Figure 11.18). As with the nodes of a packet-switching network, the bridges or routers of an internet need to make routing decisions based on knowledge of the topology and conditions of the internet. In simple internets, a fixed routing scheme is possible. However, in more complex internets, a degree of dynamic cooperation is needed among the routers. In particular, the router must avoid portions of the network that have failed and should avoid portions of the network that are congested. In order to make such dynamic routing decisions, routers exchange routing information using a special protocol for that purpose. Information is needed about the status of the internet, in terms of which networks can be reached by which routes, and the delay characteristics of various routes.

In considering the routing function of routers, it is important to distinguish two concepts:

- *Routing information:* information about the topology and delays of the internet.
- *Routing algorithm:* the algorithm used to make a routing decision for a particular datagram, based on current routing information.

A router–router protocol can be used for the purpose of exchanging routing information. In general, however, such protocols do not assume or dictate a particular routing algorithm. A general-purpose protocol will provide sufficient information to support a variety of routing algorithms.

Autonomous Systems

In order to proceed in our discussion of router–router protocols, we need to introduce the concept of an **autonomous system.** An autonomous system is an internet connected by homogeneous routers; generally the routers are under the administrative control of a single entity. An **interior router protocol** (IRP) passes routing information between routers within an autonomous system. The protocol used with the autonomous system does not need to be implemented outside of the system. This flexibility allows IRPs to be custom-tailored to specific applications and requirements.

It may happen, however, that an internet will be constructed of more than one autonomous system. For example, all of the local area networks at a site, such as a military base or campus, could be linked by routers to form an autonomous system. This system might be linked through a wide-area network to other autonomous systems. The situation is illustrated in Figure 11.21. In this case, the routing algorithms and routing tables used by routers in different autonomous systems may differ. Nevertheless, the routers in one autonomous system need at least a minimal level of information concerning networks outside the system that can be reached. The protocol used to pass routing information between routers in different autonomous systems is referred to as an **exterior router protocol** (ERP).

We can expect that an ERP will need to pass less information and be simpler than an IRP, for the following reason. If a datagram is to be transferred from a host in one autonomous system to a host in another autonomous system, a router in the first system need only determine the target autonomous system and devise a route to get into that target system. Once the datagram enters the

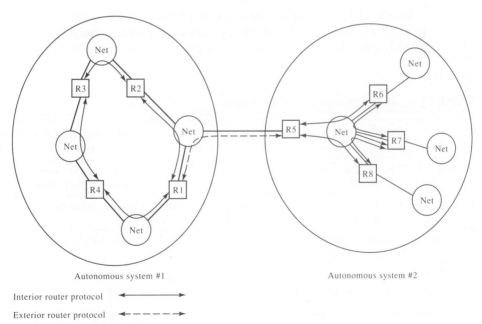

FIGURE 11.21.   Application of exterior and interior routing protocols.

target autonomous system, the routers within that system can cooperate to finally deliver the datagram. For this reason, more progress has been made on standardizing on an ERP than on an IRP. In the next portion of this section, we look at the most widely used ERP. This will be followed by a discussion of a recently developed IRP.

Exterior Gateway Protocol

The Exterior Gateway Protocol (EGP) [MILL84] was developed for use in conjunction with internets that employ the TCP/IP protocol suite, although the concepts are applicable to any internet.

Functions

The EGP was designed to allow routers, called gateways, in different autonomous systems to cooperate in the exchange of routing information. The protocol operates in terms of commands and responses, which are sent inside IP datagrams. The repertoire of commands and responses is summarized in Table 11.5.

Three functional procedures are involved in EGP:

Neighbor acquisition
Neighbor reachability
Network reachability

Two routers are considered to be neighbors if they share the same subnetwork. If the two routers are in different autonomous systems, they may wish to exchange routing information. For this purpose, it is necessary to first per-

TABLE 11.5 EGP Commands and Responses

Name	Command Interpretation	Name	Corresponding Response Interpretation
Request	Request gateway become a neighbor	Confirm Refuse	Confirm neighbor relationship Refuse neighbor relationship
Cease	Request termination of neighbor relationship	Cease-ack	Confirm termination
Hello	Request neighbor confirm neighbor reachability	I-H-U	Confirm reachability
Poll	Request neighbor provide network reachability information	Update	Provide network reachability update
		Error	Error

form **neighbor acquisition.** In essence, neighbor acquisition occurs when two neighboring routers in different autonomous systems agree to regularly exchange routing information. A formal acquisition procedure is needed since one of the routers may not wish to participate. For example, the router may be overburdened and does not want to be responsible for traffic coming in from outside the system. In the neighbor acquisition process, one router sends a request message to the other, which may either accept or refuse the offer. The protocol does not address the issue of how one router knows the address or even the existence of another router, nor how it decides that it needs to exchange routing information with that particular router. These issues must be dealt with at configuration time or by active intervention of a network manager.

To perform neighbor acquisition, one router sends a Request command to another. If the target router accepts the request, it returns a Confirm response. Otherwise, it returns a Refuse response. After a neighbor relationship has been established, either side may terminate the relationship with a Cease message, for which the appropriate response is a Cease-ack message.

Once a neighbor relationship is established, the **neighbor reachability** procedure is used to maintain the relationship. Each partner needs to be assured that the other partner still exists and is still engaged in the neighbor relationship. For this purpose, the two routers periodically exchange Hello and I-H-U (I heard you) messages. Either router may issue a Hello command, and the partner router is obligated to reply as soon as possible with an I-H-U response.

The final procedure specified by EGP is **network reachability.** As with neighbor reachability, network reachability involves a periodic command/response pair. In this case, one router sends a Poll command, and its partner responds with an Update response. The Update response contains a list of networks that can be reached by the responding router, together with an estimate of the "distance" of each network. This distance typically is expressed in terms of the number of router hops. On the basis of this information, the requesting router can build up a routing table based on determining the shortest path to each destination router.

Formats

Figure 11.22 illustrates the formats of all of the EGP messages. Each message type begins with a ten-octet header containing the following fields:

- *EGP Version Number:* identifies version of EGP.
- *Type:* message type.
- *Code:* provides additional information about the message. In effect, it identifies a subtype of message.
- *Status:* provides message-dependent status information.
- *Checksum:* Checksum of the entire EGP message. This is the same checksum used for IP.

Neighbor acquisition

Neighbor reachability

Poll

Error response/indication

FIGURE 11.22. EGP formats.

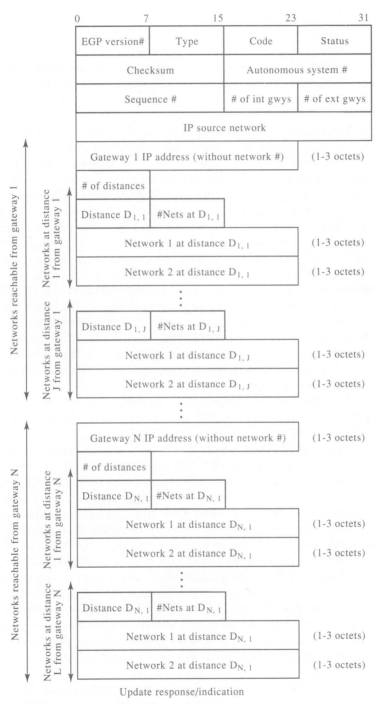

FIGURE 11.22.   (continued).

- *Autonomous System Number:* assigned number identifying the particular autonomous system.
- *Sequence Number:* used to synchronize commands and responses. A router establishes an initial sequence number during neighbor acquisition, and may increment the number for each subsequent command. Responses contain the last sequence number received.

The **neighbor acquisition** format is used for all of the commands and responses relating to neighbor acquisition and termination (request, confirm, refuse, cease, cease-ack). The Hello Interval and Poll Interval fields specify the minimum intervals between such commands from the partner. This is used to limit the burden of responding to commands for the router. The status field is used to indicate a problem or to declare the mode of operation of the router. A router operating in passive mode will not send Hello commands, and gains neighbor reachability information only by responding to Hello commands from the other side. In active mode, a router will periodically issue Hello commands. At least one of the routers in a partnership must be in active mode.

The **neighbor reachability** format is used for the Hello/I-H-U exchange. The status field indicates whether the router is up or down. In the down state, the router is currently unable/unwilling to provide routing information.

The **poll** format is used to solicit network reachability information. The IP Source Network field contains the network number of the network about which reachability information is being requested. This network is one that is common to both autonomous systems and is usually (but not necessarily) a network to which both routers are attached. In effect, the poll message is asking the question: For all routers on the specified network, what networks can be reached by each router and what are the distances involved?

At first glance, the question seems too broad. The requesting router will necessarily want to know which networks are reachable via the responding router, but why ask about other routers? This is best explained with reference to Figure 11.21. In this example, router R1 in autonomous system 1 and router R5 in autonomous system 2 implement EGP and acquire a neighbor relationship. When R5 sends a poll request to R1, R1 responds by indicating which networks it could reach and the distances (network hops) involved. R1 also provides the same information on behalf of R2. That is, R1 tells R5 what networks are reachable via R2 at what distances. In this example, the reason that R5 does not interrogate R2 directly is that R2 does not implement EGP. Typically, most of the routers in an autonomous system will not implement EGP. Only a few routers will be assigned responsibility for communicating with routers in other autonomous systems. A final point: R1 is in possession of the necessary information about R2, since R1 and R2 share an interior router protocol (IRP).

With this background, we can now describe the **update** format. The bulk of the message consists of a number of blocks, one for each router for which a report is provided. The block begins with the internet address of the router that is the subject of that block. The remainder of the block consists of a list of reachable networks grouped according to their distance from this router. First, the number of different distances is specified. The remainder of the block consists of a number of sub-blocks, one for each distance. Each sub-block begins with a field specifying the distance, followed by a field that specifies the number of networks that are reachable at that distance. Finally, the network address of each network at that distance is listed. In Figure 11.22, the notation $D_{i,j}$ has the interpretation: the jth distance in the block for router i.

Two fields in the update message remain to be explained. These fields list the number of internal and external routers provided in this update report. All routers, of course, must directly attach to the network specified in the poll command and repeated in the update response. Internal routers are those that are in the same autonomous system as the responding router. External routers are those in other autonomous systems whose routing information is known to the responding router. This latter situation may arise when one network supports routers from more than two autonomous systems.

The **error** format is used to provide information about a variety of error conditions and may be used in response to any command. The reason field may contain one of the following identifiers:

0   unspecified
1   bad EGP header format
2   bad EGP data field format
3   reachability information unavailable
4   excessive polling rate
5   no response received to a poll

The last field of the error message contains the first 12 octets of the message that caused the error detection.

Open Shortest Path First (OSPF) Protocol

The OSPF protocol was developed as part of the networking research associated with ARPANET and the Defense Advanced Research Projects Agency (DARPA) [MOY89a, MOY89b, BOULE89]. OSPF has also been proposed as an international standard. OSPF is intended for use as an interior routing protocol.

The history of interior routing protocols on the DARPA internet, mirrors that of packet-switching protocols on ARPANET. Recall that ARPANET began with a protocol based on the Bellman–Ford algorithm. The resulting protocol required each node to exchange *path delay information* with its neighbors. Information about a change in network conditions would gradually ripple through the network. A second generation protocol was based on Dijkstra's algorithm and required each node to exchange *link delay information* with all other nodes using flooding. It was found that this latter technique was more effective.

Similarly, the initial interior routing protocol on the DARPA internet was the Routing Information Protocol (RIP), which is essentially the same protocol as the first-generation ARPANET protocol. This protocol requires each router to transmit its entire routing table. Although the algorithm is simple and easy to implement, as the internet expands, routing updates grow larger and consume significantly more network bandwidth. Accordingly, OSPF operates in a fashion similar to the revised ARPANET routing algorithm: each router only transmits descriptions of its local link. This information is transmitted to all of the other routers of which it is aware. Every router receiving the update packet must acknowledge it to the sender. Such updates produce a minimum of routing traffic because link descriptions are small and rarely need to be refreshed.

OSPF provides least-cost routing through a fully user-configurable routing metric that can be set to express any function of delay, data rate, dollar cost, or other factors. OSPF is able to equalize loads over several equal-cost paths.

The topological description of the internet is somewhat more complex than that of a packet-switching network. The database of the topology of an autonomous system, from which routing tables are calculated, is a directed graph. The vertices of the graph are two types: routers and networks. A network vertex is termed transit if it can carry data that neither originates nor terminates on a host on that network; otherwise, it is a stub network. Graph edges are also of two types:

- A graph edge connects two router vertices when they are connected to each other by a direct point-to-point link.
- A graph edge connects a router vertex to a network vertex when the router has an interface on the network.

Figure 11.23 shows an example of an autonomous system, and Figure 11.24 is the resulting directed graph. The mapping is straightforward:

- Two routers joined by a point-to-point line are represented in the graph as being directly connected by a pair of edges, one in each direction (e.g., routers 6 and 10).
- When multiple routers are attached to a network (such as a LAN or a packet-switching network), the directed graph shows all routers bidirectionally connected to the network vertex (e.g., routers 1, 2, 3, and 4 connected to network 3).
- If a single router is attached to a network, the network will appear in the graph as a stub connection (e.g., network 7).
- A host computer can be directly connected to a router, in which case it is depicted in the corresponding graph (e.g., host 1).
- If a router is connected to other autonomous systems, then the path cost to each network in the other systems must be obtained by some exterior routing protocol (ERP). Each such network is represented on the graph by a stub and an edge to the router with the known path cost (e.g., networks 12 through 15).

FIGURE 11.23.   A sample autonomous system [MOY89].

A cost is associated with the output side of each router interface. This cost is configurable by the system administrator. Arcs on the graph are labelled with the cost of the corresponding router output interface. Arcs having no labelled cost have a cost of 0. Note that arcs leading from networks to routers always have cost 0; they are significant nonetheless.

A database corresponding to the directed graph is maintained by each router. It is pieced together from link state messages from other routers in the internet. Using Dijkstra's algorithm, a router calculates the shortest path to all destination networks. The result for router 6 of Figure 11.24 are shown as a tree in Figure 11.25. The tree gives the entire route to any destination network or host. However, only the next hop to the destination is used in the forwarding process. The resulting routing table for router 6 is shown in Table 11.6.

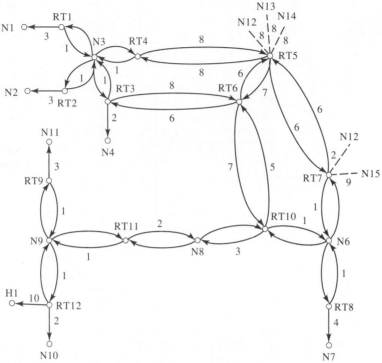

FIGURE 11.24.   The resulting directed graph [MOY89].

The table includes entries for routers advertising external routes (routers 5 and 7). For external networks whose identity is known, entries are also provided.

CONNECTION-ORIENTED INTERNETWORKING

ISO standard ISO/TR 10029 specifies the architecture and functioning of a connection-mode internetworking facility, using ISO 8208 (X.25) as the network layer protocol. We examine the protocol architecture of this approach, and then look at the functions that must be performed by the routers.

Protocol Architecture for Connection-Oriented Internetworking

Figure 11.26 illustrates the protocol activity for transferring data from a DTE attached to a packet-switching network, through a router, to a DTE attached

FIGURE 11.25.   The SPF tree for router RT6 [MOY89].

to a LAN which has been enhanced with the use of X.25. The lower portion of the figure shows the format of the data unit being processed at various points during the transfer.

To begin, from the network layer's point of view, data is presented to the network layer by the transport layer (t1). This is in the form of a data unit consisting of a transport protocol header and data from the transport layer user. This block of data is received by the packet level protocol of X.25, which appends a packet header (t2) to form an X.25 packet. The header will include the virtual circuit number of the virtual circuit that connects host A to the router. The packet is handed down to the data link layer protocol (LAP-B), which appends a link header and trailer (t3), and transmits the resulting frame to DCE X (t4). At the DCE, the link header and trailer are stripped off and the result is passed up to the packet level (t5). The packet is transferred across the network and through DCE Y to the router, which appears as just another DTE to the network. Eventually, we reach the packet level at t9 in the router. At this point, the packet is relayed onto the LAN. This will involve going through the LAN protocol layers (logical link control, medium access control) on trans-

TABLE 11.6   Routing Table for Router RT6

Destination	Next Hop	Distance
N1	RT3	10
N2	RT3	10
N3	RT3	7
N4	RT3	8
N6	RT10	8
N7	RT10	12
N8	RT10	10
N9	RT10	11
N10	RT10	13
N11	RT10	14
H1	RT10	21
RT5	RT5	6
RT7	RT10	8
N12	RT10	10
N13	RT5	14
N14	RT5	14
N15	RT10	17

mission and reception. Note that on this hop, an X.25 virtual circuit is set up on top of LLC.

Several points are worth noting:

- There is no encapsulation by the router. The same layer 3 header format is reused.
- There is no true end-to-end protocol. Each hop constitutes a single virtual circuit controlled by X.25.
- Because of the 12-bit virtual circuit number field in X.25, the router can handle a maximum of 4096 connections.

Operation of an X.25 Router

We can describe the operation of the router by considering the following areas:

- Virtual call setup.
- Data and interrupt transfer.
- Virtual call clearing.
- Reset.
- Restart.

FIGURE 11.26. X.25 internetwork relay operation.

Virtual Call Setup

Let us consider the configuration of Figure 11.26 and suppose that DTE A wishes to set up a logical network connection to DTE B. The process begins when the transport layer isues a request to the network layer for a virtual circuit to DTE B. This request is mapped into a Call Request packet. It is at this point that we see the distinction between global addresses and subnetwork attachment point addresses. The request from the transport layer will refer to the global internet address. It will be conveyed as an optional user facility known as *called address extension* in the Call Request packet. In addition, the Call Request packet includes as a parameter *called DTE address*; this parameter appears in the packet header. In this case, the called DTE address is the subnetwork attachment point address for the router on network X.

What has happened is this. The network service user has requested a logical connection to DTE B. This request passes down to the network-level entity in A, which is an X.25 packet level module. The network entity makes a routing decision that the connection can be set up through the router. So, the X.25 protocol sets up a virtual circuit to the router, using the Call Request packet. The called DTE address parameter of the Call Request packet is used by the local DCE to set up a virtual circuit to the remote DCE, which then issues an Incoming Call packet to the router.

When an Incoming Call packet arrives at a DTE, it will normally accept or reject the connection promptly. If the connection is accepted, a Call Accepted packet is issued. In the case of the router, however, this activity must be deferred until it can be determined if the virtual call can be set up all the way to DTE B. Therefore, upon receipt of the Call Request packet, the router performs the following tasks:

1. Makes a routing decision on the basis of the calling address parameter. This parameter was generated as part of the transport request primitive in A, and carried in the call user data field of the Incoming Call packet. In this case, there is no need for a hop to another router. Rather, the destination DTE is B, which is attached to a subnetwork to which this router is attached.
2. Select a free virtual circuit number on the LAN side and associate it with the virtual circuit number of the incoming call on the packet-switching network side.
3. Issue a Call Request packet onto the LAN with the subnetwork attachment point address of B in the called DTE address field. A match is made of optional user facilities.
4. If DTE B accepts the call, the router will soon receive a Call Connected packet on the virtual circuit across the LAN. It then transmits a Call Accepted packet on the logical channel corresponding to the original Incoming Call packet on the packet-switching network side.

Data and Interrupt Transfer

Once the virtual call is set up, the router peforms a mapping function between the virtual circuit numbers on the two sides. Incoming data packets on one virtual circuit are relayed and retransmitted on the other virtual circuit. The router may need to perform segmentation if there is a difference in maximum packet size. When a packet must be segmented, it is broken up into two or more smaller packets forming a complete packet sequence, using the M bit.

When an Interrupt packet is received by a DTE, it responds with an Interrupt Confirmation packet. The originating DTE may not send another Interrupt packet until it receives a confirmation to the outstanding one. Since this confirmation is end-to-end, the router must obey the following procedure:

1. When an Interrupt packet is received on one virtual circuit, an Interrupt packet is transmitted on the matching virtual circuit.
2. When an Interrupt Confirmation packet is received on the second virtual circuit, the router transmits an Interrupt Confirmation packet on the first virtual circuit.

Virtual Call Clearing

The virtual call clearing process is not a cooperative function between DTEs. Rather, either DTE may clear the virtual circuit; the other side is merely informed that the clearing has occurred. Accordingly, the router behaves as follows: When a Clear Indication packet is received on a virtual circuit, the router issues a Clear Confirmation packet on that virtual circuit and issues a Clear Request packet on the matching virtual circuit.

Reset

A reset may be initiated by either a DTE or a router. In the former case, the router will receive a Reset Indicator packet on a virtual circuit. It will respond by issuing a DTE Reset Confirmation on that virtual circuit and a Reset Request on the matching virtual circuit.

If the router needs to reset a virtual call, it issues a Reset Request on both of the virtual circuits that are part of that virtual call.

Restart

When a router receives a Restart Indication on the interface to one network it responds as follows:

1. The router issues a DTE Restart Confirmation on that interface.
2. For each virtual circuit that had existed on that interface, the router issues a Clear Request packet on the matching virtual circuit on the other network interface.

Similarly, a router may itself initiate a restart by issuing a Restart Request packet on one subnetwork interface. It must then also issue a Clear Request packet on the other interface for each virtual circuit that was destroyed by the restart.

11.8

RECOMMENDED READING

Two special issues of the *Journal on Selected Areas in Communications* provide a number of worthwhile papers on internetworking [GREE90, BUX87]. [GERL88] is a special issue of *IEEE Network* devoted to bridges. [PARU90] is a thoughtful discussion of the implications of high-speed networking and future trends in distributed processing for internetworking. [CERF78] remains one of the best overall discussions of the design issues related to internetworking.

The definitive study of the topics in this chapter is [PERL92]. [WHIT92] is a relatively short but worthwhile treatment, with special emphasis on addressing issues.

11.9

PROBLEMS

11.1 Compare virtual circuit relay and IP. What are the principal strengths and weaknesses of each?

11.2 In Figure 11.26, X.25 is used across a LAN. Note that there are no DCEs, although CCITT has defined X.25 as a DTE-to-DCE protocol. What has happened is this: ISO has issued an extension of X.25 that allows it to be used in a "DTE-to-DTE mode" across a network. What changes are needed in the protocol for this application?

11.3 What are the pros and cons of intermediate reassembly of an internet segmented datagram versus reassembly at the final destination?

11.4 In the case of the ISO internet protocol, the checksum needs to be recalculated at routers because of changes to the internet PDU header, such as a change in PDU lifetime field. In this case, it is certainly possible to recalculate the checksum from scratch. However, because of the nature of the algorithm, some time may be saved by a shorter procedure. Suggest such a procedure. Hint: Suppose that the value in octet k is changed by Z = new_value-old_value. If X and Y denote the checksum values held in octets n and n + 1, respectively, then what adjustments must be made to X and Y as a function of Z?

11.5 Repeat the previous problem for the checksum used in the TCP/IP protocol suite.

11.6 Assume a local network is to be attached to a long-haul X.25 network via a single station which appears to the X.25 network as a single DTE. What gateway logic in the station would allow other local network stations to have access to the X.25 network?

11.7 An IP datagram is to be segmented. Which options in the option field need to be copied into the header of each segment, and which need only be retained in the first segment?

11.8 Because of segmentation, an IP datagram can arrive in pieces, not necessarily in the right order. The IP layer at the receiving host must accumulate these segments until the original datagram is reconstituted.

　　a. Consider that the IP layer creates a buffer for assembling the datagram. As assembly proceeds the buffer will consist of data and "holes" between the data. Describe an algorithm for reassembly based on this concept.

　　b. For the algorithm above, it is necessary to keep track of the holes. Describe a simple mechanism for doing this.

11.9 A transport layer message consisting of 1500 bits of data and 160 bits of header is sent to an internet layer which appends another 160 bits of header. This is then transmitted through two networks, each of which uses a 24-bit packet header. The destination network has a maximum packet size of 800 bits. How many bits, including headers, are delivered to the network layer protocol at the destination?

11.10 The ICMP format includes the first 64 bits of the datagram data field. What might be the purpose of including these bits?

11.11 The architecture suggested by Figure 11.16 is to be used. What functions could be added to the ISs to alleviate some of the problems caused by the mismatched local and long-haul networks?

11.12 Would the spanning tree approach be good for an internet including routers?

11.13 Should internetworking be concerned with a network's internal routing? Why or why not?

APPENDIX 11A

The ISO Checksum Algorithm

The ISO internetwork protocol standard uses an error-detecting code, or checksum, originally specified in [FLET82], and referred to as the Fletcher checksum. This code is also used in the ISO Class 4 transport protocol discussed in Chapter 12. In both cases, a 16-bit checksum is included as a field in each PDU. The checksum is initially calculated by the sender and placed in the outgoing PDU. The receiver applies the same algorithm to the entire header, now including the 16-bit checksum, and should get a zero result if there are no errors.

11A1   Modulo 255 Addition

The Fletcher checksum is based on treating the data to be checked as a sequence of 8-bit unsigned integers and performing mod 255 addition on those integers. With mod 255 addition, the sum of any two numbers is found by performing addition and finding the remainder after division by 255. Thus:

$$254 + 253 \ (\text{mod } 255) = 507 - 255 = 252$$

This scheme is equivalent to performing one's complement addition on the numbers treated as 8-bit unsigned binary integers. With one's complement addition, if there is a carry out of the leftmost digit, then the carry digit is added back to the sum; this is known as *end-around carry*. For example:

$$
\begin{array}{r}
11111110 = 254 \\
+\ 11111101 = 253 \\
\hline
111111011 = 507 \\
1 \\
\hline
11111100 = 252
\end{array}
$$

In the original description of the algorithm, Fletcher suggested that either a mod 255 or 256 addition could be used. Because there appears to be a slight advantage, in terms of error-detecting power in using mod 255, this option was chosen for the ISO standards. Unfortunately, mod 255 addition is computationally more complex than mod 256 addition [NAKA88, COCK87].

11A2   Generating the Checksum

The algorithm is based on producing two octets calculated on the octets of the data to be checked (henceforth referred to as *message*). The two values are

- The sum, modulo 255, of every octet in the message.
- The sum, modulo 255, of every octet weighted (reversely) by its position in the message.

That is:

$$C0 = \sum_{i=1}^{L} B(i)$$

$$C1 = \sum_{i=1}^{L} (L - i + 1) \times B(i)$$

where

$$
\begin{aligned}
C0 &= \text{first check octet} \\
C1 &= \text{second check octet} \\
L &= \text{length of message in octets} \\
B(i) &= \text{value of } i\text{th octet}
\end{aligned}
$$

For convenience, the checksum calculation is performed on the entire message, including the fields that will contain the two check octets. These fields are initialized to zero. Thus, if the two checksum positions are n and $n + 1$, then the two summations above are performed with $B(n) = B(n + 1) = 0$.

Finally, we would like to set the values of the checksum octets so that the results of the algorithm is zero. That is, we need

$$C0' = 0 = \sum_{i=1}^{L} B(i) = C0 + B(n) + B(n + 1)$$

$$C1' = 0 = \sum_{i=1}^{L} (L - i + 1) \times B(i)$$

$$= C1 + (L - n + 1) \times B(n) + (L - n) \times B(n + 1)$$

where $C0$ and $C1$ are the calculations made with the checksum positions set to zero, and $C0'$ and $C1'$ are the same calculations made after the checksum positions have been set to their proper values. Solving, we obtain

$$B(n) = (L - n) \times C0 - C1$$
$$B(n) = C1 - (L - n + 1) \times C0$$

11A3   Checking the Checksum

Upon receipt of the message, the receiver performs the calculations for $C0$ and $C1$ with the received values, including the received values of the checksum positions. If the result is $C0 = C1 = 0$, then the checksum calculation has succeeded and no errors are assumed.

14A4   Motivation

The most commonly used error-detection algorithm is the cyclic redundancy check (CRC), described in Chapter 4. The CRC has several proven, desirable properties with regard to the kind and number of errors that it can detect. Furthermore, it may be conveniently and efficiently implemented in hardware [SKLO89]. Although the Fletcher checksum is not as powerful, it can be shown that, assuming all bit errors are equally likely, the Fletcher checksum

- Detects all single-bit errors.
- Detects all double-bit errors.
- Fails to detect only 0.000019% of all burst errors of length not exceeding 16.
- Fails to detect only 0.0015% of all larger burst errors.

For the internet and transport protocols, the main drawback of the CRC is that software implementations are relatively inefficient due to the number of computations required. The advantage of the Fletcher checksum is that it is relatively simple to implement and operates relatively efficiently. Nevertheless, it has quite good error-detection properties [FLET82]. Also, in the case of the internet protocol, the recalculation of the checksum after a few octets have been modified is a relatively simple matter. Recalculation with a CRC is considerably more complex.

CHAPTER 12

Transport Protocols

The transport protocol is the keystone of the whole concept of a computer-communications architecture. Lower-layer protocols are needed, to be sure, but they are less important pedagogically and to designers for a number of reasons. For one thing, lower-level protocols are better understood and, on the whole, less complex than transport protocols. Also, standards have settled out quite well for most kinds of layer 1 to 3 transmission facilities, and there is a large body of experience in their use.

Viewed from the other side, upper level protocols are also of lesser importance. The transport protocol provides the basic end-to-end service of transferring data between users. Any process or application can be programmed to access directly the transport services without going through session and presentation layers. Indeed, this is the normal mode of operation for DOD's transport protocols.

The author's conviction of the importance of the transport protocol, together with the remarkable complexity of such protocols, has led to a rather long chapter. For this, the reader's indulgence is begged. We begin by looking at the services that one might expect from a transport protocol. Next, we examine the protocol mechanisms required to provide these services. We find that most of the complexity relates to connection-oriented services. As might be expected, the less the network service provides, the more the transport protocol must do. We then look briefly at the types of network services that might be provided. Then, two sets of protocol standards are examined. Finally, the concept of lightweight transport protocols is introduced.

12.1

TRANSPORT SERVICES

We begin by looking at the kinds of services that a transport protocol can or should provide to higher-level protocols. Figure 12.1 places the concept of

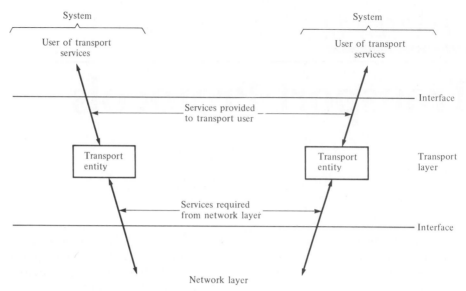

FIGURE 12.1.   Transport entity context.

transport services in context. In a system, there is a transport entity which provides services to transport users, which might be an application process or a session protocol entity. This local transport entity communicates with some remote transport entity, using the services of some lower layer, such as the network layer.

We have already mentioned that the general service provided by a transport protocol is the end-to-end transport of data in a way that shields the user from the details of the underlying communications systems. To be more specific, we must consider the specific services that a transport protocol can provide. The following categories of service are useful for describing the transport service:

- Type of service.
- Grade of service.
- Data transfer.
- User interface.
- Connection management.
- Expedited delivery.
- Status reporting.
- Security.

Type of Service

Two basic types of service are possible: connection-oriented and connectionless or datagram service. A connection-oriented service provides for the establishment, maintenance, and termination of a logical connection between transport users. This has, so far, been the most common type of protocol service available and has a wide variety of applications. The connection-oriented service generally implies that the service is reliable.

The strengths of the connection-oriented approach are clear. It allows connection-related features such as flow control, error control, and sequenced delivery. Connectionless service, however, is more appropriate in some contexts. At lower layers (internet, network), connectionless service is more robust (e.g., see discussion in Section 8.2). In addition, it represents a "least common denominator" of service to be expected at higher layers. Further, even at transport and above there is justification for a connectionless service. There are instances in which the overhead of connection establishment and maintenance is unjustified or even counterproductive. Some examples, listed in [CHAP82]:

- *Inward data collection:* involves the periodic active or passive sampling of data sources, such as sensors, and automatic self-test reports from security equipment or network components. In a real-time monitoring situation, the loss of an occasional data unit would not cause distress, since the next report should arrive shortly.
- *Outward data dissemination:* includes broadcast messages to network users, the announcement of a new node or the change of address of a service, and the distribution of real-time clock values.
- *Request-response:* applications in which a transaction service is provided by a common server to a number of distributed users, and for which a single request-response sequence is typical. Use of the service is regulated at the application level, and lower level connections are often unnecessary and cumbersome.
- *Real-time applications:* such as voice and telemetry, involving a degree of redundancy and/or a real-time transmission requirement. These must not have connection-oriented functions such as retransmission.

Thus, there is a place at the transport level for both a connection-oriented and a connectionless type of service.

Quality of Service

The transport protocol entity should allow the transport user to specify the quality of transmission service to be provided. The transport entity will attempt to optimize the use of the underlying link, network, and internet resources to the best of its ability, to provide the collective requested services.

Examples of services that might be requested:

- Acceptable error and loss levels.
- Desired average and maximum delay.
- Desired average and minimum throughput.
- Priority levels.

Of course, the transport entity is limited to the inherent capabilities of the underlying service. For example, IP does provide a quality of service parameter. It allows specification of eight levels of precedence or priority and a binary specification for normal or low delay, normal or high throughput, and normal or high reliability. Thus, the transport entity can "pass the buck" to the internetwork entity, which is still dependent on the underlying transmission facilities. Another example: X.25 provides for throughput class negotiation as an optional user facility. The network may alter flow control parameters and the amount of network resources allocated on a virtual circuit to achieve desired throughput.

The transport layer may also resort to other mechanisms to try to satisfy user requests, such as splitting one transport connection among multiple virtual circuits to enhance throughput.

The user of the quality of service feature needs to recognize that

- Depending on the nature of the transmission facility, the transport entity will have varying degrees of success in providing a requested grade of service.
- There is bound to be a trade-off among reliability, delay, throughput, and cost of services.

Nevertheless, certain applications would benefit from, or even require, certain qualities of service and, in a hierarchical or layered architecture, the easiest way for an application to extract this quality of service from a transmission facility is to pass the request down to the transport protocol.

Examples of applications that might request particular qualities of service:

- A file transfer protocol might require high throughput. It may also require high reliability to avoid retransmissions at the file transfer level.
- A transaction protocol (e.g., data-base query) may require low delay.
- An electronic mail protocol may require multiple priority levels.

One approach to providing a variety of qualities of service is to include a quality of service facility within the protocol. We have seen this with IP and will see that transport protocols to be discussed later follow the same approach. An alternative is to provide a different transport protocol for different classes of traffic. Four types of transport protocol are suggested in [MCFA79]:

- A reliable connection-oriented protocol.
- A less reliable connectionless protocol.
- A speech protocol, requiring sequenced, timely delivery.
- A real-time protocol that requires high reliability and timeliness.

Data Transfer

The whole purpose, of course, of a transport protocol is to transfer data between two transport entities. Both user data and control data must be transferred, either on the same channel or separate channels. Full-duplex service must be provided. Half-duplex and simplex modes may also be offered to support peculiarities of particular users.

User Interface

It is not clear that the exact mechanism of the user interface to the transport protocol should be standardized. Rather, it should be optimized to the station environment. As examples, a transport entity's services could be invoked by

- Procedure calls.
- Passing of data and parameters to a process through a mailbox.
- Use of direct memory access (DMA) between a host user and a front-end processor containing the transport entity.

A few characteristics of the interface may be specified however. For example, a mechanism is needed to prevent the user from swamping the transport entity with data. A similar mechanism is needed to prevent the transport entity from swamping a user with data. Another aspect of the interface has to do with the timing and significance of confirmations. Consider: A transport user passes data to a transport entity to be delivered to a remote user. The local transport entity can acknowledge receipt of the data immediately, or it can wait until the remote transport entity reports that the data have made it through to the other end. Perhaps the most useful interface is one that allows immediate acceptance or rejection of requests, with later confirmation of the end-to-end significance.

Connection Management

When connection-oriented service is provided, the transport entity is responsible for establishing and terminating connections. A symmetric connection establishment procedure should be provided, which allows either user to initiate connection establishment. An asymmetric procedure may also be provided to support simplex connections.

Connection termination can be either abrupt or graceful. With an abrupt termination, data in transit may be lost. A graceful termination prevents either side from shutting down until all data have been delivered.

Expedited Delivery

A service similar to that provided by priority classes is the expedited delivery of data. Some data submitted to the transport service may supersede data submitted previously. The transport entity will endeavor to have the transmission facility transfer the data as rapidly as possible. At the receiving end, the transport entity will interrupt the user to notify it of the receipt of urgent data. Thus the expedited data service is in the nature of an interrupt mechanism, and is used to transfer occasional urgent data, such as a break character from a terminal or an alarm condition. In contrast, a priority service might dedicate resources and adjust parameters such that, on average, higher priority data are delivered more quickly.

Status Reporting

A status reporting service allows the transport user to obtain or be notified of information concerning the condition or attributes of the transport entity or a transport connection. Examples of status information:

• Performance characteristics of a connection (e.g., throughput, mean delay).
• Addresses (network, transport).
• Class of protocol in use.
• Current timer values.
• State of protocol "machine" supporting a connection.
• Degradation in requested quality of service.

Security

The transport entity may provide a variety of security services. Access control may be provided in the form of local verification of sender and remote verification of receiver. The transport service may also include encryption/decryption of data on demand. Finally, the transport entity may be capable of routing through secure links or nodes if such a service is available from the transmission facility.

12.2

PROTOCOL MECHANISMS

It is the purpose of this section to make good on our claim that a transport protocol may need to be very complex. For purposes of clarity we present the transport protocol mechanisms in an evolutionary fashion. We begin with a network service that makes life easy for the transport protocol and define the required mechanisms. As the network service is made progressively less capable, the transport protocol becomes progressively more complex.

The ISO has defined three types of network service:

• *Type A:* network connections with acceptable residual error rate and acceptable rate of signaled failures.
• *Type B:* network connections with acceptable residual error rate but unacceptable rate of signaled failures.
• *Type C:* network connections with residual error rate not acceptable to the transport service user.

In this context, an error is defined as a lost or duplicated network protocol data unit. If the error is caught and corrected by the network service in a fashion that is transparent to the transport entity, no damage is done. If the network service detects an error, cannot recover, and signals the transport entities, this is known as a signaled failure. An example would be the notification by X.25 that a RESET has occurred. Finally, there are residual errors—those that are not corrected and for which the transport entity is not notified.

Type A provides a reliable network service. This makes life easy for the transport protocol designer. It is well to examine this case, because it helps to clarify the basic transport mechanisms. We will then see that most of the complexity of a transport protocol occurs when the underlying service is unreliable.

Let us consider three subcases of Type A, which present progressively greater difficulties to the transport service:

• Reliable, sequencing network service with arbitrary message size.
• Reliable, nonsequencing network service with arbitrary message size.
• Reliable, nonsequencing network service with maximum message size.

An example of the first case would be reliable X.25 service. The second and third cases might, for example, be reliable datagram services.

In what follows, we will concern ourselves primarily with the most stringent requirement for a transport protocol: The user of the transport service requires a reliable, sequenced, connection-oriented service. It should be clear to the reader what the implications would be of less stringent requirements.

We now consider each of the five types of network service (three subcases of Type A; Type B; Type C).

Reliable Sequencing Network Service

In this case, we assume that the network service will accept messages of arbitrary length and will, with virtually 100% reliability, deliver them in sequence to the destination. These assumptions allow the development of the simplest possible transport protocol. Four issues need to be addressed:

• Addressing.
• Multiplexing.
• Flow control.
• Connection establishment/termination.

Addressing

The issue concerned with addressing is simply this: a user of a given transport entity wishes to either establish a connection with or make a connectionless data transfer to a user of some other transport entity. The target user needs to be specified by all of the following:

• User identification.
• Transport entity identification.
• Station address.
• Network number.

Recalling our discussion in Section 10.1, user addresses can be either flat or hierarchical. Regardless, the transport protocol must be able to derive the information listed above from the user address. Typically, the user address is specified as (*Station, Port*). The *Port* variable represents a particular user. Generally, there will be a single transport entity at each station, so a transport entity identification is not needed. If more than one transport entity is present, there is usually only one of each type. In this latter case, the address should include a designation of the type of transport protocol (e.g., TCP, User Datagram). In the case of a single network, *Station* identifies an attached network device. In the case of an internet, *Station* subsumes a network number which can be derived at the internet layer.

Since routing is not a concern of the transport layer, it simply passes the *Station* portion of the address down to the network service. *Port* is included in a transport header, to be used at the destination by the destination transport protocol.

One question remains to be addressed: How does the initiating transport user know the address of the destination transport user? We discussed this problem briefly in Section 10.1, and elaborate here. Two static and two dynamic strategies suggest themselves:

1. The user must know the address it wishes to use ahead of time. This is basically a system configuration function.
2. Some commonly used services are assigned "well-known addresses."
3. A name server is provided. The user requests a service by some generic or global name. The request is sent to the name server, which does a directory lookup and returns an address. The transport entity then proceeds with the connection.
4. In some cases, the target user is to be a process that is spawned at request time. The initiating user can send a process request to a well known address. The user at that address is a privileged system process that will spawn the new process and return an address.

To see that these are distinct cases, we give an example of each:

1. A process may be running that is only of concern to a limited number of transport users. A process in a station may collect statistics on performance. From time to time, a central network management routine connects to the process to obtain the statistics. These processes generally are not, and should not be, well known and accessible to all.
2. Examples of commonly used services are time sharing and word processing.
3. Some services may be commonly used, but their location may change from time to time. For example, a data entry process may be moved from one station to another on a local network to balance load. The names of such "movable" processes can be kept in a directory, with the addresses updated when a move occurs.
4. A programmer has developed a private application (e.g., a simulation program) that will execute on a remote mainframe but be invoked from a local

minicomputer. An RJE-type request can be issued to a remote job-management process which spawns the simulation process.

Multiplexing

We now turn to the concept of multiplexing, which also was discussed in general terms in Section 10.1. With respect to the interface between the transport protocol and higher-level protocols, the transport protocol performs a multiplexing/demultiplexing function. That is, multiple users employ the same transport protocol, and are distinguished by port numbers or service access points.

The transport entity may also perform a multiplexing function with respect to the network services that it uses. Recall that we defined upward multiplexing as the multiplexing of multiple (N) connections on a single (N-1) connection, and downward multiplexing as the splitting of a single (N) connection among multiple (N-1) connections.

Consider, for example, a transport entity making use of an X.25 service. Why should the transport entity employ upward multiplexing? There are, after all, 4095 virtual circuits available. In the typical case, this is more than enough to handle all active transport users. However, most X.25 networks base part of their charge on virtual circuit connect time, since each virtual circuit consumes some node buffer resources. Thus, if a single virtual circuit provides sufficient throughput for multiple transport users, upward multiplexing is indicated.

On the other hand, downward multiplexing or splitting might be used to improve throughput. If, for example, each X.25 virtual circuit is restricted to a 3-bit sequence number, only seven packets can be outstanding at a time. A larger sequence space might be needed for high-delay networks. Of course, throughput can only be increased so far. If there is a single station-node link over which all virtual circuits are multiplexed, the throughput of a transport connection cannot exceed the data rate of that link.

Flow Control

The OSI document [ISO84] defines flow control as a function for the control of the data flow within a layer or between adjacent layers. Whereas flow control is a relatively simple mechanism at the link layer, it is a rather complex mechanism at the transport layer, for two main reasons:

- Flow control at the transport level involves the interaction of transport users, transport entities, and the network service.
- The transmission delay between transport entities is generally long compared to actual transmission time and, what is worse, variable.

Figure 12.2 illustrates the first point. Transport user A wishes to send data to transport user B over a transport connection. We can view the situation as

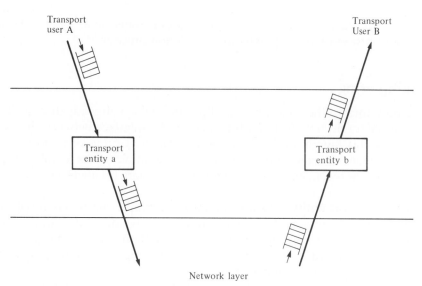

FIGURE 12.2.   Queuing representation of connection-oriented data transfer.

involving four queues. A generates data and queues it up to send. A must wait to send that data until

- It has permission from *B* (peer flow control).
- It has permission from its own transport entity (interface flow control).

As data flow down from A to transport entity a, a queues the data until it has permission to send it on from b and the network service. The data are then handed to the network layer for delivery to b. The network service must queue the data until it receives permission from b to pass them on. Finally, b must await B's permission before delivering the data to their destination.

To see the effects of delay, consider the possible interactions depicted in Figure 12.3. When a user wishes to transmit data, it sends these data to its transport entity (e.g., using a SEND call). This triggers two events. The transport entity generates one or more transport protocol data units (TPDUs) and passes these on to the network service. It also in some way acknowledges to the user that it has accepted the data for transmission. At this point, the transport entity can exercise flow control across the user–transport interface by simply withholding its acknowledgment. The transport entity is most likely to do this if the entity itself is being held up by a flow control exercised by either the network service or the target transport entity.

In any case, once the transport entity has accepted the data, it sends out a TPDU. Some time later, it receives an acknowledgment that the data have been received at the remote end. It then sends a confirmation to the sender.

At the receiving end, a TPDU arrives at the transport entity. It unwraps the data and sends them on (e.g., by an Indication primitive) to the destination

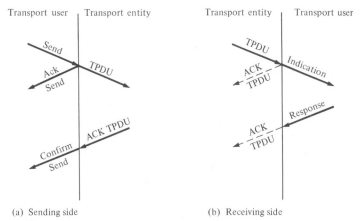

Transport user | Transport entity   Transport entity | Transport user

Send
Ack
TPDU
Send

ACK TPDU
Confirm
Send

TPDU
ACK TPDU
Indication

ACK TPDU
Response

(a) Sending side   (b) Receiving side

FIGURE 12.3.   User–transport interaction.

user. When the user accepts the data, it issues an acknowledgment (e.g., in the form of a RESPONSE primitive). The user can exercise flow control over the transport entity by withholding its response.

Now, the target transport entity has two choices regarding acknowledgment. Either it can issue an acknowledgment as soon as it has correctly received the TPDU (the usual practice), or it can wait until it knows that the user has correctly received the data before acknowledging. The latter course is the safer. In the latter case, the send confirmation is in fact a confirmation that the destination user received the data. In the former case, it merely confirms that the data made it through to the remote transport entity.

With the discussion above in mind, we can cite two reasons why one transport entity would want to restrain the rate of TPDU transmission over a connection from another transport entity:

• The user of the receiving transport entity cannot keep up with the flow of data.
• The receiving transport entity itself cannot keep up with the flow of TPDUs.

How do such problems manifest themselves? Well, presumably a transport entity has a certain amount of buffer space. Incoming TPDUs are added to the buffer. Each buffered TPDU is processed (i.e., examine the transport header) and the data are sent to the user. Either of the two problems mentioned above will cause the buffer to fill up. Thus the transport entity needs to take steps to stop or slow the flow of TPDUs to prevent buffer overflow. This requirement is not so easy to fulfill, because of the annoying time gap between sender and receiver. We return to this point in a moment. First, we present four ways of coping with the flow control requirement. The receiving transport entity can

1. Do nothing.
2. Refuse to accept further TPDUs from the network service.

3. Use a fixed sliding-window protocol.
4. Use a credit scheme.

Alternative 1 means that the TPDUs that overflow the buffer are discarded. The sending transport entity, failing to get an acknowledgment, will retransmit. This is a shame, since the advantage of a reliable network is that one never has to retransmit. Furthermore, the effect of this maneuver is to exacerbate the problem! The sender has increased its output to include new TPDUs plus retransmitted old TPDUs.

The second alternative is a backpressure mechanism that relies on the network service to do the work. When a buffer of a transport entity is full, it refuses additional data from the network service. This triggers flow control procedures within the network that throttle the network service at the sending end. This service, in turn, refuses additional TPDUs from its transport entity. It should be clear that this mechanism is clumsy and coarse-grained. For example, if multiple transport connections are multiplexed on a single network connection (virtual circuit), flow control is exercised only on the aggregate of all transport connections. Remarkably, there is at least one transport protocol that uses this strategy: the EHKP4 protocol standard developed in West Germany [MEIJ82].

The third alternative is already familiar to you from our discussions of link layer protocols. The key ingredients, recall, are

• The use of sequence numbers on data units.
• The use of a window of fixed size.
• The use of acknowledgments to advance the window.

With a reliable network service, the sliding window technique would actually work quite well. For example, consider a protocol with a window size of 7. Whenever the sender receives an acknowledgment to a particular TPDU, it is automatically authorized to send the succeeding seven TPDUs (of course, some may already have been sent). Now, when the receiver's buffer capacity gets down to seven TPDUs, it can withhold acknowledgment of incoming TPDUs to avoid overflow. The sending transport entity can send at most seven additional TPDUs and then must stop. Since the underlying network service is reliable, the sender will not time out and retransmit. Thus, at some point, a sending transport entity may have a number of TPDUs outstanding for which no acknowledgment has been received. Since we are dealing with a reliable network, the sending transport entity can assume that the TPDUs will get through and that the lack of acknowledgment is a flow control tactic. This tactic would not work well in an unreliable network, since the sending transport entity would not know whether the lack of acknowledgment is due to flow control or a lost TPDU.

The fourth alternative, a credit scheme, provides the receiver with a greater degree of control over data flow. Although it is not strictly necessary with a reliable network service, a credit scheme should result in a smoother traffic

FIGURE 12.4. Example of credit allocation mechanism.

flow. Further, it is a more effective scheme with an unreliable network service, as we shall see.

The credit scheme decouples acknowledgment from flow control. In fixed sliding-window protocols, such as X.25, the two are synonymous. In a credit scheme, a TPDU may be acknowledged without granting new credit, and vice versa. Figure 12.4 illustrates the protocol (compare Figure 5.5). For simplicity, we show a data flow in one direction only. In this example, data TPDUs are numbered sequentially modulo 8. Initially, through the connection establishment process, the sending and receiving sequence numbers are synchronized and A is granted a credit allocation of 7. A advances the trailing edge of its window each time that it transmits and advances the leading edge only when it is granted credit.

Figure 12.5 shows the view of this mechanism from the sending and receiving sides; of course, both sides take both views because data may be exchanged in both directions. From the sending point of view, sequence numbers fall into four regions:

- *Data sent and acknowledged:* Beginning with the initial sequence number used on this connection through the last acknowledged number.

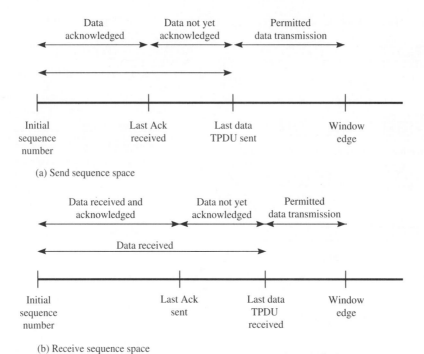

FIGURE 12.5.   Sending and receiving flow control perspectives.

- *Data sent but not yet acknowledged:* Represents data that have already been transmitted and the sender is awaiting acknowledgment.
- *Permitted data transmission:* The window of allowable transmissions, based on unused credit allocated from the other side.
- *Unused and unusable numbers:* Numbers above the window.

From the receiving point of view, the concern is for received data and for the window of credit that has been allocated. Note that the receiver is not required to immediately acknowledge incoming TPDUs, but may wait and issue a cumulative acknowledgment for a number of TPDUs; this is true for both TCP and the ISO transport protocol.

In both the credit allocation scheme and the sliding window scheme, the receiver needs to adopt some policy concerning the amount of data it permits the sender to transmit. The conservative approach is to only allow new TPDUs up to the limit of available buffer space. If this policy were in effect in Figure 12.4, the first credit message implies that *B* has five free buffer slots, and the second message that *B* has seven free slots.

A conservative flow control scheme may limit the throughput of the transport connection in long-delay situations. The receiver could potentially increase throughput by optimistically granting credit for space it does not have. For example, if a receiver's buffer is full but it anticipates that it can release space for two TPDUs within a round-trip propagation time, it could immediately send a credit of 2. If the receiver can keep up with the sender, this scheme may increase throughput and can do no harm. If the sender is faster than the receiver, however, some TPDUs may be discarded, necessitating a retransmission. Since retransmissions are not otherwise necessary with a reliable network service, an optimistic flow control scheme will complicate the protocol.

Connection Establishment and Termination

Even with a reliable network service, there is a need for connection establishment and termination procedures to support connection-oriented service. Connection establishment serves three main purposes:

- It allows each end to assure that the other exists.
- It allows negotiation of optional parameters (e.g., TPDU size, window size, quality of service).
- It triggers allocation of transport entity resources (e.g., buffer space, entry in connection table).

Connection establishment is by mutual agreement and can be accomplished by a simple set of user commands and control TPDUs, as shown in the state diagram of Figure 12.6. To begin, a user is in an IDLE state (with respect to the transport entity). The user can signal that it will passively wait for a request with a LISTEN command. A server program, such as time sharing or a file transfer application, might do this. The user may change its mind by sending a CLOSE command.

After the LISTEN command is issued, the transport entity creates a connection object of some sort (i.e., a table entry) that is in the LSTN state. If an RFC (request for connection) TPDU is received that specifies the listening user, then a connection is opened. To do this, the transport entity:

- Signals the user that a connection is open.
- Sends an RFC as confirmation to the remote transport entity.
- Puts the connection object in an OPEN state.

A user may open a connection by issuing an OPEN command, which triggers the transport entity to send an RFC. The reception of a matching RFC establishes the connection. The connection is prematurely aborted if the local user issues a CLOSE command or the remote transport entity refuses the connection by sending a CLS TPDU.

Figure 12.7 shows the robustness of this protocol. Either side can initiate a connection. Further, if both sides initiate the connection at about the same time, it is established without confusion.

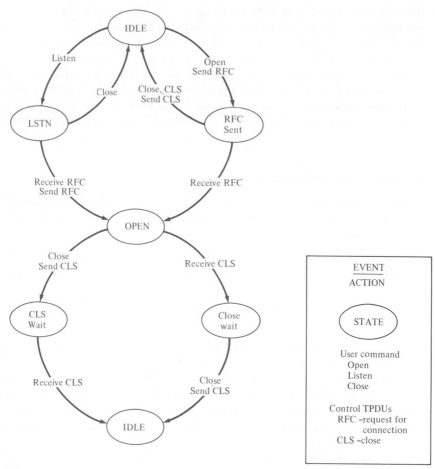

FIGURE 12.6.   Simple connection state diagram.

The reader may ask what happens if an RFC comes in while the requested user is idle (not listening). Three courses may be followed:

- The transport entity can reject the request by sending a CLS.
- The request can be queued until a LISTEN is issued by the user.
- The transport entity can interrupt or otherwise signal the user to notify it of a pending request.

Note that if the latter mechanism is used, a Listen command is not strictly necessary, but may be replaced by an Accept command, which is a signal from the user to the transport entity that it accepts the request for connection.

Connection termination is handled similarly. Either side, or both sides, may initiate a close. The connection is closed by mutual agreement. This strategy allows for either abrupt or graceful termination. To achieve the latter, a con-

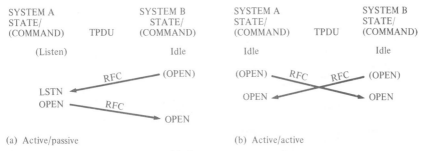

FIGURE 12.7. Connection establishment sequence of events.

nection in the CLS WAIT state must continue to accept data TPDUs until a CLS is received.

Reliable Nonsequencing Network Service

In this case, we assume that the network service will accept messages of arbitrary length and will, with virtually 100% reliability, deliver them to the destination. However, we now assume that the TPDUs may arrive out of sequence. This seemingly trivial change has a number of consequences.

The first consequence is that sequence numbers are required on TPDUs for connection-oriented service. We employ them with a reliable sequencing network service for flow control purposes. Here they are required to permit the transport entity to deliver data in sequence.

Equally important, the transport entity must keep track of control TPDUs, both in relationship to each other and to data TPDUs. Examples of this requirement are seen in flow control and in connection establishment and termination.

First, consider flow control. A transport entity may sometimes find it desirable to decrease outstanding offered credit on a connection, because expected resources did not become available, or because resources had to be reallocated to serve another connection. If sequencing is not guaranteed, a situation such as that shown in Figure 12.8 might arise. After transport entity A has sent TPDU 1, B responds with a new credit allocation of 5. A short time later, and before additional TPDUs arrive, B discovers a potential shortfall and sends a reduced credit allocation of 3. However, this allocation overtakes the earlier one and arrives first. It appears to A that B has initially granted an allocation of 3 and then obtained additional resources, and increased the allocation to 5. Thus, while B is not prepared to receive any more TPDUs at this point, A feels entitled to send two additional TPDUs. The solution to this problem is to number credit allocations sequentially.

Now consider connection establishment. Figure 12.6 shows that after a transport entity has sent an RFC, it expects to receive either a CLS (connection reject) or RFC (connection accept) from the target entity. The target transport

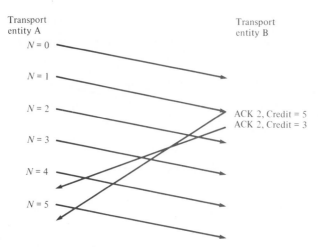

FIGURE 12.8. Example of flow control with a nonse-
quenced network service.

entity, having received the opening RFC, might respond with RFC, followed
by a number of TPDUs. One of these TPDUs could arrive back at the initiating
entity prior to the RFC. The best policy would seem to be for the initiating
transport entity to queue these TPDUs until the RFC is received that confirms
the connection.

Just as data may arrive before a connection is officially open, they may also
arrive after the connection has closed. The following may occur. After a transport entity has sent its last data TPDU, it sends a CLS. The CLS may arrive
before the last data TPDU. One way to avoid a problem is for the CLS TPDU
to contain the next sequence number after the last data TPDU sent on this
connection. Then, the receiving transport entity, upon receiving a CLS, will
wait if necessary for late-arriving data TPDUs before closing the connection.

Reliable Nonsequencing Network
Service with Maximum TPDU Size

We now add another limitation to the capability of the network service: It will
only accept TPDUs of some maximum size for transfer. Presumably, this size
is chosen to optimize network performance.

We need to distinguish two types of data transfer required by the user:
stream oriented and block oriented. A stream-oriented interface between transport and the user accepts data as if they were a continuous stream of bits and
reproduces the stream at the other end without conveying any information
about the breakpoints in the stream submitted by the sender. This interface
might serve voice and real-time applications.

A more common occurrence is a transport user that sends data in blocks.
For convenience, we refer to a block of data presented to transport as a *letter*.
If a letter exceeds the maximum allowable TPDU size, the transport entity must

segment the letter before transmission, to be reassembled at reception prior to delivery to the user. Because our network is nonsequencing, segments may arrive out of order. Worse, segments from different letters may be interchanged en route.

A simple solution to this problem is to number each letter sequentially and to number each segment sequentially within each letter. This, however, is an unnecessary duplication of the TPDU sequence numbering function. A moment's thought should make it clear that all that is required is an end-of-letter (EOL) flag. As TPDUs arrive at the destination transport entity, they are reordered. Each sequential set of TPDUs, starting with the first TPDU after an EOL, and including all TPDUs through the next EOL, are treated as a unit. The data from this unit, stripped of transport headers, are delivered as a single letter to the user.

A variation on the foregoing approach is to apply the sequence numbers to the data rather than the TPDUs. An example of this was discussed in Chapter 11, namely the segmentation and reassembly technique for IP.

Failure-Prone Network Service

We now turn to what may strike the reader as an unusual sort of network service. This is a connection-oriented network service and, while it delivers data reliably (though not necessarily in sequence), it suffers from network failures that cause it to reset or restart network connections. Thus TPDUs may be lost, but the loss is reported to the transport entities affected. The reader might visualize an X.25 network service being provided by a relatively unreliable underlying network.

In any case, the transport entity must now cope with the problem of recovering from known loss of data and/or network connections. The sequence numbering scheme provides an effective tool. In the normal course of events, TPDUs need not be acknowledged, since the network service is reliable. However, acknowledgment takes place from time to time in connection with the flow control scheme. We show this mechanism also deals with network failure.

First, consider a connection reset, such as the X.25 RESET command will cause. The network service will signal the transport entity that a reset has occurred on one or more transport connections. The transport entity realizes that it has perhaps lost some incoming TPDUs in transit, and that some already-transmitted TPDUs may not reach their destination. Two actions are indicated:

- Issue a control TPDU to the other end that acknowledges a reset condition and gives the number of the last TPDU received.
- Refrain from issuing new data TPDUs until a corresponding reset control TPDU is received from the other end.

A more serious condition is the loss of an underlying network connection, such as an X.25 RESTART causes. In this case, the side that first initiated the connection should issue a request to the network service for a new network connection and then issue a control TPDU to the other side that identifies the new network connection for the ongoing transport connection. Following this, both sides must resynchronize with the use of reset control TPDUs.

Unreliable Network Service

The most difficult case for a transport protocol is that of an unreliable network service. The problem is not just that TPDUs are occasionally lost, but that TPDUs may arrive out of sequence due to variable transit delays. As we shall see, elaborate machinery is required to cope with these two interrelated network deficiencies. We shall also see that a discouraging pattern emerges. The combination of unreliability and nonsequencing creates problems with every mechanism we have discussed so far. Generally, the solution to each problem raises new problems. Although there are problems to be overcome for protocols at all levels, it seems that there are more difficulties with a reliable connection-oriented transport protocol than any other sort of protocol.

Six issues need to be addressed:

- Retransmission strategy.
- Duplicate detection.
- Flow control.
- Connection establishment.
- Connection termination.
- Crash recovery.

Retransmission Strategy

Two events necessitate the retransmission of a TPDU. First, the TPDU may be damaged in transit but nevertheless arrive at its destination. If a frame check sequence is included with the TPDU, the receiving transport entity can detect the error and discard the TPDU. The second contingency is that a TPDU fails to arrive. In either case, the sending transport entity does not know that the TPDU transmission was unsuccessful. To cover this contingency, we require that a positive acknowledgment (ACK) scheme be used: The receiver must acknowledge each successfully received TPDU. For efficiency, we do not require one ACK per TPDU. Rather, a cumulative acknowledgment can be used, as we have seen many times in this book. Thus the receiver may receive TPDUs numbered 1, 2, and 3, but only send ACK 3 back. The sender must interpret ACK 3 to mean that number 3 and all previous TPDUs have been successfully received.

If a TPDU does not arrive successfully, no ACK will be issued and a retransmission is in order. To cope with this situation, there must be a timer associated with each TPDU as it is sent. If the timer expires before the TPDU is acknowledged, the sender must retransmit.

So the addition of a timer solves that problem. Next problem: At what value should the timer be set? If the value is too small, there will be many unnecessary retransmissions, wasting network capacity. If the value is too large, the protocol will be sluggish in responding to a lost TPDU. The timer should be set at a value a bit longer than the round trip delay (send TPDU, receive ACK). Of course this delay is variable even under constant network load. Worse, the statistics of the delay will vary with changing network conditions.

Two strategies suggest themselves. A fixed timer value could be used, based on an understanding of the network's typical behavior. This suffers from an inability to respond to changing network conditions. If the value is set too high, the service will always be sluggish. If it is set too low, a positive feedback condition can develop, in which network congestion leads to more retransmissions, which increase congestion.

An adaptive scheme has its own problems [ZHAN86]. Suppose that the transport entity keeps track of the time taken to acknowledge data TPDUs and sets its retransmission timer based on the average of the observed delays. This value cannot be trusted for three reasons:

- The peer entity may not acknowledge a TPDU immediately. Recall that we gave it the privilege of cumulative acknowledgments.
- If a TPDU has been retransmitted, the sender cannot know whether the received ACK is a response to the initial transmission or the retransmission.
- Network conditions may change suddenly.

Each of these problems is a cause for some further tweaking of the transport algorithm, but the problem admits of no complete solution. There will always be some uncertainty concerning the best value for the retransmission timer.

Incidentally, the retransmission timer is only one of a number of timers needed for proper functioning of a transport protocol. These are listed in Table 12.1, together with a brief explanation. Further discussion will be found in what follows.

Duplicate Detection

If a TPDU is lost and then retransmitted, no confusion will result. If however, an ACK is lost, one or more TPDUs will be retransmitted and, if they arrive successfully, be duplicates of previously received TPDUs. Thus the receiver must be able to recognize duplicates. The fact that each TPDU carries a se-

TABLE 12.1 Transport Protocol Timers

Retransmission timer	Retransmit an unacknowledged TPDU
Reconnection timer	Minimum time between closing one connection and opening another with the same destination address
Window timer	Maximum time between ACK/CREDIT TPDUs
Retransmit-RFC timer	Time between attempts to open a connection
Persistence timer	Abort connection when no TPDUs are acknowledged
Inactivity timer	Abort connection when no TPDUs are received

quence number helps but, nevertheless, duplicate detection and handling is no easy thing. There are two cases:

- A duplicate is received prior to the close of the connection.
- A duplicate is received after the close of the connection.

Notice that we say "a" duplicate rather than "the" duplicate. From the sender's point of view, the retransmitted TPDU is the duplicate. However, the retransmitted TPDU may arrive before the original TPDU, in which case the receiver views the original TPDU as the duplicate. In any case, two tactics are needed to cope with a duplicate received prior to the close of a connection:

- The receiver must assume that its acknowledgment was lost and therefore must acknowledge the duplicate. Consequently, the sender must not get confused if it receives multiple ACKs to the same TPDU.
- The sequence number space must be long enough so as not to "cycle" in less than the maximum possible TPDU lifetime.

Figure 12.9 illustrates the reason for the latter requirement. In this example, the sequence space is of length 8. For simplicity, we assume a sliding-window protocol with a window size of 3. Suppose that A has transmitted data TPDUs 0, 1, and 2 and receives no acknowledgments. Eventually, it times out and retransmits TPDU 0. B has received 1 and 2, but 0 is delayed in transit. Thus B does not send any ACKs. When the duplicate TPDU 0 arrives, B acknowledges 0, 1, and 2. Meanwhile, A has timed out again and retransmits 1, which B acknowledges with another ACK 2. Things now seem to have sorted themselves out and data transfer continues. When the sequence space is exhausted, A cycles back to sequence number 0 and continues. Alas, the old TPDU 0 makes a belated appearance and is accepted by B before the new TPDU 0 arrives.

It should be clear that the untimely emergence of the old TPDU would have caused no difficulty if the sequence numbers had not yet wrapped around. The problem is: How big must the sequence space be? This depends on, among other things, whether the network enforces a maximum packet lifetime, and the rate at which TPDUs are being transmitted. Fortunately, each addition of a single bit to the sequence number field doubles the sequence space, so it is rather easy to select a safe size. As we shall see, the standard transport protocols allow stupendous sequence spaces.

A more subtle problem is posed by TPDUs that continue to rattle around after a transport connection is closed. If a subsequent connection is opened between the same two transport entities, a TPDU from the old connection could arrive and be accepted on the new connection! Similarly, a delayed ACK can enter a new connection and cause problems.

There are a number of approaches to this particular problem. We mention several of the more promising. First, the sequence numbering scheme can be extended across connection lifetimes. This requires that a transport entity remember the last sequence number that it used on transmission for each terminated connection. Then, when a new connection to a transport entity is

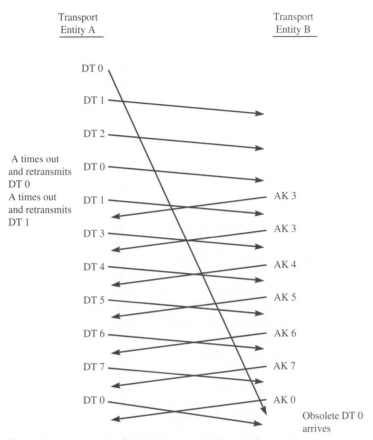

FIGURE 12.9.   Example of incorrect duplicate detection.

attempted, the RFC contains the sequence number to be used to begin data transfer. Of course, this procedure is symmetric, with each side responsible for declaring the sequence number with which it will commence transmission.

A second approach is to provide a separate transport connection identifier, and use a new identifier with each new connection.

The procedures above work fine unless a system crash occurs. In that case, the system will not remember what sequence number or connection identifier was used last. An alternative is to simply wait a sufficient time between connections to assure that all old TPDUs are gone. Then, even if one side has experienced a crash, the other side can refuse a connection until the reconnection timer expires. This, of course, may cause unnecessary delays.

Flow Control

The credit allocation flow control mechanism described earlier is quite robust in the face of an unreliable network service and requires little enhancement.

We assume that the credit allocation scheme is tied to acknowledgments in the following way: To both acknowledge TPDUs and grant credit, a transport entity sends a control TPDU of the form (ACK N, CREDIT M), where ACK N acknowledges all data TPDUs through number N, and CREDIT M allows TPDUs number N + 1 though N + M to be transmitted. This mechanism is quite powerful. Consider that the last control TPDU issued by B was (ACK N, CREDIT M). Then:

- To increase or decrease credit to X when no additional TPDUs have arrived, B can issue (ACK N, CREDIT X).
- To acknowledge a new TPDU without increasing credit, B can issue (ACK N + 1, CREDIT M − 1).

If an ACK/CREDIT TPDU is lost, little harm is done. Future acknowledgments will resynchronize the protocol. Further, if no new acknowledgments are forthcoming, the sender times out and retransmits a data TPDU, which triggers a new acknowledgment. However, it is still possible for deadlock to occur. Consider a situation in which B sends (ACK N, CREDIT 0), temporarily closing the window. Subsequently, B sends (ACK N, CREDIT M), but this TPDU is lost. A is awaiting the opportunity to send data and B thinks that it has granted that opportunity. To overcome this problem, a window timer can be used. This timer is reset with each outgoing ACK/CREDIT TPDU. If the timer ever expires, the protocol entity is required to send an ACK/CREDIT TPDU, even if it duplicates a previous one. This breaks the deadlock and also assures the other end that the protocol entity is still alive.

An alternative or supplemental mechanism is to provide for acknowledgments to the ACK/CREDIT TPDU. With this mechanism in place, the window timer can have a quite large value without causing much difficulty.

Connection Establishment

As with other protocol mechanisms, connection establishment must take into account the unreliability of a network service. Recall that a connection establishment calls for the exchange of RFCs, a procedure sometimes referred to as a *two-way handshake*. Suppose that A issues an RFC to B. It expects to get an RFC back, confirming the connection. Two things can go wrong: A's RFC can be lost or B's answering RFC can be lost. Both cases can be handled by use of a retransmit-RFC timer. After A issues an RFC, it will reissue the RFC when the timer expires.

This gives rise, potentially, to duplicate RFCs. If A's initial RFC was lost, there are no duplicates. If B's response was lost, then B may receive two RFCs from A. Further, if B's response was not lost, but simply delayed, A may get two responding RFCs. All of this means that A and B must simply ignore duplicate RFCs once a connection is established.

Now, consider that a duplicate RFC may survive past the termination of the connection. Figure 12.10 depicts the problem that may arise. An old RFC X

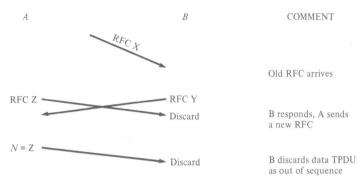

FIGURE 12.10. Example of a two-way handshake.

(request for connection, sequence number begins at X) arrives at B after the connection is terminated. B assumes that this is a fresh request and responds with RFC Y. Meanwhile, A has decided to open a new connection with B and sends RFC Z. B discards this as a duplicate. Subsequently, A initiates data transfer with a TPDU numbered Z. B rejects the TPDU as being out of sequence.

The way out of this problem is for each side to acknowledge explicitly the other's RFC and sequence number. The procedure is known as a *three-way handshake* [TOML75]. The revised connection state diagram is shown in the upper part of Figure 12.11. A new state (RFC Received) is added. In this state, the transport entity hesitates during connection opening to assure that any RFC which was sent has also been acknowledged before the connection is declared open. In addition to the new state, there is a new control TPDU (RST) to reset the other side when a duplicate RFC is detected.

Figure 12.12 illustrates typical three-way handshake operations. Under normal conditions, an RFC includes the sending sequence number. The responding RFC acknowledges that number and includes the sequence number for the other side. The initiating transport entity acknowledges the RFC/ACK in its first data TPDU. Next is shown a situation in which an old RFC X arrives at B after the close of the relevant connection. B assumes that this is a fresh request and responds with RFC Y, ACK X. When A receives this message, it realizes that it has not requested a connection and therefore sends a RST, ACK Y. Note that the ACK Y portion of the RST message is essential so that an old duplicate RST does not abort a legitimate connection establishment. The final example shows a case in which an old RFC, ACK arrives in the middle of a new connection establishment. Because of the use of sequence numbers in the acknowledgments, this event causes no mischief.

The upper part of Figure 12.11 does not include transitions in which RST is sent. This was done for simplicity. The basic rule is: Send an RST if connection state is not yet OPEN and an invalid ACK (one which does not reference something that was sent) is received. The reader should try various combinations of

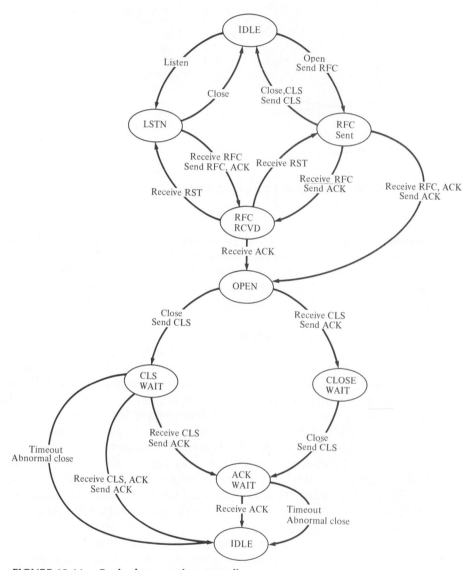

FIGURE 12.11.   Revised connection state diagram.

events to see that this connection establishment procedure works in spite of any combination of old and lost TPDUs.

Connection Termination

As with connection establishment, the connection termination procedure must cope with old and lost control TPDUs. Figure 12.11 indicates that a similar

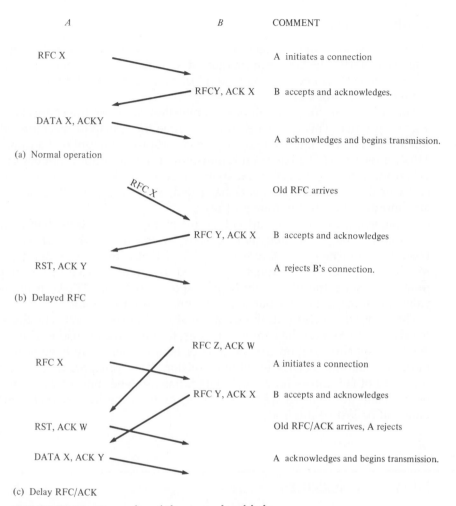

FIGURE 12.12. Examples of three-way handshake.

solution is adopted. Each side must explicitly acknowledge the CLS TPDU of the other. To avoid confusion, sequence numbers are used as follows:

- CLS contains the sequence number plus one of the last data TPDU sent.
- ACK contains the sequence number received in the CLS.

Timeout procedures are included to allow a transport entity to complete its closing if the other side appears uncooperative. The problem may be lost TPDUs rather than a failure at the other end. Therefore, one or more retransmissions are advisable before signaling an abnormal close.

Crash Recovery

When the system upon which a transport entity is running fails and subsequently restarts, the state information of all active connections is lost. The affected connections become "half-open" since the side that did not fail does not yet realize the problem.

The still active side of a half-open connection can close the connection using a give-up timer. This timer measures the time the transport machine will continue to await an acknowledgment (or other appropriate reply) of a transmitted TPDU after the TPDU has been retransmitted the maximum number of times. When the timer expires, the transport entity assumes that the other transport entity or the intervening network has failed, closes the connection, and signals an abnormal close to the transport user.

In the event that a transport entity fails and quickly restarts, half-open connections can be terminated more quickly by the use of the RST TPDU. The failed side returns a RST X to every TPDU X that it receives. When the RST X reaches the other side, it must be checked for validity based on the sequence number X, since the RST could be in response to an old TPDU. If the reset is valid, the transport entity performs an abnormal termination.

These measures clean up the situation at the transport level. The decision as to whether to reopen the connection is up to the transport users. The problem is one of synchronization. At the time of failure, there may have been one or more outstanding TPDUs in either direction. The transport user on the side that did not fail knows how much data it has received, but the other user may not, if state information were lost. Thus, there is the danger that some user data will be lost or duplicated.

12.3

NETWORK SERVICES

To function, a transport protocol must make use of the services of some lower-level network-oriented protocol, such as X.25 or IP. In this section we look first at the primitives that might be used to implement the transport/network interface, and then discuss the relationship of these primitives to the types of network service provided.

Service Primitives

Table 12.2 lists a set of primitives that might be used to provide a network service to a transport entity. This list is based on that specified by ISO [WARE83].

At minimum, the network service must provide a means of delivering TPDUs to a remote correspondent. The transport entity uses N-DATA.request to transfer data to the network service for transmission. The network ser-

TABLE 12.2 Network Service Primitives

Required:

N-DATA.request ([to network address]; [from network address]; data)
N-DATA.indication ([to network address]; [from network address]; data)

Required for connection-oriented service:

N-CONNECT.request (to network address; from network address; security; quality of service)
N-CONNECT.indication (to network address; from network address; security; quality of service)
N-CONNECT.response ( )
N-CONNECT.confirm ( )
N-DISCONNECT.request ( )
N-DISCONNECT.indication ( )

Additional Useful Primitives:

N-DATA-ACKNOWLEDGE.request ( )
N-DATA-ACKNOWLEDGE.indication ( )
N-EXPEDITED-DATA.request (data)
N-EXPEDITED-DATA.indication (data)
N-RESET.request ( )
N-RESET.indication ( )
N-RESET.response ( )
N-RESET.confirmation ( )

vice passes up received data using N-DATA.indication. If the service is not connection-oriented, address information must be included in the primitive invocation.

If the network service is connection-oriented, additional primitives are needed: N-CONNECT.request signals a request by a transport entity to open a connection. N-CONNECT.indication presents this request to the correspondent transport entity identified in the connection request. A transport entity signals its willingness to accept the connection with N-CONNECT.response. This willingness is communicated to the initiating transport entity with N-CONNECT.confirm. N-DISCONNECT.request and N-DISCONNECT.indication are used to terminate a connection. Please note that these primitives are concerned with the establishment and termination of a network connection (e.g., an X.25 virtual circuit) between two transport entities. These entities may then use this connection to establish one or more transport connections on behalf of transport users.

Additional primitives may be provided by the network service. Although not strictly necessary, these primitives enhance the capability and efficiency of the transport protocol. The N-DATA-ACKNOWLEDGE primitives permit the local exercise of flow control across the transport/network interface in both directions. N-EXPEDITED-DATA provides direct support of the transport expedited data feature. Finally, the N-RESET primitives allow the transport entity to force a reset of the network connection.

Relationship to Type of Network

It is important to realize that there is not a unique correspondence between reliability and whether a network service is connection oriented. A connection-oriented service might be reliable, in which case the techniques described above for a reliable sequencing network service would suffice for the transport protocol. On the other hand, the service might be unreliable, calling for a far more complex transport protocol.

Similarly, an unreliable connectionless service will require a complex transport protocol. However, if the connectionless service is reliable, the transport mechanisms associated with a reliable nonsequencing network service will be adequate.

12.4

THE ISO TRANSPORT STANDARDS

In this section we look at a family of transport protocols developed by ISO as an international standard [ISO86a,b]. This protocol family seems destined to achieve near-universal acceptance outside DOD.

The Transport Protocol Family

In order to handle a variety of user service requirements and available network services, ISO has defined five classes of transport protocol:

- *Class 0:* simple class.
- *Class 1:* basic error recovery class.
- *Class 2:* multiplexing class.
- *Class 3:* error recovery and multiplexing class.
- *Class 4:* error detection and recovery class.

These classes are related to the three types of network service defined in Section 12.2 as follows. Classes 0 and 2 are used with Type A networks; Classes 1 and 3 are used with Type B networks; and Class 4 is used with Type C networks. Table 12.3 lists the functions of the various protocol classes.

Class 0 was developed by CCITT and is oriented for teletex, a text-transmission upgrade to Telex. It provides the simplest kind of transport connection. It provides a connection with flow control based on network-level flow control, and connection release based on the release of the network connection.

Class 1 was also developed by CCITT and is designed to run on an X.25 network and provide minimal error recovery (network-signaled errors). The

TABLE 12.3   Functions of ISO Transport Protocol Classes[a]

Protocol Mechanism	Variant	0	1	2	3	4
Assignment to network connection		*	*	*	*	*
TPDU transfer		*	*	*	*	*
Segmenting and reassembling		*	*	*	*	*
Concatenation and separation			*	*	*	*
Connection establishment		*	*	*	*	*
Connection refusal		*	*	*	*	*
Normal release	Implicit	*				
	Explicit		*	*	*	*
Error release		*		*		
Association of TPDUs with transport connection		*	*	*	*	*
DT TPDU numbering	Normal	*	m(1)	m	m	
	Extended		o(1)	o	o	
Expedited data transfer	Network normal		m	(1)	*	*
	Network expedited		ao			
Reassignment after failure			*		*	
Retention until acknowledgment of TPDUs	Conf. receipt		ao			
	AK		m		*	*
Resynchronization			*		*	
Multiplexing and demultiplexing				*	*	*
Explicit flow control	With			m	*	*
	Without	*	*	o		
Checksum	Use of					*
	Nonuse of	*	*	*	*	o
Frozen references			*		*	*
Retransmission on timeout						*
Resequencing						*
Inactivity control						*
Treatment of protocol errors		*	*	*	*	*
Splitting and recombining						*

[a]Symbols used in this table are as follows:

*Procedure always included in class.

[m]Negotiable procedure whose implementation in equipment is mandatory.

[o]Negotiable procedure whose implementation in equipment is optional.

[ao]Negotiable procedure whose implementation in equipment is optional and where use depends on availability within the network service.

(1)Not applicable in Class 2 when nonuse of explicit flow control is selected.

key difference from Class 0 is that TPDUs are numbered. This allows the protocol to resynchronize after an X.25 RESET and to reassign a transport connection after an X.25 RESTART. Flow control is still provided by the network layer. Expedited data transfer is also provided.

Class 2 is an enhancement to Class 0 that still assumes a highly reliable network service. The key enhancement is the ability to multiplex multiple transport connections onto a single network connection. A corollary enhancement is the provision of explicit flow control, since a single network connection flow control mechanism does not allow individual flow control of transport connections. A credit allocation scheme is used.

Class 3 is basically the union of the Class 1 and 2 capabilities. It provides the multiplexing and flow control capabilities of Class 2. It also contains the resynchronization and reassignment capabilities of Class 1, which are needed to cope with failure-prone networks.

Class 4 assumes that the underlying network service is unreliable. Thus most if not all of the mechanisms described in Section 12.2 must be included.

Transport Services

The transport service specification is the same for all classes. This is to be expected, since one of the main points of the transport service is to provide end-to-end data transfer independent of the nature of the underlying network. The ISO specification is in the form of just four primitive types and 10 primitives. These are listed in Table 12.4. Figure 12.13 displays the sequences in which these primitives are used. (*Note:* The use of $\sim$ indicates the lack of a defined time relationship between two primitives.)

TABLE 12.4   ISO Transport Service Primitives

T-CONNECT.request (Called Address, Calling Address, Expedited Data Option, Quality of Service, Data)

T-CONNECT.indication (Called Address, Calling Address, Expedited Data Option, Quality of Service, Data)

T-CONNECT.response (Quality of Service, Responding Address, Expedited Data Option, Data)

T-CONNECT.confirm (Quality of Service, Responding Address, Expedited Data Option, Data)

T-DISCONNECT.request (Data)
T-DISCONNECT.indication (Disconnect Reason, Data)

T-DATA.request (Data)
T-DATA.indication (Data)

T-EXPEDITED-DATA.request (Data)
T-EXPEDITED-DATA.indication (Data)

FIGURE 12.13.   ISO transport services—primitive sequences.

The first two primitive types are concerned with connection management. The T-CONNECT primitives are used to establish a connection. Quality of service refers to certain characteristics of a transport connection as observed between the endpoints. The term actually refers to a collection of parameters, having to do with speed or accuracy/reliability characteristics during the three phases of a connection (Table 12.5). The transport entity will either provide the requested quality of service, or indicate in the indication and confirm primitives a lesser quality of service that can be provided. The quality-of-service parameters related to performance are

- *Establishment delay:* maximum acceptable delay between a T-CONNECT.request and the corresponding T-CONNECT.confirm.
- *Establishment failure probability:* acceptable proportion of connection establishment attempts that fail.
- *Throughput:* maximum and average throughput values that the user expects to produce.
- *Transit delay:* maximum and average delay values desired.
- *Residual error rate:* desired maximum rate of lost data units.
- *Transfer failure probability:* probability that the actual performance will be

TABLE 12.5   Classification of Quality-of-Service Parameters

Phase	Performance Criterion	
	Speed	Accuracy/Reliability
TC establishment	TC establishment delay	TC establishment failure probability
Data transfer	Throughput Transit delay	Residual error rate Resilience of the TC Transfer failure probability
TC release	TC release delay	TC release failure probability

worse than the expected performance for throughput, transit delay, and residual error rate.

- *Release delay:* maximum acceptable delay between issuance of T-DISCONNECT.request and the successful release of the connection at the peer transport user.
- *Release failure probability:* probability that the release delay will exceed the requested maximum.
- *Resilience:* probability of a connection release initiated by the transport service provider.

In addition, there are two other quality-of-service parameters:

- *Protection:* protection of a connection against passive monitoring and/or modification, replay, addition, or deletion.
- *Priority:* specifies the relative priority of connections with respect to (1) the order in which connections have their quality of service downgraded, if necessary and (2) the order in which connections are broken to recover resources, if necessary.

T-DISCONNECT provides for an abrupt connection termination. Termination can be initiated by either side or by one of the transport entities. T-DISCONNECT can also be used by the local transport entity or the remote addressee to reject a connection attempt.

The remaining primitives are concerned with data transfer. T-DATA and T-EXPEDITED data are used to transfer data over a transport connection. The latter attempts to expedite delivery of the data.

Protocol Formats

The ISO protocol [ISO86a] makes use of 10 types of transport protocol data units (TPDUs):

- Connection request (CR).
- Connection confirm (CC).
- Disconnect request (DR).
- Disconnect confirm (DC).
- Data (DT).
- Expedited data (ED).
- Acknowledgment (AK).
- Expedited acknowledgment (EA).
- Reject (RJ).
- TPDU error (ER).

By this time, the use of these TPDUs should be self-explanatory. In this section we confine ourselves to a discussion of the formats and field values of the various TPDUs. In the next subsection, we discuss the protocol mechanisms that are implemented with these TPDU types.

Each TPDU consists of three parts: a fixed header, a variable header, and a data field. The latter two optionally may not be present in a TPDU. The fixed header contains the frequently occurring parameters (Figure 12.14), and the variable header contains optional or infrequently occurring parameters (Table 12.5).

The fixed headers of the various TPDU types are similar. The fields, not all of which occur in all types, can be defined briefly:

- *Length indicator (LI) (8 bits):* length of the header (fixed plus variable) excluding the LI field, in octets.
- *TPDU code (4 bits):* type of TPDU.
- *Credit (CDT) (4 bits):* flow control credit allocation. Initial credit is granted in CR and CC, subsequent credit is granted in AK. As an option, a 16-bit credit field is used with AK, and is appended after the YR-TU-NR field.
- *Source reference (16 bits):* reference used by the transport entity to identify the transport connection uniquely in its own system.
- *Destination reference (16 bits):* reference used by the peer transport entity to identify the transport connection uniquely in its own system.
- *Class (4 bits):* protocol class.
- *Option (4 bits):* specifies normal (7-bit sequence number, 4-bit credit) or extended (31-bit sequence number, 16-bit credit) flow control fields. Also specifies whether explicit flow control is to be used in Class 2.
- *Reason (8 bits):* reason for requesting a disconnect or rejecting a connection request. The reasons are listed in Table 12.6.
- *EOT (1 bit):* used when a block of user data has been segmented into multiple TPDUs. It is set to 1 on the last TPDU.
- *TPDU-NR (7 bits):* send sequence number of a DT TPDU. It is normally modulo 2^7, but may be extended by three octets to be modulo 2^{31}.
- *EDTPDU-NR (7 bits):* send sequence number of a ED TPDU.

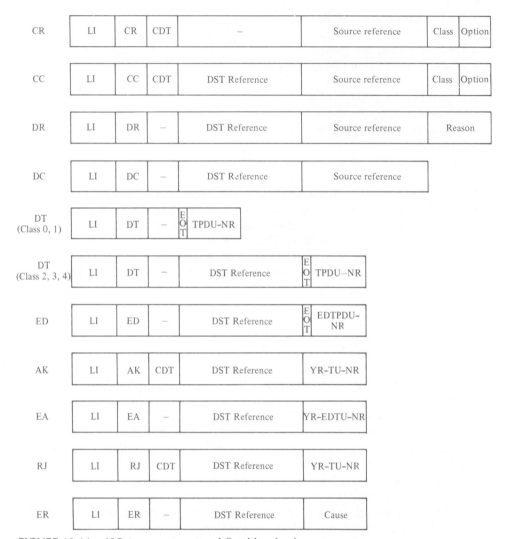

FIGURE 12.14.   ISO transport protocol fixed header formats.

- *YR-TU-NR (8 bits):* the next expected DT sequence number.
- *YR-EDTU-NR (8 bits):* the next expected ED sequence number.
- *Cause (8 bits):* reason for rejection of a TPDU (Table 12.6).

The variable header consists of a sequence of additional parameters. Each parameter field consists of three subfields: a parameter code (8 bits), a parameter length (8 bits), and the parameter value (one or more octets). Most of the parameters are used by CC and CR in the connection establishment process. The parameters are:

TABLE 12.6   ISO Transport Protocol Variable Header Parameters[a]

	CR	CC	DR	DC	DT	ED	AK	EA	RT	ER
Calling TSAP ID	X	X								
Called TSAP ID	X	X								
TPDU size	X	X								
Version number	X	X								
Security parameter	X	X								
Checksum	4	4	4	4	4	4	4	4	4	
Additional option selection	X	X								
Alternative protocol class	X	X								
Acknowledge time	4	4								
Throughput	X	X								
Residual error rate	X	X								
Priority	X	X								
Transmit delay	X	X								
Reassignment time	1, 3	1, 3								
Additional information				X						
Subsequence number							4			
Flow control confirmation							4			
Invalid TPDU										X

[a]4, class 4 only; 1, 3, classes 1 and 3 only.

- *Calling TSAP ID:* service access point that identifies the calling transport user.
- *Called TSAP ID:* service access point that identifies the called transport user.
- *TPDU size:* maximum TPDU size in octets. The range of options is from 128 to 8192 in powers of 2.
- *Version number:* version of protocol to be followed. This accommodates future revisions to the standard.
- *Security parameter:* user-defined.
- *Checksum:* result of checksum algorithm (defined in an appendix to chapter 14) for the entire TPDU. The checksum is used only for Class 4 and, within that class, it is mandatory for all CR TPDUs, and for all TPDUs when the checksum option is selected.
- *Additional option selection:* used to specify use or nonuse of certain options (Table 12.7).
- *Alternative protocol class:* specifies whether only the requested protocol class is acceptable, or that some other class is also acceptable.
- *Acknowledge time:* an estimate of the time taken by the entity to acknowledge a DT TPDU. This helps the other entity select a value for its retransmission timer.
- *Throughput:* specifies the user's throughput requirements in octets per second. Eight values are specified: the target and minimum acceptable values for both maximum throughput and average throughput; in both the calling-called direction and the called-calling direction.

TABLE 12.7   ISO Transport Parameter Values

Reason for Disconnect Request	Reason for TPDU Error
Not specified	Not specified
Congestion at TSAP	Invalid parameter code
Session entity not attached to TSAP	Invalid TPDU error
Address unknown	Invalid parameter value
Normal user-initiated disconnect	
Remote transport entity congestion	**Negotiated Options**
Connection negotiation failed	Network expedited in Class 1
Duplicate source reference	Acknowledgment in Class 1
Mismatch references	Checksum in Class 4
Protocol error	Transport expedited data service
Reference overflow	
Request refused on this network connection	
Header or parameter length invalid	

- *Residual error rate:* expresses the target and minimum rate of unreported user data loss.
- *Priority:* priority of this connection.
- *Transit delay:* specifies the user's delay requirements in milliseconds. Four values are specified: the target and maximum acceptable transit delay in both directions.
- *Reassignment time:* amount of time an entity will persist in attempts to reconnect after a network connection is broken.
- *Additional information:* related to the clearing of the connection. User defined.
- *Subsequence number:* number of the AK. It is used to assure that AKs with the same YR-TU-NR are processed in correct sequence.
- *Flow control confirmation:* echoes parameter values in the last AK TPDU received. It contains the values of the YR-TU-NR, CDT, and Subsequence Number fields.
- *Invalid TPDU:* the bit pattern of the rejected TPDU up to and including the octet that caused the rejection.

Protocol Mechanisms

The purpose of this section is to highlight the key transport protocol mechanisms. Much of what was discussed in Section 12.2 is applicable, so only a brief commentary is provided. The following topics are considered:

- Connection establishment.
- Data transfer.
- Connection termination.

Connection Establishment

The connection establishment phase requires, at minimum, the exchange of a CR and a CC TPDU. This two-way handshake suffices for Classes 0 through 3. For Class 4, a third TPDU is needed to acknowledge the CC; this may be an AK, DT, or ED.

The purpose of this phase is to establish a transport connection with agreed-upon characteristics. If the establishment attempt is successful, these characteristics are defined by the parameters of the CC. Prior to success, there may be a period of negotiation. In some cases, the calling entity specifies options (e.g., other classes are acceptable), and the called entity selects one in the CC. In other cases, the calling entity proposes a value (e.g., maximum TPDU size), and the calling entity may accept it (CC) or reject it (DR). The parameters involved in this latter process are listed in Table 12.5.

A transport connection involves four different types of identifiers:

- User identifier (service access point).
- Transport/network address.
- Transport protocol identifier.
- Transport connection identifier.

Since there may be more than one user of the transport entity, a user identifier is needed to allow the transport entity to multiplex data transfers to multiple users. This identifier must be passed down from the transport user, and included in CC and CR TPDUs. The transport/network address identifies the station on which the transport entity is located. This address, or a corresponding name, is passed down from the transport user. The address is not needed in any TPDU, but must be passed down to the network protocol entity for its use. Normally, there will be only one transport protocol entity in a station. However, more than one entity, each of a different type, might be resident in one station. In the latter case, the protocol must be identified to the network service. We saw this facility in use in IP. Finally, each transport connection is given a unique identifier (similar to an X.25 virtual-circuit number) by each of the two transport entities involved. This identifier is used in all TPDUs. It allows the transport entity to multiplex multiple transport connections on a single network connection.

Data Transfer

Normal data transfer over a connection is accomplished using DTs. Each data unit may be self contained. Alternatively, if the user data plus DT header exceeds the maximum TPDU size, the transport entity may segment the letter and send it out as a sequence of TPDUs. The last TPDU in sequence has the EOT bit set.

DTs are numbered sequentially. This is used in Classes 2 through 4 for flow control. A credit-allocation scheme is used. The initial credit is set in the CC and CR TPDUs. Subsequent credit is granted with an AK. Note that acknowledgments are in separate TPDUs, and never piggybacked onto DTs. At first glance, this might seem inefficient since an entire TPDU is needed for flow control. This is not so for two reasons:

- The transport entity may choose not to acknowledge every single DT, but only acknowledge in bunches. Thus no overhead for piggybacking is wasted in the DT.
- A sort of piggybacking is possible. A transport entity may concatenate multiple TPDUs (e.g., a DT and an AK) into one unit to be passed to the network service. Thus several TPDUs will be efficiently handled as a single packet by the network.

In Class 4, sequence numbers are also used for resequencing DTs that arrive out of order. Another mechanism unique to Class 4 is the DT checksum. If an error is detected, an ER is returned. Other reasons for ER, for all classes, are listed in Table 12.5.

Expedited data transfer uses the ED and EA data units. Sequence numbers are used, but only one ED may be outstanding at a time. The sender must receive an EA before sending another ED. The reader may ask how a transport entity expedites data. The answer may strike some as clumsy and inefficient, but it is just one more example of the limitations and complexities with which a transport protocol must cope. In Classes 1 through 4, an ED is sent before any DTs queued for that connection. In Class 4, we must contend with the problem that being sent out first does not mean being delivered first. Therefore, the Class 4 entity suspends the transfer of new DTs (although pending DTs will go out) until an EA is received. In effect, the connection is shut down to accommodate this one piece of data.

Connection Termination

An abrupt termination is achieved by the exchange of a DR and a DC. When a transport entity receives a disconnect request from its user, it discards any pending DTs and issues the DR. The entity that receives the DR issues a DC, discards any pending DTs, and informs its user.

12.5

TCP and UDP

The TCP/IP protocol suite includes two transport-level protocols: the Transmission Control Protocol (TCP), which is connection-oriented, and the User Datagram Protocol (UDP), which is connectionless.

TCP Services

TCP is designed to provide reliable communication between pairs of processes (TCP users) across a variety of reliable and unreliable networks and internets. Functionally, it is equivalent to Class 4 ISO Transport [GROE86]. In contrast to the ISO model, TCP is stream oriented. That is, TCP users exchange streams of data. The data are placed in allocated buffers and transmitted by TCP in segments (TPDUs). TCP supports security and precedence labeling. In addition, TCP provides two useful facilities for labeling data: push and urgent:

- *Data stream push:* Ordinarily, TCP decides when sufficient data has accumulated to form a TPDU for transmission. The TCP user can require TCP to transmit all outstanding data up to and including that labeled with a push flag. On the receiving end, TCP will deliver these data to the user in the same manner. A user might request this if it has come to a logical break in the data.
- *Urgent data signaling:* This provides a means of informing the destination TCP user that significant or "urgent" data is in the upcoming data stream. It is up to the destination user to determine appropriate action.

Tables 12.8 and 12.9 list the TCP service request (user to TCP) and service response (TCP to user) primitives. Several comments are in order.

The two passive open commands correspond to the LISTEN command of Figure 12.11. They signal the user's willingness to accept a connection request. The active open with data is analogous to the X.25 fast select facility.

Source port and *destination port* are essentially transport service access points. *Destination address* identifies the network and station address of the remote TCP entity. *Timeout* permits the user to set up a timeout for all data submitted to TCP. If data are not successfully delivered within the timeout, TCP will abort the connection.

TCP Header Format

TCP uses only a single type of TPDU, called a TCP segment. The header is shown in Figure 12.15a. Because one header must serve to perform all protocol mechanisms, it is rather large. Whereas the ISO fixed header is from five to seven octets long, the TCP header is a minimum of 20 octets long. The fields are

- *Source port (16 bits):* identifies source service access point.
- *Destination port (16 bits):* identifies destination service access point.
- *Sequence number (32 bits):* sequence number of the first data octet in this segment except when SYN is present. If SYN is present, it is the initial sequence number (ISN) and the first data octet is ISN + 1.
- *Acknowledgment number (32 bits):* a piggybacked acknowledgment. Contains the sequence number of the next octet that the TCP entity expects to receive.
- *Data offset (4 bits):* number of 32-bit words in the header.

TABLE 12.8   TCP Service Request Primitives

UNSPECIFIED-PASSIVE-OPEN (source-port, [timeout], [timeout-action], [precedence], [security-range])

Listen for connection attempts at specified security and precedence levels from any remote user.

FULL-PASSIVE-OPEN (source-port, destination-port, destination-address, [timeout], [timeout-action], [precedence], [security-range])

Listen for connection attempts at specified security and precedence levels from specified user.

ACTIVE-OPEN (source-port, destination-port, destination-address, [timeout], [timeout-action], [precedence], [security])

Request connection at particular security and precedence levels.

ACTIVE-OPEN W/DATA (source-port, destination-port, destination-address, [timeout], [timeout-action], [precedence], [security], data, data-length, push-flag, urgent-flag)

Request connection at particular security and precedence levels and transmit data with the request.

SEND (local-connection-name, data, data length, push-flag, urgent-flag, [timeout], [timeout-action])

Causes data to be transferred across named connection.

ALLOCATE (local-connection-name, data length)

Issue incremental allocation for receive data to TCP.

CLOSE (local-connection-name)

Close connection gracefully.

ABORT (local-connection-name)

Close connection abruptly.

STATUS (local-connection-name)

Report connection status.

- *Reserved (6 bits):* reserved for future use.
- *Flags (6 bits):*
  URG: urgent pointer field significant.
  ACK: acknowledgment field significant.
  PSH: push function.
  RST: reset the connection.
  SYN: synchronize the sequence numbers.
  FIN: no more data from sender.
- *Window (16 bits):* flow control credit allocation, in octets. Contains the number of data octets beginning with the one indicated in the acknowledgment field which the sender is willing to accept.

TABLE 12.9 TCP Service Response Primitives

OPEN-ID (local-connection-name, source-port, destination-port, destination address)

Informs user of connection name assigned to pending connection requested in an OPEN primitive.

OPEN-FAILURE (local-connection-name)

Reports failure of an active OPEN request.

OPEN-SUCCESS (local-connection-name)

Reports completion of an active OPEN request.

DELIVER (local-connection-name, data, data-length, urgent-flag)

Reports arrival of data.

CLOSING (local-connection-name)

Reports that remote TCP user has issued a CLOSE.

TERMINATE (local-connection-name, description)

Reports that connection has been terminated and no longer exists.

STATUS-RESPONSE (local-connection-name, source-port, source-address, destination-port, destination-address, connection-state, receive-window, send-window, amount-waiting-ack, amount-waiting-receipt, urgent-state, precedence, security, timeout)

Reports current status of connection.

ERROR (local-connection-name, description)

Reports service-request or internal error.

(a) Transmission control protocol (TCP)

(b) User datagram protocol (UDP)

FIGURE 12.15.   DOD transport protocol header formats.

- *Checksum (16 bits):* the one's complement of the sum modulo $2^{16} - 1$ of all the 16-bit words in the segment plus a pseudo-header, described below.
- *Urgent Pointer (16 bits):* points to the octet following the urgent data. This allows the receiver to know how much urgent data are coming.
- *Options (Variable):* at present, only one option is defined, which specifies the maximum TPDU size that will be accepted.

Several of the fields in the TCP header warrant further elaboration. The *source port* and *destination port* specify the sending and receiving users of TCP. As with IP, there are a number of common users of TCP that have been assigned numbers. These numbers should be reserved for that purpose in any implementation. Other port numbers must be arranged by agreement between communicating parties.

The *sequence number* and *acknowledgment number* are bound to octets rather than to entire segments. For example, if a segment contains sequence number 1000 and include 600 octets of data, the sequence number refers to the first octet in the data field; the next segment in logical order will have sequence number 1600. Thus, TCP is logically stream oriented: It accepts a stream of octets from the user, groups them into segments as it sees fit, and numbers each octet in the stream.

The *checksum* field applies to the entire segment plus a *pseudo-header* prefixed to the header at the time of calculation (at both transmission and reception). The pseudo-header includes the following fields from the IP header: source and destination internet address and protocol, plus a segment length field (Figure 12.16). By including the pseudo-header, TCP protects itself from misdelivery by IP. That is, if IP delivers a segment to the wrong host, even if the segment contains no bit errors, the receiving TCP entity will detect the delivery error.

The reader may feel that some items are missing from the TCP header, and that is indeed the case. TCP is designed specifically to work with IP. Hence, some user parameters are passed down by TCP to IP for inclusion in the IP header. The relevant ones are

- Precedence: a 3-bit field.
- Normal-delay/low-delay.
- Normal-throughput/high-throughput.
- Normal-reliability/high-reliability.
- Security: an 11-bit field.

It is worth observing that this TCP/IP linkage means that the required minimum overhead for every data unit is actually 40 octets.

TCP Mechanisms

Connection Establishment

Connection establishment in TCP always uses a three-way handshake. When the SYN flag is set, the TPDU is essentially a request for connection (RFC), and

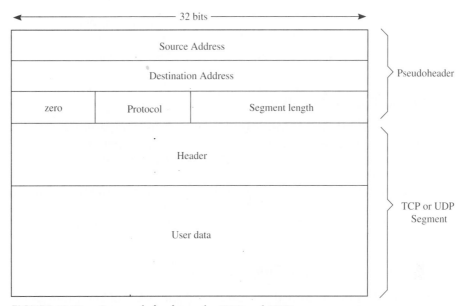

FIGURE 12.16. Scope of checksum for TCP and UDP.

functions as explained in Section 12.2. To initiate a connection, an entity sends an RFC X, where X is the initial sequence number. The receiver responds with RFC Y, ACK X by setting both the SYN and ACK flags. Finally, the initiater responds with ACK Y. If both sides issue crossing RFCs, no problem results: Both sides respond with ACKs.

Data Transfer

Although data are transferred in TPDUs over a transport connection, data transfer is viewed logically as consisting of a stream of octets. Hence every octet is numbered, modulo 2^{32}. Each TPDU contains the sequence number of the first octet in the data field. Flow control is exercised using a credit allocation scheme in which the credit is a number of octets rather than a number of TPDUs. In principle, this numbering scheme is more flexible than the ISO/NBS approach and gives the transport entity tighter control over its buffers. In practice, the two seem to provide equivalent performance.

As was mentioned, data are buffered by the transport entity on both transmission and reception. TCP normally exercises its own discretion as to when to construct a TPDU for transmission and when to release received data to the user. The PUSH flag is used to force the data so far accumulated to be sent by the transmitter and passed on by the receiver. This serves an end-of-letter function.

The user may specify a block of data as urgent. TCP will designate the end of that block with an urgent pointer and send it out in the ordinary data stream. The receiving user is alerted that urgent data are being received.

If, during data exchange, a TPDU arrives which is apparently not meant for the current connection, the RST flag is set on an outgoing TPDU. Examples of this situation are delayed duplicate SYNs and an acknowledgment of data not yet sent.

Connection Termination

The normal means of terminating a connection is a graceful close. Each transport user must issue a CLOSE primitive. The transport entity sets the FIN bit on the last TPDU that it sends out, which also contains the last of the data to be sent on this connection.

An abrupt termination occurs if the user issues an ABORT primitive. In this case, the entity abandons all attempts to send or receive data and discards data in its transmission and reception buffers. An RST TPDU is sent to the other side.

TCP Implementation Policy Options

The TCP standard provides a precise specification of the protocol to be used between TCP entities. However, certain aspects of the protocol admit several possible implementation options. Although two implementations that choose alternative options will be interoperable, there may be performance implications. The design areas for which options are specified are the following:

- Send policy.
- Deliver policy.
- Accept policy.
- Retransmit policy.
- Acknowledge policy.

Send Policy

In the absence of pushed data and a closed transmission window (see Figure 12.5a), a sending TCP entity is free to transmit data at its own convenience. As data are issued by the user, they are buffered in the transmit buffer. TCP may construct a segment for each batch of data provided by its user or it may wait until a certain amount of data accumulates before constructing and sending a segment. The actual policy will depend on performance considerations. If transmissions are infrequent and large, there is low overhead in terms of segment generation and processing. On the other hand, if transmissions are frequent and small, then the system is providing quick response.

One danger of frequent, small transmission is known as the silly window syndrome, which is explained in Problem 12.22.

Deliver Policy

In the absence of a Push, a receiving TCP entity is free to deliver data to the user at its own convenience. It may deliver data as each in-order segment is received, or it may buffer data from a number of segments in the receive buffer before delivery. The actual policy will depend on performance considerations. If deliveries are infrequent and large, the user is not receiving data as promptly as may be desirable. On the other hand, if deliveries are frequent and small, there may be unnecessary processing both in TCP and in the user software, as well as an unnecessary number of operating-system interrupts.

Accept Policy

When all data segments arrive in order over a TCP connection, TCP places the data in a receive buffer for delivery to the user. It is possible, however, for segments to arrive out of order. In this case, the receiving TCP entity has two options:

- *In-order:* Accept only segments that arrive in order; any segment that arrives out of order is discarded.
- *In-window:* Accept all segments that are within the receive window (see Figure 12.5b).

The in-order policy makes for a simple implementation but places a burden on the networking facility, as the sending TCP must time out and retransmit segments that were successfully received but discarded because of misordering. Furthermore, if a single segment is lost in transit, then all subsequent segments must be retransmitted once the sending TCP times out on the lost segment.

The in-window policy may reduce transmissions but requires a more complex acceptance test and a more sophisticated data storage scheme to buffer and keep track of data accepted out of order.

For class 4 ISO transport (TP4), the in-window policy is mandatory.

Retransmit Policy

TCP maintains a queue of segments that have been sent but not yet acknowledged. The TCP specification states that TCP will retransmit a segment if it fails to receive an acknowledgment within a given time. A TCP implementation may employ one of three retransmission strategies:

- *First-only:* Maintain one retransmission timer for the entire queue. If an acknowledgment is received, remove the appropriate segment or segments from the queue and reset the timer. If the timer expires, retransmit the segment at the front of the queue and reset the timer.
- *Batch:* Maintain one retransmission timer for the entire queue. if an acknowledgment is received, remove the appropriate segment or segments from the queue and reset the timer. If the timer expires, retransmit all segments in the queue and reset the timer.
- *Individual:* Maintain one timer for each segment in the queue. If an acknowledgment is received, remove the appropriate segment or segments from the

queue and destroy the corresponding timer or timers. If any timer expires, retransmit the corresponding segment individually and reset its timer.

The first-only policy is efficient in terms of traffic generated, since only lost segments (or segments whose ACK was lost) are retransmitted. Because the timer for the second segment in the queue is not set until the first segment is acknowledged, however, there can be considerable delays. The individual policy solves this problem at the expense of a more complex implementation. The batch policy also reduces the likelihood of long delays but may result in unnecessary retransmissions.

The actual effectiveness of the retransmit policy depends in part on the accept policy of the receiver. If the receiver is using an in-order accept policy, then it will discard segments received after a lost segment. This fits best with batch retransmission. If the receiver is using an in-window accept policy, then a first-only or individual retransmission policy is best. Of course, in a mixed network of computers, both accept policies may be in use.

The ISO TP4 specification outlines essentially the same options for a retransmit policy without mandating a particular one.

Acknowledge Policy

When a data segment arrives that is in sequence, the receiving TCP entity has two options concerning the timing of acknowledgment:

- *Immediate:* When data are accepted, immediately transmit an empty (no data) segment containing the appropriate acknowledgment number.
- *Cumulative:* When data are accepted, record the need for acknowledgment, but wait for an outbound segment with data on which to piggyback the acknowledgment. To avoid long delay, set a window timer (see Table 12.1); if the timer expires before an acknowledgment is sent, transmit an empty segment containing the appropriate acknowledgment number.

The immediate policy is simple and keeps the sending TCP entity fully informed, which limits unnecessary retransmissions. However, this policy results in extra segment transmissions, namely, empty segments used only to ACK. Furthermore, the policy can case a further load on the network. Consider that a TCP entity receives a segment and immediately sends an ACK. Then the data in the segment are released to the application, which expands the receive window, triggering another empty TCP segment to provide additional credit to the sending TCP entity.

Because of the potential overhead of the immediate policy, the cumulative policy is typically used. Recognize, however, that the use of this policy requires more processing at the receiving end and complicates the task of estimating round-trip delay by the sending TCP entity.

The ISO TP4 specification outlines essentially the same options for an acknowledge policy without mandating a particular one.

User Datagram Protocol

In addition to TCP, there is one other transport-level protocol that is in common use as part of the TCP/IP protocol suite: the user datagram protocol (UDP).

UDP provides a connectionless service for application-level procedures. Thus UDP is basically an unreliable service; delivery and duplicate protection are not guaranteed. However, this does reduce the overhead of the protocol and may be adequate in many cases. An example of the use of UDP is in the context of network management, as described in Chapter 15.

UDP sits on top of IP. Because it is connectionless, UDP has very little to do. Essentially, it adds a port addressing capability to IP. This is best seen by examining the UDP header, shown in Figure 12.15b. The header includes a source port and destination port. The length field contains the length of the entire UDP segment, including header and data. The checksum is the same algorithm used for TCP and IP. For UDP, the checksum applies to the entire UDP segment plus a pseudo-header prefixed to the UDP header at the time of calculation and is the same one used for TCP (Figure 12.16). If an error is detected, the segment is discarded and no further action is taken.

The checksum field in UDP is optional. If it is not used, it is set to zero. However, it should be pointed out that the IP checksum applies only to the IP header and not to the data field, which in this case consists of the UDP header and the user data. Thus, if no checksum calculation is performed by UDP, then no check is made on the user data.

12.6

LIGHTWEIGHT TRANSPORT PROTOCOLS

A Problem with Existing Transport Protocols

As you might expect, a tremendous amount of research, development, and real-world experience have gone into the transport protocols that are currently in widespread use, notably the ISO and TCP/IP versions. However, two trends have led to a need for a new approach:

- The most common configuration for computer networking is now an internet; isolated networks are becoming increasingly rare. Accordingly, the transport protocol is usually supported by an internet protocol.
- The data rates on both LANs (e.g., FDDI) and WANs (e.g., use of T-1 trunks in packet-switching networks, and the approach of broadband ISDN, as described in Chapter 16), are significantly greater than those that existed when current transport protocols were designed.

The upshot is that a conventional transport protocol, especially when bound to an internet protocol, produces a processing overhead that appears to be out of proportion with the high-speed networks that it must traverse. The protocols are too complex to be implemented directly in silicon. As software modules, their performance is severely limited by processor speed, memory access times, buffer management overhead, and packet formats designed for functionality rather than performance.

Note that in the above paragraph, we used the phrase "appears to be" rather than "is." Although the problem stated above is generally recognized in the design community, there is a sharp difference of opinion about the best way to proceed. In essence, there are two approaches:

• Improve the performance of existing protocols.
• Design new protocols with the net networking environment clearly in mind.

The former position is advocated by a number of researchers who have demonstrated that improvements in implementation and in integration of communications software with operating-system software can lead to improvements in performance [VAZQ88, HEAT89]. Supporters of this approach feel that the experience gained with existing complex protocols should be retained and that an implementation in silicon unnecessarily retards the evolution and refinement of these protocols. One example of such an approach is the concept of header prediction [CLAR89, STRA89]. Those involved in the project report on a statistical analysis that shows that in specific situations, parts of the packet headers of standard communication protocols follow each other with at least 90 percent certainty. This feature can be used to reduce processing. Once a certain amount of processing is done on one packet, a quick bit comparison with a future packet can determine whether the same processing steps can be skipped for that packet. Such a scheme involves no change to the protocol and no loss of functionality.

Other researchers feel that new protocols that combine internet and transport functionality and that are specifically designed with high-speed networks in mind offer the best hope for providing adequate performance. The resulting protocols have been termed lightweight transport protocols.[1] Examples of experimental lightweight transport protocols include VMTP [CHER89a, WILL89], LNTP [CHAN88], high-speed transport protocol [SABN89], GAM-T [MINE89], Delta-T [WATS89], and XTP [WHAL89, COHN88, COHN89, CHES88, HIND89, PE89]. In the remainder of this section, we examine XTP, which is the best documented and which is the most likely one of these protocols to become an international standard.

---

[1]It is interesting to note that similar concepts have arisen in the areas of communication protocols, computer architecture, and operating systems at about the same time. In the area of computer architecture, the reduced instruction set computer (RISC) approach has led to improved processor speed by streamlining processor architecture. In the area of operating systems, the lightweight process, or thread, which is a unit of dispatching within a normal process, has led to reduced processing overhead in the operating system. These two concepts are discussed at length in [STAL93c] and [STAL92b], respectively.

Xpress Transfer Protocol (XTP)

XTP combines the functionality of transport and internet protocols to produce a streamlined protocol that requires minimum processing and that allows for parallel processing of some functions. In this subsection, we highlight some of the key features of XTP.

Frame Design

Two types of packet formats are used in XTP: information packets and control packets (Figure 12.17). A common header format and a common trailer format is used for both packet formats, and both header and trailer are fixed size to simplify processing. The trailer consists simply of a checksum that covers the preceding segment. A header checksum is placed at the end of the header. The advantage of these placements is that the checksum functions are performed during or after transmission or reception of the preceding bits. So, on transmission, the code is calculated while the preceding bits of the packet are actually being transmitted and then tacked on to the end of the transmission. This opportunity for parallel processing can be exploited if the algorithm is implemented in silicon as separate processing elements that function in parallel. In contrast, both TCP and TP place a checksum for the entire segment in the header, preceding part of the data to be checked.

Table 12.10 defines the individual fields of the XTP packets. Table 12.11 lists the individual packet types that can be constructed from the two packet formats.

Receiver Responses

Most protocols require the receiver to ACK data and allow the receiver some latitude in the timing of issuing ACKs. XTP provides a bit in the header (options field) for requesting a control packet that reports status (flow, error, and rate parameters). Except for detected errors, when the receiver may autonomously generate advisory control messages, receiver responses are controlled by the peer sender. The sender is thus able to adjust the rate and timing of responses from the receiver to suit the application traffic.

Internet Routing

In a high-speed internet, it is important that the forwarding function of the router be performed rapidly. To aid in this process a route field is included in the XTP header. This has a zero value for logical connections that span a single network. If the connection spans multiple networks and hence goes through one or more routers, the field is used as follows. When an initial connection-opening packet (a FIRST packet; see Table 12.11), arrives at a router from a source (which may be a router), the router analyzes the address field which contains the global destination address and makes a routing decision. An exit port is determined and placed in a routing table. The index to that table is

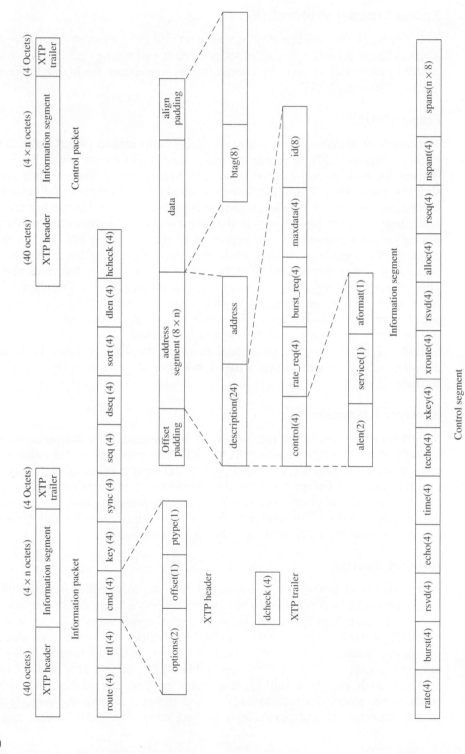

FIGURE 12.17. XTP packet formats.

590

returned to the source in the Xroute field of a control packet. Subsequent DATA packets from the source contained the assigned index in the Route field. As a result, the router can make an immediate routing decision on the basis of a table lookup. If there is a path through several routers, the route value changes at each router.

TABLE 12.10   XTP Fields

	XTP Header (40 octets)
Route	Provides the basis for packet forwarding through an internet router. The value is used by a router as an index into a routing table. On each hop, the value in the route field is changed for use by the next router.
Time to live (ttl)	Maximum remaining lifetime of the packet in the internet, expressed in 100-nanosecond clock ticks.
Command (CMD) Options	Set of options for enabling/disabling various functions, such as error detection, packet retransmission, multicast addressing, and interpretation of Sort field. Also includes bit to indicate whether first 8 octets of user data are tag information.
Offset	Specifies the amount of padding, if any, at the beginning of the information segment.
Ptype	Indicates type of packet; see Table 12.12.
Key	Logical connection, or context, identifier. It is an end-to-end value generated at one host and communicated unchanged through internet routers to a destination host. Each side of a connection may assign its own key value to the connection. Once keys have been exchanged (see Xkey, below), each side uses the key of the other side in transmissions.
Sync	Used to synchronize XTP, in conjunction with Echo field. Sender can transmit a unique number and notice when that value is returned. The sender can conclude that packets sent prior to the one containing the particular sync value have probably had enough time to arrive at the remote receiver.
Sequence (Seq)	The 32-bit end-to-end sequence number for the context (connection).
Dseq	Equal to one plus the highest sequence number transferred from XTP to the application.
Sort	Associates a value with each packet to direct the order of input and output operations. The field represents either a priority or a clock time, which is interpreted as a deadline.
Dlen	The length of the information or control segment in octets.
Hcheck	Error-detection checksum calculated over the header, not including the route and ttl fields.
	XTP Trailer (4 octets)
Dcheck	Error-detection checksum calculated over the information segment or control segment.

TABLE 12.10   (continued)

	Information Segment
Offset padding	Optional padding at the beginning of an information segment.
Address segment	
Descriptor	
Control	
Alen	Length of the address segment in octets.
Service	Indicates kind of traffic expected: connection, transaction, unacknowledged datagram, acknowledged datagram, isochronous stream, or bulk data.
Aformat	Address format used. Options include ISO standard, TCP/IP standard, and source routing format.
Rate_req	Sender's initial desired data flow rate in octets per second.
Burst_req	Indicates the expected output burst size in bytes.
Maxdata	Length in octets of the largest information segment that the sender expects to transmit.
Id	MAC address of the originator of the FIRST or PATH packet.
Address	Specifies the two endpoints (source and destination) for the FIRST or PATH packet.
Data	User data from higher layer.
btag	Optional higher-level control information.
Align padding	Optional padding at the end of an information segment.

	Control Segment
Rate	Maximum acceptable transmission rate in octets per second.
Burst	Maximum number of octets receiver will accept per burst of packets.
Rsvd	Reserved for future use.
Echo	Copy of value in most recently received Sync field.
Time	Time field of a received control segment is copied to the Techo field of an outgoing control response. Used by a host to determine round-trip delay.
Techo	Returned time value.
Xkey	Exchange key. Value assigned to a logical connection by the side that did not originate the connection and returned to the other side for future use (refer to key in XTP header).
Xroute	Exchange route. Functions in manner similar to Xkey, for internet routers. In this case, the exchange is done on a hop-by-hop basis, rather than end-to-end (refer to route in XTP header).
Rsvd	Reserved for future use.
Alloc	Other side may send octets up to but not including this sequence number.
Rseq	Sequence number expected on next incoming packet; one past the highest consecutive sequence number received without error.
Nspan	Number of pairs in Spans array.
Spans	Up to 16 pairs of sequence numbers. Each sequence number pair identifies a span of packets that has been successfully received. This selective acknowledgment identifies gaps of packets that must be retransmitted.

TABLE 12.11   XTP Packet Types

Packet Type	Segment Type	Definition
DATA	Information	Contains user data.
CNTL	Control	Used by receiver to return status (e.g., flow, error, and rate parameters). Sent in response to a packet with Sreq command bit set. Used by sender when resynchronizing with the receiver.
FIRST	Information	Initiates context establishment. Contains address segment and may contain user data.
PATH	Information	Consists of header, address segment, and trailer. It is used to thread a path through an internet and may be used to locate a router or to recover from router or connection failure.
DIAG	Information	Indicates error conditions at receiver or router (e.g., destination unknown).
MAINT	Undefined	Gathers end-to-end diagnostic data (e.g., end-to-end route, hop times).
MGMT	Undefined	Network management information.
ROUTE	Information	Used for route control. Sent by host to request that route by released. Sent by router to acknowledge that route has been released.
RCNTL	Control	Router-generated control packet.

At any given time, a single route is set up between a source/destination pair. Any number of logical connections may be multiplexed on the same route. Each logical connection is identified by the Key field in the header, which functions in a manner similar to virtual circuit numbers in X.25.

Flow and Error Control

Flow and error control are applied on a logical-connection basis, end to end. The technique is essentially a sliding-window strategy. However, to improve efficiency, selective retransmission is allowed. At any time, the destination is prepared to accept packets within some window of sequence numbers. If packets are lost or arrive out of order, gaps will develop in the received sequence. The destination is able to inform the source of the existence of such gaps (using the Span field in the Control Segment; see Table 12.10). The source then selectively retransmits the missing packets.

Rate Control

In addition to flow control on a per-connection basis, XTP provides for rate control to be used over each route. The rate may be controlled separately in each direction. XTP routers assign a maximum packet rate to each new router, and return this value to the source computer along with the new Route value in a control packet. The rate is applied to all traffic from the source computer along the route. This feature has a number of benefits:

- If the source system generates a large load on a particular route by initiating more connections, those connections must share the assigned rate, thus avoiding a surge at the router.
- If a source system wants to find a new path through the internet and obtain a new or additional rate, it can do so.
- The router may regulate assigned rates upward or downward in response to the observed load and available resources.
- A rate-based system uses fewer network packets than a scheme that achieves rate control with a moving window flow control scheme.
- The space required in an XTP router to administer rate control in this manner is related to the number of active source/destination pairs through the router. This is a much smaller number than the number of active connections, which would be the case if the protocol architecture required intervention on a connection basis.

Connection Control

In XTP, multi-packet exchange sequences provide user applications with both a transport-level virtual-circuit (connection-oriented) and a transport-level datagram (acknowledged connectionless) service. For the former, connection establishment is illustrated in Figure 12.18a. A connection request is contained in a FIRST packet, which may also include user data. When this is received, the destination replies with a control packet, which either rejects or accepts the connection. In the latter case, the destination may either indicate that the connection is to remain open, or that it is ready to close the connection. If the destination indicates a desire to close the connection, the source will confirm this in a control packet. Otherwise, the two sides may exchange data for a period, and use a three-way handshake to terminate the connection later on.

A two-way handshake is used for a transport-level datagram service or the basis for a simple request/response operation, as illustrated in Figure 12.18b. In this case, the source includes an indication that the connection is to be closed in the FIRST packet. The receiver acknowledges in a control packet. The advantage of this mode is that the destination doesn't have to wait to close the context after issuing the closing control packet.

Comparison with TCP/IP and TP4/CLNP

It is interesting and instructive to compare the approach taken by XTP on the one hand with that taken by TCP/IP and TP4/CLNP on the other. The comparison in the following list is based on an analysis in [GERM92]. The emphasis

(a) Three-packet connection-mode handshake

(b) Two-packet transaction-mode handshake

FIGURE 12.18.   XTP operation.

is on a comparison of XTP with TCP/IP; TP4/CLNP is only mentioned when it is substantially different from TCP/IP. The following differences can be noted:

- *Connection establishment:* XTP is more efficient, using only three packets to open a connection, deliver a block of data, and close the connection. TCP requires six segments to achieve the same results.
- *Priority:* In XTP, a user may open several connections, each at a different priority. Packets on higher-priority connections are given precedence and may leapfrog packets on lower-priority connections. For example, a file transfer may be given a lower priority than a message from a real-time application. There is no comparable facility in TCP. Furthermore, there is no indication in the TCP standard that an urgent segment on one connection will be processed before non-urgent segments queued up on other connections.

- *Header size:* The XTP header is fixed length, while the TCP header is variable length. In addition, each field in the XTP header is 4 octets long, while the fields in the TCP header are of various lengths. The use of fixed lengths simplifies processing and therefore speeds it up.
- *Addressing:* In XTP, addresses only appear in the FIRST control packet establishing the connection. Thereafter a simple numeric KEY in the header is used to identify the connection. This considerably simplifies the processing. TCP does not use connection identifiers, but TP4 does.
- *Flow control window size:* For flow control, all three protocols use a credit-allocation scheme. In both XTP and TCP, sequence numbers refer to octets of user data. The XTP Alloc field is a 32-bit field, which means that a credit of $2^{32} \approx 4$ gigabytes or 32 gigabits may be transmitted in a burst. TCP uses a Window field of only 16 bits, limiting the credit to 64 kbytes, or about 0.5 megabit. TP4 also uses a Credit field of only 16 bits; however, in the case of TP4, the credit refers to TPDUs rather than bytes. With a maximum TPDU size of 8192 octets, this works out to a maximum credit for TP4 of about 0.5 gigabyte or 4 gigabits. The limitation in TCP can have an effect on performance. For example, an FDDI network can transmit a burst of 0.5 megabit in about 5 ms. If the round-trip time is substantially longer than 5 ms, then the burst transmission time for FDDI will be substantially less than its theoretical rate of 100 Mbps. For a single FDDI network, the round-trip delay should cause no problem. However, if multiple FDDI networks are connected by high-speed links and bridges on a continental scale, such delays could be on the order of 30 ms.
- *Checksum:* The TCP checksum is in the header. Thus two sweeps of the data are required: one for checksum calculation and one for copying the octets to the network. XTP has two checksums: one for the information or control segment and one for the header. Both checksums are positioned after the data that they check, allowing computation "on the fly." The TP4 checksum uses the relatively complex Fletcher algorithm. TCP's checksum is simpler, based on the ADD function. XTP's checksums are the simplest, based on the XOR function. Thus, the processing burden for checksum calculation is the least for XTP. Finally, both XTP and TP4 allow for disabling the use of the checksum; the checksum is always required in TCP.
- *Acknowledgment:* TCP specifies that the receiver should decide when to send an ACK. An implementation must make a compromise between a short round-trip time and a high throughput. XTP specifies that the decision when to send an ACK rests with the sender. The receiver only sends an ACK when the SREQ flag in the Options field of the incoming XTP header is set. This allows the sending application to tailor acknowledgment behavior to its requirements.
- *Selective retransmission:* Only XTP allows selective transmission of missing packets, using the Spans field in the control segment. With this feature, an XTP entity can send out a long burst of packets, then ask for receiver status (using SREQ) and retransmit only missing packets.

12.7

RECOMMENDED READING

A good account of transport protocols can be found in [MCQU78]. Other sources are [SUNS81], [GARL77], and chapters in [SPRA91] and [TANE88]. The ISO and TCP standards are discussed in detail in [STAL90a] and [STAL90c] respectively. [PART88] contains reprints of a number of key papers dealing with specific transport protocol design issues.

Good survey articles of lightweight transport protocols include [PORT91] and [DOER90]. [STRA92] provides exhaustive coverage of XTP. Other worthwhile introductions to XTP include [WEAV91] and [SAND90].

12.8

PROBLEMS

12.1 It is common practice in most transport protocols (indeed, most protocols at all levels) for control and data to be multiplexed over the same logical channel on a per-user-connection basis. An alternative is to establish a single control transport connection between each pair of communicating transport entities. This connection would be used to carry control signals relating to all user transport connections between the two entities. Discuss the implications of this strategy.

12.2 The discussion of flow control with a reliable network service referred to a backpressure mechanism utilizing a lower-level flow control protocol. Discuss the disadvantages of this strategy.

12.3 Two transport entities communicate across a reliable network. Let the normalized time to transmit a TPDU equal 1. Assume that the end-to-end propagation delay is 3, and that it takes a time 2 to deliver data from a received TPDU to the transport user. The sender initially granted a credit of seven TPDUs. The receiver uses a conservative flow control policy, and updates its credit allocation at every opportunity. What is the maximum achievable throughput?

12.4 Draw diagrams similar to Figure 12.7 for the following (assume a reliable sequenced network service):
  a. Connection termination: active/passive.
  b. Connection termination: active/active.
  c. Connection rejection.
  d. Connection abortion: user issues an OPEN to a listening user, and then issues a CLOSE before any data are exchanged.

12.5 With a reliable sequencing network service, are TPDU sequence numbers strictly necessary? What, if any, capability is lost without them?

12.6 Consider a failure-prone network service that suffers a reset. Should the transport entity allow for the possibility of duplicate TPDUs as a result of the transport-level reset mechanism?

12.7 The discussion of retransmission strategy made reference to three problems associated with dynamic timer calculation. What modifications to the strategy would help to alleviate those problems?

12.8 Consider a transport protocol that uses a connection-oriented network service. Suppose that the transport protocol uses a credit allocation flow control scheme, and the network protocol uses a sliding window scheme. What relationship, if any, should there be between the dynamic window of the transport protocol and the fixed window of the network protocol?

12.9 In a network that has a maximum packet size of 128 bytes, a maximum packet lifetime of 30 s, and an 8-bit packet sequence number, what is the maximum data rate per connection?

12.10 Is a deadlock possible using only a two-way handshake instead of a three-way handshake? Give an example or prove otherwise.

12.11 Why is there not a T-DATA.confirm primitive in Table 12.4?

12.12 In the ISO protocol, why is the Source Reference field included in CR, CC, DR, and DC, but not the other TPDUs?

12.13 Compare the PUSH and URGENT mechanisms of TCP with the expedited data mechanism of ISO. How do they differ?

12.14 Why is UDP needed? Why can't a user program directly access IP?

12.15 Listed below are four strategies that can be used to provide a transport user with the address of the destination transport user. For each one, describe an analogy with the Postal Service user.
   a. Know the address ahead of time.
   b. Make use of a "well-known address."
   c. Use a name server.
   d. Addressee is spawned at request time.

12.16 In a credit flow control scheme, what provision can be made for credit allocations that are lost in transit?

12.17 What happens in Figure 12.6 if an RFC comes in while the requested use in IDLE? Is there any way to get the attention of the user when it is not listening?

12.18 In Section 12.2, it was pointed out that an adaptive, or dynamic, calculation of the retransmission timer may be desirable. One approach would be to simply take the average of observed round-trip times over a number of segments and then set the transmission timer equal to a value slightly greater than the average. If the average accurately predicts future round-trip delays, then the resulting retransmission timer will yield good performance. The simple averaging method can be expressed as follows:

$$ARTT(K + 1) = \frac{1}{K + 1} \sum_{i=1}^{K+1} RTT(i)$$

where $RTT(K)$ is the round-trip time observed for the Kth transmitted segment, and $ARTT(K)$ is the average round-trip time for the first K segments. This expression can be rewritten as follows:

$$ARTT(K + 1) = \frac{K}{K + 1} ARTT(K) + \frac{1}{K + 1} RTT(K + 1)$$

a. The TCP standard recommends the following formulas for estimating round-trip time and setting the retransmission timer:

$$SRTT(K + 1) = \alpha \times SRTT(K) + (1 - \alpha) \times RTT(K + 1)$$
$$RXT(K + 1) = MIN(UBOUND, MAX(LBOUND, \beta \times SRTT(K + 1)))$$

where $SRTT$ is referred to as the smoothed round-trip time, $RXT(K)$ is the retransmission timer value assigned after the first K segments, UBOUND and LBOUND are pre-chosen fixed upper and lower bounds on the timer value, and α and β are constants. The recommended initial values for a new connection are $RTT = 0$ seconds and $RXT = 3$ seconds.

Now, assume that the observed round-trip times for the first 20 segments on a connection have the following values; 1, 2, 3, 4, 5, 6, 7, 8, 9, 10, 10, 10, 10, 10, 10, 10, 10, 10, 10, 10. Show the values for $ARRT(K)$, $SRTT(K)$, and $RXT(K)$ for this sequence. For the latter two parameters, include results for $\alpha = 0.25, 0.75,$ and 0.875.

b. Repeat part (a) for the sequence 20, 19, 18, 17, 16, 15, 14, 13, 12, 11, 10, 10, 10, 10, 10, 10, 10, 10, 10, 10.

c. What function do α and β perform, and what is the effect of higher and lower values of each? Compare RTT and ARTT.

12.19 The technique specified in the TCP standard and described in the previous problem enables a TCP entity to adapt to changes in round-trip time. However, it does not cope well with a situation in which the round-trip time exhibits a relatively high variance. To cope with this, Von Jacobsen proposed a refinement to the standard algorithm that has now been officially adopted for use with TCP. The algorithm can be summarized as follows:

$$SRTT(K + 1) = (1 - \gamma) \times SRTT(K) + \gamma \times RTT(K + 1)$$
$$ERR(K + 1) = RTT(K + 1) - SRTT(K)$$
$$SDEV(K + 1) = SDEV(K) + \gamma \times (|ERR(K + 1)| - SDEV(K))$$
$$(1 - \gamma) \times SDEV(K) + \gamma \times |ERR(K + 1)|$$
$$RXT(K + 1) = SRTT(K + 1) + 2 \times SDEV(K + 1)$$

where $SDEV$ is the smoothed estimate of deviation of round-trip time and ERR is the difference between the predicted and observed values of round-trip time.

a. Show the values of $SRTT(K)$ and $RXT(K)$ for the same sequences used in parts (a) and (b) of the preceding problem.

b. Compare Von Jacobsen's algorithm with the original TCP algorithm. What does the Von Jacobsen algorithm do? How is it superior to the original algorithm?

12.20 The Von Jacobsen algorithm is quite effective in tracking the round-trip time until there is a period in which the variability of round-trip times is high or until there is a need to retransmit segments due to timer expiration.

    a. What problems does retransmission cause in estimating round-trip time?

    b. Suggest and justify a way to compensate for retransmissions. Hint: The approach mandated for TCP, known as Karn's algorithm, is as follows: Follow the Von Jacobsen algorithm until a timer expires, necessitating retransmission. Then use a different strategy until an acknowledgment arrives before a timer expires. Now all you need to do is come up with this alternative strategy.

12.21 The primary objective of developing a dynamic retransmission timer algorithm is to coordinate the needs of sender and receiver so that the sender is not delivering data either too quickly or too slowly for the receiver. A dynamic retransmission timer has the side effect of helping to cope with network congestion. As network congestion increases, retransmission timers will lengthen, thereby reducing the total network load. However, dynamic timers alone are insufficient to fully cope with severe network congestion. Since the details of the network level are hidden from TCP, it is difficult for TCP to shape its behavior to respond to congestion. However, the fact that retransmission timers are lengthening gives the TCP entity some feel for the degree of congestion.

    a. TCP mandates the use of a congestion window, whose size is altered to respond to congestion. At any time, TCP acts as if its window size is

        allowed_window = MIN [received_credit, congestion_window].

    During periods of normal traffic, the congestion window is the same as the actual window. Suggest a strategy for altering the congestion window during periods of congestion. Hint: Review the binary-exponential backoff technique used for CSMA/CD LANs.

    b. When a period of congestion appears to be over, we would like to restore transmission to the use of the actual window. However, it is best to avoid an abrupt transition to the full window, as this might reawaken congestion. Suggest a conservative approach.

12.22 A poor implementation of TCP's sliding-window scheme can lead to extremely poor performance. There is a phenomenon known as the Silly Window Syndrome (SWS), which can easily cause degradation in performance by several factors of ten. As an example of SWS, consider an application that is engaged in a lengthy file transfer, and that TCP is transferring this file in 200-octet segments. The receiver initially provides a credit of 1000. The sender uses up this window with 5 segments of 200 octets. Now suppose that the receiver returns an acknowledgment to each segment and provides an additional credit of 200 octets for every received segment. From the receiver's point of view, this opens the window back up to 1000 octets. However, from the sender's point of view, if the first acknowledgment arrives after five segments have been sent, a window of only 200 octets becomes available. Assume that at some point, the receiver calculates a window of 200 octets but has only 50 octets to send until it reaches a "push" point. It therefore sends 50 octets in one segment, followed by 150 octets in the next segment, and then resumes transmission of 200-octet segments. What might now happen to cause a performance problem? State the SWS in more general terms.

12.23 TCP mandates that both the receiver and the sender should incorporate mechanisms to cope with SWS.

    a. Suggest a strategy for the receiver. Hint: Let the receiver "lie" about

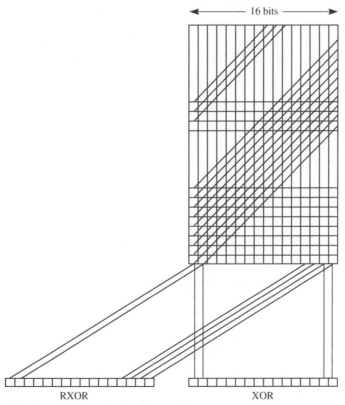

FIGURE 12.19. XTP checksum scheme.

how much buffer space is available under certain circumstances. State a reasonable rule of thumb for this.

b. Suggest a strategy for the sender. Hint: Consider the relationship between the maximum possible send window and what is currently available to send.

12.24 The 32-bit XTP checksum function is defined as the concatenation of two 16-bit functions: XOR and RXOR, defined as follows. Consider the block of data to be checked as a block of 16-bit words. The XOR function is defined as

1. Initially set the XOR result to zero.
2. For each 16-bit word, exclusive-OR (XOR) the word into the result.

The RXOR function is defined as

1. Initially set the RXOR result to zero.
2. For each 16-bit word, rotate the result left by one bit, then exclusive-OR (XOR) the word into the result.

Figure 12.19 on the previous page illustrates the XTP checksum. Note that the XOR function is a vertical redundancy check, or vertical parity (Figure 4.5).

a. Will this checksum detect all errors caused by an odd number of error bits? Explain.

b. Will this checksum detect all errors caused by an even number of error bits? If not, characterize the error patterns that will cause the checksum to fail.

CHAPTER 13

Session Services and Protocols

The transport layer, as we have seen, presents difficult technical problems. But there is universal agreement that transport protocols are needed, and, fortunately, existing standards are solidifying and being accepted. What do we have above transport? Let us consider this from the top down.

At the application level, users should be able to write their own applications that invoke the computer network functionality through a transport, session, or presentation interface, as appropriate. In addition, certain "utility-grade" applications, such as electronic mail, should be standardized and made available universally. This is widely accepted in principle. Also widely accepted, in principle, is the need for presentation services. A notable example here is a virtual terminal protocol. Some protocols seem to span both application and presentation levels. Examples are electronic mail and file transfer protocols.

Whereas the OSI model calls for the inclusion of a session layer, the TCP/IP architecture sets its face against a "session layer" as such, feeling that some of its presumed functions (e.g., graceful close) should be performed by transport and that other functions are peculiar to the processes or applications that wish to communicate. The non-DOD standards organizations have had some trouble pinning down a session layer standard, in part because of the lack of strong motivation for its existence.

This chapter examines the session layer. We begin with a general discussion of session characteristics and requirements. The following two sections examine the standard developed by ISO. In describing this standard, we will notice a marked contrast with the discussion of transport protocols in the preceding chapter. Our primary concern at the transport layer was the complexity of the transport protocol mechanisms required to provide a reliable service. At the session layer, such elaborate mechanisms are not needed; when a session protocol data unit is sent, we are guaranteed that it will be delivered reliably. Instead, the focus at the session layer is with defining a variety of data exchange services that might (or might not!) be useful to applications. Accordingly, although the session protocol is straightforward, the ISO session services are rich and complex.

SESSION CHARACTERISTICS

This section discusses session protocols in terms of principles and objectives, rather than a specific standard.

Few session protocols exist at the present time. Much of the original work that has led to the OSI concept of a session layer was done by a group of designers at Honeywell [BACH79], in the context of OSI and Honeywell's own communications architecture [HONE82]. This same general approach was pursued by ISO (NEUM83), (EMMO83) in developing a specific session protocol standard. What follows is based on the model of the session layer as reflected in the above efforts.

The essential purpose of a session protocol is to provide a user-oriented connection service. The transport protocol is responsible for creating and maintaining a logical connection between endpoints. A session protocol provides a "user interface" by "adding value" to the basic connection service. Let us consider some of the value-added features. We can group them into the following categories:

- Session establishment and maintenance.
- Dialogue management.
- Recovery.

Session Establishment and Maintenance

The minimum service that a session protocol entity provides its users is the establishment, maintenance, and termination of sessions. When two users wish to establish a connection, their respective entities will create a session that is mapped onto a transport connection and negotiate the parameters of the session (e.g., data unit size; see below for further examples).

Let us refer to the unit of data exchanged between a session user and a session protocol entity as a record. The session entity accepts records from the user and encapsulates each into a session protocol data unit (SPDU). SPDUs are, in turn, handed over the local transport entity to be sent over a transport connection in a sequence of transport protocol data units (TPDUs). The data are received on the other side and delivered to the user in the proper order. The sending transport entity may, at its discretion, segment SPDUs into multiple TPDUs if the SPDU size is too large. Alternatively, multiple records may be blocked into a single TPDU for efficiency of transmission. In any case, the receiving entity recovers the original records and passes these on to the receiving user.

The simplest relationship between sessions and transport connections is one to one. It might be desirable to multiplex multiple sessions onto a single transport connection. This reduces the processing burden and amount of state information required of the transport entity. However, caution must be observed. For example, a session supporting inquiry/response should not be multiplexed with a session supporting a file transfer, since the sending of the inquiry text may be significantly delayed when entering a long transport queue of file text from the other session. Furthermore, if the receiving session entity is forced, for any reason, to stop receiving the file transfer text, the receiving queue may soon fill up. This will cause the source queue to fill up as well and any text from the inquiry session multiplexed with the halted session may remain trapped in it.

A session might also be split between two transport connections. This could facilitate the transfer of expedited or interrupt data.

Dialogue Management

The session entity may impose a structure on the interaction or dialogue between users. There are three possible modes of dialogue: two-way simultaneous, two-way alternate, and one-way.

The two-way simultaneous mode is a full-duplex type of operation. Both sides can simultaneously send data. Once this mode is agreed upon in the session negotiation phase, there is no specific dialogue management task required. This would probably be the most common mode of dialogue.

Similarly, the one-way mode requires no specific dialogue management mechanism once it is established. All user data flows in one direction only. An example of this is if data are to be sent to a temporarily inactive user, and are accepted by a "receiver server," whose only task is to accept data on behalf of other local users and store them. Note that the characteristic of being one-way is not absolute. There is a two-way dialogue required to establish the session. During data transfer, the receiving session entity may transmit acknowledgments and other control information. Furthermore, the receiving session user may need to send back some interrupt data. For example, the receiver may need to halt reception temporarily because of a local system problem.

The most complex of the three modes is two-way alternate. In this case, the two sides take turns sending data. An example of the use of this mode is for inquiry/response applications. The session entity enforces the alternating interaction by informing each user when it is its turn. This is actually a three-step process:

- The user who has the turn informs its session entity when it has completed its turn.
- The sending session entity sends any outstanding data to the receiving entity and then informs the receiving entity that the turn is being passed.
- The receiving entity passes up any outstanding data to its user and then informs the user that it is its turn.

An economical means of accomplishing this process is to mark the data with a delimiter. Specifically, the sending user includes a delimiter in the last record of its turn. Let us call the sequence of records sent during one user's turn a *session interaction unit*. Then, on the last record of its turn, the user would include an end-of-interaction unit (I) delimiter. This delimiter is, in effect, a token that is passed to the other user.

With two-way alternate, the user is prevented from sending normal data unless it is its turn. However, a user may send interrupt data to, for example, demand the turn. As an example of the use of the demand-turn mechanism, consider a user who has requested data and is viewing them as they scroll onto a screen. The user may wish to abort the transmission once the first few lines have been viewed.

Another form of dialogue management is the *quarantine service*. This service allows a sending session user to supply a number of blocks of data to the session service and request that the session service refrain from delivering any of the data until receiving an explicit release from the user, at which time all of the quarantined data is delivered. The sending user may also request that all currently quarantined data be discarded. An example of the use of this service is for support of terminal-to-host interaction; a screen-full of data may be supplied to session in multiple blocks, but only be delivered for display when all of the data is available. This service places a buffering requirement on the session service, in effect removing that requirement from the application layer.

Recovery

Another potential feature of a session protocol is a recovery support service similar to the checkpoint/restart mechanisms used in file management.

This feature could be provided by defining a *session recovery unit*, which corresponds to the interval between checkpoints. Each user specifies the point at which a recovery unit ends, and the recovery units are numbered sequentially. To recover lost data (e.g., following a disk fault or a paper break on a printer), a user can issue a command to recover, using the recovery unit number to identify the point to which the session should be backed up.

Once a session has been backed up, some form of recovery will generally be attempted. This is a complex function, which would doubtless extend beyond the bounds of the session layer, and will not be pursued in detail here.

One fundamental point does need to be mentioned, namely, the degree of responsibility of the session protocol entities. When the session is backed up to the beginning of a session recovery unit, the session protocol entities may be requested to retransmit all records from that point forward. If so, the session entity must maintain a copy of each record. To avoid unbounded storage requirements, the user should periodically issue a release command, so that some prior session recovery units can be discarded. Alternatively, the session entity might only be required to remember the records of the current recovery unit.

FIGURE 13.1.   Session delimited data units.

On the other hand, the session entity may only be required to discard outstanding records and back up its recovery-unit counter to the point indicated, with the primary recovery responsibilities being handled at higher levels. In this case, there does not seem much point in having any recovery feature in the session layer.

Figure 13.1 indicates that a session recovery unit is made up of one or more records. However, there is no need for a defined relationship between session recovery units and session interaction units.

13.2

OSI SESSION SERVICE DEFINITION

In this section, we look at the definition of OSI session services developed and standardized by ISO and CCITT. The discussion is based on the most recent version of the standard, which is contained in the 1988 CCITT Recommendation X.215.

Session Services

Table 13.1 lists all of the services provided by OSI session. The OSI document sums up the services provided to a session-service user (SS-user) by the session service as consisting of the following:

1. Establish a connection with another SS-user, exchange data with that user in a synchronized manner, and release the connection in an orderly manner.
2. Negotiate for the use of tokens to exchange data, synchronize and release the connection, and to arrange for data exchange to be half-duplex or full-duplex.
3. Establish synchronization points within the dialogue and, in the event of errors, resume the dialogue from an agreed synchronization point.
4. Interrupt a dialogue and resume it later at a prearranged point.

We will examine the use of tokens in the next subsection. The remainder of the above points are explained in what follows.

As was mentioned in Section 13.1, the minimum service to be provided is the establishment, maintenance, and termination of connections, and the OSI standard certainly includes this service. In addition, OSI session provides a

TABLE 13.1   OSI Session Service

Primitive and Parameters	Description
Session Connection Establishment Phase	
S-CONNECT.request (identifier, calling SSAP, called SSAP, quality of service, requirements, serial number, token, data) S-CONNECT.indication (identifier, calling SSAP, called SSAP, quality of service, requirements, serial number, token, data) S-CONNECT.response (identifier, responding SSAP, result, quality of service, requirements, serial number, token, data) S-CONNECT.confirm (identifier, responding SSAP, result, quality of service, requirements, serial number, token, data)	Used to establish a connection between two session users. Allows users to negotiate tokens and parameters to be used for the connection.
Data Transfer Phase	
Data Transfer Related	
S-DATA.request (data) S-DATA.indication (data)	Allows the transfer of normal SSDUs over a session connection, in either half-duplex or full-duplex mode.
S-EXPEDITED-DATA.request (data) S-EXPEDITED-DATA.indication (data)	Allows the transfer of expedited SSDUs containing up to 14 octets of user data over a session connection, free from the token and flow control constraints of the other data transfer services.
S-TYPED-DATA.request (data) S-TYPED-DATA.indication (data)	Allows the transfer of SSDUs over a session connection, independent of the assignment of the data token. Thus, data may be sent against the normal flow in half-duplex mode.
S-CAPABILITY-DATA.request (data) S-CAPABILITY-DATA.indication (data) S-CAPABILITY-DATA.response (data) S-CAPABILITY-DATA.confirm (data)	Used when activity services are available. Allows users to exchange data while not within an activity.
Token Management Related	
S-TOKEN-GIVE.request (tokens, data) S-TOKEN-GIVE.indication (tokens, data)	Used to surrender one or more specific tokens to the other user.

608

TABLE 13.1 (continued)

Token Management Related	
S-TOKEN-PLEASE.request (tokens, data) S-TOKEN-PLEASE.indication (tokens, data)	Allows a user to request a token currently assigned to the other user. Thus, this service is only used for a particular token when the other user possesses that token.
S-CONTROL-GIVE.request (data) S-CONTROL-GIVE.indication (data)	Allows a user to surrender all available tokens to the other user. This service is part of the activity management service.

Synchronization Related	
S-SYNC-MINOR.request (type, serial number, data) S-SYNC-MINOR.indication (type, serial number, data) S-SYNC-MINOR.response (serial number, data) S-SYNC-MINOR.confirm (serial number, data)	Allows the user to define minor sync points in the flow of SSDUs. The requestor may request explicit confirmation that the minor sync point has been received by the other user.
S-SYNC-MAJOR.request (serial number, data) S-SYNC-MAJOR.indication (serial number, data) S-SYNC-MAJOR.response (serial number, data) S-SYNC-MAJOR.confirm (serial number, data)	Allows the user to define major sync points in the flow of SSDUs, which completely separates the flow before and after the major sync point.
S-RESYNCHRONIZE.request (type, serial number, tokens, data) S-RESYNCHRONIZE.indication (type, serial number, tokens, data) S-RESYNCHRONIZE.response (serial number, tokens, data) S-RESYNCHRONIZE.confirm (serial number, tokens, data)	Used to set the session connection to a previous synchronization point, but no further back than the last major sync point. The state of the connection at that point is restored.

Exception-Reporting Related	
S-P-EXCEPTION-REPORT.indication (reason)	Notifies the user of exception conditions or session protocol errors.
S-U-EXCEPTION-REPORT.request (reason, data) S-U-EXCEPTION-REPORT.indication (reason, data)	Allows a user to report an exception condition when the data token is assigned to the other user.

Activity Related	
S-ACTIVITY-START.request (activity ID, data) S-ACTIVITY-START.indication (activity ID, data)	Used to indicate that a new activity is entered.

TABLE 13.1 (continued)

Activity Related	
S-ACTIVITY-INTERRUPT.request (reason, data) S-ACTIVITY-INTERRUPT.indication (reason ID, data) S-ACTIVITY-INTERRUPT.response (data) S-ACTIVITY-INTERRUPT.confirm (data)	Allows an activity to be abnormally terminated with the implication that the work so far achieved is not to be discarded and may be resumed later.
S-ACTIVITY-RESUME.request (activity ID, old activity ID, serial number, old session connection ID, data) S-ACTIVITY-RESUME.indication (activity ID, old activity ID, serial number, old session connection ID, data)	Used to indicate that a previously interrupted activity is reentered.
S-ACTIVITY-DISCARD.request (reason, data) S-ACTIVITY-DISCARD.indication (reason ID, data) S-ACTIVITY-DISCARD.response (data) S-ACTIVITY-DISCARD.confirm (data)	Allows an activity to be abnormally terminated with the implication that the work so far achieved is to be discarded.
S-ACTIVITY-END.request (serial number, data) S-ACTIVITY-END.indication (serial number, data)	Used to end an activity.
Session Connection Release Phase	
S-RELEASE.request (data) S-RELEASE.indication (data) S-RELEASE.response (result, data) S-RELEASE.confirm (result, data)	Allows the session connection to be released after all in-transit data have been delivered and accepted by both users. If the negotiated release option is selected during connection setup, the user receiving a release request may refuse the release and continue the session.
S-U-ABORT.request (data) S-U-ABORT.indication (data)	Releases a session in a way that will terminate any outstanding service requests. This service will cause the loss of undelivered SSDUs.
S-P-ABORT.indication (reason)	Used by the session service provider to indicate the release of a connection for internal reasons. This service will cause the loss of undelivered SSDUs.

variety of ways of structuring the dialogue that takes place over a session connection. The simplest of these facilities is the ability to choose two-way simultaneous (full-duplex) or two-way alternate (half-duplex) operation.

The OSI session service also provides an optional facility for labeling the data stream with *synchronization points*, which serve two purposes. First, synchronization points can be used to clearly isolate portions of the dialogue. Second, synchronization points can be used in error recovery. Two types of synchronization points are defined: *major synchronization points* and *minor synchronization points*. The relationship is illustrated in Figure 13.2a. Major synchronization points are used to structure the exchange of data into dialogue units. The characteristic of a dialogue unit is that all data within it is completely separated from all data before and after it. When a user defines a major synchronization point, the user may not send more data until that synchronization point is acknowledged by the destination user. For recovery purposes, it is not possible to back up beyond the last major synchronization point. Thus the two purposes mentioned above are achieved. First, since the completion of one dialogue unit must be acknowledged before the next begins, the dialogue unit can be used by the session user to define application-oriented functions. For example, if a sequence of files is to be transferred, each file could be segregated

(a) Example of a structured dialogue unit

(b) Example of a structured activity

FIGURE 13.2.   Session interaction structure.

into a separate dialogue unit. Thus the sender could be assured that a particular file had been received and accepted before attempting to send another file.
Second, the dialogue units defines the limit of recovery. For example, in a
transaction processing application, each transaction could be equated with a
dialogue unit. When a transaction is complete and acknowledged, each side
can purge any recovery information that had been saved for the purpose of
permitting backup to the beginning of that transaction.

Minor synchronization points are used to structure the exchange of data
within a dialogue. They provide more flexibility in the recovery facility. A session user may define one or more minor synchronization points within a dialogue unit, and need not wait for acknowledgment before proceeding. At any
point, it is possible to resynchronize the dialogue to any previous minor synchronization point within the current dialogue unit, or, of course, to resynchronize to the beginning of the dialogue unit (most recent major synchronization point). This permits the session user to make a tradeoff: With frequent
synchronization points, backup and recovery can be speeded up at the expense
of saving frequent checkpoints.

Figures 13.3 through 13.5 give some insight into the applicability of minor
and major synchronization points. Figure 13.3 shows the use of minor synchronization points in a half-duplex dialogue. At any time, only one session
user is transmitting data. To mark a synchronization point, the sending user
issues an S-Sync-Minor.request. This is indicated by point A on the diagram.
This results in an S-Sync-Minor.indication being issued to the other session
user, indicated by point B. The result is to define a minor synchronization
point such that all events prior to A at one end correspond to events prior to

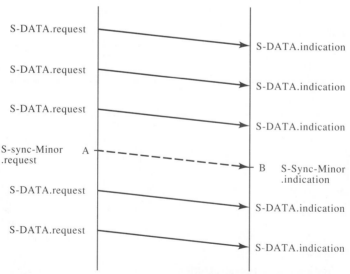

FIGURE 13.3.   Minor synchronization of half-duplex dialogue.

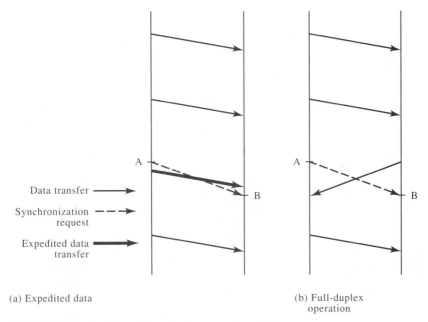

Data transfer ──────▶

Synchronization ── ── ▶
request

Expedited data ━━━▶
transfer

(a) Expedited data

(b) Full-duplex
operation

FIGURE 13.4.   Inadequacies of minor synchronization.

B on the other end, and all events after A at one end correspond to events after B on the other end. Thus a clean separation in the dialogue has been defined.

Now consider Figure 13.4, which shows two inadequacies in the use of minor synchronization. One difficulty relates to expedited data. When the transport service provides for expedited data, then the use of session expedited data will result in the transfer of the corresponding session service data unit (SSDU) as transport expedited data. Therefore, it is possible for an expedited SSDU to be issued after an ordinary SSDU but be delivered earlier than the ordinary SSDU. In part (a) of the figure, we see a situation in which the sending user issues an S-Sync-Minor.request followed by an S-Expedited-Data.request. In this case, the expedited data arrive before the S-Sync-Minor.indication. Thus we have an event (expedited data) that occurs after A and prior to B, and the synchronization point does not provide a clean separation of the dialogue.

Figure 13.4b shows the inadequacy of minor synchronization with respect to full-duplex operation. In this case, one user requests a minor synchronization point, which is established at A and B on the two sides. The other user issues an S-DATA.request prior to B, which is not received until after A. Again, the separation is not clean.

The use of major synchronization points overcomes both of these problems. Two rules stated in the session service standard are relevant:

1. After making the S-Sync-Major.request, the requestor is not able to initiate any services, except for S-Token-Give.request, S-Activity-Interrupt.request,

S-Activity-Discard.request, S-U-Abort.request, or S-Resynchronize.request until the S-Sync-Major.confirm is received.

2. Expedited data transfer services initiated by the acceptor after issuing a S-Sync-Major.response are not indicated before the S-Sync.Major.confirm.

Let us consider the implication of these two rules, using Figure 13.5 (based on a figure in [KNOW87]). When a user requests a major synchronization point (the requestor) with an S-Sync-Major.request, it may not transfer data or expedited data until it receives the corresponding S-Sync.Major.confirm. Thus, there is no danger of expedited data from the requestor overtaking the synchronization request.

Next, consider that the side that receives the S-Sync-Major.indication (the acceptor) issues an S-Sync-Major.response followed by an S-Expedited-Data.request. If the transport expedited data service is available, the expedited data may arrive before the synchronization confirmation. Rule 2 above is designed to prevent this. To explain how this rule is implemented, we must briefly refer to the session protocol, which is examined later in this chapter. When a session user issues an S-Sync-Major.response, the session protocol will issue a corresponding session protocol data unit (SPDU), known as a *major sync*

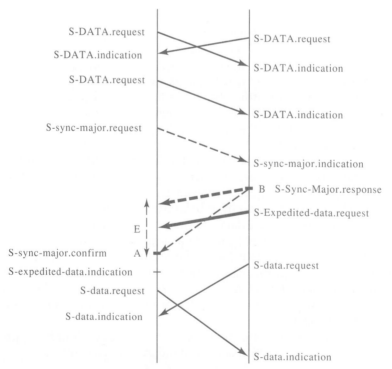

FIGURE 13.5. Major synchronization.

point SPDU. In addition, if transport expedited data service is available, the session protocol will issue a *Prepare SPDU* which will be transferred as transport expedited data. Any session expedited data received by the session protocol on the other side will be held and delivered in an S-Expedited-Data.indication only after the issuance of the S-Sync-Major.confirm. The period of time during which this could occur is indicated by the range E in Figure 13.5.

Thus, the major synchronization point capability deals effectively with expedited data. Full-duplex operation is also effectively handled. The requesting user will not issue any data between the S-Sync-Major.request and the S-Sync-Major.confirm, and the accepting user will not issue any data between the S-Sync-Major.indication and the S-Sync-Major.response. Thus, points A and B in the figure define a major synchronization point which cleanly separates the dialogue.

In the OSI standard, it is not the responsibility of the session layer to save any data that has already been transmitted. The session service will simply mark the data stream as requested with a serial number; numbers are assigned sequentially. When resynchronization occurs, the session layer decrements the sequence number back to the point of resynchronization. If it is desired to retransmit data that had been previously transmitted, it is the responsibility of the session user to have saved that data and to present it to the session service again.

One additional level of structuring is available as an option: the activity. An activity is defined as a logical unit of work, consisting of one or more dialogue units (Figure 13.2b). They key feature of an activity is that it can be interrupted and later resumed. For example, if a very long data base transfer is taking place and one machine or the other needs to interrupt this process (e.g., to go down for system maintenance or to handle a higher-priority task), then the activity is stopped by the session service, which remembers the last serial number used so that the activity may later be resumed with the same structure of synchronization points intact. Again, it is the responsibility of the session user to save any other context information that will be needed for resumption.

The relationship between an activity and a session connection is not fixed. As indicated in Figure 13.6a, it is possible to make a one-to-one correspondence. In this case, a new activity begins a new session connection, and when the activity is completed, the session connection is terminated. It is also possible to perform multiple activities in sequence over a single session connection (Figure 13.6b). This approach may be desirable if session establishment is time-consuming or resource-consuming. If two session users know that they will engage in a sequence of activities, then it makes sense to maintain the session connection. Finally, a single activity can span multiple session connections (Figure 13.6c). If an activity is interrupted, and it is not anticipated that it will be resumed immediately, then it makes sense to break the connection to free up resources and begin a new connection when the users are prepared to resume the activity.

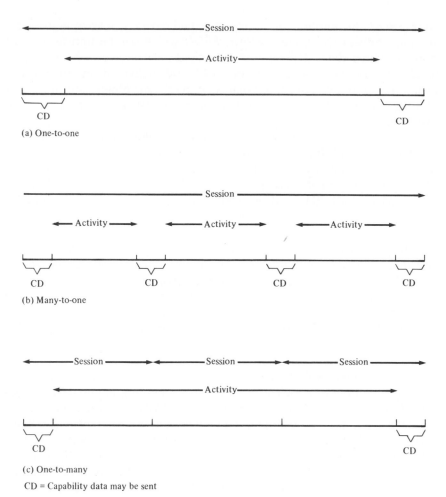

FIGURE 13.6. Relationship of activities and sessions.

A final feature illustrated in Figure 13.6 is the use of *capability data*. If two users choose to make use of the activity option, then data may normally only be exchanged when an activity is in progress. Capability data is a mechanism by which such users can exchange a small amount of acknowledged data over a session connection when no activity is in progress. For example, this feature could be used to transmit control information without going through the overhead of setting up an activity.

The Use of Tokens

In the context of the OSI standard, a token is an attribute of a session connection that is dynamically assigned to one user at a time and that grants that user the exclusive right to invoke certain services. Put another way, there are certain services which can only be invoked by the current token holder. A simple example is a token that grants the right to transmit data. As illustrated in Figure 13.7, this token enforces a half-duplex mode of operation. Only the holder of the token can send data. At any time, the token holder can pass the token to the other user, at which time the other user becomes the possessor of the right to transmit.

The token mechanism is used in the ISO session service to structure the dialogue. Four tokens are defined:

- *Data token:* used to manage a half-duplex connection.
- *Synchronize-minor token:* used to govern the setting of minor synchronization points.
- *Major/activity token:* used to govern the setting of major synchronization points and to manage the activity structure.
- *Release token:* used to govern the release of connections.

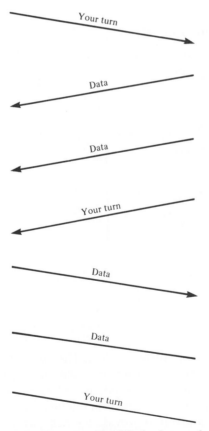

FIGURE 13.7.   Simplified token exchange.

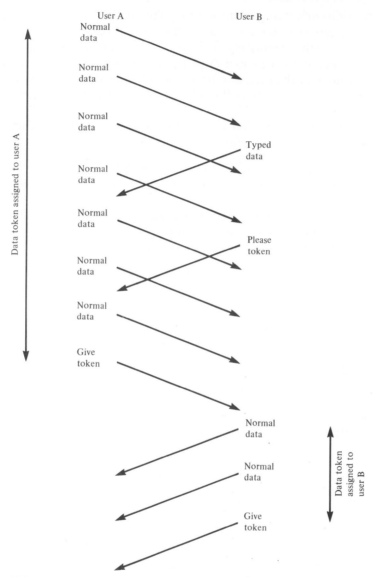

FIGURE 13.8.   Two-way alternate service.

Associated with the token mechanism are three services. The give-token service allows a user to pass a token to the other user of a session connection. The please-token service allows a user who does not possess a token to request it. The give-control service is used to pass all tokens from one user to another.

Figure 13.8 shows the use of the data token to provide the half-duplex mode of operation. In this example, the token is initially possessed by User A, who is free to transmit data. User B may not transmit normal data, but may transmit a small amount of what is referred to as typed data. An example of typed data would be the transmission of a break character from a terminal to halt the flow of data from an application. User B may request the data token at any time, but the token is relinquished only at User A's discretion.

Each of the four tokens is always in one of two states:

- *Not available:* All four of the tokens are optional and their use must be negotiated during connection establishment. In the case of the data and release tokens, their unavailability means that the corresponding services (data transfer, release) are always available to both users. In the case of the synchronization-minor and major/activity tokens, their unavailability means that the corresponding services (synchronization, activities) are unavailable to both users.
- *Available:* An available token is assigned to one of the two users, who then has the exclusive right to use the associated service.

Table 13.2 summarizes the use of the session tokens and their relationship to session services. Note that, with the exception of the release service, each service listed in the table requires the use of a particular token, and may require the use of additional tokens if they are available. The restrictions appear to be reasonable ones. For example, in the case of half-duplex operation, only the holder of the data token can set synchronization points.

Service Primitives and Parameters

Like the OSI transport service specification, each type of session service primitive (Table 13.1) appears in one or more of variations (request, indication, re-

TABLE 13.2   The Use of OSI Session Tokens

		Token		
Function	Data	Minor Sync	Major Sync	Release
Transfer SSDU (half-duplex)	M	—	—	—
Transfer capability data	I	I	M	—
Set minor sync point	I	M	—	—
Set major sync point	I	I	M	—
Start activity	I	I	M	—
Resume activity	I	I	M	—
Interrupt activity	—	—	M	—
Discard activity	—	—	M	—
End activity	I	I	M	—
Release connection	I	I	I	I

M = Mandatory; token must be available and assigned to user to perform function
I = If available; if token is available, it must be assigned to user to perform function

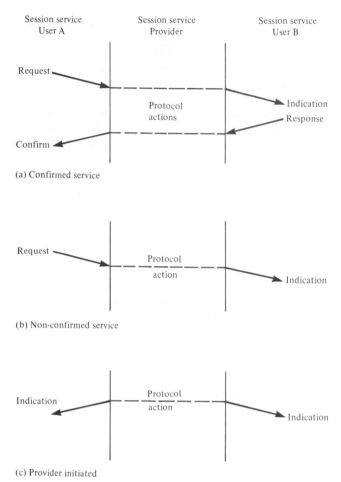

(a) Confirmed service

(b) Non-confirmed service

(c) Provider initiated

FIGURE 13.9.   Session service primitives.

sponse, confirm), depending on the requirements of the service (see Table 10.6).

Figure 13.9 indicates the ways that these variations may be combined in the session service. A service action on the part of one of the session users usually results in action between the two session protocol entities at the two ends of the session connection. This protocol action is invisible to the session user and only manifests itself as a resultant service primitive (indication or confirm). *Confirmed services* are those for which the user invoking the service expects an acknowledgment from the peer user at the other end of the connection. Examples are connection establishment, synchronization actions, and activity-related actions. In the case of connection establishment, the interaction is used for parameter negotiation as well as acknowledgment. *Nonconfirmed services* require no acknowledgment. An example of this is data transfer. In this case, the data are delivered to the session service provider by a request primitive and delivered by the service provider to the other user by an indication primitive. The session protocol making use of transport guarantees the delivery of the data, and therefore there is no need to confirm that delivery to the sender of the data. *Provider-initiated services* are initiated by the session provider in response to an exception condition that it has detected.

For the connection establishment phase, the S-CONNECT primitives are used. The parameters that are provided are

- *Identifier;* a unique identifier of this connection.
- *Calling and called SSAP:* service access points that serve as the address of the session users.
- *Quality of service:* a list of parameters that are negotiated as part of the connection establishment process (Table 13.3). For the most part, these parameters are passed down to the transport service, and were defined in Section 12.4. The session provider indicates the quality of service that can be provided on the basis of the transport service. There are two additional parameters. The extended-control parameter allows a user to make use of the resynchronize, abort, activity interrupt, and activity discard services when normal flow is congested. The optimized-dialogue parameter permits the session protocol to concatenate multiple session service requests and send them as a unit. These services are provided only if both sides agree. Finally, some parameters are prearranged and therefore do not appear in the session connection negotiation.

TABLE 13.3   ISO Session Quality of Service Parameters

Parameter	Negotiate/ Prearranged	Performance/ Other	Passed to Transport
SC establishment delay	P	P	Yes
SC establishment failure probability	P	P	Yes
Throughput	N	P	Yes
Transit delay	N	P	Yes
Residual error rate	N	P	Yes
Transfer failure probability	P	P	Yes
SC release delay	P	P	Yes
SC release failure probability	P	P	Yes
SC protection	N	O	Yes
SC priority	N	O	Yes
SC resiliance	P	P	Yes
Extended control	N	O	No
Optimized dialogue transfer	N	O	No

SC = Session connection

- *Requirements:* a list of functional options that may be requested; these are summarized below. One side proposes the list in the request primitive; only those that also appear in the response primitive are provided.
- *Serial number:* when synchronization services are to be employed, this is the proposed initial serial number.
- *Token:* a list of the initial side to which the available tokens are assigned.
- *Data:* contains session user data.

The data transfer phase involves primitives for the transfer of data and for the structuring of the dialogue. Each data unit that is delivered to the session service provider is to be delivered to the other user as quickly as possible. Thus, there is no quarantine service provided.

The remainder of the primitives are largely self-explanatory. Several points are worth mentioning. The type parameter in the S-SYNC-Major primitive indicates whether an explicit acknowledgment is required. The activity identifier is used for interrupting and later resuming activities.

Session Functional Units

As you might be able to gather, the session service tries to be all things to all people. The result is that a full-blown implementation of the session standard is not only complex but unnecessary for virtually all applications. Thus, it is likely that only subsets of the session service will be provided by particular implementations. The standard anticipates this and tries to impose some order by introducing the concept of session functional units. The services supported by each of these functional units are indicated in Table 13.4. Note that when a functional unit implies the availability of a token, services concerned with the management of that token are provided in order to be able to request and transfer the available token; the tokens involved are also indicated in the table.

Each functional unit is a logical grouping of services. The definition of functional units allows the following:

- Higher-layer entities (applications, presentation entities) may specify which functional units they require. This alerts the session service that it need not attempt to provide other functional units. Furthermore, if the session service is unable to provide the requested functional units, this can be reported to the session user.
- During the session connection establishment phase, the two session entities negotiate the use of functional units, using the Requirements parameter in the S-CONNECT primitive.

The minimum requirement is support of the kernel functional unit, which provides the basic session services required to establish a session connection, transfer normal data, and release the session connection.

There are a few restrictions on the selection of functional units:

- It is not possible to select both the half-duplex and duplex functional units. Clearly, only one mode of operation is possible at a time.

TABLE 13.4   Session Functional Units

Functional Unit	Service(s)	Token Use
Kernel (non-negotiable)	Session connection Normal data transfer Orderly release U-Abort P-Abort	—
Negotiated release	Orderly release Give tokens Please tokens	Release token
Half-duplex	Give tokens Please tokens	Data token
Duplex	No additional services	—
Expedited data	Expedited data transfer	—
Typed data	Typed data transfer	—
Capability data exchange	Capability data exchange	—
Minor synchronize	Minor synchronization point Give tokens Please tokens	Synchronize-minor token
Major synchronize	Major synchronization point Give tokens Please tokens	Major/activity token
Resynchronize	Resynchronize	—
Exceptions	Provider exception reporting User exception reporting	—
Activity management	Activity start Activity resume Activity interrupt Activity discard Activity end Give tokens Please tokens Give control	Major/activity token

- The capability data exchange functional unit can only be selected when the activity management functional unit has been selected. The reverse is not true; that is, it is not necessary to select the capability data exchange functional unit if the activity management functional unit has been selected.
- The exceptions functional unit can only be selected when the half-duplex functional unit has been selected.

OSI SESSION PROTOCOL DEFINITION

In the CCITT recommendations, the OSI session service occupies 82 pages, whereas the OSI session protocol occupies 143 pages. This is a clue to the observer that the session protocol, in its full glory, may be quite a bear to implement. However, for our purposes, we are principally concerned with explaining the functionality of the session protocol and its relationship to the session service above and the transport service below. From that point of view, happily, things are reasonably straightforward.

It is the job of the session protocol to bridge the gap between the services provided by the transport layer and those required by the session user. In essence, the transport layer provides three services:

- Establishment, maintenance, and release of a transport service with certain quality-of-service characteristics.
- Reliable transfer of data.
- Reliable transfer of expedited data.

The session service, as we have seen, provides a variety of services relating to the management and structuring of the exchange of data. Hence, it is the job of the session protocol to provide these structuring mechanisms on top of these transport services. In one sense, it appears that the session protocol standard is far more elaborate than the transport protocol standard. For example, the transport protocol includes 10 types of TPDUs while the session protocol includes 36 types of SPDUs. One reason for this complexity is that the session protocol standard has resulted from the merger of various ISO and CCITT endeavors and is anything but cleanly designed.

In another sense, however, this appearance of complexity is misleading. In the transport protocol, elaborate mechanisms are needed to deal with the unreliability and variable-delay problems that are faced. The session protocol is provided with a rather straightforward service. The complexity is in the session service, with its many session service primitives and its abundance of rules for how these primitives are to be used to provide the rich set of session services. The session protocol basically provides a rather straightforward mapping of session service primitives into session protocol data units, and makes use of the comparatively simple, reliable interface to the transport layer to exchange these primitives.

Protocol Data Units and Mechanisms

As with most protocol, the session protocol is best explained by focusing on the collection of PDUs that are used; these are listed in Table 13.5, with an explanation of the parameters in Table 13.6. For the most part, these SPDUs represent a one-to-one mapping with session service primitive pairs

TABLE 13.5   Session Protocol Data Units, Parameters, and Functions

SPDU	Parameters*	Function
Connect	Connection ID, protocol options, maximum TSDU size, version number, initial serial number, token setting, user requirements, calling SSAP, called SSAP, user data, data overflow	Initiate session connection
Accept	Connection ID, protocol options, maximum TSDU size, version number, initial serial number, token setting, token, user requirements, calling SSAP, responding SSAP, enclosure item, user data	Establish session connection
Overflow Accept	Maximum TSDU size, version number	Request remainder of the S-CONNECT.request user data
Connect Data Overflow	Enclosure item, user data	Send subsequent segments of the S-CONNECT.request user data
Refuse	Connection ID, transport disconnect, user requirements, version number, enclosure item, reason	Reject connection request
Finish	Transport disconnect, enclosure item, user data	Initiate orderly release
Disconnect	Enclosure item, user data	Acknowledge orderly release
Not Finished	Enclosure item, user data	Reject orderly release
Abort	Transport disconnect, error code, enclosure item, user data	Abnormal connection release
Abort Accept	—	Acknowledge abort
Data Transfer	Enclosure item, user data	Transfer normal data
Expedited	User data	Transfer expedited data
Typed Data	Enclosure item, user data	Transfer typed data
Capability Data	Enclosure item, user data	Transfer capability data
Capability Data ACK	Enclosure item, user data	Acknowledge capability data
Give Tokens	Token, enclosure item, user data	Transfer tokens
Please tokens	Token, enclosure item, user data	Request token assignment
Give Tokens Confirm	Enclosure item, user data	Transfer all tokens
Give Tokens Ack	—	Acknowledge all tokens

TABLE 13.5   (continued)

SPDU	Parameters*	Function
Minor Sync Point	Confirm required flag, serial number, enclosure item, user data	Define minor sync point
Minor Sync ACK	Serial number, enclosure item, user data	Acknowledge minor sync point
Major Sync Point	End of activity flag, serial number, enclosure item, user data	Define major sync point
Major Sync ACK	Serial number, enclosure item, user data	Acknowledge major sync point
Resynchronize	Token settings, resync type, serial number, enclosure item, user data	Resynchronize
Resynchronize ACK	Token settings, serial number, enclosure item, user data	Acknowledge resynchronize
Prepare	Type	Notify type SPDU is coming
Exception Report	SPDU bit pattern	Protocol error detected
Exception Data	Reason, enclosure item, user data	Put protocol in error state
Activity Start	Activity ID, enclosure item, user data	Signal beginning of activity
Activity Resume	Connection ID, old activity ID, New activity ID, serial number, enclosure item, user data	Signal resumption of activity
Activity Interrupt	Reason, enclosure item, user data	Interrupt activity
Activity Interrupt ACK	Enclosure item, user data	Acknowledge interrupt
Activity Discard	Reason, enclosure item, user data	Cancel activity
Activity Discard ACK	Enclosure item, user data	Acknowledge cancellation
Activity End	Serial number, enclosure item, user data	Signal activity end
Activity End ACK	Serial number, enclosure item, user data	Acknowledge activity end

*See Table 13.6 for explanation of parameters.

TABLE 13.6 Session Protocol Parameters

Connection ID

Enables SS-users to identify this specific session connection. The value consists of portions defined by the calling and called SS-users.

Protocol Options

Indicates whether or not the initiator is able to receive extended concatenated SPDUs. Certain SPDUs may be concatenated and transmitted as a single unit by the transport layer. Basic concatenation allows two SPDUs to be concatenated. Extended concatenation allows more than two SPDUs to be concatenated.

Maximum TSDU Size

The maximum transport service data unit size. This is the maximum of an SPDU or concatenation of SPDUs.

Version Number

Indicates which versions of this protocol are supported. Version 1 limits the size of user data to 512 octets. Version 2 imposes no restrictions on the length of user data.

Initial Serial Number

Required if minor synchronize, major synchronize, or resynchronize functional unit is proposed.

Token Setting

Initial token position for each token available on this connection.

User Requirements

List of functional units to be supported on this connection.

Calling SSAP

Identifies the calling session user.

Called SSAP

Identifies the called session user.

User Data

Session user data.

Data Overflow

This flag is present if there is more than 10,240 octets of user data to be transmitted with the session connection establishment. The first 10,240 octets are sent in the Connect SPDU; the remainder are sent in one or more Connect Data overflow SPDUs.

Token

Identifies tokens being passed or requested.

Responding SSAP

Identifies the session user that actually responds to a connection request.

Enclosure Item

Used when a session service data unit is segmented into more than one SPDU. This parameter indicates whether the SPDU that contains it is the beginning, an intermediate, or the ending SPDU in the sequence.

Transport Disconnect

Used in the Finish SPDU to indicate whether or not the transport connection is to be retained after the termination of the associated session connection.

Error Code

Contains implementation-defined value related to a protocol error.

(Table 13.7). That is, for each request-indication or response-confirm pair (see Figure 13.9), a single SPDU is used to convey the information. There are two classes of exceptions to this rule:

1. In some cases, more than one possible SPDU exists, to reflect more than one possible response to a service request. The exceptions are

   - S-CONNECT.response, S-CONNECT.confirm: The Accept and Refuse SPDUs indicate acceptance or refusal of a connection request, respectively.
   - S-RELEASE.response, S-RELEASE.confirm: The Disconnect and Not Finished SPDUs indicate acceptance or refusal of an orderly release request, respectively.

2. If the transport protocol imposes a maximum size on the data that it will accept in a single transport service request (maximum TSDU size), then it may be necessary for the session protocol to segment session data into smaller block for transmission. This in turn leads to two cases.
   a. For the following SPDUs, multiple SPDUs of the same type are used to carry the session data:

      - Refuse
      - Finish
      - Disconnect
      - Not Finished
      - Abort
      - Data Transfer
      - Typed Data
      - Capability Data
      - Capability Data ACK
      - Give Tokens
      - Please Tokens
      - Give Tokens Confirm
      - Minor Sync Point
      - Minor Sync ACK

TABLE 13.7 Relationship Between Session Service (SS) Primitives and Session Protocol Data Units (SPDUs)

SS Primitive →	SPDU →	SS Primitive
S-CONNECT.request	CONNECT and (0 or 1) OVERFLOW ACCEPT and (0 or more) CONNECT DATA OVERFLOW	S-CONNECT.indication

TABLE 13.7   (continued)

SS Primitive →	SPDU →	SS Primitive
S-CONNECT.response	ACCEPT or REFUSE	S-CONNECT.confirm
S-DATA.request	DATA TRANSFER	S-DATA.response
S-EXPEDITED-DATA.request	EXPEDITED DATA	S-EXPEDITED-DATA.indication
S-TYPED-DATA.request	TYPED DATA	S-TYPED-DATA.indication
S-CAPABILITY-DATA.request	CAPABILITY DATA	S-CAPABILITY-DATA.indication
S-CAPABILITY-DATA.response	CAPABILITY DATA ACK	S-CAPABILITY-DATA.confirm
S-TOKEN-GIVE.request	GIVE TOKENS	S-TOKEN-GIVE.indication
S-TOKEN-PLEASE.request	PLEASE TOKENS	S-TOKEN-PLEASE.indication
S-CONTROL-GIVE.request	GIVE TOKENS CONFIRM	S-CONTROL-GIVE.indication
S-SYNC-MINOR.request	MINOR SYNC POINT	S-SYNC-MINOR.indication
S-SYNC-MINOR.response	MINOR SYNC ACK	S-SYNC-MINOR.confirm
S-SYNC-MAJOR.request	MAJOR SYNC POINT	S-SYNC-MAJOR.indication
S-SYNC-MAJOR.response	MAJOR SYNC ACK	S-SYNC-MAJOR.confirm
S-RESYNCHRONIZE.request	RESYNCHRONIZE	S-RESYNCHRONIZE.indication
S-RESYNCHRONIZE.response	RESYNCHRONIZE ACK	S-RESYNCHRONIZE.confirm
S-U-EXCEPTION-REPORT.request	EXCEPTION DATA	S-U-EXCEPTION-REPORT.indication
S-ACTIVITY-START.request	ACTIVITY START	S-ACTIVITY-START.indication
S-ACTIVITY-RESUME.request	ACTIVITY RESUME	S-ACTIVITY-RESUME.indication
S-ACTIVITY-INTERRUPT.request	ACTIVITY INTERRUPT	S-ACTIVITY-INTERRUPT.indication
S-ACTIVITY-INTERRUPT.response	ACTIVITY INTERRUPT ACK	S-ACTIVITY-INTERRUPT.confirm
S-ACTIVITY-DISCARD.request	ACTIVITY DISCARD	S-ACTIVITY-DISCARD.indication
S-ACTIVITY-DISCARD.response	ACTIVITY DISCARD ACK	S-ACTIVITY-DISCARD.confirm
S-ACTIVITY-END.request	ACTIVITY END	S-ACTIVITY-END.indication
S-ACTIVITY-END.response	ACTIVITY END ACK	S-ACTIVITY-END.confirm
S-RELEASE.request	FINISH	S-RELEASE.indication
S-RELEASE.response	DISCONNECT or NOT FINISHED	S-RELEASE.confirm
S-U-ABORT.request	ABORT	S-U-ABORT.indication

- Major Sync Point
- Major Sync ACK
- Resynchronize
- Resynchronize ACK
- Exception Data
- Activity Start
- Activity Resume
- Activity Interrupt
- Activity Interrupt ACK
- Activity Discard
- Activity Discard ACK
- Activity End
- Activity End ACK

b. If the S-CONNECT.request primitive, because it includes user data, is too large to be contained in a Connect SPDU, then the Connect SPDU includes a data overflow parameter indicating that more user data is to follow. The called session protocol entity returns an Overflow Accept SPDU, and the calling session protocol entity sends as many Connect Data Overflow SPDUs as are necessary to transfer the user data. Only when all of the data has been transferred will the called entity issue an Accept SPDU to complete the session connection establishment.

Ignoring these complications, the most complex relationship between session service primitives and SPDUs occurs at connection establishment time. Figure 13.10 depicts the possible sequence of events. A request for a connection by a user triggers a Connect SPDU by the user's session protocol entity. The SPDU contains those parameters that were contained in the S-CONNECT.request and that need to be communicated to the other user. These include connection id, serial number, token selections, requirements parameters, calling and called SSAP, and, finally, those quality-of-service parameters that are negotiated between the users (extended control and optimized dialogue), referred to as protocol options. This information is transmitted via the SPDU to the other session protocol entity, which delivers the connection request and associated parameters in an S-CONNECT.indication primitive. The user accepts the connection and negotiates the parameters with a response primitive, which triggers the transmission of an Accept SPDU back to the other side, where a confirm primitive is generated.

A session user may refuse a connection because of congestion, unavailability of the desired application, or other reasons. This is reported to the session protocol entity with a response primitive in which the result parameter indicates the reason for refusal. The session protocol then sends a Refuse SPDU back to the calling side, which sends a confirm primitive to the calling user, indicating that the connection is refused and specifying the reason.

A third alternative sequence is that the called session user accepts the connection request, but proposes session parameters (e.g., no use of synchroni-

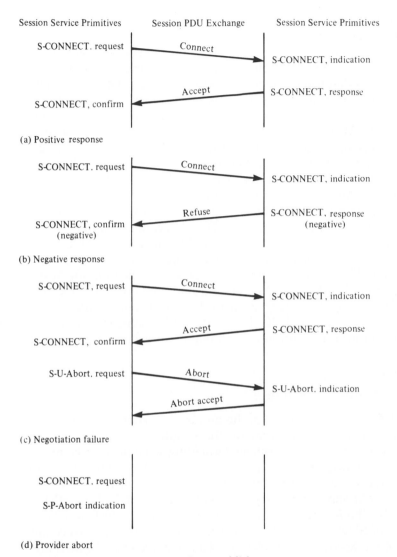

FIGURE 13.10.   Session connection establishment.

zation) unacceptable to the calling user. In this case, the calling user will abort the connection as soon as it is confirmed, and the called user will be informed. Note in Figure 13.10c that both an Abort and an Abort Accept SPDU are used. The latter is needed so that the session protocol entity that initiated the abort knows that the other side is ready for a new session connection and, if desired, that the transport connection can now be terminated.

Finally, a session provider can refuse to establish a connection, because of inability to set up a transport connection, inability to provide the desired quality of service, or some other reason. In this case, no SPDUs are employed, since the action is purely local.

Most of the other SPDUs are largely self-explanatory. However, some additional comments will be useful. In the case of the data transfer SPDU, the typical case is that each unit of data (session service data unit, SSDU) received from a session user is encapsulated with a session header and transmitted. If, however, there is a size restriction on data units to be presented to the transport layer (TSDUs), as indicated in the Connect and Accept SPDUs, then the session entity may need to segment the user's data and send it out in two or more Data-transfer SPDUs. In this latter case, the enclosure item parameter is used to indicate whether or not a Data-transfer SPDU is the last one of a group that carries a single SSDU. The receiving session entity will buffer the user data from incoming SPDUs until the last one in a group is received and then transfer all of the data to the user in an S-Data.indication primitive.

The Prepare SPDU is only used when the transport expedited flow option is available. It notifies the recipient session protocol entity of the imminent arrival of a certain SPDU. The SPDUs that may be so signalled include Resynchronize, Activity Interrupt, Activity Discard, and Activity End. In some cases, this alert will allow the session entity to discard some incoming SPDUs which arrive prior to the anticipated SPDU. In all cases, it is useful as a means of preparing the recipient for the occurrence of an important event.

Session Protocol Formats

As can be seen from Table 13.5, the number of parameters that is sent with an SPDU varies widely. Furthermore, the length of parameters is variable. The ISO standard provides a flexible formatting scheme to accommodate these variations. Unfortunately, because the final standard represents the merger of several independent efforts, the scheme is unnecessarily complex.

Figure 13.11 shows the general structure of an SPDU. Each SPDU has up to four fields. The first field is the SPDU identifier (SI), which specifies one of the 34 types of SPDUs. The next field is the length indicator, which specifies the length of the header. If the SPDU contains any parameters, then the next field contains these parameters, using a structure described below. Finally, there may be a field for session user information.

The parameter field may take on one of several general forms, depending on the way in which particular parameters are expressed. In its simplest form, a parameter is expressed with three subfields: a parameter identifier, a length indicator, and the parameter value. This form is known as a PI unit, and the SPDU may contain one or more such units. Alternatively, related parameters may be expressed in a PGI unit, which consists of a parameter group identifier, a length indicator, and either a single parameter value or one or more PI units. As was said, this is a complicated way of achieving a simple purpose, namely, the listing of parameters within a single SPDU. Figure 13.12 gives examples of the formats that appear within the standard.

SI = SPDU identifer
LI = Length indicator
PGI/PI-Field = One or more PGI and/or PI units
PGI = Parameter group identifer
PV = Parameter value
PI-Field = One or more PI units
PI = Parameter identifer

FIGURE 13.11.   SPDU format.

(a) No parameters

(b) Single parameter

(c) Single PGI with single parameter

(d) Single PGI with several parameters

(e) Two PGIs

FIGURE 13.12.   SPDU encoding examples.

Transport Connections

Session connections must be mapped into transport connections by the session protocol entity. The ISO standard contains specific guidance on the way this is to be done. Most important is the requirement that a transport connection be dedicated to a single session connection. There seems good justification for this restriction. For one thing, different session connections may require different quality of service, which will influence the parameters used to set up the transport connection. Also, if several session connections share a transport connection, neither the session user or the session protocol entity has much control over how the transport service allocates resources to meet the dynamic data transfer demands of several session connections.

If a transport connection provides expedited service, then Abort, Abort Accept, Expedited Data, and Prepare SPDUs are sent using the service. If this service is not available, the Abort and Abort Accept are sent using normal transport data transfer service, and the Expedited Data and the Prepare SPDUs cannot be sent.

Finally, when a session is terminated, the session protocol entity that initially set up the corresponding transport connection has the option of terminating that connection or not. If the transport connection is retained, then it may be used to support a new session connection request, provided that it meets the required quality of service.

13.4

RECOMMENDED READING

Very little has been written about session protocols. [NBS80] is a good general discussion. [EMMO83] summarizes the ISO standard. [CANE86], which explains various obscure points in the ISO standard, is an instructive analysis of the difficulties in interpreting a standards document.

13.5

PROBLEMS

13.1 Assume that a session layer is making use of a reliable transport layer. The transport layer guarantees that data will be delivered in sequence, but makes no guarantee about timing. Thus multiple session recovery units, as defined in Section 13.1, may be outstanding. Might there be a problem when the sending user requests that the current recovery unit be cancelled?

13.2 A session recovery unit is defined by one of the two session users. Yet it would seem that recovery must involve backing up the data streams of both users. What mechanisms are required to achieve the required cooperation?

13.3 A session user issues an S-Release.request. Before the provider can issue the paired S-Release.indication to the other user, the other user issues an S-Release.request. Eventually, both users receive an S-Release.indication, and both respond with an S-Release.response. However, by this time the session provider has already released the connection, since the standard specifies that the release is to take place if a "release collision" is detected. Is there any problem with this?

13.4 Show the mapping of all session service primitives into session protocol data units, in the manner of Figure 13.10.

13.5 Indicate the restrictions for the session protocol imposed by the token restrictions defined for the session service (Table 13.2).

13.6 It was stated in the chapter that the ISO session standard does not include a quarantine service. But consider the use of the enclosure parameter with the Data Transfer and Typed Data SPDUs. Isn't this a quarantine mechanism?

13.7 The Abort Accept SPDU adds complexity to the protocol which may not be desirable for small systems. Can we do without it?

13.8 The ISO session protocol states that, when a session connection is released, the corresponding transport connection may be maintained and reused provided that transport expedited flow control is not available on the connection. Suggest a reason for the restriction.

13.9 If a transport connection is retained, the standard further states that the side which issues the Connect SPDU to set up a new session connection on an old transport connection must be the same side that originally requested the transport connection. Suggest a reason for this restriction.

CHAPTER 14

Presentation Facilities

Presentation facilities deal with the representation of information of concern to applications. In general, we can consider two categories of presentation facilities:

- Those concerned with data to be transferred between application entities in different systems. Presentation facilities may provide a representation to be used for the transfer of information as well as mechanisms for translating between local representations and the representation used for information exchange. Examples of such facilities include encryption and compression.
- Those concerned with data structures that applications refer to in their communication. An example of such a facility is one concerned with the representation of management information for network management.

We begin this chapter with a brief introduction to presentation concepts. Then, we examine Abstract Syntax Notation One (ASN.1), which has become an all-important universal language for defining representations. Next, we look at an example of a translation facility, namely encryption. Finally, we look at the concept of virtual terminal protocols.

14.1

PRESENTATION CONCEPTS

Table 14.1 defines some key terms which are relevant to a discussion of ASN.1, and Figure 14.1 illustrates the underlying concepts.

For purposes of this discussion, a communications architecture in an end system can be considered to have two major components. The data transfer component is concerned with the mechanisms for the transfer of data between end systems. In the case of the TCP/IP protocol suite, this component would consist of TCP or UDP on down. In the case of the OSI architecture, this component would consist of the session layer on down. The application component is the user of the data transfer component and is concerned with the end user's application. In the case of the TCP/IP protocol suite, this component would consist of an application, such as SNMP, FTP, SMTP, or TELNET. In the case of OSI, this component actually consists of the application layer, which is composed of a number of application service elements and the presentation layer.

TABLE 14.1   Presentation Layer Terms

Abstract Syntax	Describes the generic structure of data independent of any encoding technique used to represent the data. The syntax allows data types to be defined and values of those types to be specified.
Data Type	A named set of values. A type may be simple, which is defined by specifying the set of its values, or structured, which is defined in terms of other types.
Encoding	The complete sequence of octets used to represent a data value.
Encoding Rules	A specification of the mapping from one syntax to another. Specifically, encoding rules determine algorithmically, for any set of data values defined in an abstract syntax, the representation of those values in a transfer syntax.
Presentation Context	A combination of abstract syntax and transfer syntax that can be used for the transfer of data using the presentation service.
Transfer Syntax	The way in which data are actually represented in terms of bit patterns while in transit between presentation entities.

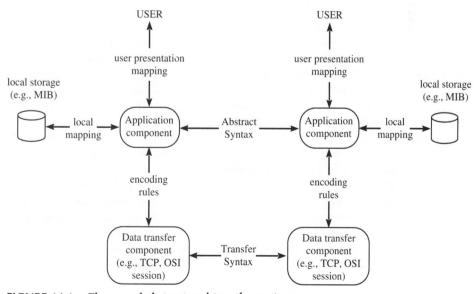

FIGURE 14.1.   The use of abstract and transfer syntaxes.

As we cross the boundary from the application to the data transfer component, there is a significant change in the way the data are viewed. For the data transfer component, the data received from an application are specified as the binary value of a sequence of octets. This binary value can be directly assembled into service data units (SDUs) for passing between layers and into protocol data units (PDUs) for passing between protocol entities within a layer. The application component, however, is concerned with a user's view of data. In general, that view is one of a structured set of information, such as text in a document, a personnel file, an integrated database, or a visual display of image information. The user is primarily concerned with the semantics of data. The application component must provide a representation of this data that can be converted to binary values; that is, it must be concerned with the syntax of the data.

The approach illustrated in Figure 14.1 to support application data is as follows. For the application component, information is represented in an abstract syntax that deals with data types and data values. The abstract syntax formally specifies data independently from any specific representation. Thus, an abstract syntax has many similarities to the data type definition aspects of conventional programming languages such as Pascal, C, and Ada, and to grammars such as Backus-Naur Form (BNF). Application protocols describe their PDUs in terms of an abstract syntax.

This abstract syntax is used for the exchange of information between application components in different systems. The exchange consists of application-level PDUs, which contain protocol control information and user data. Within a system, the information represented using an abstract syntax must be mapped into some form for presentation to the human user. Similarly, this abstract syntax must be mapped into some local format for storage. For example, such a mapping is used in the case of network management information. In addition, it is becoming common to use an abstract syntax to define the data elements in local storage. Thus, the abstract syntax notation is employed by a user to define network management information; the application must then convert this definition to a form suitable for local storage.

The component must also translate between the abstract syntax of the application and a transfer syntax that describes the data values in a binary form, suitable for interaction with the data transfer component. For example, an abstract syntax may include a data type of character; the transfer syntax could specify ASCII or EBCDIC encoding.

The transfer syntax thus defines the representation of the data to be exchanged between data transfer components. The translation from abstract syntax to the transfer syntax is accomplished by means of encoding rules that specify the representation of each data value of each data type.

This approach for the exchange of application data solves the two problems that relate to data representation in a distributed, heterogeneous environment:

- There is a common representation for the exchange of data between differing systems.
- Internal to a system, an application uses some particular representation of data. The abstract/transfer syntax scheme automatically resolves differences in representation between cooperating application entities.

The fundamental requirement for selection of a transfer syntax is that it support the corresponding abstract syntax. In addition, the transfer syntax may have other attributes that are not related to the abstract syntaxes that it can support. For example, an abstract syntax could be supported by any one of four transfer syntaxes, which are the same in all respects except that one provides data compression, one provides encryption, one provides both, and one provides neither. The choice of which transfer syntax to use would depend on cost and security considerations.

14.2

ABSTRACT SYNTAX NOTATION ONE (ASN.1)

One of the most significant developments in computer communications in recent years is the development of ASN.1. ASN.1 is now widely used both in the development of OSI-related standards and TCP/IP-related standards. It is used to define the format of protocol data units (PDUs), the representation of distributed information, and operations performed on transmitted data. A basic understanding of ASN.1 is essential for those who wish to study and work in this field.

ASN.1 Concepts

The basic building block of an ASN.1 specification is the module. We begin this section by looking at the top-level structure of the module. Then we introduce some lexical conventions used in ASN.1 definitions. Next, the data types defined in ASN.1 are described. Finally, examples of the use of ASN.1 are given.

Module Definition

ASN.1 is a language that can be used to define data structures. A structure definition is in the form of a named module. The name of the module can then be used to reference the structure. For example, the module name can be used as an abstract syntax name; an application can pass this name to the presentation service to specify the abstract syntax of the application PDUs that the application wishes to exchange with a peer application entity.

```
ModuleDefinition ::= modulereference DEFINITIONS "::=" BEGIN ModuleBody END
ModuleBody ::= AssignmentList | empty
AssignmentList ::= Assignment | AssignmentList Assignment
Assignment ::= Typeassignment | Valueassignment
Typeassignment ::= typereference "::=" Type
Valueassignment ::= valuereference Type "::="Value
Type ::= BuiltinType | DefinedType
BuiltinType ::= BooleanType | IntegerType | BitStringType | OctetStringType | NullType |
                SequenceType | SequenceOfType | SetType | SetOfType | ChoiceType |
                SelectionType | TaggedType | AnyType | ObjectIdentifierType |
                CharacterStringType | UsefulType | EnumeratedType | RealType
Value ::= BuiltinValue | DefinedValue
BuiltinValue ::= BooleanValue | IntegerValue | BitStringValue | OctetStringValue | NullValue |
                SequenceValue | SequenceOfValue | SetValue | SetOfValue | ChoiceValue |
                SelectionValue | TaggedValue | AnyValue | ObjectIdentifierValue |
                CharacterStringValue | EnumeratedValue | RealValue
DefinedValue ::= Externalvaluereference | valuereference
BooleanType ::= BOOLEAN
BooleanValue ::= TRUE | FALSE
IntegerType ::= INTEGER | INTEGER {NamedNumberList}
NamedNumberList ::= NamedNumber | NamedNumberList, NamedNumber
NamedNumber ::= identifier(SignedNumber) | identifier(DefinedValue)
SignedNumber ::= number | -number
IntegerValue ::= SignedNumber | identifier
BitStringType ::= BIT STRING | BIT STRING {NamedBitList}
NamedBitList ::= NamedBit | NamedBitList, NamedBit
NamedBit ::= identifier(number) | identifier(DefinedValue)
BitStringValue ::= bstring | hstring | {IdentifierList} | {
IdentifierList ::= Identifier | IdentifierList, identifier
OctetStringType ::= OCTETSTRING
OctetStringValue ::= bstring | hstring
NullType ::= NULL
NullValue ::= NULL
SequenceType ::= SEQUENCE {ElementTypeList) | SEQUENCE {
ElementTypeList ::= ElementType | ElementTypeList, ElementType
ElementType ::= NamedType | NamedType OPTIONAL | NamedType DEFAULT Value |
                COMPONENTS OF Type
NamedType ::= identifier Type | Type | SelectionType
SequenceValue ::= {ElementValueList} | { }
```

FIGURE 14.2.   BNF grammar for ASN.1.

Modules have the basic form

<modulereference> DEFINITIONS ::=
    BEGIN
        EXPORTS
        IMPORTS
        AssignmentList
    End

The modulereference is a module name followed optionally by an object identifier to identify the module. The EXPORTS construct indicates which definitions in this module may be imported by other modules. The IMPORTS

```
ElementValueList ::= NamedValue | ElementValueList, NamedValue
SequenceOfType ::= SEQUENCE OF Type | SEQUENCE
SequenceOfValue ::= { ValueList} | {
SetType ::= SET{ElementTypeList} | SET
SetValue ::= {ElementValueList} | {
SetOfType ::= SET OF Type | SET
SetOfValue ::= {ValueList} | { }
ChoiceType ::= CHOICE {AlternativeTypeList}
AlternativeTypeList ::= NamedType | AlternativeTypeList, NamedType
ChoiceValue ::= NamedValue
SelectionType ::= identifier < Type
SelectionValue ::= NamedValue
TaggedType ::= Tag Type | Tag IMPLICIT Type
Tag ::= [Class ClassNumber]
ClassNumber ::= number | DefinedValue
Class ::= UNIVERSAL | APPLICATION | PRIVATE | empty
TaggedValue ::= Value
AnyType ::= ANY | ANY DEFINED BY identifier
AnyValue ::= Type Value
ObjectIdentifierType ::= OBJECT IDENTIFIER
ObjectIdentifierValue {ObjIdComponentList} | {DefinedValue ObjIdComponent List}
ObjIdComponentList ::= ObjIdComponent | ObjIdComponent ObjIdComponentList
ObjIdComponent ::= NameForm | NumberForm | NameAndNumberForm
NameForm ::= identifier
NumberForm ::= number | DefinedValue
NameAndNumberForm ::= identifier(NumberForm)
CharacterStringType ::= typereference
CharacterStringValue ::= cstring
UsefulType ::= typereference
EnumeratedType ::= ENUMERATED {Enumeration}
Enumeration ::= NamedNumber | NamedNumber, Enumeration
EnumerationValue ::= identifier
RealType ::= REAL
RealValue ::= NumericRealValue | SpecialRealValue
NumericRealValue ::= {Mantissa, Base, Exponent} | 0
Mantissa ::= SignedNumber
Base::=21 10
Exponent ::= SignedNumber
SpecialRealValue ::= PLUS-INFINITY | MINUS-INFINITY
```

FIGURE 14.2. BNF grammar for ASN.1 (continued).

construct indicates which type and value definitions from other modules are to be imported into this module. Neither the IMPORTS nor EXPORTS constructs may be included unless the object identifier for the module is included. Finally, the assignment list consists of type assignments, value assignments, and macro definitions. Macro definitions are discussed later in this section. Type and value assignments have the form

<name> ::= <description>

Figure 14.2 defines the syntax for ASN.1 in Backus-Naur Form (BNF). The easiest way to describe the syntax is by example. First, we need to specify some lexical conventions.

Lexical Conventions

ASN.1 structures, types, and values are expressed in a notation similar to that of a programming language. The following lexical conventions are followed:

1. Layout is not significant; multiple spaces and blank lines can be considered as a single space.
2. Comments are delimited by pairs of hypens (--) at the beginning and end of the comment or by a pair of hyphens at the beginning of the comment and the end of the line as the end of the comment.
3. Identifiers (names of values and fields), type references (names of types), and module names consist of upper- and lower-case letters, digits, and hyphens.
4. An identifier begins with a lower-case letter.
5. A type reference or a module name begins with an upper-case letter.
6. A built-in type consists of all capital letters. A built-in type is a commonly used type for which a standard notation is provided.

Abstract Data Types

ASN.1 is a notation for abstract data types and their values. A type can be viewed as a collection of values. The number of values that a type may take on may be infinite. For example, the type INTEGER has an infinite number of values.

We can classify types into four categories:

- *Simple:* These are atomic types, with no components.
- *Structured:* A structured type has components.
- *Tagged:* These are types derived from other types.
- *Other:* This category includes the CHOICE and ANY types, defined later in this section.

Every ASN.1 data type, with the exception of CHOICE and ANY, has an associated tag. The tag consists of a class name and a nonnegative integer tag number. There are four classes of data types, or four classes of tag:

- *Universal:* Generally useful, application-independent types and construction mechanisms; these are defined in the standard and are listed in Table 14.2.
- *Application-Wide:* Relevant to a particular application; these are defined in other standards.
- *Context-Specific:* Also relevant to a particular application, but applicable in a limited context.
- *Private:* Types defined by users and not covered by any standard.

A data type is uniquely identified by its tag. ASN.1 types are the same if and only if their tag numbers are the same. For example, UNIVERSAL 4 refers to OctetString, which is of class UNIVERSAL and has tag number 4 within the class.

A **simple type** is one defined by directly specifying the set of its values. We may think of these as the atomic types; all other types are built up from the simple types. The simple data types in the UNIVERSAL class can be grouped into several categories, as indicated in Table 14.2; these are not "official" categories in the standard but are used here for convenience.

The first group of simple types can be referred to, for want of a better word, as basic types. The Boolean type is straightforward. The Integer type is the set of positive and negative integers and zero. In addition, individual integer values can be assigned names to indicate a specific meaning. The BitString is an ordered set of zero or more bits; individual bits can be assigned names. The

TABLE 14.2   Universal Class Tag Assignments

Tag	Type Name	Set of Values
Basic Types		
UNIVERSAL 1	BOOLEAN	TRUE or FALSE.
UNIVERSAL 2	INTEGER	The positive and negative whole numbers, including zero.
UNIVERSAL 3	BIT STRING	A sequence of zero or more bits.
UNIVERSAL 4	OCTET STRING	A sequence of zero or more octets.
UNIVERSAL 9	REAL	Real numbers.
UNIVERSAL 10	ENUMERATED	An explicit list of integer values that an instance of a data type may take.
Object Types		
UNIVERSAL 6	OBJECT IDENTIFIER	The set of values associated with information objects allocated by this standard.
UNIVERSAL 7	Object descriptor	Each value is human-readable text providing a brief description of an information object.
Character String Types		
UNIVERSAL 18	NumericString	Digits 0 through 9, space.
UNIVERSAL 19	PrintableString	Printable characters.
UNIVERSAL 20	TeletexString	Character set defined by CCITT Recommendation T.61.
UNIVERSAL 21	VideotextString	Set of alphabetic and graphical characters defined by CCITT Recommendations T.100 and T.101.
UNIVERSAL 22	IA5String	International alphabet five (equivalent to ASCII).
UNIVERSAL 25	GraphicString	Character set defined by ISO 8824.
UNIVERSAL 26	VisibleString	Character set defined by ISO 646 (equivalent to ASCII).
UNIVERSAL 27	GeneralString	General character string.

TABLE 14.2 (continued)

Miscellaneous Types		
UNIVERSAL 5	NULL	The single value NULL. Commonly used where several alternatives are possible but none of them apply.
UNIVERSAL 8	EXTERNAL	A type defined in some external document. It need not be one of the valid ASN.1 types.
UNIVERSAL 23	UTCTime	Consists of the date, specified with a two-digit year, a two-digit month, and a two-digit day, followed by the time, specified in hours, minutes, and optionally seconds, followed by an optional specification of the local time differential from universal time.
UNIVERSAL 24	GeneralizedTime	Consists of the date, specified with a four-digit year, a two-digit month, and a two-digit day, followed by the time, specified in hours, minutes, and optionally seconds, followed by an optional specification of the local time differential from universal time.
UNIVERSAL 9-15	Reserved	Reserved for addenda to the ASN.1 standard.
UNIVERSAL 28-	Reserved	Reserved for addenda to the ASN.1 standard.
Structured Types		
UNIVERSAL 16	SEQUENCE and SEQUENCE-OF	Sequence: defined by referencing a fixed, ordered list of types; each value is ordered list of values, one from each component type. Sequence-of: defined by referencing a single existing type; each value is an ordered list of zero or more values of the existing type.
UNIVERSAL 17	SET and SET-OF	Set: defined by referencing a fixed, unordered list of types, some of which may be declared optional; each value is an unordered list of values, one from each component type. Set-of: defined by referencing a single existing type; each value is an unordered list of zero or more values of the existing type.

actual value of a BitString can be specified as a string of either binary or hexadecimal digits. Similarly, an OctetString can be specified as a string of either binary or hexadecimal digits. The Real data type consists of numbers expressed in scientific notation (mantissa, base, exponent); that is,

$$M \times B^E$$

The mantissa (M) and the exponent (E) may take on any integer values, positive or negative; a base (B) of 2 or 10 may be used.

Finally, the Enumerated type consists of an explicitly enumerated list of integers, together with an associated name for each integer. The same functionality can be achieved with the Integer type by naming some of the integer values; but, because of the utility of this feature, a separate type has been defined. Note, however, that although the values of the enumerated type are integers, they do not have integer semantics. That is, arithmetic operations should not be performed on enumerated values.

Object types are used to name and describe information objects. Examples of information objects are standards documents, abstract and transfer syntaxes, data structures, and managed objects. In general, an information object is a class of information (e.g., a file format) rather than an instance of such a class (e.g., an individual file). The Object identifier is a unique identifier for a particular object. Its value consists of a sequence of integers. The set of defined objects has a tree structure, with the root being the object referring to the ASN.1 standard. Starting with the root of the object identifier tree, each object identifier component value identifies an arc in the tree. The Object descriptor is a human-readable description of an information object.

ASN.1 defines a number of character string types. The values of each of these types consist of a sequence of zero or more characters from a standardized character set.

There are some miscellaneous types that have also been defined in the UNIVERSAL class. The Null type is used in places in a structure where a value may or may not be present. The Null type is simply the alternative of no value being present at that position in the structure. An External type is one whose values are unspecified in the ASN.1 standard; it is defined in some other document or standard and can be defined using any well-specified notation. UTCTime and GeneralizedTime are two different formats for expressing time. In both cases, either a universal or local time may be specified.

Structured types are those consisting of components. ASN.1 provides four structured types for building complex data types from simple data types:

- SEQUENCE
- SEQUENCE OF
- SET
- SET OF

The Sequence and Sequence-of types are used to define an ordered list of values of one or more other data types. This is analogous to the record structure found in many programming languages, such as COBOL. A Sequence consists of an ordered list of elements, each specifying a type and, optionally, a name. The notation for defining the sequence type is as follows:

SequenceType ::= SEQUENCE {ElementTypeList} | SEQUENCE { }

ElementTypeList ::= ElementType | ElementTypeList,ElementType

ElementType ::=
     NamedType |
     NamedType OPTIONAL |
     NamedType DEFAULT Value |
     COMPONENTS OF Type

A NamedType is a type reference with or without a name. Each element definition may be followed by the keyword OPTIONAL or DEFAULT. The OPTIONAL keyword indicates that the component element need not be present in a sequence value. The DEFAULT keyword indicates that, if the component element is not present, then the value specified by the DEFAULT clause will be assigned. The COMPONENTS OF clause is used to define the inclusion, at this point in the ElementTypeList, of all the ElementType sequences appearing in the referenced type.

A Sequence-of consists of an ordered, variable number of elements, all of one type. A Sequence-of definition has the following form:

SequenceOfType ::= SEQUENCE OF Type | SEQUENCE

The notation SEQUENCE is to be interpreted as SEQUENCE OF ANY; the type ANY is explained in a later subsection.

A Set is similar to a Sequence, except that the order of the elements is not significant; the elements may be arranged in any order when they are encoded into a specific representation. A Set definition has the following form:

SetType ::= SET {ElementTypeList} | SET { }

Thus, a set may include optional, default, and component-of clauses.

A Set-of is an unordered, variable number of elements, all of one type. A Set-of definition has the following form:

SetOfType ::= SET OF Type | SET

The notation SET is to be interpreted as SET OF ANY; the type ANY is explained in a later subsection.

The term **tagged type** is somewhat of a misnomer since all data types in ASN.1 have an associated tag. The ASN.1 standard defines a tagged type as follows:

> A type defined by referencing a single existing type and a tag; the new type is isomorphic to the existing type, but is distinct from it. In all encoding schemes a value of the new type can be distinguished from a value of the old type.

Tagging is useful to distinguish types within an application. It may be desired to have several different type names, such as Employee_name and Customer_name, that are essentially the same type. For some structures, tagging is needed to distinguish component types within the structured type. For example, optional components of a SET or SEQUENCE type are typically given distinct context-specific tags to avoid ambiguity.

There are two categories of tagged types: implicitly tagged types and explicitly tagged types. An implicitly tagged type is derived from another type by *replacing* the tag (old class name, old tag number) of the old type with a new tag (new class name, new tag number). For purposes of encoding, only the new tag is used.

An explicitly tagged type is derived from another type by *adding* a new tag to the underlying type. In effect, an explicitly tagged type is a structured type with one component, the underlying type. For purposes of encoding, both the new and old tags must be reflected in the encoding.

An implicit tag results in shorter encodings, but an explicit tag may be necessary to avoid ambiguity if the tag of the underlying type is indeterminate (e.g., if the underlying type is CHOICE or ANY).

The **CHOICE** and **ANY types** are data types without tags. The reason for this is that when a particular value is assigned to the type, then a particular type must be assigned at the same time. Thus, the type is assigned at "run time."

The CHOICE type is a list of alternative known types. Only one of these types will actually be used to create a value. It was stated earlier that a type can be viewed as a collection of values. The CHOICE type is the union of the sets of values of all of the component types listed in the CHOICE type. This type is useful when the values to be described can be of different types depending on circumstance, and all the possible types are known in advance.

The notation for defining the CHOICE type is as follows:

ChoiceType ::= CHOICE {AlternativeTypeList}

AlternativeTypeList ::= NamedType | AlternativeTypeList, NamedType

The ANY type describes an arbitrary value of an arbitrary type. The notation is simply

AnyType ::= ANY

This type is useful when the values to be described can be of different types but the possible types are not known in advance.

Subtypes

A subtype is derived from a parent type by restricting the set of values defined for a parent type. That is, the set of values for the subtype is a subset of the set of values for the parent type. The process of subtyping can extend to more than one level; that is, a subtype may itself be a parent of an even more restricted subtype.

Six different forms of notation for designating the values of a subtype are provided in the standard. Table 14.3 indicates which of these forms can be

TABLE 14.3 Applicability of Subtype Value Sets

Type (or derived from such a type by tagging)	Single Value	Contained Subtype	Value Range	Size Constraint	Permitted Alphabet	Inner Subtyping
Boolean	✓	✓				
Integer	✓	✓	✓			
Enumerated	✓	✓				
Real	✓	✓	✓			
Object Identifier	✓	✓				
Bit String	✓	✓		✓		
Octet String	✓	✓		✓		
Character String Types	✓	✓		✓	✓	
Sequence	✓	✓				✓
Sequence-of	✓	✓		✓		✓
Set	✓	✓				✓
Set-of	✓	✓		✓		✓
Any	✓	✓				
Choice	✓	✓				✓

applied to particular parent types. The remainder of this subsection provides an overview of each form.

A **single value subtype** is an explicit listing of all of the values that the subtype may take on. For example:

SmallPrime ::= INTEGER (2 | 3 | 5 | 7 | 11 | 13 | 17 | 19 | 23 | 29)

In this case, SmallPrime is a subtype of the built-in type INTEGER. As another example:

Months ::= ENUMERATED {january (1),
                                         february (2),
                                         march (3),
                                         april (4),
                                         may (5),
                                         june (6),
                                         july (7),
                                         august (8),
                                         september (9),
                                         october (10),
                                         november (11),
                                         december (12)}

First-quarter ::= Months (january | february | march)
Second-quarter ::= Months (april | may | june)

First-quarter and Second-quarter are both subtypes of the enumerated type Months.

A **contained subtype** is used to form new subtypes from existing subtypes. The contained subtype includes all of the values of the subtypes that it contains. For example:

First-half ::= Months (INCLUDES First-quarter | INCLUDES Second-quarter)

A contained subtype may also include listing explicit values:

First-third ::= Months (INCLUDES First-quarter | april)

A **value range subtype** applies only to INTEGER and REAL types. It is specified by giving the numerical values of the endpoints of the range. The special values PLUS-INFINITY and MINUS-INFINITY may be used. The special values MIN and MAX may be used to indicate the minimum and maximum allowable values in the parent. Each endpoint of the range is either closed or open. When open, the specification of the endpoint includes the less-than symbol ("<"). The following are equivalent definitions:

PositiveInteger ::= INTEGER (0<..PLUS-INFINITY)
PositiveInteger ::= INTEGER (1..PLUS-INFINITY)
PositiveInteger ::= INTEGER (0<..MAX)
PositiveInteger ::= INTEGER (1..MAX)

The following are equivalent:

NegativeInteger ::= INTEGER (MINUS-INFINITY..<0)
NegativeInteger ::= INTEGER (MINUS-INFINITY..−1)
NegativeInteger ::= INTEGER (MIN..<0)
NegativeInteger ::= INTEGER (MIN..−1)

The **permitted alphabet constraint** may only be applied to character string types. A permitted alphabet type consists of all values (strings) that can be constructed using a sub-alphabet of the parent type. Examples:

TouchToneButtons ::= IA5String (FROM
            ("0" | "1" | "2" | "3" | "5" | "6" | "7" | "8" | "9" | "*" | "#"))
DigitString ::= IA5String (FROM
            ("0" | "1" | "2" | "3" | "5" | "6" | "7" | "8" | "9"))

A **size constraint** limits the number of items in a type. It can only be applied to the string types (bit string, octet string, character string) and to Sequence-of and Set-of types. The item that is constrained depends on the parent type, as follows:

Type	Unit of Measure
bit string	bit
octet string	octet
character string	character
sequence-of	component value
set-of	component value

As an example of a string type, Recommendation X.121 specifies that international data numbers, which are used for addressing end systems on public data networks, including X.25 networks, should consist of at least 5 digits but not more than 14 digits. This could be specified as follows:

ItlDataNumber ::= DigitString (SIZE (5..10))

Now consider a parameter list for a message that may include up to 12 parameters:

ParameterList ::= SET SIZE (0..12) OF Parameter

An **inner type constraint** can be applied to the sequence, sequence-of, set, set-of, and choice types. An inner subtype includes in its value set only those values from the parent type that satisfy one or more constraints on the presence and/or values of the components of the parent type. This is a rather complex subtype, and only a few examples are given here.

Consider a protocol data unit (PDU) that may have four different fields, in no particular order:

```
PDU ::= SET { alpha     [0]   INTEGER,
              beta      [1]   IA5String OPTIONAL,
              gamma     [2]   SEQUENCE OF Parameter,
              delta     [3]   BOOLEAN }
```

To specify a test that requires the Boolean to be false and the integer to be negative:

TestPDU ::= PDU (WITH COMPONENTS {..., delta (FALSE), alpha (MIN...<0)})

To further specify that the beta parameter is to be present and either 5 or 12 characters in length:

FurtherTestPDU ::= TestPDU (WITH COMPONENTS {..., beta (SIZE (5 | 12) PRESENT})

As another example, consider the use of inner subtyping on a sequence-of construct:

Text-block ::= SEQUENCE OF VisibleString
Address ::= Text-block (SIZE (1..6) | WITH COMPONENT (SIZE (1..32)))

This indicates that the address consists of from 1 to 6 text blocks and that each text block is from 1 to 32 characters in length.

Data Structure Example

Figure 14.3, taken from the ASN.1 standard, is an example that defines the structure of a personnel record. Part a of the figure depicts the personnel record informally by giving an example of a specific record. Such a display might correspond to the user presentation in Figure 14.1.

In part b, we see the formal description, or abstract syntax, of the data structure. In the notation, a structure definition has the form

<type name> ::= <type definition>

A simple example is

SerialNumber ::= INTEGER

There are no simple types defined in the example. A similar construction is

EmployeeNumber ::= [APPLICATION 2] IMPLICIT INTEGER

This definition makes use of the universal type Integer, but the user has chosen to give the type a new tag. The use of the term [APPLICATION 2] gives the tag (class and tag number) for this new type. Because the designation IMPLICIT is present, values of this type will be encoded only with the tag APPLICATION 2. If the designation were not present, then the values would be

Name: John P Smith
Title: Director
Employee Number: 51
Date of Hire: 17 September 1971
Name of Spouse: Mary T Smith
Number of Children: 2

Child Information
    Name: Ralph T Smith
    Date of Birth: 11 November 1957

Child Information
    Name: Susan B Jones
    Date of Birth: 17 July 1959

(a) Informal description of personnel record

PersonnelRecord ::= [APPLICATION 0] IMPLICIT SET {
        Name,
        title [0] VisibleString,
        number EmployeeNumber,
        dateOfHire [l] Date,
        nameOfSpouse [2] Name,
        children [3] IMPLICIT SEQUENCE OF ChildInformation DEFAULT { } }

ChildInformation ::= SET {
        Name,
        dateOfBirth [0] Date}

Name ::= [APPLICATION l] IMPLICIT SEQUENCE {
        givenName VisibleString,
        initial VisibleString,
        familyName VisibleString }

EmployeeNumber ::= [APPLICATION 2] IMPLICIT INTEGER

Date ::= [APPLICATION 3] IMPLICIT VisibleString — YYYYMMDD

(b) ASN.l description of the record structure

{   {givenName "John", initial "P", familyName "Smith" },
title   "Director"
number   51
dateOfHire   "19710917
nameOfSpouse   {givenName "Mary", initial "T", familyName "Smith"},
children
{ {   {givenName "Ralph", initial "T", familyName "Smith"},
    dateOfBirth   " 19571111" },
{   {givenName "Susan". initial "B", familyName "Jones"},
    dateOfBirth   "19590717" } } }

(c) ASN.l description of a record value

FIGURE 14.3.   Example of use of ASN.1.

encoded with both the APPLICATION and UNIVERSAL tags. The use of the implicit option results in a more compact representation. In some applications, compactness may be less important than other considerations, such as the ability to carry out type checking. In the latter case, explicit tagging can be used by omitting the word IMPLICIT.

The definition of the Date type is similar to that of EmployeeNumber. In this case, the type is a character string consisting of characters defined in ISO 646, which is equivalent to ASCII. The double hyphen indicates that the rest of the line is a comment; the format of the Date type will not be checked other than to determine that the value is an ISO 646 character string.

The type of Name is the Sequence type. In this case, each of the three elements in the sequence is named. ChildInformation is of the SET type. Note that no name is given to the first element of the set but that the second element is given the name dateOfBirth. The second element is the data type Date, defined elsewhere. This data type is used in two different locations, here and in the definition of PersonnelRecord. In each location, the data type is given a name and a context-specific tag, [0] and [1] respectively. This follows the general rule: When an implicit or explicit tag is defined, but only the tag number is provided, then the tag's class defaults to context specific.

Finally, the overall structure, PersonnelRecord, is defined as a Set with five elements. Associated with the last element is a default value of a null sequence, to be used if no value is supplied.

Figure 14.3c is an example of a particular value for the personnel record, expressed in the abstract syntax.

PDU Example

As another example, consider the ASN.1 specification of the format of the protocol data units for the SNMPv2 protocol (described in Chapter 15). The specification from the standard is reproduced in Figure 14.4.

One new construct in this example is the CHOICE type. This is used to describe a variable selected from a collection. Thus, any instance of the type PDU will be one of seven alternative types. Note that each of the choices is labeled with a name. Six of the PDUs defined in this fashion have the same format but different labels. The format consists of a sequence of four elements. The second element, error-status, enumerates 19 possible integer values, each with a label. The last element, variable-binding, is defined as having syntax VarBindList, which is defined later in the same set of definitions.

The BulkPDU definition is also a sequence of four elements, but it differs from the other PDUs.

VarBindList is defined as a Sequence-Of construct consisting of some number of elements of syntax VarBind, with a size constraint of up to 2147483647, or $2^{31}-1$ elements. Each element, in turn, is a sequence of two values; the first is a name, and the second is a choice among five elements.

```
SMP-PDU DEFINITIONS ::= BEGIN

PDUs ::= CHOICE {get-request          GetRequest-PDU,
                 get-next-request     GetNextRequest-PDU,
                 get-bulk-request     GetBulkRequest-PDU,
                 response             Response-PDU,
                 set-request          SetRequest-PDU,
                 inform-request       InformRequest-PDU,
                 trap                 SNMPv2-Trap-PDU  }


GetRequest-PDU          ::=     [0] IMPLICIT PDU
GetNextRequest-PDU      ::=     [1] IMPLICIT PDU
GetBulkRequest-PDU      ::=     [5] IMPLICIT PDU
Response-PDU            ::=     [2] IMPLICIT PDU
SetRequest-PDU          ::=     [3] IMPLICIT PDU
InformRequest-PDU       ::=     [6] IMPLICIT PDU
SNMPv2-Trap PDU         ::=     [7] IMPLICIT PDU


PDU ::= SEQUENCE {request-id Integer 32.
                  error-status INTEGER {              --sometimes ignored
                     noError (0),
                     tooBig (1),
                     noSuchName (2),                  --for proxy compatibility
                     badValue (3),                   --for proxy compatibility
                     readOnly (4),                   --for proxy compatibility
                     genError (5),
                     noAccess (6),
                     wrongType (7),
                     wrongLength (8),
                     wrongEncoding (9),
                     wrongValue (10),
                     noCreation (1 1),
                     inconsistentValue (12),
                     resourceUnavailable (13),
                     commitFailed (14),
                     undoFailed (15),
                     authorizationError (16),
                     notWritable (17)     },
                     inconsistentName (18)},
                  error-index INTEGER (0..2147483647),   --sometimes ignored
                  variable-binding VarBindList }          --values are sometimes ignored

BulkPDU ::= SEQUENCE {                               --MUST be identical in structure to PDU
                  request-id        Integer32,
                  non-repeaters     INTEGER (0..max-bindings),
                  max-repetitions   INTEGER (0..max-bindings),
                  variable-binding  VarBindList   }    --values are ignored

VarBind ::= SEQUENCE {name ObjectName,
                  CHOICE {value           ObjectSyntax,
                     unspecified          NULL,        --in retrieval requests
                     noSuchObject [0]     IMPLICIT NULL,
                     noSuchInstance [1]   IMPLICIT NULL,
                     endOfMibView [2]     IMPLICIT NULL } }

VarBindList ::= SEQUENCE (SIZE (0..max-bindings)) OF VarBind

END
```

FIGURE 14.4.   SNMPv2 PDU format definitions.

ASN.1 Marco Definitions

Included in the ASN.1 specification is the ASN.1 macro notation. This notation allows the user to extend the syntax of ASN.1 to define new types and their values. The subject of ASN.1 macros is a complex one, and this section serves only to introduce the subject.

Let us begin with several observations:

1. There are three levels that must be carefully distinguished:

   - The macro notation, used for defining macros.
   - A macro definition, expressed in the macro notation and used to define a set of macro instances.
   - A macro instance, generated from a macro definition by substituting values for variables.

2. A macro definition functions as a Super Type, generating a class of macro instances that function exactly like a basic ASN.1 type.[1]

3. A macro definition may be viewed as a template that is used to generate a set of related types and values.

4. The macro is used to extend the ASN.1 syntax but does not extend the encoding. Any type defined by means of a macro instance is simply an ASN.1 type and is encoded in the usual manner.

5. In addition to the convenience of defining a set of related types, the macro definition enables the user to include semantic information with the type.

We begin with a description of the general format of a macro definition. Then we look at an example. Finally, the overall macro definition process is defined.

Macro Definition Format

A macro definition has the following general form:

```
<macroname> MACRO ::=
BEGIN
   TYPE NOTATION ::= <new-type-syntax>
   VALUE NOTATION ::= <new-value-syntax>
   <supporting-productions>
END
```

The macroname is written in all upper-case letters. A new ASN.1 type is defined by writing the name of the type, which begins with a capital letter, followed by the macroname, followed by a definition of the type dictated by the form of the macro body.

The type and value notations and the supporting productions are all specified using Backus-Naur Form (BNF). The new-type-syntax describes the new

---

[1] The ASN.1 standard uses the term *basic ASN.1 type* to refer to any ASN.1 type that is not a macro instance.

type. The new-value-syntax describes the values of the new type. The supporting-productions provide any additional grammar rules for either the type or value syntax, that is, any nonterminals within the new-type-syntax and/or new-value-syntax are expanded in the supporting-productions.

When specific values are substituted for the variables or arguments of a macro definition, a macro instance is formed. This macro instance has two results. First, it generates a representation of a basic ASN.1 type, called the **returned type.** Second, it generates a representation of a generic ASN.1 value, that is, a representation of the set of values that the type may take. This generic value is called the **returned value.**

Macro Example[2]

Suppose we wish to represent a pair of integers and to be able to refer to it as an ASN.1 type in various places within an ASN.1 module. We can define a new ASN.1 type:

Pair-integers ::= SEQUENCE (INTEGER, INTEGER)

We may also have a need for a type that represents pairs whose first member is an integer and whose second member is an octet string:

Pair-integer-octet-string ::= SEQUENCE (INTEGER, OCTET STRING)

It may happen that there is a need for a number of paired structures in our module, and a large collection of defined types is assembled:

Pair-integers, Pair-octet-strings, Pair-printable-strings, Pair-booleans, Pair-object-identifiers, Pair-integer-octet-string, Pair-integer-character-string, Pair-reals, Pair-integer-real, Pair-real-integer

And so on. We may also need pairs that contain pairs:

Pair-integer-Pair-octet-strings, Pair-integer-Pair-reals, Pair-Pair-integers-Pair-integers

If such a proliferation is occurring, much of our module definition is taken up with such definitions. It is therefore preferable to find a simple representation of the concept "pairs of types."

To begin, we need a macro name to represent this concept, and we choose PAIRA. By convention, macro names are in all upper-case letters; they can be used freely anywhere a basic ASN.1 type may be used. Next, we need a general format for representing types. This can simply be "PAIRA (type,type)" as the way of expressing a macro instance, with "type" being an argument for which any ASN.1 type or any macro name may be substituted. When the substitution is made, the ASN.1 type returned by the macro instance is defined to

---

[2]This example is found in the ASN.1 standard. The narrative description is based on a discussion in [REIN88].

be SEQUENCE {type,type}. We also need to be able to express values for the new type, and we choose the format (value, value).

For example, consider this fragment of an ASN.1 module:

SET {PAIRA (INTEGER, INTEGER), OCTET STRING)

By "executing" the macro and performing the substitution, we have the following result:

SET {SEQUENCE {INTEGER, INTEGER}, OCTET STRING)

One value of this type written using the macro instance value representation is

{ (4, 20), "April 20"}

The same value using the ASN.1 value representation is

{ {4, 20}, "April 20"}

Admittedly, in this example, there is virtually no savings in using the macro definition versus directly using ASN.1 notation. We can, however, come up with a more "human-readable" form. We will call this new macro simply PAIR. The type definition format for a macro instance will be of the form

PAIR TYPE-X = type TYPE-Y = type

with a corresponding value notation:

(X = value, Y = value)

In this case, the definition

SET {PAIR TYPE-X = INTEGER TYPE-Y = INTEGER), OCTET STRING)

yields the following type result:

{ (X = 4, Y = 20), "April 20"}

Let us look at two more macro instances from the PAIR macro:

T1 ::= PAIR   TYPE-X = INTEGER
                 TYPE-Y = BOOLEAN
T2 ::= PAIR   TYPE-X = VisibleString
                 TYPE-Y = T1

Then a value of type T1 might be

(X = 3, Y = TRUE)

and a value of type T2 might be

(X = "Name", Y = (X = 4, Y = FALSE))

Figure 14.5 is the macro definition for PAIR. As with all macro definitions, it has two major parts. The first part defines the **type notation.** This part sim-

```
PAIR MACRO ::=
BEGIN
    TYPE NOTATION ::=
            "TYPE-X" "=" type (Local-type-1)        --Expects any ASN.l type and assigns it
                                                    --to the variable Local-type- 1
            "TYPE-Y" "=" type (Local-type-2)        --Expects a second ASN.l type and assigns it
                                                    --to the variable Local-type-2


    VALUE NOTATION ::=
        "("
        "X" "=" value (Local-value-1 Local-type-1)          --Expects a value for the type in
                                                            --Local-type-1 and assigns it
                                                            --to the variable Local-value-1

        "Y" "=" value (Local-value-2 Local-type-2)          --Expects a value for the type in
                                                            --Local-type-2 and assigns it
                                                            --to the variable Local-value-2

        <VALUE SEQUENCE {Local-type-1, Local-type-2}
            ::={Local-value-1. Local-value-2}>      --This "embedded definition" returns
                                                    --the final value as the value of a
                                                    --sequence of the two types

        ")"
END
```

FIGURE 14.5. ASN.1 MACRO example.

ply defines the syntax for type definition to be used in a macro instance and does not define the resulting type. The production includes the following key elements:

1. Character strings enclosed in quotation marks are to be reproduced exactly in the macro instance that declares a variable to be of the type of this macro.
2. An argument is any non-terminal in the macro definition other than non-terminals of types local-type-reference or local-value-reference. Such terms are variables, for which a substitution is made to form the macro instance.
3. The keyword TYPE is used to specify that each macro instance contains, at this point, using standard ASN.1, some ASN.1 type name.

The second major part of the macro definition is the **value notation.** This part determines the type of the macro instance and also defines the syntax for specifying values of the macro instance. The production includes the following key elements:

1. Character strings enclosed in quotation marks are to be reproduced exactly in specifying a value for a type defined by a macro instance.
2. An argument is any non-terminal in the macro definition other than non-terminals of types local-type-reference or local-value-reference. Such terms are variables, for which a substitution is made to form the macro instance.
3. The keyword VALUE is used to specify that each macro instance contains at this point, using standard ASN.1, some value of a type specified in the macro defintion.

4. The keyword VALUE is used to mark the place in the macro definition where the actual type of the macro is specified. The type appearing immediately after VALUE is the macro's returned type; that is, any value derived from the macro is encoded as a value of that type.

Macros Versus Defined Types

The ASN.1 macro facility provides tools for

1. Defining new types.
2. Representing those types.
3. Representing values of those types.
4. Encoding specific values of those types.

A similar capability already exists with ASN.1, which allows for the construction of defined types, either from built-in types or recursively from built-in types and defined types. The macro facility differs from the ASN.1 defined type capability in the following respects:

1. The macro facility allows the definition of a family of types. Each new type generated by a macro definition (a macro instance) is closely related to other types generated from the same macro. In contrast, there is no particular relationship between one basic ASN.1 defined type and other defined types.
2. A defined type is represented in a set way from the strings symbolizing the types from which it is constructed. A macro instance is represented in whatever way the writer of the macro chooses. Thus, the syntax of a type defined via macro instance can be chosen to correspond closely to the notation used within the particular application for which the macro was written. Furthermore, the macro instance may include commentary or semantic narrative. In this way, types defined by a macro may be more readable and more writeable.
3. In basic ASN.1, the representation of a value of a type is derived from the representation of the type in a relatively straightforward manner. The two representations are isomorphic; that is, they have similar or identical structure. This isomorphism is not required with a macro definition. The returned type and the returned generic value may have quite different syntaxes. Again, this allows for more readable and writeable values.

Macro Paradigm

Figure 14.6 illustrates the ASN.1 macro paradigm from conception through implementation to encoding. let us follow the steps of this diagram.

1. Starting with a concept to be represented, a set of types is chosen that adequately represents the concept. We have referred informally to this set of types as a Super Type.

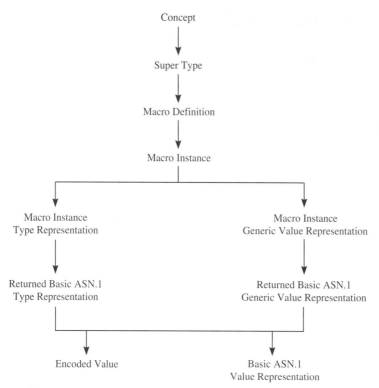

FIGURE 14.6. ASN.1 macro paradigm.

2. A macro definition, which is a concrete realization of a Super Type, is written according to the rules of the ASN.1 macro definition notation.
3. The macro definition is parameterized so that any of the types in the Super Type may be generated via the substitution of arguments when writing a particular instance of the macro definition.
4. A macro instance defines an ASN.1 type, and since any ASN.1 type has a defined type representation as well as a defined generic value representation, a macro instance provides a type representation and a generic value representation for the new ASN.1 type being defined.
5. The final result of the macro instance is returned as an argument and specifies the basic ASN.1 type representation. Since this is isomorphic to the corresponding generic value representation, the latter is also implicitly returned.
6. A specific value of the type defined by the macro instance can be encoded using the equivalent ASN.1 encoding and can be represented using the basic ASN.1 value representation.

Figure 14.7 illustrates the process of defining the PAIR macro.

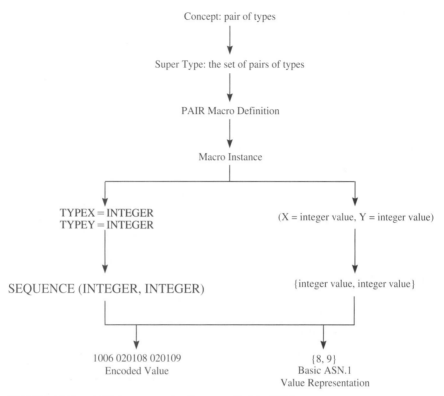

FIGURE 14.7.   ASN.1 macro paradigm applied to PAIR.

SNMPv2 OBJECT-TYPE Macro

Another example of a macro is illustrated in Figure 14.8. This macro is defined in the SNMPv2 standard (discussed in Chapter 15) and is used to define management objects. A management object is an individual variable or item of management information stored in a management information base. Thus, this is an example of the use of ASN.1 to specify the syntax of locally maintained data that are used by a distributed application.

The type notation portion of this macro consists of eight parts:

- The SYNTAX clause specifies the ASN.1 syntax type of this object. Object-Syntax defines a subset of ASN.1 types that may be used to define managed objects; its definition is not shown.
- The UNITS clause can be used to specify what units a numerical value has.
- The MAX-ACCESS clause is used to specify the access privileges for this object. Some objects are not accessible by remote users but are used by the local system for data structuring purposes. Other objects may be read-only, read-write, or read-create.
- The STATUS clause indicates the current status of this object with respect to whether it is part of the most recent standard.

```
OBJECT-TYPE MACRO ::= BEGIN
TYPE NOTATION                    ::= "SYNTAX" type (ObjectSyntax)
                                 UnitsPart
                                 "MAX-ACCESS" Access
                                 "STATUS" Status
                                 "DESCRIPTION" Text
                                 ReferPart
                                 IndexPart
                                 DefValPart

VALUE NOTATION ::= value (VALUE ObjectName)

UnitsPart ::= "UNITS" Text | empty

Access ::="not-accessible" | "read-only" | "read-write" | "read-create"

Status ::= "current" | "deprecated" | "obsolete"

ReferPart ::= "REFERENCE" Text | empty

IndexPart  ::=  "INDEX"  "{"IndexTypes"}"|"AUGMENTS"  "{"Entry"}"|empty

IndexTypes ::= IndexType | IndexTypes "," IndexType

IndexType ::= "IMPLIED" Index | Index

Index ::= value (indexobject ObjectName)        --use the SYNTAX value of the correspondent
                                                --OBJECT-TYPE invocation

Entry ::= value (entryobject ObjectName)        --use the INDEX value of the correspondent
                                                --OBJECT-TYPE invocation

DefValPart ::= "DEFVAL" "{" value (Defval ObjectSyntax) "}" | empty

END
```

FIGURE 14.8.   SNMPv2 macro for object definition.

- The DESCRIPTION clause is used to provide a textual description of the object.
- The REFERENCE clause is used to provide a cross-reference to another portion of the management information base.
- The INDEX clause is used if this object refers to a tabular structure. The clause lists the object or objects that serve as indexes into the table.
- The AUGMENTS clause is used to specify that this object refers to a tabular structure that is to be appended to another tabular structure.
- The DEFVAL clause is used to provide a default value for this object, to be supplied upon creation of the object by the local system.

The value of an object is an identifier, ObjectName, which provides a unique reference for the object.

An example of the use of this macro is the following SNMPv2 object definition:

```
snmpEventNotifyIntervalRequested OBJECT-TYPE
    SYNTAX          Integer32
    UNITS           "seconds"
    MAX-ACCESS      read-create
    STATUS          current
    DESCRIPTION
        "The requested interval for retransmission of Inform PDUs generated
        on behalf of this entry.

        This variable will be the actual interval used unless the snmp-
        EventNotifyMinInterval is greater than this object, in which case the
        interval shall be equal to snmpEventNotifyMinInterval."
    DEFVAL {30}
    ::= {snmpEventNotifyEntry 2}
```

Basic Encoding Rules

ASN.1 specifies the syntax or format of information in an abstract representation. To actually store or exchange information, it needs to be encoded as a bit pattern. The most common encoding specification for translating from an abstract syntax to a bit pattern is known as Basic Encoding Rules (BER). BER describes a method for encoding values of each ASN.1 type as a string of octets.

Encoding Structure

The Basic Encoding Rules define one or more ways to encode any ASN.1 value as an octet string. The encoding is based on the use of a type-length-value (TLV) structure. That is, any ASN.1 value can be encoded as a triple with the following components:

- Type: indicates the ASN.1 type, as well as the class of the type and whether the encoding is primitive or constructed, as explained later in this chapter.
- Length: indicates the length of the actual value representation.
- Value: the representation of the value of the ASN.1 type as a string of octets.

This structure is recursive: For any ASN.1 value that consists of one or more components, the "value" portion of its TLV encoding itself consists of one or more TLV structures.

Figure 14.9 illustrates the structure of the TLV encoding, and Figure 14.10 illustrates its use for the example personnel record value. There are three methods for encoding an ASN.1 value:

- Primitive, definite-length encoding.
- Constructed, definite-length encoding.
- Constructed, indefinite-length encoding.

(a) Encoding of each value

(b) Identifier Field

(c) Length Field

FIGURE 14.9.   BER encoding of values.

Identifier	Length	Contents
Personnel Record 60	8185	
Name 61	10	
Visible-String 1A	04	"John"
Visible-String 1A	01	"P"
Visible-String 1A	05	"Smith"
Title A0	0A	
Visible-String 1A	08	"Director"
Employee Number 42	01	33
Date of Hire A1	0A	
Date 43	08	"19710917"
Name of Spouse A2	12	
Name 61	10	
Visible-String 1A	04	"Mary"
Visible-String 1A	01	"T"
Visible-String 1A	05	"Smith"
[3] A3	42	
Set 31	1F	
Name 61	11	
Visible-String 1A	05	"Ralph"
Visible-String 1A	01	"T"
Visible-String 1A	05	"Smith"
Date of Birth A0	0A	
Date 43	08	"19571111"
Set 31	1F	
Name 61	11	
Visible String 16	05	"Susan"
Visible-String 16	01	"B"
Visible-String 1	05	"Jones"
Date of Birth A0	0A	
Date 43	08	"19590717"

FIGURE 14.10.   BER encoding for example of Figure 14.3.

The method chosen depends on the ASN.1 type of the value to be encoded and whether or not the length of the value is known based on the type. Table 14.4 summarizes the possibilities.

The **primitive, definite-length encoding** method can be used for simple types and types derived from simple types by implicit tagging. The BER format consists of three fields:

- *Identifier:* This field encodes the tag (class and tag number) of the ASN.1 type of the value. The first two bits indicate one of the four classes. The next bit is zero to indicate that this is a primitive encoding. The remaining five bits of the first octet can encode a tag number that distinguishes one data type from another within the designated class. For tags whose number is greater than or equal to 31, those five bits contain the binary value 11111, and the actual tag number is contained in the last seven bits of one or more additional octets. The first bit of each additional octet is set to 1, except for the last octet, in which it is set to 0.
- *Length:* This field specifies the length in octets of the contents field. If the length is less than 128, the length field consists of a single octet beginning with a zero. If the length is greater than 127, the first octet of the length field contains a seven-bit integer that specifies the number of additional length octets; the additional octets contain the actual length of the contents field.
- *Contents:* This field directly represents the ASN.1 value as a string of octets. Details for particular types are given later in this section.

The **constructed, definite-length encoding** method can be used for simple string types, structured types (Sequence, Sequence-of, Set, Set-of), types derived from simple string types and structured types by implicit tagging, and any type defined by explicit tagging. This encoding method requires that the length of the value be known in advance. The BER format consists of three fields:

- *Identifier:* As described for primitive, definite-length encoding, except that the P/C bit is set to 1 to indicate that this is constructed encoding.
- *Length:* As described for primitive, definite-length encoding.

TABLE 14.4   BER Encoding Methods

	Primitive, Definite-Length Encoding	Constructed, Definite-Length Encoding	Constructed, Indefinite-Length Encoding
Simple non-string types	✔		
Simple string types	✔	✔	✔
Structured types		✔	✔
Explicit tagging		✔	✔

- *Contents:* This field contains the concatenation of the complete BER encodings (identifier, length, contents) of the components of the value. There are three cases:

  1. Simple strings and types derived from simple strings by implicit tagging: the concatenation of the BER encodings of consecutive substrings of the value.
  2. Structured types and types derived from structured types by implicit tagging: the concatenation of the BER encodings of components of the value.
  3. Types defined by explicit tagging: the BER encoding of the underlying value.

The **constructed, indefinite-length encoding** method can be used for simple string types, structured types, types derived from simple string types and structured types by implicit tagging, and any type defined by explicit tagging. This encoding method does not require that the length of the value be known in advance. The BER format consists of four fields:

- *Identifier:* As described for constructed, indefinite-length encoding.
- *Length:* One octet, with the value 80_{16}.
- *Contents:* As described for constructed, indefinite-length encoding.
- *End-of-contents:* Two octets, with the value 0000_{16}.

Contents Encoding

Table 14.5 summarizes the rules for encoding for the various ASN.1 types. The table gives only a concise definition of the rules; for more detail, the reader should consult the standard.

Most of the encoding rules for ASN.1 types are relatively straightforward. For some types, a few additional comments are warranted.

Integer values are represented using two's-complement notation. This notation can be briefly summarized as follows.[3] Consider an integer in two's complement representation stored in an N-bit field. There are two cases: nonnegative and negative.

Nonnegative numbers are represented as follows. The leftmost (most significant) bit is zero, and the remaining bits are the binary form of the magnitude of the number. A negative number whose magnitude is X and for which X has a value of less than or equal to 2^{N-1} is represented by calculating $2^N - X$. For all negative numbers, the leftmost bit has a value 1. Thus, this bit functions as a sign bit.

If an N-bit sequence of binary digits $b_{N-1}b_{N-2} \cdots b_1b_0$ is interpreted as a two's complement representation, the value can be calculated as follows:

$$\text{Value} = -b_{N-1}2^{N-1} + \sum_{i=0}^{N-2} b_i 2^i$$

[3]For a more complete discussion of two's complement representation and two's complement arithmetic, see [STAL93c].

TABLE 14.5 BER Encoding Rules

ASN.1 type	BER encoding rules	Example Value	Encoding of example value[1]
BOOLEAN	Primitive. A single octet with a content of zero for FALSE and a non-zero content for TRUE.	TRUE	01 01 FF
INTEGER	Primitive. Two's complement representation with the minimum number of octets.	−129	02 02 FF 7F
ENUMERATED	Same as the integer value with which it is associated.		
REAL	Primitive. If the value of zero, there are no contents octets. Otherwise, the first contents octet indicates whether the base is 10, 2, 8, or 16, or a special real value (+∞, −∞). If base is 10, first contents octet also specifies one of three ISO 6093 character encoding schemes for the remaining contents octets. If base is 2, 8, or 16, first contents octet also specifies length of exponent, sign of mantissa, and scaling factor to align implied decimal point of mantissa with octet boundary; following the first contents octet are zero or one additional octets to specify exponent length, followed by octets for the exponent, followed by octets for the mantissa.	0	09 00

BIT STRING	Primitive or constructed. For primitive encoding, the contents consist of an initial octet followed by zero or more subsequent octets. The actual bit string begins with the first bit of the second octet and continues through as many octets as necessary. The first octet indicates how many bits in the last octet are unused.
	
	    For constructed encoding, the bit string is broken up into substrings; each substring except the last must be a multiple of 8 bits in length. Each substring may be encoded as primitive or constructed, but usually the primitive encoding is used.
		"0110111001 01110111"	primitive:
			03 04 06 6E 5D C0
			
			constructed:
			23 09
			    03 03 00 6E 5D
			    03 02 06 C0

Type	Description	Value / Definition	Encoding
OCTET STRING	Primitive or constructed. For primitive encoding, the contents octets are identical to the value of the octet string. For constructed encoding, the octet string is broken up into substrings; each substring may be encoded as primitive or constructed, but usually the primitive encoding is used.	01 23 45 67	primitive: 04 04 01 23 45 67 constructed: 24 08 04 02 01 23 04 02 34 56
NULL	Primitive. There are no contents octets.	null	05 00
SEQUENCE	Constructed. The contents octets are the concatenation of the BER encodings of the values of the components of the sequence in order of definition. If the value of a component with the OPTIONAL or DEFAULT qualifier is absent from the sequence, no encoding is included for that component. If the value of a component with the DEFAULT qualifier is the default value, then encoding of that component may or may not be included.	definition: SEQUENCE (INTEGER, INTEGER) value: (3, 8)	30 06 02 01 03 02 01 08
SEQUENCE OF	Constructed. The contents octets are the concatenation of the BER encodings of the values of the occurrences in the collection, in the order of occurrence.	definition: SEQUENCE OF (INTEGER) value: (3,8)	30 06 02 01 03 02 01 08
SET	Constructed. The contents octets are the concatenation of the BER encodings of the values of the components of the sequence in any order. If the value of a component with the OPTIONAL or DEFAULT qualifier is absent from the sequence, no encoding is included for that component. If the value of a component with the DEFAULT qualifier is the default value, then encoding of that component may or may not be included.	definition: SET (INTEGER, INTEGER) value: (3,8)	31 06 02 01 03 02 01 08

TABLE 14.5 (continued)

ASN.1 type	BER encoding rules	Example Value	Encoding of example value[1]

SET OF	Constructed. The contents octets are the concatenation of the BER encodings of the values of the occurrences in the collection, in any order.	definition: SET OF (INTEGER)
		
		value: (3,8)
			31 06
			  02 01 03
			  02 01 08

CHOICE	Primitive or constructed. The encoding of the CHOICE value is the encoding of the chosen alternative.		
IMPLICIT tag	Primitive or constructed. The encoding of the tag field replaces the underlying tag value. The encoding of the length and contents octets are the same as for the underlying value.	definition: [17] IMPLICIT BOOLEAN value: TRUE	91 01 FF
EXPLICIT tag	Constructed. The contents octets are the complete BER encoding of the underlying value.	definition: [17] BOOLEAN value: TRUE	B1 03 01 01 FF
ANY	Primitive or constructed. The encoding of the ANY value is the encoding of the actual value.		
OBJECT IDENTIFIER	Primitive. The first two components are combined using the formula $(X \times 40) + Y$ to form the first subidentifier. Each subsequent component forms the next subidentifier. Each subidentifier is encoded as a nonnegative integer using as few 7-bit blocks as possible. The blocks are packed in octets with the first bit of each octet equal to one except for the last octet of each subidentifier.	{2 100 3}	06 03 81 34 03
Character String	Primitive or constructed. Encoded as if it had been declared [UNIVERSAL x] IMPLICIT OCTET STRING.	"Jones"	1A 05 4A 6F 6E 65 73

[1]All encodings are depicted using hexadecimal notation

The largest negative number that can be represented is -2^{N-1}, and the largest positive integer that can be represented is $2^{N-1} - 1$. Thus, in a single octet, the range of numbers that can be represented is $-128 \le \text{value} \le 127$.

An important characteristic of the two's complement representation is the way in which an N-bit number is padded out to form an M-bit number, where $M > N$. For nonnegative numbers, the representation is padded out by adding additional 0's to the left. For negative numbers, the representation is padded out by adding additional 1's to the left.

BER dictates that the minimum number of octets be used for representing integers. Thus, if the value is between -128 and $+127$, only a single octet is used. Note that care must be taken for unsigned variables, such as counters and gauges. If a 32-bit counter has a value of 2^{31} or greater, then five octets rather than four will be needed to encode it. For example, in the SNMP structure of management information, the counter type is defined as follows:

Counter ::= [APPLICATION 1]IMPLICIT INTEGER (0..4294967295)

This defines an unsigned 32-bit integer with a maximum value of $2^{32} - 1$.

Now consider a 32-bit counter that has its maximum value of $FFFFFFFF_{16}$. The correct encoding, in hexadecimal, is

41 05 00 FF FF FF FF

The identifier octet specifies that this is an application class type with tag number 1. The length octet specifies that the value length is five octets. Because of the use of two's complement representation, the value cannot be encoded in four octets.

For the simple **string types,** the encoding can either be primitive or constructed. For the constructed encoding, the string is broken up into a number of substrings, each of which is encoded using BER rules. Since these rules are recursive, each substring can be further subdivided into sub-substrings using the constructed encoding.

The way in which a string is broken up into substrings is arbitrary and at the convenience of the encoding process. That is, the boundaries that define the substrings are arbitrary.

An **object identifier** consists of a sequence of integers. The BER encoding packs the first two integers into a single subidentifier. Thus, an identifier consisting of N integers has $N - 1$ subidentifiers.

The reason that the first two integers can be combined is that the first integer always takes on the value 0, 1, or 2, and the second integer must be less than 40 if the first integer is 0 or 1. The packing formula is

$$Z = (X \times 40) + Y$$

where X is the first integer, Y is the second integer, and Z is the resulting subidentifier value. The result can be summarized as follows:

Subidentifer Value	First Integer	Second Integer
$0 \leq Z \leq 39$	0	Z
$40 \leq Z \leq 79$	1	$Z - 40$
$80 \leq Z$	2	$Z - 80$

14.3

ENCRYPTION AND AUTHENTICATION CODES

One of the most important automated tools for computer security is encryption. Encryption is a process that conceals meaning by changing intelligible messages into unintelligible messages. Encryption can be by means of either a code or a cipher. A code system uses a predefined table or dictionary to substitute a meaningless word or phrase for each message or part of a message. The simplest code would substitute another letter for each letter of the alphabet. A cipher uses a computable algorithm that can translate any stream of message bits into an unintelligible cryptogram. Because cipher techniques lend themselves more readily to automation, it is these techniques that are used in contemporary computer and network security facilities. This section discusses only cipher techniques.

We begin by looking at the traditional approach to encryption, now known as conventional encryption. We then look at a new and quite useful technique known as public-key encryption. The remainder of the section deals with the use of encryption and similar techniques to achieve message authentication.

Conventional Encryption

Figure 14.11 illustrates the conventional encryption process. The original intelligible message, referred to as *plaintext,* is converted into apparently random nonsense, referred to as *ciphertext.* The encryption process consists of an algorithm and a key. The key is a relatively short bit string that controls the algorithm. The algorithm will produce a different output depending on the specific key being used at the time. Changing the key radically changes the output of the algorithm.

Once the ciphertext is produced, it is transmitted. Upon reception, the ciphertext can be transformed back to the original plaintext by using a decryption algorithm and the same key that was used for encryption.

The security of conventional encryption depends on several factors. First, the encryption algorithm must be powerful enough so that it is impractical to decrypt a message on the basis of the ciphertext alone. Beyond that, the security of conventional encryption depends on the secrecy of the key, not the secrecy of the algorithm. That is, it is assumed that it is impractical to decript a message on the basis of the ciphertext *plus* knowledge of the encryption/decryption

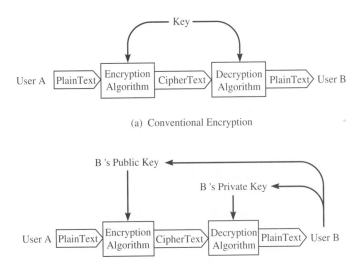

(a) Conventional Encryption

(b) Public Key Encryption

FIGURE 14.11.   Encryption.

algorithm. In other words, we don't need to keep the algorithm secret; we only need to keep the key secret.

This feature of conventional encryption is what makes it feasible for widespread use. The fact that the algorithm need not be kept secret means that manufacturers can, and have, developed low-cost chip implementations of data encryption algorithms. These chips are widely available and incorporated into a number of products. With the use of conventional encryption, the principal security problem is maintaining the secrecy of the key.

The most widely used encryption scheme is based on the data encryption standard (DES), adopted in 1977 by the National Bureau of Standards. For DES, data are encrypted in 64-bit blocks using a 56-bit key. Using the key, the 64-bit input is transformed in a series of steps into a 64-bit output. The same steps, with the same key, are used to reverse the encryption.

Public-Key Encryption

One of the major difficulties is with conventional encryption schemes is the need to distribute the keys in a secure manner. A clever way around this requirement is an encryption scheme that, surprisingly, does not require key distribution. This scheme, known as public-key encryption and first proposed in 1976, is illustrated in Figure 14.11b.

For conventional encryption schemes, the keys used for encryption and decryption are the same. This is not a necessary condition. Instead, it is possible to develop an algorithm that uses one key for encryption and a companion but different key for decryption. Furthermore, it is possible to develop algorithms such that knowledge of the encryption algorithm plus the encryption key is not sufficient to determine the decryption key. Thus the following technique will work:

1. Each end system in a network generates a pair of keys to be used for encryption and decryption of messages that it will receive.
2. Each system publishes its encryption key by placing it in a public register or file. This is the public key. The companion key is kept private.
3. If A wishes to send a message to B, it encrypts the message using B's public key.
4. When B receives the message, it decrypts it using B's private key. No other recipient can decrypt the message since only B knowns B's private key.

As you can see, public-key encryption solves the key distribution problem, since there are no keys to distribute! All participants have access to public keys, and private keys are generated locally by each participant and therefore need never be distributed. As long as a system controls its private key, its incoming communication is secure. At any time, a system can change its private key and publish the companion public key to replace its old public key.

A main disadvantage of public-key encryption compared to conventional encryption is that algorithms for the former are much more complex. Thus, for comparable size and cost of hardware, the public-key scheme will provide much lower throughput.

Table 14.6 summarizes some of the important aspects of conventional and public-key encryption.

TABLE 14.6   Conventional and Public-Key Encryption

Conventional Encryption	Public-Key Encryption
Needed to Work:	**Needed to Work:**
1. The same algorithm with the same key can be use for encryption and decryption.	1. One algorithm is used for encryption and decryption with a pair of keys, one for encryption and one for decryption.
2. The sender and receiver must share the algorithm and the key.	2. The sender and receiver must each have one of the matched pair of keys.
Needed for Security:	**Needed for Security:**
1. The key must be kept secret.	1. One of the two keys must be kept secret.
2. It must be impossible or at least impractical to decipher a message if no other information is available.	2. It must be impossible or at least impractical to decipher a message if no other information is available.
3. Knowledge of the algorithm plus samples of ciphertext must be insufficient to determine the key.	3. Knowledge of the algorithm plus one of the keys plus samples of ciphertext must be insufficient to determine the other key.

Message Authentication

Encryption protects against passive attack (eavesdropping). A different requirement is to protect against active attack (falsification of data and transactions). Protection against such attacks is known as message authentication.

A message, file, document, or other collection of data is said to be authentic when it is genuine and came from its alleged source. Message authentication is a procedure that allows the communicating parties to verify that received messages are authentic. The two important aspects are to verify that the contents of the message have not been altered and that the source is authentic. We may also wish to verify a message's timeliness (it has not been artifically delayed and replayed) and sequence relative to other messages flowing between two parties.

Authentication Using Conventional Encryption

It is possible to perform authentication simply by the use of conventional encryption. If we assume that only the sender and receiver share a key (which is as it should be), then only the genuine sender would be able to successfully encrypt a message for the other participant. Furthermore, if the message includes an error-detection code and a sequence number, the receiver is assured that no alterations have been made and that sequencing is proper. If the message also includes a timestamp, the receiver is assured that the message has not been delayed beyond that normally expected for network transit.

Digital Signature Using Public-Key Encryption

Authentication using conventional encryption protects two parties exchanging messages from any third party. However, it does not protect the two parties against each other. Several forms of dispute between the two are possible.

For example, suppose that John sends an authenticated message to Mary, using the scheme of Figure 14.11a. Consider the following disputes that could arise:

1. Mary may forge a different message and claim that it came from John. Mary would simply have to create a message and encrypt it using the key that John and Mary share.
2. John can deny sending the message. Since it is possible for Mary to forge a message, there is no way to prove that John did in fact send the message.

Both of these scenarios are of legitimate concern. An example of the first scenario: An electronic funds transfer takes place, and the receiver increases the amount of funds transferred and claims that the larger amount had arrived from the sender. An example of the second scenario: An electronic mail message contains instructions to a stockbroker for a transaction that subsequently turns out badly. The sender pretends that the message was never sent.

In situations where there is not complete trust between sender and receiver, something more than authentication is needed. The most attractive solution to this problem is the digital signature. The digital signature is analogous to the handwritten signature. It must have the following properties:

• It must be able to verify the author and the date and time of the signature.
• It must be able to authenticate the contents at the time of the signature.
• The signature must be verifiable by third parties, to resolve disputes.

Thus the digital signature function includes the authentication function.

A variety of approaches has been proposed for the digital signature function. In this section, we look at the use of public-key encryption for providing authentication and digital signature.

Figure 14.12a illustrates a simple digital signature scheme using public-key encryption. This scheme exploits an important characteristic of all public-key encryption algorithms: The two keys can be used in either order. That is, one can encrypt with the public key and decrypt with the matching private key, or encrypt with the private key and decrypt with the matching public key. Figure 14.12a illustrates the latter application. Note what is happening. *A* prepares a message to *B* and encrypts it using *A*'s private key before transmitting it. *B* can decrypt the message using *A*'s public key. Because the message was encrypted using *A*'s private key, only *A* could have prepared the message. Therefore, the entire encrypted message serves as the signature. In addition, it is impossible to alter the message without access to *A*'s private key, so the message is authenticated.

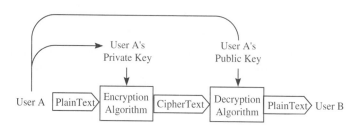

(a) Simple Digital Signature Scheme Providing Authentication

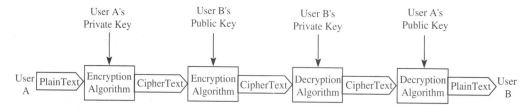

(b) Digital Signature Scheme Providing Authentication and Secrecy

FIGURE 14.12.   Digital signature using public-key system.

In the preceding scheme, the entire message is encrypted. While this validates both author and contents, it would require a great deal of storage. Each document would have to be kept in plaintext to be used for practical purposes. A copy also would have to be keyed in ciphertext so the origin and contents could be verified in case of a dispute. A more efficient way of achieving the same results is to encrypt only a portion of the document. A minimal portion would include the sender's name, the receiver's name, a sequence number, and a checksum. If this portion of the message is encrypted with the sender's private key, it serves as a signature that verifies origin, content, and sequencing.

It is important to emphasize that the encryption process just described does not provide secrecy. That is, the message being sent is safe from alteration but not safe from eavesdropping. This is obvious in the case of a signature based on a portion of the message, since the rest of the message is transmitted in the clear. Even in the case of complete encryption, as shown in Figure 14.12a, there is no protection of secrecy since any observer can decrypt the message using the sender's public key.

It is, however, possible to provide both the digital signature function, which includes authentication, and secrecy by a double use of the public-key scheme. This is illustrated in Figure 14.12b. In this case, we begin, as before, by encrypting a message using the sender's private key. This provides the digital signature. Next, we encrypt again, using the receiver's public key. The final ciphertext can only be decrypted by the intended receiver, who alone possesses the matching private key. Thus secrecy is provided. The disadvantage of this approach is that the public-key algorithm, which is complex, must be exercised four times rather than two in each communication.

Message Authentication Without Message Encryption

We have seen several schemes for message authentication that rely on encryption of the entire message. In this section, we examine several other approaches. In all of these approaches, an authentication tag is generated and appended to each message for transmission. The message itself is not encrypted and can be read at the destination independent of the authentication function at the destination.

Because the approaches discussed in this section do not encrypt the message, message secrecy is not provided. Since conventional encryption will provide authentication, and since it is widely used with readily available products, why not simply use such an approach, which provides both secrecy and authentication? [DAVI90] suggests three situations in which message authentication without secrecy is preferable:

1. There are a number of applications in which the same message is broadcast to a number of destinations, for example, notification to users that the network is now unavailable or an alarm signal in a control center. It is cheaper and more reliable to have only one destination responsible for monitoring authenticity. Thus, the message must be broadcast in plaintext with an as-

sociated message authentication tag. The responsible system performs authentication. If a violation occurs, the other destination systems are alerted by a general alarm.

2. Another possible scenario is an exchange in which one side has a heavy load and cannot afford the time to decrypt all incoming messages. Authentication is carried out on a selective basis, messages being chosen at random for checking.

3. Authentication of a computer program in plaintext is an attractive service. The computer program can be executed without having to decrypt it every time, which would be wasteful of processor resources. However, if a message authentication tag were attached to the program, it could be checked whenever assurance is required of the integrity of the program.

Thus there is a place for both authentication and encryption in meeting security requirements.

Message Authentication Code

One authentication technique involves the use of a secret key to generate a small block of data, known as a message authentication code, that is appended to the message. This technique assumes that two communicating parties, say A and B, share a common secret key K_{AB}. When A has a message to send to B, it calculates the message authentication code as a function of the message and the key: $MAC_M = F(K_{AB}, M)$. The message plus code are transmitted to the intended recipient. The recipient performs the same calculation on the received message, using the same secret key, to generate a new message authentication code. The received code is compared to the calculated code (Figure 14.13). If we assume that only the receiver and the sender know the identity of the secret key, and if the received code matches the calculated code, then

1. The receiver is assured that the message has not been altered. If an attacker alters the message but does not alter the code, then the receiver's calculation of the code will differ from the received code. Since the attacker is assumed not to know the secret key, the attacker can not alter the code to correspond to the alterations in the message.

2. The receiver is assured that the message is from the alleged sender. Since no one else knows the secret key, no one else could prepare a message with a proper code.

3. If the message includes a sequence number (such as is used with X.25, HDLC, TCP, and the ISO transport protocol), then the receiver can be assured of the proper sequence, since an attacker can not successfully alter the sequence number.

A number of algorithms could be used to generate the code. The National Bureau of Standards, in its publication *DES Modes of Operation*, recommends the use of the DES algorithm. The DES algorithm is used to generate an encrypted version of the message, and the last number of bits of ciphertext are used as the code. A 16- or 32-bit code is typical.

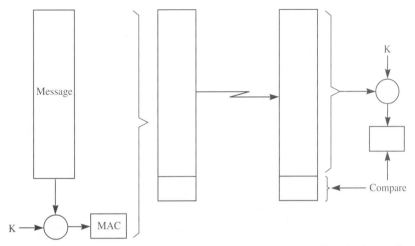

FIGURE 14.13.   Message authentication using a message authentication code (MAC).

The process just described is similar to encryption. One difference is that the authentication algorithm need not be reversible, as it must for decryption. It turns out that because of the mathematical properties of the authentication function, it is less vulnerable to being broken than encryption.

One-Way Hash Function

A variation on the message authentication code that has received much attention recently is the one-way hash function. As with the message authentication code, a hash function accepts a variable-size message M as input and produces a fixed-size tag H(M), sometimes called a message digest, as output. To authenticate a message, the message digest is sent with the message in such a way that the message digest is authentic.

Figure 14.14 illustrates three ways in which the message digest can be authenticated. The message digest can be encrypted using conventional encryption (part (a)); if it is assumed that only the sender and receiver share the encryption key, then authenticity is assured. The message can also be encrypted using public-key encryption (part (b)). The public-key approach has two advantages: It provides a digital signature as well as message authentication, and it does not require the distribution of keys to communicating parties.

These two approaches have an advantage over approaches that encrypt the entire message, in that less computation is required. Nevertheless, there has been interest in developing a technique that avoids encryption altogether. Several reasons for this interest are pointed out in [TSUD92]:

• Encryption software is quite slow. Even though the amount of data to be encrypted per message is small, there may be a steady stream of messages into and out of a system.

FIGURE 14.14.   Message authentication using a one-way hash function.

- Encryption hardware costs are non-negligible. Low-cost chip implementations of DES are available, but the cost adds up if all nodes in a network must have this capability.
- Encryption hardware is optimized toward large data sizes. For small blocks of data, a high proportion of the time is spent in initialization/invocation overhead.
- Encryption algorithms may be covered by patents. Some encryption algorithms, such as the RSA public-key algorithm, are patented and must be licensed, adding a cost.
- Encryption algorithms may be subject to export control. This is true of DES.

Figure 14.14c shows a technique that uses a hash function but not encryption for message authentication. This technique assumes that two communicating parties, say A and B, share a common secret value S_{AB}. When A has a message to send to B, it calculates the hash function over the concatenation of the secret value and the message: $MD_M = H(S_{AB}\|M)$.[4] It then sends $[M\|MD_M]$ to B. Since B possesses S_{AB}, it can recompute $H(S_{AB}\|M)$ and verify MD_M. Since the secret value itself is not sent, it is not possible for an attacker to modify an intercepted message. As long as the secret value remains secret, it is also not possible for an attacker to generate a false message.

This third technique, using a shared secret value, is the one adopted for SNMPv2 (described in Chapter 15).

Hash Function Requirements

The purpose of a hash function is to produce a "fingerprint" of a file, message, or other block of data. To be useful for message authentication, a hash function H must have the following properties, adapted from a list in [NECH91]:

1. H can be applied to a block of data of any size.
2. H produces a fixed-length output.
3. $H(x)$ is relatively easy to compute for any given x, making both hardware and software implementations practical.
4. For any given code m, it is computationally infeasible to find x such that $H(x) = m$.
5. For any given block x, it is computationally infeasible to find $y \neq x$ with $H(y) = H(x)$.
6. It is computationally infeasible to find any pair (x, y) such that $H(x) = H(y)$.

The first three properties are requirements for the practical application of a hash function to message authentication.

The fourth property is the "one-way" property: It is easy to generate a code given a message but virtually impossible to generate a message given a code. This property is important if the authentication technique involves the use of a secret value (Figure 14.14c). The secret value itself is not sent; however, if the hash function is not one-way, an attacker can easily discover the secret value: If the attacker can observe or intercept a transmission, the attacker obtains the message M and the hash code $MD_M = H(S_{AB}\|M)$. The attacker then inverts the hash function to obtain $S_{AB}\|M = H^{-1}(MD_M)$. Since the attacker now has both M and $S_{AB}\|M$, it is a trivial matter to recover S_{AB}.

The fifth property guarantees that an alternative message hashing to the same value as a given message cannot be found. This prevents forgery when an encrypted hash code is used (Figure 14.14b and c). If this property were not true, an attacker would be capable of the following sequence: First, observe or intercept a message plus its encrypted hash code; second, generate an unen-

----

[4]$\|$ denotes concatenation.

crypted hash code from the message; third, generate an alternate message with the same hash code.

A hash function that satisfies the first five properties in the preceding list is referred to as a weak hash function. If the sixth property is also satisfied, then it is referred to as a strong hash function. The sixth property protects against a sophisticated class of attack known as the birthday attack.[5]

In addition to providing authentication, a message digest also provides data integrity. It performs the same function as a frame check sequence: If any bits in the message are accidentally altered in transit, the message digest will be in error.

The MD5 Message-Digest Algorithm

The MD5 message-digest algorithm was developed by Ron Rivest at M.I.T. (the R in the RSA (Rivest–Shamir–Adelman) public-key encryption algorithm). The algorithm takes as input a message of arbitrary length and produces as output a 128-bit message digest. Before looking at the details of MD5, it will be of help to motivate the complexity of MD5 to look at two simple examples of hash functions.

Simple Hash Functions

All hash functions operate using the following general principles. The input (message, file, etc.) is viewed as a sequence of n-bit blocks. The input is processed one block at a time in an iterative fashion to produce an n-bit hash function.

One of the simplest hash functions is to take the bit-by-bit exclusive-or (XOR) of every block. This can be expressed as follows:

$$C_i = b_{i1} \oplus b_{i2} \oplus \ldots \oplus b_{im}$$

where

C_i = ith bit of the hash code, $1 \le i \le n$

m = number of n-bit blocks in the input

b_{ij} = ith bit in jth block

$\oplus$ = XOR operation

Figure 14.15 illustrates this operation. Figure 14.16a is a C program that produces a 128-bit hash code. This type of code produces a simple parity for each bit position and is known as a longitudinal redundancy check. It is reasonably effective for random data as a data integrity check. Each 128-bit hash value is equally likely. Thus, the probability that a data error will result in an unchanged hash value is 2^{-128}. With more predictably formatted data, the function is less effective. For example, in most normal text files, the high-order bit

---

[5]See [DAVI90] or [NECH91] for a discussion of birthday attacks.

	bit 1	bit 2	• • •	bit n
block 1	b_{11}	b_{21}		b_{n1}
block 2	b_{12}	b_{22}		b_{n2}
	•	•	•	•
	•	•	•	•
	•	•	•	•
block m	b_{1m}	b_{2m}		b_{nm}
hash code	C_1	C_2		C_n

FIGURE 14.15.   Simple hash function using bitwise XOR.

```
main (int argc, char *argv [ ] ) {
        unsigned long hash [4] = (0, 0, 0, 0), data [4];
        FILE *fp;
        int i;
        if ((fp == fopen (argv [1], "rb")) != NULL)  {
            while ((fread (data, 4,,4, fp) != NULL)
                for (i=0; i<4; i++)
                    hash [i] ^= data [i];
            fclose (fp);
            for (i=0; i<4; i++)
                printf ("%081x", hash [i] );
            printf ("\n");
} }
```
                            (a) XOR of every 128-bit block

```
main (int argc, char *argv [ ] ) {
        unsigned long hash [4] = (0, 0, 0, 0), data [4];
        FILE *fp;
        int i;
        if ((fp == fopen (argv [1], "rb")) != NULL) {
            while ((fread (data, 4,,4, fp) != NULL)
                for (i=0; i<4; i++)
                    hash [i] ^= data [i];
                    hash [i] = hash [i] >>l^ hash [i] <<31;
                    }
            fclose (fp);
            for (i=0; i<4; i++)
                printf ("%081x", hash [i] );
            printf ("\n");
} }
```
                        (b) Rolling each longword 1 bit to the right

FIGURE 14.16.   Simple hash functions [SCHN91].

of each octet is always zero. Therefore, 16 bits in the hash will always be zero, and the effectiveness is reduced to 2^{-112}.

A simple way to improve matters is to perform a one-bit circular shift, or rotation on the hash value after each block is processed, as shown in Figure 14.16b. This has the effect of "randomizing" the input more completely and overcoming any regularities that appear in the input.

Although the second program provides a good measure of data integrity, it is virtually useless for data security. Consider the following task of a potential attacker: Given a hash code, produce a message that yields that hash code. The attacker would simply need to prepare the desired message and then append a 128-bit block that forces the new message plus block to yield the desired hash code.

Thus we need a hash algorithm that is a much more complex function of the input bits.

MD5 Algorithm Description

The MD5 algorithm produces a 128-bit hash code, or message digest, of an input file. The algorithm was designed for speed, simplicity, and compactness on a 32-bit architecture. The algorithm processes the input in 512-bit blocks.

The algorithm consists of the following five steps:

• Step 1: Append Padding Bits

The message is padded so that its length is congruent to 448 modulo 512. That is, the length of the padded message is 64 bits less than an integer multiple of 512 bits. Padding is always added, even if the message is already of the desired length. For example, if the message is 448 bits long, it is padded by 512 bits to a length of 960 bits. Thus, the number of padding bits is in the range of 1 to 512.

The padding consists of a single 1-bit followed by the necessary number of 0-bits.

• Step 2: Append Length

A 64-bit representation of the length of the original message (before the padding) is appended to the result of step 1. If the original length is greater than 2^{64}, then only the low-order 64 bits of the length are used. The inclusion of a length value at the end of the message makes a type of attack known as a padding attack more difficult [TSUD92].

The outcome of the first two steps yeilds a message that is an integer multiple of 512 bits in length. Equivalently, the result is a multiple of 16 32-bit words. Let M[0 . . . N-1] denote the words of the resulting message, with N an integer multiple of 16.

• Step 3: Initialize MD Buffer

A 128-bit buffer is used to intermediate and final results of the hash function. The buffer can be represented as four 32-bit registers (A, B, C, D). These registers are initialized to the following hexadecimal values (low-order octets first):

```
A = 01   23   45   67
B = 89   AB   CD   EF
C = FE   DC   BA   98
D = 76   54   32   10
```

- **Step 4: Process Message in 128-Bit (16-Word) Blocks**

The heart of the algorithm makes use of four functions. Each function takes three 32-bit words as input and produces a 32-bit word output. Each function performs a set of bitwise logical operations; that is, the nth bit of the output is a function of the nth bit of the three inputs. The functions are

$$F(X, Y, Z) = (X \cdot Y) + (X' \cdot Z)$$
$$G(X, Y, Z) = (X \cdot Z) + (Y \cdot Z')$$
$$H(X, Y, Z) = X \oplus Y \oplus Z$$
$$I(X, Y, Z) = Y \oplus (X + Z')$$

where the logical operators (AND, OR, NOT, XOR) are represented by the symbols ($\cdot$, $+$, $'$, $\oplus$). Function F is a conditional function: If X then Y else Z. Function H produces a parity bit. Table 14.7a is a truth table of the four functions.

TABLE 14.7 Key Elements of MD5

(a) Truth table of logical functions

X	Y	Z	F	G	H	I
0	0	0	0	0	0	1
0	0	1	1	0	1	0
0	1	0	0	1	1	0
0	1	1	1	0	0	1
1	0	0	0	0	1	1
1	0	1	0	1	0	1
1	1	0	1	1	0	0
1	1	1	1	1	1	0

(b) Table T, constructed from the sine function

T[1] = D76AA478	T[17] = F61E2562	T[33] = FFFA3942	T[49] = F4292244
T[2] = E8C7B756	T[18] = C040B340	T[34] = 8771F681	T[50] = 432AFF97
T[3] = 242070DB	T[19] = 265E5A51	T[35] = 69D96122	T[51] = AB9423A7
T[4] = C1BDCEEE	T[20] = E9B6C7AA	T[36] = FDE5380C	T[52] = FC93A039
T[5] = F57C0FAF	T[21] = D62F105D	T[37] = A4BEEA44	T[53] = 655B59C3
T[6] = 4787C62A	T[22] = 02441453	T[38] = 4BDECFA9	T[54] = 8F0CCC92
T[7] = A8304613	T[23] = D8A1E681	T[39] = F6BB4B60	T[55] = FFEFF47D
T[8] = FD469501	T[24] = E7D3FBC8	T[40] = BEBFBC70	T[56] = 85845DD1
T[9] = 698098D8	T[25] = 21E1CDE6	T[41] = 289B7EC6	T[57] = 6FA87E4F
T[10] = 8B44F7AF	T[26] = C33707D6	T[42] = EAA127FA	T[58] = FE2CE6E0
T[11] = FFFF5BB1	T[27] = F4D50D87	T[43] = D4EF3085	T[59] = A3014314
T[12] = 895CD7BE	T[28] = 455A14ED	T[44] = 04881D05	T[60] = 4E0811A1
T[13] = 6B901122	T[29] = A9E3E905	T[45] = D9D4D039	T[61] = F7537E82
T[14] = FD987193	T[30] = FCEFA3F8	T[46] = E6DB99E5	T[62] = BD3AF235
T[15] = A679438E	T[31] = 676F02D9	T[47] = 1FA27CF8	T[63] = 2AD7D2BB
T[16] = 49B40821	T[32] = 8D2A4C8A	T[48] = C4AC5665	T[64] = EB86D391

The algorithm also makes use of a 64-element table T[1 . . . 64] constructed from the sine function. The ith element of T, denoted $T[i]$, has the value equal to the integer part of $2^{32} \times$ abs(sin(i)), where i is in radians. Since abs(sin(i)) is a number between 0 and 1, each element of T is an integer that can be represented in 32 bits. The table provides a "randomized" set of 32-bit patterns, which should eliminate any regularities in the input data. Table 14.7b lists the values of T.

Figure 14.17 defines the processing algorithm. The expression $(X <<< s)$ denotes the 32-bit value obtained by performing a circular shift of X left by s bit positions.

- **Step 5: Output**

  The message digest produced as output is stored in A, B, C, D.

The MD5 algorithm has the property that every bit of the hash code is a function of every bit in the input. The complex repetition of the basic functions (F, G, H, I) produces results that are well mixed; that is, it is unlikely that two messages chosen at random, even if they exhibit similar regularities, will have the same hash code. The author of MD5 conjectures that the difficulty of generating two messages with the same MD5 digest is on the order of 2^{64} operations, and the difficulty of generating a message that produces a given digest is on the order of 2^{128} operations.

14.4

VIRTUAL TERMINAL PROTOCOLS: TELNET AND THE ISO STANDARD

Most of our discussion has implicitly assumed that communication is between "peer" entities, that is, entities of roughly equal capabilities that wish to do roughly similar kinds of things. There are exceptions to this rule, and perhaps the most significant is the case of terminal-to-application communication.

One's first impression is that this type of communication is outside the scope of a computer–communications architecture. In the case of a terminal directly connected to a computer, the computer will have an I/O driver that handles the terminal and a mechanism for communication between that driver and the application program. If the terminal and computer are connected via a network, the network must transparently pass the data between the terminal and a computer I/O port. This seems to be a requirement since a number of terminal devices do not have the capability of implementing the various OSI layers.

There is, however, a problem in this approach that relates to one of the advertised benefits of a computer network. Specifically, a user at a terminal would like to be able to access resources and applications on a variety of computers. Furthermore, the user does not want to be limited to using the terminals and computers of a single vendor. What does this imply? Usually, in order to be able to use a terminal from one vendor with a host from another vendor,

```
/* Process each 16-word (512-bit) block. */
For i = 0 to N/16-1 do
/* Copy block i into X. */
    For j = 0 to 15 do
        Set X[j] to M[i* 16+j].
end /* of loop on j */


/* Save A as AA, B as BB, C as CC, and D as DD. */
AA = A
BB = B
CC = C
DD = D


/* Round 1. */
/* Let [abcd k s i] denote the operation          a = b + ((a + F(b.c.d) + X[k] + T[i])≪s).*/
/* do the following 16 operations. */
[ABCD    0   7   1]   [DABC    1  12   2]   [CDAB    2  17   3]   [BCDA    3  22   4]
[ABCD    4   7   5]   [DABC    5  12   6]   [CDAB    6  17   7]   [BCDA    7  22   8]
[ABCD    8   7   9]   [DABC    9  12  10]   [CDAB   10  17  11]   [BCDA   11  22  12]
[ABCD   12   7  13]   [DABC   13  12  14]   [CDAB   14  17  15]   [BCDA   15  22  16]


/* Round 2. */
/* Let [abcd k s i] denote the operation          a = b + ((a + G(b.c.d) + X[k] + T[i])≪s).*/
/* do the following 16 operations. */
[ABCD    1   5  17]   [DABC    6   9  18]   [CDAB   11  14  19]   [BCDA    0  20  20]
[ABCD    5   5  21]   [DABC   10   9  22]   [CDAB   15  14  23]   [BCDA    4  20  24]
[ABCD    9   5  25]   [DABC   14   9  26]   [CDAB    3  14  27]   [BCDA    8  20  28]
[ABCD   13   5  29]   [DABC    2   9  30]   [CDAB    7  14  31]   [BCDA   12  20  32]


/* Round 3. */
/* Let [abcd k s i] denote the operation          a = b + ((a + H(b.c.d) + X[k] + T[i])≪s).*/
/* do the following 16 operations. */
[ABCD    5   4  33]   [DABC    8  11  34]   [CDAB   11  16  35]   [BCDA   14  23  36]
[ABCD    1   4  37]   [DABC    4  11  38]   [CDAB    7  16  39]   [BCDA   10  23  40]
[ABCD   13   4  41]   [DABC    0  11  42]   [CDAB    3  16  43]   [BCDA    6  23  44]
[ABCD    9   4  45]   [DABC   12  11  46]   [CDAB   15  16  47]   [BCDA    2  23  48]


/* Round 4. */
/* Let [abcd k s i] denote the operation          a = b + ((a + I(b.c.d) + X[k] + T[i])≪s).*/
/* do the following 16 operations. */
[ABCD    0   6  49]   [DABC    7  10  50]   [CDAB   14  15  51]   [BCDA    5  21  52]
[ABCD   12   6  53]   [DABC    3  10  54]   [CDAB   10  15  55]   [BCDA    1  21  56]
[ABCD    8   6  57]   [DABC   15  10  58]   [CDAB    6  15  59]   [BCDA   13  21  60]
[ABCD    4   6  61]   [DABC   11  10  62]   [CDAB    2  15  63]   [BCDA    9  21  64]


/* Then increment each of the four registers by the value it had before this block was started. */
A = A + AA
B = B + BB
C = C + CC
D = D + DD


end /* of loop on i */
```

FIGURE 14.17.   Basic MD5 update algorithm.

a special host software package must be built to accommodate the foreign terminal. Now consider a network with N types of terminals and M types of hosts. For complete connectivity, each host type must contain a package for handling each terminal type. In the worst case, MN I/O packages must be developed. Furthermore, if a new type of host is acquired, it must be equipped with N new I/O packages. If a new type of terminal is acquired, each host must be equipped with a new I/O package, for a total of M new packages. This is not the type of situation designed to encourage multivendor interoperability.

To solve this problem, some sort of virtual terminal protocol (VTP) is needed. In the remainder of this section, we first examine the general principles of a VTP and then introduce two approaches: TELNET and the ISO VTP standards.

Generalized Virtual Terminal Protocols

As the name implies, VTP is a protocol, a set of conventions for communication between peer entities. It includes the following functions:

- Establishing and maintaining a connection between two application-level entities.
- Controlling a dialogue for negotiating the allowable actions to be performed across the connection.
- Creating and maintaining a data structure that represents the "state" of the terminal.
- Translating between actual terminal characteristics and a standardized representation.

The first two functions are in the nature of session control (layer 5); the latter two are presentation control (layer 6) functions. The principal purpose of the VTP is to transform the characteristics of a real terminal into a standardized form or virtual terminal. Because of the wide differences in capabilities among terminals, it is unreasonable to attempt to develop a single virtual terminal type. Four classes are of interest:

- *Scroll mode:* These are terminals with no local intelligence, including keyboard-printer and keyboard-display devices. Characters are transmitted as they are entered, and incoming characters are printed or displayed as they come in. On a display, as the screen fills, the top line is scrolled off.
- *Page mode:* These are keyboard-display terminals with a cursor-addressable character matrix display. Either user or host can modify random-accessed portions of the display. I/O can be a page at a time.
- *Form/data entry mode:* These are similar to page mode terminals, but allow definition of fixed and variable fields on the display. This permits a number of features, such as transmitting only the variable part, and defining field attributes to be used as validity checks.
- *Graphics mode:* These allow the creation of arbitrary two-dimensional patterns.

For any VTP, there are basically four phases of operation:

- *Connection management:* includes session-layer-related functions, such as connection request and termination.
- *Negotiation:* used to determine a mutually agreeable set of characteristics between the two correspondents.
- *Control:* exchange of control information and commands (e.g., defining the attributes of a field).
- *Data:* transfer of data between two correspondents.

Figure 14.18 illustrates the process involved. Upon user input, the characteristics of a real terminal are transformed into the agreed format, or "virtual terminal." These formatted data are transmitted over a network to a host system. In the host computer, the virtual terminal structure is translated into the terminal format normally used by the host. The reverse process is performed for host-to-terminal traffic. Thus, a virtual terminal service must understand the virtual terminal format and be able to employ a data-transfer mechanism, such as that provided in the OSI architecture.

A useful feature of a virtual terminal service is the ability to negotiate about the characteristics of the virtual terminal or the details of the data transfer. This allows users and processes to define a remote terminal access service that provides service as close as possible to what the terminal user expects.

Figure 14.19 relates the virtual terminal service to the OSI architecture. Terminals are connected locally to a device that may be a terminal cluster controller, some other sort of communications processor, or a general-purpose computer. Some terminal-handler software module is needed to communicate with the terminals; this is usually part of the operating system. The purpose of this

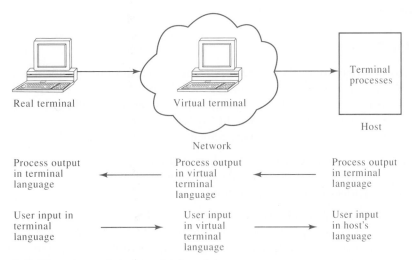

FIGURE 14.18.   Virtual terminal model.

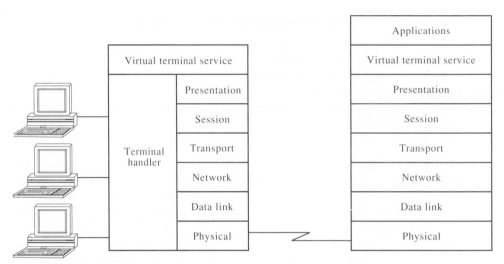

FIGURE 14.19. Architecture for virtual terminal service.

module is to link the terminal user to some application in the system. In this case, the user is linked to the virtual terminal service. This service is at the application layer of the OSI architecture and makes use of the lower six layers of OSI to establish a connection with a virtual terminal service module on a remote computer. On the remote computer, the virtual terminal service module provides an interface to various applications. To the application, terminal traffic coming in through the virtual terminal service appears to be coming from a local terminal through the usual terminal-handler software. Thus, for both the user and the application, it appears as though the user is locally connected to the remote computer.

TELNET

One of the first attempts to develop a true virtual terminal protocol is TELNET, which was developed as part of the TCP/IP protocol suite and is still widely used. Although this protocol is primarily intended for scroll-mode terminals, it embodies the principles one would expect in a VTP.

TELNET is built on three main principles:

- The concept of a network virtual terminal (NVT).
- A symmetric view of terminals and processes.
- The principle of negotiated options.

The NVT is an imaginary device that provides an intermediate representation of a canonical terminal. If the communicating entity is a process, a module is needed (Server TELNET) to convert between the NVT representation and the process representation. If the communicating entity is a terminal, a module is needed (User TELNET) to map the characteristics of the terminal into those of NVT.

Communication can occur between two terminals, two processes, or a process and a terminal. It is expected that the communication will be over a TCP connection. TELNET enforces two-way alternate mode of communication to accommodate half-duplex terminals. TELNET assumes that the ASCII code will be used. Table 14.8 lists the ASCII control codes that are part of the NVT keyboard.

Each TELNET connection begins with a negotiated option phase. Four commands are used in this phase: WILL, WONT, DO, DONT. WILL X is sent by either party to indicate that party's desire (offer) to begin performing option X; DO X and DONT X are positive and negative acknowledgments, respectively. DO X is sent to indicate a desire (request) that the other party begin performing option X; WILL X and WONT X are the positive and negative response. This mechanism is a general one and can be used to negotiate any sort of

TABLE 14.8   TELNET Parameters

ASCII Control Codes		Registered Options		
Null				
Line feed	0	Binary transmission	18	Logout
Carriage return	1	Echo	19	Byte macro
Bell	2	Reconnection	20	Data entry terminal
Backspace	3	Suppress go ahead	21	SUPDUP
Horizontal tab	4	Approximate message size	22	SUPDUP output
Vertical tab	5	Status	23	Send location
Form feed	6	Timing mark	24	Terminal type
	7	Remote-controlled	25	End of record
TELNET Commands		transmission and echoing	26	TACACS user identification
End of subnegotiation	8	Output line width	27	Output marking
NOP	9	Output page size	28	Terminal location number
Data mark	10	Output carriage-return	29	TELNET 3270 regime
Break		disposition	30	X.3 PAD
Interrupt process	11	Output horizontal tab stops	31	Negotiate about window size
Abort output	12	Output horizontal tab	32	Terminal speed
Are you there		disposition	33	Remote flow control
Erase character	13	Output formfeed	34	Linemode
Erase line		disposition	35	X display location
Go ahead	14	Output vertical tab stops	36	Environment option
Beginning of	15	Output vertical tab	37	Authentication option
subnegotiation		disposition	38	Encryption option
Will	16	Output line feed disposition	255	Extended options list
Wont	17	Extended ASCII		
Do				
Dont				
Interpret as command				

binary option (an option that is either on or off). Certain options are considered common enough to be registered and assigned codes (Table 14.8). Additional options may be encoded at the discretion of individual communicating entities. The registered options fall into three general classes of control:

- Physical terminal (8 to 17): control or accommodate physical characteristics of the real terminal.
- TELNET (0, 2, 3, 5, 255): concerned with controlling operation of TELNET connections.
- Operating system and processes (1, 4, 6): concerned with nonterminal users of TELNET.

Option 7 is an elaborate scheme for dealing with the propagation delays experienced with remote echoing. It combines the functions of all three option classes and is discussed in [DAVI77].

In addition to the negotiation phase, there are other times when control information needs to be exchanged. This is achieved by the use of commands inserted into the data stream and preceded by an escape character (interpret as command, or IAC). This is, unfortunately, a clumsy mechanism since it requires the TELNET entity to scan all input for the escape character. Table 14.8 lists the TELNET commands. Most are self-explanatory or have already been discussed. Among the remaining commands:

- *Interrupt process:* interrupts the operation of a remote process. This function is invoked when a user believes the process is looping or when an unwanted process has been activated.
- *Abort output:* allows a process that is generating output to run to completion without sending the output to the user's terminal. This function also clears any output already produced but not yet printed on the user's terminal.
- *Are you there:* gives the user some visible evidence that the system is still up and running.

The ISO Virtual Terminal Standard

The ISO virtual terminal service is an application-layer service defined within the framework of the open systems interconnection (OSI) model. The standard defines a module for a virtual terminal, which is an abstract representation of a real terminal. The standard defines operations that can be performed, such as reading text from the virtual keyboard, writing text on the virtual screen, and moving a cursor to a particular position on the virtual screen. The standard also defines a virtual terminal protocol for the exchange of data and control messages between a terminal and an application via the virtual terminal service. The protocol standard specifies the display data stream structure and the control messages by which the two sides can agree on the details of the terminal capabilities to be supported.

Rather than defining a single virtual terminal for all possible applications, the standard provides its users with the tools to define a virtual terminal suited to the application at hand and the physical limitations of the terminal. For example, if the physical terminal is monochrome, then the two sides agree not to use color information.

The structure of the ISO standard is suggested by Figure 14.20. A virtual terminal is modeled as being made up of several parts, all of which reside in the conceptual communications area, which is an abstraction used to model the interaction between two systems. A separate copy is maintained by each communicating entity, and it forms the basis for the protocol between the two sides. The Virtual Terminal Protocol (DIS 9041) is specified in terms of inter-actions between protocol entities in the two systems that affect the objects in the conceptual communications area. Each entity provides a Virtual Terminal Service (DIS 9040) to its user. The service user can be thought of as a local mapping from a real terminal or application to the virtual terminal context.

Table 14.9 lists some of the key aspects of the ISO standard. We examine each of these in turn.

Classes of Service

The ISO standard provides different classes of service. Each class meets the needs of a specific range of applications and terminal functions. So far, Basic, Forms, and Graphics classes have been identified. Of these, only the Basic class is fully defined and supported by vendors. We can expect to see the other classes available in the next few years.

The Basic class is a character-oriented service. In its simplest form, it meets the terminal access requirements of applications such as line editing and op-

FIGURE 14.20.   The structure of the virtual terminal environment.

TABLE 14.9   Aspects of the ISO Virtual Terminal Service

Classes of Service	Echo Control
Basic	Local echo
Forms	Remote echo
Graphics	
	Parameters
Modes of Operation	Display objects
Two-way alternate	Device objects
Two-way simultaneous	Control objects
Delivery Control	
No delivery control	
Simple delivery control	
Quarantine delivery control	

erating system command language interaction, which can be satisfied with simple scroll-mode terminals. The basic class also supports page-mode terminals and provides for the exchange of data in blocks instead of character-at-a-time. An extension to the basic class provides a primitive set of forms-related services. It allows the definition and addressing of individual fields and the transmission of selected fields. With this capability, the service can transfer just the variable fields on a form. However, there is no facility for defining or using field attributes.

The Forms class is designed to handle all of the operations associated with forms-mode terminals, such as the 3720 terminals. This would allow any forms-mode terminal from any vendor to interact with forms-mode applications on any host from any vendor. Finally, the Graphics class will deal with graphics and image-processing terminals.

Modes of Operation

The virtual terminal standard supports two modes of operation: two-way alternate (half duplex) and two-way simultaneous (full duplex). When a terminal sets up a connection to a host, the mode of operation is agreed upon between the two virtual service modules.

Recall that the two-way alternate mode enforces the discipline that only one side at a time can transmit. This prevents the situation in which data from the computer begin to appear on the terminal display screen while the user is entering text from the keyboard. The two-way alternate mode is typical of synchronous forms-mode terminals such as the 3270. Most normal enquiry/response applications are naturally two-way alternate, for example.

The two-way simultaneous mode permits both sides to transmit at the same time. An example of the utility of this would be the control terminal for a complex real-time system such as a process control plant. For such an application, the terminal must be capable of being updated rapidly with status changes even if the operator is typing in a command.

Delivery Control

Delivery control allows one side to control delivery of data to the other side to co-ordinate multiple actions. Normally, any data entered at a terminal are automatically delivered to the application on the other side as soon as possible, and any data transmitted by the application are delivered to the terminal as soon as possible. In some cases, however, one side may require explicit control over when certain data are delivered to its peer.

For example, suppose a user is logged on to a time-sharing system via the virtual terminal service. The time-sharing system may issue a single prompt character (e.g., ">") when it is ready for the next command. However, the terminal side of the virtual terminal service may choose to deliver data to the terminal for display only after several characters have been received, rather than one character at a time. Since this single prompt character must be displayed, and since the terminal side cannot reasonably be expected to know what the prompt character is, some mechanism is needed to force delivery. Another example is the use of special "function keys," which are often found on terminals and which can be set up to perform multiple actions, resulting in the transmission of multiple messages to the host. Sometimes it is desirable that all of the functions of the key are presented to the peer user simultaneously.

Three types of delivery control can be specified with any transmission:

- *No delivery control:* This is the default type. In this case data are made available to the peer at the convenience of the implementation of the virtual terminal service.
- *Simple delivery control:* In this case, the service user (terminal or application) can issue a request that all undelivered data be delivered. The invoking side may also, optionally, request acknowledgement of the delivery to the other side.
- *Quarantine delivery control:* This requires that the remote virtual terminal service module hold all incoming data until they are explicitly released for delivery by the other side. For example, an application could send a screenfull of data in several small blocks but instruct the other side to defer delivery so that the entire screen update is displayed at once. Another example is the function key action mentioned previously.

Echo Control

Echo control is concerned with the control of how characters typed on a keyboard will cause updates to a display (Figure 14.21). In real terminals, characters typed on the keyboard may be displayed on the screen locally by the ter-

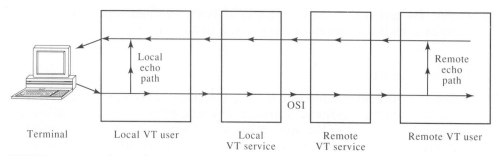

FIGURE 14.21.   Echo paths (ISO 9040).

minal as they are typed or may be "echoed back" to the display by the computer. The former option is less flexible but is often chosen when the communication link is half duplex and echoing back would therefore not be practical. The latter option is used where the communication line is full duplex and where greater control over the screen is required. For example, a time-sharing system may wish to suppress the display of the terminal user's password and identification code but display all other characters.

Virtual Terminal Parameters

A major feature of the service is the use of terminal parameters. These are similar to those used in TELNET in that they provide a way of defining various characteristics of the terminal. However, the parameters available in the ISO standard are much more complex and powerful than those of TELNET. They allow the user to define various characteristics of displayable characters, such as font, size, intensity, color, and so on. Control objects can be defined that are used to control formatting on the display and to trigger various events such as ringing an alarm. Characteristics of other devices such as printers can also be specified.

Table 14.10 lists the parameters that have been defined for the basic class service.

14.5

RECOMMENDED READING

A thorough presentation of ASN.1 is to be found in [STEE90]. Two quite useful documents are [KALI91] and [GAUD89].

Excellent treatments of encryption and authentication can be found in [PFLE89] and [DAVI90]. The use of a message digest for authentication is discussed in [TSUD92], [WAYN91], [GONG89], and [JUEN85].

TELNET is examined in detail in [STAL90c]. The ISO virtual terminal service is discussed in [KNOW87] and [TANG92].

TABLE 14.10   Directed Graph of Virtual Terminal Parameters (ISO 9040).

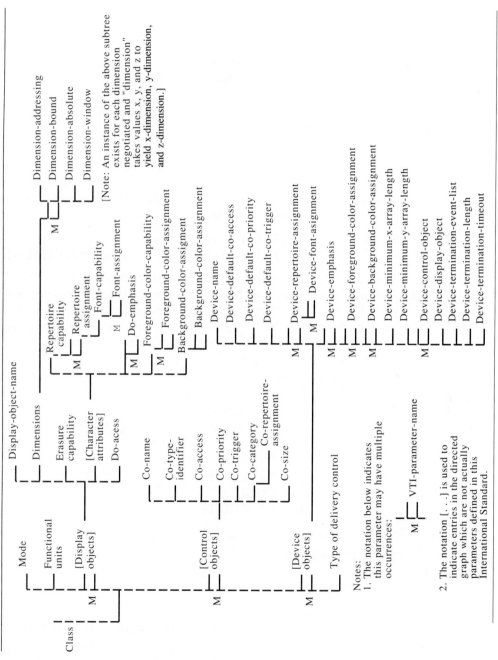

697

14.6

PROBLEMS

14.1 a. Consider the following definitions:

ExpeditedDataAcknowledgment ::= SET {
          destRef [0] Reference,
          yr-tu-nr [1] TPDUnumber,
          checkSum [2] CheckSum OPTIONAL }
NormalEA ::= ExpeditedDataAcknowledgment
     (WITH COMPONENTS {
        destRef,
        yr-tu-ner (0..127) }

  Find an equivalent expression for defining NormalEA.
 b. Consider the following definition:

ExtendedEA ::= ExpeditedDataAcknowledgment
      (WITH COMPONENTS {..., checkSum PRESENT})

  Find an equivalent expression for defining ExtendedEA.
 c. Define a new type, EA, based on ExpeditedDataAcknowledgment, with the restriction that either the checksum is absent, in which case yr-tu-nr must be in the range of 0 to 127, or the checksum is present, in which case there is no additional constraint on yr-tu-nr.

14.2 Given the following definition:

TypH ::= SEQUENCE {
        r INTEGER,
        s BOOLEAN,
        t INTEGER OPTIONAL }

 which of the following values are valid?

valH1 TypH ::= {r -5,s TRUE, t 0}
valH2 TypH ::= {10, FALSE}
valH3 TypH ::= {t 1, r 2, s TRUE}

14.3 Given the following definitions:

T1 ::= SEQUENCE {X1,
      b BOOLEAN }
X1 ::= CHOICE {y INTEGER, z REAL }

 would the identifiers for T1 be: y, z, b?

14.4 Define an IA5String-based type that contains only either "A" or "B" characters and is restricted to a maximum length of 10 chars.

14.5 Figure 14.22 contains the ASN.1 specification of the protocol data units used in the application standard Remote Operations Service Element (ROSE). Provide a narrative description.

Remote_Operations_APDUs DEFINITIONS ::= BEGIN

ROSEapdus ::= CHOICE {roiv-apdu [1] IMPLICIT ROIVapdu,
                       rors-apdu [2] IMPLICIT RORSapdu,
                       roer-apdu [3] IMPLICIT ROERapdu,
                       rorj-apdu [4] IMPLICIT RORJapdu }

ROIVapdu ::= SEQUENCE {invokeID InvokedIDType,
                        linked-ID IMPLICIT InvokedIDType OPTIONAL,
                        operation-value OPERATION,
                        argument ANY DEFINED BY operation-value OPTIONAL }

InvokedIDType ::= INTEGER

RORSapdu ::= SEQUENCE {InvokeID InvokedIDType,
                       SEQUENCE { operation-value OPERATION,
                                  result ANY DEFINED BY operation-value
                                } OPTIONAL }

ROERapdu ::= SEQUENCE {InvokeID InvokeIDType,
                       error-value ERROR,
                       parameter ANY DEFINED BY error-value OPTIONAL }

RORJapdu ::= SEQUENCE {InvokeID CHOICE {InvokeIDTYPE. NULL}.
                       problem CHOICE { [0] IMPLICIT GeneralProblem,
                                        [1] IMPLICIT InvokeProblem,
                                        [2] IMPLICIT ReturnResultProblem,
                                        [3] IMPLICIT ReturnErrorProblem } }

GeneralProblem ::= INTEGER { unrecognizedAPDU (0),
                             mistypedAPDU (1)
                             badlyStructuredAPDU (2)}

InvokeProblem ::= INTEGER { duplicateInvocation (0),
                            unrecognizedOperation (1),
                            mistypedArgument (2),
                            resourceLimitation (3),
                            initiatorReleasing (4),
                            unrecognisedLinkedID (5),
                            linkedResponseUnexpected (6),
                            unexpectedChildOperation (7) }

ReturnResultProblem ::= INTEGER { unrecognisedInvocation (0),
                                  resultResponseUnexpected (1),
                                  mistypedResult (2) }

ReturnErrorProblem ::= INTEGER { UnrecognisedInvocation (0),
                                 errorResponseUnexpected (1),
                                 unrecognisedError (2),
                                 unexpectedError (3),
                                 mistypedParameter (4) }

END

FIGURE 14.22.   ASN.1 definition of ROSE PDUs.

14.6 Encode the bit string '0900000009'H in BER using
   a. Primitive form.
   b. Constructed form.

14.7 Show the BER encoding of the following integers:
   a. −27066   **f.** 127
   b. −129   **g.** 128
   c. −128   **h.** 255
   d. −1   **i.** 256
   e. 0

14.8 Show the BER encoding for the following value:

   e REAL ::= {2918189707, 2, −26}

14.9 Show the BER encoding for the following value. Use the ASCII code in Table 2.1, which is equivalent to IA5.

   story IA5String ::= "Once upon a time . . . happily ever after."

14.10 Show the BER encoding for the following value:

   weatherReporting OBJECT IDENTIFIER ::= {2 6 6 247 1}

14.11 Given the following definitions:

   TypA ::= SET {p BOOLEAN, q INTEGER, r BIT STRING}

   valA TypA ::= {p TRUE, r '83F'H, q −7}

   provide three alternative BER encodings of valA.

14.12 Given the following definitions:

   Readings ::= SEQUENCE OF INTEGER (−100..60)
   medicineHatReadings ::= {−5, −4, 4, 15, 20, 24, 29, 28, 20, 15, 3, −2}

   provide a BER encoding of medicineHatReadings

14.13 Given the following definition:

   OneOrSeveralIntegers ::= CHOICE {
                                   one   INTEGER,
                                   several SEQUENCE OF
                                   INTEGER }

   provide the BER encodings for the following values of OneOrSeveral-Integers:
   a. one −129
   b. several {−129, 0}

14.14 Describe how a protocol converter in a digital PBX architecture (Figure 7.17) can be used to implement a virtual terminal protocol.

14.15 A TELNET implementation attempts to buffer characters and send them out in blocks in TCP segments. What problems might this cause and what is the solution?

CHAPTER 15

Distributed Applications

All of the protocols and functions described so far in Part II are geared toward one objective: the support of distributed applications that involve the interaction of multiple independent systems. In the OSI model, such applications occupy the application layer and are directly supported by the presentation layer. In the TCP/IP protocol suite, such applications typically rely on TCP or UDP for support.

In this chapter, we examine three quite different applications that give the reader a feel for the range and diversity of applications supported by a communications architecture. The first, network management, is itself a support-type application, designed to assure the effective monitoring and control of a distributed system. The specific protocol that is examined in the Simple Network Management Protocol, version 2 (SNMPv2), which is designed to operate in both the TCP/IP and OSI environments. Next, we examine file transfer, using the ISO standard, File Transfer, Access, and Management (FTAM), as an example. Finally, electronic mail applications are considered, with the CCITT standard X.400 used as an example.

15.1

NETWORK MANAGEMENT: SNMPv2

Networks and distributed processing systems are of critical and growing importance in business, government, and other organizations. Within a given organization, the trend is toward larger, more complex networks supporting more applications and more users. As these networks grow in scale, two facts become painfully evident:

- The network and its associated resources and distributed applications become indispensable to the organization.
- More things can go wrong, disabling the network or a portion of the network or degrading performance to an unacceptable level.

A large network cannot be put together and managed by human effort alone. The complexity of such a system dictates the use of automated network management tools. The urgency of the need for such tools is increased, and the difficulty of supplying such tools is also increased, if the network includes equipment from multiple vendors. In response, standards that deal with network management have been developed, covering services, protocols, and management information bases.

This section begins with an introduction to the overall concepts of standardized network management. The remainder of the section is devoted to a discussion of SNMPv2, which is an extension of SNMP, the most widely used network management standard.

Network Management Systems

A network management system is a collection of tools for network monitoring and control that is integrated in the following senses:

- A single operator interface with a powerful but user-friendly set of commands for performing most or all network management tasks.
- A minimal amount of separate equipment. That is, most of the hardware and software required for network management are incorporated into the existing user equipment.

A network management system consists of incremental hardware and software additions implemented among existing network components. The software used in accomplishing the network management tasks resides in the host computers and communications processors (e.g., front-end processors, terminal cluster controllers). A network management system is designed to view the entire network as a unified architecture, with addresses and labels assigned to each point and the specific attributes of each element and link known to the system. The active elements of the network provide regular feedback of status information to the network control center.

A network management system consists of the following key elements:

- Management station, or manager.
- Agent.
- Management information base.
- Network management protocol.

The **management station** is typically a stand-alone device but may be a capability implemented on a shared system. In either case, the management station serves as the interface for the human network manager into the network management system. The management station will have, at minimum:

- A set of management applications for data analysis, fault recovery, and so on.

- An interface by which the network manager may monitor and control the network.
- The capability of translating the network manager's requirements into the actual monitoring and control of remote elements in the network.
- A database of network management information extracted from the databases of all the managed entities in the network.

The other active element in the network management system is the **agent.** Key platforms, such as hosts, bridges, routers, and hubs, may be equipped with agent software so that they may be managed from a management station. The agent responds to requests for information from a management station, responds to requests for actions from the management station, and may asynchronously provide the management station with important but unsolicited information.

The means by which resources in the network may be managed is to represent these resources as objects. Each object is, essentially, a data variable that represents one aspect of the managed agent. The collection of objects is referred to as a **management information base** (MIB). The MIB functions as a collection of access points at the agent for the management station. These objects are standardized across systems of a particular class (e.g., bridges all support the same management objects). A management station performs the monitoring function by retrieving the value of MIB objects. A management station can cause an action to take place at an agent or can change the configuration settings of an agent by modifying the value of specific variables.

The management station and agents are linked by a **network management protocol.** The protocol used for the management of TCP/IP networks is the simple network management protocol (SNMP). For OSI-based networks, the common management information protocol (CMIP) is being developed. An enhanced version of SNMP, known as SNMPv2, is intended for both TCP/IP- and OSI-based networks. Each of these protocols includes the following key capabilities:

- *Get:* enables the management station to retrieve the value of objects at the agent.
- *Set:* enables the management station to set the value of objects at the agent.
- *Notify:* enables an agent to notify the management station of significant events.

In a traditional centralized network management scheme, one host in the configuration has the role of a network management station; there may be possibly one or two other management stations in a backup role. The remainder of the devices on the network contain agent software and an MIB, to allow monitoring and control from the management station. As networks grow in size and traffic load, such a centralized system is unworkable. Too much burden is placed on the management station, and there is too much traffic, with reports from every single agent having to wend their way across the entire network to headquarters. In such circumstances, a decentralized, distributed approach works best (e.g., Figure 15.1). In a decentralized network management scheme, there may be multiple top-level management stations, which might be referred to as management servers. Each such server might directly manage a portion of the total pool of agents. However, for many of the agents, the management server delegates responsibility to an intermediate manager. The intermediate manager plays the role of manager to monitor and control the agents under its responsibility. It also plays an agent role to provide information and accept control from a higher-level management server. This type of architecture spreads the processing burden and reduces total network traffic.

Simple Network Management Protocol Version 2 (SNMPv2)

In August of 1988, the specification for SNMP was issued and rapidly became the dominant network management standard. A number of vendors offer stand-alone network management workstations based on SNMP, and most vendors of bridges, routers, workstations, and PCs offer SNMP agent packages that allow their products to be managed by an SNMP management station.

As the name suggests, SNMP is a simple tool for network management. It defines a limited, easily implemented management information base (MIB) of scalar variables and two-dimensional tables, and it defines a streamlined protocol to enable a manager to get and set MIB variables and to enable an agent to issue unsolicited notifications, called *traps*. This simplicity is the strength of SNMP. SNMP is easily implemented and consumes modest processor and network resources. Also, the structure of the protocol and the MIB is sufficiently straightforward that it is not difficult to achieve interoperability among management stations and agent software from a mix of vendors.

With its widespread use, the deficiencies of SNMP became increasingly apparent; these include both functional deficiencies and a lack of a security facility. As a result, an enhanced version, known as SNMPv2, was issued in 1993. SNMPv2 has quickly gained support, and a number of vendors had announced products within months of the issuance of the standard.

The Elements of SNMPv2

Surprisingly, SNMPv2 does not provide network management at all! SNMPv2 instead provides a framework on which network management applications can be built. Those applications, such as fault management, performance monitoring, accounting, and so on, are outside the scope of the standard.

What SNMPv2 does provide is, to use a contemporary term, the infrastructure for network management. Figure 15.2 is an example of a configuration that illustrates that infrastructure.

The essence of SNMPv2 is a protocol that is used to exchange management information. Each "player" in the network management system maintains a

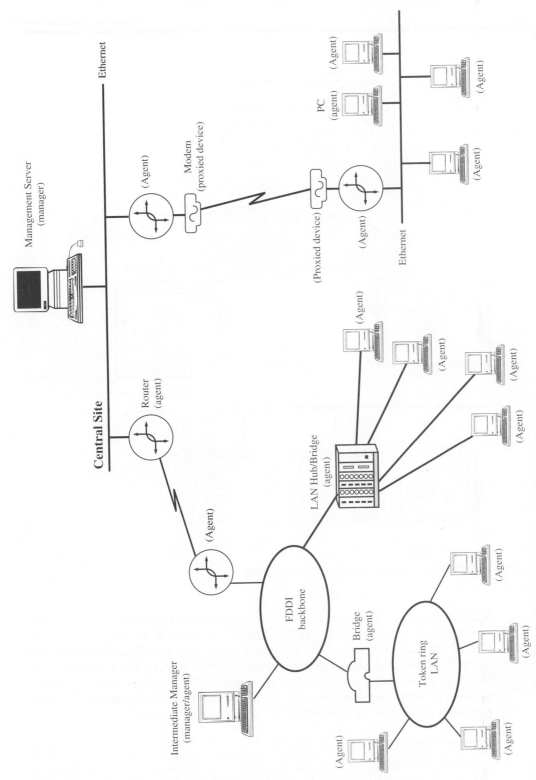

FIGURE 15.1. Example distributed network management configuration.

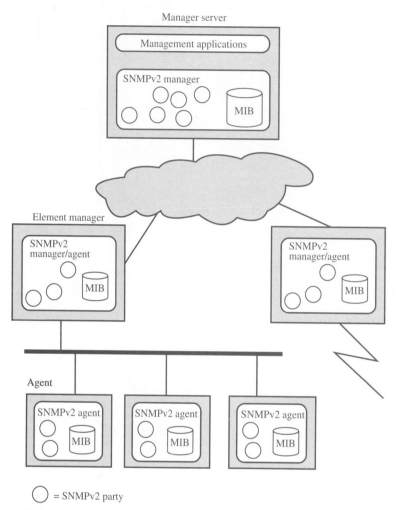

FIGURE 15.2.   SNMPv2-managed configuration.

local database of information relevant to network management, known as the management information base (MIB). The SNMPv2 standard defines the structure of this information and the allowable data types; this definition is known as the structure of management information (SMI). We can think of this as the language for defining management information. The standard also supplies a number of MIBs that are generally useful for network management.[1] In addition, new MIBs may be defined by vendors and user groups.

---

[1]There is a slight fuzziness about the term MIB. In its singular form, the term MIB can be used to refer to the entire database of management information at a manager or an agent. It can also be used in singular or plural form to refer to a specific defined collection of management information that is part of an overall MIB. Thus, the SNMPv2 standard includes the definition of three MIBs and incorporates, by reference, an MIB defined in SNMP.

At least one system in the configuration must be responsible for network management. It is here that any network management applications are housed. There may be more than one of these management stations, to provide redundancy or simply to split up the duties in a large network. Most other systems act in the role of agent. An agent collects information locally and stores it for later access by a manager. The information includes data about the system itself and may also include traffic information for the network or networks to which the agent attaches.

SNMPv2 will support either a highly centralized network management strategy or a distributed one. In the latter case, some systems operate both in the role of manager and of agent. In its agent role, such a system will accept commands from a superior management system. Some of those commands relate to the local MIB at the agent. Other commands require the agent to act as a proxy for remote devices. In this case, the proxy agent assumes the role of manager to access information at a remote agent and then assumes the role of an agent to pass that information on to a superior manager.

All of these exchanges take place using the SNMPv2 protocol, which is a simple request/response type of protocol. Typically, SNMPv2 is implemented on top of the user datagram protocol (UDP), which is part of the TCP/IP protocol suite. It can also be implemented on top of the ISO transport protocol.

The final ingredient noted in Figure 15.2 is that of party. The actual exchange of information takes place between two parties. The use of parties allows systems to define access control and security policies that differ depending on the combination of manager, agent, and desired information. This gives the user considerable flexibility in setting up a network management system and assigning various levels of authorization to different persons. This concept is explored in more detail later in this section.

Structure of Management Information

The structure of management information (SMI) defines the general framework within which an MIB can be defined and constructed. The SMI identifies the data types that can be used in the MIB and how resources within the MIB are represented and named. The philosophy behind SMI is to encourage simplicity and extensibility within the MIB. Thus, the MIB can store only simple data types: scalars and two-dimensional arrays of scalars, called tables. The SMI does not support the creation or retrieval of complex data structures. This philosophy is in contrast to that used with OSI systems management, which provides for complex data structures and retrieval modes to support greater functionality. SMI avoids complex data types and structures to simplify the task of implementation and to enhance interoperability. MIBs will inevitably contain vendor-created data types and, unless tight restrictions are placed on the definition of such data types, interoperability will suffer.

There are actually three key elements in the SMI specification. At the lowest level, the SMI specifies the data types that may be stored. Then the SMI specifies a formal technique for defining objects and tables of objects. Finally, the

TABLE 15.1   Allowable Data Types in SNMPv2

Data Type	Description
INTEGER	Integers in the range of -2^{31} to $2^{31} - 1$.
UInteger32	Integers in the range of 0 to $2^{32} - 1$.
Counter32	A non-negative integer that may be incremented modulo 2^{32}.
Counter64	A non-negative integer that may be incremented modulo 2^{64}.
Gauge32	A non-negative integer that may increase or decrease but shall not exceed a maximum value. The maximum value can not be greater than $2^{32} - 1$.
TimeTicks	A non-negative integer that represents the time, modulo 2^{32}, in hundredths of a second.
OCTET STRING	Octet strings for arbitrary binary or textual data; may be limited to 255 octets.
IpAddress	A 32-bit internet address.
NsapAddress	An OSI address. The first octet contains a binary value in the range of 0 to 20 that indicates the length of the address. The remaining octets contain the actual address.
BIT STRING	An enumeration of named bits.
OBJECT IDENTIFIER	Administratively assigned name to object or other standardized element. Value is a sequence of up to 128 non-negative integers.

SMI provides a scheme for associating a unique identifier with each actual object in a system, so that data at an agent can be referenced by a manager.

Table 15.1 shows the data types that are allowed by the SMI. This is a fairly restricted set of types. For example, real numbers are not supported. However, it is rich enough to support most network management requirements.

The SNMPv2 specification includes a template, known as an ASN.1 (Abstract Syntax Notation One) macro, which provides the formal model for defining objects. That template was illustrated in Figure 14.8. Figure 15.3 shows how this template is used to define objects and tables of objects.

The first three productions serve to define a table, grokTable, stored at an agent. As with all SNMPv2 tables, grokTable is organized as a sequence of rows, or entries, each of which has the same sequence of objects; in this case, each row consists of four objects. The INDEX clause specifies that the object grokIndex serves as an index into the table; each row of the table will have a unique value of grokIndex.

```
grokTable OBJECT-TYPE
    SYNTAX        SEQUENCE OF GrokEntry
    MAX-ACCESS       not-accessible
    STATUS           current
    DESCRIPTION
        "The (conceptual) grok table."
    ::= { adhocGroup 2 }

grokEntry OBJECT-TYPE
    SYNTAX           GrokEntry
    MAX-ACCESS       not-accessible
    STATUS           current
    DESCRIPTION
        "An entry (conceptual row) in the
        grok table."
    INDEX            { grokIndex }
    ::= { grokTable 1 }

GrokEntry ::= SEQUENCE {
    grokIndex        INTEGER,
    grokIPAddress    IpAddress,
    grokValue        Counter32,
    grokStatus       RowStatus }

grokIndex OBJECT-TYPE
    SYNTAX           INTEGER
    MAX-ACCESS       not-accessible
    STATUS           current
    DESCRIPTION
        "The auxiliary variable used to
        identify instances of the columnar
        objects in the grok table."
    ::= { grokEntry 1 }
```

```
grokIPAddress OBJECT-TYPE
    SYNTAX           IpAddress
    MAX-ACCESS       read-create
    STATUS           current
    DESCRIPTION
        "The Ip address to send grok packets
        to."
    ::= { grokEntry 2 }

grokCount OBJECT-TYPE
    SYNTAX           Counter32
    MAX-ACCESS       read-only
    STATUS            current
    DESCRIPTION
        "The total number of grok packets
        sent so far."
    DEFVAL {0}
    ::= { grokEntry 3 }

grokStatus OBJECT-TYPE
    SYNTAX           RowStatus
    MAX-ACCESS       read-create
    STATUS           current
    DESCRIPTION
        "The status object used for creating,
        modifying, and deleting a conceptual
        row instance in the grok table."
    DEFVAL { active }
    ::= { grokEntry 4 }
```

FIGURE 15.3.   An example of an SNMPv2 table.

The access type of grokIPAddress is read-create, which means that the object is read-write and that the object may be assigned a value by a manager at the time that the row containing this object is created by a manager. Each row of the table maintains a counter for the number of grok packets sent to the grokIPAddress specified for that row. The grokCount object is read-only; its value cannot be altered by a manager but is maintained by the agent within which this table resides. The grokStatus object is used in the process of row creation and deletion. The algorithm for row creation and deletion is rather complex. In essence, a RowStatus type of object is used to keep track of the state of a row during the process of creation and deletion.

Each object definition includes a value, which is a unique identifier for that object. For example, the value for grokEntry is {grokTable 1}, which means that the identifier for grokEntry is the concatenation of the identifier for grokTable and 1. The objects in an MIB are organized in a tree structure, and the identifier of an object is found by walking the tree from its root to the position of the object in the tree structure. For scalar objects, this scheme provides a unique identifier for any given object instance. For objects in tables, there is one instance of each object for each row of the table, so a further qualification is needed. What is done is to concatenate the value of the INDEX object to the identifier of each object in the table.

Protocol Operation

The heart of the SNMPv2 framework is the protocol itself. The protocol provides a straightforward, basic mechanism for the exchange of management information between manager and agent.

The basic unit of exchange is the message, which consists of an outer message wrapper and an inner protocol data unit (PDU). The outer message header deals with security and is discussed later in this section.

Seven types of PDUs may be carried in an SNMP message. The general formats for these are illustrated informally in Figure 15.4; the formal ASN.1 definition was provided in Figure 14.4. Several fields are common to a number of PDUs. The request-id field is an integer assigned such that each outstanding request can be uniquely identified. This enables a manager to correlate income responses with outstanding requests. It also enables an agent to cope with duplicate PDUs generated by an unreliable transport service. The variable-bindings field contains a list of object identifiers; depending on the PDU, the list may also include a value for each object.

The GetRequest-PDU, issued by a manager, includes a list of one or more object names for which values are requested. If the get operation is successful, then the responding agent will send a Response-PDU. The variable-bindings

PDU type	request-id	0	0	variable-bindings

(a) GetRequest-PDU, GetNextRequest-PDU, SetRequest-PDU, SNMPv2-Trap-PDU, InformRequest-PDU

PDU type	request-id	error-status	error-index	variable-bindings

(b) Response-PDU

PDU type	request-id	non-repeaters	max-repetitions	variable-bindings

(c) GetBulkRequest-PDU

name1	value1	name2	value2	• • •	namen	valuen

(d) variable bindings

FIGURE 15.4.   SNMPv2 PDU formats.

list will contain the identifier and value of all retrieved objects. For any variables that are not in the relevant MIB view, its identifier and an error code are returned in the variable-bindings list. Thus, SNMPv2 permits partial responses to a GetRequest, which is a significant improvement over SNMP. In SNMP, if one or more of the variables in a GetRequest is not supported, the agent returns an error message with a status of noSuchName. In order to cope with such an error, the SNMP manager must either return no values to the requesting application, or it must include an algorithm that responds to an error by removing the missing variables, resending the request, and then sending a partial result to the application.

The GetNextRequest-PDU also is issued by a manager and includes a list of one or more objects. In this case, for each object named in the variable-bindings field, a value is to be returned for the object that is next in lexicographic order, which is equivalent to saying next in the MIB in terms of its position in the tree structure of object identifiers. As with the GetRequest-PDU, the agent will return values for as many variables as possible. One of the strengths of the GetNextRequest-PDU is that it enables a manager entity to discover the structure of an MIB view dynamically. This is useful if the manager does not know *a priori* the set of objects that is supported by an agent or that is in a particular MIB view.

One of the major enhancements provided in SNMPv2 is the GetBulkRequest PDU. The purpose of this PDU is to minimize the number of protocol exchanges required to retrieve a large amount of management information. The GetBulkRequest PDU allows an SNMPv2 manager to request that the response be as large as possible given the constraints on message size.

The GetBulkRequest operation uses the same selection principle as the GetNextRequest operation; that is, selection is always of the next object instance in lexicographic order. The difference is that, with GetBulkRequest, it is possible to specify that multiple lexicographic successors be selected.

In essence, the GetBulkRequest operation works in the following way. The GetBulkRequest includes a list of $(N + R)$ variable names in the variable-bindings list. For each of the first N names, retrieval is done in the same fashion as for GetNextRequest. That is, for each variable in the list, the next variable in lexicographic order plus its value is returned; if there is no lexicographic successor, then the named variable and a value of endOfMibView are returned. For each of the last R names, multiple lexicographic successors are returned.

The GetBulkRequest PDU has two fields not found in the other PDUs: non-repeaters and max-repetitions. The non-repeaters field specifies the number of variables in the variable-bindings list for which a single lexicographic successor is to be returned. The max-repetitions field specifies the number of lexicographic successors to be returned for the remaining variables in the variable bindings list. To explain the algorithm, let us define the following:

L = number of variable names in the variable-bindings field of the Get-BulkRequest PDU.

N = the number of variables, starting with the first variable in the variable-bindings field, for which a single lexicographic successor is requested.

R = the number of variables, following the first N variables, for which multiple lexicographic successors are requested.

M = the number of lexicographic successors requested for each of the last R variables.

The following relationships hold:

N = MAX[MIN (non-repeaters, L),0]
M = MAX[max-repetitions, 0]
$R = L - N$

The effect of the MAX operator is that if the value of either non-repeaters or max-repetitions is less than zero, a value of 0 is substituted.

If N is greater than 0, then the first N variables are processed as for Get-NextRequest. If R is greater than 0 and M is greater than 0, then for each of the last R variables in the variable bindings list, the M lexicographic successors are retrieved. That is, for each variable:

- Obtain the value of the lexicographic successor of the named variable.
- Obtain the value of the lexicographic successor to the object instance retrieved in the previous step.
- Obtain the value of the lexicographic successor to the object instance retrieved in the previous step.
- And so on, until M object instances have been retrieved.

If, at any point in this process, there is no lexicographic successor, then the endOfMibView value is returned, paired with the name of the last lexicographic successor or, if there were no successors, with the name of the variable in the request.

Using these rules, the total number of variable-binding pairs that can be produced is $N + (M \times R)$. The order in which the last $(M \times R)$ of these variable binding pairs are placed in the Response PDU can be expressed as follows:

for i ::= 1 **to M do**
   for r ::= 1 **to R do**
      retrieve i-th successor of (N+r)-th variable;

The effect of this definition is that the successors to the last R variables are retrieved row by row, rather than retrieving all of the successors to the first variable, followed by all of the successors to the second variable, and so on. This matches with the way in which conceptual tables are lexicographically ordered, so that if the last R values in the GetBulkRequest are columnar objects of the same table, then the Response will return conceptual rows of the table.

The GetBulkRequest operation removes one of the major limitations of SNMP, which is its inability to efficiently retrieve large blocks of data. Moreover, this use of this operator can actually enable reducing the size of management applications that are supported by the management protocol, realizing further efficiencies. These is no need for the management application to concern itself with some of the details of packaging requests. It need not perform a trial-and-error procedure to determine the optimal number of variable bindings to put in a request PDU. Also, if a request is too big, even for GetBulk-Request, the agent will send back as much data as it can, rather than simply sending a tooBig error message. Thus, the manager simply has to retransmit the request for the missing data; it does not have to figure out how to repackage the original request into a series of smaller requests.

The SetRequest-PDU is issued by a manager to request that the values of one or more objects be altered. The receiving SNMPv2 entity responds with a Response-PDU containing the same request-id. The SetRequest operation is atomic: Either all of the variables are updated or none are. If the responding entity is able to set values for all of the variables listed in the incoming variable-bindings list, then the Response-PDU includes the variable-bindings field, with a value supplied for each variable. If at least one of the variable values cannot be supplied, then no values are returned, and no values are updated. In the latter case, the error-status code indicates the reason for the failure, and the error-index field indicates the variable in the variable-bindings list that caused the failure.

The SNMPv2-Trap PDU is generated and transmitted by an SNMPv2 entity acting in an agent role when an unusual event occurs. It is used to provide the management station with an asynchronous notification of some significant event. The variable-bindings list is used to contain the information associated with the trap message. Unlike the GetRequest, GetNextRequest, GetBulk-Request, SetRequest, and InformRequest PDUs, the SNMPv2-Trap PDU does not elicit a response from the receiving entity; it is an unconfirmed message.

The InformRequest-PDU is sent by an SNMPv2 entity acting in a manager role, on behalf of an application, to another SNMPv2 entity acting in a manager role, to provide management information to an application using the latter entity. As with the SNMPv2-Trap-PDU, the variable-bindings field is used to convey the associated information. The manager receiving an InformRequest acknowledges receipt with a Response-PDU.

For both the SNMPv2-Trap and the InformRequest, various conditions can be defined that indicate when the notification is generated; and the information to be sent is also specified.

SNMPv2 Management Information Base

The objects defined as part of SNMPv2 are organized into three MIBs: the SNMPv2 MIB, the manager-to-manager MIB, and the party MIB. Each MIB is in turn organized into a number of groups. A group is simply a related collection of objects. Typically, implementations are characterized in terms of which groups they implement. An implementation is said to include a group if all of the objects in-that group are supported. This provides a concise way for vendors and customers to gain a mutual understanding of what management information is supported by the vendor's product.

The **SNMPv2 MIB** defines objects that descibe the behavior of an SNMPv2 entity. This information enables a manager to monitor the amount of SNMPv2-related activity at an agent and the amount of dedicated SNMPv2-related resources at the agent. This MIB contains five groups: SNMPv2 statistics, SNMPv1 statistics, object resource, traps, and set.

The SNMPv2 statistics group provides basic instrumentation of the SNMPv2 entity. It consists of counters used to record the number of incoming and outgoing SNMPv2 messages, broken down into successful messages plus those that suffered various error conditions. The SNMPv1 statistics group includes several objects that are useful if an SNMPv2 entity also implements SNMPv1. The object resources group enables an SNMPv2 entity acting in an agent role to describe its dynamically configurable object resources; essentially, this group consists of a table with one entry for each resource, with a text description of the resource. The trap group consists of objects that allow the SNMPv2 entity, when acting in an agent role, to be configured to generate SNMPv2-Trap-PDUs. Finally, the set group consists of a single object, snmpSetSerialNo, that is used to solve two problems that can occur with the use of the set operation. First, multiple set operations on the same MIB object may be issued by a manager, and it may be essential that these operations be performed in the order that they were issued, even if they are reordered in transmission. And second, concurrent use of set operations by multiple managers may result in an inconsistent or inaccurate database. The snmpSetSerialNo is an integer-valued object that obeys the following rules. If the value of the object is K and a set operation is received that attempts to assign K to this object, then the object is incremented to $(K + 1) \bmod 2^{31}$, and the operation succeeds. If any other value is used, the operation fails.

The snmpSet object can be used in the following way: When a manager wishes to set one or more object values in an agent, it first retrieves the value of snmpSet object. It then issues a SetRequest PDU whose variable binding list includes the snmpSet object with its current value. If two or more managers issue SetRequests using the same value of snmpSet, the first to arrive at the agent will succeed (assuming no other problems exist), resulting in an increment of snmpSet; the remaining set operations will fail due to an inconsistent snmpSet value.

The **manager-to-manager (M2M) MIB** is specifically provided to support the distributed management architecture. It enables a superior manager to define events that a subordinate manager will use as triggers for sending alert-type messages to the superior manager. The M2M MIB may be used to allow an intermediate manager to function as a remote monitor of network media traffic. It may also be used to allow an intermediate manager to report on activities at the intermediate manager or at subordinate agents. This MIB consists of two groups: the alarm group and the event group. The alarm group is used to define a set of threshold alarms. Each threshold alarm specifies some object in the local MIB that is to be monitored. When the value of that object crosses a threshold, then an event is triggered. Typically, the triggered event is an InformRequest-PDU that is to be sent to a superior manager. Each alarm in the alarm group points to an entry in the event group, which in turn defines the information that is to be sent with that InformRequest-PDU.

The **Party MIB** relates to security, which is discussed next.

SNMPv2 Security

The new security features of SNMPv2 are designed to provide, in essence, three security-related services: privacy, authentication, and access control.

Privacy is the protection of transmitted data from eavesdropping or wiretapping. Privacy requires that the contents of any message be disguised in such a way that only the intended recipient can recover the original message.

A message, file, document, or other collection of data is said to be authentic when it is genuine and came from its alleged source. Message authentication is a procedure that allows communicating parties to verify that received messages are authentic. The two important aspects are to verify that the contents of the message have not been altered and that the source is authentic. We may also wish to verify a message's timeliness (it has not been artifically delayed and replayed) and sequence relative to other messages flowing between two parties.

In the context of network management, the purpose of access control is to ensure that only authorized users have access to a particular management information base and that access to and modification of a particular portion of data are limited to authorized individuals and programs.

Before examining these three services, we need to introduce the concept of party and look at the message structure for SNMPv2.

SNMPv2 Parties

It is essential for secure communication to identify specifically a source and a destination for any exchange. Authentication depends on the source: It is the responsibility of the source to include information in any message that assures that the origin is authentic, and it is the responsibility of the source to perform the required functions to ensure message integrity. However, message privacy, which is achieved by encryption, depends on the destination. That is, encryption must be done in such a way that only the intended destination can perform the decryption. Finally, access control depends on both source and destination. That is, each destination may have a distinct access policy for each potential source.

Thus, each message must identify both the source and destination. Furthermore, it is insufficient to equate the source with a sending SNMPv2 entity and the destination with a receiving SNMPv2 entity. Each SNMPv2 entity may behave differently, from a security point of view, depending on the identity of the other SNMPv2 entity involved in an exchange. Put another way, the role of an SNMPv2 entity depends on the context of its operation. The concept of role is captured in SNMPv2 as the SNMPv2 **party.** A party is defined as an execution context of an SNMPv2 protocol entity. Any protocol entity may include multiple-party identities.

The way in which parties are handled is as follows. Each SNMPv2 entity maintains a database with information that represents all SNMPv2 parties known to it. This includes

- *Local parties:* The set of parties whose operation is realized by the local SNMPv2 entity; that is, the set of "roles" for this SNMPv2 entity.
- *Proxied parties:* The set of parties for proxied entities that this SNMPv2 entity represents.
- *Remote parties:* The set of parties whose operation is realized by other SNMPv2 entities with which this SNMPv2 entity is capable of interacting.

Message Format

In SNMPv2, information is exchanged between a management station and an agent in the form of a message. Each message includes a message header, which contains security-related information, and one of a number of types of protocol data units. The message structure is depicted in Figure 15.5.

The header consists of five fields. The **srcParty** identifies the party at a manager or agent that is sending this message. The **dstParty** identifies the party at a manager or agent to whom the message is sent. The **context** may indicate that this exchange relates to an access to an MIB local to the agent; in this case, the context value serves to identify a portion of the agent's MIB, known as an MIB view. An MIB view is simply a subset of the MIB at the agent, which is the subject of this protocol exchange. Otherwise, the context value indicates that this exchange involves access to a third system by means of a proxy relationship; in this case, the context value serves to identify the proxied device and the access control privileges associated with accessing that proxied device. In either case, the combination of source party, destination party, and context value is used to determine the access control privileges for this exchange. The **authInfo** field contains information relevant to the authentication protocol. The **privDst** field repeats the object identifier of the destination party.

If the message is non-secure (not authenticated and not private), then the authInfo field consists of an ASN.1 (Abstract Syntax Notation One) encoding of an octet string of zero length. If the message is authenticated but not private, then the authInfo field contains information needed for authentication.

When privacy is provided, then the entire message, including header and PDU but excluding the privDst field, is encrypted. The privDst field must remain unencrypted so that the destination SNMPv2 entity can determine the destination party and therefore determine the privacy characteristics of the message.

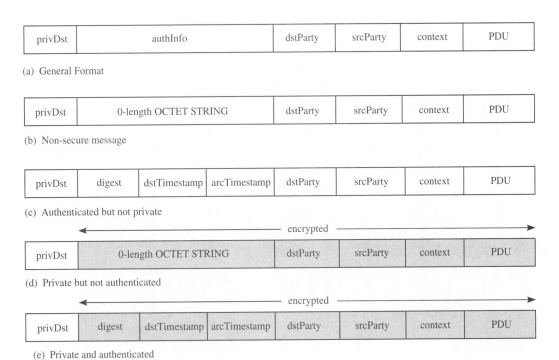

FIGURE 15.5.   SNMPv2 message formats.

Figure 15.6a shows the general procedure for message transmission. Authentication if performed first, if needed, followed by encryption, if needed. Figure 15.6b shows the general procedure for message reception. If the message is encrypted, decryption is performed first. Then, if the message is authenticated, the receiver performs the appropriate authentication algorithm. Finally, access control is performed to determine if the source party is authorized to perform the requested management operation for this context and destination party.

Privacy

For each party known to an SNMPv2 entity, the party database contains three variables whose significance is specific to the privacy protocol:

- *partyPrivProtocol:* Indicates the privacy protocol and mechanism by which all messages received by this party are protected from disclosure. The value noPriv indicates that messages received by this party are not protected from disclosure.
- *partyPrivPrivate:* A secret value needed to support the privacy protocol. It may be conventional-encryption key or the private key in a public-key encryption scheme.

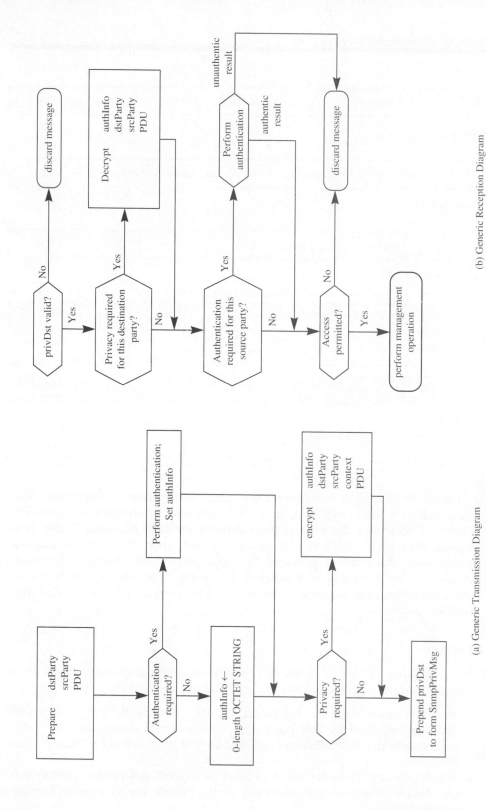

(a) Generic Transmission Diagram

(b) Generic Reception Diagram

FIGURE 15.6. Transmission and reception of secure SNMP messages.

- *partyPrivPublic:* Represents any public value that may be needed to support the privacy protocol. It may be a public key in a public-key encryption scheme.

The specific privacy mechanism chosen for the current version of secure SNMPv2 is the symmetric privacy protocol. It provides for protection from disclosure of a received message (i.e., only the intended recipient and the sender are able to read the message). The mechanism for providing such protection is conventional encryption, which requires that the source and destination parties share the same encryption key. The Data Encryption Standard (DES) is the encryption algorithm used. The database structure, however, allows for the use of other conventional encryption schemes as well as public-key encryption schemes.

Authentication

For each party known to an SNMPv2 entity, the party database contains five variables whose significance is specific to the authentication protocol:

- *partyAuthProtocol:* Indicates the authentication protocol and mechanism used by this party to authenticate the origin and integrity of its outgoing messages. The value noAuth indicates that messages generated by this party are not authenticated.
- *partyAuthClock:* Represents a current time as kept locally for this party.
- *partyAuthPrivate:* A secret value needed to support the authentication protocol. It may be a secret value used in a message digest, a conventional-encryption key, or the private key in a public-key encryption scheme.
- *partyAuthPublic:* Represents any public value tht may be needed to support the authentication protocol. It may be a public key in a public-key encryption scheme.
- *partyAuthLifetime:* An administrative upper bound on acceptable delivery delay for messages generated by this party.

The specific authentication mechanism chosen for the current version of secure SNMPv2 is the MD5 digest authentication protocol. It provides for the verification of the integrity of a received message (i.e., the message received is the message sent), for authentication of the origin of the message, and for the timeliness of message delivery.

In essence, the authentication procedure is as follows. A message digest is computed over the message to be sent prefixed by a secret value, using the MD5 message algorithm described in Chapter 14. The message, plus the message digest (but not the secret value), is transmitted. On reception, the message digest is recomputed using the incoming message and a local copy of the secret value. If the incoming message digest matches the calculated message digest, the received message is declared authentic. The use of the message digest guarantees integrity, and the use of a secret value guarantees origin authentication.

We now turn to the details of the authentication protocol, considering first transmission and then reception. To support authentication, the message header in a transmitted SNMPv2 message includes an authentication-information field, which consists of three components:

- *authDigest:* Represents the digest computed over an appropriate portion of the message, plus the secret value (partyAuthPrivate).
- *authSrcTimestamp:* Represents the time of generation of this message according to the partyAuthClock of the SNMPv2 party that is the source party. The granularity of the clock and therefore of this timestamp is one second.
- *authDstTimestamp:* Represents the time of generation of this message according to the partyAuthClock of the SNMPv2 party that is the destination party. Note that this is the value of the destination party clock stored at the source SNMPv2 entity.

The procedure to be followed for authentication upon reception is somewhat more complex to describe than that for message generation, since various error-checking functions must be taken into account. Suppose that a message is sent from party a on one system to party b on another system. The message authentication process consists of the following steps:

1. If the authSrcTimestamp value does not satisfy the criterion for timeliness, the message is rejected. The timeliness criterion states that the message must be received within a reasonable period of time that does not exceed an administratively set value. This criterion can be expressed as follows. A message is timely if

$$\text{partyAuthClock.a} - \text{authTimestamp} \leq \text{partyAuthLifetime.a}$$

   Put another way, the age of the message at the time of receipt must be less than the maximum allowable lifetime.
2. The authDigest value is extracted and temporarily stored. The authDigest value is temporarily set to the secret value. The message digest is computed over an appropriate portion of the message, plus the secret value (partyAuthPrivate) and compared to the value that was stored (the value that arrived in the incoming message). If the two values match, the message is accepted as authentic.

The relationship between partyAuthClock, partyAuthLifetime, and authSrcTimestamp is illustrated in Figure 15.7. Part (a) of the figure shows the relationship that exists for a message that is authentic in terms of timeliness. Part (b) shows the case of an unauthentic message. Part (c) illustrates the fact that the timestamp of the incoming message may actually exceed the current value of partyAuthClock for the sending party as maintained at the destination. From a logical point of view, this indicates that a message arrives "before" it is sent. Of course, this logical impossibility is due to a mismatch in clocks. When this condition occurs, the clock at the destination is advanced to equal the incoming timestamp. Similarly, to keep the clocks synchronized in

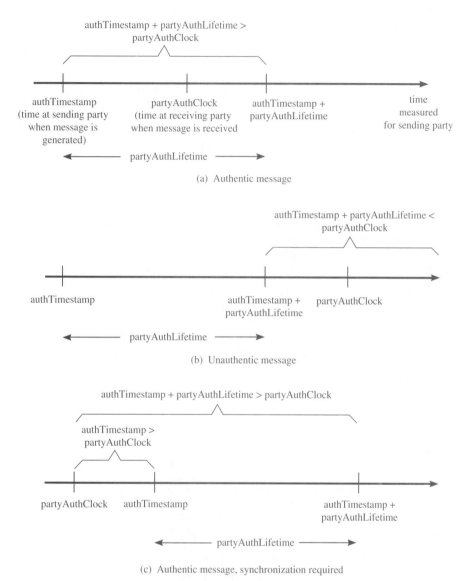

(a) Authentic message

(b) Unauthentic message

(c) Authentic message, synchronization required

FIGURE 15.7.   Authentication timeliness requirement.

the other direction, the partyAuthClock of the receiving party is compared to authDstTimestamp and advanced if necessary to equal the incoming time-stamp.

The lifetime value for a party should be chosen to be as small as possible given the accuracy of the clocks involved, round-trip communication delays, and the frequency with which clocks are synchronized. If the lifetime value is set too small, authentic messages will be rejected as unauthentic. On the other hand, a large lifetime increases the vulnerability to malicious delays of messages.

It is important to note that the generation of the message depends on the values of the source party that are stored by the sending SNMPv2 entity, where the source party resides, while the authentication of the message at the destination depends on the party values *for the source party* that are stored at the receiving SNMPv2 entity, where the destination party resides. The values in the two instances may therefore differ.

Clock Synchronization

When a message is transmitted, it includes the value of both the sending and receiving party clocks. Upon message reception, authentication depends on the timeliness of the message with reference to the source timestamp.

When a party is first configured, its clock is set to zero. The clock then increments once per second. There are, however, two versions of a party's clock: one stored with the party information at the management station and one stored with the party information at the agent. Thus there is the potential for drift between the two versions, which could adversely affect authentication.

For any pair of parties, four possible conditions can occur that require correction:

1. The manager's version of the agent's clock is greater than the agent's version of the agent's clock. This creates the risk of a false rejection of a message from the agent to the manager.
2. The manager's version of the manager's clock is greater than the agent's version of the manager's clock. This creates the risk of a false acceptance of a message from the manager to the agent.
3. The agent's version of the agent's clock is greater than the manager's version of the agent's clock. This creates the risk of a false acceptance of a message from the agent to the manager.
4. The agent's version of the manager's clock is greater than the manager's version of the manager's clock. This creates the risk of a false rejection of a message from the manager to the agent.

Now let us consider the case in which an agent receives a message from a manager. If the authSrcTimestamp in the message exceeds the agent's value of partyAuthClock for the sending manager party, that clock is advanced and condition 2 is corrected. If the authDstTimestamp in the message exceeds the agent's value of partyAuthClock for the receiving agent party, the clock is advanced and condition 1 is corrected. To complete this line of reasoning, consider the case in which a manager receives a message from an agent. If the authSrcTimestamp in the message exceeds the agent's value of partyAuthClock for the sending agent party, the clock is advanced and condition 3 is corrected.

If the authDstTimestamp in the message exceeds the agent's value of party-AuthClock for the receiving manager party, the clock is advanced and condition 4 is corrected.

At first glance, the effects of these clock updates would appear to eliminate the need for explicit, manager-directed clock synchronization, since all four clock skew conditions are corrected when messages are exchanged. However, in most cases of manager–agent interaction, the interaction is in the form of a manager request and an agent response. It is intended that a trap message, which originates at the agent, is to be used sparingly. If there has been a considerable lapse of time between requests from a particular manager party to a particular agent party, then clock drift may have created condition 4 with a substantial difference in the two clock values. The result is that any request by the manager will be rejected. Accordingly, it remains necessary for the manager to perform clock synchronization on all manager party clocks, but it is not necessary to synchronize agent party clocks. For this purpose, the manager periodically retrieves the manager party clock values from agents and advances its clocks as necessary.

Access Control

Management information at a system is stored as a collection of objects that represents manageable resources. These objects are arranged in a tree structure to form the management information base (MIB) at the system.

For purposes of access control, the concepts of MIB view and view subtree are used. A view subtree consists of a node in the MIB tree plus all of its subordinate elements. Each view subtree in the MIB view is specified as being included or excluded. That is, the MIB view either includes or excludes all objects contained in that subtree. This specification technique provides a flexible but concise means of defining an MIB view.

Access control is determined by information in the Party MIB. This MIB consists of four groups: party database, contexts, access privileges, and MIB view. The best way to describe the purpose of each of these groups is to consider their use during message transmission.

Consider that a message is sent from a manager to an agent. The message header includes the fields srcParty, dstParty, and context. The party database group at the agent contains information about each local and remote party known to the agent. The party information includes authentication parameters that need to be applied to srcParty and privacy parameters that need to be applied to dstParty. The context group consists of a table with one entry for each context known to the agent. Each entry specifies whether the context is local, in which case the appropriate MIB view must be used, or remote, in which case the proxied device is indicated. The MIB view group is referenced by the contexts group. The appropriate entry defines a subset of the local MIB that is accessible through this context. Finally, the access privileges database group contains the aclTable. Each entry in the table has a unique combination of srcParty, dstParty, and context and indicates which management operations (which PDUs) are allowed for this combination.

FILE TRANSFER: FTAM

In this section, we first present the general principles of file transfer protocols, then look at the ISO standard.

Architecture

The purpose of a file transfer protocol (FTP) is to transfer a file or a portion of a file from one system to another, under command of an FTP user. Depending on its scope of responsibility, the FTP may be a pure application protocol in the OSI sense, or it may also have presentation functionality, and even some elements of a session layer.

Figure 15.8 shows a view of FTP as an application-level protocol. Here, FTP is viewed as the top layer of a seven-layer communications architecture that is supported by the station's operating system. Typically, FTP is used interactively by an on-line user. The user's communication with FTP is mediated by the operating system, which contains I/O drivers. If the user on system *A* wishes access to a file on system *B*, then *A*'s FTP establishes a connection to *B*'s FTP. This is, of course, a logical connection. The actual path for control and user data is through the layers of the architecture.

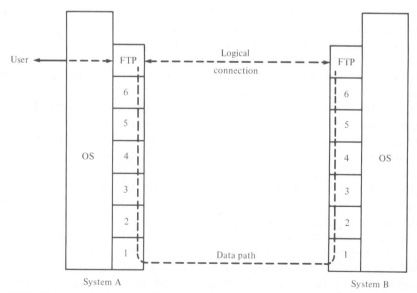

FIGURE 15.8.   Architectural context of a file transfer protocol.

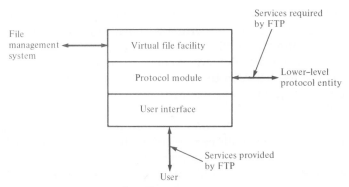

FIGURE 15.9. Generic FTP structure.

The user connects to the local FTP in order to transfer all or part of a file. There are three possibilities. The user at A may wish a file at B to be transferred to A. This would give the user local access to the contents of the file. The user may have prepared a file locally (at A) and wish it sent to B. Finally, the user may request that a file be exchanged between B and a third system, C. This is referred to as a third-party transfer and involves the FTP entities at A, B, and C.

FTP must interact with three entities, as depicted in Figure 15.9. First, there must be a user interface to accept requests from an interactive user or, possibly, a program. Of course, this interaction only takes place at the requesting system. The remote FTP in a file transfer event does not interact with a user. Second, FTP must be able to communicate with other FTPs to achieve file transfer. Typically, this is done by interfacing to a lower-level protocol entity. Finally, to transfer a file, FTP must be able to get at the file. For this, an interface is needed to the local file management system.

Consideration of this last interface reminds us that a general-purpose FTP must operate in a heterogeneous environment. Because different systems may have different file formats and structures, FTP must have knowledge of the local file system or, at least, rely on an entity that does. Before suggesting an effective way of handling this situation, let us consider what it is that is to be transferred. There are three possibilities.

- *The data in the file:* If just the actual data in the file are sent, we are not really dealing with a file transfer. This is more in the nature of a message exchange or electronic mail facility.
- *The data plus the file structure:* This, at minimum, is what is usually meant by a file transfer protocol.
- *The data, file structure, and all its attributes:* Examples of attributes are an access control list, an update history, and a list of indices for an indexed sequential file facility.

If the FTP operates somewhere on a spectrum bounded by the last two items, it must have knowledge of the local file structure and format, and it must understand the incoming file structure and format. To avoid the $M \times N$ problem discussed in the section on virtual terminal protocols, a similar solution may be adopted: the virtual file. Thus a general-purpose virtual file structure is defined. Only virtual files are exchanged between FTPs. Locally, a transformation is needed between the virtual file format and the local file format. This transformation can be implemented in the FTP or provided by a presentation protocol.

A virtual file structure should be simple enough that files can be exchanged between identical file systems with minimum overhead. On the other hand, it must be complex enough to be able to represent accurately a variety of dissimilar file systems. In general, a virtual file, or any file for that matter, consists of the following:

- A filename, that allows it to be referenced unambiguously.
- Other descriptive attributes which express common properties of the file, such as size, accounting information, history, and so on; these might be referred to as management attributes.
- Attributes describing the logical structure and dimensions of the data stored in the file; these might be referred to as structural attributes.
- Any data forming the contents of the file.

A wide variety of file structures are in common use, including sequential, indexed sequential, hierarchical, network, and relational. A simple example of

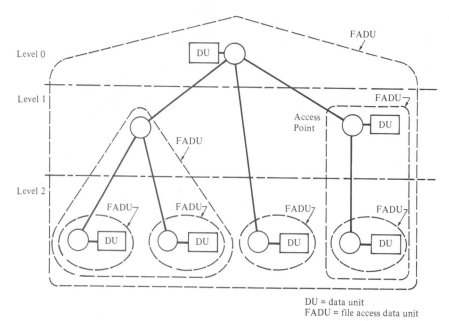

DU = data unit
FADU = file access data unit

FIGURE 15.10.   Virtual file structure.

a hierarchical virtual file structure is shown in Figure 15.10. The key building block of this virtual file is a *file access data unit* (FADU). The FADU is the unit on which operations on the file content are performed. Operations include read, write, insert, and delete. The file exhibits a tree structure, where each node of the tree defines a subtree that is an FADU. The highest-level (level 0) FADU encompasses the entire file. The lowest-level FADUs represent the leaves of the tree. The smallest unit of a file's contents on which filestore operations can be performed is the *data unit* (DU). Each data unit is associated with a node of the file access structure. An example of a data unit is a record in a file. In that case, the internal structure of the data unit (i.e., in terms of fields and groups of fields) is not specified. However, certain attributes of the file may be part of the virtual file structure. These may include access control parameters, and the identity of index keys.

Characteristics

As is usually the case with any protocol, file transfer protocols can be characterized by the services they provide and the protocol mechanisms they employ. Table 15.2 contains a list of relevant service and protocol features for file transfer protocols, suggested in [NBS80c]. We will briefly consider each feature in turn.

Service Features

In the typical computer system, there is some *access control* mechanism to protect the file system. A user must have an ID and password to gain access to the system at all. Then individual files may maintain access control lists with specific permissions (read, write) by user. This capability must be extended across the network. The simplest way, perhaps, is to require the user to do a remote log-in and be identified at the system. In a controlled network environ-

TABLE 15.2   File Transfer Protocol Features

Service Features	Protocol Features
Access control	Transmission of commands
Processing mode	File attributes
File naming	Negotiation
Alternative operations	Text formatting
File management	Security
Error recovery	Statistics
Flow control	
File structuring	
Status reports	

ment, there might be a network-wide access control mechanism. In any case, the mechanism must be mediated by the FTP.

The normal *processing mode* of a file transfer is immediate. That is, when the transfer is requested, FTP will endeavor to achieve the transfer right away and report back. If, however, the transfer is not urgent, the user could indicate that the transfer could take place in a background mode.

A *file naming* facility is needed to identify the source and destination station and the source and destination file. At a minimum, the user must specify the network name of the station and a file name that is locally significant (local to the system on which the file resides). This requires the user to know the syntax and semantics of file naming conventions at each system of interest. A better service is one that involves standardized syntax for file names, although semantics may still differ (e.g., modifiers such as SOURCE and OBJECT may have particular significance). A virtual file name would then be used, to be translated locally by FTP. Again, in a controlled network environment, one might hope for a network-wide file system, with a common syntax and semantics, in which the user need not even know the location of a file.

The basic operation of FTP is to duplicate a file and send it to another system, where it is stored with a new local name. *Alternative operations* include: transfer of a portion of a file, copy a file only if an empty destination file already exists, and append a file to the contents of a destination file.

An FTP can mediate user access to certain *file management* facilities, either local or remote. Although file management is not properly a part of a file transfer protocol, certain minimal services seem warranted. The following three are found in most file transfer protocols: file allocation (define a new file and allocate space), file deletion, and listing file names in a directory.

An *error recovery* facility would provide for recovery from errors or failure in the file system or operating system. The mechanism to be used is checkpointing. Checkpoint locations are transferred along with the file. The number of unacknowledged checkpoints can be controlled by a sliding window protocol. When an error is detected, the file transfer can be backed up to any acknowledged checkpoint. This mechanism could be implemented entirely in FTP, or rely on the session layer for checkpoint transmission and acknowledgment.

A simple stop-and-wait *flow-control* scheme is a useful addition to an FTP. This mechanism allows the transfer to be temporarily halted and resumed later. This feature provides the ability to mount tapes during the transfer and allows system resources such as disks to be preempted by a higher priority task without aborting a transfer in progress.

We have already discussed the need for a *file structuring* service with an FTP. A hierarchical or tree structure file description will have the most general applicability.

File transfers can be lengthy processes, particularly if performed in background mode. *Status reports* should be provided that indicate the start and completion of a transfer. The user should be able to interrogate FTP to determine the current status of any ongoing file transfer.

Protocol Features

A fundamental feature of a file transfer protocol is the *transmission of commands*. An FTP entity must communicate with a peer counterpart to coordinate and control the data transfer. Control information could be exchanged over the same session as the file data, or it could be accomplished over a separate session. In a third-party transfer, mechanisms must be in place to provide for the coordination among three FTP entities.

The source FTP must communicate *file attributes* to the recipient system. This is so even if a fully general virtual file structure is used. The reason is that, at the receiving end, the virtual file must be transformed into a local real file. The nature of that transformation may depend on attributes of the original source file. For example, if the destination system only uses the ASCII character code and the source file is non-ASCII text, this attribute needs to be known so that either the source or destination FTP can invoke a conversion function.

A flexible file transfer protocol is bound to have a number of options, for example, use of checkpointing, flow control, buffer size, and so on. A process of *negotiation* is required for two FTP entities to agree on a common level of service.

In text files, there will be certain control codes that affect the format of the text (e.g., vertical and horizontal spacing). A *text formatting* mechanism indicates which control codes are in the file and how they are to be interpreted. Thus systems using different text format control conventions can intelligibly exchange text files.

In addition to specific access control mechanisms that control access to files by identified users, files may be designated with a *security* label. FTP must cooperate with the file system's security mechanism to maintain security. Specifically, FTP must match the security level of the file to the security level of the session.

Finally, *statistics* can be gathered by FTP to provide information to a central control authority and to provide the user with information to be used when allocating local resources.

The ISO FTAM Standard

As an example, we briefly describe a recently adopted ISO standard [ISO87], [LEWA83], known as file transfer, access, and management (FTAM). The FTAM standard is quite complex; this section is intended only to give the reader a general appreciation of its features. The standard is organized into three parts:

- Virtual filestore definition.
- File service definition.
- File protocol specification.

Virtual Filestore Definition

The virtual filestore in FTAM is defined in terms of the structure of files, the attributes that can be assigned to files; and the allowable actions on files and file elements.

There are four aspects of the *structure of a file,* each conveying different information about the file:

- *File access structure:* describes the composition of the file from file access data units (FADUs). The file access structure is that depicted in Figure 15.10. Thus, the current version of the standard is limited to hierarchical or simpler types of file structures. Later revisions may also include network and relational structures.
- *Presentation structure:* describes the abstract syntaxes of the data units (DUs) which are defined within the file access structure. The presentation structure expresses the data unit in terms of the syntactic arrangement of data elements. However, it is not possible to access the individual data elements within a data unit by means of FTAM; the data unit is accessed as a whole. The definition of presentation syntax may be useful for checkpointing and for providing guidance to the presentation layer.
- *Transfer structure:* describes the serialization of the FADUs for communication purposes. The transfer structure specifies the way in which a structured file is transferred as a series of data element values.
- *Identification structure:* describes the naming of the nodes in the file access structure and the identification of FADUs to be transferred.

Each file has associated with it a number of properties, known as *attributes.* Two classes of attributes are defined: file attributes and activity attributes. File attributes represent properties of the file itself, independent of any FTAM action occurring over an ISO session connection. These attributes distinguish a file from bulk data by providing the kind of file management information normally associated with a data base or file management system. Three groups of file attributes are defined in FTAM. The kernel group is the minimum that must be supported; it provides the basic information needed for the act of file transfer. The storage group defines concepts related to the physical storage of files. It is concerned with physical properties of the file, such as size, as well as information about accessors. The security group provides for file-related security information. The attributes are listed in Table 15.3. Some of them merit further definition:

- *Contents type:* indicates the internal structure of the file (unstructured, flat, hierarchical) and the data type (text, binary).
- *Permitted actions:* lists those actions (defined below) which are permitted on this file.
- *Access control:* list of permitted actions by identity of accessor.
- *Encryption name:* name of the algorithm used to encrypt the file contents.

TABLE 15.3   FTAM Attributes

File Attributes	Activity Attributes
Kernel Group	
Filename	Active contents type
Contents Type	Current Access Request
	Current Location
	Current Processing Mode
	Current Application Entity Title
Storage Group	
Storage Account	Current Account
Date and Time of Creation	Current Access Context
Date and Time of Last Modification	Current Concurrency Control
Date and Time of Last Read Access	
Date and Time of Last Attribute Modification	
Identity of Creator	
Identity of Last Modifier	
Identity of Last Reader	
Identity of Last Attribute Modifier	
File Availability	
Permitted Actions	
Filesize	
Future Filesize	
Security Group	
Access Control	Active Legal Qualifications
Encryption Name	Current Initiator Identity
Legal Qualifications	Current Access Passwords

- *Legal qualifications:* character string conveying information about the legal status of the file and its use.

The other class of attributes are activity attributes. These are relevant only to the file service session in progress. There is a different set of values for file activity attributes for each file service connection. As with file attributes, activity attributes are divided into kernel, storage, and security groups. Among these are:

- *Current access context:* indicates the view of the file's access structure for the purpose of communication (hierarchical, flat, unstructured)
- *Current concurrency control:* indicates the restrictions on parallel access to the file for particular actions.

Table 15.4 lists the *allowable actions on files and file elements.* Some actions are defined on a complete file; these fall within the scope of file management. The other actions are related to the access of individual file access data units within a file.

TABLE 15.4   Allowable Actions on FTAM Files

Actions on Complete Files

Create file	Creates new file; establishes its attributes
Select file	Creates relationship between initiator and file
Change attribute	Changes a current file attribute
Read attribute	Gets value of requested attribute
Open file	Establishes suitable regime for the performance of the actions for file access on the selected file. File may be opened for read or read/write.
Close file	Terminates the open regime.
Delete file	Deletes the selected file.
Deselect file	Terminates file selection.

Actions for File Access

Locate	Locates specified FADU
Read	Locates and reads an FADU
Insert	Inserts FADU relative to current location
Replace	Replaces currently located FADU
Extend	Adds data to the end of the DU associated with the root node of the currently located FADU
Erase	Specified FADU is erased

File Service Definition

Whereas the virtual filestore definition defines the structure of files and the allowable actions on those files, the file service definition defines the services available to users for accessing and manipulating the virtual files.

The FTAM service and its supporting protocol are concerned with creating, in a series of stages, a working environment in which the user's desired activities can take place. The dialogue must, in turn:

- Allow the user and the filestore provider to establish each other's identity.
- Identify the file which is needed and establish the user's authority to access the file.
- Establish the attributes describing the file structure which is to be accessed on this occasion and establish controls on the concurrent access of the file by other users;
- Allow the user to access the attributes or contents of the currently selected file.

These steps build up various parts of an operational context. The period for which some part of the contextual information is valid is called a *regime*. As progressively more contextual detail is established, a nest of corresponding regimes is built up; this nesting is shown in Figure 15.11. In essence, the regime determines the state of the FTAM service provider with respect to a given

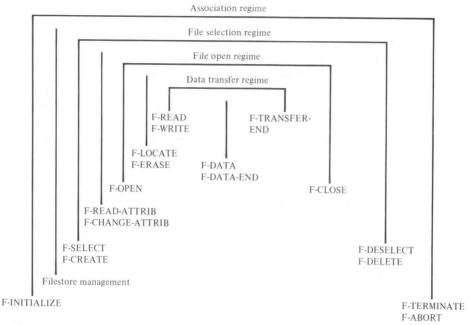

FIGURE 15.11.   FTAM file service regimes and primitives.

user connection and therefore the services that can be provided at a given point in time.

As usual, the services provided by FTAM are defined as a set of primitives and parameters. Table 15.5 shows the primitives. They may be grouped as follows:

- *FTAM regime control:* these services are used to create and terminate a connection by which the user can access the virtual file.
- *File selection regime control:* identify a unique file to which subsequent operations will apply. The file may be selected from among existing files, or it may be created.
- *File management:* allows the user to inspect or modify attributes of the selected file.
- *File open regime control:* assigns a file to a user for access purposes. Concurrency controls may be exercised.
- *Grouping control:* allows the user to indicate the start and end of a set of primitives that are to be processed and responded to as a group.
- *Access to file content:* identify a unique location within a file structure (i.e., the position of a particular FADU) to which subsequent operations apply.
- *Bulk data transfer:* used for the transfer of one or more data units. The procedure begins with the user issuing either an F-READ.request or an F-WRITE.request. This causes a sequence of F-DATA.requests followed by an

TABLE 15.5   FTAM Service Primitives

FTAM Regime Control
F-INITIALIZE request/indication/response/confirm
F-TERMINATE request/indication/response/confirm
F-U-ABORT request/indication
F-P-ABORT indication

File Selection Regime Control
F-SELECT request/indication/response/confirm
F-DESELECT request/indication/response/confirm
F-CREATE request/indication/response/confirm
F-DELETE request/indication/response/confirm

File Management
F-READ-ATTRIB request/indication/response/confirm
F-CHANGE-ATTRIB request/indication/response/confirm

File Open Regime Control
F-OPEN request/indication/response/confirm
F-CLOSE request/indication/response/confirm

Grouping Control
F-BEGIN-GROUP request/indication/response/confirm
F-END-GROUP request/indication/response/confirm

Access to File Content
F-LOCATE request/indication/response/confirm
F-ERASE request/indication/response/confirm

Bulk Data Transfer
F-READ request/indication
F-WRITE request/indication
F-DATA request/indication
F-DATA-END request/indication
F-TRANSFER-END request/indication/response/confirm
F-CANCEL request/indication/response/confirm

Checkpointing and Restarting
F-CHECK request/indication/response/confirm
F-RESTART request/indication/response/confirm

F-DATA-END.request by the sender of the data. The procedure is completed by the user issuing an F-TRANSFER-END.request.

- *Checkpointing and restarting:* allows the sender of data to establish marks in the flow of data for the purpose of subsequent restart. Restarting involves backing up to a checkpoint and retransmitting data from that point.

File Protocol Specification

The FTAM protocol provides a rather direct support of the FTAM service. By and large, there is a one-to-one mapping from service primitives to protocol data units. The FTAM protocol will set up a session connection and insert checkpoints in the flow of data.

15.3

ELECTRONIC MAIL: X.400

One of the deadliest wasters of time in the office is a phenomenon known as "telephone tag." Mr. X calls Ms. Y, who is away from her desk. Some time later Y returns the call but X is out or on another line. X is now "it" and must return Y's return to X's call. And so on. . . . Independent studies have shown that over 70 percent of all business telephone calls do not reach the intended recipient on the first try [MARI79]. The problem is that the caller and callee must both be at their phones and available to answer at the same time. If the caller could simply write a note and leave it on the callee's desk, the problem could be avoided. Electronic mail provides a way to do this.

Electronic mail addresses another problem as well: the office paper explosion. Offices generate a tremendous amount of paperwork, most of it in the form of internal memos and reports: over 80 percent of all business documents are textual and/or numeric (no graphics) and originate and remain within the same organization [POTT77].

Electronic mail, also known as a computer-based message system (CBMS), is a facility that allows users at terminals to compose and exchange messages. The messages need never exist on paper unless the user (sender or recipient) desires a paper copy of the message. Some electronic mail systems serve only users on a single computer; others provide service across a network of computers. In this section, we briefly look at the functionality of single-system electronic mail, then turn our attention to the more interesting (for this book) case of network electronic mail. Finally, the CCITT X.400 family of standards is described.

Single-System Electronic Mail

The simplest, and by far the most common, form of electronic mail is the single-system facility. This facility allows all the users of a shared computer system to exchange messages. Each user is registered on the system and has a unique identifier, usually the person's last name. Associated with each user is a mailbox. The electronic mail facility is an application program available to any user logged on to the system. A user may invoke the electronic mail facility, prepare a message, and "send" it to any other user on the system. The act of sending simply involves putting the message in the recipient's mailbox. The mailbox is actually an entity maintained by the file management system, and is in the nature of a file directory. One mailbox is associated with each user. Any "incoming" mail is simply stored as a file under that user's mailbox directory. The user may later go and fetch that file to read the message. The user reads messages by invoking the mail facility and "reading" rather than "sending." In most systems, when the user logs on, he or she is informed if there is any new mail in that user's mailbox.

A basic electronic mail system performs four functions:

- *Creation:* A user creates and edits a message, generally using a rudimentary editing capability. Most systems also allow the user to create a message using the system editor or a word processor, and then incorporate the resulting file as the body of the message.
- *Sending:* The user designates the recipient (or recipients) of the message, and the facility stores the message in the appropriate mailbox(es).
- *Reception:* The intended recipient may invoke the electronic mail facility to access and read the delivered mail.
- *Storage:* Both sender and recipient may choose to save the message in a file for more permanent storage.

Because we are interested in the networking aspects of electronic mail, the topic of basic user services will not be further pursued here. More detail can be found in [HIRS85] and [BARC81].

Network Electronic Mail

With a single-system electronic mail facility, messages can only be exchanged among users of that particular system. Clearly, this is too limited. In a distributed environment, we would like to be able to exchange messages with users attached to other systems. Thus, we would like to treat electronic mail as an application-layer protocol that makes use of lower-layer protocols to transmit messages.

Figure 15.12 suggests the internal system architecture required. Let us refer to a single-system mail facility as a *native mail* facility. For native mail, three major modules are needed. Users will interact with native mail via terminals; hence, terminal-handling software is needed. Mail is stored as files in the file system, so file-handling software is needed. Finally, there must be a native mail package that contains all the logic for providing mail-related services to users.

To extend this system to *network mail*, two more modules are needed. Since we are going to communicate across some sort of network or transmission system, communication I/O logic is needed; in the most general case, this would encompass layers 1 through 6 of the OSI model. Mail transfer logic is also needed, that knows how to invoke the communications function, to specify the network address of the recipient, and to request whatever communication services are needed (e.g., priority). Note in the figure that the user does not directly interact with the mail transfer module. Ideally, the user interface for local and remote mail should be the same. If the user designates a local recipient, the message is stored in a local mailbox. If a remote recipient is designated, the native mail module passes the message to the mail transfer mod-

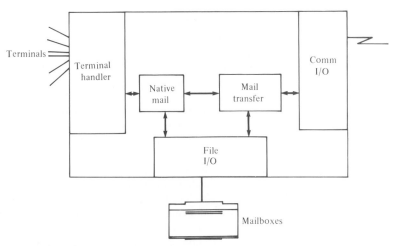

FIGURE 15.12.   Conceptual structure of electronic mail system.

ule for transmission across the network. Incoming mail from the network is routed to the appropriate mailbox and henceforth treated the same as other messages in the mailbox.

Many vendors now offer a network version of their basic electronic mail facility. However, this will only allow the user to send mail to users on systems of the same vendor. As in other areas, standards are needed. It is to these standards that we now turn our attention.

The CCITT X.400 Family of Standards

In 1984, CCITT issued a family of standards for Message Handling Systems (MHS) that encompass the requirements of what we have referred to as network electronic mail; the standards were substantially revised in 1988. The standards do not deal with the user interface or the services available directly to the user (what we have referred to as native mail). They do, however, specify what services are available for use in sending messages across the network and thus provide the base for building the user interface.

Table 15.6 lists the nine recommendations that comprise the X.400 family. All of the recommendations fit into the framework of an MHS model, which is described in X.400. We describe that model first, and then look at some of the key aspects of the specifications of services and protocols.

MHS Functional Model

X.400 defines a functional model for the message handling system, as shown in Figure 15.13. This model provides a framework for all of the other recommendations. The model defines a number of key components (Table 15.7).

**TABLE 15.6   The CCITT X.400 Family of Standards for
Message Handling Systems**

Number	Title	Description
X.400	System and Service Overview	Defines the message-handling system model consisting of user agents and message-transfer agents, discusses naming and addressing, defines interpersonal messaging and message transfer services, and discussed protocols for implementation.
X.402	Overall Architecture	Defines the overall architecture and serves as a technical introduction to it.
X.403	Conformance Testing	Specifies the criteria for acceptance of an implementation as conforming to the X.400 family of recommendations.
X.407	Abstract Service Definition Conventions	Defines techniques for formally specifying the distributed information processing tasks that arise in Message Handling.
X.408	Encoded Information Type Conversion Rules	Specifies the conversion between different types of encoded information to allow dissimilar devices to exchange messages. The encoded information types that are handled include Telex, Teletex, ASCII terminals, facsimile, and videotex.
X.411	Message Transfer Layer	Defines the conceptual layer service provided by the message transfer layer and the message transfer protocol.
X.413	Message Store: Abstract Service Definition	Defines the services provided by the message store.
X.419	Protocol Specifications	Defines the protocols for accessing the Message Transfer System, for accessing a Message Store, and that are used between Message Transfer Agents to provide for the distributed operation of the MTS.
X.420	Interpersonal Messaging System	Defines the services provided by Interpersonal Messaging and the procedures for providing those services.

The actual work of message transfer is done in the message transfer system, which consists of an interconnected set of message transfer agents (MTAs). The **message transfer agent** accepts messages from a user agent (UA) for delivery to other UAs or to a message store (MS). Sometimes the MTA that accepts submission of a message delivers it directly to the destination UA or MS. In other cases, it is necessary for the message to be relayed through a series of MTAs to the destination. For example, if only some MTAs have access to the proper long-distance communication paths, a message addressed to a distant

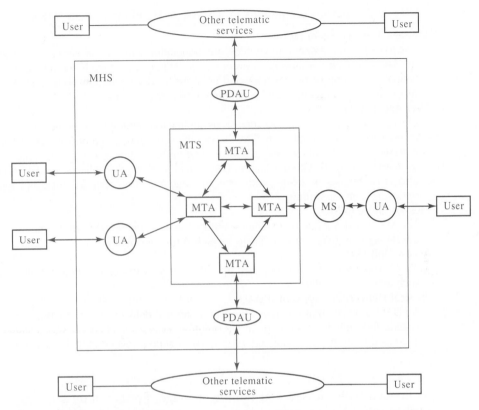

MHS = Message handlng system
MTS = Message transfer system
MTA = Message transfer agent
MS = Message store
UA = User agent
AU = Access unit
PDAU = Physical delivery access unit

FIGURE 15.13.   X.400 MHS functional model.

UA might be relayed in several stages. Using relays also eliminates the need to have all UAs and MTAs available on a 24-hour basis. The store-and-forward action makes it feasible to treat electronic mail components like any other office equipment that gets turned off at night.

The other elements of the message handling system are users of the message transfer system. The **user agent** operates on behalf of a user. The UA submits messages to an MTA for transmission across the network. The X.400 series specifies the interaction of the UA with MTA and other UA entities but does not specify the interaction between the UA and its user.

The **message store** is a concept that was introduced in the 1988 version of the standard. One of the drawbacks of the 1984 scheme, which had no message store, was that if a remote UA was off-line for a period of time, it could

TABLE 15.7 Basic Components of a Message Handling System (MHS)

Message Transfer Agent (MTA)

The MTA is a functional entity which, in cooperation with similar entities, conveys messages through the message transfer system. When a message is submitted, the MTA validates the submission envelope and performs housekeeping functions, such as recording submission time and generating a message identifier.

User Agent (UA)

Operates on behalf of the user (person or application program that originates and receives messages). It interacts directly with the user, performs functions for preparing messages and submitting messages for routing to the destination(s). In the process, the source UA interacts with destination UAs, which perform the delivery function. The UAs also assist the user in dealing with other message functions, such as filing, replying, retrieving, and forwarding.

Message Store (MS)

The MS provides a mailbox facility. Messages may be delivered from the message transfer system (MTS) into the MS to be picked up later by a UA.

Access Unit (AU)

An AU provides a gateway between the MHS and an external communications service, such as Telex or Teletex.

Physical Delivery Access Unit (PDAU)

A PDAU is an AU that provides access to a physical delivery system such as the postal system. It produces a hard copy of the message contents together with an envelope addressed using the electronic addressing information provided by the originator.

---

be flooded with messages at the log-on stage. Furthermore, a message delivered to the UA is "trapped" in that UA system; it causes problems for users on the move, who may want to access their mailbox from terminals at different locations or from a portable terminal. The MS concept is designed to alleviate these problems.

The functionality defined for the message store can be summarized as follows [CHIL90]:

- One MS acts on behalf of one user (i.e., one originator/response address).
- When a UA subscribes to an MS, all messages destined for the UA are delivered to the MS; when a message is delivered to an MS the role of the message transfer system (MTS) in the transfer process is complete. Note that the MS does not store submitted messages, only delivered messages.
- It is possible to request an alert when a certain message arrives.
- Message submission from the UA to its MTA, via the MS, is transparent.
- Users are provided with general message management facilities such as selective message retrieval, delete, and list.

In effect, the MS specification is just a standardized definition of how otherwise local UA functions have been taken over by a separate system, and accessed via a protocol.

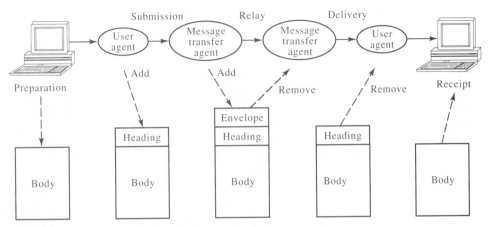

FIGURE 15.14.   X.400 message flow.

Finally, various **access units** (AUs) allow MHS users to communicate with other message-based systems. The rules for coded information conversion are defined, making it possible to standardize the conversion of message contents for transfer of messages between dissimilar systems.

Figure 15.14 suggests the way in which messages are constructed and transmitted. The user prepares the *body* of a message outside of the scope of X.400, using some sort of word processor or editor. The user presents this body to the user agent software, together with a description, which might include recipient, subject, and priority. The user agent appends a *header* containing this qualifying information to the *message,* forming a complete message. This message is submitted to a message transfer agent. The MTA appends an *envelope* to the message; the envelope contains the source and destination addresses plus other control information needed for relaying the message through the network.

The X.400 Protocol Architecture

The message-handling protocols defined in the X.400 series are located in the application layer of the OSI model. Table 15.8 lists the protocols in the X.400 family.

An example of the use of these protocols is shown in Figure 15.15. User A sends a message to User B and User C. The message is handed over to User A's UA, which *submits* the message after putting it in an envelope. The envelope is, in effect the header of a P3 protocol data unit. The MTAs take over the *transfer* of the message until it reaches an MTA which can make a *delivery* of the message. The routing of the message among the MTAs is accomplished with the P1 protocol. The recipient User B gets delivery directly to B's UA, via protocol P3, where it can be directly read. For recipient User C, a copy of the message is delivered into C's MS from where it can later be retrieved via protocol P7.

The P1 protocol is used to transfer a message from the originator's MTA to the recipient's MTA through zero or more intermediate MTAs. The protocol is also used, if the service has been requested, for transferring a notification of delivery or nondelivery back to the originator's MTA. Of course, if the originator and recipient share the same MTA, then this protocol is not needed.

Three types of protocol data units are defined: user, delivery report, and probe. The user PDU consists of the user agent sublayer PDU plus a header, known as the *envelope* (Figure 15.16). The envelope contains the information needed for handling the message, including a network name for the recipient that will allow routing, a unique identifier, and information on how to process the PDU, such as the priority and whether a delivery report is required. The delivery report includes a header that consists of a unique identifier, the name of the originator that submitted the message to which this report refers, and

TABLE 15.8   MHS Protocols (X.419)

Message Transfer Protocol (P1)
>   P1 provides for relaying messages and other interactions among the various message transfer agents. It thus serves as the backbone switching protocol.

Remote UA Access Protocol (P3)
>   P3 enables a user agent (UA) that is remote from its message transfer agent (MTA) to obtain access to the message transfer service for submission from the UA and retrieval from the MTA. In effect, P3 is a remote procedure call protocol.

MS Access Protocol (P7)
>   P7 enables a user agent to interact with a message store, providing in effect a mailbox facility.

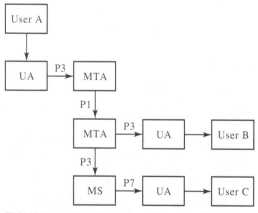

FIGURE 15.15.   Example of how the X.400 protocols can be used [MANR89].

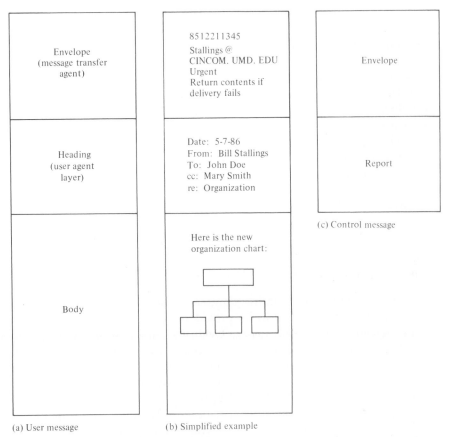

(a) User message

(b) Simplified example

FIGURE 15.16.   X.400 message structure.

trace information, which indicates the route that the delivery report followed. The body of the delivery report PDU includes the identifier of the original user PDU plus information about the delivery. This may include such items as the trace of the original user PDU, billing information, and, of course, whether delivery was successful.

The probe PDU is similar to the envelope portion of a user PDU. Its purpose is to determine if a particular delivery is possible without actually sending a user message. Delivery reports will be returned on probe PDUs.

Figure 15.16 also indicates the presence of a message heading. The heading is transparent to the message transfer agent and to the various protocols (P1, P3, P7). However, the format of the message heading is specified for use by user agents. The heading contains the following fields:

- Message ID.
- Originator.
- Authorizing users.

- Primary recipients.
- Copy recipients.
- Blind copy recipients.
- Replies to message.
- Obsoletes messages.
- Related messages.
- Subject.
- Expiry time.
- Reply time.
- Reply recipients.
- Importance.
- Sensitivity.
- Auto forwarded.
- Extensions.

X.400 Services

As with most communications standards, the X.400 series specifies not only protocols but the services to be provided to users. In this case the users are either terminal users who invoke electronic mail facilities, or application programs that exchange messages. The services are grouped into message transfer services and interpersonal messaging services.

For both sets of services, the services are divided into three categories: basic, essential optional, and additional optional. *Basic* services are inherent in the message handling system and must be implemented. The remaining services are known as optional user facilities which may be invoked at the option of the user, in some cases on a per-message basis and in others for an agreed contractual period. *Essential optional user facilities* must be offered by the service provider; that is, the provider must offer the option, but it is up to the user to select or not select the option. Finally, *additional optional user facilities* may or may not be offered by the provider.

Table 15.9 lists the services provided by the message transfer agent. The layer attempts to deliver messages to one or more intended recipients, and can be asked to notify the originator's UAE of the success or failure of each attempt. This layer may also invoke presentation-layer transformations on behalf of the user agent sublayer. The originator may request that delivery take place no earlier than a specified time. The recipient may request that a message be temporarily held in the system prior to delivery. In addition, the originator may designate a message as urgent.

Interpersonal messaging services are provided by the user agent, and are listed in Table 15.10. In this case optional services receive two designations, one for origination and one for reception. Note that many of the services that are additional (need not be offered) for origination are essential for reception. For example, UAs are not required to allow a user to mark a message as pri-

TABLE 15.9   Message Transfer Layer Services (X.401)

Basic Services

Access management	Enables UA to submit and have messages delivered to it
Content type indication	Specified by originating UA
Converted indication	Specifies any conversions performed on message being delivered
Submission/delivery time stamp	Submission and delivery time are supplied with each message
Message identification	Unique identifier for each message
Nondelivery notification	Message cannot be delivered
Registered encoded information types	Allows UA to specify types that can be delivered to it
Original encoded information types	Specified by submitting UA and supplied to receiving UA

Essential Optional Services

Alternate recipient allowed	Deliver to alternate if designated recipient cannot be found
Deferred delivery	Deliver no sooner than specified date and time
Deferred delivery cancellation	Abort delivery of deferred message
Delivery notification	Notify originator of successful delivery
Disclosure of other recipients	Disclose list of recipients to recipient
Grade of delivery selection	Request urgent, normal, or nonurgent
Multi-destination delivery	Specify more than one recipient
Conversion prohibition	Prevents MTS from conversion
Probe	Determines if a message could be deliverable

Additional Optional Services

Prevention of non-delivery notification	Suppress potential nondelivery notice
Return of contents	Return message contents if nondelivery
Explicit conversion	Specifies particular conversion
Implicit conversion	Perform necessary conversion on all messages without explicit instruction
Alternate recipient assignment	Requests designation of requesting UA as alternate recipient
Hold for delivery	Requests that messages intended for this UA be held in MTS until later time

vate, but must be able to appropriately handle a received message marked private. There are many services at this sublayer. Among the most fundamental are specification of primary and secondary recipients and the subject of the message. Other services have to do with how to handle the message and instructions for notification.

TABLE 15.10   Interpersonal Messaging Services (X.401)

Basic Services

IP-message identification	Assign reference identifier to each message content sent or received
Typed body	Allows nature and attributes of message body to be conveyed along with body.

Essential Optional Services
(for both origination and reception)

Originator indication	Identifies the user that sent message
Primary and copy recipients indication	Allows UA to specify primary and secondary recipients
Replying IP-message indication	Specifies an earlier message to which this is a reply
Subject indication	Description of message

Additional (for origination) and Essential
(for reception) Optional Services

Blind copy recipient indication	List of recipients whose identities are not to be disclosed to primary or copy recipients
Auto-forwarded indication	Marks a message as containing an automatically-forwarded message
Authorizing users indication	Indicates one or more persons who authorized the message
Expiry date indication	Conveys a date and time after which the originator considers the message invalid
Cross-referencing indication	Specifies one or more other messages related to this one
Importance indication	Specifies low, normal, or high
Obsoleting indication	Specifies previous messages that are obsolete and superseded by this one
Sensitivity indication	Specifies personal, private, or company-confidential
Reply request indication	Asks for response; may also specify date and time and other recipients
Forwarded IP-message indication	Marks a message as containing a forwarded message
Body part encryption indication	Body part of message is encrypted
Multi-part body	Enables sending message with multiple parts, each with its own attributes

Additional Optional Services
(for both origination and reception)

Nonreceipt notification	Requests that originator be informed if message is not received by its intended recipient
Receipt notification	Requests that originator be notified of receipt of message by intended recipient

15.4

RECOMMENDED READING

[STAL93d] provides a comprehensive and detailed examination of network management protocol standards, including SNMP, SNMPv2, and the OSI standards; the book also provides an overview of network management technology. [STAL93f] contains reprints of key recent papers on network management technology and standards. One of the few textbooks on the subject of network management is [TERP91]. [BALL92] provides a relatively nontechnical treatment of the issues confronting the network user and/or system manager who must deal with the specific problems of managing and using networks. [KUAF92] is a discussion of network management oriented toward products rather than basic principles and standards. [LEIN93] is a practical discussion of the key functional areas of network management, plus an overview of the major standards.

For an analysis of issues relating to file transfer protocols, see [DAY81]. A discussion of the ISO FTAM standard can be found in [LINI89]; it is also well treated in [KNOW87], [HENS90], and [VALE92].

A quite thorough presentation of X.400 is contained in [PLAT91]. [HENS90] also provides a good discussion of the 1988 X.400 standards; a somewhat briefer presentation is in [CHIL90]. [MANR89] explains the rather substantial differences between the 1984 and 1988 versions of X.400.

15.5

PROBLEMS

15.1 The formats for SNMPv2 PDUs depicted in Figure 15.4 show that each PDU begins with a PDU type field. But this field is not shown in the ASN.1 definition depicted in Figure 14.4. Explain.

15.2 The original (version 1) specification of SNMP has the following definition of a new type:

Gauge ::= [APPLICATION 2] IMPLICIT INTEGER (0..4294967295)

The standard includes the following explanation of the semantics of this type:

> This application-wide type represents a non-negative integer, which may increase or decrease, but which latches at a maximum value. This standard specifies a maximum value of 2^{32-1} (4294967295 decimal) for gauges.

Unfortunately, the word *latch* is not defined, and has resulted in two different interpretations. The SNMPv2 standard cleared up the ambiguity with the following definition:

The value of a Gauge has its maximum value whenever the information being modeled is greater than or equal to that maximum value; if the information being modeled subsequently decreases below the maximum value, the Gauge also decreases.

    a. What is the alternative interpretation?

    b. Discuss the pros and cons of the two interpretations.

15.3 User A requests a third-party file transfer between B and C. What logical connections (e.g., A-B, B-C, C-A) are necessary for this transfer?

15.4 There are two file transfer protocols in use on ARPANET: the file transfer protocol (FTP) and the trivial file transfer protocol (TFTP). The former makes use of TELNET, which makes use of TCP. The latter simply makes use of the user datagram protocol (UDP). What features would you expect to be lacking in TFTP?

15.5 Draw a time sequence diagram of FTAM primitives showing the sequence of events in a successful file transfer.

15.6 Indicate how PDUs can be used to implement the FTAM service primitives.

15.7 There is not an end-to-end transport connection between the originator and recipient of a message. Why not?

15.8 Protocol P1 provides that a message envelope and its contents be transmitted from one MTAE to another. The standard specifies that the message envelope and the message content be transmitted as a single P1 PDU. Several other mechanisms are possible. The sending MTAE could transmit the message envelope first, wait for approval from the second MTAE, and then transmit the message content. A third method is to transmit the message envelope first, one parameter at a time, waiting for a positive acknowledgment after each parameter. For example, the recipient list might be transmitted first, then handling instructions, and so on. Discuss the relative advantages and disadvantages of each method.

15.9 Electronic mail systems differ in the manner in which multiple recipients are handled. In some systems, the originating UA or MTA makes all the necessary copies and these are sent out independently. An alternative approach is to determine the route for each destination first. Then a single message is sent out on a common portion of the route and copies are only made when the routes diverge; this process is referred to as mail-bagging. Discuss the relative advantages and disadvantages of the two methods.

PART IV

INTEGRATED SERVICES DIGITAL NETWORKS

Perhaps the most important development in the computer–communication industry over the next decade will be the evolution of the integrated services digital network (ISDN). The ISDN will have a dramatic effect on communications providers, component manufacturers, and both personal and business users. Although the technology of and standards for ISDN are still evolving, a clear picture of the architecture, design approaches, and services of the ISDN is emerging. A discussion of ISDN ties together many of the concepts used throughout the book and is an appropriate culmination to our study of data and computer communications.

Chapter 16 looks specifically at the architecture of ISDN and the higher-speed broadband ISDN. Chapter 17 looks at the two most important outgrowths of the ISDN effort: frame relay and cell relay.

CHAPTER 16

ISDN and Broadband ISDN

We have but one more topic to address in this book, and that topic represents in some sense a culmination of all the technologies and techniques that we have explored. The *integrated services digital network* (ISDN) is a projected worldwide public telecommunications network that will service a wide variety of user needs. The ISDN will be defined by the standardization of user interfaces, and will be implemented as a set of digital switches and paths supporting a broad range of traffic types and employing many of the concepts already discussed in this book. Actually, there will be multiple ISDNs, implemented within national boundaries, but from the user's point of view, there will be a single worldwide service.

A number of small-scale ISDN facilities have been developed, but the promised extension of ISDN to encompass worldwide public telecommunications is some years off. Meanwhile, the characteristics of ISDN are defined by an evolving set of standard (being developed on a truly massive scale, both in terms of content and participants. Thus, this chapter provides only a preview of the evolving ISDN.

The chapter begins by looking at a concept that serves as the foundation for ISDN: the integrated digital network (IDN). Next, we provide an overview of ISDN by viewing it from several perspectives. The next two sections concentrate on the two areas that have received the most attention, both technically and in terms of standards; these are the transmission structure and user access to ISDN. This is followed by a discussion of the protocols that have been defined to support user access.

Finally, the chapter looks at the next, fast approaching, generation of ISDN, known as broadband ISDN.

THE INTEGRATED DIGITAL NETWORK

Public telephone and telecommunications networks are rapidly evolving to the exclusive use of digital technology. The ways in which these networks employ digital technology are listed in Table 16.1. The movement toward digital technology has been "pushed" by the competitive desire to lower cost and improve quality of voice transmission and networking services. As the use of distributed processing and data communications has grown, this evolution of an all-digital network has been "pulled" by the need to provide a framework for ISDN.

The evolution of the existing telecommunications networks and specialized carrier facilities to integrated digital networks is based on two technological developments: digital switching and digital transmission. Both of these developments are, of course, well established. The first T-carrier system was introduced into commercial service by AT&T in 1962, and the first large-scale time-division digital switch, the Western Electric 4ESS, was introduced in 1976. More important than the benefits of either of these two technologies however, was the revolutionary idea that the functions of transmission and switching could be integrated to form an *integrated digital network* (IDN). The idea was proposed as early as 1959 [VAUG59] and is in the process of being implemented worldwide [DORR83, COOK84].

To understand the implications of an IDN, consider Figure 16.1. Traditionally, the transmission and switching systems of a telephone network have been

TABLE 16.1   Use of Digital Technology in Public
Telecommunications Networks

Switching
   The circuit-switching nodes of the network make use of digital time-division switching techniques rather than analog space-division switching techniques.

Trunk (Carrier) Transmission
   Digital transmission technology is used on the multiplexed trunks between switches, although either analog or digital signaling may be used. Each trunk carries multiple voice and/or data channels using synchronous time-division multiplexing.

Subscriber Loop
   Digital transmission technology may also be used between the subscriber and the switch to which the subscriber attaches over the "subscriber loop." This implies that digitized voice is employed and that full-duplex digital transmission over the subscriber loop is used.

Control Signaling
   Common channel signaling over a packet-switched network embedded into the public telecommunications network is used. Packets contain messages used for routing, monitoring, and control.

designed and administered by functionally separate organizations. The two systems are referred to by the operating telephone companies as outside plant and inside plant, respectively. In the analog network, incoming voice lines are modulated and multiplexed at the end office and sent out over an FDM line. As you know, the constituent signals may pass through one or more intermediate switching centers before reaching the destination end office (Figure 8-24). At each switching center, the incoming FDM carrier has to be demultiplexed and demodulated by an FDM channel bank before being switched by a space-division switch. After switching, the signals have to be multiplexed and modulated again to be transmitted. This repeated process results in an accumulation of noise, as well as cost.

When both the transmission and switching systems are digital, integration as in Figure 16.1b can be achieved. Incoming voice signals are digitized using PCM and multiplexed using TDM. Time-division digital switches along the way can switch the individual signals without decoding them. Furthermore, separate multiplex/demultiplex channel banks are not needed at the intermediate offices, since that function is incorporated into the switching system.

Figure 16.2 gives a simple example that suggests the architectures that are involved in the analog and digital switching approaches. Consider an intermediate switch in a circuit-switched network that has six voice channels (labeled A, B, C, D, E, F) of data coming in on one trunk (Figure 16.2a). Based on the calls that are currently established, three of the channels are to be switched out on one trunk (A, B, E) and three channels on another trunk

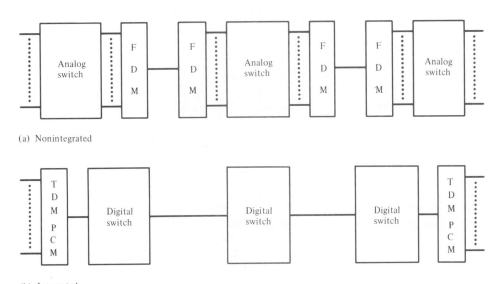

(a) Nonintegrated

(b) Integrated

FIGURE 16.1.   The integration of transmission and switching.

(a) General block diagram

(b) Digital time division switch

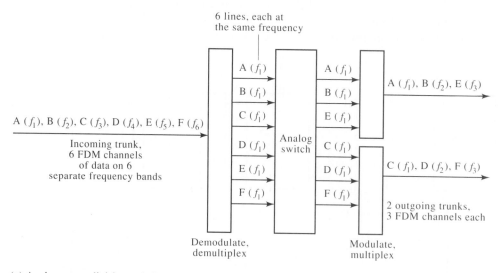

(c) Analog space-division switch

FIGURE 16.2.   Example of digital versus analog switching.

(C, D, F). All three trunks link to other switches, and all three trunks are multiplexed to carry multiple channels of data. In the case of a digital system (Figure 16.2b), the voice signals are digitized and transmitted as a stream of bits. On a multiplexed trunk, bits from various voice signals are interleaved using time-division multiplexing (TDM). Thus, the incoming trunk has bits from six different voice channels interleaved in time. Inside the digital switch, a technique such as TDM bus switching, discussed in Chapter 7, is employed to extract the slots of data from the incoming stream and route them to the appropriate outgoing stream.

The architecture for the equivalent analog system is considerably more complex (Figure 16.2c). Each voice signal occupies a frequency band of about 4 kHz. The incoming trunk requires a bandwidth of at least 24 kHz, and each voice signal occupies one channel centered on a unique frequency (f_1 for channel A, f_2 for channel B, etc.). These channels must be fed into a space-division analog switch. However, such a switch is only capable of switching signals from a collection of input lines to a collection of output lines. For general operation, any input line must be connectable to any output line; therefore, all inputs and outputs must be at the same frequency. Thus, the frequency-division multiplexed (FDM) input must be demultiplexed, and each signal must be returned to the base voice frequency (f_1) to provide input to the switch. The switch routes the incoming data to the appropriate output lines, with each output line dedicated to a particular output trunk. For each trunk, the associated lines must pass through a modulator/multiplexer to produce an FDM signal for transmission over the outgoing trunk.

The conversion of telecommunications networks to digital transmission and digital switching is well under way. Much less well developed is the extension of digital service to the end user. Telephones are still sending analog data to the end office where they must be digitized. Lower-speed (<56 kbps) end-user digital service is commonly available via leased lines at present, and higher speed leased services are being introduced [HOLM83]. The provision of switched digital service over the local loop [KELC83], [HARR86], [ERIK86] will eventually lead to an end-to-end switched digital telecommunications network.

This evolution has been driven by the need to provide economic voice communications. The resulting network, however, is also well suited to meet the growing variety of digital data service needs. Thus the IDN will combine the coverage of the geographically extensive telephone network with the data carrying capacity of digital data networks in a structure called the *integrated services digital network* (ISDN). In this latter context, the "integrated" of ISDN refers to the simultaneous carrying of digitized voice and a variety of data traffic on the same digital transmission links and by the same digital exchanges. The key to ISDN is the small marginal cost for offering data services on the digital telephone network, with no cost or performance penalty for voice services already carried on the IDN.

TABLE 16.2   CCITT Recommendation I.120 (1988)

1 Principles of ISDN

1.1   The main feature of the ISDN concept is the support of a wide range of voice and non-voice applications in the same network. A key element of service integration for an ISDN is the provision of a range of services (see Part II of the I-Series in this Fascicle) using a limited set of connection types and multipurpose user-network interface arrangements (see Parts III and IV of the I-Series in Fascicle III.8).

1.2   ISDNs support a variety of applications including both switched and non-switched connections. Switched connections in an ISDN include both circuit-switched and packet-switched connections and their concatenations.

1.3   As far as practicable, new services introduced into an ISDN should be arranged to be compatible with 64 kbit/s switched digital connections.

1.4   An ISDN will contain intelligence for the purpose of providing service features, maintenance and network management functions. This intelligence may not be sufficient for some new services and may have to be supplemented by either additional intelligence within the network, or possibly compatible intelligence in the user terminals.

1.5   A layered protocol structure should be used for the specification of the access to an ISDN. Access from a user to ISDN resources may vary depending upon the service required and upon the status of implementation of national ISDNs.

1.6   It is recognized that ISDNs may be implemented in a variety of configurations according to specific national situations.

2 Evolution of ISDNs

2.1   ISDNs will be based on the concepts for telephone IDNs and may evolve by progressively incorporating additional functions and network features including those of any other dedicated networks such as circuit-switching and packet-switching for data so as to provide for existing and new services.

2.2   The transition from an existing network to a comprehensive ISDN may require a period of time extending over one or more decades. During this period arrangements must be developed for the networking of services on ISDNs and services on other networks (see Part V).

2.3   In the evolution towards an ISDN, digital end-to-end connectivity will be obtained via plant and equipment used in existing networks, such as digital transmission; time-division multiplex switching and/or space-division multiplex switching. Existing relevant recommendations for these constituent elements of an ISDN are contained in the appropriate series of recommendations of CCITT and of CCIR.

2.4   In the early stages of the evolution of ISDNs, some interim user-network arrangements may need to be adopted in certain countries to facilitate early penetration of digital service capabilities. Arrangements corresponding to national variants may comply partly or wholly with I-Series Recommendations. However, the intention is that they not be specifically included in the I-Series.

2.5   An evolving ISDN may also include at later stages switched connections at bit rates higher and lower than 64 kbit/s.

16.2

OVERVIEW OF ISDN

ISDN Concept

The concept of ISDN is best introduced by considering it from several different viewpoints:

- Principles of ISDN.
- Evolution of ISDN.
- The user interface.
- Objectives.
- Benefits.
- Services.

Principles of ISDN

Standards for ISDN are being defined by CCITT, a topic that we explore later in this section. Table 16.2, which is the complete text one of the ISDN-related standards, states the principles of ISDN from the point of view of CCITT. Let us look at each of these points in turn.

1. *Support of voice and nonvoice applications using a limited set of standardized facilities.* This principle defines both the purpose of ISDN and the means of achieving it. The ISDN will support a variety of services related to voice communications (telephone calls) and nonvoice communications (digital data exchange). These services are to be provided in conformance with standards (CCITT recommendations) that specify a small number of interfaces and data transmission facilities.
2. *Support for switched and nonswitched applications.* ISDN will support both circuit switching and packet switching. In addition, ISDN will support nonswitched services in the form of dedicated lines.
3. *Reliance on 64-kbps connections.* ISDN is intended to provide circuit-switched and packet-switched connections at 64 kbps. This is the fundamental building block of ISDN. This rate was chosen because, at the time, it was the standard rate for digitized voice, and hence was being introduced into the evolving IDNs. Although this data rate is useful, it is unfortunately restrictive to rely solely on it. Future developments in ISDN will permit greater flexibility.
4. *Intelligence in the network.* An ISDN is expected to be able to provide sophisticated services beyond the simple setup of a circuit-switched call.
5. *Layered protocol architecture.* The protocols being developed for user access to ISDN exhibit a layered architecture and can be mapped into the OSI model. This has a number of advantages:

- Standards already developed for OSI-related applications may be used on ISDN. An example is X.25 level 3 for access to packet-switching services in ISDN.
- New ISDN-related standards can be based on existing standards, reducing the cost of new implementations. An example is LAP-D, which is based on LAP-B.
- Standards can be developed and implemented independently for various layers and for various functions within a layer. This allows for the gradual implementation of ISDN services at a pace appropriate for a given provider or a given customer base.

6. *Variety of configurations.* More than one physical configuration is possible for implementing ISDN. This allows for differences in national policy (single-source versus competition), in the state of technology, and in the needs and existing equipment of the customer base.

Evolution of ISDN

As we discussed earlier, ISDN evolves from and with the integrated digital network (IDN). The evolution of the IDN has been driven by the need to provide economic voice communications. The resulting network, however, is also well suited to meet the growing variety of digital data service needs. Whereas the "I" in IDN refers to the integration of digital transmission and switching facilities, the "I" in ISDN refers to the integration of a variety of voice and data transmission services.

Table 16.2 gives the CCITT view of the way in which ISDN will evolve. Let us look at each of these points in turn.

1. *Evolution from telephone IDNs.* The intent is that the ISDN evolve from the existing telephone networks. Two conclusions can be drawn from this point. First, the IDN technology developed for and evolving within existing telephone networks forms the foundation for the services to be provided by ISDN. Second, although other facilities, such as third-party (not the telephone provider) packet-switched networks and satellite links, will play a role in ISDN, the telephone networks will have the dominant role. Although packet switching and satellite providers may be less than happy with this interpretation, the overwhelming prevalence of telephone networks dictates that these networks form the basis of ISDN.
2. *Transition of one or more decades.* The evolution to ISDN will be a slow process. This is true of any migration of a complex application or set of applications from one technical base to a newer one. The introduction of ISDN services will be done in the context of existing digital facilities and existing services. There will be a period of coexistence in which connections and perhaps protocol conversion will be needed between alternative facilities and/or services.

3. *Use of existing networks.* This point is simply an elaboration of point 2. For example, ISDN will provide a packet-switched service. For the time being, the interface to that service will be X.25. With the introduction of fast packet switching (see discussion of broadband ISDN later in this chapter) and more sophisticated virtual call control, there may need to be a new interface in the future.

4. *Interim user-network arrangements.* Primarily, the concern here is that the lack of digital subscriber loops might delay introduction of digital services, particularly in developing countries. With the use of modems and other equipment, existing analog facilities can support at least some ISDN services.

5. *Connections at other than 64 kbps.* The 64-kbps data rate was chosen as the basic channel for circuit switching. With improvements in voice digitizing technology, this rate is unnecessarily high. On the other hand, this rate is too low for many digital data applications. Thus, other data rates will be needed.

The details of the evolution of ISDN facilities and services will vary from one nation to another, and indeed from one provider to another in the same country. These points simply provide a general description, from CCITT's point of view, of the process.

The User Interface

Figure 16.3 is a conceptual view of the ISDN from a user or customer point of view. The user has access to the ISDN by means of a local interface to a "digital

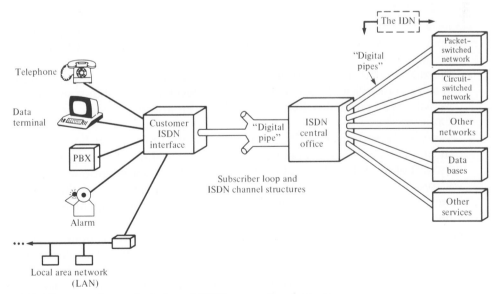

FIGURE 16.3. Conceptual view of ISDN connection features.

pipe" of a certain bit rate. Pipes of various sizes will be available to satisfy differing needs. For example, a residential customer may require only sufficient capacity to handle a telephone and a videotex terminal. An office will undoubtedly wish to connect to the ISDN via an on-premise digital PBX, and will require a much higher capacity pipe.

At any given point in time, the pipe to the user's premises has a fixed capacity, but the traffic on the pipe may be a variable mix up to the capacity limit. Thus a user may access circuit-switched and packet-switched services, as well as other services, in a dynamic mix of signal types and bit rates. To provide these services, the ISDN will require rather complex control signals to instruct it how to sort out the time-multiplexed data and provide the required services. These control signals will also be multiplexed onto the same digital pipe.

An important aspect of the interface is that the user may, at any time, employ less than the maximum capacity of the pipe, and will be charged according to the capacity used rather than "connect time." This characteristic significantly diminishes the value of current user design efforts that are geared to optimize circuit utilization by use of concentrators, multiplexers, packet switches, and other line sharing arrangements.

Objectives

Activities currently under way are leading to the development of a worldwide ISDN. This effort involves national governments, data processing and communications companies, standards organizations, and others. Certain common objectives are, by and large, shared by this disparate group. We list here the key objectives:

- *Standardization:* It is essential that a single set of ISDN standards be provided to permit universal access and to permit the development of cost-effective equipment.
- *Transparency:* The most important service to be provided is a transparent transmission service. This permits users to develop applications and protocols with the confidence that they will not be affected by the underlying ISDN.
- *Separation of competitive functions:* It must be possible to separate out functions that could be provided competitively as opposed to those that are fundamentally part of the ISDN. In most countries, a single, government-owned entity will provide all services. Some countries desire (in the case of the United States, require) that certain enhanced services be offered competitively (e.g., videotex, electronic mail).
- *Leased and switched services:* The ISDN should provide dedicated point-to-point services as well as switched services. This will allow the user to optimize his or her implementation of switching and routing techniques.
- *Cost-related tariffs:* The price for ISDN service should be related to cost, and independent of the type of data being carried. One type of service should not be in the position of subsidizing others.

- *Smooth migration:* The conversion to ISDN will be gradual, and the evolving network must coexist with existing equipment and services. Thus ISDN interfaces should evolve from current interfaces, and provide a migration path for users.
- *Multiplexed support:* In addition to providing low-capacity support to individual users, multiplexed support must be provided to accommodate user-owned PBX and local network equipment.

There are, of course, other objectives that could be named. Those listed above are certainly among the most important and widely accepted, and help to define the character of the ISDN.

Benefits

The principal benefits to the user can be expressed in terms of cost savings and flexibility. The integration of voice and a variety of data on a single transport system means that the user does not have to buy multiple services to meet multiple needs. The efficiencies and economies of scale of an integrated network allows these services to be offered at lower cost than if they were provided separately. Further, the user needs to bear the expense of just a single access line to these multiple services.

The requirements of various users can differ greatly in a number of ways: for example, information volume, traffic pattern, response time, and interface types. The ISDN will allow the user to tailor the service purchased to actual needs to a degree not possible at present.

Services

The ISDN will provide a variety of services, supporting existing voice and data applications as well as providing for applications now being developed. The most important in the latter category are

- *Facsimile:* service for the transmission and reproduction of graphics, handwritten, and printed material. This type of service has been available for many years, but has suffered from a lack of standardization and the limitations of the analog telephone network. Digital facsimile standards (CCITT Group 3) are now available and can be used to transmit a page of data at 64 kbps in 5 s.
- *Teletex:* service that enables subscriber terminals to exchange correspondence. Communicating terminals are used to prepare, edit, transmit, and print messages. Transmission is at a rate of one page in 2 s at 9.6 kbps.
- *Videotex:* An interactive information retrieval service. A page of data can be transmitted in one second at 9.6 kbps.

Table 16.3 shows the type of services that could be supported by ISDN. These services fall into the broad categories of voice, digital data, text, and image. Most of these services can be provided with a transmission capacity of 64 kbps or less. This rate, as we shall see, will be the standard ISDN rate

TABLE 16.3 Candidate Services for Integration

Bandwidth	Service			
	Telephony	Data	Text	Image
Digital voice (64 kbps)	Telephone Leased circuits Information retrieval (by voice analysis and synthesis)	Packet-switched data Circuit-switched data Leased circuits Telemetry Funds transfer Information retrieval Mailbox Electronic mail Alarms	Telex Teletex Leased circuits Videotex Information retrieval Mailbox Electronic mail	 Facsimile Information retrieval Surveillance
Wide band (>64 kbps)	Music	High-speed computer communication		TV conferencing Teletext Videophone Cable TV distribution

offered to the user. Some services require considerably higher data rates and may be provided by high speed facilities outside the ISDN (e.g., cable TV distribution plants). However, these higher-speed services may intersect with the ISDN and make use of high-capacity ISDN links for part of a transmission path.

One of the key aspects of the ISDN will be that it is an "intelligent network." By use of a flexible signaling protocol, the ISDN will provide a variety of network facilities for each service. Table 16.4 gives some examples of planned facilities.

Architecture

Figure 16.4 is a block diagram of the ISDN. ISDN supports a completely new physical connecter for users, a digital subscriber loop (link from end user to central or end office), and modifications to all central office equipment.

The area to which most attention has been paid by standards organizations is that of user access. A *common physical interface* will be defined to provide, in essence, a DTE-DCE connection. The same interface should be usable for telephone, computer terminal, and videotex terminal. Protocols are needed for the exchange of control information between user device and the network. Provision must be made for high-speed interfaces to, for example, a digital PBX or a LAN.

The subscriber loop portion of today's telephone network consists of twisted pair links between the subscriber and the central office, carrying 4-kHz analog signals. Under the ISDN, one or two twisted pairs will be used to provide a basic full-duplex digital communications link.

The digital central office will connect the numerous ISDN subscriber loop signals to the IDN. In addition to providing access to the circuit-switched network, the central office will provide subscriber access to dedicated lines, packet-switched networks, and time-shared transaction-oriented computer services. Multiplexed access via digital PBX and LAN must also be accommodated.

Standards

Although a number of standards organizations are involved in various aspects of ISDN, the controlling body is the International Telegraph and Telephone Consultative Committee (CCITT). The development of ISDN is governed by a set of recommendations issued by CCITT, called the I-series of recommendations. These recommendations, or standards, were first issued in 1984. A more complete set was issued in 1988.

It is enlightening to look at the history of CCITT's interest in ISDN. In 1968, CCITT established Special Study Group D (forerunner of today's Study Group XVIII, which has ISDN responsibility within CCITT) to look at a variety of issues related to the use of digital technology in the telephone network. At

TABLE 16.4 Basic and Additional Facilities for ISDN Services

Telephony	Data	Teletex	Videotex	Facsimile
		Basic		
National toll access	Automatic dialed call	Incoming call not disturbing local mode	Information retrieval by dialogue with a database	Automatic dialed call
International toll access	Manual dialed call	Message printed on operator demand		Manual dialed call
Malicious call blocking	Automatic answer	Message presentation as in the original		Automatic answer
		Day and hour automatic indication		
		Additional		
Transfer call	Direct call	Delayed messages	Transactions (e.g. reservation, shopping)	Delayed delivery
Abbreviated dialing	Closed user group	Abbreviated address		Multiple destination
Rerouting to verbal announcements	Closed user group with outgoing access	Multiple address		
Intermediate call	Calling line identification	Charging indication	Message box service between users	Code, speed, and format conversion for different terminals
Conference call	Called line identification	Telex access	Loading of software from a data base to a terminal	
Camp-on busy	Abbreviated address calling	Graphic mode		
Barring outgoing toll traffic	Barred incoming call		Loading of special character set	
	Multiaddress calling			
Hot line	Detailed billing			
Detailed billing	Transfer call			
Automatic wake-up	Call charging indication			

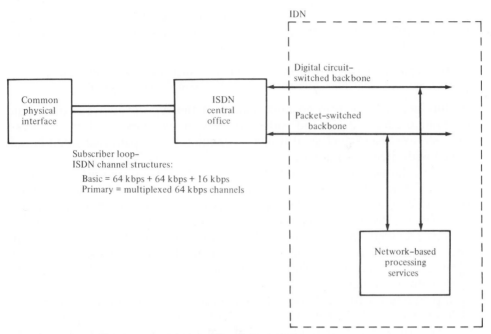

FIGURE 16.4.   Block diagram of ISDN functions.

each Plenary Assembly, the study group was given assignments for the next four-year study period. The first and principal question assigned over this period is shown in Table 16.5. The titles of the first question reflect the evolution of CCITT interest. The focus shifts from digital technology to integrated digital networks (IDN) to ISDN.

In 1968, Study Group D was set up to study all questions related to the standardization of transmission of pulse-code-modulated (PCM) voice and to coordinate work going on in other groups relating to digital networking. Even

TABLE 16.5   Question 1 as Assigned to Special Study Group D (1969–1976) and to Study Group XVIII (1977–1992)

Study Period	Title of Question 1
1969–1972	Planning of digital systems
1973–1976	Planning of digital systems and integration of services
1977–1980	Overall aspects of integrated digital network and integration of services
1981–1984	General network aspects of an integrated services digital network (ISDN)
1985–1988	General question on ISDN
1989–1992	General aspects of ISDN

at this early stage, there was a vision of an ISDN. Recommendation G.702, issued in 1972, contained the following definition of an integrated services digital network:

> An integrated digital network in which the same digital switches and digital paths are used to establish for different services, for example, telephony, data.

At this point, there was no information on the type of network that could integrate digital switches and paths, nor how the network could integrate various services. Nevertheless, it was a recognition of the path that could be followed with digital technology.

During the next study period (1973–1976), there were continuing advances in digital transmission technology. In addition, digital switching equipment began to emerge from the laboratory. Thus the construction of integrated digital networks became a real possibility. Accordingly, the 1976 set of recommendations included specifications dealing with digital switching as well as the specification of a new control signaling scheme designed for use in the forthcoming digital networks. The first question for this period also specifically deals with the integration of services.

In planning for the 1977–1980 study period, CCITT recognized that the evolution toward a digital network was under way and was more important than the standardization of individual digital systems and equipment. Thus the focus was on the integration aspects of the digital network and on the integration of services on an IDN. Two key developments that emerged during this study period were

- The integration of services is based on providing a standardized user-network interface that allows the user to request various services through a uniform set of protocols.
- ISDN will evolve from the digital telephone network.

At the end of this period, the first ISDN standard emerged, entitled Integrated Services Digital Network (ISDN), which was just a general statement of principles and objectives. No other standards on ISDN were issued in 1980; at this point, only the general concept of an ISDN had been developed.

As the next period began (1981–1984), ISDN was declared the major concern of CCITT for the upcoming study period. A set of recommendations was published in 1984. This initial set of specifications was incomplete and, in some cases, internally inconsistent. Nevertheless, the specification of ISDN by 1984 was sufficient for manufacturers and service providers to begin to develop ISDN-related equipment and to demonstrate ISDN-related services and networking configurations. The 1984 series included this definition of ISDN, retained in the 1988 documents:

> An ISDN is a network, in general evolving from a telephony IDN, that provides end-to-end digital connectivity to support a wide range of services, including voice and non-voice services, to which users have access by a limited set of standard multi-purpose user-network interfaces.

Work on the I-series and related recommendations continued in the 1985–1988 period. At the beginning of this period, CCITT was significantly restructured to give a number of its study groups a part of future ISDN work. The dominant function of CCITT became the study of ISDN matters. The 1988 version of the I-series recommendations were sufficiently detailed to make preliminary ISDN implementations possible in the late 1980s.

The 1984 standards contained recommendations in series I.100 through I.400. Some updates and expansions occurred in this series in the 1984-1988 period. The I.500 and I.600 series were left for further study in 1984, and some preliminary work was ready for 1988. Revised standards in all these areas were issued in 1992.

16.3

TRANSMISSION STRUCTURE

ISDN Channels

The digital pipe between the central office and the ISDN user will be used to carry a number of communication channels. The capacity of the pipe, and therefore the number of channels carried may vary from user to user. The transmission structure of any access link will be constructed from the following types of channels:

- *B channel:* 64 kbps.
- *D channel:* 16 or 64 kbps.
- *H channel:* 384, 1536, and 1920 kbps.

The B channel is the basic user channel. It can be used to carry digital data, PCM-encoded digital voice, or a mixture of lower-rate traffic, including digital data and digitized voice encoded at a fraction of 64 kbps. In the case of mixed traffic, all traffic must be destined for the same endpoint. Three kinds of connections can be set up over a B channel:

- *Circuit-switched:* this is equivalent to switched digital service available today. The user places a call and a circuit-switched connection is established with another network user. An interesting feature is that, unlike X.21, the call establishment dialogue does not take place over the B channel, but is done over the D, as explained below.
- *Packet-switched:* the user is connected to a packet-switching node, and data is exchanged with other users via X.25.
- *Semipermanent:* this is a connection to another user set up by prior arrangement, and not requiring a call establishment protocol. This is equivalent to a leased line.

The designation of 64 kbps as the standard user channel rate highlights the fundamental contradiction in standards activities. This rate was chosen as the most effective for digitized voice, yet the technology has progressed to the point at which 32 kbps or even less will produce equally satisfactory voice reproduction. To be effective, a standard must freeze the technology at some defined point. Yet by the time the standard is approved, it may already be obsolete.

The D channel serves two purposes. First, it carries signalling information to control circuit-switched calls on associated B channels at the user interface. In addition, the D channel may be used for packet-switching or low-speed (e.g., 100 bps) telemetry at times when no signalling information is waiting. Table 16.6 summarizes the types of data traffic to be supported on B and D channels.

H channels are provided for user information at higher bit rates. The user may use such a channel as a high-speed trunk or subdivide the channel according to the user's own TDM scheme. Examples of applications include fast facsimile, video, high-speed data, high-quality audio, and multiple information streams at lower data rates.

These channel types are grouped into transmission structures that are offered as a package to the user. The best-defined structures at this time are the basic channel structure (basic access) and the primary channel structure (primary access), which are depicted in Figure 16.5.

The basic channel structure consists of two full-duplex 64 kbps B channels and a full-duplex 16-kbps D channel. The total bit rate, by simple arithmetic, is 144 kbps. However, framing, synchronization, and other overhead bits bring the total bit rate on a basic access link to 192 kbps. Figure 16.6 shows the frame structure for basic access. Each frame of 48 bits includes 16 bits from each of the B channels and 4 bits from the D channel. The functions of the remaining bits are explained in Section 16.5.

The basic service is intended to meet the needs of most individual users, including residential and very small offices. It allows the simultaneous use of voice and several data applications, such as packet-switched access, a link to a

TABLE 16.6   ISDN Channel Functions

B Channel (64 kbps)	D Channel (16 kbps)
Digital voice	Signaling
64 kbps PCM	Basic
Low bit rate (32 kbps)	Enhanced
High-speed data	Low-speed data
Circuit-switched	Videotex
Packet-switched	Teletex
Other	Terminal
Facsimile	Telemetry
Slow-scan video	Emergency services
	Energy management

FIGURE 16.5.   ISDN channel structures.

central alarm service, facsimile, videotex, and so on. These services could be accessed through a single multifunction terminal or several separate terminals. In either case, a single physical interface is provided. Most existing two-wire local loops can support this interface [GIFF86].

In some cases one or both of the B channels remain unused. This results in a $B + D$ or D interface, rather than the $2B + D$ interface. However, to simplify the network implementation, the data rate at the interface remains at 192 kbps. Nevertheless, for those subscribers with more modest transmission requirements, there may be a cost savings in using a reduced basic interface.

The primary service is intended for users with greater capacity requirements, such as offices with a digital PBX or a local network. Because of differences in the digital transmission hierarchies used in different countries, it was not possible to get agreement on a single data rate. The United States, Canada, and Japan make use of a transmission structure based on 1.544 Mbps; this corresponds to the T1 transmission facility using the DS-1 transmission format. In Europe, 2.048 Mbps is the standard rate. Both of these data rates are provided

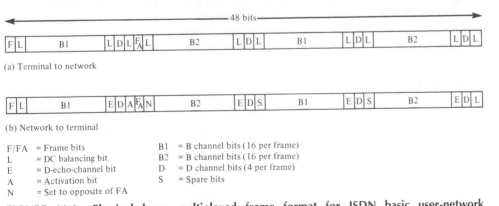

FIGURE 16.6.   Physical layer multiplexed frame format for ISDN basic user-network interface.

as a primary interface service. Typically, the channel structure for the 1.544-Mbps rate will be 23 B channels plus one 64-kbps D channel and, for the 2.048-Mbps rate, 30 B channels plus one 64-kbps D channel. Again, it is possible for a customer with lower requirements to employ fewer B channels, in which case the channel structure is $nB + D$, where n ranges from 1 to 23 or 1 to 30 for the two primary services. Also, a customer with high data rate demands may be provided with more than one primary physical interface. In this case, a single D channel on one of the interfaces may suffice for all signalling needs, and the other interfaces may consist solely of B channels ($24B$ or $31B$).

The primary interface may also be used to support H channels. Some of these structures include a 64-kbps D channel for control signaling. When no D channel is present, it is assumed that a D channel on another primary interface at the same subscriber location will provide any required signaling. The following structures are recognized:

- *Primary rate interface H0 channel structures:* This interface supports multiple 384-kbps H0 channels. The structures are $3H0 + D$ and $4H0$ for the 1.544-Mbps interface and $5H0 + D$ for the 2.048-Mbps interface.
- *Primary rate interface H1 channel structures:* The H11 channel structure consists of one 1536-kbps H11 channel. The H12 channel structure consists of one 1920-kbps H12 channel and one D channel.
- *Primary rate interface structures for mixtures of B and H0 channels:* Consists of zero or one D channels plus any possible combination of B and H0 channels up to the capacity of the physical interface (e.g., $3H0 + 5B + D$ and $3H0 + 6B$).

The user interface consists of some number of B channels and one D channel. The B channel can be used to support a circuit to another end user or some value-added service provided by a third party (e.g., a data base system). The B channel can also provide a link to a packet-switching network node. In this figure, the packet-switching network is provided by the ISDN provider; it is also possible to set up a circuit across ISDN to a third-party packet-switching network. In all of these cases, the D channel is used to exchange control messages between the user and the ISDN local exchange. These messages set up, maintain, and terminate B-channel connections.

Subscriber Loop Technology

The extension of digital links to the end users is an essential part of ISDN evolution: The subscriber loop must support the channel structure being developed.

One intermediate technique for providing access is *data over voice*. On an analog link, voice occupies the frequency spectrum below 4 kHz. A data rate of 8 to 16 kbps can be supported by appropriate modulation of the digital signal onto a carrier at a band above 4 kHz.

To provide true full-duplex digital service, three approaches are possible. The first makes use of two twisted pairs (four-wire) per subscriber. Each

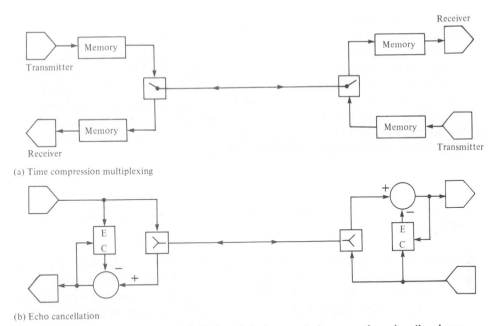

(a) Time compression multiplexing

(b) Echo cancellation

FIGURE 16.7. Techniques for full-duplex digital transmission over the subscriber loop.

twisted pair is operated in simplex fashion. This technique is technically simple, but doubles the amount of cable needed to serve hundreds of millions of residential subscribers.

What is really desired is a means of transmitting full-duplex digital data over a single twisted pair. This would allow the introduction of ISDN services making use of the large installed base of twisted-pair local loop. Two approaches to achieving this are illustrated in Figure 16.7 [KADE81]. The first method, known as time compression multiplexing [BOSI82], or the ping-pong protocol, was described in Chapter 7. In this technique, data are transmitted in one direction at a time, with transmission alternating between the two directions. To achieve the desired subscriber data rate, the subscriber's bit stream is divided into equal segments, compressed in time to a higher transmission rate, and transmitted in bursts which are expanded at the other end to the original rate. A short quiescent period is used between bursts going in opposite directions to allow the line to settle down; this results in a data rate requirement of 2.25 times the data rate as seen by the subscribers.

The alternative method is known as echo cancellation. In this technique, digital transmission is allowed to proceed in both directions within the same bandwidth simultaneously. This procedure introduces a technical difficulty known as echo. Echo is the feedback of the transmitted signal to the receiver. This echo primarily occurs from the local attachment of the transmitter-receiver to the two-wire local loop. The technique used to overcome this problem is echo cancellation [LIN90], [MURA90], [MESS84], [MESS86]. A replica of the echo signal is generated at the transmitting end and is subtracted from the incoming signal. This effectively cancels the echo. This technique has the disadvantage of requiring complex digital signal processing circuitry, but avoids the need to transmit at a signalling rate more than double the subscriber rate. With the continued advances in VLSI circuitry, the cost of echo cancellation is dropping, and has become the preferred technique [GERW84], [LECH86].

The above comments apply to twisted-pair connections. Ultimately, optical fiber connections will be used [FINN89b]. For these, FDM or time-compression multiplexing are the most attractive options.

16.4

USER ACCESS

To define the requirements for ISDN user access, an understanding of the anticipated configuration of user premises equipment and of the necessary standard interfaces is critical. The first step is to group functions that may exist on the user's premises. Figure 16.8 shows the CCITT approach to this task, using:

* *Functional groupings:* certain finite arrangements of physical equipment or combinations of equipment.
* *Reference points:* conceptual points used to separate groups of functions.

The architecture on the subscriber's premises is broken up functionally into groupings separated by reference points. This permits interface standards to be developed at each reference point. This effectively organizes the standards work and provides guidance to the equipment providers. Once stable interface standards exist, technical improvements on either side of an interface can be made without impact on adjacent functional groupings. Finally, with stable interfaces, the subscriber is free to procure equipment from different suppliers for the various functional groupings, so long as the equipment conforms to the relevant interface standards.

Network termination 1 (NT1) includes functions associated with the physical and electrical termination of the ISDN on the user's premises; these correspond to OSI layer 1. The NT1 may be controlled by the ISDN provider and forms a boundary to the network. This boundary isolates the user from the transmission technology of the subscriber loop and presents a physical connector interface for user device attachment. In addition, the NT1 performs line maintenance functions such as loopback testing and performance monitoring. The NT1 supports multiple channels (e.g., 2B + D); at the physical level, the bit streams of these channels are multiplexed together, using synchronous time-division multiplexing. Finally, the NT1 interface might support multiple devices in a multidrop arrangement. For example, a residential interface might include a telephone, personal computer, and alarm system, all attached to a single NT1 interface via a multidrop line.

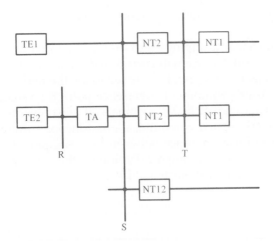

R,S,T – Reference interface points
TE1 – Subscriber terminel type 1
TE2 – Subscriber terminal type 2
TA – Terminal adapter
NT1 – Network termination 1
NT2 – Network termination 2
Nt12 – Combined network termination 1 and 2

**FIGURE 16.8.   ISDN   reference   points   and
functional groupings.**

Network termination 2 (NT2) is an intelligent device that can perform
switching and concentration functions; it may include functionality up through
layer 3 of the OSI model. Examples of NT2 are a digital PBX, a terminal controller, and a LAN. An example of a switching function is the construction of
a private network using semipermanent circuits among a number of sites. Each
site could include a PBX that acts as a circuit switch or a host computer that
acts as a packet switch. The concentration function simply means that multiple
devices, attached to a digital PBX, LAN, or terminal controller, may transmit
data across ISDN.

Network termination 1, 2 (NT12) is a single piece of equipment that contains
the combined functions of NT1 and NT2. This points out one of the regulatory
issues associated with ISDN interface development. In many countries, the
ISDN provider will own the NT12 and provide full service to the user. In the
United States, there is a need for a network termination with a limited number
of functions to permit competitive provision of user premises equipment.
Hence the user premises network functions are split into NT1 and NT2.

Terminal equipment refers to subscriber equipment that makes use of ISDN.
Two types are defined. **Terminal equipment type 1** (TE1) refers to devices that
support the standard ISDN interface. Examples are digital telephones, integrated voice/data terminals, and digital facsimile equipment. **Terminal equipment type 2** (TE2) encompasses existing non-ISDN equipment. Examples are
terminals with a physical interface such as EIA-232-D and host computers with

an X.25 interface. Such equipment requires a **terminal adaptor** (TA) to plug into an ISDN interface.

The definitions of the functional groupings also define, by implication, the reference points. **Reference point T** (terminal) corresponds to a minimal ISDN network termination at the customer's premises. It separates the network provider's equipment from the user's equipment. **Reference point S** (system) corresponds to the interface of individual ISDN terminals. It separates user terminal equipment from network-related communications functions. **Reference point R** (rate) provides a non-ISDN interface between user equipment that is not ISDN-compatible and adaptor equipment. Typically, this interface will comply with an older interface standard, such as EIA-232-D.

16.5

ISDN PROTOCOLS

ISDN Protocol Architecture

The development of standards for ISDN includes, of course, the development of protocols for interaction between ISDN users and the network and for interaction between one ISDN user and another. It would be desirable to fit these new ISDN protocols into the OSI framework, and to a great extent this has been done. However, there are certain requirements for ISDN that are not met within the current structure of OSI [DUC85]. Examples of these are

- *Multiple related protocols:* The primary example of this is the use of a protocol on the D channel to set up, maintain, and terminate a connection on a B channel.
- *Multi-media calls:* ISDN will allow a call to be set up that allows information flow consisting of multiple types, such as voice, data, facsimile, and control signals.
- *Multipoint connections:* ISDN will allow conference calls.

These and other functions are not directly addressed in the current OSI specification. However, the basic 7-layer framework appears valid even in the ISDN context and the issue is more one of specific functionality at the various layers. The issue of the exact relationship between ISDN and OSI remains one for further study.

Figure 16.9 suggests the relationship between OSI and ISDN. As a network, ISDN is essentially unconcerned with user layers 4-7. These are end-to-end layers employed by the user for the exchange of information. Network access is concerned only with layers 1–3. Layer 1, defined in I.430 and I.431, specifies the physical interface for both basic and primary access. Since B and D channels are multiplexed over the same physical interface, these standards apply to both types of channels. Above this layer, the protocol structure differs for the two channels.

Application	End-to-end user signaling						
Presentation							
Session							
Transport							
Network	Call control I.451/Q.931	X.25 packet level	(Further study)				X.25 packet level
Data Link	LAPD(I.441/Q.921)				Frame Relay		LAPB
Physical	I.430 basic interface + I.431 primary interface						
	Signal	Packet	Telemetry	Circuit switched	Semipermanent	Packet switched	
	D channel			B channel			

FIGURE 16.9. ISDN protocol architecture at the user–network interface.

For the D channel, a new data link layer standard, LAPD (Link Access Protocol, D Channel) has been defined. This standard is based on HDLC, modified to meet ISDN requirements. All transmission on the D channel is in the form of LAPD frames that are exchanged between the subscriber equipment and an ISDN switching element. Three applications are supported: control signaling, packet-switching, and telemetry. For **control signaling,** a call control protocol has been defined (I.451/Q.931). This protocol is used to establish, maintain, and terminate connections on B channels. Thus it is a protocol between the user and the network. Above layer 3, there is the possibility for higher-layer functions associated with user-to-user control signaling. These are a subject for further study. The D channel can also be used to provide **packet switching** services to the subscriber. In this case, the X.25 level 3 protocol is used, and X.25 packets are transmitted in LAPD frames. The X.25 level 3 protocol is used to establish virtual circuits on the D channel to other users and to exchange packetized data. The final application area, **telemetry,** is a subject for further study.

The B channel can be used for circuit switching, semipermanent circuits, and packet-switching. For **circuit switching,** a circuit is set up on a B channel on demand. The D-channel call control protocol is used for this purpose. Once the circuit is set up, it may be used for data transfer between the users. A **semipermanent circuit** is a B-channel circuit that is set up by prior agreement between the connected users and the network. As with a circuit-switched connection, it provides a transparent data path between end systems.

With either a circuit-switched connection or a semipermanent circuit, it appears to the connected stations that they have a direct full-duplex link with each other. They are free to use their own formats, protocols, and frame synchronization. Hence, from the point of view of ISDN, layers 2 through 7 are not visible or specified.

In the case of **packet-switching,** a circuit-switched connection is set up on a B channel between the user and a packet-switched node using the D-channel control protocol. Once the circuit is set up on the B channel, the user may employ X.25 layers 2 and 3 (see Chapter 8) to establish a virtual circuit to another user over that channel and to exchange packetized data. As an alternative, the recently defined frame relay service may be used. Frame relay can also be used over H channels.

Some of the protocols shown in Figure 16.9 are summarized in the remainder of this section. First, we look at the way in which packet-switched and circuit-switched connections are set up. Next, we examine the control signaling protocol and then LAPD. Finally, the physical layer specifications are reviewed. Because of its importance, frame relay is discussed in depth in Chapter 17.

ISDN Connections

ISDN provides four types of service for end-to-end communication:

- Circuit-switched cells over a B channel.
- Semipermanent connections over a B channel.
- Packet-switched calls over a B channel.
- Packet-switched calls over the D channel.

Circuit-Switched Calls

The network configuration and protocols for circuit switching involve both the B and D channels. The B channel is used for the transparent exchange of user data. The communicating users may use any protocols they wish for end-to-end communication. The D channel is used to exchange control information between the user and the network for call establishment and termination, and access to network facilities.

The B channel is serviced by an NT1 or NT2 using only layer 1 functions. On the D channel, a three-layer network access protocol is used and is explained below. Finally, the process of establishing a circuit through ISDN involves the cooperation of switches internal to ISDN to set up the connection. These switches interact using Signaling System Number 7, which is examined later in this chapter.

Semipermanent Connections

A semipermanent connection between agreed points may be provided for an indefinite period of time after subscription, for a fixed period, or for agreed periods during a day, week, or other interval. As with circuit-switched connections, only Layer 1 functionality is provided by the network interface. The call control protocol is not needed since the connection already exists.

Packet-Switched Calls Over a B Channel

The ISDN must also permit user access to packet-switched services for data traffic (e.g., interactive) that is best serviced by packet switching. There are two possibilities for implementing this service: Either the packet-switching capability is furnished by a separate network, referred to as a packet-switched public data network (PSPDN), or the packet-switching capability is integrated into ISDN. In the former case, the service is provided over a B channel. In the latter case, the service may be provided over a B or D channel. We first examine the use of a B channel for packet-switching.

When the packet-switching service is provided by a separate PSPDN, the access to that service is via a B channel. Both the user and the PSPDN must therefore be connected as subscribers to the ISDN. In the case of the PSPDN, one or more of the packet-switching network nodes, referred to as packet handlers, are connected to ISDN. We can think of each such node as a traditional X.25 DCE supplemented by the logic needed to access ISDN. That is, the ISDN subscriber assumes the role of an X.25 DTE, the node in the PSPDN to which it is connected functions as an X.25 DCE, and the ISDN simply provides the connection from DTE to DCE. Any ISDN subscriber can then communicate, via X.25, with any user connected to the PSPDN, including

- Users with a direct, permanent connection to the PSPDN.
- Users of the ISDN that currently enjoy a connection, through the ISDN, to the PSPDN.

The connection between the user (via a B channel) and the packet handler with which it communicates may be either semipermanent or circuit-switched. In the former case, the connection is always there and the user may freely invoke X.25 to set up a virtual circuit to another user. In the latter case, the D channel is involved, and the following sequence of steps occur (Figure 16.10);

- The user requests, via the D-channel call control protocol (I.451/Q.931), a circuit-switched connection on a B channel to a packet handler.
- The connection is set up by ISDN and the user is notified via the D channel call control protocol.
- The user sets up a virtual circuit to another user via the X.25 call establishment procedure on the B channel (described in Section 3.2). This requires that first a data link connection, using LAPB, must be set up between the user and the packet handler.
- The user terminates the virtual circuit using X.25 on the B channel.
- After one or more virtual calls on the B channel, the user is done and signals via the D channel to terminate the circuit-switched connection to the packet switching node.
- The connection is terminated by ISDN.

Figure 16.11 shows the configuration involved in providing this service. In the figure, the user is shown to employ a DTE device that expects an interface to an X.25 DCE. Hence, a terminal adapter is required. Alternatively, the X.25

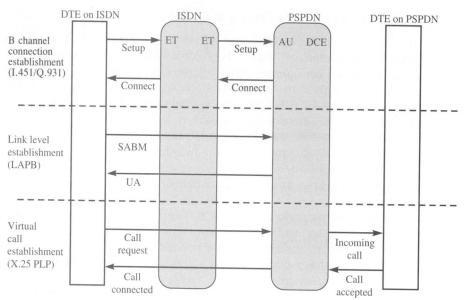

FIGURE 16.10.   Virtual call setup.

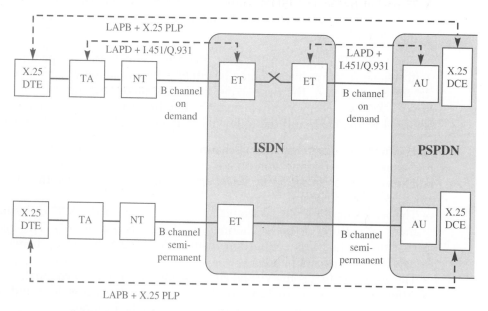

AU	ISDN access unit
TA	Terminal adapter
NT	Network termination 2 and/or 1
ET	Exchange termination
PLP	Packet-level procedure
PSPDN	Packet-switched public data network

FIGURE 16.11.   Access to PSPDN for packet-mode service.

capability can be an integrated function of an ISDN TE1 device, dispensing with the need for a separate TA.

When the packet-switching service is provided by ISDN, the packet-handling function is provided within the ISDN, either by separate equipment or as part of the exchange equipment. The user may connect to a packet handler either by a B channel or the D channel. On a B channel, the connection to the packet handler may be either switched or semipermanent, and the same procedures described above apply for switched connections. In this case, rather than establish a B-channel connection to another ISDN subscriber that is a PSPDN packet handler, the connection is to an internal element of ISDN that is a packet handler.

Packet-Switched Calls Over a D Channel

When the packet-switching service is provided internal to the ISDN, it can also be accessed on the **D channel.** For D-channel access, ISDN provides a semipermanent connection to a packet-switching node within the ISDN. The user employs the X.25 level 3 protocol as is done in the case of a B-channel virtual call. Here, the level 3 protocol is carried by LAPD frames. Since the D channel is also used for contol signaling, some means is needed to distinguish between X.25 packet traffic and ISDN control traffic. This is accomplished by means of the link layer addressing scheme, as explained below.

Figure 16.12 shows the configuration for providing packet-switching within ISDN. The packet-switching service provided internal to the ISDN over the B and D channels is logically provided by a single packet-switching network. Thus virtual calls can be set up between two D-channel users, two B-channel users, and between a B and D channel user. In addition, it will be typical to also provide access to X.25 users on other ISDNs and PSPDNs by appropriate interworking procedures. One common approach is the use of X.75, which specifies an interworking scheme between two public X.25 networks.

A Standard for Common Channel Signaling: I.451

CCITT has developed a standard, I.451, for common channel signaling. The primary application of this standard is for the Integrated Services Digital Network.

In OSI terms, I.451 is a layer 3, or network layer, protocol. As Figure 16.13 indicates, I.451 relies on a link layer protocol to transmit messages over the D channel.

Messages

I.451 specifies procedures for establishing connections on the B channels that share the same physical interface to ISDN as the D channel. It also provides user-to-user control signaling over the D channel.

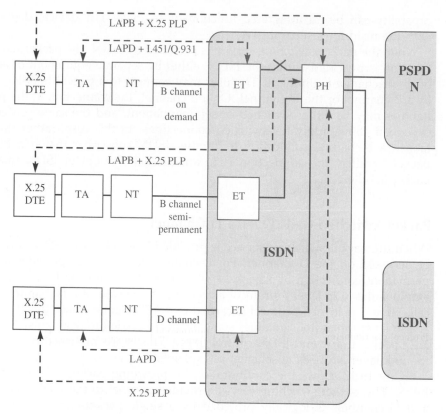

TA   Terminal adapter
NT   Network termination 2 and/or 1
ET   Exchange termination
PLP   Packet-level procedure
PSPDN   Packet-switched public data network
PH   Packet handling function

FIGURE 16.12.   **Access to ISDN for packet-mode service.**

FIGURE 16.13.   **Call control communications architecture.**

The process of establishing, controlling, and terminating a call occurs as a result of control signaling messages exchanged between the user and the network over a D channel. A common format is used for all messages defined in I.451, illustrated in Figure 16.14a. Three fields are common to all messages:

- *Protocol discriminator:* used to distinguish messages for user-network control from other message types. Other sorts of protocols may share the common signaling channel.
- *Call reference:* identifies the user-channel call to which this message refers. As with X.25 virtual circuit numbers, it has only local significance. The call reference field comprises 3 subfields. The length subfield specifies the length of the remainder of the field in octets. This length is one octet for a basic rate interface, and two octets for a primary rate interface. The flag indicates which end of the LAP-D logical connection initiated the call.
- *Message type:* identifies which I.451 message is being sent. The contents of the remainder of the message depend on the message type.

(a) General message format

(b) Single-octet information element format (type 1)

(c) Single-octet information element format (type 2)

(d) Variable-length information element format

FIGURE 16.14. I.451 formats.

Following these three common fields, the remainder of the message consists of a sequence of zero or more information elements, or parameters. These contain additional information to be conveyed with the message. Thus, the message type specifies a command or response, and the details are provided by the information elements. Some information elements must always be included

TABLE 16.7   I.451 Messages

Message	Application	Function
Call/Access-Connection Establishment Messages		
ALERTing	C, P, U	Sent by called user and by network to calling user to indicate that called user alerting has been initiated.
CALL PROCeeding	C, P, U	Sent by called user and by network to calling user to indicate that requested establishment has been initiated.
CONNect	C, P, U	Sent by called user and by network to calling user to indicate call/access-connection acceptance by the called user.
CONNect ACKnowledge	C, P, U	Sent by network to called user to indicate the user has been awarded the call/access connection
PROGRESS	C, P	Sent by user or network to indicate progress of a call/access connection in the event of interworking.
SETUP	C, P, U	Sent by calling user and by network to called user to request call/access-connection establishment.
SETUP ACKnowledge	C, U	Sent by network to calling user and called user to network to indicate that call establishment has been initiated but additional information may be required.
Call Information Phase Messages		
RESume	C	Sent by user to request resumption of previously suspended call.
RESume ACKnowledge	C	Sent by network to indicate that requested call has been reestablished.
RESume REJect	C	Sent by network to indicate failure to resume suspended call.
SUSPend	C	Sent by user to request suspension of a call.
SUSPend ACKnowledge	C	Sent by network to indicate that call has been suspended.
SUSPend REJect	C	Sent by network to indicate failure of requested call suspension.
USER INFOrmation	C, U	Sent by user to network and then by network to another user to transfer information between the two users.

TABLE 16.7   continued

Message	Application	Function
Call/Access-Connection Clearing Messages		
DISConnect	C, P	Sent by user or network to indicate call/access connection is completed and the receiver is invited to release the channel and call/access connection reference.
RELease	C, P, U	Sent by either user or network to indicate that the channel and call reference are to be released.
RELease COMplete	C, P, U	Sent by either user or network to indicate acceptance of RELease message and that the channel and call reference are released.
Miscellaneous Messages		
CONgestion CONtrol	C, U	Sent by network or user to set or release flow control on USER INFORMATION messages.
FACility	C	Sent by user to request a network facility and by network when activation of a facility requires user agreement.
INFOrmation	C, U	Sent by network or user to provide additional information.
NOTIFY	C	Sent by user or network to indicate information pertaining to a call.
RESTART	G	Sent by user or network to request the recipient to restart (i.e., return to idle condition) the indicated channel or interface.
RESTART ACKNOWLEDGE	G	Sent by user or network to indicate that the requested restart is complete.
STATUS	C, P, U, G	Sent by user or network in response to a STATUS ENQUIRY or at any time to report an error condition.
STATUS ENQUIRY	C, P, U	Sent by user or network to solicit STATUS message from peer entity.

C = Messages for circuit-mode connection control
P = Messages for packet-mode access connection control
U = Messages for user-to-user signaling not associated with circuit-switched calls
G = Messages used with the global call reference

with a given message (mandatory), and others are optional (additional). Three formats for information elements are used, as indicated in Figure 16.14b through d.

Table 16.7 lists all of the I.451 messages. The messages can be grouped along two dimensions. Messages apply to one of four applications: circuit-mode control, packet-mode access connection control, user-to-user signaling not associated with circuit-switched calls, and messages used with the global call reference. In addition messages perform functions in one of four categories: call establishment, call information, call clearing, and miscellaneous.

Circuit-mode control refers to the functions needed to set up, maintain, and clear a circuit-switched connection on a user channel. This function corresponds to call control in existing circuit-switching telecommunications networks. **Packet-mode access connection control** refers to the functions needed to set up a circuit-switched connection (called an access connection in this context) to an ISDN packet-switching node; this connects the user to the packet-switching network provided by the ISDN provider. **User-to-user signaling messages** allow two users to communicate without setting up a circuit-switched connection. A temporary signaling connection is established and cleared in a manner similar to the control of a circuit-switched connection. Signaling takes place over the signaling channel and thus does not consume user-channel resources. Finally, **global call reference** refers to the functions that enable user or network to return one or more channels to an idle condition.

Call establishment messages are used to initially set up a call. This group includes messages between the calling terminal and the network (SETUP, SETUP ACK, CALL PROC, CONN, PROGRESS) and between the network and the called terminal (SETUP, ALERT, CONN, CONN ACK, PROGRESS). These messages support the following services:

- Set up a user-channel call in response to user request.
- Provide particular network facilities for this call.
- Inform calling user of the progress of the call establishment process.

Once a call has been set up, but prior to the disestablishment (termination) phase, **call information** phase messages are sent between user and network. One of the messages in this group allows the network to relay, without modification, information between the two users of the call. The nature of this information is beyond the scope of the standard, but it is assumed that it is control signaling information that can't or should not be sent directly over the user-channel circuit. The remainder of the messages allow users to request the suspension and later resumption of a call. When a call is suspended, the network remembers the identity of the called parties and the network facilities supporting the call, but deactivates the call so that no additional charges are incurred and so that the corresponding user channel is freed up. Presumably, the resumption of a call is quicker and cheaper than the origination of a new call.

Call clearing messages are sent between user and network in order to terminate a call. Finally, there are some **miscellaneous** messages that may be sent between user and network at various stages of the call. Some may be sent during call setup; others may be sent even though no calls exist. The primary function of these messages is to negotiate network features (supplementary services).

Circuit-Switched Call Example

Figure 16.15, taken from I.451, is an example of the use of the protocol to set up a user-channel circuit-switched telephone call. We will follow this example through to give the reader an idea of the use of the I.451 protocol. The example is for the placement of a telephone call, but the sequence would be similar for a computer-to-computer or terminal-to-computer data call.

The process begins when a calling subscriber lifts the handset. The ISDN-compatible telephone insures that the signaling channel is active before itself generating a dial tone (not shown). When the subscriber keys in the called number (not shown), the telephone set accumulates the digits, and when all are keyed in, sends a SETUP message over the signaling channel to the exchange. The SETUP message includes the destination number, a channel identification which specifies which user channel is to be used, and any requested network services or facilities (e.g., reverse charging).

The SETUP message triggers two activities at the local exchange. First, using internal control signaling, the local exchange sends a message through the network that results in designating a route for the requested call and allocating resources for that call. Second, the exchange sends back a CALL PROC message indicating that call setup is underway. The exchange may also request more information from the caller (via SETUP ACK and INFO). When the internal control message reaches the remote exchange, it sends a SETUP message to the called telephone. The called telephone accepts the call by sending an ALERT message to the network and generating a ringing tone. The ALERT message is transmitted all the way back to the calling telephone set. When the called party lifts the handset, the telephone sends a CONN message to the network. The local exchange sends a CONN ACK message to its subscriber and forwards the CONN message to the calling exchange, and it in turn forwards it to the calling telephone. The circuit is now available for the called and calling telephone.

Because the call setup process makes use of common channel signaling, other channels are undisturbed, and the fact that all of the user channels are engaged does not prevent the signaling channel dialogue. For example, even if all of a user's channels are assigned to circuits, an incoming call request will be presented to the user via the signaling channel; the user can, if desired, put a call in progress on hold in order to use the corresponding user channel for the new call.

Once the circuit is set up, full duplex 64-kbps data streams are exchanged via the user channel between the two end users. Additional signaling messages, such as call information phase messages, may be transmitted during this period.

Call termination begins when one of the telephone users hangs up. This causes a DISC message to be sent from the telephone to the exchange. The exchange responds with a REL message and when the telephone sends REL

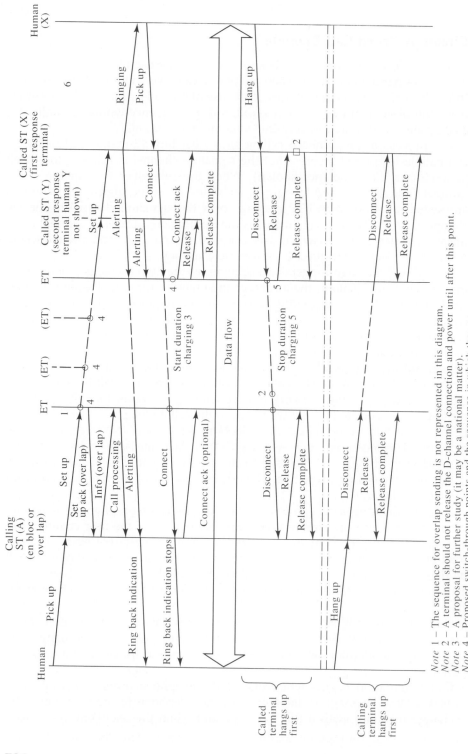

Note 1 – The sequence for overlap sending is not represented in this diagram.
Note 2 – A terminal should not release the D-channel connection and power until after this point.
Note 3 – A proposal for further study (it may be a national matter).
Note 4 – Proposed switch-through points and the sequence in which they ocurr.
Note 5 – Proposed network release points and the sequence.
Note 6 – The interactions between the human and the terminals are shown for illustration only.

FIGURE 16.15. Procedure for an I.451 call.

COM the user channel is released. The complementary action takes place at the other telephone-network interface.

LAP-D

All traffic over the D channel employs a link-layer protocol known as LAP-D (Link Access Protocol–D Channel).

LAP-D Services

The LAP-D standard provides two forms of service to LAP-D users: the unacknowledged information transfer service and the acknowledged information transfer service. The **unacknowledged information transfer service** simply provides for the transfer of frames containing user data with no acknowledgement. The service does not guarantee that data presented by one user will be delivered to another user, nor does it inform the sender if the delivery attempt fails. The service does not provide any flow control or error control mechanism. This service supports both point-to-point (deliver to one user) or broadcast (deliver to a number of users). This service allows for fast data transfer and is useful for management procedures such as alarm messages and messages that need to be broadcast to multiple users.

The **acknowledged information transfer service** is the more common one, and is similar to the service offered by LAP-B and HDLC. With this service, a logical connection is established between two LAP-D users prior to the exchange of data.

LAP-D Protocol

The LAP-D protocol is based on HDLC. Both user information and protocol control information and parameters are transmitted in frames. Corresponding to the two types of service offered by LAP-D, there are two types of operation:

- *Unacknowledged operation:* Layer 3 information is transferred in unnumbered frames. Error detection is used to discard damaged frames, but there is no error control or flow control.
- *Acknowledged operation:* Layer 3 information is transferred in frames that include sequence numbers that are acknowledged. Error control and flow control procedures are included in the protocol. This type is also referred to in the standard as multiple-frame operation.

These two types of operation may coexist on a single D channel.

Both types of operation make use of the frame format illustrated in Figure 16.16. This format is identical to that of HDLC (Figure 5.13) with the exception of the address field.

To explain the address field, we need to consider that LAP-D has to deal with two levels of multiplexing. First, at the subscriber site, there may be mul-

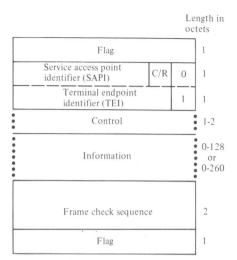

FIGURE 16.16.   LAP-D format.

tiple user devices sharing the same physical interface. Second, within each user device, there may be multiple types of traffic: specifically, packet-switched data and control signaling. To accommodate these levels of multiplexing, LAP-D employs a two-part address, consisting of a terminal endpoint identifier (TEI) and a service access point identifier (SAPI).

Typically, each user device is given a unique **terminal endpoint identifier (TEI).** It is also possible for a single device to be assigned more than one TEI. This might be the case for a terminal concentrator. TEI assignment occurs either automatically when the equipment first connects to the interface, or manually by the user. In the latter case, care must be taken that multiple equipment attached to the same interface do not have the same TEI. The advantage of the automatic procedure is that it allows the user to change, add, or delete equipment at will without prior notification to the network administration. Without this feature, the network would be obliged to manage a data base for each subscriber that would need to be updated manually. Table 16.8a shows the assignment of TEI numbers.

The **service access point identifier (SAPI)** identifies a layer 3 user of LAP-D, and thus corresponds to a layer 3 protocol entity within a user device. Four specific values have been assigned, as shown in Table 16.8b. A SAPI of 0 is used for call control procedures for managing B channel circuits; the value 16 is reserved for packet-mode communication on the D channel using X.25 level 3; and a value of 63 is used for the exchange of layer 2 management information. The most recent assignment, made in 1988 is the value of 1 for packet-mode communication using I.451: this could be used for user-user signaling. Finally, values in the range 32 to 62 have tentatively been reserved to support frame-relay connections, as described in Chapter 17.

TABLE 16.8   SAPI and TEI Assignments

(a) TEI Assignments

TEI Value	User Type
0 – 63	Nonautomatic TEI assignment user equipment
64 –126	Automatic TEI assignment user equipment
127	Used during automatic TEI assignment

(b) SAPI Assignments

SAPI Value	Related Layer 3 or Management Entity
0	Call control procedures
1	Reserved for packet mode communication using I.451 call control procedures
16	Packet communication conforming to X.25 level 3
32 – 62	Frame-relay connection
63	Layer 2 management procedures
All others	Reserved for future standardization

For acknowledged operation, LAP-D follows essentially the same procedures described for HDLC in Chapter 5. For unacknowledged operation, the user information (UI) frame is used to transmit user data. When a LAP-D user wishes to send data, it passes the data to its LAP-D entity, which passes the data in the information field of a UI frame. When this frame is received, the information field is passed up to the destination user. There is no acknowledgment returned to the other side. However, error detection is performed and frames in error are discarded.

Physical Layer

The ISDN physical layer is presented to the user at either reference point S or T (Figure 16.8). The mechanical interface was described in Chapter 4.

The electrical specification depends on the specific interface. For the basic access interface, pseudoternary coding is used (Figure 3.2). Recall that with pseudoternary, the line signal may take one of three levels. This is not as efficient as a two-level code, but it is reasonably simple and inexpensive. At the relatively modest data rate of the basic access interface, this is a suitable code.

For the higher-speed primary access interface, a more efficient coding scheme is needed. For the 1.544-Mbps data rate, the B8ZS code is used, while for the 2.048-Mbps data rate, the HDB3 code is used (Figure 3.5). There is no particular advantage of one over the other; the specification reflects historical usage.

The functional specification for the physical layer includes the following functions:

- Full-duplex transmission of B-channel data.
- Full-duplex transmission of D-channel data.
- Full-duplex transmission of timing signals.
- Activation and deactivation of physical circuit.
- Power feeding from the network termination to the terminal.
- Terminal identification.
- Faulty terminal isolation.
- D-channel contention access.

The final function is required when multiple TE1 terminals share a single physical interface (i.e., a multipoint line). In that case, no additional functionality is needed to control access in the B channels, since each channel is dedicated to a particular circuit at any given time. However, the D channel is available for use by all the devices for both control signalling and for packet transmission. For incoming data, the LAP-D addressing scheme is sufficient to sort out the proper destination for each data unit. For outgoing data, some sort of contention resolution protocol is needed to assure that only one device at a time attempts to transmit.

The D-channel contention-resolution algorithm has the following elements:

1. When a subscriber device has no LAP-D frames to transmit, it transmits a series of binary ones on the D channel. According to the signal encoding scheme that is used, this corresponds to the absence of line signal.
2. The network, on receipt of a D-channel bit, reflects back the binary value as a *D-echo bit* (see Figure 16.6).
3. When a terminal is ready to transmit an LAP-D frame, it listens to the stream of incoming D-echo bits. If it detects a string of 1-bits of length equal to a threshold value X_i, then it may transmit. Otherwise, the terminal must assume that some other terminal is transmitting and wait.
4. It may happen that several terminals are monitoring the D-echo stream and begin to transmit at the same time, causing a collision. To overcome this condition, a transmitting station monitors the D-echo bits and compares them to its transmitted bits. If a discrepancy is detected, the terminal ceases to transmit and returns to a listen state.

The electrical characteristics of the interface (i.e.,1-bit = absence of signal) are such that any user equipment transmitting a 0-bit will override user equipment transmitting a 1-bit at the same instant. This arrangement ensures that one device will be guaranteed successful completion of its transmission.

The algorithm also includes a primitive priority mechanism based on the threshold value X_i. Signalling information is given priority over packet information. Within each of these two priority classes, a station begins at normal priority and then is reduced to lower priority after a transmission. It remains at the lower priority until all other terminals have had an opportunity to transmit. The values of X_i are 11 and 10 for signal information and 9 and 8 for packet information.

With the above background, we can return to Figure 16.6 and describe the overhead bits in the D channel frame. Recall that pseudoternary coding is used. Each frame begins with a framing bit that is always transmitted as a positive pulse. This is followed by a DC-balancing bit that is set as a negative pulse to balance the voltage. These bits provide a means of synchronizing the frame. The remaining balance bits in the frame follow the rule: The balance bit is set to binary zero if the number of binary zeros following the previous balance bit is odd; otherwise it is set to one. The remaining bits in the frame format are easily explained. The activation bit is used to activate user equipment. The echo bit reflects the most recently transmitted D bit from the terminal.

16.6

BROADBAND ISDN

In 1988, as part of its I-series of recommendations on ISDN, CCITT issued the first two recommendations relating to broadband (B-ISDN):I.113, *Vocabulary of Terms for Broadband Aspects of ISDN,* and I.121, *Broadband Aspects of ISDN.* These documents represent the level of consensus reached among the participants concerning the nature of the future B-ISDN, as of late 1988. They provide a preliminary description and a basis for future standardization and development work. Some of the important notions developed in these documents are presented in Table 16.9.

CCITT modestly defines B-ISDN as "a service requiring transmission channels capable of supporting rates greater than the primary rate." Behind this innocuous statement lie plans for a network and set of services that will have far more impact on business and residential customers than ISDN. With B-

TABLE 16.9   Noteworthy Statements in I.113 and I.121

Broadband: A service or system requiring transmission channels capable of supporting rates greater than the primary rate.

The term B-ISDN is used for convenience in order to refer to and emphasize the broadband aspects of ISDN. The intent, however, is that there be one comprehensive notion of an ISDN which provides broadband and other ISDN services.

Asynchronous transfer mode (ATM) is the target transfer mode solution for implementing a B-ISDN. It will influence the standardization of digital hierarchies and multiplexing structures, switching and interfaces for broadband signals.

B-ISDN will be based on the concepts developed for ISDN and may evolve by progressively incorporating additional functions and services (e.g., high quality video applications).

The reference configuration defined in I.411 is considered sufficiently general to be applicable not only for a basic access and a primary rate access but also to a broadband access. Both reference points S and T are valid for broadband accesses.

ISDN, services, especially video services, requiring data rates orders of magnitude beyond those that can be delivered by ISDN will become available. To contrast this new network and these new services to the original concept of ISDN, that original concept is now being referred to as **narrowband ISDN.**

With both demand (user interest) and supply (the technology for high-speed networking) evolving rapidly, the usual four-year cycle would be fatal to hopes of developing a standardized high-speed network utility. To head off the possibility of a fragmentation of effort and a proliferation of non-standard products and services, CCITT issued an interim set of 1990 draft Recommendations on B-ISDN. The set of thirteen documents provides, for the first time, a detailed and specific master plan for the broadband revolution.

Broadband ISDN Architecture

B-ISDN differs from a narrowband ISDN in a number of ways. To meet the requirement for high-resolution video, an upper channel rate of on the order of 150 Mbps is needed. To simultaneously support one or more interactive services and distributive services, a total subscriber line rate of about 600 Mbps is needed. In terms of today's installed telephone plant, this is a stupendous data rate to sustain. The only appropriate technology for widespread support of such data rates is optical fiber. Hence, the introduction of B-ISDN depends on the pace of introduction of fiber subscriber loops.

Internal to the network, there is the issue of the switching technique to be used. The switching facility has to be capable of handling a wide range of different bit rates and traffic parameters (e.g., burstiness). Despite the increasing power of digital circuit-switching hardware and the increasing use of optical fiber trunking, it is difficult to handle the large and diverse requirements of B-ISDN with circuit-switching technology. For this reason, there is increasing interest in some type of fast packet-switching as the basic switching technique for B-ISDN. This form of switching readily supports a new user–network interface protocol known as asynchronous transfer mode (ATM), which is examined in Chapter 17.

Functional Architecture

Figure 16.17 depicts the functional architecture of B-ISDN. As with narrowband ISDN, control of B-ISDN is based on common-channel signaling. Within the network, an SS7, enhanced to support the expanded capabilities of a higher-speed network, will be used. Similarly, the user-network control signaling protocol will be an enhanced version of I.451/Q.931.

B-ISDN must of course support all of the 64-kbps transmission services, both circuit-switching and packet-switching, that are supported by narrowband ISDN. This protects the user's investment and facilitates migration from narrowband to broadband ISDN. In addition, broadband capabilities are provided for higher data rate transmission services. At the user–network interface, these

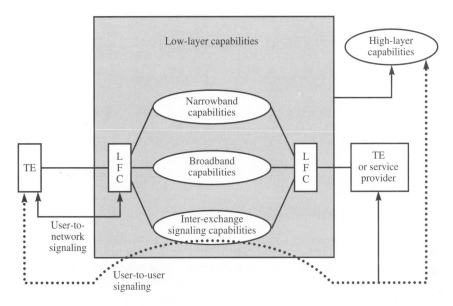

LFC - Local function capabilities
TE - Terminal equipment

FIGURE 16.17. B ISDN architecture.

capabilities will be provided with the connection-oriented asynchronous transfer mode (ATM) facility.

User–Network Interface

The reference configuration defined in I.411 is considered general enough to be used for B-ISDN. Figure 16.18, which is almost identical to Figure 16.8, shows the reference configuration for B-ISDN. In order to clearly illustrate the broadband aspects, the notations for reference points and functional groupings are appended with the letter B (e.g., B-NT1, T_B). The broadband functional groups are equivalent to the functional groups defined in I.411 and are discussed below. Interfaces at the R reference point may or may not have broadband capabilities.

Transmission Structure

In terms of data rates available to B-ISDN subscribers, three new transmission services are defined. The first of these consists of a full-duplex 155.52-Mbps service. The second service defined is asymmetrical, providing transmission from the subscriber to the network at 155.52 Mbps and in the other direction at 622.08 Mbps. And the highest-capacity service yet defined is a full-duplex 622.08-Mbps service.

A data rate of 155.52 Mbps can certainly support all of the narrowband ISDN services. That is, it readily supports one or more basic or primary rate inter-

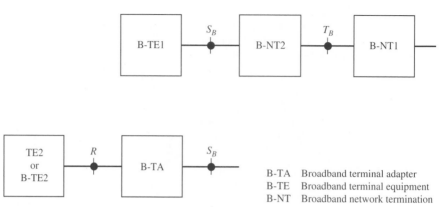

FIGURE 16.18.   B ISDN reference configurations.

faces. In addition, it can support most of the B-ISDN services. At that rate, one or several video channels can be supported, depending on the video resolution and the coding technique used. Thus, the full-duplex 155.52-Mbps service will probably be the most common B-ISDN service.

The higher data rate of 622.08 Mbps is needed to handle multiple video distribution, such as might be required when a business conducts multiple simultaneous videoconferences. This data rate makes sense in the network-to-subscriber direction. The typical subscriber will not initiate distribution services and thus would still be able to use the lower, 155.52-Mbps service. The full-duplex 622.08-Mbps service would be appropriate for a video distribution provider.

The 1988 document (I.121) discussed the need for a 150-Mbps and 600-Mbps data rate service. The specific rates chosen for the 1990 documents were designed to be compatible with defined digital transmission services.

The 1988 document also included a list of specific channel data rates to be supported within these services. The 1990 documents drop all reference to channel rates. This allows the user and the network to negotiate any channel capacity that can fit in the available capacity provided by the network. Thus, B-ISDN becomes considerably more flexible and can be tailored precisely to a wide variety of applications.

Broadband ISDN Protocols

The protocol architecture for B-ISDN introduces some new elements not found in the ISDN architecture, as depicted in Figure 16.19. For B-ISDN, it is assumed that the transfer of information across the user–network interface will use what is referred to as asynchronous transfer mode (ATM). ATM is, in essence, a form of packet transmission across the user–network interface in the same way that X.25 is a form of packet transmission across the user–network interface. One difference between X.25 and ATM is that X.25 includes control signaling on the same channel as data transfer, whereas ATM makes use of com-

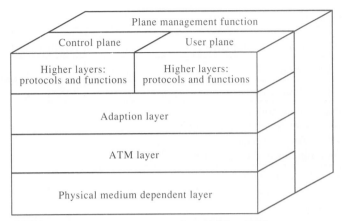

FIGURE 16.19.   B-ISDN protocol model for ATM.

mon-channel signaling. Another difference is that X.25 packets may be of varying length, whereas ATM packets are of fixed size, referred to as cells.

The decision to use ATM for B-ISDN is a remarkable one. This implies that B-ISDN will be a packet-based network, certainly at the interface and almost certainly in terms of its internal switching. Although the recommendation also states that B-ISDN will support circuit-mode applications, this will be done over a packet-based transport mechanism. Thus, ISDN, which began as an evolution from the circuit-switching telephone network, will transform itself into a packet-switching network as it takes on broadband services.

Two layers of the B-ISDN protocol architecture relate to ATM functions. There is an ATM layer common to all services that provides packet transfer capabilities and an ATM adaptation layer (AAL) that is service dependent. The AAL maps higher-layer information into ATM cells to be transported over B-ISDN, then collects information from ATM cells for delivery to higher layers. The use of ATM creates the need for an adaptation layer to support information transfer protocols not based on ATM. Two examples listed in I.121 are PCM voice and LAP-D. PCM voice is an application that produces a stream of bits. To employ this application over ATM, it is necessary to assemble PCM bits into packets (called cells in the recommendation) for transmission and to read them out on reception in such a way as to produce a smooth, constant flow of bits to the receiver. For LAP-D, it is necessary to map LAP-D frames into ATM packets; this will probably mean segmenting one LAP-D frame into a number of packets on transmission and reassembling the frame from packets on reception. By allowing the use of LAP-D over ATM, all of the existing ISDN applications and control signaling protocols can be used on B-ISDN.

The protocol reference model makes reference to three separate planes:

User Plane: Provides for user information transfer, along with associated controls (e.g., flow control, error control).

TABLE 16.10   Functions of the B-ISDN Layers

	Higher-Layer Functions	Higher Layers	
Layer Management	Convergence	CS	AAL
	Segmentation and reassembly	SAR	
	Generic flow control Cell header generation/extraction Cell VPI/VCI translation Cell multiplex and demultiplex	ATM	
	Cell rate decoupling HEC header sequence generation/verification Cell delineation Transmission frame adaptation Transmission frame generation/recovery	TC	Physical layer
	Bit timing Physical medium	PM	

CS = Covergence sublayer
SAR = Segmentation and reassembly sublayer
AAL = ATM adaptation layer
ATM = Asynchronous transfer mode
TC = Transmission control sublayer
PM = Physical medium sublayer

- *Control Plane:* Performs call control and connection control functions.
- *Management Plane:* Includes plane management, which performs management functions related to a system as a whole and provides coordination between all the planes, and layer management, which performs management functions relating to resources and parameters residing in its protocol entities.

The 1988 I.121 Recommendation contains the protocol reference model depicted in Figure 16.19, but provides virtually no detail on the functions to be performed at each layer. The 1990 documents include a more detailed description of functions to be performed, as illustrated in Table 16.10.

16.7

RECOMMENDED READING

A detailed technical treatment of ISDN can be found in [STAL92b]. Other book-length treatments include [HELG91], [KESS90], and [VERM90]. [STAL92c] contains reprints of a number of the key papers. Special issues on broadband ISDN include [HORN92], [WU91], [COUD88], and [LEON89].

16.8

PROBLEMS

16.1 Is an IDN necessary for an ISDN? Sufficient? Explain.

16.2 It was mentioned that user-implemented multidrop lines and multiplexers may disappear. Explain why.

16.3 Does Figure 16.1 suggest why long distance telephone charges are more a function of time than they are of distance?

16.4 Refer to Figure 16.4. Why should not the subscriber pay for the cost of his local loop by the month, just as is currently charged?

16.5 An ISDN customer has offices at a number of sites. A typical office is served by two 1.544-Mbps digital pipes. One provides circuit-switched access to the ISDN; the other is a leased line connecting to another user site. The on-premises equipment consists of a CBX aligned with packet-switching node logic. The user has three requirements:

- Telephone service.
- A private packet-switched network for data.
- Video teleconferencing at 1.544 Mbps.

How might the user allocate capacity optimally to meet these requirements?

16.6 Figure 16.6 indicates that an ISDN basic access frame has 32 B bits and 4 D bits. Suppose that more bits were used, say 160 B bits and 20 D bits per frame. Would this reduce the percentage overhead and therefore the basic access bit rate? If so, discuss any potential disadvantages.

16.7 Under what circumstances would user layer 3 on the B channel not be null?

16.8 Compare the addressing schemes in HDLC, LLC, and LAP-D:
   a. Are the SAPI of LAP-D and the SAP of LLC the same thing?
   b. Are the TEI of LAP-D and the MAC-level address of IEEE 802 the same thing?
   c. Why are two levels of addressing needed for LAP-D and LLC, but only one level for HDLC?
   d. Why does LLC need a source address, but LAP-D and HDLC do not?

16.9 What is the percentage overhead on the basic channel structure?

16.10 From Figure 16.9, it would appear that layers 4–7 of the OSI model are little affected by ISDN. Would you expect this? Why or why not?

16.11 In the United States, there has been considerable thought given to the types of telecommunication services that should be subject to government regulation of price and quality, and those that should be offered competitively with little or no regulation. Two important efforts in this regard are the Computer Inquiry II by the Federal Communications Commission (FCC) and the Modification of Final Judgement (MFJ) which resulted in the break-up of AT&T. In Computer Inquiry II, the FCC defined the following terms:

Basic Service   limited to the common carrier offering of transmission capacity for the movement of information

Enhanced Service   any offering over the telecommunications network that is more than a basic transmission service. Such services employ computer processing applications that act on the format, content, code, protocol or similar aspects of the subscriber's transmitted information; provide the subscriber additional, different, or restructured information; or involve subscriber interaction with stored information.

The MFJ produced the following definitions:

Telecommunication   the transmissions, between or among points specified by the user,

Service   of information of the user's choosing, without change in the form or content of the information as seen and received, by means of electromagnetic transmission, with or without benefit of any closed transmission medium, including all instrumentalities, facilities, apparatus, and services (including the collection, storage, forwarding, switching, and delivery of such information) essential to such transmission

Information Service   a capability for generating, acquiring, storing, transforming, processing, retrieving, utilizing, or making available information which may be conveyed via telecommunications, except that such service does not include any use of such capability for the management, control, or operation of a telecommunications system or the management of a telecommunications service.

Compare these two pairs of definitions with these definitions from I.112:

Bearer Service   a type of telecommunication service that provides the capability for the transmission of signals between user-network interfaces.

Teleservice   a type of telecommunication service that provides the complete capability, including terminal equipment functions, for communication between users according to protocols established by agreement between Administrations and/or RPOAs.

16.12 X.25 and most other layer 3 protocols provide techniques for flow control and error control. Why are such features not provided in I.451?

CHAPTER 17

Frame Relay and Cell Relay

Perhaps the most important development in communications networking over the past few years has been the introduction of frame relay and cell relay capabilities into various networking and communications products. Frame relay represents the first major improvement in packet-switching technology in over twenty years. Cell relay, which follows the same evolutionary path as frame relay, is seen by many in the industry to be equivalent to networking nirvana. Indeed, it is hard to overstate the enthusiasm generated by these two technologies.

Frame relay and cell relay are outgrowths of the work on ISDN and BISDN, respectively, so they are treated here rather than in Part II of this book. We begin by placing these two technologies in context, then examine each in detail.

17.1

Communication Switching Techniques

Figure 17.1 describes a spectrum of switching techniques available to transport information across a network. The two extreme ends of the spectrum represent the two traditional switching techniques: circuit switching and packet switching; the remaining techniques are of more recent vintage. In general, the techniques toward the left end of the line provide transmission with little or no variability and with minimal processing demands on attached stations, while techniques toward the right end provide increased flexibility to handle varying bit rates and unpredictable traffic at the expense of increasing processing complexity.

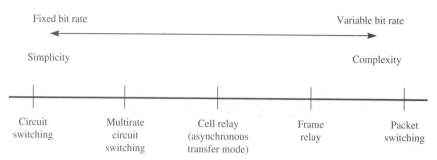

FIGURE 17.1. Sprectrum of switching techniques [PRYC91].

Circuit Switching

Circuit switching is the traditional technique used for telephone networks and is the basic technology for narrowband ISDN. The essence of circuit-switching is the establishment of a fixed-capacity circuit for the complete duration of a connection. To accommodate different data-rate requirements and/or multiple users at an endpoint, a number of circuits can be multiplexed in a fixed, synchronous time-division multiplexing structure.

When the standards work on broadband ISDN (B-ISDN) began in the mid-1980s, it was generally assumed by most participants that some form of synchronous time-division multiplexing (TDM) technique would be used, as is the case with the basic and primary rate access methods for ISDN. Under this approach, the interface structure that was proposed was

$$j \times H4 + k \times H2 + 1 \times H1 + m \times H0 + n \times B + D$$

where D, B, H0, and H1 (H11 or H12) are narrowband ISDN channels and H2 and H4 are new B-ISDN fixed-rate channels. H2 would be in the range of 30 to 45 Mbps and H4 in the range of 120 to 140 Mbps.

Although the synchronous TDM approach is a natural extension of narrowband ISDN, it does not provide the best model for BISDN. There are two basic disadvantages of the synchronous approach. First, it does not provide a flexible interface for meeting a variety of needs. At the high data rates offered by B-ISDN, there could be a wide variety of applications, and many different data rates, that need to be switched. One or two fixed-rate channel types do not provide a structure that can easily accommodate this requirement. Furthermore, many data (as opposed to voice or video) applications are bursty in nature and can more efficiently be handled with some sort of packet-switching approach.

The second disadvantage of the synchronous approach for high-speed transmission is that the use of multiple high data rates (e.g., a number of H2 and H4 channels) complicates the switching system. It would require switches that can handle data streams of multiple high data rates. This is in contrast to narrow-band ISDN, which has just the 64-kbps data stream to switch.

Multirate Circuit Switching

An enhancement of the traditional synchronous TDM approach has been investigated that seeks to provide more flexibility. This technique is known as multirate circuit switching. The transmission technique for multirate circuit switching is the same as that for pure circuit switching. The enhancement provided by multirate circuit switching is the ability to construct a connection consisting of multiple, synchronized circuits. For example, the video codecs developed for narrowband ISDN, and standardized by Recommendation H.261, can operate at bit rates that are multiples of the 64-kbps B-channel circuit rate.

The multirate circuit-switching approach does provide some increased level of flexibility at the cost of increased switching and access complexity. It does support a variety of applications that require different sustained data rates. However, it still does not provide an efficient means of supporting bursty traffic.

Packet Switching

The long-haul circuit-switched telecommunications network was originally designed to handle voice traffic, and the majority of traffic on these networks continues to be voice. A key characteristic of circuit-switched networks is that resources within the network are dedicated to a particular call. For voice connections, the resulting circuit will enjoy a high percentage of utilization since, most of the time, one party or the other is talking. However, as the circuit-switched network began to be used increasingly for data connections, two shortcomings became apparent.

- In a typical terminal-to-host data connection, much of the time the line is idle. Thus, with data connections, a circuit-switched approach is inefficient.
- In a circuit-switched network, the connection provides for transmission at constant data rate. Thus each of the two devices that are connected must transmit and receive at the same data rate as the other. This limits the utility of the network in interconnecting a variety of host computers and terminals.

Traditional packet switching, based on X.25, overcomes these shortcomings. However, X.25 is itself limited in two areas. First, because of the considerable overhead in the protocol, it is difficult to implement an X.25-based network to support applications that require high data rates. Secondly, because of the variable delay in delivering packets, X.25 is not suitable for applications, such as voice, that require a constant bit rate.

Frame Relay

Packet switching was developed at a time when digital long-distance transmission facilities exhibited a relatively high error rate compared to today's facilities. As a result, there is a considerable amount of overhead built into packet-switching schemes to compensate for errors. The overhead includes additional bits added to each packet to enhance redundancy and additional processing at the end stations and the intermediate network nodes to detect and recover from errors.

With modern, high-speed telecommunications systems, this overhead is unnecessary and counterproductive. It is unnecessary because the rate of errors has been dramatically lowered, and any remaining errors can easily be caught by logic in the end systems that operate above the level of the packet-switching logic. It is counterproductive because the overhead involved soaks up a significant fraction of the high capacity provided by the network.

To take advantage of the high data rates and low error rates of contemporary networking facilities, frame relay was developed. Whereas the original packet-switching networks were designed with a data rate to the end user of about 64 kbps, frame relay networks are designed to operate at user data rates of up to 2 Mbps. The key to achieving these high data rates is to strip out most of the overhead involved with error control.

Cell Relay

Cell Relay, also known as asynchronous transfer mode (ATM), is in a sense a culmination of all of the developments in circuit switching and packet switching over the past twenty years. One useful way to view cell relay is as an evolution from frame relay. Both frame relay and ATM take advantage of the reliability and fidelity of modern digital facilities to provide faster packet switching than X.25. Like frame relay and X.25, cell relay allows multiple logical connections to be multiplexed over a single physical interface. As with frame relay, there is no link-by-link error control or flow control with cell relay. As with frame relay, cell relay provides minimum overhead for error control, depending on the inherent reliability of the transmission system and on higher layers of logic to catch and correct remaining errors. The most obvious difference between cell relay and frame relay is that frame relay uses variable-length packets, called frames, and cell relay uses fixed-length packets, called cells. By using a fixed packet length, the processing overhead is reduced even further for cell relay compared to frame relay. The result is that cell relay is designed to work in the range of 100s and 1000s of Mbps, compared to the 2 Mbps of frame relay.

Another way to view cell relay is as an evolution from multirate circuit switching. With multirate circuit switching, only fixed data rate channels are available to the end system. Cell relay allows the definition of virtual channels with data rates that are dynamically defined at the time that the virtual channel is created. By using small, fixed-size cells, cell relay is so efficient that it can offer a constant data rate channel even though it is using a packet-switching technique. Thus cell relay extends multirate circuit switching to allow multiple channels with the data rate of each channel dynamically set on demand.

17.2

FRAME MODE BEARER SERVICE AND PROTOCOL

CCITT has published two recommendations for frame relay:

- *233: ISDN Frame Mode Bearer Services* (1991).
- *370: Congestion Management for the Frame Relaying Bearer Service.* (1991).

The work on frame relay is more developed in the United States, where ANSI has issued three standards:

- *ANSI T1.606: Architectural Framework and Service Description for Frame-Relaying Bearer Service* (1990).
- *Draft ANSI T1.617:* Signaling Specification for Frame Relay Bearer Service (1991).
- *ANSI T1.618: Core Aspects of Frame Protocol for Use with Frame Relay Bearer Service* (1991).

It is anticipated that the final CCITT recommendations will be closely aligned with the current ANSI standards. This section draws on all of these documents, using the ANSI specifications for details not provided by CCITT.

Motivation

The traditional approach to packet switching, as discussed in Chapter 8, is X.25. Several key features of the X.25 approach are

- Call control packets, used for setting up and clearing virtual circuits, are carried on the same channel and same virtual circuit as data packets. In effect, inband signaling is used.
- Multiplexing of virtual circuits takes place at layer 3.
- Both layer 2 and layer 3 include flow-control and error-control mechanisms.

This approach results in considerable overhead. Figure 17.2a indicates the flow of data link frames required for the transmission of a single data packet from source end system to destination end system and the return of an acknowledgment packet. At each hop through the network, the data link control protocol involves the exchange of a data frame and an acknowledgment frame.

(a) Packet-switching network

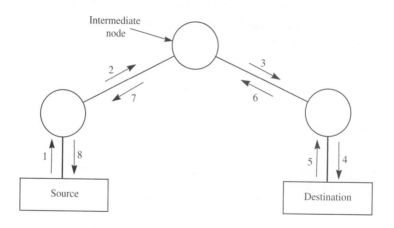

(b) Frame relay network

FIGURE 17.2. Packet switching versus frame relay: source sending, destination responding.

Furthermore, at each intermediate node, state tables must be maintained for each virtual circuit to deal with the call management and flow control/error control aspects of the X.25 protocol.

All of this overhead may be justified when there is a significant probability of error on any of the links in the network. This approach may not be the most appropriate for ISDN. On the one hand, ISDN employs reliable digital transmission technology over high-quality, reliable transmission links, many of which are optical fiber. On the other hand, with ISDN, high data rates can be achieved, especially with the use of H channels. In this environment, the overhead of X.25 is not only unnecessary, but degrades the effective utilization of the high data rates available with ISDN.

Frame relaying is designed to eliminate as much as possible of the overhead of X.25. The key differences of frame relaying from a conventional X.25 packet-switching service are

- Call control signaling is carried on a separate logical connection from user data. Thus, intermediate nodes need not maintain state tables or process messages relating to call control on an individual per-connection basis.
- Multiplexing and switching of logical connections take place at layer 2 instead of layer 3, eliminating one entire layer of processing.
- There is no hop-by-hop flow control and error control. End-to-end flow control and error control are the responsibility of a higher layer, if they are employed at all.

Figure 17.2b indicates the operation of frame relay, in which a single user data frame is sent from source to destination, and an acknowledgment, generated at a higher layer, is carried back in a frame.

Let us consider the advantages and disadvantages of this approach. The principal potential disadvantage of frame relaying, compared to X.25, is that we have lost the ability to do link-by-link flow and error contol. (Although frame relay does not provide end-to-end flow and error control, this is easily provided at a higher layer.) In X.25, multiple virtual circuits are carried on a single physical link, and LAPB is available at the link level for providing reliable transmission from the source to the packet-switching network and from the packet-switching network to the destination. In addition, at each hop through the network, the link control protocol can be used for reliability. With the use of frame relaying, this hop-by-hop link control is lost. However, with the increasing reliability of transmission and switching facilities, this is not a major disadvantage.

The advantage of frame relaying is that we have streamlined the communications process. The protocol functionality required at the user–network interface is reduced, as is the internal network processing. As a result, lower delay and higher throughput can be expected. Preliminary results indicate a reduction in frame processing time of an order of magnitude [BUSH89], and the CCITT recommendation (I.233) indicates that frame relay is to be used at access speeds up to 2 Mbps. Thus, we can expect to see frame relaying supplant X.25 as ISDN matures.

The ANSI standard T1.606 lists four examples of applications that would benefit from the frame-relay service used over a high-speed H channel:

1. *Block-interactive data applications:* An example of a block-interactive application would be high-resolution graphics (e.g., high-resolution videotex, CAD/CAM). The pertinent characteristics of this type of application are low delays and high throughput.
2. *File transfer:* The file transfer application is intended to cater to large file transfer requirements. Transit delay is not as critical for this application as

it is, for example, in the first application. High throughput might be necessary in order to produce reasonable transfer times for large files.

3. *Multiplexed low-bit rate:* The multiplexed low-bit-rate application exploits the multiplexing capability of the frame-relaying service in order to provide an economical access arrangement for a large group of low-bit-rate applications. An example of one such low-bit-rate application is given in (4) below. The low-bit-rate sources may be multiplexed onto a channel by an NT function.

4. *Character-interactive traffic:* An example of a character-interactive traffic application is text editing. The main characteristics of this type of application are short frames, low delays, and low throughput.

Frame Relay Architecture

Figure 17.3 depicts the protocol architecture for frame relay. As in other areas of ISDN, we need to consider two separate planes of operation: a control (C) plane, which is involved in the establishment and termination of logical connections, and a user (U) plane, which is responsible for the transfer of user data between subscribers. Thus, C-plane protocols are between a subscriber and the network, while U-plane protocols provide end-to-end functionality.

For the actual transfer of information between end users, the U-plane protocol is Q.922. Q.922 is a new recommendation, issued in 1992, that is an en-

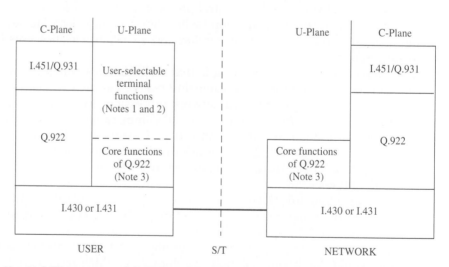

Note 1: Q.922 is one protocol that may be used. Other standard or proprietary protocols may be used.
Note 2: Additional requirements may be placed on terminal depending on the congestion control and
throughput enforcement used. One mechanism that can satisfy the congestion control requirements
is for the terminal to implement a dynamic window algorithm.
Note 3: Additional functions may be needed for throughput monitoring and enforcement.

FIGURE 17.3.   Frame relay protocol architecture.

hanced version of LAPD (I.441/Q.921). Only the core functions of Q.922 are used for frame relay:

- Frame delimiting, alignment and transparency.
- Frame multiplexing/demultiplexing using the address field.
- Inspection of the frame to ensure that it consists of an integer number of octets prior to zero bit insertion or following zero bit extraction.
- Inspection of the frame to ensure that it is neither too long nor too short.
- Detection of transmission errors.
- Congestion control functions.

The last function listed above is new to Q.922 and is discussed in a later section. The remaining functions listed above are also core functions of I.441/Q.921.

The core functions of Q.922 in the U plane constitute a sublayer of the data link layer. This provides the bare service of transferring data link frames from one subscriber to another, with no flow control or error control. Above this, the user may choose to select additional data link or network-layer end-to-end functions. These are not part of the ISDN service. Based on the core functions, ISDN offers frame relaying as a connection-oriented link layer service with the following properties:

- Preservation of the order of frame transfer from one edge of the network to the other.
- Nonduplication of frames.
- A small probability of frame loss.

In the control plane, Q.922 is used to provide a reliable data link control service, with error control and flow control, for the delivery of I.451/Q.931 messages.

As can be seen, this architecture reduces to the bare minimum the amount of work accomplished by the network. User data are transmitted in frames with virtually no processing by the intermediate network nodes, other than to check for errors and to route based on connection number. A frame in error is simply discarded, leaving error recovery to higher layers.

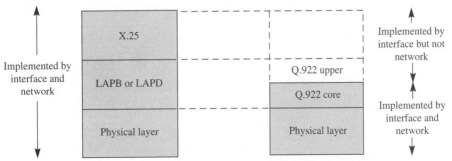

FIGURE 17.4.   A comparison of X.25 and frame relay protocol stacks.

Figure 17.4 compares the protocol architecture of frame relay to that of X.25. The packet-handling functions of X.25 operate at layer 3 of the OSI model. At layer 2, either LAPB or LAPD is used, depending on whether the protocol is operating on a B channel or D channel. Table 17.1 provides a functional comparison of X.25 and frame relay, and Figure 17.5 illustrates that comparison.

TABLE 17.1 Comparison of X.25 Packet Switching and Frame Relay

Function	X.25 in ISDN (X.31)	Frame Relay
Flag generation/recognition	X	X
Transparency	X	X
FCS generation/recognition	X	X
Recognize invalid frames	X	X
Discard incorrect frames	X	X
Address translation	X	X
Fill interframe time	X	X
Multiplexing of logical channels	X	X
Manage V(S) state variable	X	
Manage V(R) state variable	X	
Buffer packets awaiting acknowledgment	X	
Manage retransmission timer T1	X	
Acknowledge received I-frames	X	
Check received N(S) against V(R)	X	
Generation of REJ (rejection message)	X	
Respond to P/F (poll/final) bit	X	
Keep track of number of retransmissions	X	
Act upon reception of REJ	X	
Respond to RNR (receiver not ready)	X	
Respond to RR (receiver ready)	X	
Management of D bit	X	
Management of M bit	X	
Management of Q bit	X	
Management of P(R)	X	
Detection of out-of-sequence packets	X	
Management of network layer RR	X	
Management of network layer RNR	X	

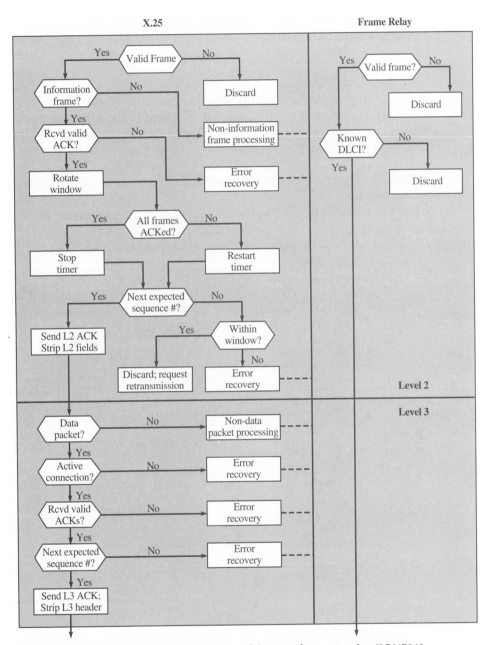

FIGURE 17.5. Simplified model of X.25 and frame relay processing [JONE91].

As can be seen, the processing burden on the network for X.25 is considerably higher than for frame relay.

User Data Transfer

The operation of frame relay for user data transfer is best explained by beginning with the frame format, illustrated in Figure 17.6a. The format is similar to that of LAPD and LAPB with one obvious omission: There is no control field. This has the following implications:

- There is only one frame type, used for carrying user data. There are no control frames.
- It is not possible to use in-band signaling; a logical connection can only carry user data.
- It is not possible to perform flow control and error control, since there are no sequence numbers.

The flag and frame check sequence (FCS) fields function as in LAPD and LAPB. The information field carries higher-layer data. If the user selects to

(a) Frame format

(b) Address field-2 octets (default)

(c) Address field-3 octets

(d) Address field-4 octets

C/R   Command/response; use in application-specific
EA   Address field extension
DE   Discard eligibility indicator
BECN   Backward explicit congestion notification
FECN   Forward explicit congestion notification
DLCI   Data link connection identifier

FIGURE 17.6. Frame relay formats.

implement additional data link control functions end-to-end, then a data link frame can be carried in this field. Specifically, a common selection will be to use enhanced LAPD, as defined in Q.922, to perform functions above the core functions of Q.922. Thus the entire LAPD frame would be carried in the information field. Note that the protocol implemented in this fashion is strictly between the end subscribers and is transparent to ISDN.

The address field has a default length of 2 octets and may be extended to 3 or 4 octets. It carries a data link connection identifier (DLCI) of 10, 17, or 24 bits. The DLCI serves the same function as the virtual circuit number in X.25: It allows multiple logical frame relay connections to be multiplexed over a single channel. As in X.25, the connection identifier has only local significance: Each end of the logical connection assigns its own DLCI from the pool of locally unused numbers, and the network must map from one to the other. The alternative, using the same DLCI on both ends, would require some sort of global management of DLCI values.

For D-channel frame relay, a 2-octet address field is assumed, and the DLCI values are limited to the range 480–1007. This is equivalent to an SAPI of 32–62. Thus frame relay frames can be multiplexed with LAPD frames on the D channel, and the two types of frames are distinguished on the basis of bits 8 to 3 in the first octet of the address field.

The length of the address field, and hence of the DLCI, is determined by the address field extension (EA) bits. The C/R bit is application-specific and is not used by the standard frame relay protocol. The remaining bits in the address field have to do with congestion control and are discussed below.

Network Function

The frame-relaying function performed by ISDN, or any network that supports frame relaying, consists of the routing of frames with the format of Figure 17.6a, based on their DLCI values.

Figure 17.7 suggests the operation of a frame handler in a situation in which a number of users are directly connected to the same frame handler over different physical channels. The operation could just as well involve relaying a frame through two or more frame handlers. In this figure, the decision-making logic is shown conceptually as a separate module, the frame relay contol point. This module is responsible for making routing decisions.

Typically, routing is controlled by entries in a connection table based on DLCI that map incoming frames on one channel to another. The frame handler switches a frame from an incoming channel to an outgoing channel based on the appropriate entry in the connection table and translates the DLCI in the frame before transmission. For example, incoming frames from TE B on logical connection 306 are retransmitted to TE D on logical connection 342. This technique has been referred to as chained-link path routing [LAI88]. The figure also shows the multiplexing function: Multiple logical connections to TE D are multiplexed over the same physical channel.

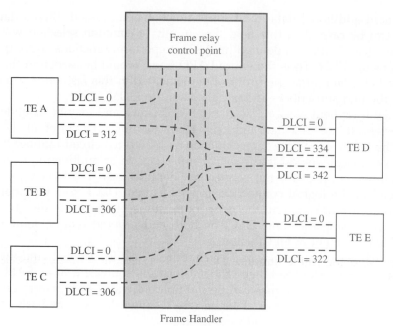

FIGURE 17.7.   Frame handler operation.

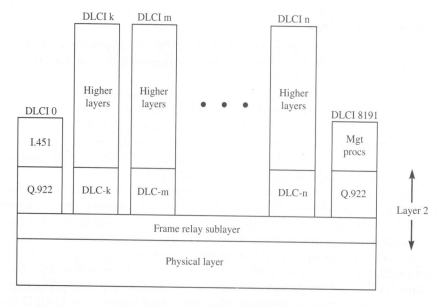

FIGURE 17.8.   Multiplexing at the frame relay sublayer.

Note also that all of the TEs have a logical connection to the frame relay control point with a value of DLCI = 0. These connections are reserved for in-channel call control, to be used when I.451/Q.931 on the D channel is not used for frame relay call control.

As part of the frame relay function, the FCS of each incoming frame is checked. When an error is detected, the frame is simply discarded. It is the responsibility of the end users to institute error recovery above the frame relay protocol.

Figure 17.8 is another view of the protocols involved in frame relay, this time from the point of view of the individual frame relay connections. There is a common physical layer and frame relay sublayer. An optional layer 2 data link control protocol may be included above the frame relay sublayer. This selection is application-dependent and may differ for different frame relay connections (DLC-i). If frame relay call control messages are carried in frame relay frames, these are carried on DLCI 0, which provides a frame relay connection between the user and the frame handler. DLCI 8191 is dedicated to management procedures.

17.3

FRAME RELAY CONGESTION CONTROL

In Section 8.5, we discussed the potentially disastrous effects of congestion on the ability of network nodes to sustain throughput. To summarize that discussion, Figure 17.9 illustrates the effects of congestion in general terms. As the load on a network increases, a region of mild congestion is reached, where the queueing delays at the nodes result in increased end-to-end delay and reduced capability to provide desired throughput. When a point of severe congestion is reached, the classic queueing response results in dramatic growth in delays and a collapse in throughput.

It is clear that these catastrophic events must be avoided, which is the task of congestion control. The object of all congestion control techniques is to limit queue lengths at the frame handlers so as to avoid throughput collapse.

Frame Relay and Congestion Control

CCITT, in I.370, defines the objectives for frame relay congestion control to be the following:

- Minimize frame discard.
- Maintain, with high probability and minimum variance, agreed-upon quality of service.
- Minimize the possibility that one end user can monopolize network resources at the expense of other end users.

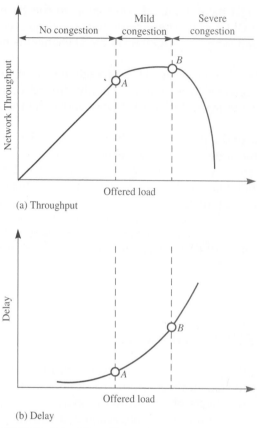

(a) Throughput

(b) Delay

FIGURE 17.9. The effects of congestion.

- Be simple to implement and place little overhead on either end user or network.
- Create minimal additional network traffic.
- Distribute network resources fairly among end users.
- Limit spread of congestion to other networks and elements within the network.
- Operate effectively regardless of the traffic flow in either direction between end users.
- Have minimum interaction or impact on other systems in the frame-relaying network.
- Minimize the variance in quality of service delivered to individual frame relay connections during congestion (e.g., individual logical connections should not experience sudden degradation when congestion approaches or has occurred).

The challenge of congestion control is particularly acute for a frame relay network because of the limited tools available to the frame handlers. The frame relay protocol has been streamlined in order to maximize throughput and efficiency. A consequence of this is that a frame handler cannot control the flow of frames coming from a subscriber or an adjacent frame handler using the typical sliding-window flow-control protocol, such as is found in LAPD.

Congestion control is the joint responsibility of the network and the end users. The network (i.e., the collection of frame handlers) is in the best position to monitor the degree of congestion, while the end users are in the best position to control congestion by limiting the flow of traffic. With the above in mind, we can consider two general congestion-control strategies: congestion avoidance and congestion recovery.

Congestion avoidance procedures are used at the onset of congestion to minimize the effect on the network. Thus, these procedures would be initiated at or prior to point A in Figure 17.9 to prevent congestion from progressing to point B. Near point A, there would be little evidence available to end users that congestion is increasing. Thus, there must be some **explicit signaling** mechanism from the network that will trigger the congestion avoidance.

Congestion recovery procedures are used to prevent network collapse in the face of severe congestion. These procedures are typically initiated when the network has begun to drop frames due to congestion. Such dropped frames will be reported by some higher layer of software (e.g., Q.922) and serve as an **implicit signaling** mechanism. Congestion recovery procedures operate around point B and within the region of severe congestion, as shown in Figure 17.9.

CCITT and ANSI consider congestion avoidance with explicit signaling and congestion recovery with implicit signaling to be complementary forms of congestion control in the frame relaying bearer service.

Congestion Avoidance with Explicit Signaling

For explicit signaling, two bits in the address field of each frame are provided. Either bit may be set by any frame handler that detects congestion. If a frame handler receives a frame in which one or both of these bits are set, it must not clear the bits before forwarding the frame. Thus, the bits constitute signals from the network to the end user. The two bits are

- **Backward explicit congestion notification (BECN):** Notifies the user that congestion avoidance procedures should be initiated where applicable for traffic in the opposite direction of the received frame. It indicates that the frames that the user transmits on this logical connection may encounter congested resources.
- **Forward explicit congestion notification (FECN):** Notifies the user that congestion avoidance procedures should be initiated where applicable for

traffic in the same direction as the received frame. It indicates that this frame, on this logical connection, has encountered congested resources.

Let us consider how these bits are used by the network and the user. First, for the **network response,** it is necessary for each frame handler to monitor its queueing behavior. If queue lengths begin to grow to a dangerous level, then either FECN or BECN bits or a combination should be set to try to reduce the flow of frames through that frame handler. The choice of FECN or BECN may be determined by whether the end users on a given logical connection are prepared to respond to one or the other of these bits. This may be determined at configuration time. In any case, the frame handler has some choice as to which logical connections should be alerted to congestion. If congestion is becoming quite serious, all logical connections through a frame handler might be notified. In the early stages of congestion, the frame handler might just notify users for those connections that are generating the most traffic.

In an appendix to ANSI T1.618, a procedure for monitoring queue lengths is suggested. The frame handler monitors the size of each of its queues. A cycle begins when the outgoing circuit goes from idle (queue empty) to busy (non-zero queue size, including the current frame). The average queue size over the previous cycle and the current cycle is calculated. If the average size exceeds a threshold value, then the circuit is in a state of incipient congestion, and the congestion avoidance bits should be set on some or all logical connections that use that circuit. By averaging over two cycles instead of just monitoring current queue length, the system avoids reacting to temporary surges that would not necessarily produce congestion.

The average queue length may be computed by determining the area (product of queue size and time interval) over the two cycles and dividing by the time of the two cycles. This algorithm is illustrated in Figure 17.10.

The **user response** is determined by the receipt of BECN or FECN signals. The simplest procedure is the response to a BECN signal: The user simply reduces the rate at which frames are transmitted until the signal ceases. The response to an FECN is more complex, since it requires the user to notify its peer user on this connection to restrict its flow of frames. The core functions used in the frame relay protocol do not support this notification. Therefore, it must be done at a higher layer, such as the transport layer. The flow control could also be accomplished by Q.922 or some other link control protocol implemented above the frame relay sublayer (Figure 17.3). Q.922 is particularly useful, since it includes an enhancement to LAPD that permits the user to adjust window size.

Congestion Recovery with Implicit Signaling

Implicit signaling occurs when the network discards a frame and this fact is detected by the end user at a higher layer, such as Q.922. When this occurs, the end user software may deduce that congestion exists. For example, in a

The algorithm makes use of the following variables:

t = current time
t_i = time of ith arrival or departure event
f_{qi} = number of frames in the system after the event
T_0 = time at the beginning of the previous cycle
T_1 = time at the beginning of the current cycle

The algorithm consists of three components:

1. Queue Length Update: Beginning with $q_0 := 0$.
   If the ith event is an arrival event. $q_i := q_{i-1} + 1$
   If the ith event is a departure event, $q_i := q_{i-1} - 1$

2. Queue Area (integral) update:

   Area of the previous cycle $= \displaystyle\sum_{t_i \in [T_0, T_1)} q_{i-1} \, (t_i - t_{i-1})$

   Area of the current cycle $= \displaystyle\sum_{t_i \in [T_1, t)} q_{i-1} \, (t_i - t_{i-1})$

3. Average Queue Length Update
   Average queue length over the two cycles

   $$= \frac{\text{Area of the two cycles}}{\text{Time of the two cycles}} = \frac{\text{Area of the two cycles}}{t - T_0}$$

FIGURE 17.10.   Queue length averaging algorithm.

data link control protocol such as Q.922, when a frame is dropped because of buffer overflow in the network, the following frame will generate a REJECT frame from the receiving end point. Thus, a higher-layer procedure can be used to provide flow control to recover from congestion.

The ANSI standard suggests that a user that is capable of varying the flow-control window size use this mechanism in response to implicit signaling. Let us assume that the layer-2 window size, W, can vary between the parameters W_{min} and W_{max} and is initially set to W_{max}. In general, we would like to reduce W as congestion increases to gradually throttle the transmission of frames. Three classes of adaptive window schemes based on response to the receipt of a REJECT frame have been suggested [CHEN89, DOSH88]:

1.1   Set $W = $ Max $[W - 1, W_{min}]$
1.2   Set $W = W_{min}$
1.3   Set $W = $ Max $[\alpha W, W_{min}]$, where $0 < \alpha < 1$

Successful transmissions (measured by receipt of acknowledgments) may indicate that the congestion has gone away and window size should be increased. Two possible approaches:

2.1   Set $W = $ Min $[W + 1, W_{max}]$ after N consecutive successful transmissions
2.2   Set $W = $ Min $[W + 1, W_{max}]$ after W consecutive successful transmissions

A study reported in [CHEN89] suggests that the use of strategy 1.3 with $\alpha = 0.5$ plus strategy 2.2 provides good performance over a wide range of network parameters and traffic patterns.

So far, we have talked about the user role in congestion recovery. The network role, of course, is to discard frames as necessary. One bit in the address field of each frame can be used to provide guidance:

- **Discard eligibility (DE):** Indicates a request that a frame should be discarded in preference to other frames in which this bit is not set, when it is necessary to discard frames.

The DE capability makes it possible for the user to temporarily send more frames than it is allowd to on average. In this case, the user sets the DE bit on the excess frames. The network will forward these frames if it has the capacity to do so.

The DE bit also can be set by a frame handler. The network can monitor the influx of frames from the user and use the DE bit to protect the network with flexible "firewalls." That is, if the frame handler to which the user is directly connected decides that the input is potentially excessive, it sets the DE bit on each frame and then forwards it further into the network.

The DE bit can be used in such a way as to provide guidance for the discard decision and at the same time as a tool for providing a guaranteed level of service. This tool can be used on a per-logical-connection basis to ensure that heavy users can get the throughput they need without penalizing lighter users. The mechanism works as follows: Each user can negotiate a **committed information rate (CIR)** (in bits per second) at connection setup time. The requested CIR represents the user's estimate of its "normal" traffic during a busy period; the granted CIR, which is less than or equal to the requested CIR, is the network's commitment to deliver data at that rate in the absence of errors. The frame handler to which the user's station attaches then performs a metering function (Figure 17.11). If the user is sending data at less than the CIR, the incoming frame handler does not alter the DE bit. If the rate exceeds the CIR, the incoming frame handler will set the DE bit on the excess frames and then forward them; such frames may get through or may be discarded if congestion is encountered. Finally, a maximum rate is defined, such that any frames above the maximum are discarded at the entry frame handler.

This procedure, in theory, could be exercised on a continuous basis. In practice, the practical approach is for the frame handler to measure traffic over each logical connection for a time interval Tc that is set by the network. Accordingly, two additional parameters may be negotiated. The **committed burst size (Bc)** is the maximum committed amount of data that the network commits to deliver over a logical connection during an interval Tc. The **excess burst size (Be)** is the maximum amount of data by which a user can exceed Bc during an interval Tc; these data are delivered with lower probability than the data within Bc.

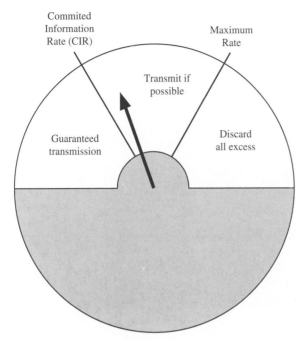

FIGURE 17.11.   Operation of the CIR [JONE91].

The ANSI specification suggests the use of a leaky bucket algorithm for monitoring flow (illustrated in Figure 17.12). The frame handler records the cumulative amount of data sent by each user in a counter C. The counter is decremented at a rate of Bc every Tc time units. Of couse, the counter is not allowed to become negative, so the actual assignment is $C \leftarrow$ MIN $[C, Bc]$. Whenever the counter value exceeds Bc but is less than $Bc + Be$, incoming data are in excess of the committed burst size and are forwarded with the DE bit set. If the counter reaches $Bc + Be$, all incoming frames are discarded until the counter has been decremented.

17.4

ASYNCHRONOUS TRANSFER MODE

ATM Overview

Figure 17.13 shows the overall hierarchy of function in an ATM-based network. This hierarchy is seen from the point of view of the internal network functions needed to support ATM as well as the user-network functions. The ATM layer

Be = Excess
Burst Size
(set DE and forward)

Bc = Commited
Burst Size
(forward)

Limit C to Bc + Be;
Discard any incoming data
while C is at its threshold.

C = counter; increment
with incoming data

Decrement C by MIN [C, Bc] every Tc time units

CIR = Bc/Tc

FIGURE 17.12.   Leaky bucket algorithm.

Higher Layers		
ATM layer	Virtual channel level	
	Virtual path level	
Physical layer	Transmission path level	
	Digital section level	
	Regenerator section level	

FIGURE 17.13.   ATM transport hierarchy.

consists of virtual channel and virtual path levels; these are discussed in the next subsection.

- *Transmission path level:* Extends between network elements that assemble and disassemble the payload of a transmission system. For end-to-end communication, the payload is end user information. For user-to-network communication, the payload may be signaling information. Cell delineation and header error control functions are required at the end points of each transmission path.

- *Digital section:* Extends between network elements that assemble and disassemble a continuous bit or byte stream. This refers to the exchanges or signal transfer points in a network that are involved in switching data streams.
- *Regenerator section level:* A portion of a digital section. An example of this level is a repeater that is used to simply regenerate the digital signal along a transmission path that is too long to be used without such regeneration; no switching is involved.

Virtual Channels and Virtual Paths

Logical connections in ATM are referred to as virtual channel connections (VCC). A VCC is analogous to a virtual circuit in X.25 or a frame relay logical connection. It is the basic unit of switching in B-ISDN. A VCC is set up between two end users through the network and a variable-rate, full-duplex flow of fixed-size cells is exchanged over the connection. VCCs are also used for user–network exchange (control signaling) and network–network exchange (network management and routing).

For ATM, a second sublayer of processing has been introduced that deals with the concept of virtual path (Figure 17.14). A virtual path connection (VPC) is a bundle of VCCs that have the same endpoints. Thus all of the cells flowing over all of the VCCs in a single VPC are switched together.

The virtual path concept was developed in response to a trend in high-speed networking in which the control cost of the network is becoming an increasingly higher proportion of the overall network cost [BURG91]. The virtual path technique helps contain the control cost by grouping connections sharing common paths through the network into a single unit. Network management actions can then be applied to a small number of groups of connections instead of a large number of individual connections.

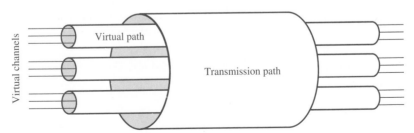

FIGURE 17.14.   ATM connection relationships.

Several advantages can be listed for the use of VPCs:

- *Simplified network architecture:* Network transport functions can be separated into those related to an individual logical connection (VCC) and those related to a group of logical connections (VPC).
- *Increased network performance and reliability:* The network deals with fewer, aggregated entities.
- *Reduced processing and short connection setup time:* Much of the work is done when the VPC is set up. By reserving capacity on a VPC in anticipation of later call arrivals, new virtual channel connections can be established by executing simple control functions at the endpoints of the VPC; no call processing is required at transit nodes. Thus, the addition of new VCCs to an existing VPC involves minimal processing.

FIGURE 17.15. Call establishment using virtual paths [BURG91].

- *Enhanced network services:* the VPC is used internal to the network but is also visible to the end user. Thus, the user may define closed user groups or closed networks of virtual-channel bundles.

Figure 17.15 suggests in a general way the call establishment process using VCCs and VPCs. The process of setting up a VPC is decoupled from the process of setting up an individual VCC:

- The VPC control mechanisms include calculating routes, allocating capacity, and storing connection state information.
- For an individual VCC setup, control involves checking that there is a VPC to the required destination node with sufficient available capacity to support the VCC, with the appropriate quality of service, and then storing the required state information (VCC/VPC mapping).

The terminology of virtual paths and virtual channels used in the standard is a bit confusing and is summarized in Table 17.2. Whereas most of the ISDN

TABLE 17.2   Virtual Path/Virtual Connection Terminology

Virtual Channel (VC)	A generic term used to describe unidirectional transport of ATM cells associated by a common unique identifier value.
Virtual Channel Link	A means of unidirectional transport of ATM cells between a point where a VCI value is assigned and the point where that value is translated or terminated.
Virtual Channel Identifier (VCI)	Identifies a particular VC link for a given VPC.
Virtual Channel Connection (VCC)	A concatenation of VC links that extends between two points where the adaptation layer is accessed. VCCs are provided for the purpose of user—user, user-network, or network-network information transfer. Cell sequence integrity is preserved for cells belonging to the same VCC.
Virtual Path	A generic term for a bundle of VC links; all the VC links in a bundle have the same endpoints.
Virtual Path Link	A group of VC links, identified by a common value of VPI, between a point where a VPI value is assigned and the point where that value is translated or terminated.
Virtual Path Identifier (VPI)	Identifies a particular VP link.
Virtual Path Connection (VPC)	A concatenation of VP links that extends between the point where the VCI values are assigned and the point where those values are translated or removed, i.e., extending the length of a bundle of VC links that share the same VPI. VPCs are provided for the purpose of user—user, user-network, or network-network information transfer.

and B-ISDN concepts that we deal with in this book relate only to the user–network interface, the concepts of virtual path and virtual channel are defined in the CCITT Recommendations with reference to both the user–network interface and the internal network operation.

Virtual Channel Connection Uses

The end points of a VCC may be end users, network entities, or an end user and a network entity. In all cases, cell sequence integrity is preserved within a VCC; that is, cells are delivered in the same order in which they are sent. Let us consider examples of the three uses of a VCC:

- *Between end users:* Can be used to carry end-to-end user data; can also be used to carry control signaling between end users, as explained below. A VPC between end users provides them with an overall capacity; the VCC organization of the VPC is up to the two end users, provided the set of VCCs does not exceed the VPC capacity.
- *Between an end user and a network entity:* Used for user-to-network control signaling, as discussed below. A user-to-network VPC can be used to aggregate traffic from an end user to a network exchange or network server.
- *Between two network entities:* Used for network traffic management and routing functions. A network-to-network VPC can be used to define a common route for the exchange of network management information.

Virtual Path/Virtual Channel Characteristics

As yet, many of the details of the virtual-path/virtual-channel concept have not been worked out. Interim Recommendation I.150 lists the following as characteristics of virtual channel connections:

Quality of service: A user of a VCC is provided with a Quality of Service specified by parameters such as cell loss ratio (ratio of cells lost to cells transmitted) and cell delay variation.
- *Switched and semipermanent virtual channel connections:* Both switched connections, which require call-control signaling, and dedicated channels can be provided.
- *Cell sequence integrity:* The sequence of transmitted cells within a VCC is preserved.
- *Traffic parameter negotiation and usage monitoring:* Traffic parameters can be negotiated between a user and the network for each VCC. The input of cells to the VCC is monitored by the network to ensure that the negotiated parameters are not violated.

The types of traffic parameters that can be negotiated would include average rate, peak rate, burstiness, and peak duration. The network may need a number of strategies to deal with congestion and to manage existing and requested

VCCs. At the crudest level, the network may simply deny new requests for VCCs to prevent congestion. Additionally, cells may be discarded if negotiated parameters are violated or if congestion becomes severe. In an extreme situation, existing connections might be terminated.

I.150 also lists characteristics of VPCs. The first four characteristics listed are identical to those for VCCs. That is, quality of service, switched and semipermanent VPCs, cell sequence integrity, and traffic parameter negotiation and usage monitoring are all also characteristics of a VPC. There are a number of reasons for this duplication. First, this provides some flexibility in how the network service manages the requirements placed upon it. Second, the network must be concerned with the overall requirements for a VPC, and within a VPC, may negotiate the establishment of virtual channels with given characteristics. Finally, once a VPC is set up, it is possible for the end users to negotiate the creation of new VCCs. The VPC characteristics impose a discipline on the choices that the end users may make.

In addition, a fifth characteristic is listed for VPCs:

Virtual channel identifier restriction with a VPC: One or more virtual channel identifiers, or numbers, may not be available to the user of the VPC, but may be reserved for network use. Examples would be VCCs used for network management.

Control Signaling

In narrowband ISDN, the D channel is provided for control signaling of calls on B and H channels. In B-ISDN, with its ATM interface, there is no simple fixed-rate structure of H, B, and D channels. Thus, a more flexible arrangement for control signaling is needed. The requirement is further complicated by the need for the establishment and release of two types of entities: VCCs and VPCs.

For VCCs, I.150 specifies four methods for providing an establishment/release facility. One or a combination of these methods will be used in any particular network.

1. **Semipermanent VCCs** may be used for user-to-user exchange. In this case, no control signaling is required.
2. If there is no preestablished call control signaling channel, then one must be set up. For that purpose, a control signaling exchange must take place between the user and the network on some channel. Hence we need a permanent channel, probably of low data rate, that can be used to set up VCCs that can be used for call control. Such a channel is called a **meta-signaling channel,** since the channel is used to set up signaling channels.
3. The meta-signaling channel can be used to set up a VCC between the user and the network for call control signaling. This **user-to-network signaling virtual channel** can then be used to set up VCCs to carry user data.

4. The meta-signaling channel can also be used to set up a **user-to-user signaling virtual channel.** Such a channel must be set up within a preestablished VPC. It can then be used to allow the two end users, without network intervention, to establish and release user-to-user VCCs to carry user data.

For VPCs, three methods are defined in I.150:

1. A VPC can be established on a **semipermanent** basis by prior agreement. In this case, no control signaling is required.
2. VPC establishment/release may be **customer controlled.** In this case, the customer uses a signaling VCC to request the VPC from the network.
3. VPC establishment/release may be **network controlled.** In this case, the network establishes a VPC for its own convenience. The pay may be network-to-network, user-to-network, or user-to-user.

ATM Cells

The asynchronous transfer mode makes use of fixed-size cells, consisting of a 5-octet header and a 48-octet information field (Figure 17.16a). In the 1988 document (I.121), the header fields and header size are undefined, and it had not yet been decided to use fixed-size cells. The definitive decision to use fixed-size cells is documented in the 1990 Recommendations.

There are several advantages to the use of small, fixed-size cells. First, the use of small cells may reduce queueing delay for a high-priority cell, since it waits less if it arrives slightly behind a lower-priority cell that has gained access to a resource (e.g., the transmitter). Secondly, it appears that fixed-size cells can be switched more efficiently, which is important for the very high data rates of ATM. For a discussion of these issues, see [PARE88].

Header Format

Figure 17.16b shows the header format at the user–network interface (S or T reference point). Figure 17.16c shows the cell header format internal to the network. The generic flow-control field, which performs end-to-end functions, is not retained. Instead, the virtual path identifier field is expanded from 8 to 12 bits. This allows support for an expanded number of VPCs internal to the network, to include those supporting subscribers and those required for network management.

The **generic flow-control field** does not appear in the cell header internal to the network, but only at the user–network interface. Hence, it can be used for control of cell flow only at the local user–network interface. Although the details of its application are for further study, two general functions are under consideration: flow control across a T interface and medium access control across an S or T interface (see Figure 16.20).

The field could be used to assist the customer in controlling the flow of traffic for different qualities of service. One candidate for the use of this field is a

(a) Overall Cell Structure

(b) Header format at user-network interface

(c) Header format at network node interface

FIGURE 17.16. ATM cell format.

multiple-priority-level indicator to control the flow of information in a service-dependent manner. In any case, the GFC mechanism is used to alleviate short-term overload conditions in the network.

As with the basic rate interface to ISDN, multiple terminals may share a single access link to B-ISDN. The GFC mechanism supports both point-to-point and point-to-multipoint configurations. In the former case, the GFC can be used to contol the flow from an individual TE. In the latter case, the GFC can only provide aggregate flow control. However, the GFC might also be used for some sort of medium access control when multiple terminals share a common bus medium attachment at the user–network interface.

I.150 lists as a requirement for the GFC mechanism that all terminals be able to get access to their assured capacities. This includes all constant bit rate (CBR) terminals as well as the variable bit rate (VBR) terminals that have an element of guaranteed capacity.

The **virtual path identifier** (VPI) constitutes a routing field for the network. It is 8 bits at the user–network interface and 12 bits at the network–network interface, allowing for more virtual paths to be supported within the network. The **virtual channel identifier** (VCI) is used for routing to and from the end user. Thus, it functions much as a service access point.

The **payload type** field indicates the type of information in the information field. A value of 00 indicates user information; that is, information from the next higher layer. Other values are for further study. Presumably, network management and maintenance values will be assigned. This field allows the insertion of network-management cells on to a user's VCC without impacting user's data. Thus, it could provide in-band control information.

The **cell loss priority** is used to provide guidance to the network in the event of congestion. A value of 0 indicates a cell of relatively higher priority, which should not be discarded unless no other alternative is available. A value of 1 indicates that this cell is subject to discard within the network. The user might employ this field so that extra information may be inserted into the network, with a CLP of 1, and delivered to the destination if the network is not congested. The network set this field to 1 for any data cell that is in violation of a traffic agreement. In this case, the switch that does the setting realizes that the cell exceeds the agreed traffic parameters but that that switch is capable of handling the cell. At a later point in the network, if congestion is encountered, this cell has been marked for discard in preference to cells that fall within agreed traffic limits.

Header Error Control

Each ATM cell includes an 8-bit header error-control field (HEC) that is calculated based on the remaining 32 bits of the header. The polynomial used to generate the code is $X^8 + X^2 + X + 1$. In most existing protocols that include an error-control field, such as LAPD and LAPB, the data that serve as input to the error code calculation are in general much longer than the size of the resulting error code. This allows for error detection. In the case of ATM, the input to the calculation is only 32 bits, compared to 8 bits for the code. The fact that that input is relatively short allows the code to be used not only for error detection but, in some cases, for actual error correction. This is because there is sufficient redundancy in the code to recover from certain error patterns.

Figure 17.17 depicts the operation of the HEC algorithm at the receiver. At initialization, the receiver's error-correction algorithm is in the default mode for single-bit error correction. As each cell is received, the HEC calculation and comparison are performed. As long as no errors are detected, the receiver remains in error-correction mode. When an error is detected, the receiver will correct the error if it is a single-bit error or will detect that a multibit error has occurred. In either case, the receiver now moves to detection mode. In this mode, no attempt is made to correct errors. The reason for this change is to recognize that a noice burst or other event might cause a sequence of errors. The receiver remains in detection mode as long as errored cells are received. When a header is examined and found not to be in error, the receiver switches back to correction mode. The flowchart of Figure 17.18 shows the consequence of errors in the cell header.

The error-protection function provides both recovery from single-bit header errors and a low probability of the delivery of cells with errored headers under bursty error conditions. The error characteristics of fiber-based transmission systems appear to be a mix of single-bit errors and relatively large burst errors [PRYC91]. For some transmission systems, the error-correction capability, which is more time-consuming, might not be invoked.

Figure 17.19, from I.432, indicates how random bit errors impact the probability of occurrence of discarded cells and valid cells with errored headers.

FIGURE 17.17.   HEC operation at receiver.

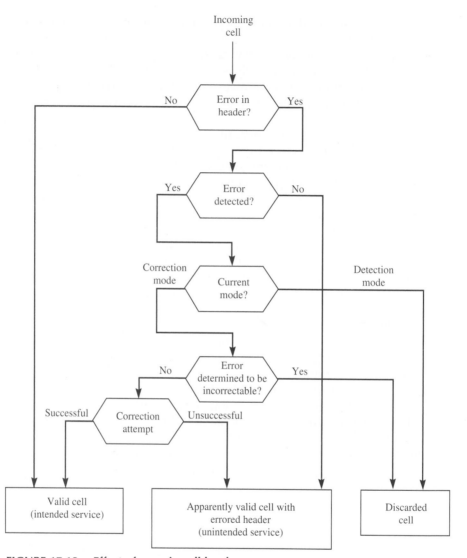

FIGURE 17.18.   **Effect of error in cell header.**

17.5

RECOMMENDED READING

[GROS91] and [HEND91] provide concise overviews of frame relay. Interesting examinations of frame relay congestion control issues are to be found in [GOLD91], [BERG91], [CHEN89], and [DOSH88]. [MARS91] discusses interworking issues related to frame relay. [SILL92] is a special issue devoted to applications of frame relay in public and private networks.

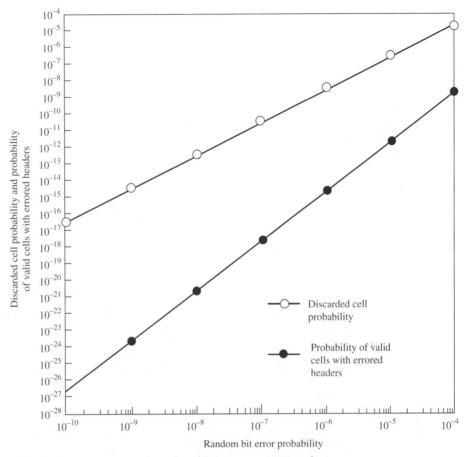

FIGURE 17.19. Impact of random bit errors on HEC performance.

Both [PRYC91] and [HAND91] provide in-depth coverage of ATM. Two interesting overviews of ATM are [XXX00] and [MINZ89]. The virtual path/virtual channel approach of ATM is examined in [SATO91] and [BURG91]. [ECK91] and [BAE91] discuss various approaches to flow control and congestion control in ATM networks. [DECI92], [SOHR91a], and [SOHR91b] are all special issues devoted to congestion control in ATM networks.

17.6

PROBLEMS

17.1 One method of transmitting ATM cells is as a continuous stream of cells, with no framing imposed; therefore, the transmission is simply a stream of bits, with all bits being part of cells. Since there is no external frame, some other form of synchronization is needed. This can be achieved using the HEC function. The requirement is to assure that the receiver knows the beginning and ending cell boundaries and does not drift with respect to the sender. Draw a state diagram for the use of the HEC to achieve cell synchronization, and explain its functionality.

17.2 Although ATM does not include any end-to-end error-detection and control functions on the user data, it is provided with an HEC field to detect and correct header errors. Let us consider the value of this feature. Suppose that the bit error rate of the transmission system is B. If errors are uniformly distributed, then the probability of an error in the header is

$$\frac{h}{h + i} \times B$$

and the probability of error in the data field is

$$\frac{i}{h + i} \times B$$

where h is the number of bits in the header and i is the number of bits in the data field.

a. Suppose that errors in the header are not detected and not corrected. In that case, a header error may result in a misrouting of the cell to the wrong destination; therefore, i bits will arrive at an incorrect destination, and i bits will not arrive at the correct destination. What is the overall bit error rate $B1$? Find an expression for the multiplication effect on the bit error rate: $M1 = B1/B$.

b. Now suppose that header errors are detected but not corrected. In that case, i bits will not arrive at the correct destination. What is the overall bit error rate $B2$? Find an expression for the multiplication effect on the bit error rate: $M2 = B2/B$.

c. Now suppose that header errors are detected and corrected. What is the overall bit error rate $B3$? Find an expression for the multiplication effect on the bit error rate: $M3 = B1/B$.

d. Plot $M1$, $M2$, and $M3$ as a function of header length, for $i = 48 \times 8 = 384$ bits. Comment on the results.

17.3 One key design decision for ATM was whether to use fixed- or variable-length cells. Let us consider this decision from the point of view of efficiency. We can define transmission efficiency as

$$N = \frac{\text{Number of information octets}}{\text{Number of information octets} + \text{number of overhead octets}}$$

a. Consider the use of fixed-length packets. In this case, the overhead consists of the header octets. Define:

L = Data field size of the cell in octets.
H = Header size of the cell in octets.

X = Number of information octets to be transmitted as a single message. Derive an expression for N. Hint: The expression will need to use the operator $|\bullet|$, where $|Y|$ = the smallest integer greater than or equal to Y.

b. If cells have variable length, then overhead is determined by the header, plus the flags to delimit the cells or an additional length field in the header. Let Hv = additional overhead octets required to enable the use of variable-length cells. Derive an expression for N in terms of X and H.

c. Let $H = 5$ and $Hv = 2$. Plot N versus message size for fixed- and variable-length cells. Comment on the results.

17.4 Another key design decision for ATM is the size of the data field for fixed-size cells. Let us consider this decision from the point of view of efficiency and delay.

a. Assume that an extended transmission takes place, so that all cells are completely filled. Derive an expression for the efficiency N as a function of H and L.

b. Packetization delay is the delay introduced into a transmission stream by the need to buffer bits until an entire packet is filled before transmission. Derive an expression for this delay as a function of L and the data rate R of the source.

c. Common data rates for voice coding are 32 kbps and 64 kbps. Plot packetization delay as a function of L for these two data rates; use a left-hand Y axis with a maximum value of 2 ms. On the same graph, plot transmission efficiency as a function of L; use a right-hand Y axis with a maximum value of 100%. Comment on the results.

GLOSSARY

Some of the terms in this glossary are from the *Glossary of Telecommunication Terms*, FED-STD-1037A, National Communications Systems, 1986. These are indicated in the text by an asterisk.

Aloha.   A medium access control technique for multiple access transmission media. A station transmits whenever it has data to send. Unacknowledged transmissions are repeated.

Amplitude.   The size or magnitude of a voltage or current waveform.

Amplitude modulation.*   A form of modulation in which the amplitude of a carrier wave is varied in accordance with some characteristic of the modulating signal.

Amplitude-shift keying.   Modulation in which the two binary values are represented by two different amplitudes of the carrier frequency.

Analog data.*   Data represented by a physical quantity that is considered to be continuously variable and whose magnitude is made directly proportional to the data or to a suitable function of the data.

Analog signal.   A continuously varying electromagnetic wave that may be propagated over a variety of media.

Analog transmission.   The transmission of analog signals without regard to content. The signal may be amplified, but there is no intermediate attempt to recover the data from the signal.

Angle modulation.*   Modulation in which the angle of a sine wave carrier is varied. Phase and frequency modulation are particular forms of angle modulation.

Application layer.   Layer 7 of the OSI model. This layer determines the interface of the system with the user.

Asynchronous transmission.   Transmission in which each information character is individually synchronized (usually by the use of start elements and stop elements).

Attenuation.   A decrease in magnitude of current, voltage, or power of a signal in transmission between points.

Automatic repeat request. A feature that automatically initiates a request for retransmission when an error in transmission is detected.

Balanced transmission. A transmission mode in which signals are transmitted as a current that travels down one conductor and returns on the other. For digital signals, this technique is known as differential signaling, with the binary value depending on the voltage difference.

Bandlimited signal. A signal all of whose energy is contained within a finite frequency range.

Bandwidth.* The difference between the limiting frequencies of a continuous frequency spectrum.

Baseband. Transmission of signals without modulation. In a baseband local network, digital signals (1's and 0's) are inserted directly onto the cable as voltage pulses. The entire spectrum of the cable is consumed by the signal. This scheme does not allow frequency-division multiplexing.

Bell operating companies. Before divestiture, the 22 Bell operating companies (BOCs) were AT&T subsidiaries that built, operated, and maintained the local and intrastate networks and provided most of the day-to-day service for customers. After divestiture, the BOCs retain their identity within seven regional companies and are responsible for local service as defined by local access and transport areas (LATAs).

Bit stuffing. The insertion of extra bits into a data stream to avoid the appearance of unintended control sequences.

Bridge. A device that links two homogeneous packet-broadcast local networks. It accepts all packets from each network addressed to devices on the other, buffers them, and retransmits them to the other network.

Broadband. The use of coaxial cable for providing data transfer by means of analog (radio-frequency) signals. Digital signals are passed through a modem and transmitted over one of the frequency bands of the cable.

Broadcast. The simultaneous transmission of data to a number of stations.

Broadcast address. An address that designates all entities within a domain (e.g., network, internet).

Broadcast communication network. A communication network in which a transmission from one station is broadcast to and received by all other stations.

Bus.* One or more conductors that serve as a common connection for a related group of devices.

Carrier. A continuous frequency capable of being modulated or impressed with a second (information carrying) signal.

CATV. Community Antenna Television. CATV cable is used for broadband local networks, and broadcast TV distribution.

Cellular radio. The use of low-power radio transmitters arranged in a honeycomb pattern, to permit reuse of a frequency multiple times in a small area.

Checksum. An error-detecting code based on a summation operation performed on the bits to be checked.

Circuit switching. A method of communicating in which a dedicated communications path is established between two devices through one or more intermediate switching nodes. Unlike packet switching, digital data are sent as a continuous stream of bits. Bandwidth is guaranteed, and delay is essentially limited to propagation time. The telephone system uses circuit switching.

Coaxial cable. A cable consisting of one conductor, usually a small copper tube or wire, within and insulated from another conductor of larger diameter, usually copper tubing or copper braid.

Codec. Coder-decoder. Transforms analog data into a digital bit stream (coder), and digital signals into analog data (decoder).

Collision. A condition in which two packets are being transmitted over a medium at the same time. Their interference makes both unintelligible.

Common carrier. In the United States, companies that furnish communication services to the public. The usual connotation is for long-distance telecommunications services. Common carriers are subject to regulation by federal and state regulatory commissions.

Common channel signaling. Technique in which network control signals (e.g., call request) are separated from the associated voice or data path by placing the signaling from a group of voice or data paths on a separate channel dedicated to signaling only.

Communications architecture. The hardware and software structure that implements the communications function.

Communication network. A collection of interconnected functional units that provides a data communications service among stations attached to the network.

Connectionless data transfer. A protocol for exchanging data in an unplanned fashion and without prior coordination (e.g., datagram).

Connection-oriented data transfer. A protocol for exchanging data in which a logical connection is established between the endpoints (e.g., virtual circuit).

Contention. The condition when two or more stations attempt to use the same channel at the same time.

Crosstalk.* The phenomenon in which a signal transmitted on one circuit or channel of a transmission system creates an undesired effect in another circuit or channel.

CSMA. Carrier Sense Multiple Access. A medium access control technique for multiple-access transmission media. A station wishing to transmit first senses the medium and transmits only if the medium is idle.

CSMA/CD. Carrier Sense Multiple Access with Collision Detection. A refinement of CSMA in which a station ceases transmission if it detects a collision.

Current-mode transmission. A transmission mode in which the transmitter alternately applies current to each of two conductors in a twisted pair to represent logic 1 or 0. The total current is constant and always in the same direction.

Cyclic redundancy check.   An error detecting code in which the code is the remainder resulting from dividing the bits to be checked by a predetermined binary number.

Data circuit-terminating equipment.   In a data station, the equipment that provides the signal conversion and coding between the data terminal equipment (DTE) and the line. The DCE may be separate equipment or an integral part of the DTE or of intermediate equipment. The DCE may perform other functions that are normally performed at the network end of the line.

Datagram.   In packet switching, a self-contained packet, independent of other packets, that does not require acknowledgment, and that carries information sufficient for routing from the originating data terminal equipment (DTE), without relying on earlier exchanges between the DTEs and the network.

Data link layer.   Layer 2 of the OSI model. Converts unreliable transmission channel into reliable one.

Data terminal equipment (DTE).*   Equipment consisting of digital end instruments that convert the user information into data signals for transmission, or reconvert the received data signals into user information.

Decibel.   A measure of the relative strength of two signals. The number of decibels is 10 times the log of the ratio of the power of two signals, or 20 times the log of the ratio of the voltage of two signals.

Delay distortion.   Distortion of a signal occurring when the propagation delay for the transmission medium is not constant over the frequency range of the signal.

Demand-assignment multiple access.   A technique for allocating satellite capacity, based on either FDM or TDM, in which capacity is granted on demand.

Differential encoding.   A means of encoding digital data on a digital signal such that the binary value is determined by a signal change rather than a signal level.

Digital data.   Data consisting of a sequence of discrete elements.

Digital private branch exchange.   A local network based on the private branch exchange (PBX) architecture. Provides an integrated voice/data switching service.

Digital signal.   A discrete or discontinuous signal, such as voltage pulses.

Digital switch.   A star topology local network. Usually refers to a system that handles only data but not voice.

Digital transmission.   The transmission of digital data, using either an analog or digital signal, in which the digital data is recovered and repeated at intermediate points to reduce the effects of noise.

Digitize.*   To convert an analog signal to a digital signal.

DOD Protocol architecture. A communications architecture that has evolved from the ARPANET project and DOD standardization activities.

Encapsulation. The addition of control information by a protocol entity to data obtained from a protocol user.

Error detecting code.* A code in which each expression conforms to specific rules of construction, so that if certain errors occur in an expression, the resulting expression will not conform to the rules of construction and thus the presence of the errors is detected.

Error rate.* The ratio of the number of data units in error to the total number of data units.

Fast select. An option of the X.25 virtual call that allows the inclusion of data in the call setup and call clearing packets.

Flow control. The function performed by a receiving entity to limit the amount or rate of data that is sent by a transmitting entity.

Frame check sequence. An error-detecting code inserted as a field in a block of data to be transmitted. The code serves to check for errors upon reception of the data.

Frequency. Rate of signal oscillation in hertz.

Frequency-division multiple access. A technique for allocating capacity on a satellite channel using fixed-assignment FDM.

Frequency-division multiplexing. The division of a transmission facility into two or more channels by splitting the frequency band transmitted by the facility into narrower bands, each of which is used to constitute a distinct channel.

Frequency modulation. Modulation in which the frequency of an alternating current is the characteristic varied.

Frequency-shift keying. Modulation in which the two binary values are represented by two different frequencies near the carrier frequency.

Full-duplex transmission. Data transmission in both directions at the same time.

Gateway. A device that connects two systems, especially if the systems use different protocols. For example, a gateway is needed to connect two independent local networks, or to connect a local network to a long-haul network.

Half-duplex transmission. Data transmission in either direction, one direction at a time.

HDLC (high-level data link control). A very common bit-oriented data link protocol (OSI layer 2) issued by ISO. Similar protocols are ADCCP, LAP-B, and SDLC.

Header.   System-defined control information that precedes user data.

High-speed local network (HSLN).   A local network designed to provide high throughput between expensive, high-speed devices, such as mainframes and mass storage devices.

Impulse noise.   A high-amplitude, short-duration noise pulse.

Integrated services digital network.   A planned worldwide telecommunication service that will use digital transmission and switching technology to support voice and digital data communication.

Intermodulation noise.   Noise due to the nonlinear combination of signals of different frequencies.

Internet.   A collection of packet-switched and broadcast networks that are connected together via gateways.

Internet protocol.   An internetworking protocol that provides connectionless service across multiple packet-switched networks.

Internetworking.   Communication among devices across multiple networks.

Local area network (LAN).   A general-purpose local network that can serve a variety of devices. Typically used for terminals, microcomputers, and minicomputers.

Local loop.   Transmission path, generally twisted pair, between the individual subscriber and the nearest switching center of the public telecommunications network.

Local network.   A communication network that provides interconnection of a variety of data communicating devices within a small area.

Longitudinal redundancy check.   The use of a set of parity bits for a block of characters such that there is a parity bit for each bit position in the characters.

Manchester encoding.   A digital signaling technique in which there is a transition in the middle of each bit time. A 1 is encoded with a high level during the first half of the bit time; a 0 is encoded with a low level during the first half of the bit time.

Medium access control (MAC).   For broadcast networks, the method of determining which device has access to the transmission medium at any time. CSMA/CD and token are common access methods.

Message switching.   A switching technique using a message store-and-forward system. No dedicated path is established. Rather, each message contains a destination address and is passed from source to destination through intermediate nodes. At each node, the entire message is received, stored briefly, and then passed on to the next node.

Microwave.   Electromagnetic waves in the frequency range of about 2 to 40 GHz.

Modem. Modulator/Demodulator. Transforms a digital bit stream into an analog signal (modulator), and vice versa (demodulator).

Modulation.* The process, or result of the process, of varying certain characteristics of a signal, called a carrier, in accordance with a message signal.

Multicast address. An address that designates a group of entities within a domain (e.g., network, internet).

Multiplexing. In data transmission, a function that permits two or more data sources to share a common transmission medium such that each data source has its own channel.

Multipoint. A configuration in which more than two stations share a transmission path.

Network layer. Layer 3 of the OSI model. Responsible for routing data through a communication network.

Network terminating equipment. Grouping of ISDN functions at the boundary between the ISDN and the subscriber.

Noise. Unwanted signals that combine with and hence distort the signal intended for transmission and reception.

Nonreturn to zero. A digital signaling technique in which the signal is at a constant level for the duration of a bit time.

Optical fiber. A thin filament of glass or other transparent material through which a signal-encoded light beam may be transmitted by means of total internal reflection.

Packet assembler/disassembler. A device used with an X.25 network to provide service to asynchronous terminals.

Packet switching. A method of transmitting messages through a communication network, in which long messages are subdivided into short packets. The packets are then transmitted as in message switching. Usually, packet switching is more efficient and rapid than message switching.

Parity bit.* A check bit appended to an array of binary digits to make the sum of all the binary digits, including the check bit, always odd or always even.

PBX. Private branch exchange. A telephone exchange on the user's premises. Provides a switching facility for telephones on extension lines within the building and access to the public telephone network. May be manual (PMBX) or automatic (PABX). A digital PBX that also handles data devices without modems is called a CBX.

Phase. The relative position in time within a single period of a signal.

Phase modulation. Modulation in which the phase angle of a carrier is the characteristic varied.

Phase-shift keying. Modulation in which the phase of the carrier signal is shifted to represent digital data.

Physical layer. Layer 1 of the OSI model. Concerned with the electrical, mechanical, and timing aspects of signal transmission over a medium.

Piggybacking. The inclusion of an acknowledgment to a previously received packet in an outgoing data packet.

Point-to-point. A configuration in which two stations share a transmission path.

Poll and select. The process by which a primary station invites secondary stations, one at a time, to transmit (poll), and by which a primary station requests that a secondary receive data (select).

Presentation layer. Layer 6 of the OSI model. Concerned with data format and display.

Protocol. A set of rules that govern the operation of functional units to achieve communication.

Protocol data unit. A block of data exchanged between two entities via a protocol.

Public data network. A government-controlled or national monopoly packet-switched network. This service is publicly available to data processing users.

Pulse code modulation. A process in which a signal is sampled, and the magnitude of each sample with respect to a fixed reference is quantized and converted by coding to a digital signal.

Residual error rate. The error rate remaining after attempts at correction are made.

Ring. A local network topology in which stations are attached to repeaters connected in a closed loop. Data are transmitted in one direction around the ring, and can be read by all attached stations.

RS-232-C. A physical layer interface standard for the interconnection of equipment, established by EIA.

RS-449/422-A/423-A. A set of physical layer standards developed by EIA and intended to replace RS-232-C. RS-422-A and RS-423-A specify electrical characteristics; RS-449 specifies mechanical, functional, and procedural characteristics.

Satellite-switched time-division multiple access (SS/TDMA). A form of TDMA in which circuit switching is used to dynamically change the channel assignments.

Service access point. A means of identifying a user of the services of a protocol entity. A protocol entity provides one or more SAPs for use by higher-level entities.

Session layer. Layer 5 of the OSI model. Manages a logical connection (session) between two communicating processes or applications.

Simplex transmission. Data transmission in one preassigned direction only.

Single channel per carrier. A technique for allocating satellite capacity in which the bandwidth is divided into a number of individual voice-frequency channels.

Sliding-window technique. A method of flow control in which a transmitting station may send numbered packets within a window of numbers. The window changes dynamically to allow additional packets to be sent.

Space-division switching. A circuit-switching technique in which each connection through the switch takes a physically separate and dedicated path.

Spectrum. Refers to an absolute range of frequencies. For example, the spectrum of CATV cable is now about 5 to 400 MHz.

Star. A topology in which all stations are connected to a central switch. Two stations communicate via circuit switching.

Statistical time-division multiplexing. A method of TDM in which time slots on a shared transmission line are allocated to I/O channels on demand.

Stop and wait. A flow control protocol in which the sender transmits a block of data and then awaits an acknowledgment before transmitting the next block.

Switched communication network. A communication network consisting of a network of nodes connected by point-to-point links. Data are transmitted from source to destination through intermediate nodes.

Synchronous time-division multiplexing. A method of TDM in which time slots on a shared transmission line are assigned to I/O channels on a fixed, predetermined basis.

Synchronous transmission. Data transmission in which the time of occurrence of each signal representing a bit is related to a fixed time frame.

TDM bus switching. A form of time-division switching in which time slots are used to transfer data over a shared bus between transmitter and receiver.

Telematics. User-oriented information transmission services. Includes Teletex, Videotex, and facsimile.

Teletex. A text communications service that provides message preparation and transmission facilities.

Teletext. A one-way information retrieval service. A fixed number of information pages are repetitively broadcast on unused portions of a TV channel bandwidth. A decoder at the TV set is used to select and display pages.

Thermal noise. Statistically uniform noise due to the temperature of the transmission medium.

Time-division multiple access. A synchronous TDM scheme for satellite capacity allocation.

Time-division multiplexing. The division of a transmission facility into two or more channels by allotting the facility to several different information channels, one at a time.

Time-division switching. A circuit-switching technique in which time slots in a time-multiplexed stream of data are manipulated to pass data from an input to an output.

Time-multiplexed switching (TMS). A form of space-division switching in which each input line is a TDM stream. The switching configuration may change for each time slot.

Time-slot interchange (TSI). The interchange of time slots within a time-division multiplexed frame.

Token bus. A medium access control technique for bus/tree. Stations form a logical ring, around which a token is passed. A station receiving the token may transmit data and then must pass the token on to the next station in the ring.

Token ring. A medium access control technique for rings. A token circulates around the ring. A station may transmit by seizing the token, inserting a packet onto the ring, and then retransmitting the token.

Topology. The structure, consisting of paths and switches, that provides the communications interconnection among nodes of a network.

Transmission medium. The physical path between transmitters and receivers in a communications system.

Transport layer. Layer 4 of the OSI model. Provides reliable, transparent transfer of data between endpoints.

Tree. A local network topology in which stations are attached to a shared transmission medium. The transmission medium is a branching cable emanating from a headend, with no closed circuits. Transmissions propagate throughout all branches of the tree, and are received by all stations.

Twisted pair. A transmission medium consisting of two insulated wires arranged in a regular spiral pattern.

Unbalanced transmission. A transmission mode in which signals are transmitted on a single conductor. Transmitter and receiver share a common ground.

Value-added network. A privately owned packet-switched network whose services are sold to the public.

Videotex. A two-way information retrieval service accessible to terminals and TV sets equipped with a special decoder. Pages of information at a central resource are retrieved interactively over a switched telephone line connection.

Virtual circuit. A packet-switching service in which a connection (virtual circuit) is established between two stations at the start of transmission. All packets follow the same route, need not carry a complete address, and arrive in sequence.

X.21.   A network access standard for connecting stations to a circuit-switched network. Includes OSI layers 1–3 functionality.

X.25.   A network access standard for connecting stations to a packet-switched network. Includes OSI layers 1–3 functionality.

X.75.   An internetworking protocol that provides virtual circuit service across multiple X.25 networks.

REFERENCES

Abbo84   Abbott, G. F. "Digital Space Division: A Technique for Switching High-Speed Data Signals." *IEEE Communications Magazine*, April 1984.

Abra70   Abramson, N. "The ALOHA System—Another Alternative for Computer Communications." *Proceedings, Fall Joint Computer Conference*, 1970.

Amor80   Amoroso, F. "The Bandwidth of Digital Data Signals." *IEEE Communications Magazine*, November 1980.

Anon88   Anonymous. "SEL Claims Mark for Optical Transmission." *Electronics*, March 3, 1988.

Ansi90   American National Standards Institute. *Dictionary for Information Systems*. X3.172–1990.

Aoya88   Aoyama, T.; Daumer, W.; and Modena, G., eds. *Voice Coding for Communications*. Special issue of the IEEE Journal on Selected Areas in Communications, February 1988.

Bach79   Bachman, C., and Canepa, M. *The Session Control Layer of an Open System Interconnection*. International Organization for Standardization OSIC/TG 6/79-10, 1979.

Back88   Backes, F. "Transparent Bridges for Interconnection of IEEE 802 LANs." *IEEE Network*, January 1988.

Bae91   Bae, J., and Suda, T. "Survey of Traffic Control Schemes and Protocols in ATM Networks." *Proceedings of the IEEE*, February 1991.

Ball92   Ball, L. *Cost-Efficient Network Management*. New York: McGraw-Hill, 1992.

Barc81   Barcomb, D. *Office Automation*. Bedford, MA: Digital Press, 1981.

Bart86   Bartee, T. *Digital Communications*, Indianapolis, IN: Howard W. Sams & Co., 1986.

Basc87   Basch, E., editor. *Optical-Fiber Transmission*. Indianapolis, IN: Howard W. Sams, 1987.

Bede86   Bederman, S. "Source Routing." *Data Communications*, February 1986.

Bell86   Bell, P., and Jabbour, K. "Review of Point-to-Point Network Routing Algorithms." *IEEE Communications Magazine*, January, 1986.

Bell90   Bellcore (Bell Communications Research). *Telecommunications Transmission Engineering, Third Edition*. Three volumes. 1990.

Bell91   Bellamy, J. *Digital Telephony*. New York: Wiley, 1991.

Berg91   Bergman, W. "Narrowband Frame Relay Congestion Control." *Proceedings, Tenth Annual Phoenix Conference on Computers and Communications*, March 1991.

BERT80 Bertine, H. U. "Physical Level Protocols." *IEEE Transactions on Communications,* April 1980.

BERT92 Bertsekas, D., and Gallager, R. *Data Networks.* Englewood Cliffs, NJ: Prentice-Hall, 1992.

BHAR83 Bhargava, V. "Forward Error Correction Schemes for Digital Communications." *IEEE Communications Magazine,* January 1983.

BHUS85 Bhushan, B., and Opderbeck, H. "The Evolution of Data Switching for PBX's." *IEEE Journal on Selected Areas in Communications,* July 1985.

BOGG80 Boggs, D.; Shoch, J.; Taft, E.; and Metcalfe, R. "Pup: An Internetwork Architecture." *IEEE Transactions on Communications,* April 1980.

BOSI82 Bosik, B., and Kartalopoulos, S. "A Time Compression Multiplexing System for a Circuit Switched Digital Capability." *IEEE Transactions on Communications,* September 1982.

BOUL89 Boule, R., and Moy, J. "Inside Routers: a Technology Guide for Network Builders." *Data Communications,* 21 September 1989.

BROD83 Brodd, W. "HDLC, ADCCP, and SDLC: What's the Difference?" *Data Communications,* August 1983.

BROO83 Broomell, G., and Heath, J. "Classification Categories and Historical Development of Circuit Switching Topologies." *ACM Computing Surveys,* June 1983.

BURG91 Burg, J., and Dorman, D. "Broadband ISDN Resource Management: The Role of Virtual Paths." *IEEE Communications Magazine,* September 1991.

BUSH89 Bush, J. "Frame-Relay Services Promise WAN Bandwidth on Demand." *Data Communications,* July 1989.

BUX83 Bux, W.; Closs, F.; Kummerle, H.; and Mueller, H. "Architecture and Design of a Reliable Token-Ring Network." *IEEE Journal on Selected Areas in Communications,* November 1983.

BUX87 Bux, W.; Grillo, D.; and Maxemchuk, N., editors. Interconnection of Local Area Networks. Special issue of *IEEE Journal on Selected Areas in Communications,* December 1987.

BYTE85 Bytex Corporation. *Autoswitch Technical Manual,* 1985.

CANE86 Caneschi, F. "Hints for the Interpretation of the ISO Session Layer." *Computer Communication Review.* July/August 1986.

CARG89 Cargill, C. *Information Technology Standardization: Theory, Process, and Organizations.* Bedford, MA: Digital Press, 1989.

CAST88 Castiel, D. "Satellite Links for the Masses: The Final Frontier." *Data Communication,* November 1988.

CERF78 Cerf, V., and Kristein, P. T. "Issues in Packet-Network Interconnection." *Proceedings of the IEEE,* November 1978.

CERF83 Cerf, V., and Lyons, R. "Military Requirements for Packet-Switched Networks and Their Implications for Protocol Standardization." *Computer Networks,* October 1983.

CERN84 Cerni, D. *Standards in Process: Foundations and Profiles of ISDN and OSI Studies.* National Telecommunications and Information Administration, Report 84-170, December 1984.

CHAN76 Chang, K. Y. "Transmission of Analog, Video, and Digital Signals Over Analog-Repeatered Coaxial Lines." *IEEE Transactions on Communications,* September 1976.

CHAN88 Chanson, S.; Ravindran, K.; and Robinson, J. "The Design and Tuning of a Transport Protocol for Local Area Networks." *Proceedings, IEEE INFOCOM '88,* March 1988.

CHAP82 Chapin, A. "Connectionless Data Transmission." *Computer Communication Review*, April 1982.

CHAP83 Chapin, A. "Connections and Connectionless Data Transmission." *Proceedings of the IEEE*, December 1983.

CHAR79 Charransol, P.; Hauri, J.; Athenes, C.; and Hardy, D. "Development of a Time Division Switching Network Usable in a Very Large Range of Capacities." *IEEE Transactions on Communications*, July 1979.

CHEN89 Chen, K.; Ho, K.; and Saksena, V. "Analysis and Design of a Highly Reliable Transport Architecture for ISDN Frame-Relay Networks." *IEEE Journal on Selected Areas in Communications*, October 1989.

CHER89a Cheriton, D., and Williamson, C. "VMTP as the Transport Layer for High-Performance Distributed Systems." *IEEE Communications Magazine, June 1989.*

CHER89b Cherukuri, R., and Derby, J. "Frame Relay: Protocols and Private Network Applications." *Proceedings, IEEE INFOCOM '89,* April 1989.

CHES88 Chesson, G. "XTP/PE Overview." *Proceedings, 13 Conference on Local Computer Networks,* October 1988.

CHIL90 Chilton, P. *X.400: The Messaging and Interconnection Medium for the Future.* Oxford, England: NCC Publications, 1990.

CHU73 Chu, W. "Asynchronous Time-Division Multiplexing Systems," In *Computer Communication Networks* (ed. Abramson and Kuo). Englewood Cliffs, NJ, Prentice-Hall, 1973.

CLAI88 Clair, M., and Orlov, M. "Is It Wise for Users to Run Ethernet Over Existing Nonshielded Twisted Pair?" *Network World*, January 11, 1988.

CLAR89 Clark, D.: Jacobson, V.; Romkey, J.; and Salwen, H. "An Analysis of TCP Processing Overhead." *IEEE Communications Magazine*, June 1989.

COCH88 Cochrane, P., and Brain, M. "Future Optical Fiber Transmission Technology and Networks." *IEEE Communications Magazine*, November 1988.

COCK87 Cockburn, A. "Efficient Implementation of the OSI Transport-Protocol Checksum Algorithm Using 8/16-Bit Arithmetic." *Computer Communications Review*, July/August 1987.

COHN88 Cohn, M. "A Lightweight Transfer Protocol for the U.S. Navy Safenet Local Area Network Standard." *Proceedings, 13th Conference on Local Computer Networks*, October 1988.

COHN89 Cohn, M. "A Case for XTP." *Data Communications,* July 1989.

COLE90 Cole, G. *Implementing OSI Networks.* New York: Wiley, 1990.

COME91 Comer, D. *Internetworking with TCP/IP: Principles, Protocols, and Architecture.* Englewood Cliffs, NJ: Prentice-Hall, 1991.

COOK84 Cooke, R. "Intercity Limits: Looking Ahead to All-Digital Networks and No Bottlenecks." *Data Communications*, March 1984.

COOP84 Cooper, E. *Broadband Network Technology.* Mountain View, CA: Sytek Press, 1984.

COOV85 Coover, E. "Notes from Mid-revolution: Searching for the Perfect PBX." *Data Communications,* August 1985.

COOV89 Coover, E., ed. *Digital Private Branch Exchanges.* Los Alamitos, CA: IEEE Computer Society Press, 1989.

COUC90 Couch, L. *Digital and Analog Communication Systems, Third Edition.* New York: Macmillan, 1990.

COUD88 Coudreuse, J.; Sincoskie, W.; and Turner, J., editors. Special Issue on Broadband Packet Communications. *IEEE Journal on Selected Areas in Communications,* December 1988.

CROC83 Crochiere, R. E., and Flanagan, J. L. "Current Perspectives in Digital Speech." *IEEE Communications Magazine,* January 1983.

CROC89 Crockett, B. "The Changing Role of Satellite in Telecommunications." *Telecommunications,* June 1989.

CYPS91 Cypser, R. *Communications for Cooperating Systems: OSI, SNA, and TCP/IP.* Reading, MA: Addison-Wesley, 1991.

DAVI73 Davies, D. W., and Barber, D. L. *Communication Networks for Computers.* New York: Wiley, 1973.

DAVI77 Davidson, J.; Hathaway, W.; Postel, J.; Mimno, N.; Thomas, R.; and Walden, D. "The ARPANET Telnet Protocol: Its Purpose, Principles, Implementation, and Impact on Host Operating System Design." *Proceedings, Fifth Data Communications Symposium,* 1977.

DAVI90 Davies, D., and Price, W. *Security for Computer Networks.* New York: Wiley, 1990.

DAY81 Day, J. "Terminal, File Transfer, and Remote Job Protocols for Heterogeneous Computer Networks." In *Protocols and Techniques for Data Communication Networks* (ed. F. F. Kuo). Englewood Cliffs, NJ: Prentice-Hall, 1981.

DAYT89 Dayton, R. *Guide to Integrating Digital Services.* New York: McGraw-Hill, 1989.

DCA85 Defense Communications Agency. *DDN Protocol Handbook.* December 1985.

DEAT79 Deaton, G. "Flow Control in Packet-Switched Networks with Explicit Path Routing." *Proceedings, Conference on Flow Control in Computer Networks,* Paris, 1979.

DECI82a Decina, M. "Managing ISDN Through International Standards Activities." *IEEE Communications Magazine,* September 1982.

DECI82b Decina, M. "Progress Towards User Access Arrangements in Integrated Services Digital Networks." *IEEE Transactions on Communications,* September 1982.

DECI92 Decina, M., and Trecordi, V., editors. *Special Issue on Traffic Management and Congestion Control for ATM Networks.* IEEE Network, September 1992.

DHAS86 Dhas, C., and Konangi, U. "X.25: An Interface to Public Packet Networks." *IEEE Communications Magazine,* September 1986.

DIJK59 Dijkstra, E. "A Note on Two Problems in Connection with Graphs." *Numerical Mathematics,* October 1959.

DINE80 Dineson, M. A., and Picazo, J. J. "Broadband Technology Magnifies Local Network Capability." *Data Communications,* February 1980.

DIXO83 Dixon, R.; Strole, N.; and Markov, J. "A Token-ring Network for Local Data Communications." *IBM Systems Journal.* Nos. 1/2, 1983.

DIXO88 Dixon, R., and Pitt, D. "Addressing, Bridging, and Source Routing." *IEEE Network,* January 1988.

DOER90 Doeringer, W., et al. "A Survey of Light-Weight Transport Protocols for High-Speed Networks." *IEEE Transactions on Communications,* November 1990.

DOLA84 Dolan, M. "A Minimal Duplex Connection Capability in the Top Three Layers of the OSI Reference Model." *Proceedings, SIGCOMM '84,* June 1984.

DORR83 Dorros, I. "Telephone Nets Go Digital." *IEEE Spectrum,* April 1983.

DOSH88 Doshi, B., and Nguyen, H. "Congestion Control in ISDN Frame-Relay Networks." *AT&T Technical Journal,* November/December 1988.

DUC85 Duc, N., and Chew, E. "ISDN Protocol Architecture." *IEEE Communications Magazine,* March 1985.

ECK91 Eckberg, A.; Doshi, B.; and Zoccolillo, R. "Controlling Congestion in B-ISDN/ATM: Issues and Strategies." *IEEE Communications Magazine,* September 1991.

EIA69 Electronic Industries Association. *EIA Standard RS-232-C Interface Between Data*

Terminal Equipment and Data Communication Equipment Employing Serial Binary Data Interchange, October, 1969.

EIA71 Electronic Industries Association. *Application Notes for EIA Standard RS-232-C*, May 1971.

EMMO83 Emmons, W., and Chandler, H. "OSI Session Layer Services and Protocols." *Proceedings of the IEEE*, December 1983.

ENNI82 Ennis, G.; Kaufman, D.; and Biba, K. *DOD Protocol Reference Model*, Sytek, TR-82026, September 1982.

ENNI83 Ennis, G. "Development of the DOD Protocol Reference Model." *Proceedings, SIGCOMM '83 Symposium*, 1983.

ENOM85 Enomoto, O.; Kohashi, T.; Aomori, T.; Kadota, S.; Oka, S.; and Fujita, K. "Distributed Microprocessors Control Architecture for Versatile Business Communications." *IEEE Journal on Selected Areas in Communications*, July 1985.

ERIK86 Eriksen, S. "The How and Where of Switched 56-kbit/s Service." *Data Communications*, August 1986.

FARM69 Farmer, W. D., and Newhall, E. E. "An Experimental Distributed Switching System to Handle Bursty Computer Traffic." *Proceedings, ACM Symposium on Problems in the Optimization of Data Communications*, 1969.

FEIT93 Feit, S. *TCP/IP: Architecture, Protocols, and Implementation*. New York: McGraw-Hill, 1993.

FIEL86 Field, J. "Logical Link Control." *IEEE Infocom 86*, April 1986.

FINN89a Finnie, G. "VSATs: A Technical Update." *Telecommunications*, February 1989.

FINN89b Finnie, G. "Lighting up the Local Loop." *Telecommunications*, January 1989.

FLET82 Fletcher, J. "An Arithmetic Checksum for Serial Transmissions." *IEEE Transactions on Communications*, January 1982.

FORB81 Forbes, V. "RF Prescribed for Many Local Links." *Data Communications*, September 1981.

FORD62 Ford, L., and Fulkerson, D. *Flows in Networks*. Princeton, NJ: Princeton University Press, 1962.

FORR86 Forrest, S. "Optical Detectors: Three Contenders." *IEEE Spectrum*, May 1986.

FRAN84 Frank, C. "Legal and Policy Ramifications of the Emerging Integrated Services Digital Network." *Journal of Telecommunication Networks*, Spring 1984.

FREE85 Freeman, R. *Reference Manual for Telecommunications Engineering*. New York: Wiley, 1985.

FREE89 Freeman, R. *Telecommunication System Engineering, Second Edition*. New York: Wiley, 1989.

FREE91 Freeman, R. *Telecommunication Transmission Handbook*. New York: Wiley, 1991.

GALL68 Gallager, R. *Information Theory and Reliable Communication*. New York: Wiley, 1968.

GARL77 Garlick, L.; Rom, R.; and Postel, J. "Reliable Host-to-Host Protocols: Problems and Techniques." *Proceedings, Fifth Data Communications Symposium*, 1977.

GAUD89 Gaudette, P. *A. Tutorial on ASN.1*. Technical Report NCSL/SNA-89/12. Gaithersburg, MD: National Institute of Standards and Technology, 1989.

GEOR82 George, F. and Young, G. "SNA Flow Control: Architecture and Implementation." *IBM Systems Journal*, Number 2, 1982.

GERL80 Gerla, M., and Kleinrock, L. "Flow Control: A Comparative Survey." *IEEE Transactions on Communications*, April 1980.

GERL84 Gerla, M. and Pazos-Rangel, A. "Bandwidth Allocation and Routing in ISDN's." *IEEE Communications Magazine*, February 1984.

GERL88 Gerla, M.; Green, L.; and Rutledge, R., editors. Special issue of *IEEE Network*, January 1988.

GERM92 Germuska, M., and Morgan, G. "Comparison of XTP with TCP/IP and ISO TP4/CLNS." *Transfer*, July/August 1992.

GERW84 Gerwin, P.; Verhoeckx, N.; and Claasen, T. "Design Considerations for a 144 kbit/s Digital Transmission Unit for the Local Telephone Network." *IEEE Journal on Selected Areas in Communications*, March 1984.

GIBS89 Gibson, J. *Principles of Digital and Analog Communications.* New York: Macmillan, 1889.

GIFF86 Gifford W. "ISDN User-Network Interfaces." *IEEE Journal on Selected Areas in Communications*, May 1986.

GITM76 Gitman, I.; Van Slyke, R.; and Frank, H. "Routing in Packet-Switching Broadcast Radio Networks." *IEEE Transactions on Communications*, August 1976.

GLEN86 Glen, D. *Networks, Signaling, and Switching for Post-Divestiture and the ISDN.* National Telecommunications and Information Administration, Report 86-191, February 1986.

GOLD91 Goldstein, F. "Congestion Control in Frame Relay Networks Using Explicit Binary Feedback." *Proceedings, Tenth Annual Phoenix Conference on Computers and Communications*, March 1991.

GONG89 Gong, L. "Using One-Way Functions for Authentication." *Computer Communications Review*, October 1989.

GOPA85 Gopal, I. "Prevention of Store-and-Forward Deadlock in Computer Networks." *IEEE Transactions on Communications*, December 1985.

GREE77 Greene, W., and Pooch, U. "A Review of Classification Schemes for Computer Communication Networks." *Computer*, November 1977.

GREE90 Green, P.; Naemura, K.; and Williamson, R., editors. Heterogeneous Computer Networks Interconnection. Special issue of *IEEE Journal on Selected Areas in Communications*, January 1990.

GREE93 Green, P. *Fiber Optic Networks.* Englewood Cliffs, NJ: Prentice-Hall, 1993.

GROE86 Groenbaek, I. "Conversion Between the TCP and ISO Transport Protocols as a Method of Achieving Interoperability Between Data Communication Systems." *IEEE Journal on Selected Areas in Communications*, March 1986.

GROS91 Grossman, D. "An Overview of Frame Relay Technology." *Proceedings, Tenth Annual Phoenix Conference on Computers and Communications*, March 1991.

HALS88 Halsall, F. *Data Communications, Computer Networks and OSI, Second Edition.* Reading, MA: Addison-Wesley, 1988.

HAMM86 Hammond, J., and O'Reilly, R. *Performance Analysis of Local Computer Networks.* Reading, MA: Addison-Wesley, 1986.

HAMN88 Hamner, M., and Samsen, G. "Source Routing Bridge Implementation." *IEEE Network*, January 1988.

HAND91 Handel, R., and Huber, M. *Integrated Broadband Networks.* Reading, MA: Addison-Wesley, 1991.

HARR86 Harrington, E.; Cipriano, G.; and Micheroni, V. "Public Switched 56-kbps Networks." *Telecommunications*, March 1986.

HART88 Hart, J. "Extending the IEEE 802.1 MAC Bridge Standard to Remote Bridges." *IEEE Network*, January 1988.

HASK87 Haskell, B.; Pearson, D.; and Yamamoto, H., eds. *Low Bit-Rate Coding of Moving Images.* Special issue of the IEEE Journal on Selected Areas in Communications, August 1987.

Heat89   Heatley, S., and Stokesberry, D. "Analysis of Transport Measurements Over a Local Area Network." *IEEE Communications Magazine,* June 1989.

Hech86   Hecht, J. "Bell Labs Transmits 8 Gbit/s Over 68.3 km." *Lasers and Applications,* May 1986.

Hegg84   Heggestad, H. "An Overview of Packet-Switching Communications." *IEEE Communications Magazine,* April 1984.

Held83   Held, G. "Strategies and Concepts for Linking Today's Personal Computers." *Data Communications,* May 1983.

Held86   Held, G. *Data Communications Networking Devices.* New York: Wiley, 1986.

Helg91   Helgert, H. *Integrated Services Digital Networks; Architectures, Protocols, and Standards.* Reading, MA: Addison-Wesley, 1991.

Hend91   Henderson, F., and McCoy, J. "Less Is Faster." *LAN Magazine,* July 1991.

Hens90   Henshall, J., and Shaw, S. *OSI Explained: End-to-End Computer Communication Standards.* New York: Ellis Horwood, 1990.

Hind83   Hinden, R.; Haverty, J.; and Sheltzer, A. "The DARPA Internet: Interconnecting Heterogeneous Computer Networks with Gateways." *Computer,* September 1983.

Hind89   Hindin, E. "XTP: A New LAN Protocol Promises Multi-Megabit/s Throughput." *Data Communications,* March 1989.

Hirs85   Hirschheim, R. *Office Automation.* Reading, MA: Addison-Wesley, 1986.

Holm83   Holmes, E. "A Closer Look at AT&T's New High-Speed Digital Services." *Data Communications,* July 1983.

Hone82   Honeywell Information Systems, Inc. *Distributed Systems Architecture,* CT37-01, 1982.

Hong86   Hong, J. "Timing Jitter." *Data Communications,* February 1986.

Hope73   Hopewell, L.; Chou, W.; and Frank, H. "Analysis of Architectural Strategies for a Large Message-Switching Network: A Case Study." *Computer,* April 1973.

Hopk80   Hopkins. G. T., and Wagner, P. E. *Multiple Access Digital Communications System.* U.S. Patent 4,210,780, July 1, 1980.

Horn92   Horn, W., editor. *ISDN Special Issue: End User Requirements and Solutions.* IEEE Communications Magazine, August 1992.

Hsie84a   Hsieh, W., and Gitman, I. "How Good Is Your Network Routing Protocol?" *Data Communications,* May 1984.

Hsie84b   Hsieh, W., and Gitman, I. "Routing Strategies in Computer Networks." *Computer,* June 1984.

Hsie84c   Hsieh, W., and Gitman, I. "How to Prevent Congestion in Computer Networks." *Data Communications,* June 1984.

Hubi92   Hubing, N., ed. *Speech and Image Coding.* Special issue of the *IEEE Journal on Selected Areas in Communications,* June 1992.

Hurl87   Hurley, B.; Seidl, C.; and Sewell, W. "A Survey of Dynamic Routing Methods for Circuit-Switched Traffic." *IEEE Communications Magazine,* September 1987.

Ieee89a   The Institute of Electrical and Electronics Engineers. *Logical Link Control.* American National Standard ANSI/IEEE Std. 802.2-1989.

Ieee89b   The Institute of Electrical and Electronics Engineers. *Token Ring Access Method and Physical Layer Specifications.* American National Standard ANSI/IEEE Std. 802.5-1989.

Ieee90a   IEEE Computer Society. *Draft IEEE Standard 802.1 (Part A): Overview and Architecture,* October 1990.

IEEE90b The Institute of Electrical and Electronics Engineers. *Carrier Sense Multiple Access with Collision Detection (CSMA/CD) Access Method and Physical Layer Specifications.* American National Standard ANSI/IEEE Std. 802.3-1990.

IEEE90c The Institute of Electrical and Electronics Engineers. *Token-Passing Bus Access Method and Physical Layer Specifications.* American National Standard ANSI/IEEE Std. 802.4-1990.

IEEE90d The Institute of Electrical and Electronics Engineers. *IEEE Standard 802.1: MAC Bridges.* September 1990.

IEEE91 The Institute of Electrical and Electronics Engineers. *IEEE 802.5, Appendix D: Multi-ring Networks (Source Routing).* 1991.

Iso84 International Organization for Standardization. *Basic Reference Model for Open Systems Interconnection,* ISO 7498, 1984.

Iso86a International Organization for Standardization. *Connection Oriented Transport Protocol Specification,* ISO 8072, 1986.

Iso86b International Organization for Standardization. *Transport Service Definition.* ISO 8072, 1986.

Iso86c International Organization for Standardization. *Basic Connection Oriented Session Service Definition.* ISO 8329, 1986.

Iso86d International Organization for Standardization. *Basic Connection Oriented Session Protocol Specification,* ISO 8327, 1986.

Iso86e International Organization for Standardization. *Protocol for Providing the Connectionless-Mode Network Service.* DIS 8473, 1986.

Iso87a International Organization for Standardization. *File Transfer, Access and Management.* DIS 8571, 1987.

Iso87b International Organization for Standardization. *Interface Connector and Contact Assignments for ISDN Basic Access Interface Located at Reference Points S and T.* ISO 8877, 1987.

Iso87c International Organization for Standardization. *Network Service Definition, Addendum 1: Connectionless-mode Transmission.* ISO 8348/Add. 1, 1987.

Iso88 International Organization for Standardization. *Protocol for Providing the Connectionless-mode Network Service (Internetwork Protocol).* ISO 8473, 1988.

JAIN88 Jain, R., and Ramakrishnan, K. "Congestion Avoidance in Computer Networks with a Connectionless Network Layer: Concepts, Goals, and Methodology." *Proceedings, Computer Networking Symposium,* April 1988.

JAYA84 Jayant, N., and Noll, P. *Digital Coding of Waveforms.* Englewood Cliffs, NJ: Prentice-Hall, 1984.

JAYA86 Jayant, N. "Coding Speech at Low Bit Rates." *IEEE Spectrum,* August 1986.

JAYA87 Jayasumana, A. "Performance Analysis of Token Bus Priority Schemes: *Proceedings, INFOCOM '87,* 1987.

JAYA90 Jayant, N. "High-Quality Coding of Telephone Speech and Wideband Audio." *IEEE Communications Magazine,* January 1990.

JEWE85 Jewett, R. "The Fourth-Generation PBX: Beyond the Integration of Voice and Data." *Telecommunications,* February 1985.

JOEL77 Joel, A. E. "What Is Telecommunications Circuit Switching?" *Proceedings of the IEEE,* September 1977.

JOEL79a Joel, A. E. "Circuit Switching: Unique Architecture and Applications." *Computer,* June 1979.

JOEL79b Joel, A. E. "Digital Switching—How it Has Developed." *IEEE Transactions on Communications,* July 1979.

JOEL85   Joel, A., ed. *Special Issue on Serving the Business Customer Using Advances in Switching Technology*. IEEE Journal on Selected Areas in Communications, July 1985.

JOHN87   Johnson, M. "Proof that Timing Requirements of the FDDI Token Ring Protocol are Satisfied." *IEEE Transactions on Communications*, June 1987.

JONE91   Jones, T.; Rehbehn, K.; and Jennings, E. *The Buyer's Guide to Frame Relay*. Networking. Herndon, VA: Netrix Corporation, 1991.

JORD85   Jordan, E., ed. *Reference Data for Engineers: Radio, Electronics, Computer, and Communications*. Indianapolis, IN: Howard Sams & Co., 1985.

JUEN85   Jueneman, R.; Matyas, S.; and Meyer, C. "Message Authentication." *IEEE Communications Magazine*, September 1985.

JUNK83   Junker, S., and Noller, W. "Digital Private Branch Exchanges." *IEEE Communications Magazine*, May 1983.

KADE81   Kaderali, F., and Weston, J. "Digital Subscriber Loops." *Electrical Communication*, Vol. 56, No. 1, 1981.

KAJI83   Kajiwara, M. "Trends in Digital Switching System Architectures." *IEEE Communications Magazine*, May 1983.

KALI91   Kaliski, B. *A Layman's Guide to a Subset of ASN.1, BER, and DER*. Report SEC-SIG-91-17, Redwood City, CA: RSA Data Security Inc. 1991.

KAMI86   Kamali, B., and Davis, G. "Modulation Codes in Digital Magnetic Recording Systems." *Proceedings, Fifth Annual International Phoenix Conference on Computers and Communications*, March 1986.

KANE80   Kane, D. A. "Data Communications Network Switching Methods," *Computer Design*, April 1980.

KASA83   Kasac, H.; Ohue, K.; Hoshino, T.; and Tsuyuki, S. "800 Mbit/s Digital Transmission System Over Coaxial Cable." *IEEE Transactions on Communications*, February 1983.

KASS79   Kasson, J. M. "Survey of Digital PBX Design." *IEEE Transactions on Communications*, July 1979.

KAUF92   Kauffels, F. *Network Management: Problems, Standards, and Strategies*. Reading, MA: Addison-Wesley, 1992.

KEIS85   Keiser, B., and Strange, E. *Digital Telephony and Network Integration*. New York: Van Nostrand Reinhold, 1985.

KELC83   Kelcourse, F., and Siegel, E. "Switched Digital Capability: An Overview." *IEEE Communications Magazine*, January 1983.

KELL84   Kelley, R.; Jones, J.; Bhatt, V.; and Pate, P. "Transceiver Design and Implementation Experience in an Ethernet-Compatible Fiber Optic Local Area Network." *Proceedings, INFOCOM 84*, 1984.

KESS89   Kessler, G. "Splitting Hairs and Bits." *Data Communications*, February 1989.

KESS90   Kessler, G. *ISDN: Concepts, Facilities, and Services*. New York: McGraw-Hill, 1990.

KESS92   Kessler, G., and Train, D. *Metropolitan Area Networks: Concepts, Standards, and Services*. New York: McGraw-Hill, 1992.

KHAN89   Khanna, A., and Zinky, J. "The Revised ARPANET Routing Metric." *Proceedings, SIGCOMM '89 Symposium*, 1989.

KIM89   Kim, B. *Current Advances in LANs, MANs, & ISDN*. Norwood, MA: Artech House, 1989.

KIMB75   Kimbleton, S., and Schneider, G. "Computer Communication Networks: Approaches, Objectives, and Performance Considerations." *ACM Computing Surveys*, September 1975.

KLEI78 Kleinrock, L. "Principles and Lessons in Packet Communications." *Proceedings of the IEEE,* November 1978.

KLEI86 Klein, M., and Balph, T. "Carrierband Is Low-Cost, Single-Channel Solution for MAP." *Computer Design,* February 1, 1986.

KNOW87 Knowles, T., Larmouth, J.; and Knightson, K. *Standards for Open Systems Interconnection.* Boston, MA: BSP Professional Books, 1987.

KOPF77 Kopf, J. "TYMNET as a Multiplexed Packet Network." *Proceedings, National Computer Conference,* 1977.

KOST84 Kostas, D. "Transition to ISDN—An Overview." *IEEE Communications Magazine,* January 1984.

KUMM80 Kummede, K., and Rudin, H. "Packet and Circuit Switching: Cost/Performance Boundaries." *Computer Networks,* No. 2, 1980.

KUMM87 Kummerle, K.; Limb, J.; and Tobagi, F. *Advanced in Local Area Networks.* New York: IEEE Press, 1987.

KUO81 Kuo, F. *Protocols and Techniques for Data Communication Networks.* Englewood Cliffs, NJ: Prentice-Hall, 1981.

LAI89 Lai, W. "Frame Relaying Service: An Overview." *Proceedings, IEEE INFOCOM '89,* April 1989.

LECH86 Lechleider, J. "Loop Transmission Aspects of ISDN Basic Access." *IEEE Journal on Selected Areas in Communications,* November, 1986.

LEIN93 Leinwand, A., and Fang, K. *Network Management: A Practical Perspective.* Reading, MA: Addison-Wesley, 1993.

LEON89 Leon-Garcia, A., editor. Special Issue on Broadband Networks. *IEEE Network,* January 1989.

LEWA83 Lewan, D., and Long, H. "The OSI File Service." *Proceedings of the IEEE,* December 1983.

LIN90 Lin, D. "Minimum Mean-Squared Error Echo Cancellation and Equalization for Digital Subscriber Line Transmission." *IEEE Transactions on Communications,* January 1990.

LINI89 Linington, P. "File Transfer Protocols." *IEEE Journal on Selected Areas in Communications,* September 1989.

LIU80 Liu, J. "Distributed Routing and Relay Management in Mobile Packet Radio Networks." *Proceedings, COMPCON FALL 80,* 1980.

MALO81 Malone, J. "The Microcomputer Connection to Local Networks." *Data Communications,* December 1981.

MANR89 Manros, C. *The X.400 Blue Book Companion.* Twickenham, England: Technology Appraisals, 1989.

MARI79 Marill, T. "Why the Telephone Is on Its Way Out and Electronic Mail Is on Its Way In." *Datamation,* August 1979.

MARS91 Marsden, P. "Interworking IEEE 802/FDDI LANs Via the ISDN Frame Relay Bearer Service." *Proceedings of the IEEE,* February 1991.

MART87 Martin, J., and Chapman, K. *SNA: IBM's Networking Solution.* Englewood Cliffs, NJ: Prentice-Hall, 1987.

MART88 Martin, J., and Leban, J. *Data Communication Technology.* Englewood Cliffs, NJ: Prentice-Hall, 1988.

MART89 Martin, J., and Chapman K. *Local Area Networks: Architectures and Implementations.* Englewood Cliffs, NJ: Prentice-Hall, 1989.

MART90 Martin, J. *Telecommunications and the Computer, Third Edition.* Englewood Cliffs, NJ: Prentice-Hall, 1990.

MccL83 McClelland, F. "Services and Protocols of the Physical Layer." *Proceedings of the IEEE*, December 1983.

McFA79 McFarland, R. "Protocols in a Computer Internetworking Environment." *Proceedings, EASCON 79*, 1979.

McNA88 McNamara, J. E. *Technical Aspects of Data Communication, Third Edition*. Bedford, MA: Digital Press, 1988.

McQu80 McQuillan, J.; Richer, I.; and Rosen, E. "The New Routing Algorithm for the ARPANET." *IEEE Transactions on Communications*. May 1980.

MEIJ82 Meijer, A., and Peeters, P. *Computer Network Architectures*, Rockville, MD: Computer Science Press, 1982.

MEIJ87 Meijer, A. *Systems Network Architecture: A Tutorial*. London: Pitman, 1987.

MESS84 Messerschmitt, D. "Echo Cancellation in Speech and Data Transmission." *IEEE Journal on Selected Areas in Communications*, March, 1984.

MESS86 Messerschmitt, D. "Design Issues in the ISDN U-Interface Transceiver." *IEEE Journal on Selected Areas in Communications*, November, 1986.

METC76 Metcalfe, R. M., and Boggs, D. R. "Ethernet: Distributed Packet Switching for Local Computer Networks." *Communications of the ACM*, July 1976.

METC77 Metcalfe, R. M.; Boggs, D. R.; Thacker, C. P.; and Lampson, B. W. *Multipoint Data Communication System with Collision Detection*. U.S. Patent 4,063,220, 1977.

METZ83 Metz, S. "The Different Flavors of SNA Compatibility." *Data Communications*, April 1983.

MIER84 Mier, E. "The ABCs of FEC." *Data Communications*, May 1984.

MIER86 Mier, E. "Light Sources and Wavelengths." *Data Communications*, February 1986.

MIER89 Mier, E. "Coming Soon to an Outlet Near You: Premises Fiber." *Data Communications*, February 1989.

MILL81 Miller, L. "An Analysis of Link Level Protocols for Error Prone Links." *Proceedings, Seventh Data Communications Symposium*, 1981.

MILL82 Miller, C. K., and Thompson, D. M. "Making a Case for Token Passing in Local Networks." *Data Communications*, March 1982.

MILL84 Mills, D. *Exterior Gateway Protocol Formal Specification*. RFC 904, April 1984. Reprinted in [DCA85].

MINE89 Minet, P. "Performance Evaluation of GAM-T-103 Real-Time Transfer Protocols." *Proceedings, IEEE INFOCOM '89*, April, 1989.

MINZ89 Minzer, S. "Broadband ISDN and Asynchronous Transfer Mode (ATM)." *IEEE Communications Magazine*, September 1989.

MOEN84 Moeneclaey, M. "Synchronizability of a General Class of PCM Formats, Including NRZ, Manchester, and Miller Coding." *IEEE Transactions on Communications*, September 1984.

MOY89a Moy, J., and Chiappa, N. "OSPF: A New Dynamic Routing Standard." *Network World*, 7 August 1989.

MOY89b Moy, J. *The OSPF Specification*. RFC 1131, October 1989. Available from the DDN Network Information Center, SRI International, Menlo Park, CA.

MUKH91 Mukherjee, B. "Integrated Voice-Data Communication Over High-Speed Fiber Optic Networks." *Computer*, 1991.

MURA87 Murakami, H.; Matsumoto, S.; Hatori, Y.; and Yamamoto, H. "15/30 Mbit/s Universal Digital TV Codec Using a Median Adaptive Predictive Coding Method." *IEEE Transactions on Communications*, June 1987.

MURA88 Murakami, H.; Hashimoto, H.; and Hatori, Y. "Quality of Band-Compressed TV Services." *IEEE Communications Magazine,* October 1988.

MURA90 Murano, K.; Unagami, S.; and Amano, F. "Echo Cancellation and Applications." *IEEE Communications Magazine,* January 1990.

NAKA88 Nakassis, A. "Fletcher's Error Detection Algorithm: How To Implement It Efficiently and How to Avoid the Most Common Pitfalls." *Computer Communications Review,* October 1988.

NAUG91 Naugle, M. *Local Area Networking.* New York: McGraw-Hill, 1991.

NBS80 National Bureau of Standards. *Features of the Transport and Session Protocols,* ICST/HLNP-80-1, March 1980.

NECH91 Nechvatal, J. *Public-Key Cryptography.* NIST Special Publication 800-2. National Institute of Standards and Technology, Gaithersburg, MD, 1991.

NETR88 Netravali, A. *Digital Pictures: Representation and Compression.* New York: Plenum Press, 1988.

OETT79 Oetting, J. "A Comparison of Modulation Techniques for Digital Radio." *IEEE Transactions on Communications,* December 1979.

ONEA80 O'Neal, J. "Waveform Encoding of Voiceband Data Signals." *Proceedings of the IEEE,* February 1980.

ORLO88 Orlov, M. "Another Twist: Twisted-Pair Ethernet May Not Be All It's Cracked Up to Be." *LAN Magazine,* August 1988.

PAOL75 Paolette, L. "AUTODIN." In *Computer Communication Networks* (ed. R. L. Grimsdale and F. F. Kuo). Leyden, The Netherlands: Noordhoff International, 1975.

PARE88 Parekh, S., and Sohraby, K. "Some Performance Trade-Offs Associated with ATM Fixed-Lenth Vs. Variable-Length Cell Formats. "Proceedings. GlobeCom, November 1988. Reprinted in [KIM89].

PART88 Partridge, C. *Innovations in Internetworking.* Norwood, MA: Artech House, 1988.

PARU90 Parulkar, G. "The Next Generation of Internetworking." Computer Communications Review, January 1990.

PE92 Protocols Engines, Inc. *XTP Protocol Definition, Revision 3.6.* Santa Barbara, CA, 1992.

PEEB87 Peebles, P. *Digital Communication Systems.* Englewood Cliffs, NJ: Prentice-Hall, 1987.

PERL84 Perlman, R. "An Algorithm for Distributed Computation of a Spanning Tree." Proceedings, Ninth Data Communications Symposium, 1984.

PERL92 Perlman, R. *Interconnections: Bridges and Routers.* Reading, MA: Addison-Wesley, 1992.

PETE61 Peterson, W., and Brown, D. "Cyclic Codes for Error Detection." *Proceedings of the IRE,* January 1961.

PFLE89 Pfleeger, C. *Security in Computing.* Englewood Cliffs, NJ: Prentice-Hall, 1989.

PICK86 Pickholtz, R. *Local Area Networks.* Rockville, MD: Computer Science Press, 1986.

PITT85 Pitt, D.; Sy, K.; and Donnan, R. "Source Routing for Bridged Local Area Networks." *Proceedings, Globecom '85,* December 1985. Reprinted in [KUMM87].

PITT87 Pitt, D., and Winkler, J. "Table-Free Bridging." *IEEE Journal on Selected Areas in Communications,* December 1987.

PLAT91 Plattner, B., et al. *X.400 Message Handling: Standards, Interworking, Applications.* Reading, MA: Addison-Wesley, 1991.

PORT91   Porta, T., and Schwartz, M. "Architectures, Features, and Implementation of High-Speed Transport Protocols." *IEEE Network Magazine*, May 1991.

POTT77   Potter, R. "Electronic Mail." *Science*, March 19,1977.

POUZ78   Pouzin, L., and Zimmermann, H. "A Tutorial on Protocols." *Proceedings of the IEEE*, November 1978.

POUZ81   Pouzin, L. "Methods, Tools, and Observations on Flow Control in Packet-Switched Data Networks." *IEEE Transactions on Communications*, April 1981.

POWE90   Powers, J., and Stair, H. *Megabit Data Communications.* Englewood Cliffs, NJ: Prentice-Hall, 1990.

PRYC91   Prycker, M. *Asynchronous Transfer Mode: Solution for Broadband ISDN.* New York: Ellis Horwood, 1991.

QUAR86   Quarterman, J., and Hoskins, J. "Notable Computer Networks." *Communications of the ACM*, October 1986.

RAJA78   Rajaraman, A. "Routing in TYMNET." *Proceedings, European Computing Conference*, 1978.

RAMA88   Ramabadroan, T., and Gaitonde, S. "A Tutorial on CRC Computations." IEEE Micro, August 1988.

RAWS78   Rawson, E. G., and Metcalfe, R. M. "Fibernet: Multimode Optical Fibers for Local Computer Networks." *IEEE Transactions on Communications*, July 1978.

REIN88   Reinstedler, J. "ASN.1 Macro Facility." *Open Systems Data Transfer*, April 1988.

RELC87   Relcom, Inc. *Carrier-Band Network Handbook, Second Edition.* Forest Grove, OR, 1987.

REY83   Rey, R., editor, *Engineering and Operations in the Bell System, Second Edition.* Murray Hill, NJ: AT&T Bell Laboratories, 1983.

RIND77   Rinde, J. "Routing and Control in a Centrally Directed Network." *Proceedings, National Computer Conference*, 1977.

RIND79a   Rinde, J. "Virtual Circuits in TYMNET II." *Proceedings, National Electronics Conference*, 1979.

RIND79b   Rinde, J., and Caisse, A. "Passive Flow Control Techniques for Distributed Networks." *Proceedings, IRIA Flow Control and Computer Networks Conference*, 1979.

ROBE74   Roberts, L. "Data by the Packet." *IEEE Spectrum*, February 1974.

ROBE75   Roberts, L. "ALOHA Packet System With and Without Slots and Capture." *Computer Communications Review*, April 1975.

ROBE78   Roberts, L. "The Evolution of Packet Switching." *Proceedings of the IEEE*, November 1978.

ROBI86   Robinson, R. "Digital Voice Compression." *Telecommunications*, February 1986.

ROBI90   Robinson, J.; Friedman, D.; and Steenstrup, M. "Congestion Control in BBN Packet-Switched Networks." *Computer Communication Review*, January 1990.

ROCH79   Rocher, E. "Taking a Fresh Look at Local Data Distribution." *Data Communications*, May 1979.

ROSS89   Ross, F. "An Overview of FDDI: The Fiber Distributed Data Interface." *IEEE Journal on Selected Areas in Communications.* September 1989.

RUDI76   Rudin, H. "On Routing and Delta Routing: A Taxonomy and Performance Comparison of Techniques for Packet-Switched Networks." *IEEE Transactions on Communications*, January 1976.

RUSH82   Rush, J. R. "Microwave Links Add Flexibility to Local Networks." *Electronics*, January 13, 1982.

RYBC80   Rybczynski, A. "X.25 Interface and End-to-End Virtual Circuit Service Characteristics." *IEEE Transactions on Communications*, April 1980.

SABN89 Sabnani, K. and Netravali, A. "A High-Speed Transport Protocol for Datagram/Virtual Circuits." *Proceedings, SIGCOMM '89 Symposium,* 1989.

SAND90 Sanders, R., and Weaver, A. "The Xpress Transfer Protocol (XTP)—A Tutorial." *Computer Communications Review,* October 1990.

SATO91 Sato, K.; Ueda, H.; and Yoshikai, M. "The Role of Virtual Path Crossconnection." *IEEE LTS,* August 1991.

SCAC86 Scace, E. "Integrated Services Digital Networks." In [BART86].

SCHN91 Schneier, B. "One-Way Hash Functions." *Dr. Dobb's Journal,* September 1991.

SCHW77 Schwartz, M. *Computer-Communication Network Design and Analysis.* Englewood Cliffs, N.J.: Prentice-Hall, 1977.

SCHW80 Schwartz, M., and Stern, T. E. "Routing Techniques Used in Computer Communication Networks." *IEEE Transactions on Communications,* April 1980.

SELV82 Selvaggi, P. "The Department of Defense Data Protocol Standardization Program." *Proceedings, EASCON 82,* 1982.

SEVC87 Sevcik, K., and Johnson, M. "Cycle Time Properties of the FDDI Token Ring Protocol." *IEEE Transactions on Software Engineering,* March 1987.

SEYE84 Seyer, M. *RS-232 Made Easy.* Englewood Cliffs, NJ: Prentice-Hall, 1984.

SHAR89 Sharma, R. "Satellite Network Design Parameters and Trade-Off Analysis." *Telecommunications,* June 1987.

SHAR89 Sharma, R. "VSAT Network Economics: A Comparative Analysis." *IEEE Communications Magazine,* February 1989.

SHEL82 Sheltzer, A.; Hinden, R.; and Brescia, M. "Connecting Different Types of Networks with Gateways." *Data Communications,* August 1982.

SHIM85 Shimayama, H.; Kato, K.; Oshima, G.; and Yano, K. "State-of-the-Art SCPC Satellite Communications Systems." *Signal,* February 1985.

SHOC78 Shoch, J. F. "Internetwork Naming, Addressing, and Routing." *Proceedings, COMPCON 78,* 1978.

SHOC82 Shoch, J. F.; Dala, Y. K.; and Redell, D. D. "Evolution of the Ethernet Local Computer Network." *Computer,* August 1982.

SHUF84 Shuford, R. "An Introduction to Fiber Optics." *Byte,* December 1984.

SHUM89 Shumate, P. "Optical Fibers Reach Into Homes." *IEEE Spectrum,* February 1989.

SIRB85 Sirbu, M., and Zwimpfer, L. "Standards Setting for Computer Communication: The Case of X.25." *IEEE Communications Magazine,* March 1985.

SKAP79 Skaperda, N. J."Some Architectural Alternatives in the Design of a Digital Switch." *IEEE Transactions on Communications,* July 1979.

SKLA88 Sklar, B. *Digital Communications: Fundamentals and Applications.* Englewood Cliffs, NJ: Prentice-Hall, 1988.

SKLO89 Sklower, K. "Improving the Efficiency of the OSI Checksum Calculation." *Computer Communication Review,* October 1989.

SLON91 Slone, J., and Drinan, A., editors. *Handbook of Local Area Networks.* New York: Auerbach, 1991.

SOHR91a Sohraby, K., editor. *Special Issue on Congestion Control in High Speed Networks. IEEE Communications Magazine,* October 1991.

SOHR91b Sohraby, K.; Fratta, L.; Gopal, K.; and Lazar, A. editors. *Special Issue on Congestion Control in High-Speed Packet Switched Networks. IEEE Journal on Selected Areas in Communications,* September 1991.

SPRA91 Spragins, J,; Hammond, J.; and Pawlikowski, K. *Telecommunications Protocols and Design.* Reading, MA.: Addison-Wesley, 1993.

STAL90a   Stallings, W. *The Business Guide to Local Area Networks*. Carmel, IN: Prentice-Hall/Sams, 1990.

STAL90b   Stallings, W. *Handbook of Computer Communications Standards, Volume 2: The TCP/IP Protocol Suite, Second Edition*, New York: Macmillan, 1990.

STAL92a   Stallings, W. *Computer Communications: Architectures, Protocols, and Standards*. Los Alamitos, CA: IEEEE Computer Society Press, 1992.

STAL92b   Stallings, W. *ISDN and Broadband ISDN, Second Edition*. New York: Macmillan, 1992.

STAL92c   Stallings, W. *Advances in ISDN and BROADBAND ISDN*. Los Alamitos, CA: IEEEE Computer Society Press, 1992.

STAL92d   Stallings, W. *Operating Systems*. New York: Macmillan, 1992.

STAL93a   Stallings, W. *Networking Standards: A Guide to OSI, ISDN, LAN, and MAN Standards*. Reading, MA.: Addison-Wesley, 1993.

STAL93b   Stallings, W. *Local and Metropolitan Area Networks, Fourth Edition*. New York: Macmillan, 1993.

STAL93c   Stallings, W. *Computer Organization and Architecture, Third Edition*, New York: Macmillan, 1993.

STAL93d   Stallings, W. *SNMP, SNMPv2, and CMIP: The Practical Guide to Network Management Standards*. Reading, MA.: Addison-Wesley, 1993.

STAL93e   Stallings, W. *Advances in Local and Metropolitan Area Networks*. Los Alamitos, CA: IEEE Computer Society Press, 1993.

STAL93f   Stallings, W. *Network Management*. Los Alamitos, CA: IEEE Computer Society Press, 1993.

STEE90   Steedman, D. *ASN.1: The Tutorial and Reference*. London: Technology Appraisals, 1990.

STIE81   Stieglitz, M. "Local Network Access Tradeoffs." *Computer Design*, October 1981.

STRA89   Strauss, P. "Header Prediction Will Boost Packet Throughput." *Data Communications*, August 1989.

STRA92   Strayer, W.; Dempsey, B.; and Weaver, A. *The Xpress Transfer Protocol*. Reading, MA.: Addison-Wesley, 1992.

STRO83   Strole, N. "A Local Communication Network Based on Interconnected Token-Access Rings: A Tutorial." *IBM Journal of Research and Development*, September 1983.

SUNS81   Sunshine, C. "Transport Protocols for Computer Networks." In [Kuo81].

TANE88   Tanenbaum, A. *Computer Networks, Second Edition*. Englewood Cliffs, NJ: Prentice-Hall, 1988.

TANG92   Tang, A., and Scoggins, S. *Open Networking with OSI*. Englewood CLiffs, NJ: Prentice-Hall, 1992.

TERP92   Terplan, K. *Communication Networks Management*. Englewood Cliffs, NJ: Prentice-Hall, 1992.

THAK86   Thaker, G., and Cain, J. "Interactions Between Routing and Flow Control Algorithms. *IEEE Transactions on Communications*, March 1986.

THUR85   Thurber, K., ed. *The LOCALNetter Designer's Handbook*. Minneapolis, MN: Architecture Technology Corporation, November 1985.

TILL90   Tillman, M., and Yen, D. "SNA and OSI: Three Strategies for Interconnection." *Communications of the ACM*, February 1990.

TOBA80   Tobagi, F. A. "Multiaccess Protocols in Packet Communication Systems." *IEEE Transactions on Communications*, April 1980.

TOML75 Tomlinson, R. "Selecting Sequence Numbers." *Proceedings ACM SIGCOMM/ SIGOPS Interprocess Communication Workshop, 1975.*

TSUD92 Tsudik, G. "Message Authentication with One-Way Hash Functions." *Computer Communications Review,* October 1992.

TYME81 Tymes, L. "Routing and Flow Control in TYMNET." *IEEE Transactions on Communications,* April 1981.

VALE92 Valenzano, A.; Demartini, C.; and Ciminiera, L. *MAP and TOP Communications: Standards and Applications.* Reading, MA: Addison-Wesley, 1992.

VAUG59 Vaughan, H. "Research Model for Time Separation Integrated Communication." *Bell System Technical Journal,* July 1959.

VAZQ88 Vazquez, et al. "Performance of OSI Transport Over Accunet and Iberpac." *Proceedings, INFOCOM '88,* March 1988.

VERM90 Verma, P., ed. *ISDN Systems: Architecture, Technology, and Applications.* Englewood Cliffs, NJ: Prentice-Hall, 1990.

VONA80 Vonarx, M. "Controlling the Mushrooming Communications Net." *Data Communications,* June 1980.

WATS89 Watson, R. "The Delta-T Transport Protocol." *Proceedings, 14th Conference on Local Computer Networks,* October 1989.

WAYN91 Wayner, P. "True Data." *Byte,* September 1991.

WEAV91 Weaver, A. "Making Transport Protocols Fast." *Proceedings, 16th Conference on Local Computer Networks.* October 1991.

WEIS78 Weissler, R.; Binder, R.; Bressler, R.; Rettberg, R.; and Walden, D. "Synchronization and Multiple Access Protocols in the Initial Satellite IMP." *Proceedings, COMPCON FALL 78,* 1978.

WERN86 Wernli, M. "The Choices in Designing a Fiber-Optic Network." *Data Communications,* June 1986.

WHAL89 Whaley, A. "The X-Press Transfer Protocol." *Proceedings, 14th Conference on Local Computer Networks,* October 1989.

WHIT92 White, G. *Internetworking and Addressing.* New York: McGraw-Hill, 1992.

WILL87 Williams, R. *Communication Systems Analysis and Design.* Englewood Cliffs, NJ: Prentice-Hall, 1987.

WILL89 Williamson, C., and Cheriton, D. "An Overview of the VMTP Transport Protocol." *Proceedings, 14th Conference on Local Computer Networks,* October 1989.

WU91 Wu, W., and Levine, A. *Special Issue: Integrated Services Digital Networks. Proceedings of the IEEE,* February 1991.

YEN83 Yen, C., and Crawford, R. "Distribution and Equalization of Signal on Coaxial Cables Used in 10 Mbps/s Baseband Local Area Networks." *IEEE Transactions on Communications,* October 1983.

YUM87 Yum, T., and Schwartz, M. "Comparison of Routing Procedures for Circuit-Switched Traffic in Nonhierarchical Networks." *IEEE Transactions on Communications,* May 1987.

ZANG91 Zanger, H., and Zanger C. *Fiber Optics: Communication and Other Applications.* New York: Macmillan, 1991.

ZHAN86 Zhang, L. "Why TCP Timers Don't Work Well." *Proceedings, SIGCOMM '86 Symposium,* August 1986.

Index

College Division
Macmillan Publishing Company
Front & Brown Streets
Riverside, NJ 08075

ORDER FORM

Ship To: **Bill to:**
(Please print or type)   (If different from shipping address)

Name _____   Name _____

Co. _____   Co. _____

Address _____   Address _____

_____   _____

City _____ St ___ Zip _____   City _____ St ___ Zip _____

Mail your order to the above address or call 800-548-9939 (in New Jersey call
609-461-6500) or Fax 609-461-9265

Shipping Method **(select one)**
_____ UPS ground
_____ 2nd Day Air
_____ Book Rate

Payment Method **(select one)**	
_____ Check	_____ Visa
_____ Bill Me	_____ MasterCard

Authorized Signature

_____   _____
Card Number   Exp Date

(continued)

**TEAR OUT THIS PAGE TO ORDER OTHER TITLES BY
WILLIAM STALLINGS:**

SEQ.	QTY.	ISBN NO.	TITLE	SINGLE COPY PRICE	TOTAL
1	_____	002-415495-4	Computer Organization & Architecture 3/e	69.00	_____
2	_____	002-415441-5	Data and Computer Communications 4/e	69.00	_____
3	_____	002-415465-2	Local and Metropolitan Area Networks 4/e	60.00	_____
4	_____	002-415433-4	Business Data Communications 2/e	49.00	_____
5	_____	002-415475-X	ISDN and Broadband ISDN 2/e	55.00	_____
6	_____	002-415481-4	Operating Systems	56.00	_____

Handbooks of Computer Communications Standards

7	_____	002-415521-7	Volume 1, The Open Systems Interconnection (OSI) Model and OSI-Related Standards, 2/e	47.00	_____
8	_____	002-415522-5	Volume 2, Local Area Network Standards, 2/e	47.00	_____
9	_____	002-415523-3	Volume 3, The TCP/IP Protocol Suite, 2/e	47.00	_____

GRAND TOTAL _____

A small shipping charge will be added. Prices subject to change without prior notification.

PSR-PSL 350-3500   FC# 1355

ACRONYMS

ANS	American National Standard
ANSI	American National Standards Institute
ASK	Amplitude-Shift Keying
CATV	Community Antenna Television
CBX	Computerized Branch Exchange
CCITT	Consultative Committee on International Telegraphy and Telephony
CRC	Cyclic Redundancy Check
CSMA	Carrier-Sense Multiple Access
CSMA/CD	Carrier-Sense Multiple Access with Collision Detection
DCE	Data Circuit-Terminating Equipment
DES	Data Encryption Standard
DOD	Department of Defense
DQDB	Distributed Queue, Dual Bus
DTE	Data Terminal Equipment
FCS	Frame Check Sequence
FDDI	Fiber Distributed Data Interface
FDM	Frequency-Division Multiplexing
FNP	Front-End Network Processor
FSK	Frequency-Shift Keying
HAM	Hybrid Access Method
HDLC	High-Level Data Link Control
IEEE	Institute of Electrical and Electronics Engineers
IP	Internet Protocol
ISO	International Standards Organization